Cross-Cultural Analysis
Methods and Applications

The European Association of Methodology (EAM) serves to promote research and development of empirical research methods in the fields of the Behavioural, Social, Educational, Health and Economic Sciences as well as in the field of Evaluation Research.
Homepage: http://www.eam-online.org

The purpose of the EAM book series is to advance the development and application of methodological and statistical research techniques in social and behavioral research. Each volume in the series presents cutting-edge methodological developments in a way that is accessible to a broad audience. Such books can be authored, monographs, or edited volumes.

Sponsored by the European Association of Methodology, the EAM book series is open to contributions from the Behavioral, Social, Educational, Health and Economic Sciences. Proposals for volumes in the EAM series should include the following: (1) Title; (2) authors/editors; (3) a brief description of the volume's focus and intended audience; (4) a table of contents; (5) a timeline including planned completion date. Proposals are invited from all interested authors. Feel free to submit a proposal to one of the members of the EAM book series editorial board, by visiting the EAM website http:// eam-online.org. Members of the EAM editorial board are Manuel Ato (University of Murcia), Pamela Campanelli (Survey Consultant, UK), Edith de Leeuw (Utrecht University) and Vasja Vehovar (University of Ljubljana).

Volumes in the series include

Davidov/Schmidt/Billiet: Cross-Cultural Analysis: Methods and Applications, 2011

Das/Ester/Kaczmirek: Social and Behavioral Research and the Internet: Advances in Applied Methods and Research Strategies, 2011

Hox/Roberts: Handbook of Advanced Multilevel Analysis, 2011

De Leeuw/Hox/Dillman: International Handbook of Survey Methodology, 2008

Van Montfort/Oud/Satorra: Longitudinal Models in the Behavioral and Related Sciences, 2007

Cross-Cultural Analysis

Methods and Applications

Edited by

Eldad Davidov
University of Zurich, Switzerland

Peter Schmidt
University of Marburg, Germany
Professor Emeritus, University of Giessen, Germany

Jaak Billiet
University of Leuven, Belgium

Routledge
Taylor & Francis Group
New York London

Routledge
Taylor & Francis Group
270 Madison Avenue
New York, NY 10016

Routledge
Taylor & Francis Group
27 Church Road
Hove, East Sussex BN3 2FA

Routledge is an imprint of Taylor & Francis Group, an Informa business

Printed in the United States of America on acid-free paper
10 9 8 7 6 5 4 3 2 1

International Standard Book Number: 978-1-84872-822-6 (Hardback) 978-1-84872-823-3 (Paperback)

Library of Congress Cataloging-in-Publication Data

Cross-cultural analysis : methods and applications / edited by Eldad Davidov, Peter Schmidt, Jaak Billiet.
p. cm. -- (European Association of Methodology series)
Includes bibliographical references and index.
ISBN 978-1-84872-822-6 (hardcover : alk. paper) -- ISBN 978-1-84872-823-3 (pbk. : alk. paper)
1. Cross-cultural studies--Research. 2. Cross-cultural studies--Methodology. I. Davidov, Eldad. II. Schmidt, Peter, 1942- III. Billiet, Jaak.

GN345.7.C728 2011
306.072'1--dc22 2010038133

Visit the Taylor & Francis Web site at
http://www.taylorandfrancis.com

and the Psychology Press Web site at
http://www.psypress.com

Contents

Preface

In recent years, the increased interest of researchers on the importance of choosing appropriate methods for the analysis of cross-cultural data can be clearly seen in the growing amount of literature on this subject. At the same time, the increasing availability of cross-national data sets, like the European Social Survey (ESS), the International Social Survey Program (ISSP), the European Value Study and World Value Survey (EVS and WVS), the European Household Panel Study (EHPS), and the Program for International Assessment of Students' Achievements (PISA), just to name a few, allows researchers currently to engage in cross-cultural research more than ever. Nevertheless, presently, most of the methods developed for such purposes are insufficiently applied, and their importance is often not recognized by substantive researchers in cross-national studies. Thus, there is a growing need to bridge the gap between the methodological literature and applied cross-cultural research. Our book is aimed toward this goal.

The goals we try to achieve through this book are twofold. First, it should inform readers about the state of the art in the growing methodological literature on analysis of cross-cultural data. Since this body of literature is very large, our book focuses on four main topics and pays a substantial amount of attention to strategies developed within the generalized latent variable approach.

Second, the book presents applications of such methods to interesting substantive topics using cross-national data sets employing theory-driven empirical analyses. Our selection of authors further reflects this structure. The authors represent established and internationally prominent, as well as younger researchers working in a variety of methodological and substantive fields in the social sciences.

CONTENTS

The book is divided into four major topics we believe to be of central importance in the literature. The topics are not mutually exclusive, but rather provide complementary strategies for analyzing cross-cultural data, all within the generalized-latent variable approach. The topics include (1) multiple group confirmatory factor analysis (MGCFA), including the comparison of relationships and latent means and the expansion of MGCFA into multiple group structural equation modeling (MGSEM); (2) multilevel analysis; (3) latent class analysis (LCA); and (4) item response theory (IRT). Whereas researchers in different disciplines tend to use different methodological approaches in a rather isolated way (e.g., IRT commonly used by psychologists or education researchers; LCA, for instance, by marketing researchers and sociologists; and MGCFA and multilevel analysis by sociologists and political scientists, among others), this book offers an integrated framework. In this framework, different cutting edge methods are described, developed, applied, and linked, crossing "methodological borders" between disciplines. The sections include methodological as well as more applied chapters. Some chapters include a description of the basic strategy and how it relates to other strategies presented in the book. Other chapters include applications in which the different strategies are applied using real data sets to address interesting, theoretically oriented research questions. A few chapters combine both aspects.

Some words about the structure of the book: Several orderings of the chapters within each section are possible. We chose to organize the chapters from general to specific; that is, each section begins with more general topics followed by later chapters focusing on more specific issues. However, the later chapters are not necessarily more technical or complex.

The first and largest section focuses especially on MGCFA and MGSEM techniques and includes nine chapters. Chapter 1, by Fons J. R. van de Vijver, is a general discussion of how the models developed in cross-cultural psychology to identify and assess bias can be identified using structural equation modeling techniques. Chapter 2, by Nick Allum, Sanna Read, and Patrick Sturgis, provides a nontechnical introduction for the application of MGCFA (including means and intercepts) to assess invariance. The method is demonstrated with an analysis of social and political trust in Europe in three rounds of the ESS. Chapter 3, by Jaehoon Lee, Todd D. Little, and Kristopher J. Preacher, discusses methodological issues that may arise when researchers conduct SEM-based differential item functioning (DIF) analysis across countries and shows techniques for conducting such analyses more accurately. In addition, they demonstrate general procedures to assess invariance and latent constructs' mean differences across countries. Holger Steinmetz's Chapter 4 focuses on the use of MGCFA to estimate mean differences across cultures, a central topic in cross-cultural research. The author gives an easy and nontechnical introduction to latent mean difference testing, explains its presumptions, and illustrates its use with data from the ESS on self-esteem. In Chapter 5, by Alain De Beuckelaer and Gilbert Swinnen, readers will find a simulation study that assesses the reliability of latent variable mean comparisons across two groups when one latent variable indicator fails to satisfy the condition of measurement invariance across groups. The main conclusion is that noninvariant measurement parameters, and in particular a noninvariant indicator intercept, form a serious threat to the robustness of the latent variable mean difference test. Chapter 6, by Eldad Davidov, Georg Datler, Peter Schmidt, and Shalom H. Schwartz tests the comparability of the measurement of human values in the second round (2004–2005) of the ESS across three countries, Belgium, the Netherlands, and Luxembourg, while accounting for the fact that the data are ordinal (ordered-categorical). They use a model for ordinal indicators that includes thresholds as additional parameters to test for measurement invariance. The general conclusions are that results are consistent with those found using MGCFA, which typically assumes the use of normally distributed, continuous data. Chapter 7 offers a simultaneous test of measurement and structural models across European countries by Bart Meuleman and Jaak Billiet and focuses on the interplay between social structure, religiosity, values, and social attitudes. The authors use ESS (round 2) data to compare these relations across 25 different European countries. Their study provides an example of how multigroup structural equation modeling (MGSEM) can be used in comparative research. A particular characteristic of their analysis is the simultaneous test of both the measurement and structural parts in an integrated multigroup model. Chapter 8, by William M. van der Veld and Willem E. Saris, illustrates how to test the cross-national invariance properties of social trust. The main difference to Chapter 3 is that here they propose a procedure that makes it possible to test for measurement invariance after the correction for random and systematic measurement errors. In addition, they propose an alternative procedure to evaluate cross-national invariance that is implemented in a software program called JRule. This software can detect misspecifications in structural equation models taking into account the power of the test, which is not taken into account in most applications. The last chapter in this section, Chapter 9, by Shaul Oreg and colleagues uses confirmatory smallest space analysis (SSA) as a complementary technique to MGCFA. The authors use samples from 17 countries to validate the resistance to change scale across these nations.

Section 2 focuses on multilevel analysis. The first chapter in this section, Chapter 10, by Bart Meuleman, demonstrates how two-level data may be used to assess context effects on anti-immigration attitudes. By doing this, the chapter proposes some refinements to existing theories on anti-immigrant sentiments and an alternative to the classical multilevel analysis. Chapter 11, by Hermann Dülmer, uses multilevel analysis to reanalyze results on the work ethic presented by Norris and Inglehart in 2004. This contribution illustrates the disadvantages of using conventional ordinary least squares (OLS) regression for international comparisons instead of the more appropriate multilevel analyses, by contrasting the results of both methods. The section concludes with Chapter 12, by Remco Feskens and Joop J. Hox, that discusses the problem of small sample sizes on different levels in multilevel analyses. To overcome this small sample size problem they explore the possibilities of using resampled (bootstrap) standard errors.

The third section focuses on LCA. It opens with Chapter 13, by Miloš Kankaraš, Guy Moors, and Jeroen K. Vermunt, that shows how measurement invariance may be tested using LCA. LCA can model any type of discrete level data and is an obvious choice when nominal indicators are used and/or it is a researcher's aim to classify respondents in latent classes. The methodological discussion is illustrated by two examples. In the first example they use a multigroup LCA with nominal indicators; in the second, a multigroup latent class factor analysis with ordinal indicators. Chapter 14, by Pascal Siegers, draws a comprehensive picture of religious orientations in 11 European countries by elaborating a multiple group latent class model that distinguishes between church religiosity, moderate religiosity, alternative spiritualities, religious indifferences, and atheism.

The final section, which focuses on item response theory (IRT), opens with Chapter 15, by Rianne Janssen, that shows how IRT techniques may be used to test for measurement invariance. Janssen illustrates the procedure with an application using different modes of data collection: paper-and-pencil and computerized test administration. Chapter 16, by Markus Quandt, explores advantages and limitations of using Rasch models for identifying potentially heterogeneous populations by using a practical application. This chapter uses a LCA. The book concludes with Chapter 17, by Jean-Paul Fox and Josine Verhagen, that shows how cross-national survey data can be properly analyzed using IRT with random item effects for handling measurement noninvariant items. Without the need of anchor items, the item characteristics differences across countries are explicitly modeled and a common measurement scale is obtained. The authors illustrate the method with the PISA data. Table 0.1 presents the chapters in the book; for each chapter a brief description of its focus is given along with a listing of the statistical methods that were used, the goal(s) of the analysis, and the data set that was employed.

DATA SETS

The book is accompanied by a Web site at http://www.psypress.com/crosscultural-analysis-9781848728233. Here readers will find data and syntax files for several of the book's applications. In several cases, for example in those chapters where data from the ESS were used, readers may download the data directly from the corresponding Web site. The data can be used to replicate findings in different chapters and by doing so get a better understanding of the techniques presented in these chapters.

INTENDED AUDIENCE

Given that the applications span a variety of disciplines, and because the techniques may be applied to very different research questions, the book should be of interest to survey researchers, social science methodologists, cross-cultural researchers, as well as scholars, graduate, and postgraduate students in the following disciplines: psychology, political science, sociology, education, marketing and economics, human geography, criminology, psychometrics, epidemiology, and public health. Readers from more formal backgrounds such as statistics and methodology may find interest in the more purely methodological parts. Readers without much knowledge of mathematical statistics may be more interested in the applied parts. A secondary audience includes practitioners who wish to gain a better understanding of how to analyze cross-cultural data for their field

TABLE 0.1

Overview

Chapter Number, Author(s), and Title	Topic, Statistical Method(s), and Goal of Analysis	Countries and Dataset
1. Fons J. R. van de Vijver *Capturing Bias in Structural Equation Modeling*	Strengths and weaknesses of structural equation modeling (SEM) to test equivalence in cross-national research 1. Theoretical framework of bias and equivalence 2. Procedures and examples to identify bias and address equivalence 3. Identification of all bias types using SEM 4. Strengths, weaknesses, opportunities, and threat (SWOT) analysis	/
2. Nick Allum, Sanna Read, and Patrick Sturgis *Evaluating Change in Social and Political Trust in Europe*	Analysis of social and political trust in European countries over time using SEM with structured means and multiple groups 1. Introduction to structured means analysis using SEM 2. Application to the ESS data	Seventeen European countries First three rounds of the ESS 2002, 2004, 2006
3. Jaehoon Lee, Todd D. Little, and Kristopher J. Preacher *Methodological Issues in Using Structural Equation Models for Testing Differential Item Functioning*	Differential item functioning (DIF) and SEM-based invariance testing Multigroup SEM with means and intercepts Mean and covariance structure (MACS) Multiple indicators multiple causes (MIMIC) model 1. Introduction to the concept of factorial invariance 2. Levels of invariance 3. The concept of differential item functioning 4. Two methods for detecting DIF	Two simulation studies

4. Holger Steinmetz *Estimation and Comparison of Latent Means Across Cultures*	Comparison of the use of composite scores and latent means in confirmatory factor analysis (CFA) with multiple groups (MGCFA), higher-order CFA, and MIMIC models 1. General discussion of observed means MGCFA, composite scores, and latent means 2. Application to ESS data measuring self-esteem in two countries using MGCFA	Two countries First round of ESS, 2002
5. Alain De Beuckelaer and Gilbert Swinnen *Biased Latent Variable Mean Comparisons due to Measurement Noninvariance: A Simulation Study*	Noninvariance of one indicator MACS SEM with latent means and intercepts Simulation study with a full factorial design varying: 1. The distribution of indicators 2. The number of observations per group 3. The noninvariance of loadings and intercepts 4. The size of difference between latent means across two groups	Two-country case Simulated data
6. Eldad Davidov, Georg Datler, Peter Schmidt, and Shalom H. Schwartz *Testing the Invariance of Values in the Benelux Countries with the European Social Survey: Accounting for Ordinality*	Invariance testing of thresholds, intercepts, and factor loadings of values in the Benelux countries with MGCFA accounting for the ordinality of the data 1. Description of the approach including MPLUS code 2. Comparison with MGCFA assuming interval data 3. Application to the ESS value scale	Three European countries Second round of ESS, 2004
7. Bart Meuleman and Jaak Billiet *Religious Involvement: Its Relation to Values and Social Attitudes*	Effects of religious involvement on values and attitudes in Europe MGCFA and multigroup structural equation model (MGSEM) 1. Specification and simultaneous test of measurement and structural models 2. Specification of structural models	Twenty-five European countries Second round of ESS, 2004

(Continued)

TABLE 0.1 (Continued)

Overview

Chapter Number, Author(s), and Title	Topic, Statistical Method(s), and Goal of Analysis	Countries and Dataset
8. William M. van der Veld and Willem E. Saris *Causes of Generalized Social Trust*	Comparative analysis of the causes of generalized social trust with a correction of random and systematic measurement errors and an alternative procedure to evaluate the fit of the model MGCFA/SEM JRule software to detect model misspecifications taking into account the power of the test 1. Description of the procedure to correct for measurement errors 2. Description of the new procedure to evaluate the fit 3. Application to ESS data on the generalized social trust scale	Nineteen European countries First round of ESS, 2002
9. Shaul Oreg and Colleagues *Dispositional Resistance to Change*	Resistance to change scale MGCFA and confirmatory SSA Invariance of measurement, comparison over 17 countries using MGCFA, and confirmatory smallest space analysis (confirmatory SSA)	Seventeen countries Data collected in 2006–2007
10. Bart Meuleman *Perceived Economic Threat and Anti-Immigration Attitudes: Effects of Immigrant Group Size and Economic Conditions Revisited*	Threat and anti-immigration attitudes Two-step approach: 1. MGCFA 2. Bivariate correlations, graphical techniques Invariance of measurements and tests of the effects of contextual variables	Twenty-one countries First round of ESS, 2002

11. Hermann Dülmer *A Multilevel Regression Analysis on Work Ethic*	Work ethic and values changes a. Test of a one-level versus a two-level CFA b. OLS-regression versus multilevel structural equation model (ML SEM) 1. Reanalysis of the Norris/Inglehart explanatory model with a more adequate method 2. Illustration of disadvantages of using an OLS-regression for international comparisons instead of the more appropriate multilevel analysis 3. Elimination of inconsistencies between the Norris/Inglehart theory and their empirical model	Fifty-three countries European Values Study (EVS) Wave III, 1999/2000; World Values Survey (WVS) Wave IV, 1999/2000; combined data sets
12. Remco Feskens and Joop J. Hox *Multilevel Structural Equation Modeling for Cross-cultural Research: Exploring Resampling Methods to Overcome Small Sample Size Problems*	Use of resampling methods to get accurate standard errors in multilevel analysis 1. MGCFA 2. SEM (with Mplus), a bootstrap procedure 3. MGSEM bootstrap procedure Test of the use of bootstrap techniques for multilevel structural equation models and MGSEM	Twenty-six European countries First three rounds of ESS, pooled data set, 2002–2006
13. Miloš Kankaraš, Guy Moors, and Jeroen K. Vermunt *Testing for Measurement Invariance with Latent Class Analysis*	Use of latent class analysis (LCA) for testing measurement invariance a. Latent class cluster model b. Latent class factor model 1. Identification of latent structures from discrete observed variables using LCA 2. Treating latent variables as nominal or ordinal 3. Estimations are performed assuming fewer distributional assumptions	Four European countries EVS, 1999/2000

(*Continued*)

TABLE 0.1 (Continued)

Overview

Chapter Number, Author(s), and Title	Topic, Statistical Method(s), and Goal of Analysis	Countries and Dataset
14. Pascal Siegers *A Multiple Group Latent Class Analysis of Religious Orientations in Europe*	Religious orientation in Europe Multiple group latent class analysis (MGLCA) Quantification of the importance of alternative spiritualities in Europe	Eleven countries Religious and moral pluralism project (RAMP), 1999
15. Rianne Janssen *Using a Differential Item Functioning Approach to Investigate Measurement Invariance*	Item response theory (IRT) and its application to testing for measurement invariance IRT model used a. strictly monotonous b. parametric c. dichotomous items 1. Introduction to IRT 2. Modeling of differential item functioning (DIF) 3. Application to a dataset	One country Paper-and-pencil and computerized test administration methods
16. Markus Quandt *Using the Mixed Rasch Model in the Comparative Analysis of Attitudes*	Use of a mixed polytomous Rasch model 1. Introduction to polytomous Rasch models 2. Their use for testing invariance of the national identity scale	Five countries International Social Survey Program (ISSP) national identity module, 2003

17. Jean-Paul Fox and A. Josine Verhagen *Random Item Effects Modeling for Cross-National Survey Data*	Random item effects modeling Normal ogive item response theory (IRT) model with country specific item parameters; multilevel item response theory (MLIRT) model 1. Properties and possibilities of random effects modeling 2. Simulation study 3. Application to the PISA data	Forty countries PISA-study 2003; Mathematics Data

of study. For example, many practitioners may want to use these techniques for analyzing consumer data from different countries for marketing purposes. Clinical or health psychologists and epidemiologists may be interested in methods of how to analyze and compare cross-cultural data on, for example, addictions to alcohol or smoking or depression across various populations. The procedures presented in this volume may be useful for their work. Finally, the book is also appropriate for an advanced methods course in cross-cultural analysis.

REFERENCE

Norris, P., and Inglehart, R. (2004). *Sacred and secular. Religion and politics worldwide.* Cambridge: Cambridge University Press.

Acknowledgments

We would like to thank all the reviewers for their work on the different chapters included in this volume and the contributors for their dedicated efforts evident in each contribution presented here. Their great cooperation enabled the production of this book. Many thanks to Joop J. Hox for his very helpful and supportive comments and to Robert J. Vandenberg and Peer Scheepers for their endorsements. Special thanks also go to Debra Riegert and Erin Flaherty for their guidance, cooperation, and continous support, to Lisa Trierweiler for the English proofreading, and to Mirjam Hausherr and Stephanie Kernich for their help with formatting the chapters. We would also like to thank the people in the production team, especially Ramkumar Soundararajan and Robert Sims for their patience and continuous support. The first editor would like to thank Jaak Billiet, Georg Datler, Wolfgang Jagodzinski, Daniel Oberski, Willem Saris, Elmar Schlüter, Peter Schmidt, Holger Steinmetz, and William van der Veld for the many interesting discussions we shared on the topics covered in this book.

Eldad Davidov, Peter Schmidt, and Jaak Billiet

Section I

MGCFA and MGSEM Techniques

1

Capturing Bias in Structural Equation Modeling

Fons J. R. van de Vijver
Tilburg University and North-West University

1.1 INTRODUCTION

Equivalence studies are coming of age. Thirty years ago there were few conceptual models and statistical techniques to address sources of systematic measurement error in cross-cultural studies (for early examples, see Cleary & Hilton, 1968; Lord, 1977, 1980; Poortinga, 1971). This picture has changed; in the last decades conceptual models and statistical techniques have been developed and refined. Many empirical examples have been published. There is a growing awareness of the importance in the field for the advancement of cross-cultural theorizing. An increasing number of journals require authors who submit manuscripts of cross-cultural studies to present evidence supporting the equivalence of the study measures. Yet, the burgeoning of the field has not led to a convergence in conceptualizations, methods, and analyses. For example, educational testing focuses on the analysis of items as sources of problems of cross-cultural comparisons, often using item response theory (e.g., Emenogu & Childs, 2005). In personality psychology, exploratory factor analysis is commonly applied as a tool to examine the similarity of factors underlying a questionnaire (e.g., McCrae, 2002). In survey research and marketing, structural equation modeling (SEM) is most frequently employed (e.g., Steenkamp & Baumgartner, 1998). From a theoretical perspective, these models are related; for example, the relationship of item response theory and confirmatory factor analysis (as derived from a general latent variable model) has been described by Brown (2006). However, from a practical perspective, the models can be seen as relatively independent paradigms; there are no recent studies in which various bias models are compared (an example of an older study in which procedures are compared that are no longer used has been described by Shepard, Camilli, & Averill, 1981).

In addition to the diversity in mathematical developments, conceptual frameworks for dealing with cross-cultural studies have been developed in cross-cultural psychology, which, again, have a slightly different focus. It is fair to say that the field of equivalence is still expanding in both conceptual and statistical directions and that rapprochement of the approaches and best practices that are broadly accepted across various fields are not just around the corner.

The present chapter relates the conceptual framework about measurement problems that is developed in cross-cultural psychology (with input from various other sciences studying cultures and cultural differences) to statistical developments and current practices in SEM vis-à-vis multigroup testing. More specifically, I address the question of the strengths and weaknesses of SEM from a conceptual bias and equivalence framework. There are few publications in which more conceptually based approaches to bias that are mainly derived from substantive studies are linked to more statistically based approaches such as developed in SEM. This chapter adds to the literature by linking two research traditions that have worked largely independent in the past, despite the overlap in bias issues addressed in both traditions. The chapter deals with the question to what extent the study of equivalence, as implemented in SEM, can address all the relevant measurement issues of cross-cultural studies. The first part of the chapter describes a theoretical framework of bias and equivalence. The second part describes various procedures and examples to identify bias and address equivalence. The third part discusses the identification of all the bias types distinguished using SEM. The fourth part presents a SWOT analysis (strengths, weaknesses, opportunities, and threats) of SEM in dealing with bias sources in cross-cultural studies. Conclusions are drawn in the final part.

1.2 BIAS AND EQUIVALENCE

The bias framework is developed from the perspective of cross-cultural psychology and attempts to provide a comprehensive taxonomy of all systematic sources of error that can challenge the inferences drawn from cross-cultural studies (Poortinga, 1989; Van de Vijver & Leung, 1997). The equivalence framework addresses the statistical implications of the bias framework and defines conditions that have to be fulfilled before inferences can be drawn about comparative conclusions dealing with constructs or scores in cross-cultural studies.

1.2.1 Bias

Bias refers to the presence of nuisance factors (Poortinga, 1989). If scores are biased, the meaning of test scores varies across groups and constructs and/or scores are not directly comparable across cultures. Different types of bias can be distinguished (Van de Vijver & Leung, 1997).

1.2.1.1 Construct Bias

There is *construct bias* if a construct differs across cultures, usually due to an incomplete overlap of construct-relevant behaviors. An empirical example can be found in Ho's (1996) work on filial piety (defined as a psychological characteristic associated with being "a good son or daughter"). The Chinese concept, which includes the expectation that children should assume the role of caretaker of elderly parents, is broader than the Western concept.

1.2.1.2 Method Bias

Method bias is the generic term for all sources of bias due to factors often described in the methods section of empirical papers. Three types of method bias have been defined, depending on whether the bias comes from the sample, administration, or instrument. Sample bias refers to systematic differences in background characteristics of samples with a bearing on the constructs measured. Examples are differences in educational background that can influence a host of psychological variables such as cognitive tests. Administration bias refers to the presence of cross-cultural conditions in testing conditions, such as ambient noise. The potential influence of interviewers and test administrators can also be mentioned here. In cognitive testing, the presence of the tester does not need to be obtrusive (Jensen, 1980). In survey research there is more evidence for interviewer effects (Lyberg et al., 1997). Deference to the interviewer has been reported; participants are more likely to display positive attitudes to an interviewer (e.g., Aquilino, 1994). Instrument bias is a final source of bias in cognitive tests that includes instrument properties with a pervasive and unintended influence on cross-cultural differences such as the use of response alternatives in Likert scales that are not identical across groups (e.g., due to a bad translation of item anchors).

1.2.1.3 Item Bias

Item bias or differential item functioning refers to anomalies at the item level (Camilli & Shepard, 1994; Holland & Wainer, 1993). According to a definition that is widely used in education and psychology, an item is biased if respondents from different cultures with the same standing on the underlying construct (e.g., they are equally intelligent) do not have the same mean score on the item. Of all bias types, item bias has been the most extensively studied; various psychometric techniques are available to identify item bias (e.g., Camilli & Shepard, 1994; Holland & Wainer, 1993; Sireci, 2011; Van de Vijver & Leung, 1997, 2011).

Item bias can arise in various ways, such as poor item translation, ambiguities in the original item, low familiarity/appropriateness of the item content in certain cultures, and the influence of culture-specific nuisance factors or connotations associated with the item wording. Suppose that a geography test is administered to pupils in all EU countries that ask for the name of the capital of Belgium. Belgian pupils can be expected to show higher scores on the item than pupils from other EU countries. The item is biased because it favors one cultural group across all test score levels.

1.2.2 Equivalence

Bias has implications for the comparability of scores (e.g., Poortinga, 1989). Depending on the nature of the bias, four hierarchically nested types of equivalence can be defined: construct, structural or functional, metric (or measurement unit), and scalar (or full score) equivalence. These four are further described below.

1.2.2.1 Construct Inequivalence

Constructs that are inequivalent lack a shared meaning, which precludes any cross-cultural comparison. In the literature, claims of construct inequivalence can be grouped into three broad types, which differ in the degree of inequivalence (partial or total). The first and strongest claim of inequivalence is found in studies that adopt a strong emic, relativistic viewpoint, according to which psychological constructs are completely and inseparably linked to their natural context. Any cross-cultural comparison is then erroneous as psychological constructs are cross-culturally inequivalent.

The second type is exemplified by psychological constructs that are associated with specific cultural groups. The best examples are culture-bound syndromes. A good example is Amok, which is specific to Asian countries like Indonesia and Malaysia. Amok is characterized by a brief period of violent aggressive behavior among men. The period is often preceded by an insult and the patient shows persecutory ideas and automatic behaviors. After this period, the patient is usually exhausted and has no recollection of the event (Azhar & Varma, 2000). Violent aggressive behavior among men is universal, but the combination of triggering events, symptoms, and lack of recollection is culture-specific. Such a combination of universal and culture-specific aspects is characteristic for culture-bound syndromes. Taijin Kyofusho is a Japanese example (Suzuki, Takei, Kawai, Minabe, & Mori, 2003; Tanaka-Matsumi & Draguns, 1997). This syndrome is characterized by an intense fear that one's body is discomforting or insulting for others by its appearance, smell, or movements. The description of the symptoms suggests a strong form of a social phobia (a universal), which finds culturally unique expressions in a country in which conformity is a widely shared norm. Suzuki et al. (2003) argue that most symptoms of Taijin Kyofusho can be readily classified as social phobia, which (again) illustrates that culture-bound syndromes involve both universal and culture-specific aspects.

The third type of inequivalence is empirically based and found in comparative studies in which the data do not show any evidence for construct comparability; inequivalence here is a consequence of the lack of cross-cultural comparability. Van Leest (1997) administered a standard personality questionnaire to mainstream Dutch and Dutch immigrants. The instrument showed various problems, such as the frequent use of colloquialisms. The structure found in the Dutch mainstream group could not be replicated in the immigrant group.

1.2.2.2 Structural or Functional Equivalence

An instrument administered in different cultural groups shows structural equivalence if it measures the same construct(s) in all these groups (it should be noted that this definition is different from the common definition of structural equivalence in SEM; in a later section I return to this confusing difference in definitions). Structural equivalence has been examined for various cognitive tests (Jensen, 1980), Eysenck's Personality Questionnaire (Barrett, Petrides, Eysenck, & Eysenck, 1998), and the five-factor model of personality (McCrae, 2002). Functional equivalence as a specific type of structural equivalence refers to identity of nomological networks (Cronbach & Meehl, 1955). A questionnaire that measures, say, openness to new cultures shows functional equivalence if it measures the same psychological constructs in each culture, as manifested in a similar pattern of convergent and divergent validity (i.e., nonzero correlations with presumably related measures and zero correlations with presumably unrelated measures). Tests of structural equivalence are applied more often than tests of functional equivalence. The reason is not statistical. With advances in statistical modeling (notably path analysis as part of SEM), tests of the cross-cultural similarity of nomological networks are straightforward. However, nomological networks are often based on a combination of psychological scales and background variables, such as socioeconomic status, education, and sex. The use of psychological scales to validate other psychological scales can lead to an infinite regression in which each scale in the network that is used to validate the target construct requires validation itself. If this issue has been dealt with, the statistical testing of nomological networks can be done in path analyses or MIMIC model (multiple indicators multiple causes; Jöreskog & Goldberger, 1975), in which the background variables predict a latent factor that is measured by the target instrument as well as the other instruments studied to address the validity of the target instrument.

1.2.2.3 Metric or Measurement Unit Equivalence

Instruments show metric (or measurement unit) equivalence if their measurement scales have the same units of measurement, but a different origin (such as the Celsius and Kelvin scales in temperature measurement). This type of equivalence assumes interval- or ratio-level scores (with the same measurement units in each culture). Metric equivalence is found when a source of bias creates an offset in the scale in one or more groups, but does not affect the relative scores of individuals within each cultural group. For example, social desirability and stimulus familiarity influence questionnaire scores more in some cultures than in others, but they may influence individuals within a given cultural group in a fairly homogeneous way.

1.2.2.4 Scalar or Full Score Equivalence

Scalar equivalence assumes an identical interval or ratio scale in all cultural groups. If (and only if) this condition is met, direct cross-cultural comparisons can be made. It is the only type of equivalence that allows for the conclusion that average scores obtained in two cultures are different or equal.

1.3 BIAS AND EQUIVALENCE: ASSESSMENT AND APPLICATIONS

1.3.1 Identification Procedures

Most procedures to address bias and equivalence only require cross-cultural data with a target instrument as input; there are also procedures that rely on data obtained with additional instruments. The procedures using additional data are more open, inductive, and exploratory in nature, whereas procedures that are based only on data with the target instrument are more closed, deductive, and hypothesis testing. An answer to the question of whether additional data are needed, such as new tests or other ways of data collection such as cognitive pretesting, depends on many factors. Collecting additional data is the more laborious and time-consuming way of establishing equivalence that is more likely to be used if fewer cross-cultural data with the target instrument are available; the cultural and linguistic distance between the cultures in the study are larger, fewer theories about the target construct are available, or when the need is more felt to develop a culturally appropriate measure (possibly with culturally specific parts).

1.3.1.1 Detection of Construct Bias and Construct Equivalence

The detection of construct bias and construct equivalence usually requires an exploratory approach in which local surveys, focus group discussions, or in-depth interviews are held with members of a community are used to establish which attitudes and behaviors are associated with a specific construct. The assessment of method bias also requires the collection of additional data, alongside the target instrument. Yet, a more guided search is needed than in the assessment of construct bias. For example, examining the presence of sample bias requires the collection of data about the composition and background of the sample, such as educational level, age, and sex. Similarly, identifying the potential influence of cross-cultural differences in response styles requires their assessment. If a bipolar instrument is used, acquiescence can be assessed by studying the levels of agreement with both the positive and negative items; however, if a unipolar instrument is used, information about acquiescence should be derived from other measures. Item bias analyses are based on closed procedures; for example, scores on items are summed and the total score is used to identify groups in different cultures with a similar performance. Item scores are then compared in groups with a similar performance from different cultures.

1.3.1.2 Detection of Structural Equivalence

The assessment of structural equivalence employs closed procedures. Correlations, covariances, or distance measures between items or subtests are used to assess their dimensionality. Coordinates on these dimensions (e.g., factor loadings) are compared across cultures. Similarity of coordinates is used as evidence in favor of structural equivalence. The absence of structural equivalence is interpreted as evidence in favor of construct inequivalence. Structural equivalence techniques, as they are closed procedures, are helpful to determine the cross-cultural similarity of constructs, but they may need to be complemented by open procedures, such as focus group discussions to provide a comprehensive coverage of the definition of construct in a cultural group. Functional equivalence, on the other hand, is based on a study of the convergent and divergent validity of an instrument measuring a target construct. Its assessment is based on open procedures, as additional instruments are required to establish this validity.

1.3.1.3 Detection of Metric and Scalar Equivalence

Metric and scalar equivalence are also on closed procedures. SEM is often used to assess relations between items or subtests and their underlying constructs. It can be concluded that open and closed procedures are complementary.

1.3.2 Examples

1.3.2.1 Examples of Construct Bias

An interesting study of construct bias has been reported by Patel, Abas, Broadhead, Todd, and Reeler (2001). These authors were interested how depression is expressed in Zimbabwe. In interviews with Shona speakers, they found that:

> Multiple somatic complaints such as headaches and fatigue are the most common presentations of depression. On inquiry, however, most patients freely admit to cognitive and emotional symptoms. Many somatic symptoms, especially those related to the heart and the head, are cultural metaphors for fear or grief. Most depressed individuals attribute their symptoms to "thinking too much" (kufungisisa), to a supernatural cause, and to social stressors. Our data confirm the view that although depression in developing countries often presents with somatic symptoms, most patients do not attribute their symptoms to a somatic illness and cannot be said to have "pure" somatisation. (p. 482)

This conceptualization of depression is only partly overlapping with western theories and models. As a consequence, western instruments will have a limited suitability, particularly with regard to the etiology of the syndrome.

There are few studies that are aimed at demonstrating construct inequivalence, but studies have found that the underlying constructs were not (entirely) comparable and hence, found evidence for construct inequivalence. For example, De Jong and colleagues (2005) examined the cross-cultural construct equivalence of the Structured Interview for Disorders to of Extreme Stress (SIDES), an instrument designed to assess symptoms of Disorders of Extreme Stress Not Otherwise Specified (DESNOS). The interview aims to measure the psychiatric sequelae of interpersonal victimization, notably the consequences of war, genocide, persecution, torture, and terrorism. The interview covers six clusters, each with a few items; examples are alterations in affect regulation and impulses. Participants completed the SIDES as a part of an epidemiological survey conducted between 1997 and 1999 among large samples of survivors of war or mass violence in Algeria, Ethiopia, and Gaza. Exploratory factor analyses were conducted for each of the six clusters; the cross-cultural equivalence of the six clusters was tested in a multisample, confirmatory factor analysis. The Ethiopian sample was sufficiently large to be split up into two subsamples. Equivalence across these subsamples was supported. However, comparisons of this model across countries showed a very poor fit. The authors attributed this lack of equivalence to the poor applicability of various items in these cultural contexts; they provide an interesting table in which they compare the prevalence of various symptoms in these populations with those in field trials to assess Post-Traumatic Stress Disorder that are included in the *DSM–IV* (American Psychiatric Association 2000). The general pattern was that most symptoms were less prevalent in these three areas than reported in the manual and that there were also large differences in prevalence across the three areas. Findings indicated that the factor structure of the SIDES was not stable across samples; thus construct equivalence was not shown. It is not surprising that items with such large cross-cultural differences in endorsement rates are not related in a similar manner across cultures. The authors conclude that more sensitivity for the cultural context and the cultural appropriateness of the instrument would be needed to compile instruments that would be better able to stand cross-cultural validation. It is an interesting feature of the study that the authors illustrate how this could be done by proposing a multistep interdisciplinary method that accommodates universal chronic sequelae of extreme stress and accommodates culture-specific symptoms across a variety of cultures. The procedure illustrates how constructs with only a partial overlap across cultures require a more refined approach to cross-cultural comparisons as shared and unique aspects have to be separated. It may be noted that this approach exemplifies universalism in cross-cultural psychology (Berry et al., 2002), according to which the core of psychological constructs tends to be invariant across cultures but manifestations may take culture-specific forms.

As another example, it has been argued that organizational commitment contains both shared and culture-specific components. Most western research is based on a three-componential model (e.g., Meyer &

Allen, 1991; cf. Van de Vijver & Fischer, 2009) that differentiates between affective, continuance, and normative commitment. Affective commitment is the emotional attachment to organizations, the desire to belong to the organization and identification with the organizational norms, values, and goals. Normative commitment refers to a feeling of obligation to remain with the organization, involving normative pressure and perceived obligations by significant others. Continuance commitment refers to the costs associated with leaving the organization and the perceived need to stay. Wasti (2002) argued that continuance commitment in more collectivistic contexts such as Turkey, loyalty and trust are important and strongly associated with paternalistic management practices. Employers are more likely to give jobs to family members and friends. Employees hired in this way will show more continuance commitment. However, Western measures do not address this aspect of continuance commitment. A meta-analysis by Fischer and Mansell (2007) found that the three components are largely independent in Western countries, but are less differentiated in lower-income contexts. These findings suggest that the three components become more independent with increasing economic affluence.

1.3.2.2 Examples of Method Bias

Method bias has been addressed in several studies. Fernández and Marcopulos (2008) describe how incomparability of norm samples made international comparisons of the Trail Making Test (an instrument to assess attention and cognitive flexibility) impossible: "In some cases, these differences are so dramatic that normal subjects could be classified as pathological and vice versa, depending upon the norms used" (p. 243). Sample bias (as a source of method bias) can be an important rival hypothesis to explain cross-cultural score differences in acculturation studies. Many studies compare host and immigrant samples on psychological characteristics. However, immigrant samples that are studied in Western countries often have lower levels of education and income than the host samples. As a consequence, comparisons of raw scores on psychological instruments may be confounded by sample differences. Arends-Tóth and Van de Vijver (2008) examined similarities and differences in family support in five cultural groups in the Netherlands (Dutch mainstreamers, Turkish-, Moroccan-, Surinamese-, and Antillean-Dutch). In each group, provided support was larger than received support, parents provided and received more support than siblings, and emotional support was stronger than functional support. The cultural differences in mean scores were small for family exchange and quality of relationship, and moderate for frequency of contact. A correction for individual background characteristics (notably age and education) reduced the effect size of cross-cultural differences from 0.04 (proportion of variance accounted for by culture before correction) to 0.03 (after correction) for support and from 0.07 to 0.03 for contact. So, it was concluded that the cross-cultural differences in raw scores were partly unrelated to cultural background and had to be accounted for by background characteristics.

The study of response styles (and social desirability that is usually not viewed as a style, but also involves self-presentation tactics) enjoys renewed interest in cross-cultural psychology. In a comparison of European countries, Van Herk, Poortinga, and Verhallen (2004) found that Mediterranean countries, particularly Greece, showed higher acquiescent and extreme responding than Northwestern countries in surveys on consumer research. They interpreted these differences in terms of the individualism versus collectivism dimension. In a meta-analysis across 41 countries, Fischer, Fontaine, Van de Vijver, and Van Hemert (2009) calculated acquiescence scores for various scales in the personality, social psychological, and organizational domains. A small but significant percentage (3.1%) of the overall variance was shared among all scales, pointing to a systematic influence of response styles in cross-cultural comparisons. In presumably the largest study of response styles, Harzing (2006) found consistent cross-cultural differences in acquiescence and extremity responding across 26 countries. Cross-cultural differences in response styles are systematically related to various country characteristics. Acquiescence and extreme responding are more prevalent in countries with higher scores on Hofstede's collectivism and power distance, and GLOBE's uncertainty avoidance. Furthermore, extraversion (at the country level) is a positive predictor of acquiescence and extremity scoring. Finally, she found that English-language questionnaires tend to evoke less extremity scoring and that answering items in one's native language is associated with more extremity scoring. Cross-cultural findings on social desirability also point to the presence of systematic differences in that more affluent countries show, on average, lower scores on social desirability (Van Hemert, Van de Vijver, Poortinga, & Georgas, 2002).

Instrument bias is a common source of bias in cognitive tests. An example can be found in Piswanger's (1975) application of the Viennese Matrices Test (Formann & Piswanger 1979). A Raven-like figural inductive reasoning test was administered to high-school students in Austria, Nigeria, and Togo (educated in Arabic). The most striking findings were the cross-cultural differences in item difficulties related to identifying and applying rules in a horizontal direction (i.e., left to right). This was interpreted as bias in terms of the different directions in writing Latin-based languages as opposed to Arabic.

1.3.2.3 Examples of Item Bias

More studies of item bias have been published than of any other form of bias. All widely used statistical techniques have been used to identify item bias. Item bias is often viewed as an undesirable item characteristic that should be eliminated. As a consequence, items that are presumably biased are eliminated prior to the cross-cultural comparisons of scores. However, it is also possible to view item bias as a source of cross-cultural differences that is not to be eliminated but requires further examination (Poortinga & Van der Flier, 1988). The background of this view is that item bias, which by definition involves systematic cross-cultural differences, can be interpreted as referring to culture-specifics. Biased items provide information about cross-cultural differences on other constructs than the target construct. For example in a study on intended self-presentation strategies by students in job interviews involving 10 countries, it was found that the dress code yielded biased items (Sandal et al., in preparation). Dress code was an important aspect of self-presentation in more traditional countries (such as Iran and Ghana) whereas informal dress was more common in more modern countries (such as Germany and Norway). These items provide important information about self-presentation in these countries, which cannot be dismissed as bias but that should be eliminated.

Experiences accumulated over a period of more than 40 years after Cleary and Hilton's (1968) first study have not led to new insights as to which items tend to be biased. In fact, one of the complaints has been the lack of accumulation. Educational testing has been an important domain of application of item bias. Linn (1993), in a review of the findings, came to the sobering conclusion that no general findings have emerged about which item characteristics are associated with item bias; he argued that item difficulty was the only characteristic that was more or less associated with bias. The item bias tradition has not led to widely accepted practices about item writing for multicultural assessment. One of the problems in accumulating knowledge from the item bias tradition about item writing may be the often specific nature of the bias. Van Schilt-Mol (2007) identified item bias in educational tests (Cito tests) in Dutch primary schools using psychometric procedures. She then attempted to identify the source of the item bias, using a content analysis of the items and interviews with teachers and immigrant pupils. Based on this analysis, she changed the original items and administered the new version. The modified items showed little or no bias, indicating that she successfully identified and removed the bias source. Her study illustrates an effective, though laborious way to deal with bias. The source of the bias was often item specific (such as words or pictures that were not equally known in all cultural groups) and no general conclusions about how to avoid items could be drawn from her study.

Item bias has also been studied in personality and attitude measures. Although I do not know of any systematic comparison, the picture that emerges from the literature is one of great variability in numbers of biased items across instruments. There are numerous examples in which many or even a majority of the items turned out to be biased. If so many items are biased, serious validity issues have to be addressed, such as potential construct bias and adequate construct coverage in the remaining items. A few studies have examined the nature of item bias in personality questionnaires. Sheppard, Han, Colarelli, Dai, and King (2006) examined bias in the Hogan Personality Inventory in Caucasian and African-Americans, who had applied for unskilled factory jobs. Although the group mean differences were trivial, more than a third of the items showed item bias. Items related to cautiousness tended to be potentially biased in favor of African-Americans. Ryan, Horvath, Ployhart, Schmitt, and Slade (2000) were interested in determining sources of item bias global employee opinion surveys. Analyzing data from a 36-country study involving more than 50,000 employees, they related item bias statistics (derived from item response theory) to country characteristics. Hypotheses about specific item contents and Hofstede's (2001) dimensions were only partly confirmed; the authors found that more dissimilar countries showed more item bias. The positive relation between the size of global cultural differences and item bias may well generalize to other studies. Sandal et al. (in preparation) also found more bias between countries that are culturally further apart. If this conclusion would hold across other studies, it would imply that a larger cultural distance between countries can be expected to be associated with more valid cross-cultural differences and more item bias. Bingenheimer, Raudenbush, Leventhal, and Brooks-Gunn (2005) studied bias in the Environmental Organization and Caregiver Warmth scales that were adapted from several versions of the HOME Inventory (Bradley, 1994; Bradley, Caldwell, Rock, Hamrick, & Harris, 1988). The scales are measures of parenting climate. There were about 4000 Latino, African-American, and European American parents living in Chicago that participated. Procedures based on item response theory were used to identify bias. Biased items were not thematically clustered.

1.3.2.4 Examples of Studies of Multiple Sources of Bias

Some studies have addressed *multiple sources of bias*. Thus, Hofer, Chasiotis, Friedlmeier, Busch, and Campos (2005) studied various forms of bias in a thematic apperception test, which is an implicit measure of power and affiliation motives. The instrument was administered in Cameroon, Costa Rica, and Germany. Construct bias in the coding of responses was addressed in discussions with local informants; the discussions pointed to the equivalence of coding rules. Method bias was addressed by examining the relation between test scores and background variables such as age and education. No strong evidence was found. Finally, using loglinear models, some items were found to be biased. As another example, Meiring, Van de Vijver, Rothmann, and Barrick (2005) studied construct, item, and method bias of cognitive and personality tests in a sample of 13,681 participants who had applied for entry-level police jobs in the South African Police Services. The sample consisted of Whites, Indians, Coloreds, and nine Black groups. The cognitive instruments produced very good construct equivalence, as often found in the literature (e.g., Berry, Poortinga, Segall, & Dasen, 2002; Van de Vijver, 1997); moreover, logistic regression procedures identified almost no item bias (given the huge sample size, effect size measures instead of statistical significance were used as criterion for deciding whether items were biased). The personality instrument (i.e., the 16 PFI Questionnaire that is an imported and widely used instrument in job selection in South Africa) showed more structural equivalence problems. Several scales of the personality questionnaire revealed construct bias in various ethnic groups. Using analysis of variance procedures, very little item bias in the personality scales was observed. Method bias did not have any impact on the (small) size of the cross-cultural differences in the personality scales. In addition, several personality scales revealed low-internal consistencies, notably in the Black groups. It was concluded that the cognitive tests were suitable as instruments for multicultural assessment, whereas bias and low-internal consistencies limited the usefulness of the personality scales.

1.4 IDENTIFICATION OF BIAS IN STRUCTURAL EQUATION MODELING

There is a fair amount of convergence on how equivalence should be addressed in structural equation models. I mention here the often quoted classification by Vandenberg (2002; Vandenberg & Lance, 2000) that, if fully applied, has eight steps:

1. A global test of the equality of covariance matrices across groups.
2. A test of *configural invariance* (also labeled weak factorial invariance) in which the presence of the same pattern of fixed and free factor loadings is tested for each group.
3. A test of *metric invariance* (also labeled strong factorial invariance) in which factor loadings for identical items are tested to be invariant across groups.
4. A test of *scalar invariance* (also labeled strict invariance) in which identity of intercepts when identical items are regressed on the latent variables.
5. A test of invariance of unique variances across groups.
6. A test of invariance of factor variances across groups.
7. A test of invariance of factor covariances across groups.
8. A test of the null hypothesis of invariant factor means across groups. The latter is a test of cross-cultural differences in unobserved means.

The first test (the local test of invariance of covariance matrices) is infrequently used, presumably because researchers are typically more interested in modeling covariances than merely testing their cross-cultural invariance and the observation that covariance matrices are not identical may not be informative about the nature of the difference. The most frequently reported invariance tests involve configural, metric, and scalar invariance (Steps 2 through 4). The latter three types of invariance address relations between observed and latent variables. As these involve the measurement aspects of the model, they are also referred to as measurement invariance (or measurement equivalence). The last four types of invariance (Steps 5 through 8) address characteristics of latent variables and their relations; therefore, they are referred to as structural invariance (or structural equivalence).

As indicated earlier, there is a confusing difference in the meaning of the term "structural equivalence," as employed in the cross-cultural psychology tradition, and "structural equivalence" (or structural invariance), as employed in the SEM tradition. Structural equivalence in the cross-cultural psychology tradition addresses the question of whether an instrument measures the same underlying construct(s) in different cultural groups and is usually examined in exploratory factor analyses. Identity of factors is taken as evidence in favor of structural equivalence, which then means that the structure of the underlying construct(s) is identical across groups. Structural equivalence in the structural equation tradition refers to identical variances and covariances of structural variables (latent factors) of the model. Whereas structural equivalence addresses links between observed and latent variables, structural invariance does not involve observed variables at all. Structural equivalence in the cross-cultural psychology tradition is close to what in the SEM tradition is between configural invariance and metric invariance (measurement equivalence).

I now describe procedures that have been proposed in the SEM tradition to identify the three types of bias (construct, method, and item bias) as well as illustrations of the procedures; an overview of the procedures (and their problems) can be found in Table 1.1.

1.4.1 Construct Bias

1.4.1.1 Procedure

The structural equivalence tradition started with the question of how invariance of any parameter of a structural equation model can be tested. The aim of the procedures is to establish such invariance in a statistically

TABLE 1.1

Overview of Types of Bias and Structural Equation Modeling (SEM) Procedures to their Identification

Type of Bias	Definition	SEM Procedure for Identification	Problems
Construct	A construct differs across cultures, usually due to an incomplete overlap of construct-relevant behaviors.	Multigroup conformatory factor analysis, testing configural invariance (identity of patterning of loadings and factors).	Cognitive interviews and ethnographic information may be needed to assess whether construct is adequately captured.
Method	Generic term for all sources of bias due to factors often described in the methods section of empirical papers. Three types of method bias have been defined, depending on whether the bias comes from the sample, administration, or instrument.	Confirmatory factor analysis or path analysis of models that evaluate the influence of method factors (e.g., by testing method factors).	Many studies do not collect data about method factors, which makes the testing of method factor impossible.
Item	Anomalies at the item level; an item is biased if respondents from different cultures with the same standing on the underlying construct (e.g., they are equally intelligent) do not have the same mean score on the item.	Multigroup confirmatory factor analysis, testing scalar invariance (testing identity of intercepts when identical items are regressed on the latent variables; assumes support for configural and metric equivalence).	Model of scalar equivalence, prerequisite for a test of items bias, may not be supported. Reasons for item bias may be unclear.

rigorous manner. The focus of the efforts has been on the comparability of previously tested data. The framework does not specify or prescribe how instruments have to be compiled to be suitable for cross-cultural comparisons; rather, the approach tests corollaries of the assumption that the instrument is adequate for comparative purposes. The procedure for addressing this question usually follows the steps described before, with an emphasis on the establishment of configural, metric, and scalar invariance (weak, strong, and strict invariance).

1.4.1.2 Examples

Caprara, Barbaranelli, Bermúdez, Maslach, and Ruch (2000) tested the cross-cultural generalizability of the Big Five Questionnaire (BFQ), which is a measure of the Five Factor Model in large samples from Italy, Germany, Spain, and the United States. The authors used exploratory factor analysis, simultaneous component analysis (Kiers, 1990), and confirmatory factor analysis. The Italian, American, German, and Spanish versions of the BFQ showed factor structures that were comparable: "Because the pattern of relationships among the BFQ facet-scales is basically the same in the four different countries, different data analysis strategies converge in pointing to a substantial equivalence among the constructs that these scales are measuring" (p. 457). These findings support the universality of the five-factor model. At a more detailed level the analysis methods did not yield completely identical results. The confirmatory factor analysis picked up more sources of cross-cultural differences. The authors attribute the discrepancies to the larger sensitivity of confirmatory models.

Another example comes from the values domain. Like the previous study, it addresses relations between the (lack of) structural equivalence and country indicators. Another interesting aspect of the study is the use of multidimensional scaling where most studies use factor analysis. Fontaine, Poortinga, Delbeke, and Schwartz (2008) assessed the structural equivalence of the values domain, based on the Schwartz value theory, in a dataset from 38 countries, each represented by a student and a teacher sample. The authors found that the theoretically expected structure provided an excellent representation of the average value structure across samples, although sampling fluctuation causes smaller and larger deviations from this average structure. Furthermore, sampling fluctuation could not account for all these deviations. The closer inspection of the deviations shows that higher levels of societal development of a country were associated with a larger contrast between protection and growth values. Studies of structural equivalence in large-scale datasets open a new window on cross-cultural differences. There are no models of the emergence of constructs that accompany changes in a country, such as increases in the level of affluence. The study of covariation between social developments and salience of psychological constructs is largely uncharted domain.

A third example from the values domain comes from Spini (2003), who examined the measurement equivalence of 10 value types from the Schwartz Value Survey in a sample of 3859 students from 21 different countries. Acceptable levels of configural and metric equivalence were found for all values, except Hedonism. The hypothesis of scalar equivalence was rejected for all value types. Although the study by Fontaine et al. (2008) tested the universality of the global structure whereas Spini tested the equivalence of the separate scales, the two studies show remarkable resemblance in that structural equivalence was relatively well supported.

Arends-Tóth and Van de Vijver (2008) studied associations between well-being and family relationships among five cultural groups in the Netherlands (Dutch mainstreamers, and Turkish, Moroccan, Surinamese, and Antillean immigrants). Two aspects of relationships were studied: family values, which refer to obligations and beliefs about family relationships, and family ties that involve more behavior-related relational aspects. A SEM model was tested in which the two aspects of relationships predicted a latent factor, called well-being, which was measured by loneliness and general and mental health. Multisample models showed invariance of the regression weights of the two predictors and of the factor loadings of loneliness and health. Other model components showed some cross-cultural variation (correlations between the errors of the latent and outcome variables).

Van de Vijver (2002) examined the comparability of scores on tests of inductive reasoning in samples of 704 Zambian, 877 Turkish, and 632 Dutch pupils from the highest two grades of primary and the lowest two grades of secondary school. In addition to the two tests of inductive reasoning (employing figures and nonsense words as stimuli, respectively), three tests were administered that assessed cognitive components that are assumed to be important in inductive thinking (i.e., classification, rule generation, and rule testing). SEM was used to test the fit of a MIMIC model in which the three component tests predicted a latent factor, labeled inductive reasoning, which was measured by the two tests mentioned. Configural invariance was supported, metric equivalence invariance was partially supported, and tests of scalar equivalence showed a poor fit. It was concluded that comparability of test scores across these groups was problematic and that cross-cultural score differences were probably influenced by auxiliary constructs such as test exposure. Finally, Davidov (2008) examined invariance of a 21-item instrument measuring human values of the European Social Survey that was administered in 25 countries. Multigroup confirmatory factor analysis did not support configural and metric invariance across these countries. Metric equivalence was only established after a reduction in the number of countries to 14 and of the original 10 latent factors to seven.

1.4.2 Method Bias

1.4.2.1 Procedure

The study of method bias in SEM is straightforward. Indicators of the source of method bias, which are typically viewed as confounding variables, can be introduced in a path model, which enables the statistical evaluation of their impact. Below examples of studies in response styles are given, but other examples can be easily envisaged, such as including years of schooling, socioeconomic status indicators, or interviewer characteristics. The problem with the study of method bias is usually not the statistical evaluation but the availability of pertinent data. For example, social desirability is often mentioned as a source of cross-cultural score differences but infrequently measured; only when such data are available, an evaluation of its impact can be carried out.

1.4.2.2 Examples

Various authors have addressed the evaluation of response sets, notably acquiescence and extremity scoring (e.g., Cheung & Rensvold, 2000; Mirowsky & Ross, 1991; Watson, 1992); yet, there are relatively few systematic SEM studies of method bias compared to the numerous studies on other types of bias. Billiet and McClendon (2000) worked with a balanced set of Likert items that measured ethnic threat and distrust in politics in a sample of Flemish respondents. The authors found a good fit for a model with three latent factors: two content factors (ethnic threat and distrust in politics that are negatively correlated) with positive and negative slopes according to the wording of the items, and one uncorrelated common style factor with all positive loadings. The style factor was identified as acquiescence, given that its correlation with the sum of agreements was very high. Welkenhuysen-Gybels, Billiet, and Cambré (2003) applied a similar approach in a cross-cultural study.

1.4.3 Item Bias

1.4.3.1 Procedure

Item bias in SEM is closely associated with the test of scalar invariance. It is tested by examining invariance of intercepts when an item is regressed on its latent factor (fourth step in Vandenberg's procedure). The procedure is different from those described in the differential item functioning tradition (e.g., Camilli & Shepard, 1994; Holland & Wainer, 1993). Although it is impossible to capture the literally hundreds of procedures in this tradition that have been proposed, some basic ideas prevail. The most important is the relevance of comparing item statistics per score level. The latter are usually defined by splitting up a sample in subsamples of respondents with similar scores (such as splitting up the sample in low, medium, and high scorers). Corollaries of the assumption that equal sum scores on the (unidimensional) instrument reflect an equal standing on the latent trait are then tested. For example, the Mantel–Haenszel procedure tests whether the mean scores of persons with the same sum scores are identical across cultures (as they should be for an unbiased item). The SEM procedure tests whether the (linear) relation between observed and latent variable is identical across cultures (equal slopes and intercepts). From a theoretical point of view, the Mantel–Haenszel and SEM procedures are very different; for example, the Mantel–Haenszel procedure is based on a nonlinear relation between item score and latent trait whereas SEM employs a linear model. Also, both employ different ways to get access to the latent trait (through covariances in SEM and slicing up data in score levels in the Mantel–Haenszel procedure). Yet, from a practical point of view, the two procedures will often yield convergent results. It has been shown that using the Mantel–Haenszel is conceptually identical to assuming a Rasch model to apply to the scale and testing identity of item parameters across groups (Fischer, 1993). The nonlinear (though strictly monotonous) relation between item and latent construct score that is assumed in the Rasch model will often not differ much from the linear relation assumed by SEM. Convergence of results is therefore not surprising, in particular when items show a strong bias.

It is an attractive feature of SEM that biased items do not need to be eliminated from the instrument prior to the cross-cultural comparison (as are often done in analyses based on other statistical models). Biased items can be retained as culture-specific indicators. Partial measurement invariance allows for including both shared and nonshared items in cross-cultural comparisons. Scholderer, Grunert, and Brunsø (2005) describe a procedure for identifying intercept differences and correcting for these differences in the estimation of latent means.

1.4.3.2 Examples

Two types of procedures can be found in the literature that address item bias. In the first and most common type, item bias is part of a larger exercise to study equivalence and is tested after configural and metric equivalence have been established. The second kind of application adds information from background characteristics to determine to what extent these characteristics can help to identify bias.

De Beuckelaer, Lievens, and Swinnen (2007) provide an example of the first type of application. They tested the measurement equivalence of a global organizational survey that measures six work climate factors in 24 countries from West Europe, East Europe, North America, the Americas, Middle East, Africa, and the Asia-Pacific region; the sample comprised 31,315 employees and survey consultants. The survey instrument showed configural and metric equivalence of the six-factor structure, but scalar equivalence was not supported. Many intercept differences of items were found; the authors argued that this absence was possibly a consequence of response styles. They split up the countries in regions with similar countries or with the same language. Within these more narrowly defined regions (e.g., Australia, Canada, United Kingdom, and the United States as the English-speaking region), scalar equivalence was found. A study by Prelow, Michaels, Reyes, Knight, and Barrera (2002) provides a second example. These authors tested the equivalence of the Children's Coping Strategies Checklist in a sample of 319 European American, African-American, and Mexican American adolescents from low-income, inner-city families. The coping questionnaire consisted of two major styles, active coping and avoidant coping, each of which comprised different subscales. Equivalence was tested per subscale. Metric equivalence was strongly supported for all subscales of the coping questionnaire; yet, intercept invariance was found in few cases. Most of the salient differences in intercept were found between the African-American and Mexican American groups.

An example of the second type of item bias study has been described by Grayson, Mackinnon, Jorm, Creasey, and Broe (2000). These authors were interested in the question of whether physical disorders influence scores on the Center for Epidemiological Studies Depression Scale (CES-D) among elderly, thereby leading to false-positives in assessment procedures. The authors recruited a sample of 506 participants aged 75 or older living in their community in Sydney, Australia. The fit of a MIMIC model was tested. The latent factor, labeled depression, was measured by the CES-D items; item bias was defined as the presence of significant direct effects of background characteristics on items (so, no cultural variation was involved). Various physical disorders (such as mobility, disability, and peripheral vascular disease) had a direct impact on particular item scores in addition to the indirect path through depression. The authors concluded that the CES-D score is "polluted with contributions unrelated to depression" (p. 279). The second example is due to Jones (2003), who assessed cognitive functioning among African-American and European American older adults (>50 years) in Florida during a telephone interview. He also used a MIMIC model. Much item bias was found (operationalized here as differences in both measurement weights and intercepts of item parcels on a general underlying cognition factor). Moreover, the bias systematically favored the European American group. After correction for this bias, the size of the cross-cultural differences in scores was reduced by 60%. Moreover, various background characteristics had direct effects on item parcels, which were interpreted as evidence for item bias.

The two types of applications provide an important difference in perspective on item bias. The first approach only leads to straightforward findings if the null hypothesis of scalar equivalence is confirmed; if, as is often the case, no unambiguous support for scalar equivalence is found, it is often difficult to find reasons that are methodologically compelling for the lack of scalar equivalence. So, the conclusion can then be drawn that scalar equivalence is not supported and a close inspection of the deviant parameters will indicate those items that are responsible for the poor fit. However, such an observation usually does not suggest a substantive reason for the poor fit. The second approach starts from a more focused search for a specific antecedent of item bias. As a consequence, the results of these studies are easier to interpret. This observation is in line with a common finding in item bias studies of educational and cognitive tests (e.g., Holland & Wainer, 1993): Without specific hypotheses about the sources of item bias, a content analysis of which items are biased and unbiased hardly ever leads to interpretable results as to the reasons for the bias.

The literature on equivalence testing is still scattered and is not yet ready for a full-fledged meta-analysis of the links between characteristics of instruments, samples, and their cultures on the one hand, and levels of equivalence on the other hand; yet, it is already quite clear that studies of scalar equivalence often do not support the direct comparison of scores across countries. Findings based on SEM and findings based on other item bias techniques point in the same direction: Item bias is more pervasive than we may conveniently think and when adequately tested, scalar equivalence is often not supported. The widespread usage of analyses of (co) variance, *t*-tests, and other techniques that assume full score equivalence, is not based on adequate invariance testing. The main reason for not bothering about scalar invariance prior to comparing means across cultures is opportunistic: various studies have compared the size of cross-cultural differences before and after correction for item bias and most of these have found that item bias does not tend to favor a single group and that correction for item bias usually does not affect the size of cross-cultural differences (Van de Vijver, 2011).

1.5 STATISTICAL MODELING AND BIAS: A SWOT ANALYSIS

After the description of a framework for bias and equivalence and a description of various examples in which the framework was employed, the stage is set for an evaluation of the contribution of SEM to the study of bias and equivalence. The evaluation takes the form of a SWOT analysis (strengths, weaknesses, opportunities, and threats).

The main *strength* of SEM is the systematic manner in which invariance can be tested. There is no other statistical theory that allows for such a fine-grained, flexible, and integrated analysis of equivalence. No other older approach combines these characteristics; for example, a combination of exploratory factor analysis and item bias analysis could be used for examining the configural and scalar equivalence, respectively. However, the two kinds of procedures are conceptually unrelated. As a consequence, partial invariance is difficult to incorporate in such analyses. Furthermore, SEM has been instrumental in putting equivalence testing on the agenda of cross-cultural researchers and in stimulating the interest in cross-cultural studies.

The first *weakness* of equivalence testing using SEM is related to the large discrepancy between the advanced level of statistical theorizing behind the framework and the far from advanced level of available theories about cross-cultural similarities and differences. The level of sophistication of our conceptual models of cross-cultural differences is nowhere near the statistical sophistication available to test these differences. As a consequence, it is difficult to strike a balance between conceptual and statistical considerations in equivalence testing. The literature shows that it is tempting to use multigroup factor analysis in a mechanical manner by relying entirely on statistical, usually significance criteria to draw conclusions about levels of equivalence. An equivalence test using SEM can easily become synonymous with a demonstration that scores can be compared in a bias-free manner. In my view, there are two kinds of problems with these mechanical applications of equivalence tests. First, there are statistical problems with the interpretation of fit tests. Particularly in large-scale cross-cultural studies, the lack of convergence of information provided by the common fit statistics, combined with the absence of adequate Monte Carlo studies and experience with fit statistics in similar cases, can create problems in choosing the most adequate model. In these studies, it is difficult to tease apart fit problems due to conceptually trivial sample particulars that do not challenge the interpretation of the model as being equivalent and fit problems due to misspecifications of the model that are conceptually consequential. Secondly, equivalence testing in SEM can easily become a tool that, possibly inadvertently, uses statistical sophistication to compensate for problems with the adequacy of instruments or samples. Thus, studies using convenience samples have problems of external validity, whatever the statistical sophistication used to deal with the data. Also, it is relatively common in cross-cultural survey research to employ short instruments. Such instruments may yield a poor rendering of the underlying construct and may capitalize on item specifics, particularly in a cross-cultural framework.

In addition to statistical problems, there is another and probably more salient problem of equivalence testing in a SEM framework: Sources of bias can be easily overlooked in standard equivalence tests based on confirmatory factor analysis, thereby reaching overly liberal conclusions about equivalence. Thus, construct inequivalence cannot be identified in deductive equivalence testing (i.e., testing in which only data from a target instrument are available, as is the case in confirmatory factor analysis). There is a tendency in the literature to apply closely translated questionnaires without adequately considering adaptation issues (Hambleton, Merenda, & Spielberger, 2005). Without extensive pretesting, the use of interviews to determine the accuracy of items, or the inclusion of additional instruments to check the validity of a target instrument, it is impossible to determine whether closely translated items are the best possible items in a specific culture. Culture-specific indicators of common constructs may have been missed. The focus on using identical instruments in many cultures may lead to finding superficial similarities between cultures, because the instrument compilation may have driven the study to an emphasis on similarities. The various sources of bias (construct, method, and items) cannot be investigated adequately if only data from the target instrument are available. Various sources of bias can be studied in SEM, but most applications start from a narrow definition of bias that capitalizes on confirmatory factor analysis without considering or having additional data to address bias. It should be noted that the problem of not considering all bias sources in cross-cultural studies is not an intrinsic characteristic of SEM, but a regrettable, self-imposed limitation in its use.

A first *opportunity* of equivalence testing using SEM is its scope to establish a closer link between the statistical modeling and inference levels. The discrepancy between the widespread usage of statistical techniques that compare mean scores across countries, such as analysis of variance, and the frequent observation in SEM procedures that conditions of scalar equivalence are not fulfilled defines a clear mission for SEM researchers. A second opportunity is related to the distinction between significance and relevance. It is quite clear that blind applications of significance testing often do not yield meaningful results; however, more work is needed to identify boundaries of practical significance. How much lack of fit can be tolerated before different substantive conclusions have to be drawn?

The main *threat* is that SEM procedures remain within the purview of SEM researchers. Usage of the procedures has not (yet?) become popular among substantive researchers. There is a danger that SEM researchers keep on "preaching the gospel to the choir" by providing solutions to increasingly complex technical issues without linking questions from substantive researchers and determining how SEM can help to solve substantive problems and advance our theorizing.

1.6 CONCLUSIONS

Statistical procedures in the behavioral and social sciences are tools to improve research quality. This also holds for the role of SEM procedures in the study of equivalence and bias. In order to achieve a high quality, a combination of various types of expertise is needed in cross-cultural studies. SEM procedures can greatly contribute to the quality of cross-cultural studies, but more interaction between substantive and method researchers is needed to realize this potential. It is not a foregone conclusion that the potential of SEM procedures will materialize and that the threats of these procedures will not materialize. We need to appreciate that large-scale cross-cultural studies require many different types of expertise; it is unrealistic to assume that there are many researchers who have all the expertise required to conduct such studies. Substantive experts are needed with knowledge of the target construct, next to cultural experts with knowledge about construct in the target context, next to measurement experts who can convert substantive knowledge in adequate measurement procedures, next to statistical experts who can test bias and equivalence in a study. The strength of a chain is defined by the strength of the weakest link; this also holds for the quality of cross-cultural studies. SEM has great potential for cross-cultural studies, but it will be able to achieve this potential only in close interaction with expertise from various other domains.

REFERENCES

American Psychiatric Association. (2000). Diagnostic and Statistical Manual of Mental Disorders DSM-IV-R. Washington, DC: Author.

Aquilino, W. S. (1994). Interviewer mode effects in surveys of drug and alcohol use. *Public Opinion Quarterly, 58,* 210–240.

Arends-Tóth, J. V., & Van de Vijver, F. J. R. (2008). Family relationships among immigrants and majority members in the Netherlands: The role of acculturation. *Applied Psychology: An International Review, 57,* 466–487.

Azhar, M. Z., & Varma, S. L. (2000). Mental illness and its treatment in Malaysia. In I. Al-Issa (Ed.), *Al-Junun: Mental illness in the Islamic world* (pp. 163–185). Madison, CT: International Universities Press.

Barrett, P. T., Petrides, K. V., Eysenck, S. B. G., & Eysenck, H. J. (1998). The Eysenck personality questionnaire: An examination of the factorial similarity of P, E, N, and L across 34 countries. *Personality and Individual Differences, 25,* 805–819.

Berry, J. W., Poortinga, Y. H., Segall, M. H., & Dasen, P. R. (2002). *Cross-cultural psychology: Research and applications* (2nd ed.). New York: Cambridge University Press.

Billiet, J. B., & McClendon, M. J. (2000). Modeling acquiescence in measurement models for two balanced sets of items. *Structural Equation Modeling, 7,* 608–628.

Bingenheimer, J. B., & Raudenbush, S. W., Leventhal, T., & Brooks-Gunn, J. (2005) Measurement equivalence and differential item functioning in family psychology. *Journal of Family Psychology, 19,* 441–455.

Bradley, R. H. (1994). A factor analytic study of the infant-toddler and early childhood versions of the HOME Inventory administered to White, Black, and Hispanic American parents of children born preterm. *Child Development, 65,* 880–888.

Bradley, R. H., Caldwell, B. M., Rock, S. L., Hamrick H. M., & Harris, P. (1988). Home observation for measurement of the environment: Development of a home inventory for use with families having children 6 to 10 years old. *Contemporary Educational Psychology, 13,* 58–71.

Brown, T. A. (2006). *Confirmatory factor analysis for applied research.* New York: Guilford Press.

Camilli, G., & Shepard, L. A. (1994). *Methods for identifying biased test items.* Thousand Oaks, CA: Sage.

Caprara, G. V., Barbaranelli, C., Bermúdez, J., Maslach, C., & Ruch, W. (2000). Multivariate methods for the comparison of factor structures. *Journal of Cross-Cultural Psychology, 31,* 437–464.

Cheung, G. W., & Rensvold, R. B. (2000). Assessing extreme and acquiescence response sets in cross-cultural research using structural equations modeling. *Journal of Cross-Cultural Psychology,* 31, 160–186.

Cleary, T. A., & Hilton, T. L. (1968). An investigation of item bias. *Educational and Psychological Measurement, 28,* 61–75.

Cronbach, L. J., & Meehl, P. E. (1955). Construct validity in psychological tests. *Psychological Bulletin, 52,* 281–302.

Davidov, E. (2008). A cross-country and cross-time comparison of the human values measurements with the second round of the European Social Survey. *Survey Research Methods, 2,* 33–46.

De Beuckelaer, A., Lievens, F., & Swinnen, G. (2007). Measurement equivalence in the conduct of a global organizational survey across countries in six cultural regions. *Journal of Occupational and Organizational Psychology, 80,* 575–600.

De Jong, J. T. V. M., Komproe, I. V., Spinazzola, J., Van der Kolk, B. A., Van Ommeren, M. H., & Marcopulos, F. (2005). DESNOS in three postconflict settings: Assessing cross-cultural construct equivalence. *Journal of Traumatic Stress, 18,* 13–21.

Emenogu, B. C., & Childs, R. A. (2005). Curriculum, translation, and differential functioning of measurement and geometry items. *Canadian Journal of Education, 28,* 128–146.

Fernández, A. L., & Marcopulos, B. A. (2008). A comparison of normative data for the trail making test from several countries: Equivalence of norms and considerations for interpretation. *Scandinavian Journal of Psychology, 49,* 239–246.

Fischer, G. H. (1993). Notes on the Mantel Haenszel procedure and another chi squared test for the assessment of DIF. *Methodika, 7,* 88–100.

Fischer, R., Fontaine, J. R. J., Van de Vijver, F. J. R., &Van Hemert, D. A. (2009). An examination of acquiescent response styles in cross-cultural research. In A. Gari & K. Mylonas (Eds.), *Quod erat demonstrandum: From Herodotus' ethnographic journeys to cross-cultural research* (pp. 137–148). Athens, Greece: Pedio Books Publishing.

Fischer, R., & Mansell, A. (2009). Commitment across cultures: A meta-analytical approach. *Journal of International Business Studies* 40, 1339–1358.

Fontaine, J. R. J., Poortinga, Y. H., Delbeke, L., & Schwartz, S. H. (2008). Structural equivalence of the values domain across cultures: Distinguishing sampling fluctuations from meaningful variation. *Journal of Cross-Cultural Psychology, 39,* 345–365.

Formann, A. K., & Piswanger, K. (1979). *Wiener Matrizen-Test. Ein Rasch-skalierter sprachfreier Intelligenztest* [The Viennese Matrices Test. A Rasch-calibrated non-verbal intelligence test]. Weinheim, Germany: Beltz Test.

Grayson, D. A., Mackinnon, A., Jorm, A. F., Creasey, H., & Broe, G. A. (2000). Item bias in the center for epidemiologic studies depression scale: Effects of physical disorders and disability in an elderly community sample. *Journal of Gerontology: Psychological Sciences, 55,* 273–282.

Hambleton, R. K., Merenda, P., & Spielberger C. (Eds.). (2005). *Adapting educational and psychological tests for cross-cultural assessment* (pp. 3–38). Hillsdale, NJ: Lawrence Erlbaum.

Harzing, A. (2006). Response styles in cross-national survey research: A 26-country study. *Journal of Cross Cultural Management, 6,* 243–266.

Ho, D. Y. F. (1996). Filial piety and its psychological consequences. In M. H. Bond (Ed.), *Handbook of Chinese psychology* (pp. 155–165). Hong Kong: Oxford University Press.

Hofer, J., Chasiotis, A., Friedlmeier, W., Busch, H., & Campos, D. (2005). The measurement of implicit motives in three cultures: Power and affiliation in Cameroon, Costa Rica, and Germany. *Journal of Cross-Cultural Psychology, 36,* 689–716.

Hofstede, G. (2001). *Culture's consequences. Comparing values, behaviors, institutions, and organizations across nations* (2nd ed.). Thousand Oaks, CA: Sage.

Holland, P. W., & Wainer, H. (Eds.). (1993). *Differential item functioning.* Hillsdale, NJ: Erlbaum.

Jensen, A. R. (1980). *Bias in mental testing.* New York: Free Press.

Jones, R. N. (2003). Racial bias in the assessment of cognitive functioning of older adults. *Aging & Mental Health, 7,* 83–102.

Jöreskog, K. G., & Goldberger, A. S. (1975). Estimation of a model with multiple indicators and multiple causes of a single latent variable. *Journal of the American Statistical Association, 70,* 631–639.

Kiers, H. A. L. (1990). *SCA: A program for simultaneous components analysis.* Groningen, the Netherlands: IEC ProGamma.

Linn, R. L. (1993). The use of differential item functioning statistics: A discussion of current practice and future implications. In P. W. Holland & H. Wainer (Eds.), *Differential item functioning* (pp. 349–364). Hillsdale, NJ: Erlbaum.

Lord, F. M. (1977). A study of item bias, using item characteristic curve theory. In Y. H. Poortinga (Ed.), *Basic problems in cross-cultural psychology* (pp. 19–29). Lisse, the Netherlands: Swets & Zeitlinger.

Lord, F. M. (1980). *Applications of item response theory to practical testing problems.* Hillsdale, NJ: Erlbaum.

Lyberg, L., Biemer, P., Collins, M., De Leeuw, E., Dippo, C., Schwarz, N., & Trewin, D. (1997). *Survey measurement and process quality*. New York: Wiley.

McCrae, R. R. (2002). Neo-PI-R data from 36 cultures: Further intercultural comparisons. In R. R. McCrae & J. Allik (Eds.), *The five-factor model of personality across cultures* (pp. 105–125). New York: Kluwer Academic/Plenum Publishers.

Meiring, D., Van de Vijver, F. J. R., Rothmann, S., & Barrick, M. R. (2005). Construct, item, and method bias of cognitive and personality tests in South Africa. *South African Journal of Industrial Psychology, 31*, 1–8.

Meyer, J. P., & Allen, N. J. (1991). A three-component conceptualization of organizational commitment. *Human Resource Management Review, 1*, 61–89.

Mirowsky, J., & Ross, C. E. (1991). Eliminating defense and agreement bias from measures of the sense of control: A 2 × 2 index. *Social Psychology Quarterly, 54*, 127–145.

Patel, V., Abas, M., Broadhead, J., Todd, C., & Reeler, A. (2001). Depression in developing countries: Lessons from Zimbabwe. *British Medical Journal, 322*, 482–484.

Piswanger, K. (1975). *Interkulturelle Vergleiche mit dem Matrizentest von Formann* [Cross-cultural comparisons with Formann's Matrices Test]. Unpublished doctoral dissertation, University of Vienna, Vienna.

Poortinga, Y. H. (1971). Cross-cultural comparison of maximum performance tests: Some methodological aspects and some experiments. *Psychologia Africana, Monograph Supplement, No. 6*.

Poortinga, Y. H. (1989). Equivalence of cross cultural data: An overview of basic issues. *International Journal of Psychology, 24*, 737–756.

Poortinga, Y. H., & Van der Flier, H. (1988). The meaning of item bias in ability tests. In S. H. Irvine & J. W. Berry (Eds.), *Human abilities in cultural context* (pp. 166–183). Cambridge: Cambridge University Press.

Prelow, H. M., Michaels, M. L., Reyes, L., Knight, G. P., & Barrera, M. (2002). Measuring coping in low income European American, African American, and Mexican American adolescents: An examination of measurement equivalence. *Anxiety, Stress, and Coping, 15*, 135–147.

Ryan, A. M., Horvath, M., Ployhart, R. E., Schmitt, N., & Slade, L. A. (2000). Hypothesizing differential item functioning in global employee opinion surveys. *Personnel Psychology, 53*, 541–562.

Sandal, G. M., Van de Vijver, F. J. R., Bye, H. H., Sam, D. L., Amponsah, B., Cakar, N., . . . Kosic, A. (in preparation). *Intended Self-Presentation Tactics in Job Interviews: A 10-Country Study*.

Scholderer, J., Grunert, K. G., & Brunsø, K. (2005). A procedure for eliminating additive bias from cross-cultural survey data. *Journal of Business Research, 58*, 72–78.

Shepard, L., Camilli, G., & Averill, M. (1981). Comparison of six procedures for detecting test item bias using both internal and external ability criteria. *Journal of Educational Statistics, 6*, 317–375.

Sheppard, R., Han, K., Colarelli, S. M., Dai, G., & King, D. W. (2006). Differential item functioning by sex and race in the Hogan personality inventory. *Assessment, 13*, 442–453.

Sireci, S. (2011). Evaluating test and survey items for bias across languages and cultures. In D. M. Matsumoto & F. J. R. van de Vijver (Eds.), *Cross-cultural research methods in psychology* (pp. 216–243). Cambridge: Cambridge University Press.

Spini, D. (2003). Measurement equivalence of 10 value types from the Schwartz value survey across 21 countries. *Journal of Cross-Cultural Psychology, 34*, 3–23.

Steenkamp, J.-B. E. M., & Baumgartner, H. (1998). Assessing measurement invariance in cross-national consumer research. *Journal of Consumer Research, 25,* 78–90.

Suzuki, K., Takei, N., Kawai, M., Minabe, Y., & Mori, N. (2003). Is Taijin Kyofusho a culture-bound syndrome? *American Journal of Psychiatry, 160,* 1358.

Tanaka-Matsumi, J., & Draguns, J. G. (1997). Culture and psychotherapy. In J. W. Berry, M. H. Segall, & C. Kagitcibasi (Eds.), *Handbook of cross-cultural psychology* (Vol. 3, pp. 449–491). Needham Heights, MA: Allyn and Bacon.

Vandenberg, R. J. (2002). Toward a further understanding of and improvement in measurement invariance methods and procedures. *Organizational Research Methods, 5,* 139–158.

Vandenberg, R. J., & Lance, C. E. (2000). A review and synthesis of the measurement invariance literature: Suggestions, practices, and recommendations for organizational research. *Organizational Research Methods, 2,* 4–69.

Van de Vijver, F. J. R. (1997). Meta-analysis of cross-cultural comparisons of cognitive test performance. *Journal of Cross-Cultural Psychology, 28,* 678–709.

Van de Vijver, F. J. R. (2002). Inductive reasoning in Zambia, Turkey, and the Netherlands: Establishing cross-cultural equivalence. *Intelligence, 30,* 313–351.

Van de Vijver, F. J. R. (2011). Bias and real differences in cross-cultural differences: Neither friends nor foes. In S. M. Breugelmans, A. Chasiotis, & F. J. R. van de Vijver (Eds.), *Fundamental questions in cross-cultural psychology.* Cambridge: Cambridge University Press.

Van de Vijver F. J. R., & Fischer, R. (2009). Improving methodological robustness in cross-cultural organizational research. In R. S. Bhagat & R. M. Steers (Eds.), *Handbook of culture, organizations, and work* (pp. 491–517). Cambridge, NY: Cambridge University Press.

Van de Vijver, F. J. R., & Leung, K. (1997). *Methods and data analysis for cross-cultural research.* Newbury Park, CA: Sage.

Van de Vijver, F. J. R., & Leung, K. (2011). Equivalence and bias: A review of concepts, models, and data analytic procedures. In D. M. Matsumoto & F. J. R. van de Vijver (Eds.), *Cross-cultural research methods in psychology* (pp. 17–45). Cambridge: Cambridge University Press.

Van Hemert, D. A., Van de Vijver, F. J. R., Poortinga, Y. H., & Georgas, J. (2002). Structural and functional equivalence of the Eysenck personality questionnaire within and between countries. *Personality and Individual Differences, 33,* 1229–1249.

Van Herk, H., Poortinga, Y. H., & Verhallen, T. M. (2004). Response styles in rating scales: Evidence of method bias in data from six EU countries. *Journal of Cross-Cultural Psychology, 35,* 346–360.

Van Leest, P. F. (1997). Bias and equivalence research in the Netherlands. *European Review of Applied Psychology, 47,* 319–329.

Van Schilt-Mol, T. M. M. L. (2007). *Differential Item Functioning en itembias in de Cito-Eindtoets Basisonderwijs.* Amsterdam: Aksant.

Wasti, S. A. (2002). Affective and continuance commitment to the organization: Test of an integrated model in the Turkish context. *International Journal of Intercultural Relations, 26,* 525–550.

Watson, D. (1992). Correcting for acquiescent response bias in the absence of a balanced scale: An application to class consciousness. *Sociological Methods Research, 21,* 52–88.

Welkenhuysen-Gybels, J., Billiet, J., & Cambre, B. (2003). Adjustment for acquiescence in the assessment of the construct equivalence of Likert-type score items. *Journal of Cross-Cultural Psychology, 34,* 702–722.

2

Evaluating Change in Social and Political Trust in Europe

Nick Allum
University of Essex

Sanna Read
London School of Hygiene and Tropical Medicine and
the Helsinki Collegium for Advanced Studies

Patrick Sturgis
University of Southampton

2.1 INTRODUCTION

In social science, we typically work with measures that are laden with errors. Theories are generally couched in terms of constructs or phenomena that are unobserved or unobservable but nevertheless have empirical implications. It is these unobservable indicators that we actually analyze. Hence, an important preliminary task for an analyst is to specify the assumed relationship of observable indicators to the underlying phenomenon that is to be measured. Better still, one can test hypotheses about these relations. The focus of this volume is on cross-cultural methods; this brings with it further complexities for deriving adequate social measurement in that we cannot expect to necessarily see the same empirical patterns of observations across cultures (for instance, on a set of related questionnaire items measuring a single attitude) even where the underlying phenomenon is in fact the same. Absent some resolution of this problem, comparisons of the true differences in, say, attitudes or beliefs across cultures are problematic because of the conflation of such differences as may exist with differences in the ways in which the observable indictors "behave" across the very same cultural boundaries.

Other chapters in this volume (Chapter 7) demonstrate the use of confirmatory factor analysis (CFA) to evaluate cross-cultural comparability of measures. This chapter goes beyond the measurement model and presents methods for evaluating group mean differences on unobserved, latent variables. It is probably fair to say that the most common approach in this regard is for researchers first to evaluate the extent of metric equivalence between groups using CFA (equal factor loadings) and then test hypotheses about group mean differences using *t*-tests or analysis of variance (ANOVA) on summated scales derived from the collection of indicators shown to have invariant measurement properties across these groups (Ployhart & Oswald, 2004; Vandenberg & Lance, 2000). However, for this procedure to yield valid inferences, the items must exhibit scalar invariance—equality of intercepts. In order to evaluate this, it is necessary to model both the covariance and mean structure of the latent variable system (Meredith, 1993).

This chapter provides a nontechnical introduction to the use of CFA for cross-national comparisons that include mean structures. It should be of interest to applied social scientists who wish to utilize the methods in their own work as well as for readers who want to understand and critically evaluate literature in their substantive fields that employs this type of analysis. The method allows for the testing of hypotheses about group mean differences on unobserved, latent variables instead of manifest composite variables such as summated scales or factor score estimates. We demonstrate these techniques with an analysis of social and political trust in Europe in three waves of the European Social Survey (ESS).

2.2 COVARIANCE AND MEAN STRUCTURES

In CFA, or structural equation modeling (SEM) more generally, the interest lies in accounting for the observed pattern of covariances between manifest variables with reference to one or more latent variables. The latent variable(s) can be thought of as predictors of the observed items and the factor loadings as regression coefficients. In the example below, there is a vector of manifest indicator variables, X, that depends on a single continuous latent variable ξ. The covariance structure can be modeled without reference to means by simply assuming that the intercepts are zero. The Λ and δ are factor loadings and unique errors, respectively,

$$X = \Lambda_x \xi + \delta. \tag{2.1}$$

Interpretation is then analogous to regression analysis using standardized coefficients. However, if one wishes explicitly to examine latent means, then the mean structure must be incorporated into the model by estimating a vector, τ, of intercepts:

$$\mathbf{x} = \tau_x + \Lambda_x \xi + \delta. \tag{2.2}$$

For a model where there are multiple groups (e.g., several countries, male/female, etc.), separate parameters need to be estimated for each of these *g* groups:

$$\mathbf{x}^g = \tau_x^g + \Lambda_x^g \xi^g + \delta^g. \tag{2.3}$$

This procedure for testing hypotheses about group differences in levels of unobserved variables was originally referred to as "structured means modeling" (SMM; Sörbom, 1974), but is also known as "mean and covariance structure" analysis (MACS; Ployhart & Oswald, 2004). The key advantage over the ANOVA or *t*-test approaches more usually employed is that—in common with applications of SEM in general—relations between latent unobserved variables can be modeled after attenuating for measurement error. True group differences will emerge more clearly than they would using only observed items or summated scales because these have a higher ratio of "noise" to "signal" compared to latent variables.

Estimating this type of model when one has a hypothesis about the difference between group means entails several complications relative to multigroup CFA that uses only the covariance structure. First, there is the additional consideration of testing for equal intercepts across groups as well as factor loadings. Second, it is not possible to simultaneously estimate means of latent variables in all groups because this model is unidentified. "The reason for this lack of identification is analogous to a situation where one is told that the difference between two numbers is 10 and the task is to identify both numbers. No unique solution exists to this problem (Hancock 2004)." However, as our interest is in estimating the difference in latent means, fixing one value and estimating the other is sufficient. The usual solution is to fix at zero the latent mean, treating it as a reference group, and then all other latent group means are estimated as deviations from the reference mean (Bollen, 1989). At least one intercept also has to be fixed, usually at unity, in order to identify the model. The meaning of the intercept for each observed item is, as in standard regression, the expected score on the item for an individual who has an estimated latent factor score of zero.

Many authors have discussed the degree to which measurement equivalence needs to hold in both mean and covariance structures. Vandenberg and Lance (2000) review this literature and derive a recommended sequence for testing for invariance that seems to reflect the current consensus. The first step in a multigroup CFA where the aim is ultimately to test for latent mean differences is to test for configural invariance. That is to say, is the factor structure across groups the same? This is something of a qualitative judgment rather than a formal test. If, say, one has a set of items thought to measure a single latent attitude, then a one-factor model should fit the data in each group. If in some groups the items reflect two underlying factors, according to goodness-of-fit measures, then it is not appropriate to continue with further invariance testing. Assuming that configural invariance is obtained, the next step is to test for metric invariance. Factor loadings should be set equal across groups so that only one parameter for each loading is estimated. The fit of this model is compared with the fit of the unrestricted model that allows for freely estimated loadings in each group. At this point, researchers often find that the restricted model fits significantly worse than the unrestricted one. One should then be guided by a combination of modification indices and substantive theory in deciding which loadings that should be freed sequentially in order to obtain a better fitting model. Again, it is to a large extent a matter of judgment as to what constitutes a model that displays sufficient partial invariance to proceed to the next stage, other than at least one estimated loading should be invariant across groups in addition to the loadings that are equal due to their being fixed at unity for identification purposes (Steenkamp & Baumgartner, 1998).

Assuming that a model is found that demonstrates sufficient cross-group equivalence of factor loadings, one can then proceed to testing for scalar invariance: equality of intercepts. One intercept for each latent variable needs to be fixed at zero. This should be for the item whose factor loading is fixed at unity. The other intercepts are all constrained to be equal across groups. (Alternative strategies for identifying this model are presented in Chapter 3 of this volume). The fit of the model compared to the final one from the previous stage should be evaluated and, if, as is often the case, the fit is significantly poorer, a decision needs to be made as to which intercepts to free up. Contrary to what is sometimes assumed, Byrne, Shavelson, and Muthén (1989) show that it is not necessary to have full scalar invariance in order to validly estimate latent mean differences (But it is necessary that this situation is evaluated and recognised prior to latent means analysis. See Chapter 5). A minimum of two are required: one being fixed to zero and one constrained equal across groups. The item for which the intercepts are constrained equally should also have factor loadings constrained to be equal (Byrne et al. 1989). Finally, assuming a model is found that satisfies these conditions, one can proceed to testing for differences between the estimated latent means across groups. The standard procedure for doing this is to fix one group's mean at zero and then evaluate the overall fit of further nested models, where some or all of the other groups' latent means are set equal to the reference mean (i.e., at zero) and then this constrained model is compared with one where the group latent means are freely estimated.

A simpler, alternative type of approach in SEM that can be used for the same purpose is the multiple indicators multiple causes (MIMIC) model (Jöreskog & Goldberger, 1975). In this formulation, group membership is denoted by a dummy variable, or several dummy variables, onto which the latent variable of interest is regressed. It is not necessary explicitly to model the mean structure in this approach. Only covariances and variances are modeled and, because variables are scaled as deviations from their means over the entire sample, group differences are estimated with the dummy variable coefficients (Hancock, 2004). The great disadvantage of this approach is that strict equivalence (equal factor loadings, intercepts, and error variances) is simply assumed, rather than tested. Equal structural paths, latent variances, and covariances are also assumed equal. MIMIC models are covered in detail in Chapter 4.

2.3 SOCIAL AND POLITICAL TRUST IN EUROPE: A MULTIPLE GROUP CONFIRMATORY FACTOR ANALYSIS WITH STRUCTURED MEANS

In the remainder of this chapter, we present an analysis of European survey data on political and social trust. Social or interpersonal trust relates to beliefs held by individuals in a given society about the moral orientation and incentive structure of a diffuse, unknown "other" (Delhey & Newton, 2003; Rotter, 1967, 1980). This type of "thin" or "horizontal" trust must be differentiated from the instrumental, "particularized" trust we invest in family, friends, colleagues, acquaintances, and institutions that are known to us (Hardin, 1999; Putnam, 2000; Uslaner & Brown, 2002). While particularized trust is developed over time through direct personal experience, social trust is more akin to a core value or belief; an abstract evaluation of the moral standards of the society in which we live (Delhey & Newton, 2003). To the extent that individuals within a society are inclined to make positive evaluations of the trustworthiness of their fellow citizens, various normatively benign consequences may be expected to follow, at both the individual and societal levels, as a result. This is because social trust is postulated to facilitate cooperative behavior in the absence of information about the trustworthiness of the other. This type of diffuse trust, it is argued, can reduce social and economic transaction costs by lowering the need for contracts, legal or regulatory frameworks, and other forms of coercive authority (Hardin, 1999; Luhmann, 1979). It has been posited as the mechanism through which disconnected individuals with divergent preferences can overcome collective action problems (Arrow, 1974; Fukayama, 1995; Parsons, 1937). As Stolle puts it, trust is "a key social resource that seems to oil the wheels of the market economy and democratic politics" (Stolle, 2003, p. 19).

In addition to generalized social trust, another key concern is trust in political institutions. Institutional trust is sometimes considered as "confidence," in as much as individual citizens are generally unable to unilaterally withdraw trust from distal institutions (Luhmann, 1979, 1993). Nevertheless, political trust, as measured by eliciting evaluations of the various institutions that make up the political system, has been found to correlate with a host of positive behaviors, beliefs, and attitudes (Newton, 2007). It is also expected to vary cross-nationally and over time, according to the health of the polity (Bromley, Curtice, & Seyd, 2004; Inglehart, 1997). As one might expect, both social and political trust tend to be correlated at the individual and the aggregate country levels (Allum, Patulny, Read & Sturgis, 2010). Citizens who tend to trust undefined others also tend to have confidence in political institutions.

Having now set the methodological and substantive context for the research, we present an analysis that utilizes the methods described earlier for latent means comparisons and explore whether and how levels of social and political trust vary across and within European countries between 2002 and 2006.

2.4 DATA AND METHODS

We use the data from the three rounds available in the European Social Survey (ESS, 2009). The ESS is a biennial survey that interviews a probability sample of approximately 1500 citizens in each of between 20 and 35 countries, dependent on the wave. It began in 2002 when a total of 22 countries participated. The second and third rounds were carried out in 2004 and 2006, with 24 and 25 countries, respectively. In this study, the 17 countries that participated during all three rounds were Austria, Belgium, Denmark, Finland, France, Germany, Hungary, Ireland, the Netherlands, Norway, Poland, Portugal, Slovenia, Spain, Sweden, Switzerland, and the United Kingdom.

The ESS was designed to study the changes in institutions and attitudes, beliefs and behavior patterns in Europe. The items in the questionnaire were carefully chosen on the basis of their proven reliability and validity in previous studies. Social trust was measured using three items:

1. Would you think that most people can be trusted, or do you think that you can't be too careful in dealing with people?
2. Do you think that most people would try to take advantage of you if they got the chance or would they try to be fair?
3. Would you say that most people try to be helpful or that they are mostly looking out for themselves?

Each of these items was rated on a scale from 0 to 10 (where 0 equals low trust and 10 equals high trust).

We selected only two items measuring political trust: trust in parliament and trust in politicians. These items were asked in all three first rounds. The questionnaire also included an item for trust in political parties, but this item was not asked in the first round. The questionnaire also has items on trust in the legal system, the police, European Parliament, and the United Nations. These items were not used in this study, because, following some preliminary CFA, they appeared to measure a separate dimension of political trust. The measurement model, with factor loadings and factor covariance for social and political trust, is shown in Figure 2.1.

The measurement models were constructed using multiple group CFA with Mplus software (Muthén & Muthén, 2006). The variables were, strictly speaking ordinal, with 11 discrete points. However, we elected to regard them as continuous for the purposes of analysis because their distribution was approximately normal and maximum likelihood (ML) estimation is reasonably robust to violations of distributional assumptions in SEM (Coenders, Satorra, & Saris, 1997).

First, we wanted to create a model with equal factor loadings and intercepts across countries. We could have begun, as Byrne suggests (2001), by fitting a model to one country only. We decided not to do this because there is sufficient prior research in this area to suggest that the proposed model should fit across many European countries (Reeskens & Hooghe, 2008). However, because we expected that these constrained models may

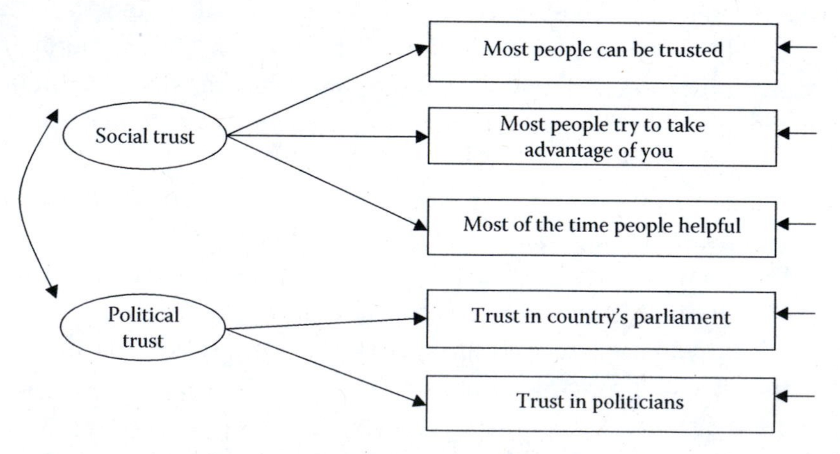

FIGURE 2.1
Schematic model for social and political trust.

not fit in all countries, we decided to find a subset of countries that provide equal factor loadings and intercepts within country in all three rounds of the ESS, rather than looking for heterogeneous patterns of partial equivalence. This approach was justifiable here for the purposes of demonstrating the method and also because we did not have any particular country that it was imperative that we include.

We accomplished this task in the following way. We started at Round 1 and fitted a model where intercepts and factor loadings were constrained to be equal across countries. Following the method of Reeskens and Hooghe (2008), we excluded the country with the highest chi-square contribution to lack of fit until a model with an acceptable fit was attained. To test the fit of the models, we used two fit indices. Steiger's (1990) root mean square error of approximation (RMSEA) is a fit index based on a noncentral chi-square distribution. Standardized root mean square residual (SRMR) describes the average discrepancy between the observed correlations and the correlations predicted by the model. The model shows an acceptable fit when RMSEA <0.08 and SRMR <0.05 (Hu & Bentler, 1999). Model testing also produces a chi-square value and its degrees of freedom. With large sample sizes, as was the case in this study, chi-square values tend be large and underestimate the fit of an overall model. Chi-square and the degrees of freedom used for calculating chi-square difference is, however, a useful tool to help assess whether or not to constrain the parameters in nested models. There is some debate over the appropriate strategy for testing fit in nested models. We adopt the view that using the combination of approximate fit indices described above is most appropriate for testing differences in the fit of nested model constraints, just as it is appropriate for other model evaluation tasks when sample sizes are very large (Mulaik, 2007).

In a second stage, the subset of countries showing acceptable fit in Round 1 for the metric and scalar equivalent models was tested on the Round 2 data. Countries with highest chi-square contribution were again excluded, one at a time, until the model showed an acceptable fit for Round 2. The same procedure was repeated for the Round 3 observations. In the end, this procedure resulted in a subset of 12 countries that showed equal factor loadings and intercepts across countries in each of the three rounds.

In the next phase of analysis, we tested the over-time measurement equivalence for social and political trust using the pooled subset of the 12 countries that demonstrated metric and scalar equivalence in all three rounds described above. Each of the three rounds of data represented the three groups in the analysis. Finally, for evaluating the real change in trust over time, we estimated latent means for social and political trust using 2002 as the baseline. In this model, the latent means for social and political trust were fixed to zero. The latent means for Round 2 and Round 3 were estimated freely. To indicate if the latent means in Round 2 and Round 3 differed from zero, 95% confidence intervals were constructed. In other words, was there a statistically significant increase or decrease in both political and social trust over the period of time? We also fit models where latent means for social and political trust in Round 2 and Round 3 were set at zero (or equal) in order to see if there were statistically significant changes between these rounds, as well as between Round 1 and the others.

A few points of explanation are in order before continuing to consider the results. First, it would, in principle, have been possible to test for changes in latent means within countries over time. However, this would have served to demonstrate the same analytic procedures as the pooled analysis so we elected only to show this pooled European over-time comparison in the chapter. Second, we did not apply weights to correct for differential population size in each country, although this can be done if it is important for analytic purposes. For this analysis, we elected not to concern ourselves with population weights. The Mplus software will allow for weights and estimate correct standard errors if this is required.

2.5 RESULTS

We started the model testing of cross-country equivalence in social and political trust with a model including 17 countries in Round 1. Because we had in mind the strategy to eliminate countries that did not exhibit scalar and metric invariance, we decided to constrain loadings and intercepts to equality across countries from the outset. This is actually rather convenient in Mplus because the default option for multiple group analysis imposes these equality constraints. The model fit for this base model (Model 1) is presented in Table 2.1.

Both fit indices, RMSEA and SRMR, are higher than the critical values for an acceptable fit, indicating that some of the countries are not metric and scalar equivalent. The country with highest contribution to chi-square

TABLE 2.1

Models to Identify a Subset of Countries with Metric and Scalar Invariance (Equal Factor Loadings and Intercepts) in Social and Political Trust

Model	χ^2	DF	RMSEA	SRMR	Country with the Highest χ^2 Contribution	χ^2 Contribution
Round 1						
1. Full model, 17 countries	2297.72	164	0.089	0.052	Netherlands	323.84
2. Excluding the Netherlands	2335.70	154	0.086	0.052	Ireland	318.50
3. Excluding the Netherlands and Ireland	1997.63	144	0.082	0.048	UK	276.98
4. Excluding the Netherlands, Ireland, and UK	1699.12	134	0.078	0.044	Austria	292.64
Round 2						
5. Subset of 14 countries (Netherlands, Ireland, and UK excluded)	1924.89	134	0.084	0.048	Austria	266.89
6. Excluding Austria	1634.40	124	0.081	0.048	Portugal	285.28
7. Excluding Portugal	1304.05	115	0.075	0.044	Spain	179.93
Round 3						
8. Subset of 12 countries (Netherlands, Ireland, UK, Austria, and Portugal excluded)	1431.53	114	0.079	0.044	Spain	245.43

Note: The countries with the highesfft chi-square contribution are excluded from the model. This was repeated in each round until the fit of the model was satisfactory (RMSEA <0.08 and SMR <0.05).

was the Netherlands. After excluding the Netherlands from the model, the model was still not within the limits of an acceptable model fit (Model 2 in Table 2.1). The highest chi-square contribution in this model was due to Ireland. The model fit was somewhat better after excluding Ireland, the SRMR value was acceptable, but the RMSEA value was still higher than 0.08 (Model 3 in Table 2.1). Of the countries, the United Kingdom contributed most to the chi-square and it was excluded in the next model. This model (Model 4 in Table 2.1) showed an acceptable fit, with RMSEA <0.08 and SRMR <0.05.

The subset of 14 countries with acceptable fit in Round 1 was used for testing for metric invariance in social and political trust in Round 2 (Model 5 in Table 2.1). The RMSEA value was higher than 0.08, and the country with the highest chi-square contribution in this model was Austria. In the next model (Model 6 in Table 2.1), Austria was excluded. The RMSEA value was still above 0.08. The next country with the highest chi-square contribution to be excluded from the model was Portugal. After excluding Portugal, the model fit well to the data according to both RMSEA and SRMR indices (Model 7 in Table 2.1). This subset of 12 countries with acceptable fit in Round 2 was tested in Round 3. The model fit well for these countries (Model 8 in Table 2.1) and this subset was taken forward into the next stage of the analysis. The factor loadings and covariance for this Model 8 are shown in Table 2.2.

TABLE 2.2

Unstandardized Coefficients (Unstandardized Coefficients Equated Across the Subset of 12 Countries and Three Rounds)

	Unstandardized Coefficients (SE)
Social trust	
Most people can be trusted	1.00 (0.000)
Most people try to take advantage of you	0.91 (0.006)
Most of the time people helpful	0.80 (0.006)
Political trust	
Trust in country's parliament	1.00 (0.000)
Trust in politicians	0.95 (0.007)
Social trust*Political trust (latent covariance)	2.20 (0.037)

The cross-time comparison of the latent factor means was carried out for the subset of 12 countries based on the cross-country analysis described above. The grouping was organized by year of data collection and the 12 countries pooled in each round. We specified a base model where equal factor loadings and equal intercepts were estimated across rounds. In this base model, the latent factor means for social and political trust in Round 1 were set to zero, and in Round 2 and Round 3 they were estimated freely. Essentially, this base model was a only a test of over-time factorial equivalence as the vector of latent means to be estimated was unrestricted except for the fixing at zero in Round 1 for identification purposes (Model 1 in Table 2.3). This model fit well to the data, with both RMSEA (0.024) and SRMR (0.01) within acceptable limits. The 95% confidence intervals, which are available as output in Mplus, indicated that for the social trust the latent factor means did not differ between Round 1 and Round 2, but the latent factor mean in Round 3 was higher compared to the two previous rounds. For political trust, the factor means in Round 2 and Round 3 were about equal and significantly lower than the factor mean in Round 1. Equating the latent means in the nested models in the way indicated by the pattern of confidence intervals confirmed this configuration of mean change over time. There is a small but significant loss of fit in imposing the mean equality constraint to political trust in Rounds 2 and 3, but given acceptable fit on approximate indices Model 6 in Table 2.3 is the preferred one. (The Mplus input file for this model is presented in Appendix 2.A.)

The changes in latent means can be interpreted on the same scale as the original observed variable used to set the scale, which is 0–10. The results indicate that social trust stays steady until 2006 when it rises by a small measure (0.11). Political trust, in contrast, declines between 2002 and 2004 (by 0.24) and thereafter remains constant. These changes are small but statistically significant.

2.6 CONCLUSIONS

In this chapter we have provided a nontechnical introduction to structured means analysis and provided an empirical example to demonstrate the method. We first established a subset of European countries for which metric and scalar equivalence were demonstrated. This enabled us

TABLE 2.3

Cross-Time Change in the Latent Factor Means of Social and Political Trust (Subset of 12 Countries Based on the Model Testing in Table 2.1)

	Estimates for Latent Factor Means in the Three Rounds (95% CI)											
Model	**Social Trust 2002**	**Social Trust 2004**	**Social Trust 2006**	**Political Trust 2002**	**Political Trust 2004**	**Political Trust 2006**	**CFI**	**RMSEA**	**χ^2**	**df**	**Model Comparison**	**χ^2(df) Difference**
1. Factor means estimated freely	0	0.02 (0.02–0.06)	0.14 (0.10–0.18)	0	−0.25 (−0.29 to −0.21)	−0.21 (−0.25 to −0.16)	1.00	0.025	360.40	24	—	—
2. Factor mean for Social trust 2 set 0	0	0	0.13 (0.10–0.16)	0	−0.26 (−0.30 to −0.22)	−0.21 (−0.25 to −0.17)	1.00	0.025	361.64	25	2 vs. 1	1.24 (1) ns
3. Factor mean for Social trust 3 set 0	0	0	0	0	−0.26 (−0.30 to −0.24)	−0.27 (−0.31 to −0.24)	1.00	0.026	417.03	26	3 vs. 2	55.39 (1)***

4. Factor means for Social trust 2 and Political trust 2 set 0	0	0	0.13 (0.09–0.16)	0	0	−0.9 (−0.12 to −0.05)	1.00	0.028	551.41	26	4 vs. 2	189.77 (1)***
5. Factor means for Social trust 2 and Political trust 3 set 0	0	0	0.20 (0.17–0.23)	0	−0.18 (−0.21 to −0.14)	0	1.00	0.025	463.62	26	5 vs. 2	101.98 (1)***
6. Factor means for Social trust 2 set 0 and Political trust 2 = Political trust 3	0	0	0.11 (0.08–0.14)	0	−0.24 (−0.27 to −0.21)	−0.24 (−0.27 to −0.21)	1.00	0.024	367.35	26	6 vs. 2	5.71 (1)*

*$p < .05$, ***$p < .001$, *ns = nonsignificant.*

Note: The chosen subset of 12 countries showed cross-country metric and scalar equivalence with satisfactory model fit (RMSEA <0.08 and SMR <0.05) in all three rounds. The latent factor means were set zero at Round 1.

to pool the national samples and move on to the question of evaluating changes over time. Although this first step was perhaps not always necessary, we included it here for the purpose of demonstrating the procedure for the reader. In the analysis we evaluated models that imposed metric and scalar invariance and showed how this can be achieved in Mplus. In our models, due to the large number of groups, we selected models that imposed full metric and scalar invariance and disposed of countries for which the model did not fit. Researchers who want to include all groups in their analysis can pursue a partial invariance strategy, which we discussed in the introduction of this chapter but did not implement here.

We also highlighted a method for selecting countries based on global fit contribution. This method is not the only way in which we could have selected countries. Rather than start with all countries and remove problematic countries, we could have started with one country and added others according to some theoretical criterion. It is more than likely that a different subset of countries would be chosen using different approaches. We believe that neither method is the "royal road" and it is for the analyst to justify the approach taken in any given context. In some ways, the preferred solution to this problem will depend on one's philosophical inclination. One can begin with the strongest assumptions and then relax them if they are untenable or start with minimal assumptions and progressively impose more. There is no statistical criterion for choosing the method to take.

Looking at changes in levels of political and social trust in Europe between 2002 and 2006, we find small but significant patterns of change. Political trust appears to decline to some extent, while social trust rises by a smaller increment. These changes are small, but according to one's theoretical or practical interest may or may not be important. From our perspective, we would probably see this as providing evidence of relative stability in perceptions of political institutions and generalized others. With only three observations, it is not really possible to validly infer a trend.

However, the advantage of evaluating shifts over time using latent means in this way is that we can be more confident than we might otherwise be that we are not simply seeing artifacts of measurement. With this control of measurement error, it is concomitantly more likely that small—but real—differences across time or any other group classification will be detected. In the present case, although we use a pooled sample of countries, we are satisfied through testing that the measures are robust both across countries and across time.

It is an empirical matter in any given case whether or not other alternative, simpler to execute methods would produce the same results and conclusions. We would recommend that straightforward ANOVA or dummy variable regression methods also be applied routinely in this type of situation and the results compared, as a form of sensitivity analysis. The main reason for this is less scientific than presentational. Simply, most audiences are more familiar with ANOVA and regression than with SEM, so it may make sense to present results in this way, if they lead to the same conclusions. However, sometimes they will not, and in these cases the SEM analysis will generally be more reliable and should be preferred. To reiterate this point: comparing latent means after having tested for scalar and metric invariance is recommended because using ANOVA and regression methods on observed variables cannot tell us whether the measures are truly comparable across groups or time and we cannot, therefore, be confident that our comparative results reflect real differences or measurement error.

REFERENCES

Allum, N., Patulny, R., Read, S., & Sturgis, P. (2010). Re-evaluating the links between social trust, political trust and civic association in Europe. In J. Stillwell, P. Norman, C. Thomas, & P. Surridge (Eds.), *Spatial and Social Disparities*, (pp. 199–216). London: Springer Verlag.

Arrow, K. J. (1974). *The limits of organization*. New York, NY: Norton.

Bollen, K. (1989). *Structural equations with latent variables*. New York, NY: Wiley.

Bromley, C., Curtice, J., & Seyd, B. (2004). *Is Britain facing a crisis of democracy?* (Working Paper 106). Oxford: Centre for Research Into Elections and Social Trends.

Byrne, B. (2001). *Structural equation modeling with AMOS: Basic concepts, applications and programming*. Mahwah, NJ: Erlbaum.

Byrne, B., Shavelson, R., & Muthén, B. (1989). Testing for the equivalence of factor covariance and mean structures: The issue of partial measurement invariance. *Psychological Bulletin, 105*(3), 456–466.

Coenders, G., Satorra, A., & Saris, W. E. (1997). Alternative approaches to structural modeling of ordinal data: A monte carlo study. *Structural Equation Modeling, 4*, 261–268.

Delhey, J., & Newton, K. (2003). Who trusts? The origins of social trust in seven societies. *European Societies, 5*(2), 93–137.

European Social Survey (2009). *Homepage*. http://www.europeansocialsurvey.org

Fukayama, F. (1995). *Trust*. New York, NY: Free Press.

Hancock, G. (2004). Experimental, quasi-experimental and non-experimental design and analysis with latent variables. In D. Kaplan (Ed.), *The SAGE handbook of quantitative methodology for the social sciences*. 317–334. Thousand Oaks, CA: Sage.

Hardin, R. (1999). Do we want to trust in government? In M. E. Warren (Ed.), *Democracy and trust* (pp. 22–41). Cambridge: Cambridge University Press.

Hu, L., & Bentler, P. M. (1999). Cutoff criteria for fit indices in covariance structure analysis: Conventional criteria versus new alternatives. *Structural Equation Modeling, 6*(1), 1–55.

Inglehart, R. (1997). *Modernization and postmodernization: Cultural, economic and political change in 43 societies.* Princeton, NJ: Princeton University Press.

Jöreskog, K. G., & Goldberger, A. S. (1975). Estimation of a model with multiple indicators and multiple causes of a single latent variable. *Journal of the American Statistical Association, 70*(351), 631–639. Retrieved from http://www.jstor.org/stable/2285946

Luhmann, N. (1979). *Trust and power.* Chichester: Wiley.

Luhmann, N. (1993). *Risk: A sociological theory.* New York, NY: A. de Gruyter.

Meredith, W. (1993). Measurement invariance, factor analysis and factorial invariance. *Psychometrika, 58,* 525–543.

Mulaik, S. (2007). There is a place for approximate fit in structural equation modelling. *Personality and Individual Differences, 42*(5), 883–891.

Muthén, B., & Muthén, L. (2006). *Mplus User's Guide.* Los Angeles, CA: Author.

Newton, K. (2007). Social and political trust. In R. J. Dalton & H.-D. Klingemann (Eds.), *The Oxford handbook of political behavior* (pp. 342–362). New York, NY: Oxford University Press.

Parsons, T. (1937). *Structure of Social Action.* New York, NY: Free Press.

Ployhart, R. E., & Oswald, F. L. (2004). Applications of mean and covariance structure analysis: Integrating correlational and experimental approaches. *Organizational Research Methods, 7*(1), 27–65.

Putnam, R. D. (2000). *Bowling alone: The collapse and revival of American community.* New York, NY: Simon and Schuster.

Reeskens, T., & Hooghe, M. (2008). Cross-cultural measurement equivalence of generalized trust. Evidence from the European social survey (2002 and 2004). *Social Indicators Research, 85*(3), 515–532. Retrieved from http://www.springerlink.com/content/g5238448u2203m8n/

Rotter, J. (1967). A new scale for the measurement of interpersonal trust. *Journal of Personality, 35*(4), 651–665.

Rotter, J. (1980). Interpersonal trust, trustworthiness, and gullibility. *American Psychologist, 35*(1), 1–7.

Sörbom, D. (1974). A general method for studying differences in factor means and factor structures between groups. *British Journal of Mathematical and Statistical Psychology, 27,* 229–239.

Steenkamp, J.-B. E. M., & Baumgartner, H. (1998). Assessing measurement invariance in cross-national consumer research. *Journal of Consumer Research, 25,* 78–90.

Steiger, J. H. (1990). Structural model evaluation and modification: An interval estimation approach. *Multivariate Behavioral Research, 25,* 173–180.

Stolle, D. (2003). The sources of social capital. In D. Stolle & M. Hooghe (Eds.), *Generating social capital: Civil society and institutions in comparative perspective.* New York, NY: Palgrave Macmillan.

Uslaner, E. M., & Brown, M. (2002). *Inequality, trust and civic engagement: A review of the literature for the Russell Sage foundation.* College Park, MD: University of Maryland.

Vandenberg, R. J., & Lance, C. E. (2000). A review and synthesis of the measurement invariance literature: Suggestions, practices, and recommendations for organizational research. *Organizational Research Methods, 3*(1), 4–70.

APPENDIX 2.A: MPLUS INPUT FILE FOR MODEL 6, TABLE 2.3

```
TITLE: ESS trust cross-country cross-time model, excluding the
   Netherlands, Ireland, UK, Austria, and Portugal
DATA: FILE IS esstrust2long.dat;
VARIABLE: NAMES ARE ESSROUND IDNO trust fair help parliament
   politicians cntry1;
USEVARIABLES ESSROUND trust fair help parliament politicians;
GROUPING IS essround (1 = round1 2 = round2 3 = round3);
MISSING = ALL (999);
MODEL:
soctrust BY trust fair help ;
poltrust BY parliament politicians;
Model round2:
[soctrust@0];
[poltrust] (1);
Model round3:
[poltrust] (1);
OUTPUT: SAMPSTAT RESIDUAL cinterval tech1;
```

3

Methodological Issues in Using Structural Equation Models for Testing Differential Item Functioning

Jaehoon Lee, Todd D. Little, and Kristopher J. Preacher
University of Kansas

3.1 INTRODUCTION

In cross-cultural studies, groups often differ in various characteristics (e.g., demographics, socioeconomic status, language, culture, etc.) and these characteristics may not be relevant to the goals of a particular study. Even when reasonable precautions have been taken to prepare a test or survey that is equivalent across cultural groups, it is possible that the attribute being measured has different conceptual meanings in different groups (de Beuckelaer, Lievens, & Swinnen, 2007) or that some items have different importance for one group more than another (Cheung & Rensvold, 1999). In such cases, observed group differences may represent measurement artifacts related to the instrument rather than true differences on a relevant construct. This disparity between observed and true group differences, in turn, adversely affects the comparability of their scores (Byrne & Stewart, 2006; de Beuckelaer et al., 2007; Raju, Laffitte, & Byrne, 2002; Vandenberg & Lance, 2000; van de Vijver & Poortinga, 1992). Thus, researchers have highlighted the importance of measurement equivalence as a prerequisite for meaningful group comparisons (Drasgow, 1984; Little, 1997; Reise, Widaman, & Pugh, 1993). Accordingly, standards established by both the American Psychological Association (APA) and the International Test Commission (ITC) have emphasized evaluation of measurement equivalence for fair use of a scale (1999).

Structural equation modeling (SEM) has been highlighted as a useful and powerful tool for assessing measurement equivalence, or equivalently factorial invariance, across different cultural groups. For example, researchers have successfully evaluated factorial invariance in questionnaires for physical and mental health (Liang, 2001; Wang, Liu, Biddle, & Spray, 2005), mood and depression (Bagozzi, 1994; Byrne & Stewart, 2006; Gregorich, 2006; Reise et al., 1993), self-concept and personality (Katsuya, 2007; Leone, van der Zee, van Oudenhoven, Perugini, & Ercolani, 2005; Marsh, Tracey, & Craven, 2006), and consumer and organizational behavior (Dholakia, Firat, & Bagozzi, 1980; Raju et al., 2002; Riordan & Vandenberg, 1994; Schaffer & Riordan, 2003; Steenkamp & Baumgartner, 1998). In this chapter, we address some methodological issues that may arise when researchers conduct the SEM analysis of factorial invariance. This chapter consists of two parts. In Part I, we (a) introduce the concept of factorial invariance, (b) review the levels of invariance, and (c) introduce the concept of differential item functioning (DIF), which refers a lack of invariance at the item level. In Part II, we (a) describe two SEM-based DIF analyses, (b) summarize two Monte Carlo studies that examine the effects of employing different scaling designs, analytic strategies, and test statistics, and (c) provide general procedural guidelines for evaluating invariance of a scale. This chapter contributes to the cross-cultural measurement literature by cautioning researchers against the use of the conventional analytic approach in DIF analysis. Throughout this chapter, we will show that an innocuous choice of identification condition in the conventional approach involves the danger of inflating Type I error for tests of DIF, and therefore any cross-cultural group comparisons can be jeopardized by falsely identified item bias.

3.2 PART I

3.2.1 Factorial Invariance

Factorial invariance, which originated from the factor analytic and SEM literatures (Meredith, 1993), has a long history in the study of group differences. The key question that factorial invariance addresses is "Are the underlying (latent) constructs measured in a comparable manner across two or more groups?" If the answer is "Yes," the indicators or items of the constructs behave similarly (psychometrically speaking) in each group. When items behave similarly, any observed differences represent "true" differences in the constructs, but not artifactual differences stemming from any differential functioning of the items. We will explain more precisely what we mean by the phrase "behave similarly" later. For now, the idea of similar behavior implies that key item parameters are statistically equivalent across two or more groups.

3.2.1.1 Mean and Covariance Structure Analysis for Factorial Invariance

Currently, mean and covariance structure (MACS; Sörbom, 1974) analysis is preferable for evaluating factorial invariance for several reasons (Little, 1997). In MACS analysis, a hypothesized factor structure is fitted simultaneously in two or more groups. Between-group equality of all parameters can be assessed, and "strong" tests for factorial invariance are possible. MACS analysis can be thought of as an extension of standard confirmatory factor analysis (CFA). That is, CFA attempts to reproduce the covariance structure that underlies a set of measured variables, while MACS analysis considers their mean structure as well. Thus, both CFA and MACS analysis are special cases of SEM.

The basic equations for MACS analysis are presented in Table 3.1. In Equation 3.1, observed examinee scores are depicted using a typical regression layout, where $\mathbf{T}$ is a $(p \times 1)$ vector of regression intercepts; Λ is a $(p \times m)$ matrix of regression slopes, or loadings, which define the associations between items and latent constructs; η is an $(m \times 1)$ vector of latent scores; and Θ is a $(p \times 1)$ vector of residual or unique factor scores. A key feature of this equation (and Equations 3.2 and 3.3) is that the parameters in each matrix are estimated uniquely in each group (denoted by the subscript g).

3.2.1.2 Levels of Factorial Invariance

Vandenberg and Lance (2000) extensively reviewed different levels of factorial invariance proposed in the literature and recommended a number of

TABLE 3.1

The Basic Equations for MACS Analysis and Levels of Invariance

Invariance Level	Equation	
Configural	$y_g = \mathbf{T}_g + \Lambda_g \eta_g + \Theta_g$	(3.1)
	$E(y_g) = \mu_{y_g} = \mathbf{T}_g + \Lambda_g \mathbf{A}_g$	(3.2)
	$\Sigma_g = \Lambda_g \Psi_g \Lambda_g' + \Theta_g$	(3.3)
Metric (weak factorial)	$y_g = \mathbf{T}_g + \Lambda \eta_g + \Theta_g$	(3.4)
	$E(y_g) = \mu_{y_g} = \mathbf{T}_g + \Lambda \mathbf{A}_g$	(3.5)
	$\Sigma_g = \Lambda \Psi_g \Lambda' + \Theta_g$	(3.6)
Scalarb (strong factorial)	$y_g = \mathbf{T} + \Lambda \eta_g + \Theta_g$	(3.7)
	$E(y_g) = \mu_{y_g} = \mathbf{T} + \Lambda \mathbf{A}_g$	(3.8)
	$\Sigma_g = \Lambda \Psi_g \Lambda' + \Theta_g$	(3.9)

Note: y is a $p \times 1$ vector of observed responses on the p items and g is an index that refers to the group. When g is present, the parameters in the associated matrix are freely estimated across groups. $E(\,)$ is the expectation operator and μ is a $p \times 1$ vector of item means. A is an $m \times 1$ vector of latent construct means. Σ is the model implied variance–covariance matrix of y.

invariance levels that could be evaluated in empirical research.* *Configural invariance* describes the situation when the parameters are estimated uniquely in each group but the pattern of free and fixed parameters is the same (or very similar). Configural invariance is determined by overall model fit and simple judgment regarding the adequacy of the hypothesized model in each group.

Different levels of factorial invariance require the parameter estimates in different matrices to be constrained across groups. In the model of *metric invariance*, the loading estimates in Λ are constrained to be equal

* The invariance levels that are not discussed here include invariance of unique factor variances, invariance of latent construct variances/covariances, and invariance of latent construct means. For a detailed discussion on factorial invariance, see Meredith (1993) and Vandenberg and Lance (2000).

across groups and therefore common values are generated that are optimal for all groups (see Equation 3.4). In order to determine whether or not metric invariance holds, we evaluate the reasonableness of the metric invariance model (i.e., the imposed equality constraints) relative to the configural invariance model. Although metric invariance suggests that two or more groups share the same unit of measurement, it does not necessarily indicate that the origins (i.e., intercepts) of the scale are equivalent across groups. Thus, this invariance level is often called *weak* factorial invariance (Meredith, 1993).

Similarly, in the model of *scalar invariance*, the intercept estimates in **T** are also constrained to be equal across groups (see Equation 3.7). We evaluate the reasonableness of the scalar invariance model by assessing the fit change from the metric invariance model. Given scalar invariance, the scale is considered to have the same unit of measurement as well as the same origin, and therefore group mean comparisons become tenable (Widaman & Reise, 1997). Thus, this invariance level is often called *strong* factorial invariance (Meredith, 1993).

3.2.1.3 Testing Factorial Invariance

As mentioned previously, invariance testing involves judging the reasonableness of the sequentially added constraints. Although one could evaluate the imposed equality constraints by assessing the χ^2 differences between two nested models (i.e., likelihood ratio [LR] test), $\Delta\chi^2$ value may not a practical test statistic because of its dependency on sample size (Brannick, 1995; Kelloway, 1995). Instead, the set of equality constraints can be evaluated by assessing the change in key global fit indices. Most recently, Meade, Johnson, and Braddy (2008) conducted a conservative simulation study (i.e., 0.01 Type I error, 0.90 power) and concluded that the optimal criterion for rejecting a hypothesized invariance model is the change in the comparative fit index (CFI) of greater than −0.002. This recommendation represents a more stringent criterion than a previous simulation study conducted by Cheung and Rensvold (2002). They recommended that a ΔCFI value less than 0.01 was sufficient evidence that a hypothesized invariance model holds with regard to a more conventional Type I error (i.e., 0.05). In addition, Chen (2007) recommended assessing changes in the root mean square error of approximation (RMSEA) and standardized root mean square residual (ΔSRMR) as well. Nevertheless, she also concluded that

ΔCFI should be the main criterion because ΔRMSEA and ΔSRMR tests tend to overreject an invariant model when sample size is small.*

Taken together, if imposing equality constraints leads to a loss in CFI that is greater than 0.002 or 0.01, then one or more of the constraints are not tenable. In such cases, a set of "offending" (i.e., noninvariant) items must be located in a scale. A variety of analyses have been proposed for this purpose in the SEM literature (e.g., Chan, 2000; Ferrando, 1996; Muthén, 1988). As we detail later, most of the analyses are influenced by how we scale the latent constructs.

3.2.2 Methods of Scaling

In any structural model, the scale of the construct needs to be identified in order to obtain a unique solution for every parameter (Bollen, 1989). There are now three useful, statistically equivalent scaling methods (Little, Slegers, & Card, 2006). When three or more items are used to measure a construct, each scaling method provides the necessary condition for identifying the scale of the construct. Because using fewer than three indicators risks underidentification and increases the probability of obtaining an infeasible solution (Bollen, 1989), our discussion focuses on situations when a researcher has three or more items for each construct.

The most common scaling method is the *marker-variable method*. This method constrains one of the loadings and a corresponding intercept, by which the other parameters are estimated (see Little et al., 2006; see also Little, in press, Chapter 3). Generally, the loading is fixed to 1 and the intercept is fixed to 0. The second common method involves fixing the variance of the construct to 1 and the mean to 0. This method is termed the *fixed-factor* or *reference-factor method*. The third method is the recently introduced *effects-coded method*. This method involves placing a set of constraints so that the loadings average 1 and the intercepts average 0. Unlike the other two methods that provide an arbitrary scale of the construct, the effects-coded method provides a scale of the construct that directly reflects the scale of its indicators (see Little et al., 2006; Little, in press).

* Information-theoretic measures of fit (e.g., Akaike information criterion, Bayesian information criterion) are also suitable for evaluating factorial invariance, but they have not been supported in the literature as being informative beyond the CFI and the other fit measures discussed here.

3.2.3 Differential Item Functioning

The concept of factorial invariance also underlies the concept of DIF; a concept originated from the item response theory (IRT) literature. The IRT includes the statistical models specialized for different types of categorical responses (e.g., binary, ordinal), and the models for binary responses can be viewed as special cases of graded response model (Samejima, 1969, 1972). Before we detail in Part II how the concept of DIF is integrated into the SEM framework, we will briefly introduce the key terms and parameters in IRT. More detailed discussion on IRT can be found in Chapters 15 through 17 in this book.

The basic assumptions in IRT are that a set of items assesses a single ability dimension (unidimensionality) but they are pairwise uncorrelated at a given value of latent ability (local independence). That is, residual variances are uncorrelated when conditioned on the common ability variance—similar to the conditional independence assumption in CFA. In the graded response model, the relationship between the latent ability (θ) and the probability of choosing a progressively increasing response category is depicted by a series of boundary response functions, $p^*_{ik}(\theta_j) = e^{a_i(\theta_j - b_{ik})} / 1 + e^{a_i(\theta_j - b_{ik})}$, where $p^*_{ik}(\theta_j)$ is the probability that an examinee j with a certain value of θ will respond to an item i at or above a response category k. For a particular item with k response categories, $k - 1$ boundary response functions are present. As observed in this equation, the boundary response functions depend on the θ parameter as well as the b and a parameters. The latter two parameters are usually termed the *attractiveness* (or *difficulty*) and *discrimination* of an item, respectively. For each item, $k - 1$ attractiveness/difficulty estimates are possible and a common value is generated for the discrimination estimates. As noted previously, if $k - 2$, the graded response model simplifies to a two-parameter model (Birnbaum, 1968; Lord & Novick, 1968; McDonald, 1967). Furthermore, if $a - 1$, this model becomes a one-parameter model (Hambleton, Swaminathan, & Rogers, 1991; Rasch, 1960).

In IRT, a lack of factorial invariance is referred to as *differential item functioning* or DIF. More specifically, DIF represents group differences in the probability of an item response after their ability scores are placed on a common scale, or "statistically matched" (Mellenbergh, 1994). When present, DIF indicates either *impact* or *item bias* depending on the source or nature of DIF (Camilli & Shepard, 1994; Zumbo, 1999). When groups

TABLE 3.2

The IRT and SEM Parameters that Determine the Type of DIF or Item Bias

Type of DIF	IRT Parameter	SEM Parameter
Uniform (i.e., a failure of scalar invariance)	Attractiveness/ difficulty (b)	Intercept (τ)
Nonuniform (i.e., a failure of metric invariance)	Discrimination (a)	Loading (λ)

truly differ in a latent ability being measured, they are expected to provide different responses on the same items. In such case, the parameter estimates of these items accurately reflect group differences in the ability or impact. In contrast, item bias occurs when different item responses are caused by factors that are irrelevant to the ability being measured. Because the conditional probability of an item response depends on the item parameters (see boundary response function described above), DIF (either impact or item bias) is present when the item parameter estimates are not invariant across groups (Raju et al., 2002).

DIF can be either uniform or nonuniform depending on what item parameter differs across groups. *Uniform DIF* is present when only the attractiveness/difficulty parameter estimates differ across groups. *Nonuniform DIF* exists when the discrimination parameter estimates differ across groups regardless of whether the attractiveness/difficulty parameter estimates are different or not. As detailed later, uniform DIF corresponds to group differences in intercepts, whereas nonuniform DIF corresponds to group differences in loadings. Table 3.2 presents the corresponding IRT and SEM parameters that determine the two types of DIF.

3.3 PART II

The links between IRT and SEM have been well demonstrated in the literature (e.g., Brown, 2006; Fleishman, Spector, & Altman, 2002; Goldstein & Wood, 1989; Kamata & Bauer, 2008; MacIntosh & Hashim, 2003; McDonald, 1999; Mellenbergh, 1994; Millsap & Yun-Tein, 2004; Muthén & Asparouhov, 2002; Muthén & Christoffersson, 1981; Muthén

& Lehman, 1988; Takane & de Leeuw, 1987). Researchers have extended these links, allowing us to test DIF within the SEM framework (e.g., Chan, 2000; Ferrando, 1996; Muthén, 1988). The most common SEM techniques employ either MACS (Sörbom, 1974) analysis or multiple indicators multiple causes (MIMIC; Jöreskog & Goldberger, 1975) analysis. The model specification and analytic strategies for each analysis are demonstrated here.

3.3.1 MACS Analysis for DIF

MACS analysis for DIF detection assumes that the responses on a given set of items reflect a single common construct. Further assuming that the covariances among the unique factor scores of this set of items are 0 in the population, the mean of an item is equal to the intercept when the construct score is zero and the covariances between each item and construct are equal to the loading (Jöreskog, 1971). The assumptions that (a) a single latent construct underlies the correlations among a set of items and that (b) off-diagonal elements in Θ_g are zero and are the analogs of, respectively, the unidimensionality and local independence assumptions in IRT. Note that in MACS DIF analysis, the local independence assumption can be violated and estimated (i.e., true population correlated residuals can be specified). In addition, multiple constructs—each with a unique set of indicators—can be included in simultaneous tests for DIF across all constructs.

The intercept parameters correspond to the attractiveness/difficulty parameters in IRT; the higher the intercept, the more attractive/difficult the item is (i.e., a higher mean response is obtained). The loading parameters correspond to the discrimination parameters; the higher the loading, the more discriminating the item is (i.e., this item better differentiates examinees of different construct scores; see Ferrando, 1996; Grayson & Marsh, 1994; Mellenbergh, 1994). As noted previously, uniform DIF exists when only the attractiveness/difficulty parameter estimates differ across groups; nonuniform DIF is present when the discrimination parameter estimates differ across groups regardless of whether or not the attractiveness parameter estimates are invariant. Thus, a lack of invariance in $\mathbf{T}$ implies uniform DIF, whereas a lack of invariance in Λ implies nonuniform DIF regardless of whether or not $\mathbf{T}$ is invariant (Chan, 2000).

3.3.2 MIMIC Analysis for DIF

Multiple indicators multiple causes (MIMIC) analysis extends the standard MACS analysis by regressing latent constructs on measured grouping variables (covariates). Muthén and colleagues (Gallo, Anthony, & Muthén, 1994; Muthén, 1988) further extended MIMIC analysis such that item responses are also regressed on the covariates (MIMIC DIF analysis). Table 3.3 shows the basic equations for MIMIC and MIMIC DIF analyses. In Equations 3.10 through 3.15, B is a $(p \times q)$ matrix of regression slopes of the responses on the covariates and Γ is an $(m \times q)$ matrix of regression slopes of the constructs on the covariates.

The regression slopes in Γ are termed the *indirect effects* and they account for (latent) group mean differences across groups. The regression slopes in B are termed the *direct effects* because they influence the responses, unmediated by the latent constructs (Bollen, 1989; Dorans & Holland, 1993; Dorans & Kulick, 1986; Jones, 2006). The direct effects indicate whether item responses differ across groups after controlling for any latent mean differences, which is the definition of DIF (Fleishman, 2005; Fleishman & Lawrence, 2003; Fleishman et al., 2002). Accordingly, DIF is evident when the direct effects are statistically significant (Grayson, Mackinnon, Jorm, Creasey, & Broe, 2000; Jones, 2006). The direct and indirect effects are conceptually illustrated in Figure 3.1. Note that because common loading parameters are assumed for different groups, MIMIC DIF analysis is limited to tests for uniform DIF.

3.3.3 Analytic Strategies

There are two analytic strategies useful for SEM DIF analysis. The first strategy tests DIF one item at a time, assuming that other items are DIF-free

TABLE 3.3

The Basic Equations for MIMIC Analysis

Analysis	Equation	
MIMIC	$y = \mathbf{T} + \Lambda\eta + \Theta$	(3.10)
	$E(y) = \mathbf{T} + \Lambda\mathbf{A}$	(3.11)
	$\eta = \mathbf{A} + \Gamma x_k + \zeta$	(3.12)
MIMIC DIF	$y = \mathbf{T} + \Lambda\eta + \mathrm{B}x_k + \Theta$	(3.13)
	$E(y) = \mathbf{T} + \Lambda\mathbf{A} + \mathrm{B}x_k$	(3.14)
	$\eta = \mathbf{A} + \Gamma x_k + \zeta$	(3.15)

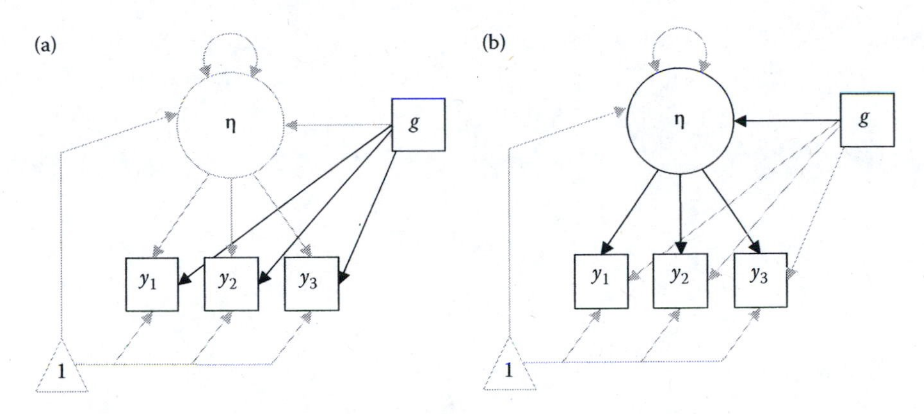

FIGURE 3.1
Direct and indirect effects in MIMIC DIF analysis. (a) Direct effects of a covariate on item responses. (b) Indirect effects of a covariate on item responses via construct.

anchors (e.g., Chan, 2000; Chen & Anthony, 2003; Finch, 2005; Gelin, 2005; Muthén & Asparouhov, 2002; Oishi, 2006; Stark, Chernyshenko, & Drasgow, 2006). In MIMIC DIF analysis, this strategy involves starting with a baseline model in which no direct effects are specified. After the fit of this baseline model is established, it is then statistically compared with each of the p models (where p = number of items), where a direct effect is allowed for only one item at a time.

To test nonuniform DIF using MACS DIF analysis, a baseline model constrains each item's loading and intercept to be equal across groups. Then, this model is compared with each of the p models in which one respective loading is freely estimated in each group. Uniform DIF is usually examined only for those items whose loadings have been found to be invariant (Steenkamp & Baumgartner, 1998), although this is not a required condition (i.e., loading and intercept invariance can be evaluated simultaneously for an item; see Stark et al., 2006). A baseline model constrains the items' loadings (except for the nonuniform DIF items) and intercepts to be equal across groups. Then, this baseline model is then compared with each of q models (where q = number of items with invariant loadings) in which one respective intercept is freely estimated in each group. Because this analytic strategy starts by constraining the parameters of interest across groups, it is termed the *constrained-baseline strategy*.

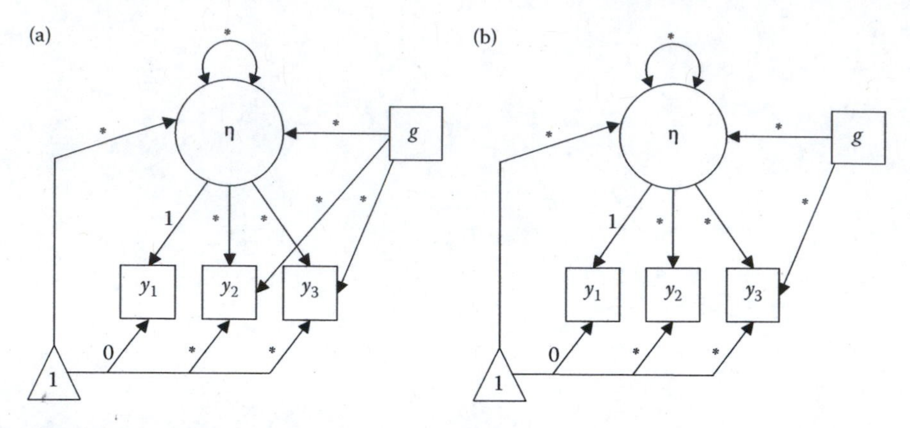

FIGURE 3.2
The free-baseline strategy for MIMIC DIF analysis. (a) Free-baseline model. (b) Model of a single restrictive direct effect. 3.2A and 3B depicts two nested MIMIC models. This example illustrates a simple case in which (a) a test includes three items and (b) the marker-variable scaling method was used for scaling. For simplicity, unique factor variances are omitted. Free parameters are marked by "*."

The second strategy tests DIF one item at a time, assuming that other items are not free from DIF (e.g., Fleishman et al., 2002; Stark et al., 2006; Woods, 2009; Woods, Oltmanns, & Turkheimer, 2009). Accordingly, this strategy starts with the baseline model in which all the parameters are freely estimated except those needed for scaling. This *free-baseline strategy* is depicted in Figures 3.2 (MIMIC DIF analysis) and 3.3 (MACS DIF analysis). For MIMIC DIF analysis, all possible direct effects except for at least one anchor are freely estimated in the baseline model (Figure 3.2a). Then, this baseline model is compared with each of the *p* models that remove one respective direct effect (Figure 3.2b).

To test nonuniform DIF, the MACS baseline model freely estimates all the loadings and intercepts in each group (Figure 3.3a). This model is compared with each of the *p* models that constrain one respective loading to be equal across groups (Figure 3.3b). Then, to test uniform DIF, the invariant loadings are constrained to be equal and this model is compared with each of the *q* models in which one respective intercept is constrained to be equal across groups (Figure 3.3c).*

* The constrained-baseline strategy is similar to the ìtop-downî approach for assessing scale-level invariance in that it starts with a model that imposes the most restrictive (or full) metric or scalar invariance. In contrast, the free-baseline strategy has similarities with the "bottom-up" approach in that it starts with the least restrictive (or partial) metric or scalar invariance model. For more details on these two approaches, see Welkenhuysen-Gybels and van de Vijver (2001).

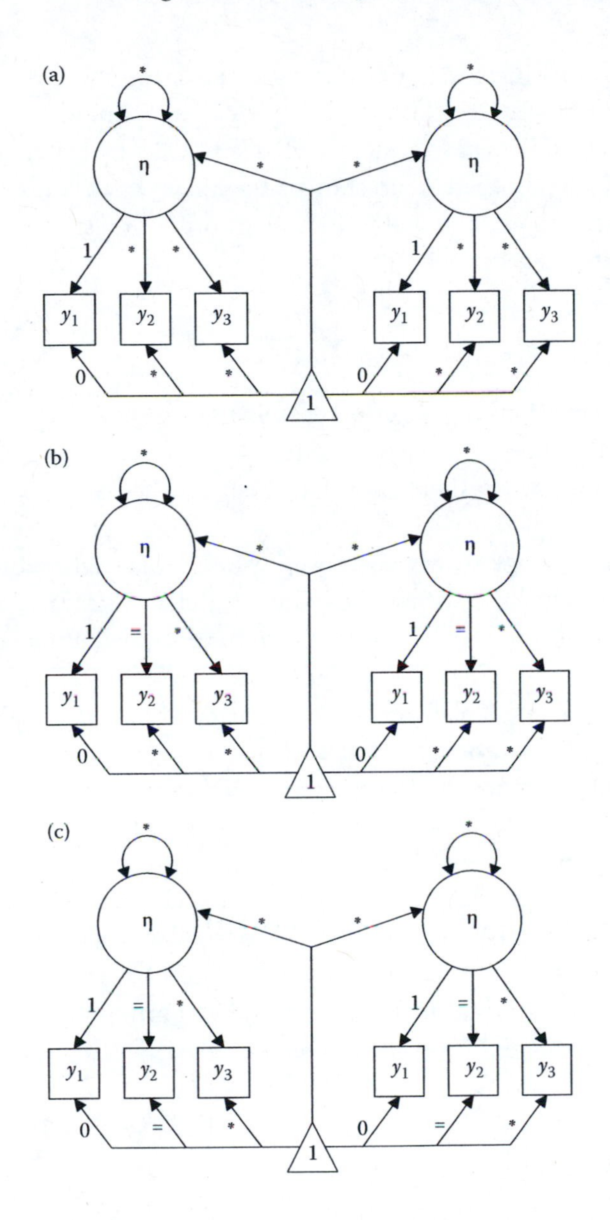

FIGURE 3.3
The free-baseline strategy for MACS DIF analysis. (a) Free-baseline model. (b) Model of a single restrictive loading. (c) Model of a set of restrictive loading and intercept. 3.3A and C depicts three nested MACS models. This example illustrates a simple case, in which (a) the scale includes three items, (b) only the second item exhibits nonuniform DIF, and (c) the marker-variable scaling method is used.

Regardless of which analytic strategy is used, the LR test is most frequently used to test DIF. Although empirical sampling distributions for other global fit indices have been provided (e.g., Cheung & Rensvold, 2002; Meade et al., 2008), there is no standard against which a researcher can compare the changes in global fit indices in order to test factorial invariance at the item level.

3.3.4 Previous Simulation Studies

Empirical evaluations of the SEM DIF analyses are scant. Recently, Stark et al. (2006) found that the constrained-baseline strategy is suitable for testing DIF only when there is no DIF item in a scale; Type I error was considerably inflated especially in uniform DIF cases. In contrast, the free-baseline strategy works fairly well; power was high enough, while Type I error was near or below the nominal alpha value. They also found that Type I error could be decreased substantially by using the Bonferroni-corrected LR test in large sample, large DIF cases. Similarly, Hernández and González-Romá (2003) showed that the constrained-baseline MACS analysis provided reasonable Type I error and power for detecting uniform DIF but power was not acceptable in the nonuniform DIF case.

For MIMIC DIF analysis, Finch (2005) reported that using the constrained-baseline strategy, Type I error was acceptable and power was very close to 1 unless a scale was relatively short and three-parameter logistic IRT model underlay the data. Using the free-baseline strategy, Woods (2009) also found that Type I error was controlled at the nominal alpha level, and power was reasonable when the focal group's sample size was equal to or greater than 100 (with reference group's sample size equal to or greater than 500).

3.3.5 Methodological Issues

The SEM DIF analyses, which are simple variations of the idea of partial factorial invariance (Raju et al., 2002), involve some methodological issues to be resolved in practice. Generally, the scaling method does not change the conclusions about overall model fit or the tests for omnibus scale-level invariance. However, when a researcher locates DIF in a scale after metric or scalar invariance has been rejected, a potential problem arises. Specifically, different scaling methods can lead to different conclusions of

DIF analysis because this post-hoc analysis relies on an examination of individual parameters.

To scale a latent construct in MACS DIF analysis, researchers conventionally fix an item's loading and intercept to be equal across groups (i.e., marker-variable method). This marker variable is termed an *anchor* in the DIF literature. In the case of MIMIC DIF analysis, researchers use an anchor or anchor set to which no direct effect is estimated. These scaling approaches essentially assume that the anchor set is truly invariant. If an invariant anchor set cannot be guaranteed or a researcher arbitrarily chooses an anchor set, other parameter estimates may be biased against invariance (Bollen, 1989; Cheung & Rensvold, 1999; Millsap, 2005). Indeed, Stark et al. (2006) found that a biased anchor set severely inflated Type I error of the MACS DIF analysis. Finch (2005) and Navas-Ara and Gómez-Benito (2002) also reported that MIMIC DIF analysis was adversely affected by a biased anchor set.

A variety of empirical solutions for choosing an invariant anchor set have been proposed in the literature (e.g., Cheung & Rensvold, 1999; Christensen, MacKinnon, Korten, & Jorm, 2001; Fleishman et al., 2002; González-Romá, Tomás, Ferreres, & Hernández, 2005; MacKinnon et al., 1999; Stark et al., 2006). However, such solutions necessarily increase the number of nested-model comparisons, which requires setting a more conservative alpha level. Even when the alpha level has been adjusted, Type I error is severely inflated if no item appears to be invariant.

3.3.6 Current Simulation Studies

In a series of simulation studies, we included scaling method as a study condition, along with other conditions commonly examined in the DIF literature. For MACS DIF analysis, three different scaling methods (i.e., marker-variable, fixed-factor,* effects-coded; see *Method of Scaling* in Part I of this chapter) were examined using the free-baseline strategy as we illustrated previously (see Figure 3.3). Because different analytic strategies have not been empirically compared for MIMIC DIF analysis, the three scaling methods were combined with two analytic strategies

* When evaluating scale-level invariance, the variance and/or mean of a construct are freely estimated in one group. In contrast, when evaluating item-level invariance, they are constrained to equality across groups. In other words, the configural invariance model is used as the baseline model when examining nonuniform DIF and uniform DIF.

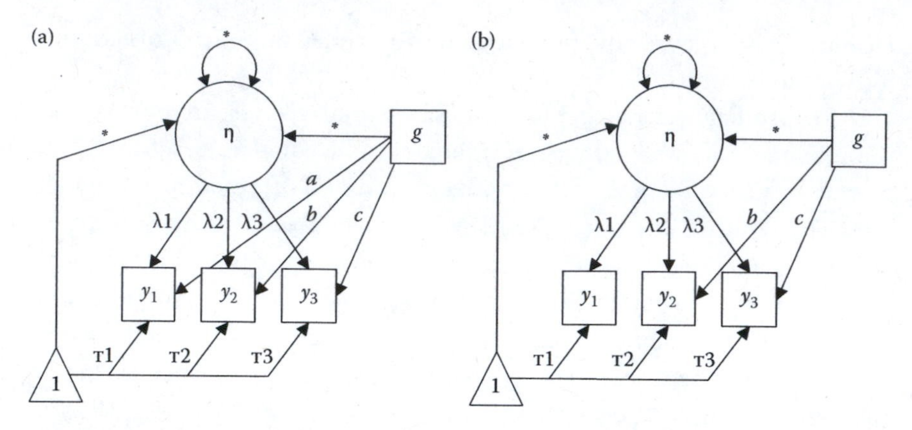

FIGURE 3.4
The effects-baseline strategy for MIMIC DIF analysis. (a) Free-baseline model. (b) Model of a single restrictive direct effect. 3.4A and B depicts two nested MIMIC models. This example illustrates a simple case, in which (a) the scale includes three items and (b) the effects-coded scaling method is used ($\Sigma_i^p \lambda_i = p, \Sigma_i^p \tau_i = 0$). A set of regression paths from the covariate g to the items (a, b, c or b, c) averages 0 ($\Sigma_i^p b_{ik} = 0$) in the effects-baseline strategy. Note that no anchor set is required for the purpose of scaling.

(i.e., constrained-baseline, free-baseline; see *Analytic Strategies for Testing DIF* in this chapter). We also tested a variant of the free-baseline strategy in which all possible direct effects are estimated as an optimal balance around a certain value (i.e., $\Sigma B_k = 0$). This *effects-baseline strategy* is theoretically appealing because there is no need for an anchor set. Figure 3.4 depicts the effects-baseline strategy used for MIMIC DIF analysis.

For both MACS and MIMIC DIF analyses, we also considered the biased anchor as a study condition. In addition, we used four different criteria for rejecting the assumption of partial factorial invariance; uncorrected and corrected critical p values for the LR test ($p = .05/n$, where n is the number of nested-model comparisons; Stark et al., 2006)* and ΔCFI values of −0.01 (Cheung & Rensvold, 2002) and −0.002 (Meade et al., 2008). The study conditions considered in the current simulation studies are presented in Table 3.4. More details on the current simulation studies and outcomes are available in Lee (2009, in preparation).

* For example, in Figure 3.3, two nested-model comparisons are possible for testing nonuniform or uniform DIF. Thus, the corrected critical p value equals .025 (=.05/2).

TABLE 3.4

The Study Conditions Examined in the Current Simulation Studies

Item Response (Scale Point)	Test Length	Sample Size ($N_F : N_R$)	Type of DIF in Anchor Item	Type of DIF in Target Item	DIF Amount	Scaling Method	Analytic Strategy[a]
Binary (2)	6 items	100 : 900	Uniform	Uniform	No	Marker-variable	Constrained-baseline
Ordinal (5)	12 items	250 : 750	Nonuniform	Nonuniform	Small	Fixed-factor	Free-baseline
		500 : 500			Large	Effects-coded	Effects-baseline

Note: The MACS study had a $2 \times 2 \times 3 \times 2 \times 2 \times 3 \times 3 \times 1^a$ factorial design (432 cells) and the MIMIC study had a $2 \times 2 \times 3 \times 2 \times 2 \times 3 \times 3 \times 3^a$ factorial design (1296 cells). Five hundred replications were made within each cell.

3.3.6.1 Simulation Results for MACS DIF Analysis

In terms of Type I error and power, the three scaling methods used for MACS DIF analysis yielded different outcomes of testing (large) DIF. The conventional marker-variable method tested DIF effectively in most conditions. Some exceptions were the conditions when nonuniform DIF (loading invariance) was located in a relatively short test (e.g., 6 items). Similarly, the fixed-factor method detected uniform DIF (intercept invariance) quite well especially when DIF was introduced in the ordinal responses. When nonuniform DIF was present in the ordinal responses, this scaling method performed marginally well unless groups differed largely in size (e.g., $N_F = 100$ vs. $N_R = 900$). In contrast, the effects-coded method was tenable only for testing uniform DIF in a short test.

We found that a biased anchor greatly deteriorated the accuracy of testing nonuniform DIF for the marker-variable and effects-coded methods. That is, neither of these scaling methods was suitable for detecting DIF in almost all conditions.

Generally, the use of ΔCFI test greatly decreased Type I error as well as power. When used with the ΔCFI value of −0.002, the fixed-factor method worked well for testing uniform DIF unless groups differed greatly in size. With the same criterion, however, the marker-variable method was tenable for testing uniform DIF only when the anchor was not contaminated by the same type of DIF. In contrast, Bonferroni-correction on the LR test statistic did reduce Type I error, while retaining reasonable power (i.e., > 0.80) to detect both nonuniform and uniform DIF. Thus, the use of Bonferroni-correction is strongly recommended when using MACS analysis for DIF detection. For example, the fixed-factor method detected uniform DIF reasonably well in almost all conditions, including the biased anchor item.

3.3.6.2 Simulation Results for MIMIC Analysis

As mentioned previously, MIMIC DIF analysis is not applicable to tests for nonuniform DIF because it presumes equal loadings across groups. Supporting this limiting assumption, power for detecting nonuniform DIF was not satisfactory in all conditions. Thus, our discussion is limited to the cases that, if present, only uniform DIF appears in a target.

Contrary to the case of MACS DIF analysis, scaling method had no impact on the accuracy of the MIMIC analysis for DIF detection. This finding was not surprising because DIF is determined by the significance of the direct effect estimate, not the invariance of the loading or intercept estimates as in the MIMIC DIF analysis.

Generally, each of three analytic strategies effectively detected uniform DIF. Type I error was below or near the nominal alpha value except in a few conditions (e.g., the constrained-baseline strategy with binary responses). Unless group sizes were largely different, power was satisfactory (i.e., > 0.80) in all conditions.

We found that the accuracy of MIMIC DIF analysis was considerably degraded by the presence of DIF in the anchor item. That is, none of the three analytic strategies was tenable for testing DIF when the anchor was biased by uniform DIF. Nevertheless, Type I error was substantially reduced by using the Bonferroni-corrected LR test. Consequently, the constrained-baseline strategy performed marginally well even with the biased, uniform DIF anchor. When the anchor had nonuniform DIF, the free-baseline strategy performed fairly well regardless of whether the Bonferroni-correction was used or not. In contrast, the ΔCFI tests markedly decreased power, making MIMIC DIF analysis useful in only a few conditions. Thus, if one cannot guarantee an anchor set devoid of uniform DIF, we recommend using the constrained-baseline strategy with the Bonferroni-corrected LR test for uniform DIF.

3.3.6.3 Summary of Simulation Results

Our simulation results indicate that MACS analysis for DIF detection should be conducted using the fixed-factor scaling method. This method consistently outperformed the marker-variable and effects-coded scaling methods. For MIMIC DIF analysis, the scaling method had no impact, but the analytic strategy did. That is, either the free-baseline or the effects-baseline strategy effectively identified uniform DIF when the anchor set was DIF-free. When the anchor set had nonuniform DIF, the free-baseline strategy outperformed the other two strategies. In contrast, when the anchor set had uniform DIF, the constrained-baseline strategy performed the best. Finally, for both MACS and MIMIC DIF analyses, the Bonferroni-correction for nested-model comparisons should be considered to improve the accuracy of these analyses, particularly when a DIF-free anchor set has not been established.

3.3.6.4 Limitations

There are several weaknesses that require readers to interpret and generalize our simulation results with caution. First, maximum likelihood (ML) estimation, which assumes normality of the measured variables, was used with binary and ordinal responses. Lubke and Muthén (2004) noted that ML estimation can lead to erroneous invariance detection when used with categorical measured variables without accounting for their nonnormality. Second, no missing values were assumed in the responses although conclusions of any DIF analysis likely depend on the amounts and the patterns of missing values. Finally, sample sizes were selected so as to represent those often observed in psychological assessment. However, in some cases, smaller samples (i.e., less than 100) may be encountered especially with low-incidence groups.

3.4 CONCLUSIONS

Factorial invariance is a critical concern in cross-cultural research. Although researchers in this field have applied different methodologies to this issue, SEM has offered an integrative framework in which factorial invariance can be evaluated at both scale and item level. For example, MACS and MIMIC analyses reflect general IRT concepts, still accounting for measurement error in the responses and offering a variety of flexible options (e.g., multiple latent constructs, more than two groups, categorical or continuous covariates). The empirical findings illustrated in this chapter bring up some methodological issues and recommendations to be considered when a researcher conducts DIF analysis using SEM.

In a series of simulation studies, we found that statistically equivalent scaling methods did not provide identical outcomes when MACS analysis was used for testing DIF. We recommend using the fixed-factor scaling method (see *Methods of Scaling* in Part I of this chapter). If a test to be analyzed is relatively short, the effects-coded method may be considered for testing uniform DIF. The scaling method does not impact the accuracy of MIMIC DIF analysis, but its analytic strategies may lead to different conclusions about DIF. Either the free-baseline or effects-baseline strategy is recommended for testing uniform DIF under favorable conditions such as comparable group sizes and a DIF-free anchor set (see *Analytic Strategies for Testing DIF* in this chapter). In less than favorable conditions, we recommend using the MACS DIF analysis.

An important issue in testing factorial invariance is the presence of DIF in the anchor set. Researchers have shown that having bias in the anchor set adversely affects invariance testing (Cheung & Rensvold, 1999; Finch, 2005; Navas-Ara & Gómez-Benito, 2002; Stark et al., 2006). Supporting this literature, we found that a biased anchor severely degraded Type I error and power of SEM DIF analyses. Nevertheless, our empirical results suggest a couple of possibilities to ameliorate these problems. That is, if used with the fixed-factor scaling method, Bonferroni-corrected LR test, and comparable large samples, the MACS DIF analysis would be a nearly fail-safe methodology for testing DIF, even when a designated anchor set is not readily available. Similarly, if accompanied by the Bonferroni-corrected LR test, constrained-baseline MIMIC analysis would produce accurate conclusions about DIF.

The critical ΔCFI values that have been suggested for scale-level invariance testing (i.e., −0.01, −0.002) were not optimal criteria for testing item-level invariance or DIF. In our simulation studies, they markedly reduced power of MACS and MIMIC DIF analyses. This is consistent with the results from the previous simulation study conducted by French and Finch (2006). They found that despite the fact that the ΔCFI test (of −0.01) has comparable power to the LR test (at .01 alpha level) for testing metric invariance in some conditions, this criterion rarely performs as well for detecting noninvariance (i.e., nonuniform DIF) of a single item.* Taken together, future efforts are needed to empirically examine the potential criterion values under a variety of DIF conditions (e.g., sample size, number of items, proportion of DIF in a scale, etc.). These criterion values should be independent from the overall fit of the baseline model, should not be influenced by model complexity, and should not be redundant with

* In supplementary analyses, we found that the critical values of RMSEA and SRMR suggested by Chen (2007) are not suitable for DIF analysis as well. When used to detect nonuniform and uniform DIF under our simulated conditions, generally they inflated Type I error above the nominal alpha level and/or provided very low power.

other fit indices (Cheung & Rensvold, 2002). Until optimal criterion values become available, we recommend using the Bonferroni-corrected LR test for testing DIF.

With regard to categorical measured variables, the use of alternative test statistics and estimation methods would provide more reliable DIF analyses. For example, the Satorra–Bentler (SB) χ^2 incorporates a scale correction, taking into account the hypothesized model and the distributional characteristics of the data (1988). Satorra and Bentler (2001) further demonstrated how to calculate SB $\Delta\chi^2$ and corresponding degrees of freedom suitable for nested-model comparisons. Another alternative is to use a robust estimation method such as weighted least square (WLS) and robust WLS (RWLS).* These methods use polychoric correlations, item means, and weight matrices to produce an asymptotic covariance matrix of measured variables, which in turn is used to estimate the loading and intercept parameters (Muthén & Asparouhov, 2002).

Combining these methodological issues and recommendations, we suggest general procedural guidelines for testing factorial invariance in a flowchart (see Figure 3.5). This testing procedure proceeds in three stages. In the first stage, omnibus metric invariance of a scale is evaluated (see *Testing Factorial Invariance* in Part I of this chapter). If metric invariance holds, then omnibus scalar invariance of the scale is evaluated in the second stage. The ΔCFI test of −0.01 (or −0.002 for high-stakes testing environments) is recommended for assessing scale-level invariance. If it is appropriate to use ML estimation, the conventional LR test will be a comparable, or better, choice (see French & Finch, 2006). Because the scaling method generally does not change conclusions about scale-level invariance, any scaling method is applicable.

If metric invariance is rejected, locating the source of noninvariance would occur within the first stage. Nonuniform DIF is examined in each item, one at a time by conducting the free-baseline MACS analysis with the fixed-factor scaling method and Bonferroni-corrected LR test (see Figure 3.3). After flagging nonuniform DIF items, loading parameters for

* In fact, WLS and RWLS are not recommended in some cases. For example, Flora and Curran (2004) noted that the WLS χ^2 is inflated, as are the parameter estimates, whereas their standard errors are negatively biased. Also, French and Finch (2006) found that the RWLS LR test provides very low power for testing scale-level metric invariance.

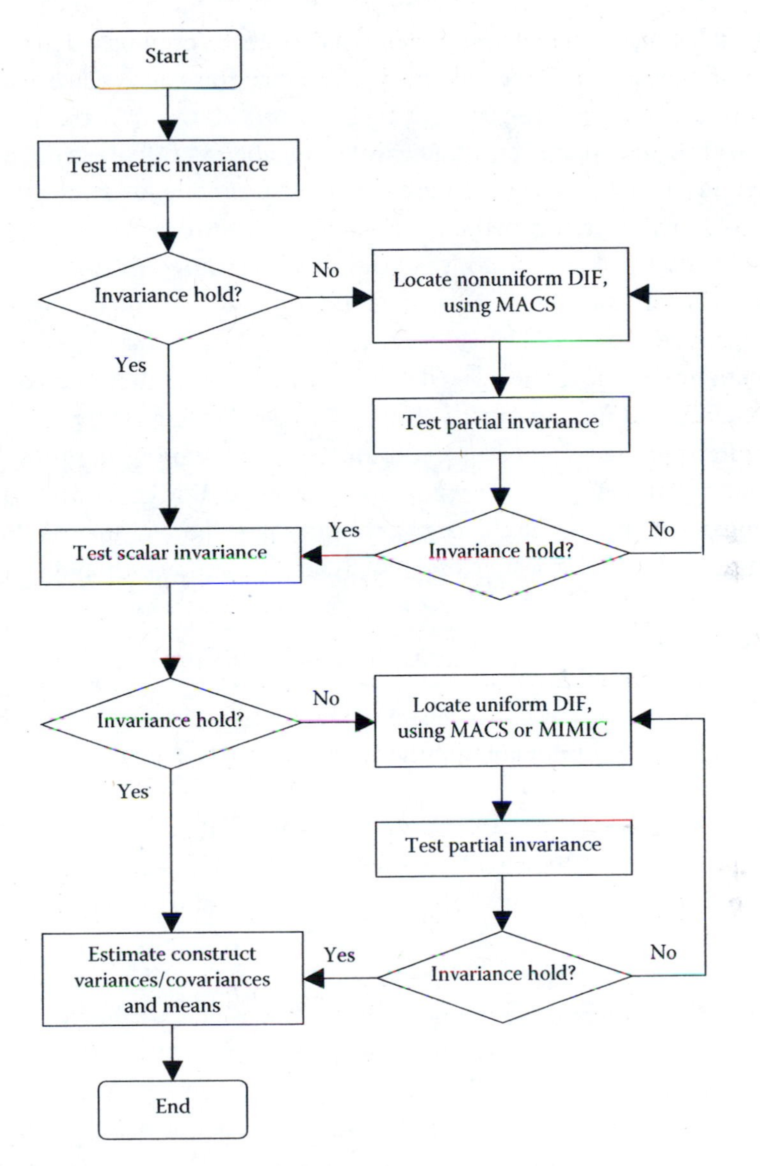

FIGURE 3.5
The procedure for testing factorial invariance in the SEM framework.

the DIF items are allowed to be freely estimated in each group and remain unconstrained throughout the next stages (i.e., partial metric invariance).

In the second stage, either MACS or MIMIC analysis is used to identify the items exhibiting uniform DIF. It should be noted that, because MIMIC analysis presumes equal loadings across groups, this analysis should be avoided if scale-level metric invariance has not been established in the first stage. If metric invariance holds, one can use the constrained-baseline MIMIC analysis with the Bonferroni-corrected LR test to detect uniform DIF in each item, one at a time. Regardless of whether full or partial metric invariance holds, one can also use the free-baseline MACS analysis with the fixed-factor scaling method and the Bonferroni-corrected LR test.

There is some debate as to what minimum number of items should be invariant. For example, as a conservative approach to employing partial metric invariance, Vandenberg and Lance (2000) recommended that loading constraints should be relaxed for only a minority of items. In contrast, Steenkamp and Baumgartner (1998) suggested that at least two (loading- and intercept-) invariant items are sufficient for meaningful group comparisons. Although we agree with the recommendation of Steenkamp and Baumgartner (1998), the choice of a minimum number of invariant items must remain the prerogative of a researcher. This choice should be based on empirical evidence as well as practical considerations (Vandenberg & Lance, 2000).

After locating DIF items, further invariance tests (e.g., construct variances/covariances, construct means) may continue in the third stage. A baseline model should maintain the constraints of partial metric and scalar invariance that have been supported in the first two stages. When used in the multiple-group case, the effects-coded scaling method provides some preferable features (see Little et al., 2006). For example, because the scale of a construct is optimally weighted by all of its indicators in the effects-coded method, this method would be more useful in practice than the fixed-factor method in which the scale is defined by a single, arbitrarily chosen anchor. Furthermore, in MACS analysis, when invariance constraints are placed on the loadings and intercepts, the effects-coded method provides the scale of a construct within each group, which is not the case with the fixed-factor method. Accordingly, we recommend using the effects-coded scaling method when testing invariance of construct parameters.

Upon completing the illustrated testing procedure, a researcher may determine the "biasedness" of the DIF items through subsequent empirical and content analyses (Zumbo, 1999). As noted previously (see *Differential Item Functioning* in Part I of this chapter), only when observed group differences are attributable to the construct-irrelevant group characteristics can DIF be considered item bias. Because groups in cross-cultural research often differ in various demographic and socioeconomic characteristics, these post-hoc analyses are strongly recommended to accomplish valid, meaningful group comparisons.

REFERENCES

American Educational Research Association, American Psychological Association, & National Council on Measurement in Education (1999). *Standards for educational and psychological testing*. Washington, DC: American Educational Research Association.

Bagozzi, R. P. (1994). The effects of arousal on the organization of positive and negative affect and cognitions: Application to attitude theory. *Structural Equation Modeling, 1*, 222–252.

Birnbaum. A. (1968). Some latent trait models and their use in inferring an examinee's ability. In F. M. Lord & M. R. Novick (Eds.). *Statistical theories of mental test scores*. Reading, MA: Addison-Wesley.

Bollen, K. A. (1989). *Structural equations with latent variables*. New York, NY: Wiley.

Brannick, M. T. (1995). Critical comments on applying covariance structure modeling. *Journal of Organizational Behavior, 16*, 201–213.

Brown, T. A. (2006). *Confirmatory factor analysis for applied research*. New York, NY: Guilford Press.

Byrne, B. M., & Stewart, S. M. (2006). The MACS approach to testing for multigroup invariance of a second-order structure: A walk through the process. *Structural Equation Modeling, 13*, 287–321.

Camilli, G., & Shepard, L. A. (1994). *Measurement methods for the social sciences series: Methods for identifying biased test items* (Vol. 4). Thousand Oaks, CA: Sage.

Chan, D. (2000). Detection of differential item functioning on the Kirton Adaptation-Innovation Inventory using multiple-group mean and covariance structure analyses. *Multivariate Behavioral Research, 35*, 169–199.

Chen, C., & Anthony, J. C. (2003). Possible age-associated bias in reporting of clinical features of drug dependence: Epidemiological evidence on adolescent-onset marijuana use. *Addiction, 98*, 71–82.

Chen, F. F. (2007). Sensitivity of goodness of fit indexes to lack of measurement invariance. *Structural Equation Modeling, 14*, 464–504.

Cheung, G. W., & Rensvold, R. B. (1999). Testing factorial invariance across groups: A reconceptualization and proposed new method. *Journal of Management, 25*, 1–27.

Cheung, G. W., & Rensvold, R. B. (2002). Evaluating goodness-of-fit indexes for testing measurement invariance. *Structural Equation Modeling, 9*, 233–255.

Christensen, H., MacKinnon, A. J., Korten, A., & Jorm, A. F. (2001). The "common cause hypothesis" of cognitive aging: Evidence for not only a common factor but also specific associations of age with vision and grip strength in a cross-sectional analysis. *Psychology and Aging, 16*, 588–599.

de Beuckelaer, A., Lievens, F., & Swinnen, G. (2007). Measurement equivalence in the conduct of a global organizational survey across countries in six cultural regions. *Journal of Occupational and Organizational Psychology, 80*, 575–600.

Dholakia, N., Firat, A. F., & Bagozzi, R. (1980). The de-Americanization of marketing thought: In search of a universal basis. In C. Lamb & P. Dunne (Eds.), *Theoretical developments in marketing* (pp. 25–29). Chicago, IL: American Marketing Association.

Dorans, N. J., & Holland, P. W. (1993). DIF detection and description: Mantel Haenszel and standardization. In P. W. Holland & H. Wainer (Eds.), *Differential item functioning* (pp. 35–66). Hillsdale, NJ: Lawrence Erlbaum.

Dorans, N. J., & Kulick, E. (1986). Demonstrating the utility of the standardization approach to assessing unexpected differential item performance on the Scholastic Aptitude Test. *Journal of Educational Measurement, 23*, 355–368.

Drasgow, F. (1984). Scrutinizing psychological tests: Measurement equivalence and equivalent relations with external variables are central issues. *Psychological Bulletin, 95*, 134–135.

Ferrando, P. J. (1996). Calibration of invariant item parameters in a continuous item response model using the extended LISREL measurement submodel. *Multivariate Behavioral Research, 31*, 419–439.

Finch, H. (2005). The MIMIC model as a method for detecting DIF: Comparison with Mantel-Haenszel, SIBTEST and the IRT likelihood ratio test. *Applied Psychological Measurement, 29*, 278–295.

Fleishman, J. A. (2005). Using MIMIC models to assess the influence of differential item functioning. Retrieved from http://outcomes.cancer.gov/conference/irt/fleishman.pdf

Fleishman, J. A., & Lawrence, W. F. (2003). Demographic variation in SF-12 scores: True differences or differential item functioning. *Medical Care, 41*, 75–86.

Fleishman, J. A., Spector, W. D., & Altman, B. M. (2002). Impact of differential item functioning on age and gender differences in functional disability. *Journal of Gerontology: Social Sciences, 57*, 275–283.

Flora, D. B., & Curran, P. J. (2004). An empirical evaluation of alternative methods of estimation for confirmatory factor analysis with ordinal data. *Psychological Methods, 9*, 466–491.

French, B. F., & Finch, H. (2006). Confirmatory factor analytic procedures for determination of measurement invariance. *Structural Equation Modeling, 13*, 378–402.

Gallo, J. J., Anthony, J. C., & Muthén, B. O. (1994). Age differences in the symptoms of depression: A latent trait analysis. *Journal of Gerontology: Psychological Sciences, 49*, 251–264.

Gelin, M. N. (2005). *Type I error rates of the DIF MIMIC approach using Jöreskog's covariance matrix with ML and WLS estimation*. Unpublished doctoral dissertation, University of British Columbia, Canada.

Goldstein, H., & Wood, R. (1989). Five decades of item response modeling. *British Journal of Mathematical and Statistical Psychology, 42*, 139–167.

González-Romá, V., Tomás, I., Ferreres, D., & Hernández, A. (2005). Do items that measure self-perceived physical appearance function differentially across gender groups of adolescents? An application of the MACS model. *Structural Equation Modeling, 12*, 157–171.

Grayson, D. A., Mackinnon, A., Jorm, A. F., Creasey, H., & Broe, G. A. (2000). Item bias in the Center for Epidemiological Studies Depression Scale: Effects of physical disorders and disability in an elderly community sample. *Journal of Gerontology: Psychological Sciences, 55B*, 273–282.

Grayson, D. A., & Marsh, H. W. (1994). Identification with deficient rank loading matrices in Confirmatory Factor Analysis: Multitrait-multimethod models. *Psychometrika, 59*, 121–134.

Gregorich, S. E. (2006). Do self-report instruments allow meaningful comparisons across diverse population groups? Testing measurement invariance using the confirmatory factor analysis framework. *Medical Care, 44*, 78–94.

Hambleton, R. K., Swaminathan, H., & Rogers, H. J. (1991). *Fundamentals of item response theory.* Newbury Park, CA: Sage.

Hernández, A., & González-Romá, V. (2003). Evaluating the multiple-group Mean and Covariance Structure analysis model for the detection of Differential Item Functioning in polytomous ordered items. *Psichotema, 15*, 322–327.

Jones, R. N. (2006). Identification of measurement differences between English and Spanish language versions of the Mini-Mental State Examination: Detecting differential item functioning using MIMIC modeling. *Medical Care, 44*, 124–133.

Jöreskog, K. G. (1971). Simultaneous factor analysis in several populations. *Psychometrika, 36*, 409–426.

Jöreskog, K. G., & Goldberger, A. S. (1975). Estimation of a model with multiple indicators and multiple causes of a single latent variable. *Journal of the American Statistical Association, 10*, 631–639.

Kamata, A., & Bauer, D. J. (2008). A note on the relation between factor analytic and item response theory models. *Structural Equation Modeling, 15*, 136–153.

Katsuya, T. (2007). Cross-cultural validity of self-construal scales: An investigation of differential item functioning using multigroup mean and covariance structure. *Japanese Journal of Behaviormetrics, 34*, 79–89.

Kelloway, E. K. (1995). Structural equation modeling in perspective. *Journal of Organizational Behavior, 16*, 215–224.

Lee, J. (2009). *Type I error and power of the MACS CFA for DIF detection: Methodological issues and resolutions.* Unpublished doctoral dissertation, University of Kansas.

Lee, J. *Type I Error and power of the MIMIC technique for DIF detection: Problem of biased anchor set and a recommended procedure.* Manuscript in preparation.

Leone, L., van der Zee, K., van Oudenhoven, J. P., Perugini, M., & Ercolani, A. P. (2005). The cross-cultural generalizability and validity of the Multicultural Personality Questionnaire. *Personality and Individual Differences, 38*, 1449–1462.

Liang, J. (2001). Assessing cross-cultural comparability in mental health among older adults. *Journal of Mental Health and Aging, 7*, 21–30.

Little, T. D. (1997). Mean and covariance structures (MACS) analyses of cross-cultural data: Practical and theoretical issues. *Multivariate Behavioral Research, 32*, 53–76.

Little, T. D. (in press). Longitudinal structural equation modeling: Individual-difference panel models. New York: Guilford press.

Little, T. D., Slegers, D. W., & Card, N. A. (2006). A non-arbitrary method of identifying and scaling latent variables in SEM and MACS models. *Structural Equation Modeling, 13*, 59–72.

Lord, F. M., & Novick, M. R. (1968). *Statistical theories of mental test scores.* Reading, MA: Addison Wesley.

Lubke, G. H., & Muthén, B. O. (2004). Applying multigroup confirmatory factor models for continuous outcomes to Likert scale data complicates meaningful group comparisons. *Structural Equation Modeling, 11*, 514–534.

MacIntosh, R., & Hashim, S. (2003). Variance estimation for converting MIMIC model parameters to IRT parameters in DIF analysis. *Applied Psychological Measurement, 27*, 372–379.

Mackinnon, A., Jorm, A. F., Christensen, H., Korten, A. E., Jacomb, P. A., & Rodgers, B. (1999). A short form of the Positive and Negative Affect Schedule: Evaluation of factorial validity and invariance across demographic variables in a community sample. *Personality and Individual Differences, 27*, 405–416.

Marsh, H. W., Tracey, D. K., & Craven, R. G. (2006). Multidimensional self-concept structure for preadolescents with mild intellectual disability: A hybrid multigroup-MIMIC approach to factorial invariance and latent mean differences. *Educational and Psychological Measurement, 66*, 795–818

McDonald, R. P. (1967). Nonlinear factor analysis. *Psychometric Monographs,* No. 15. New York, NY: Springer.

McDonald, R. P. (1999). *Test theory: Unified treatment.* Mahwah, NJ: Lawrence Erlbaum.

Meade, A. W., Johnson, E. C., & Braddy, P. W. (2008). Power and sensitivity of alternative fit indices in test of measurement invariance. *Journal of Applied Psychology, 93*, 568–592.

Mellenbergh, G. J. (1994). A unidimensional latent trait model for continuous item responses. *Multivariate Behavioral Research, 29*, 223–237.

Meredith, W. (1993). Measurement invariance, factor analysis and factorial invariance. *Psychometrika, 58*, 525–543.

Millsap, R. E. (2005). Four unresolved problems in studies of factorial invariance. In A. Maydeu-Olivares & J. J. McArdle (Eds.), *Contemporary psychometrics* (pp. 153–172). Mahwah, NJ: Lawrence Erlbaum.

Millsap, R. E., & Yun-Tein, J. (2004). Assessing factorial invariance in ordered-categorical measures. *Multivariate Behavioral Research, 39*, 479–515.

Muthén, B. O. (1988). Some uses of structural equation modeling in validity studies: Extending IRT to external variables. In H. Wainder & H. Braun (Eds.), *Test validity* (pp. 213–238). Hillsdale, NJ: Lawrence Erlbaum.

Muthén, B. O., & Asparouhov, T. (2002). *Latent variable analysis with categorical outcomes: Multiple-group and growth modeling in Mplus.* Los Angeles, CA: University of California and Muthén & Muthén.

Muthén, B. O., & Christoffersson, A. (1981). Simultaneous factor analysis of dichotomous variables in several groups. *Psychometrika, 46*, 407–419.

Muthén, B. O., & Lehman, J. (1988). Multiple group IRT modeling: Applications to item bias analysis. *Journal of Educational Statistics, 10*, 133–142.

Navas-Ara, M. J., & Gómez-Benito, J. (2002). Effects of ability scale purification on identification of DIF. *European Journal of Psychological Assessment, 18*, 9–15.

Oishi, S. (2006). The concept of life satisfaction across cultures: An IRT analysis. *Journal of Research in Personality, 40*, 411–423.

Raju, N. S., Laffitte, L. J., & Byrne, B. M. (2002). Measurement equivalence: A comparison of methods based on confirmatory factor analysis and item response theory. *Journal of Applied Psychology, 87*, 517–529.

Rasch, G. (1960). *Probabilistic models for some intelligence and attainment tests.* Danish Institute for Educational Research, Copenhagen. (Expanded edition, 1980. Chicago: The University Chicago Press).

Reise, S. P., Widaman, K. F., & Pugh, R. H. (1993). Confirmatory Factor Analysis and item response theory: Two approaches for exploring measurement invariance. *Psychological Bulletin, 114*, 552–566.

Riordan, C. R., & Vandenberg, R. J. (1994). A central question in cross-cultural research: Do employees of different cultures interpret work-related measures in an equivalent manner? *Journal of Management, 20*, 643–671.

Samejima, F. (1969). Estimation of latent ability using a response pattern of graded scores. *Psychometrika Monographs*, No. 17. New York, NY: Springer.

Samejima, F. (1972). A general model for free-response data. *Psychometrika Monographs*, No. 18. New York, NY: Springer.

Satorra, A., & Bentler, P. M. (1988). Scaling corrections for chi-square statistics in covariance structure analysis. *American Statistical Association 1988 proceedings of the business and economics section* (pp. 308–313). Alexandria VA: American Statistical Association.

Satorra, A., & Bentler, P. M. (2001). A scaled difference chi-square test statistic for moment structure analysis. *Psychometrika, 66*, 507–514.

Schaffer, B. S., & Riordan, C. M. (2003). A review of cross-cultural methodologies for organizational research: A best-practices approach. *Organizational Research Methods, 6*, 169–215.

Sörbom, D. (1974). A general method for studying differences in factor means and factor structure between groups. *British Journal of Mathematical and Statistical Psychology, 27*, 229–239.

Stark, S., Chernyshenko, O. S., & Drasgow, F. (2006). Detecting differential item functioning with confirmatory factor analysis and item response theory: Toward a unified strategy. *Journal of Applied Psychology, 91*, 1202–1306.

Steenkamp, J. E. M., & Baumgartner, H. (1998). Assessing measurement invariance in crossnational consumer research. *Journal of Consumer Research, 25*, 78–90.

Takane, Y., & de Leeuw, J. (1987). On the relationship between item response theory and factor analysis of discretized variables. *Psychometrika, 52*, 393–408.

Vandenberg, R. J., & Lance, C. E. (2000). A review and synthesis of the measurement invariance literature: Suggestions, practices, and recommendations for organizational research. *Organizational Research Methods, 3*, 4–69.

van de Vijver, F., & Poortinga, Y. H. (1992). Testing in culturally heterogeneous populations: When are cultural loadings undesirable? *European Journal of Psychological Assessment, 8*, 17–24.

Wang, C. K. J., Liu, W. C., Biddle, S. J. H., & Spray, C. M. (2005). Cross-cultural validation of the Conceptions of the Nature of Athletic Ability Questionnaire Version 2. *Personality and Individual Differences, 38*, 1245–1256.

Welkenhuysen-Gybels, J., & van de Vijver, F. (2001). A comparison of methods for the evaluation of construct equivalence in a multigroup setting. *Proceedings of the annual meeting of the American Statistical Association*. Alexandria VA: American Statistical Association.

Widaman, K. F., & Reise, S. P. (1997). Exploring the measurement invariance of psychological instruments: Applications in the substance use domain. In K. J. Bryant, M. Windle, & S. G. West (Eds.), *The science of prevention: Methodological advances from alcohol and substance abuse research* (pp. 281–324). Washington, DC: American Psychological Association.

Woods, C. M. (2009). Evaluation of MIMIC-model methods for DIF testing with comparison to two-group analysis. *Multivariate Behavioral Research, 44*, 1–27.

Woods, C. M., Oltmanns, T. F., & Turkheimer, E. (2009). Illustration of MIMIC-Model DIF Testing with the Schedule for Nonadaptive and Adaptive Personality. *Journal of Psychopathology and Behavioral Assessment, 31*, 320–330.

Zumbo, B. D. (1999). *A handbook on the theory and methods of differential item functioning (DIF): Logistic regression modeling as a unitary framework for binary and Likert-type (ordinal) item scores*. Ottawa, ON: Directorate of Human Resources Research and Evaluation, Department of National Defense.

4

Estimation and Comparison of Latent Means Across Cultures

Holger Steinmetz
University of Giessen

4.1 INTRODUCTION

One of the most often conducted kind of analysis in cross-cultural research is to compare the mean of some construct across two or more cultural populations. Although one of the long-term goals of cross-cultural research may be to understand cultural functioning with regard to underlying cultural dimensions (Hofstede, 1980; House, Javidan, Hanges, & Dorfman, 2002) or contextual factors, mean comparisons are an important first way to generate knowledge about cross-cultural differences.

Although the use of structural equation modeling has increased in the last decades, researchers still rely on traditional methods (e.g., analysis of covariance (ANOVA) and *t*-test) when comparing means. The typical procedure consists in aggregating items, for instance, from a questionnaire or telephone interview, to a composite score and comparing the composites' mean across the cultural samples. Therefore, although researchers are well aware that observed variables differ from latent variables (Borsboom, 2008), traditional analyses treat observed *means* as if they were equal to latent means. However, observed means cannot simply be equated with the latent mean of the underlying construct. As I will show later in more detail, the relationship between an observed mean and the latent mean is a function that contains two other important parameters, that is, the indicator intercept and the factor loading. Consequently, group differences on an observed composite can be solely attributed to a latent mean difference when the intercepts and loadings of the indicators are invariant (i.e., equal) across the groups.

Using a mean and covariance structure analysis (MACS) approach, the estimation of latent means is straightforward (Little, 1997; Ployhardt & Oswald, 2004). A MACS approach allows combining the estimation of latent means (and their comparison across groups) with the analysis of the factor structure, whereas the aggregation of items to a composite score avoids such an analysis. Aggregation is problematic when the referring items are conceptually different facets and, hence, measure different latent variables. Furthermore, the statistical tests conducted within the MACS framework have a much higher power compared with tests for composite mean differences using *t*-tests or ANOVA (Thompson & Green, 2006) and lead to unbiased mean estimates even under conditions of partial invariance of the indicator intercepts (Steinmetz, 2010).* Observed mean analyses, in contrast, presume full invariance of intercepts.

This chapter gives an easy and nontechnical introduction to latent mean difference testing, explains its presumptions, and provides an empirical example using cross-cultural survey data. In addition, the chapter contains the syntax codes for LISREL and Mplus and a short description of the procedure in Amos. In contrast to existing introductions to latent mean estimation, the chapter contains an overview of the different ways to identify the mean structure, and discusses mean estimation in the second-order factor analytic and MIMIC modeling framework and when considering formative measurement models. Regarding formative measurement models, the chapter explicitly discusses the recent literature and its debate about the ontological nature of such models and implications for mean analyses.

4.2 THE RELATIONSHIP BETWEEN AN OBSERVED AND A LATENT MEAN

Although researchers currently are well aware that observed variables differ from underlying latent variables, observed means seem to be unintentionally equated with latent means. Observed means are a function of the indicator intercept, factor loading, and the latent mean and, hence, cannot simply be equated with the latent mean. In a usual common factor model,

* See a contrasting view on partial invariance by De Beuckelaer (2005).

the relationship between an observed indicator and the latent variable can be described by a usual regression equation:

$$X_i = \lambda_i \xi + \delta_i, \tag{4.1}$$

where X_i is the observed indicator i (e.g., the ith item in a questionnaire, response to an interview question, or a coded observation). The ξ is a latent variable that "underlies"—that is, caused—the observed indicator with the causal strength λ_i. Finally, δ_i is the residual that denotes the amount of unexplained variance in X_i. Conceptually, this model refers to reflective or effect indicator factor model that presumes that X_i reflects (i.e., is caused by) the latent variable (Bollen & Lennox, 1991).

The model depicted in Equation 4.1 as it is applied in the majority of confirmatory factor analyses aims at the estimation of factor loadings, variances, and covariances of the latent variables and measurement errors (see Brown, 2006, for a nontechnical introduction to confirmatory factor analyses). In this regard, estimates are found that allow to explain the variances and covariances of the observed variables. Mathematical relationships between the empirical (co)variances and the model parameters serve as a way to decompose each cell of the covariance matrix to a set of model parameters. For instance, the variance of an indicator with a single factor loading can be decomposed to the product of the squared loading times the variance of the latent variable plus the measurement error (i.e., $\text{Var}(X_i) = \lambda_i^2\phi + \delta_i$). As another example, the covariance between two indicators that measure the same latent variable can be decomposed to the product of their loadings and the variance of the latent variable (i.e., $\text{Cov}(X_i, X_j) = \lambda_i\lambda_j\phi$). Hence, the only empirical information underlying the model is the variances and covariances of the indicators. Consequently, the indicators are treated in terms of deviation units, implying zero means and intercepts.

In contrast, estimating location parameters (i.e., means) requires treating indicators in terms of their original metric. Therefore, the indicator intercept τ_i has to be included as an additional model parameter:

$$X_i = \tau_i + \lambda_i \xi + \delta_i. \tag{4.2}$$

Intercepts are comparable to the constant in a regression equation. Intercepts represent the difference between the response of an individual and the expected value that results from the product of the loading and the person's position on the latent dimension. To derive the equation for the latent mean, expectancies are taken that lead to

$$E(X_i) = \tau_i + \lambda_i E(\xi) + E(\delta_i), \tag{4.3}$$

where $E(X_i)$ is the expected value (i.e., mean) of the indicator and $E(\xi)$ is the latent mean. Because the distribution of the errors has an expected value of zero (i.e., $E(\delta_i) = 0$), it can be omitted. The $E(\xi)$ is hereafter denoted as κ:

$$E(X_i) = \tau_i + \lambda_i \kappa. \tag{4.4}$$

As shown in Equation 4.4, the observed mean results not only from the latent mean but also from the factor loading and the intercept. Whereas the factor loading weights the influence of the latent mean on the indicator, the intercept is a systematic bias that is added to or subtracted from the product of the latent mean and the loading. Such biases occur when respondents give systematically higher or lower responses on an average than expected from the latent mean. When investigating diverse cultural populations, differences in intercepts can result from differences in such response biases (see Steinmetz, 2009, for a more detailed discussion of intercepts). Regarding the estimation of intercepts and means, a vector of indicator means is added to the covariance matrix of the indicators as input information. Hence, in the same way, the empirical variances and covariances are decomposed to loadings, (co)variances of the latent variable(s), and errors, and empirical indicator means are decomposed to intercepts, loadings, and latent means (see Bollen, 1989; Brown, 2006, for further details).

4.3 ASSUMPTIONS

As Equation 4.4 shows, the observed mean cannot simply be equated with the latent mean. Likewise, observed mean *differences* between two or more groups (e.g., cultures) do not necessarily indicate latent mean differences as unequal intercepts and/or factor loadings will also lead to observed differences. Figure 4.1 shows two examples in which two groups with the

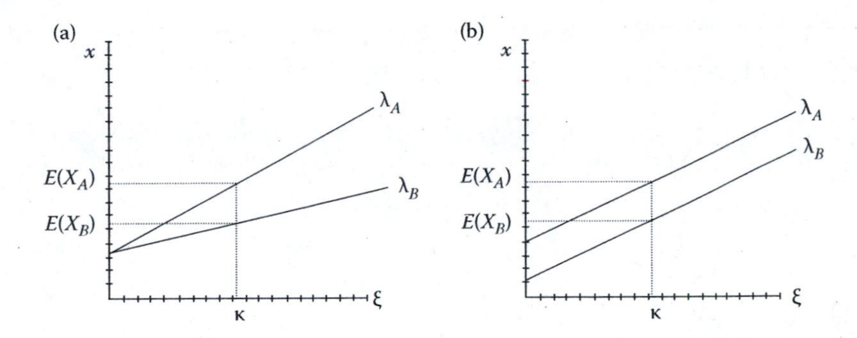

FIGURE 4.1
Relationship between latent and observed means under conditions of unequal factor loadings but equal intercepts (a) and equal factor loadings but unequal intercepts (b).

same latent mean κ show a difference in the observed mean as a result of unequal factor loadings (Figure 4.1a) and indicator intercepts (Figure 4.1b).

Therefore, it has to be shown prior to the comparison of the latent means that the groups do not significantly differ in the loadings and intercepts of the measures. The tests of these presumptions are one form of the overall tests for *measurement invariance* that concern the comparison of measurement parameters across two or more groups (Meredith, 1993; Steenkamp & Baumgartner, 1998; Vandenberg & Lance, 2000). In this regard, the equality of the factor loadings has been referred to as *metric (weak) invariance* and the equality of the intercepts signifies *scalar (strong) invariance.* Both presumptions, however, rest on the overall assumption that the analyzed groups show a comparable model structure; that is, *configural invariance.* In summary, analyses and comparisons of latent means across cultures are only warranted when the hypothesis of configural, metric, and scalar invariance cannot be rejected.

Whereas early claims of invariance concerned the full invariance of all parameters of a respective parameter matrix (e.g., the Λ matrix containing the factor loadings), the literature has somewhat agreed that *partial invariance* is a more realistic and sufficient condition. In particular, Byrne, Shavelson, and Muthén (1989) and Steenkamp and Baumgartner (1998) argued that at least two indicators have to show invariant loadings and intercepts to establish partial invariance. Other scholars, however (e.g., De Beuckelaer, 2005), argued that relying on partial invariance does not enable unbiased analyses of latent means and that full invariance is required (Chapter 3, by Lee, Little, and Preacher, and Chapter 5, by De Beuckelaer and Swinnen, in this book treat partial invariance in more detail).

4.4 PROCEDURE

MACS analyses and accompanying tests of measurement invariance are usually conducted within the multigroup confirmatory factor analysis (MGCFA) framework (an alternative will be described at the end of the chapter). In a MGCFA model, parameters of a factor model (see Equation 4.4) are separately estimated for two or more groups. However, it is possible to specify *equality constraints* that force the maximum likelihood algorithm to find the optimal noninvariant parameter value for the groups. For example, setting an equality constraint for a specific factor loading forces the algorithm to find a noninvariant estimate that delivers the best possible data fit. Tests for measurement invariance as well as the latent mean comparisons are conducted within a series of nested models in which each step contains more restrictions (i.e., equality constraints) than the step before. Consequently, the adequacy of a set of restrictions is evaluated with the chi-square difference (or likelihood ratio) test. A nonsignificant increase in the chi-square value indicates the noninvariance of the respective parameters. One problem with the chi-square difference test, however, is that its value depends on the overall fit of the former, less restricted, model (Yuan & Bentler, 2004). As a remedy, Cheung and Rensvold (2002) proposed to rely on the difference in the comparative fit index (Bentler, 1990), ΔCFI, to judge the adequacy of invariance assumptions. Based on their simulation study, which analyzed the behavior of several fit indexes, they found that the ΔCFI was the only fit index that was not correlated with its overall value of the former model. They proposed to reject the invariance hypothesis when $\Delta CFI > 0.01$.

As mentioned before, latent mean comparisons are only warranted under conditions of (partial) configural, metric, and scalar invariance. The sequence starts with testing configural invariance as the baseline. If the model fit is adequate, the factor loadings are constrained to be equal across the groups and the difference in the chi-square is evaluated. If a significant increase occurs, the equality constraints for those loadings with significant differences can be relaxed. At the next step, the intercepts are constrained to be equal. If the former step had led to one or more unequal loadings, the intercepts for those indicators are kept unconstrained. That is, indicators with significantly unequal loadings are not tested for scalar invariance. In case of a significant increase in the chi-square, noninvariant intercepts are identified and their constraints are relaxed. If this testing procedure results in at least two indicators with metric and scalar invariance, equality constraints for the latent means can be specified. A subsequent significant increase in the chi-square value indicates a latent mean difference. Recently, Saris, Satorra, and van der Veld (2009) argued that tests of a model are usually conducted without considering the power of the chi-square test to detect misspecifications. The authors noted that the power does not depend only on the size of the misspecification (i.e., deviation of the true population parameter from the sample parameter fixed to zero) but also on the sample size, the effect sizes of other parameters, and the number of indicators. Although this discussion refers to the test of overall structural equation models and not MACS, power considerations could be valuable information in the context of invariance testing.

There is some discussion, on how to proceed when the hypothesis of full invariance of a parameter matrix has been rejected. As mentioned above, partial invariance means that some parameters are allowed to differ across the groups. The question, however, arises on how to elaborate which parameters differ significantly across the groups and, hence, violate the assumption of full invariance. Initially, Byrne et al. (1989) proposed to inspect the modification indices (or univariate Lagrange multipliers) that are provided by the software (e.g., LISREL, AMOS, Mplus) for each fixed or constrained parameter. A modification index signifies the reduction of the chi-square value if the respective parameter is freely estimated. Although this procedure can be referred to as the most practical and straightforward, it is not without dangers. Modification indexes assume that the model is correct (Cheung & Rensvold, 1999). Hence, indexes calculated for the fully invariant model are more or less biased depending on the extent of noninvariance. Practically, this implies that the modification index for a respective parameter may not be trustworthy. Furthermore, the sequence by which constraints for parameters with high modification indexes (MIs) are relaxed affect the MIs for the remaining constrained parameters. It is, for instance, possible that a modification index is substantial in a certain step of the sequence and becomes negligible after relaxing the constraint for another parameter with a larger modification index. Similarly, parameters that have passed one step of the sequence again show a high MI when elements of a different parameter matrix are constrained (e.g., after successfully passing the test for metric invariance, some loadings show high-MIs when restricting the intercepts to be equal). According to Steenkamp and Baumgartner (1998), "model respecifications should be conducted cautiously and [...] we recommend that invariance constraints be relaxed only when MIs [modification indexes] are highly significant (both in absolute magnitude and in comparison with the majority of others MIs) and expected parameters change (EPCs) are substantial" (p. 81). Additional information can be obtained by inspecting the estimates of the unconstrained parameters. In this regard, descriptively large differences across groups should match the information provided by the MIs. In the case that the marker indicator that defines the scale and origin of the latent variable (see Section 4.5) is noninvariant across groups, another indicator with invariant loading and intercept has to be selected as the marker.

4.5 IDENTIFICATION

MACS analyses require additional restrictions to identify intercepts and latent means. In the same way, loadings, errors, and latent variances can only be estimated when the model is either just-identified (i.e., the number of parameters equals the number of empirical [co]variances) or over-identified (i.e., the number of parameters is smaller than the number of empirical [co]variances), intercepts and means can be estimated only when the number of empirical means equals or exceeds the number of intercepts and means. For instance, specifying a measurement model with two groups and four indicators implies 10 unknown parameters (i.e., eight intercepts and two latent means). However, there are only eight observed means as empirical information. Hence, the model is unidentified unless some restrictions are implemented. These restrictions have a further substantial meaning: Latent variables are continuous dimensions, and thus have neither a metric nor numerical values (such as a numerical mean). The scale is usually provided by fixing one factor loading to one or, alternatively, by fixing the latent variance to one. Analogously, the origin of the latent variable has to be defined in order to assign numerical values to the latent dimensions and to be able to compare those values across groups.

There are three approaches to identifying the mean structure (see Little, Slegers, & Card, 2006, for an overview). All approaches lead to identical conclusions regarding mean differences but result in different interpretations of the absolute values of means and intercepts.

First, the intercept of the marker item that is used to scale the latent variable may be fixed to zero and both means estimated (the "marker method"). As a consequence, the latent mean will be estimated as the marker mean. The remaining intercepts are estimated as the deviation of the observed mean and the $\lambda_i\kappa$ product of the referring indicator (i.e., $\tau_i = \overline{X}_i - \lambda_i\kappa$). The equality constraints that are implemented in the process of metric and scalar invariance testing assure that a potential difference in the latent mean across the groups can be attributed to the latent level and not only to differences in the marker mean.

Second, the latent means may be fixed to zero and all intercepts estimated (the "reference-group method"). As a consequence, the intercepts will be equal to their respective observed indicators (i.e., $\tau_i = \overline{X}_i - \lambda_i \times 0$). When the test for scalar invariance is conducted, the zero fixation of latent mean in one group—the "comparison group"—has to be relaxed because, otherwise, the tests for scalar and mean invariance are confounded. That means that—at the same time—both the latent mean and the intercepts would be constrained to equality, which would make it impossible to determine which constraint is wrong. Using the reference-group method, it is possible to interpret a latent mean difference in terms of the standardized effect size Glass' Δ, which belongs to the class of effect sizes of the *d*-family (Rosenthal & DiMatteo, 2001) and is often used in experimental research by dividing the mean difference between the treatment and control groups (i.e., reference group) by the standard deviation of the control group (Little et al., 2006). In the MACS analyses, Glass' Δ is gained by fixing the variance of the latent variances instead of the marker indicator to one. If the researcher finds it more comfortable to interpret effect sizes in terms of a correlation, Glass' Δ (as any effect size of the *d*-family) can be converted to *r* by using the formula:

$$r = \sqrt{\frac{d^2}{d^2 + 4}}, \tag{4.5}$$

where *d* is Glass' Δ.

Analogous to the estimation of the latent mean, the unit fixation of the latent variance in the comparison group has to be relaxed when metric invariance is tested. Otherwise, the tests of metric invariance and invariance of the latent variances are confounded. The test for mean equality can finally be conducted by constraining the mean of the comparison group to be equal to the mean of the first group.

Little et al. (2006) proposed as a third method ("effects coding method") using all intercepts in combination to identify the mean structure and all loadings to identify the covariance structure. In particular, the intercepts are constrained such that their *sum* equals zero and the loadings are constrained that their *average* equals 1. The summation of the intercepts is, for instance, established by requesting one intercept to be estimated as a function of the others (e.g., $\tau_1 = 0 - \tau_2 - \tau_3 - \tau_4$). As a result of these constraints, the latent mean is estimated as the weighted average of the observed means and the latent variance is estimated as the weighted average of the observed variances.

4.6 AN EMPIRICAL EXAMPLE

The empirical example relies on data from the European Social Survey (2002). The aim was to compare the latent means of the latent variable "self-esteem" among the Norwegian and British population. Four items were used in the MACS model: "In general I feel very positive about myself" (pstvms), "I feel what I do in life is valuable and worthwhile" (dngval), "At times I feel as if I am a failure" (flrms), and "It is hard to be hopeful about the future of the world" (nhpftr). The responses were provided on a five-point Likert scale from 1 (*agree strongly*) to 5 (*disagree strongly*). The sample sizes were $N = 2375$ (British sample) and $N = 1744$ (Norwegian sample). The analyses were based on the covariance matrices and means of the four indicators computed for both samples. The indicators *pstvms* and *dngval* were inverted in order to interpret high-numerical values in all four indicators as a reflection of a high self-esteem.

The syntax commands for LISREL and Mplus are depicted in Appendices 4.A and 4.B, respectively. Appendix 4.C contains a description of the procedure in AMOS. The LISREL code contains the covariance matrices and mean vector of the indicators. Whereas Mplus analyses usually are based on the raw data, the analyses in the present case were conducted based on an external file with the covariance matrix and mean vector. This file can be rebuilt by copying the matrices from the LISREL code into a text file. This file should contain the mean (row) vector followed by the covariance matrix, subsequently for the groups:

```
3.7642 3.8756 3.5008 2.8158 #means of group 1
0.6654        #covariance matrix of group 1
0.2030 0.5382
0.3353 0.1605 1.0788
0.1536 0.1050 0.1497 1.0491
3.6777 3.9845 3.3967 3.0573 #means of group 2
0.5862        #covariance matrix of group 2
0.1299 0.3707
0.2568 0.0957 1.0436
0.1219 0.0600 0.1388 0.9228
```

Although the identification procedure proposed by Little et al. (2006) has some advantages (e.g., interpretation of latent means in terms of average observed means), the presented analyses relied on the marker method as this is the more straightforward way. In this regard, the loading of *pstvms* was fixed to one and its intercept was fixed to zero.

Table 4.1 shows the fit indexes for the nested models that test for configural, metric, and scalar invariance as preconditions for the comparison of the latent mean. Each model contains a set of equality constraints that makes it more restrictive than the former model.* The differences in chi-square ($\Delta\chi^2$) and CFI (ΔCFI) allow a judgment of whether the respective constraint is tenable. Information provided by the modification indices as well the residuals (discussed later in detail) provide information about potential sources of noninvariance. As Table 4.1 shows, the tests for metric and scalar invariance resulted in full metric invariance of all four factor loadings (Model B) and partial scalar invariance (Model D). In particular, the intercepts of the equations for *dngval* ("I feel what I do in life is valuable and worthwhile") and *nhpftr* ("It is hard to be hopeful about the future of the world") were significantly higher in the Norwegian sample. Because of the large sample size, the statistical tests for invariance had a high power that makes it very difficult to find especially nonsignificant intercept differences. Therefore, Table 4.1 also presents the ΔCFI (Cheung & Rensvold, 2002) that enables evaluating invariance from a more practical

* An exception is Model D testing for partial scalar invariance that relaxes two constraints imposed by Model C.

TABLE 4.1

Results of the Invariance Tests

Model		Compared Model	χ^2 (df)	$\Delta\chi^2$ (Δdf)	RMSEA	CFI	ΔCFI	AIC	Conclusion
A	Configural invariance		8.27 (4)	—	0.023	0.997	—	56.27	Baseline model fits
B	Full metric invariance	A	12.05 (7)	+ 3.78 (3)	0.019	0.996	0.001	54.05	Nonsignificant increase in chi-square: Metric invariance holds
C	Full scalar invariance	B	145.05 (10)**	+ 133.00 (3)**	0.081	0.904	0.090	181.05	Significant increase in chi-square: Some intercept(s) differ
D	Partial scalar invariance	B	12.94 (8)	+ 0.89 (1)	0.017	0.996	0.000	52.94	Two intercepts are invariant
E	Invariance of latent means	D	28.73 (9)**	+ 15.79 (1)**	0.033	0.986	0.010	66.73	The latent mean differs significantly across the groups

**$p < 0.001$.

perspective. In the present example, however, the information provided by the ΔCFI corresponded to the information provided by the chi-square test. Finally, the tests for equal latent means (Model E) showed that the Norwegian sample had a significantly lower latent mean in self-esteem compared to the British sample. Applying the reference method to identify the latent means showed that the effect size of the difference, however, is small (Glass' $\Delta = 0.15$).

Table 4.2 gives a closer look into the parameter estimates of the various models and illustrates how parameters are estimated under an increasing number of equality constraints. Depicted are the observed mean (X_i), the parameters of the model (i.e., τ_i, λ_i, and κ), the fitted means; that is, the indicator means implied by the estimated parameters (see Equation 4.4), and the residuals that are the differences between each observed and fitted indicator mean. The goal of the estimator (e.g., maximum likelihood) is to minimize these residuals.

The *configural invariant* model (Model A from Table 4.1) implies no restrictions on the mean structure beyond those necessary for the identification (the first intercept is fixed to zero). Fixed or constrained parameters are underlined. Due to these constraints, the latent mean is estimated as the observed mean of the marker indicator (3.76 and 3.68). All other intercepts and loadings are optimally chosen such that the residuals are minimized and the fitted means exactly equal the observed means.

The *metrically invariant model* (Model B) imposes equality constraints on the factor loadings. These constraints have implications just for the minimization process regarding the covariance matrix. As the factor loadings are not only part of the mean equations (i.e., $E(X_i) = \tau_i + \lambda_i k$) of the indicators but also of the structural equations linking the model to the observed covariance matrix (i.e., $\mathrm{Var}(X_i) = \lambda_i^2\phi + \delta_i$), restricting loadings to be equal raises the question whether the observed (co)variances in both groups can adequately be reproduced. Regarding the mean structure, the metrically invariant model is still just-identified and the observed means can perfectly be reproduced by choosing the intercepts in such a way that the residuals are zero. As Table 4.2 shows, the intercepts change from Model A to Model B.

The test for *full scalar invariance* (Model C), causes the first strain for the mean structure. As the former model allowed finding intercept estimates separately for both groups, the algorithm could simply adapt to each

TABLE 4.2

Parameter Estimates for the Models

	Group A: British Sample						Group B: Norwegian Sample					
Indicator	$\bar{X}_i$	τ_i	λ_i	κ	**Fitted Means**	**Residuals**	$\bar{X}_i$	τ_i	λ_i	κ	**Fitted Means**	**Residuals**
Configural invariance (Model A)												
pstvms	3.76	<u>0.00</u>	<u>1.00</u>	3.76	3.76	0.00	3.68	<u>0.00</u>	<u>1.00</u>	3.68	3.68	<u>0.00</u>
dngval	3.88	1.93	0.52		3.88	0.00	3.99	2.43	0.42		3.98	0.00
flrms	3.50	0.29	0.85		3.50	0.00	3.40	0.26	0.85		3.40	0.00
nhpftr	2.82	1.24	0.42		2.82	0.00	3.06	1.45	0.44		3.06	0.00
Metric invariance (Model B)												
pstvms	3.76	<u>0.00</u>	<u>1.00</u>	3.76	3.76	0.00	3.68	0.00	1.00	3.68	3.68	0.00
dngval	3.88	2.06	<u>0.48</u>		3.88	0.00	3.99	2.21	0.48		3.99	0.00
flrms	3.50	0.30	<u>0.85</u>		3.50	0.00	3.40	0.27	0.85		3.40	0.00
nhpftr	2.82	1.22	<u>0.43</u>		2.82	0.00	3.06	1.49	0.43		3.06	0.00
Full scalar invariance (Model C)												
pstvms	3.76	<u>0.00</u>	<u>1.00</u>	3.74	3.74	0.02	3.68	<u>0.00</u>	<u>1.00</u>	3.71	3.71	−0.03
dngval	3.88	<u>2.19</u>	<u>0.47</u>		3.94	−0.06	3.99	<u>2.19</u>	<u>0.47</u>		3.92	0.06
flrms	3.50	<u>0.31</u>	<u>0.84</u>		3.47	0.03	3.40	<u>0.31</u>	<u>0.84</u>		3.44	−0.04
nhpftr	2.82	<u>1.41</u>	<u>0.41</u>		2.93	−0.11	3.06	<u>1.41</u>	<u>0.41</u>		2.92	0.14

Partial scalar invariance (Model D)												
pstvms	3.76	0.00	1.00	3.77	3.77	0.00	3.68	0.00	1.00	3.67	3.67	0.00
dngval	3.88	2.05	0.48		3.88	0.00	3.99	2.21	0.48		3.98	0.00
flrms	3.50	0.26	0.86		3.49	0.01	3.40	0.26	0.86		3.41	-0.01
nhpftr	2.82	1.20	0.43		2.82	0.00	3.06	1.49	0.43		3.06	0.00
Latent mean invariance (Model E)												
pstvms	3.76	0.00	1.00	3.72	3.72	0.04	3.68	0.00	1.00	3.72	3.72	-0.05
dngval	3.88	2.07	0.48		3.86	0.01	3.99	2.21	0.48		4.00	-0.01
flrms	3.50	0.28	0.85		3.45	0.05	3.40	0.28	0.85		3.45	-0.06
nhpftr	2.82	1.22	0.42		2.80	0.01	3.06	1.49	0.42		3.07	-0.01

Note: $\bar{X}_i$ = observed indicator mean; τ_i = indicator intercept, λ_i = factor loading; κ = latent mean; residual = difference between the observed indicator means the predicted mean (by $\tau_i + \lambda_i\kappa$); underlined estimates are constrained.

loading constraint by choosing the respective intercept that—together with the loading—reproduce the observed means. Metaphorically speaking, one can think of the intercept functioning as a valve that enables reducing the tension within a mechanical system. The fully scalar invariant model, in contrast, restricts the intercepts to be equal in both groups (i.e., closes the valve). The algorithm now has to find an optimal compromise among three options to reproduce the observed means: (a) it can change the latent mean estimate for both groups separately but this will affect all observed means in each group, (b) it can change factor loadings for both groups but this will affect the observed means and (co)variances, (c) it can change intercepts for both groups. As Table 4.2 shows, even the most optimal compromise led to implied means of *dngval* and *nhpftr* that deviate substantially from the observed means: For the British sample, the residuals for these indicators are –0.06 and –0.11 and for the Norwegian sample, the residuals are 0.06 and 0.14. For these two indicators, hence, the null hypothesis of invariance has to be rejected.

The *partially scalar invariant model* (Model D) relaxes the constraints on the intercepts for *dngval* and *nhpftr*. By finding different estimates of the intercepts for both groups ($\tau_{dngval} = 2.05$ vs. 2.21, and $\tau_{nhpftr} = 1.20$ vs. 1.49), it is possible to reproduce the observed means almost perfectly.

The *final model* (Model E) tests if—given the most optimal pattern of invariant and noninvariant loadings and intercepts resulting from the former models—the observed means could have occurred under the premise that the latent means are equal. The strain for the mean structure in this case is caused by requesting only one latent mean estimate occurring in each of the eight mean equations. Although the algorithm can adapt slightly by changing intercept and loading estimates to minimize the residuals, these changes can only occur within the limits created by the cross-group constraints. When, therefore, the observed means cannot be adequately reproduced even after the best possible compromise in estimating a single latent mean, intercepts, and loadings (simultaneously for both groups), the hypothesis of equal latent means must be rejected. In the present case, especially the observed means of *pstvms* and *flrms*, could not adequately be reproduced. This misfit shows why it is important to have at least one additional invariant intercept because otherwise, the algorithms simply could reproduce the observed means by adapting the intercepts in each group. The invariant intercepts, however, imply limits in which changes in the latent means can take place.

4.7 ESTIMATING LATENT MEANS IN SECOND-ORDER FACTOR MODELS, MIMIC MODELS, AND FORMATIVE MODELS

The subsequent section will briefly discuss three further issues relevant to the estimation of latent means: second-order factor models, MIMIC modeling, and formative measurement models.

4.8 LATENT MEAN ESTIMATION IN SECOND-ORDER FACTOR MODELS

The preceding section described in detail the relationship between an observed mean and a latent mean (see Equation 4.4) in a first-order factor model. That is, it was assumed that a single latent variable causally determines a set of observed indicators, although in practice it is rather common to have several latent variables that are allowed to covary. Sometimes, the researchers may hypothesize that the covariation among these latent variables is the result of a higher-order factor (Gerbing, Hamilton, & Freeman, 1994; Rindskopf & Rose, 1988). The mean of this higher-order factor can also be compared across groups. In the same way, Equation 4.2 describes the relationship between an observed indicator and an underlying latent variable, Equation 4.6 describes the relationship between a first-order factor and an underlying second-order factor:

$$\eta_i = \alpha_i + \gamma_i \xi + \zeta_i. \tag{4.6}$$

Here, η_i is the *i*th first-order factor caused by ξ; γ_i is the higher-order factor loading relating ξ to η_i, and ζ_i is the disturbance (i.e., the variance in η_i not explained by ξ). Finally, α_i is the intercept. Analogous to Equation 4.5, the relationship between the first-order factor mean and the second-order mean can be described by

$$E(\eta_i) = \alpha_i + \gamma_i \kappa. \tag{4.7}$$

Equation 4.7 is almost identical to Equation 4.4: κ is still the latent mean of the exogenous variable ξ. The only difference is that the "indicator" in a higher-order factor model is not an observed variable X_i but a latent variable η_i. Thus, the notation for the intercept changes from τ_i to α_i. The similarity between the lower-order structure and the higher-order structure can easily be used to describe the identification constraints in tests of metric and scalar invariance: Again, the researcher has the choice between the marker method (i.e., fixing one higher-order loading to 1 and one higher-order intercept α_i to zero, and estimate the κ's in all groups), the reference-group method (i.e., fixing the κ's to zero in all groups and estimating the intercepts α_i), or the effects coding approach (all intercepts and loadings are used in combination to identify the covariance and mean structure). Furthermore, the chosen strategy can be the same for both the lower- and higher-order level or different. For instance, Chen, Sousa, and West (2005) used the marker approach for the lower level and the reference-group approach for the higher level. Regarding the tests for measurement invariance, these authors emphasized that a test of the higher-order parameters requires invariance of the lower-order parameters. They proposed the following sequence of tests: (a) invariance of the lower-order factor loadings, (b) invariance of the higher-order factor loadings, (c) invariance of the lower-order intercepts, (d) invariance of the higher-order intercepts, and (e) invariance of the higher-order factor means.

4.9 THE MIMIC MODELING APPROACH TO MEAN ANALYSES

A multiple group modeling approach is not the only way in which means can be compared across groups. Multiple indicators multiple causes (MIMIC; Jöreskog & Goldberger, 1975; Muthén, 1989) modeling is a single-group approach (i.e., relies on a single covariance matrix) but incorporates group information in the form of observed dummy variables as covariates of the latent variable(s). In case of two groups, one dummy variable (e.g., 0 = Norwegian, 1 = British) is included that predicts the latent variable. In contrast to the multiple group approach, the indicator means are not considered (see Figure 4.2). The unstandardized coefficient of the dummy variable denotes the units by which one group differs on average from another in the latent variable and the standardized coefficient denotes the effect size of this difference (Thompson & Green, 2006). Brown (2006),

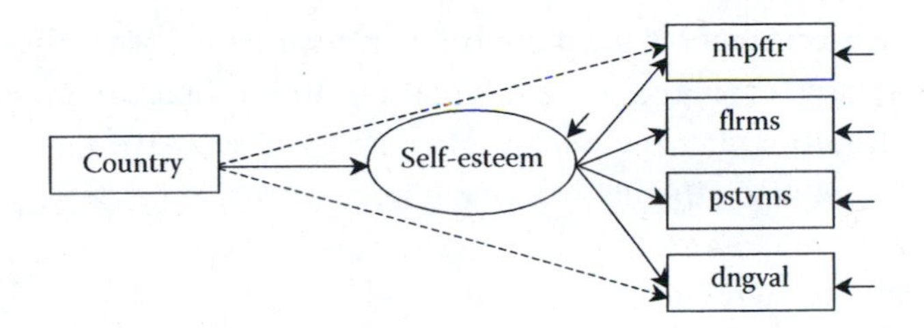

FIGURE 4.2
MIMIC model analyzing latent means across the British and Swedish sample.

however, emphasizes that the standardization should only refer to the latent variable but not to the dummy variables.

The MIMIC model depicted in Figure 4.2 is a reanalysis of the empirical example from the previous section (i.e., comparison of the British and Norwegian sample). The regression effect of the binary country variable on the latent self-esteem variable denotes the difference in the latent means. Without considering differences in intercepts (i.e., lack of direct effects of the country variable on the four indicators of self-esteem), the model did not fit the data well ($\chi^2(5) = 137.69$, $p < .001$, RMSEA (root mean square error approximation) = 0.08, CFI = .91). Inspecting the residuals (in this case, these are the deviations between the implied covariances and the empirical covariances) revealed that the covariance between the country variable and *nhpftr* and *dngval* could not be sufficiently explained by the presence of the latent variable. The modification indices underscored this interpretation, recommending the estimation of direct effects of the country variable on these two indicators (i.e., the dotted paths in Figure 4.2). This modification led to a well-fitting model ($\chi^2(3) = 8.21$, $p = 0.04$, RMSEA = 0.02, CFI = 1.0). The conclusion resulting from the MIMIC model, hence, equals the conclusion from the multiple group analysis that the countries differ in these indicators beyond a level that could be explained by differences in the latent self-esteem.

The advantage of the MIMIC approach compared to the multiple group approach is that more than one grouping variable can be addressed at one time, as well as their interaction (i.e., by incorporating a product term that results from multiplying the dummy variables). For instance, given the example of self-esteem, the researcher could address group differences between British and Norwegian individuals, women and men, as well as their interaction. In this case, incorporation of dummy variables would equal the treatment of dummy variables in multiple regression (Cohen,

Cohen, West, & Aiken, 2003). One further advantage is that the MIMIC approach requires a smaller sample size than the multiple group approach. Whereas a multiple group model implies estimating two or more models, the MIMIC approach implies just one model.

One disadvantage is that the MIMIC approach assumes that most of the parameters (i.e., factor loadings, errors, and latent (co)variances) are equal across the groups (Brown, 2006), which cannot be tested. It is, however, possible to investigate scalar invariance by testing if the dummy variable has a direct effect on the indicators of the latent variable. A significant effect denotes that, while holding the latent variable constant, the observed means differ across the groups (Brown, 2006). Marsh, Tracey, and Craven (2006) proposed combining multiple group and MIMIC analyses. In their study, they first tested for invariance of the various parameters regarding each grouping variable, and successively combined several grouping variables as well as their product terms for further analyses.

4.10 MEANS IN FORMATIVE MEASUREMENT MODELS

Formative measurement models (or formative constructs, emergent constructs) have been discussed for decades (Bollen & Lennox, 1991; Cohen, Cohen, Teresi, Marchi, & Velez, 1990; Diamantopoulos, Riefler, & Roth, 2008; Diamantopoulos & Winklhofer, 2001; Jarvis, MacKenzie, & Podsakoff, 2003; MacCallum & Browne, 1993). Whereas the typical *reflective measurement model* refers to a latent variable that is supposed to cause the observed variable (see Equation 4.1), the formative model assumes that the observed variables determine the construct. Consequently, these observed variables are denoted as *causal indicators*. Issues of latent mean estimation have mostly been discussed within the reflective model perspective (see Cole, Maxwell, Arvey, & Salas, 1993; Thompson & Green, 2006, as exceptions). Cole et al. (1993) as well as Thompson and Green (2006) argue that, in contrast to reflective models, means of formative constructs (they use the term "emergent construct") should be compared with multivariate analysis of variance (MANOVA). The current debate about the usefulness and ontological status of the formative model (Bagozzi, 2007; Bollen, 2007; Franke, Preacher, & Rigdon, 2008; Howell, Breivik, & Wilcox, 2007a, 2007b; Wilcox, Howell, & Breivik, 2008), however, leads to a deviating perspective on the adequate way of comparing means of formative constructs.

MANOVA is an observed variable method and even weighting variables does not imply any latent construct. Ontologically, such a treatment of observed variables corresponds to the idea of many scholars that a formative construct is characterized by "causal indicators [which] are combined additively to form a linear composite" (Thompson & Green, 2006, p. 121). Diamantopoulos et al. (2008) conceive causal indicators as both causal influences and integral part of the construct when they argue that "each indicator captures a specific aspect of the construct's domain" (p. 1205). Similarly, Cadogan, Souchon, and Procter (2008) note that "when specifying the content and identifying the indicators of formative models, the indicators should adequately cover the breadth of the latent variable" (p. 1265). As Borsboom, Mellenbergh, and van Heerden (2003) point out, the ontological status of such a construct is ambiguous and refers to a *constructivist* (i.e., the construct is a "construction of the human mind," p. 207) or *operationalist* (i.e., the construct is defined via the measurement operations) rather than an *entity realism* view (i.e., the construct exists beyond its measures). A researcher adhering to such a view about the construct, of course, can conduct a MANOVA with the observed variables. However, because indicators of a formative construct have been described as conceptually distinct entities "not required to have the same antecedents and consequences" (Jarvis et al., 2003, p. 203), the question is what inferences can be drawn for the whole construct by comparing means of this multivariate set of observed means? As a further caveat, MANOVA equals other observed mean techniques as it assumes equal response biases across groups, which is unlikely to be the case.

The view of formative constructs as described above was recently questioned by Howell et al. (2007b) and Wilcox et al. (2008) who argued that constructs are not inherently reflective or formative. These authors claimed that it is the relationship between an indicator and its construct that is either reflective or formative and that it is possible to measure every "formative construct" (in addition or alternatively) with reflective indicators. The important difference to the view introduced initially is that such a view implies an entity realism perspective of the latent variable. In this case, considering the mean of such a latent variable does indeed make sense. From a technical point of view, however, the question is whether inferences about the construct's mean should be based on the indicators' means and if yes, how such an inference would look like. The reason is that the mean of a formative latent variable is not an estimated parameter because it is directly implied by the means of the causal indicators and their effects on the formative construct:

$$E(\eta) = \alpha + \gamma_1 E(X_1) + \gamma_2 E(X_2) + \ldots + \gamma_n E(X_n) = \alpha + \sum_{i=1}^{n} \gamma_i E(X_i), \quad (4.8)$$

where $E(\eta)$ is the mean of the formative construct, α is the intercept of the structural equation and X_1–X_n are the n causal indicators affecting η with γ_i. Because the latent mean is not an estimated parameter, it is not possible to directly compare the groups in their construct mean. Comparing the set of observed means again raises ambiguity about the ontological status of the construct (indeed, the mean of every possible sum score can easily be compared regardless if this sum score refers to anything reasonable). Furthermore, it is possible that the same implied latent mean results from a diverse profile of mean differences in the set of causal indicators.

The solution to this problem, however, lies in the identification part of the model, which is a necessary part of every formative measurement model (Bollen & Davis, 1994; MacCallum & Browne, 1993). Because the formative measurement model has to incorporate at least two dependent latent variables or at least two reflective measures to identify the formative construct, the procedures for testing mean differences described for the usual (first- or second-order factor model above) is valid in this case, too. In this regard, a formative construct emitting paths to two dependent latent variables can be treated as a second-order factor, and the formative construct measured by two reflective indicators can bet treated as any other reflective latent variable (Wilcox et al., 2008). The only difference to the usual test of means is that the causal indicators are part of the model with the result that the latent mean is still not a model parameter. The most obvious practical solution here is to eliminate the causal indicators for the test of the latent mean and to proceed with the tests for metric, scalar, and mean invariance.

As a further possibility, means of such a latent variable may be investigated with the MIMIC approach addressed in the previous section (see Figure 4.2). In this regard, one or more dummy variables that represent the countries are included as predictors of the formative variable. An advantage of this approach is that the causal indicators do not have to be omitted from the model, more than two countries can be included, and the interaction between the country variable(s) and other predictors of the formative variable (e.g., the causal indicators) can be investigated.

4.11 CONCLUSIONS

This chapter provided an overview of approaches to estimate and compare latent means across cultures. Most notable, the MACS approach reflects the important difference between observed means and latent means. After explaining the relationship between latent and observed means and the important role of the indicator intercepts, the various tests for invariance (e.g., configural, metric, and scalar invariance) that are preconditions for a meaningful comparison of latent means were reviewed. Subsequently, the procedure of testing the various steps of invariance via equality constraints, evaluation of these tests using the chi-square difference statistic and differences in the fit indexes (e.g., ΔCFI), and the use of modification indices as means to investigate failure of a constraint were discussed. Likewise, three methods to identify the mean structure of the model (i.e., the marker method, the reference-group method, and the effects coding method) were reviewed that lead to identical results regarding the significance of latent mean differences but offer the researcher control over the precise numerical estimates the respective method delivers. The chapter illustrated these theoretical issues with an empirical example using data from the European Social Survey. Table 4.2 presented a step-by-step explanation of how the software estimates the parameters at the various steps of the invariance tests. Finally, the chapter discussed mean estimation in second-order factor models, MIMIC models, and formative measurement models.

All the issues discussed in this chapter implied idealized conditions with regard to the assumptions of any latent variable model—and, thus, MACS analyses as well. In this regard, the discussion of the issues presumed *normally distributed data, continuous scale level* of the indicators, *causal homogeneity* of the cultural population from which the ESS samples were drawn, and a nonexistence of *missing data*. In practical applications, however, these assumptions may often be violated (see Hoogland &

Boomsma, 1998, for a review of robustness in latent variable modeling). Possible targets of violations of the assumptions are the unbiasedness of the parameter estimates (i.e., the mean of a parameter's sampling distribution equals the population parameter), their standard errors, and the chi-square test. In the following, the most salient issues of concern are briefly discussed.

Normality. One of the most basic assumption of maximum likelihood estimation is multivariate normal distribution of the indicators (i.e., the joint probability distribution of the indicators is normal). Whereas maximum likelihood estimated parameters are relatively robust to nonnormality, their standard errors and chi-square statistic are biased (Finney & DiStefano, 2006). Thus, before using a MACS or MIMIC approach, researchers should screen their data for normality, and try to use univariate (Tabachnik & Fidell, 2005) or multivariate (Yuan, Chan, & Bentler, 2000) transformation methods to normalize the data or remove potential outliers. An alternative is to use the corrected chi-square statistic and robust standard errors (Satorra & Bentler, 1994) or bootstrapping (Bollen & Stine, 1992). When using the Satorra–Bentler correction in MACS analyses, care has to be taken when comparing nested models. Because the difference between two Satorra–Bentler corrected chi-square statistics is not chi-square distributed, a special formula has to be applied to test for the difference.*

Scale level. A closely connected assumption of latent variable models is that the observed indicators are measured on a continuous scale. Given that most research is conducted with Likert-type rating scales that are ordered categorical, this assumption is violated. A consequence of treating categorical indicators as continuous may be that their correlations are underestimated, which biases parameter estimates (especially when using less than five response categories, cf. Finney & DiStefano, 2006). In single group latent variable models, a polychoric, polyserial, or tetrachorical correlation matrix (instead of a covariance matrix) can be used as input matrix, and specific estimators (robust weighted least squares in Mplus or diagonally weighted least squares in LISREL) can be applied to estimate the correct parameters (Flora & Curran, 2004). In a model with ordinal data, thresholds are estimated that represent the position in

* A freeware program to calculate the Satorra-Bentler corrected chi-square difference can be downloaded from the Web site http://www.abdn.ac.uk/~psy086/dept/psychom.htm

a latent response variable that cause the selection of a certain observed response category. Given *m* response categories in the observed indicator, *m*–1 threshold parameters are estimated. In a MACS analysis, thresholds instead of intercepts are compared across groups as a goal of invariance testing (Lubke & Muthén, 2004).

As the two final points of concern, lack of *causal homogeneity* and *missing data* can bias the parameters in a MACS analysis. The causal homogeneity assumption (Muthén, 1989) means that the investigated sample is drawn from a population in which the model is valid. Causal heterogeneity, in contrast, means that the population consists of subpopulations with different model parameters (i.e., different causal effects) or even a completely different structure. Failure to account for causal (or population) heterogeneity can bias parameters or result in a low fit of the model. Remedies are mixture modeling approaches (Bauer & Curran, 2004; Gagné, 2006; Lubke & Muthén, 2005; Muthén, 2001), in which the model is estimated for a prespecified number of (unknown) subpopulations. Consequently, solutions for differing numbers of subpopulations can be compared with regard to their fit, plausibility, and differences in parameter estimates (e.g., factor loadings, latent means). Whereas traditional MACS analyses target *observed* heterogeneity (i.e., the subpopulations are indicated by a measure such as gender, culture, or education), unobserved heterogeneity refers to unknown subpopulation membership of the investigated cases, which then has to be inferred. For a more in-depth coverage of the unobserved heterogeneity issue, see Chapters 14 and 13 in this book.

Finally, nonrandom *missing data* can bias parameter estimates when the sample data departs systematically from the target population. In recent years, however, powerful methods have been investigated to address missingness, such as full information maximum likelihood (Enders, 2001; Enders & Bandalos, 2001) or multiple imputation (Schafer & Graham, 2002; Schafer & Olsen, 1998; Sinharay, Stern, & Russell, 2001).

REFERENCES

Arbuckle, J. (1999). *Amos 4.0 users guide*. Chicago, IL: SPSS.

Bagozzi, R. P. (2007). On the meaning of formative measurement and how it differs from reflective measurement: Comment on Howell, Breivik, and Wilcox (2007). *Psychological Methods, 12*, 229–237.

Bauer, D. J., & Curran, P. J. (2004). The integration of continuous and discrete latent variable models: Potential problems and promising opportunities. *Psychological Methods, 9,* 3–29.

Bentler, P. M. (1990). Comparative fit indexes in structural models. *Psychological Bulletin, 107,* 238–246.

Bollen, K. A. (1989). *Structural equations with latent variables.* New York, NY: Wiley.

Bollen, K. A. (2007). Interpretational confounding is due to misspecification, not to type of indicator: Comment on Howell, Breivik, and Wilcox (2007). *Psychological Methods, 12,* 219–228.

Bollen, K. A., & Davis, W. R. (1994). *Causal indicator models: Identification, estimation, and testing.* Unpublished paper, University of North Carolina at Chapel Hill.

Bollen, K. A., & Lennox, R. (1991). Conventional wisdom on measurement: A structural equation perspective. *Psychological Bulletin, 110,* 305–314.

Bollen, K. A., & Stine, R. A. (1992). Bootstrapping goodness-of-fit measures in structural equation modeling. *Sociological Methods & Research, 21,* 205–229.

Borsboom, D. (2008). Latent variable theory. *Measurement, 6,* 25–53.

Borsboom, D., Mellenbergh, G. J., & van Heerden, J. (2003). The theoretical status of latent variables. *Psychological Review, 110,* 203–219.

Brown, T. A. (2006). *Confirmatory factor analysis for applied research.* New York, NY: Guilford.

Byrne, B., Shavelson, R. J., & Muthén, B. (1989). Testing for the equivalence of factor covariance and mean structures: The issue of partial measurement invariance. *Psychological Bulletin, 105,* 456–466.

Cadogan, J. W., Souchon, A. L., & Procter, D. B. (2008). The quality of market-oriented behaviors: Formative index construction. *Journal of Business Research, 61,* 1263–1277.

Chen, F. F., Sousa, K. H., & West, S. G. (2005). Testing measurement invariance of second-order factor models. *Structural Equation Modeling, 12,* 471–492.

Cheung, G. W., & Rensvold, R. B. (1999). Testing factorial invariance across groups: A reconceptualization and proposed new method. *Journal of Management, 25,* 1–27.

Cheung, G. W., & Rensvold, R. B. (2002). Evaluating goodness-of-fit indexes for testing measurement invariance. *Structural Equation Modeling, 9,* 233–255.

Cohen, J., Cohen, P., West, S. G., & Aiken, L. S. (2003). *Applied multiple regression/correlation analysis for the behavioral sciences.* Mahwah, NJ: Lawrence Erlbaum.

Cohen, P., Cohen, J., Teresi, J., Marchi, M., & Velez, C. N. (1990). Problems in the measurement of latent variables in structural equations causal models. *Applied Psychological Measurement, 14,* 183–196.

Cole, D. A., Maxwell, S. E., Arvey, R. D., & Salas, E. (1993). Multivariate group comparisons of variable systems: MANOVA and structural equation modeling. *Psychological Bulletin, 114,* 174–184.

De Beuckelaer, A. (2005). *Measurement invariance issues in international management research.* Limburg, Belgium: Limburgs Universitair Centrum.

Diamantopoulos, A., Riefler, P., & Roth, K. P. (2008). Advancing formative measurement models. *Journal of Business Research, 61,* 1203–1218.

Diamantopoulos, A., & Winklhofer, H. M. (2001). Index construction with formative indicators: An alternative to scale development. *Journal of Marketing Research, 38,* 269–277.

Enders, C. K. (2001). A primer on maximum likelihood algorithms available for use with missing data. *Structural Equation Modeling, 8,* 128–141.

Enders, C. K., & Bandalos, D. L. (2001). The relative performance of full information maximum likelihood estimation for missing data in structural equation models. *Structural Equation Modeling, 8*, 430–457.

European Social Survey. (2002). *Questionnaire development report.* Unpublished report: Retrieved from http://www.europeansocialsurvey.org

Finney, S. J., & DiStefano, C. (2006). Non-normal and categorical data in structural equation modeling. In G. R. Hancock & R. O. Mueller (Eds.), *Structural equation modeling: A second course* (pp. 269–314). Greenwich, CT: Information Age.

Flora, D. B., & Curran, P. J. (2004). An empirical evaluation of alternative methods of estimation for confirmatory factor analysis with ordinal data. *Psychological Methods, 9*, 466–491.

Franke, G. R., Preacher, K. J., & Rigdon, E. E. (2008). Proportional structural effects of formative indicators. *Journal of Business Research, 61*, 1229–1237.

Gagné, P. (2006). Mean and covariance structure mixture models. In G. R. Hancock & R. O. Mueller (Eds.), *Structural equation modeling: A second course* (pp. 197–224). Greenwich, CT: Information Age.

Gerbing, D. W., Hamilton, J. G., & Freeman, E. B. (1994). A large-scale second-order structural equation model of the influence of management participation on organizational planning benefits. *Journal of Management, 20*, 859–885.

Hofstede, G. (1980). *Culture's consequences: International differences in work-related values.* Beverly Hills, CA: Sage.

Hoogland, J. J., & Boomsma, A. (1998). Robustness studies in covariance structure modeling: An overview and meta-analysis. *Sociological Methods & Research, 26*, 329–367.

House, R., Javidan, M., Hanges, P., & Dorfman, P. (2002). Understanding cultures and implicit leadership theories across the globe: An introduction to project GLOBE. *Journal of World Business, 37*, 3–10.

Howell, R. D., Breivik, E., & Wilcox, J. B. (2007a). Is formative measurement really measurement? Reply to Bollen (2007) and Bagozzi (2007). *Psychological Methods, 12*, 238–245.

Howell, R. D., Breivik, E., & Wilcox, J. B. (2007b). Reconsidering formative measurement. *Psychological Methods, 12*, 205–218.

Jarvis, C. B., MacKenzie, S. B., & Podsakoff, P. M. (2003). A critical review of construct indicators and measurement model misspecification in marketing and consumer research. *Journal of Consumer Research, 31*, 199–218.

Jöreskog, K. G., & Goldberger, A. S. (1975). Estimation of a model with multiple indicators and multiple causes of a single latent variable. *Journal of the American Statistical Association, 70*, 631–639.

Little, T. D. (1997). Mean and covariance structures (MACS) analyses of cross-cultural data: Practical and theoretical issues. *Multivariate Behavioral Research, 32*, 53–76.

Little, T. D., Slegers, D. W., & Card, N. A. (2006). A non-arbitrary method of identifying and scaling latent variables in SEM and MACS models. *Structural Equation Modeling, 13*, 59–72.

Lubke, G., & Muthén, B. (2004). Applying multigroup confirmatory factor models for continuous outcomes to Likert scale data complicates meaningful group comparisons. *Structural Equation Modeling, 11*, 514–534.

Lubke, G., & Muthén, B. (2005). Investigating population heterogeneity with factor mixture models. *Psychological Methods, 10*, 21–39.

MacCallum, R. C., & Browne, M. W. (1993). The use of causal indicators in covariance models: Some practical issues. *Psychological Bulletin, 114*, 533–541.

Marsh, H. W., Tracey, D. K., & Craven, R. G. (2006). Multidimensional self-concept structure for preadolescents with mild intellectual disabilities: A hybrid multigroup-MIMIC approach to factorial invariance and latent mean differences. *Educational and Psychological Measurement, 66*, 795–818.

Meredith, W. (1993). Measurement invariance, factor analysis and factorial invariance. *Psychometrika, 58*, 525–543.

Muthén, B. (1989). Latent variable modeling in heterogeneous populations. *Psychometrika, 54*, 557–585.

Muthén, B. (2001). Latent variable mixture modeling. In G. A. Marcoulides & R. E. Schumacker (Eds.), *New developments and techniques in structural equation modeling* (pp. 1–33). Mahwah, NJ: Lawrence Erlbaum Associates.

Ployhardt, R. E., & Oswald, F. L. (2004). Applications of mean and covariance structure analysis: Integrating correlational and experimental approaches. *Organizational Research Methods, 7*, 27–65.

Rindskopf, D., & Rose, T. (1988). Some theory and applications of confirmatory second-order factor analysis. *Multivariate Behavioral Research, 23*, 67.

Rosenthal, R., & DiMatteo, M. R. (2001). Meta-analysis: Recent developments in quantitative methods for literature reviews. *Annual Review of Psychology, 52*, 59–92.

Saris, W. E., Satorra, A., & van der Veld, W. M. (2009). Testing structural equation models or detection of misspecifications? *Structural Equation Modeling, 16*, 561–582.

Satorra, A., & Bentler, P. M. (1994). Corrections to test statistics and standard errors in covariance structure analysis. In A. von Eye & C. Clogg (Eds.), *Latent variables analysis: Applications for Developmental Research* (pp. 399–419). Thousand Oaks, CA: Sage.

Schafer, J. L., & Graham, J. W. (2002). Missing data: Our view of the state of the art. *Psychological Methods, 7*, 147–177.

Schafer, J. L., & Olsen, M. K. (1998). Multiple imputation for multivariate missing-data problems: A data analyst's perspective. *Multivariate Behavioral Research, 33*, 545–571.

Sinharay, S., Stern, H. S., & Russell, D. (2001). The use of multiple imputation for the analysis of missing data. *Psychological Methods, 6*, 317–329.

Steenkamp, J.-B. E. M., & Baumgartner, H. (1998). Assessing measurement invariance in crossnational consumer research. *Journal of Consumer Research, 25*, 78–90.

Steinmetz, H. (2010). Analyzing observed composite differences across groups: Is partial measurement invariance enough? *Unpublished Manuscript*.

Tabachnik, B. G., & Fidell, L. S. (2005). *Using multivariate statistics*. New York, NY: HarperCollins.

Thompson, M. S., & Green, S. B. (2006). Evaluating between-group differences in latent means. In G. R. Hancock & R. O. Mueller (Eds.), *Structural Equation Modeling: A Second Course* (pp. 119–169). Greenwich, CT: Information Age.

Vandenberg, R. J., & Lance, C. E. (2000). A review and synthesis of the measurement invariance literature: Suggestions, practices, and recommendations for organizational research. *Organizational Research Methods, 3*, 4–69.

Wilcox, J. B., Howell, R. D., & Breivik, E. (2008). Questions about formative measurement. *Journal of Business Research, 61*, 1219–1228.

Yuan, K.-H., & Bentler, P. M. (2004). On chi-square difference and *z* tests in mean and covariance structure analysis when the base model is misspecified. *Educational and Psychological Measurement, 64*, 737–757.

Yuan, K.-H., Chan, W., & Bentler, P. M. (2000). Robust transformation with applications to structural equation modeling. *British Journal of Mathematical and Statistical Psychology, 53*, 31–50.

APPENDIX 4.A: LISREL SYNTAX

```
********************* GREAT BRITAIN ************************

DA NI = 4  NO = 2378  NG = 2  MA = CM
CM FU
0.6654 0.2030 0.3353 0.1536
0.2030 0.5382 0.1605 0.1050
0.3353 0.1605 1.0788 0.1497
0.1536 0.1050 0.1497 1.0491
ME
3.7642 3.8756 3.5008 2.8158

LA
pstvms_r dngval_r flrms nhpftr
MO NX = 4  NK = 1  LX = FU,FI  TD = FU,FI  PH = SY,FR  TX = FU,FI
KA = FU,FI  !In addition to usual matrices, TX and KA are
added that contain intercepts and means

LK
LifeSat

VA 1 LX 1 1    !The loading of the first indicator is fixed
               !to one in order to scale the latent variable
FR LX 2 1 LX 3 1 LX 4 1

VA 0 TX 1      !The first intercept is fixed to zero
FR TX 2 TX 3 TX 4

FR KA 1        !the latent mean is estimated
FR TD 1 1 TD 2 2 TD 3 3 TD 4 4

OU ML AD = OFF  IT = 1000
```

```
******************** NORWAY *******************************

DA NI=4 NO=1744 MA=CM
CM FU
0.5862 0.1299 0.2568 0.1219
0.1299 0.3707 0.0957 0.0600
0.2568 0.0957 1.0436 0.1388
0.1219 0.0600 0.1388 0.9228

ME
3.6777 3.9845 3.3967 3.0573

LA
pstvms_r dngval_r flrms nhpftr
MO LX=IN TD=PS PH=PS TX=IN KA=IN
!The "IN" specify which parameter matrices are constrained

LK
LifeSat

FR TX 4 TX 2 !Non-invariant intercepts
OU ML AD=OFF IT=1000 ND=2 RS
```

APPENDIX 4.B: MPLUS SYNTAX

```
DATA: FILE=Mplus CM.dat;
    TYPE IS MEANS COVARIANCE;
    NGROUPS=2;
    NOBSERVATIONS=1744 2300;
VARIABLE:
    NAMES ARE pstvms dngval flrms nhpftr;
ANALYSIS:
    TYPE=meanstructure;
MODEL: !Overall model
    Selfest by pstvms dngval flrms nhpftr;
    [pstvms@0 dngval flrms nhpftr];
    Selfest;
    [Selfest];

! The following sections define the parameters for both groups
```

```
#*************************************************************

MODEL g1: !This section has to be included if one wants to
          !fix the first intercept to zero and to estimate
          !both means (Mplus' default is to estimate all
          !intercepts and fix the first mean to 0)
[pstvms@0 dngval flrms nhpftr];
!#1 (Delete/mute for scalar invariance)

 [Selfest];

#*************************************************************

MODEL g2: !This section contains the parameters the user
          !wants to estimate varying across the groups. The
          !intercepts do not have to be included as line #1
          !causes varying intercepts. The latent mean does
          !not have to be included as the mean in the second
          !group varies per default

Selfest by dngval flrms nhpftr;
!#2 (Delete/mute for metric invariance)
```

Note: This is the syntax for the configural invariance model. Testing metric invariance requires to delete/mute row #2 Testing scalar invariance requires to delete/mute row #1. Relaxing specific parameters (e.g., the two noninvariant intercepts) can be achieved by writing these parameters, for instance, "[dngval nhpftr]" in the section below "MODEL g2."

Finally, latent mean invariance is incorporated by mentioning the mean in the g2-section and providing both means (in section g1 and g2) with the same "parameter label"—in our case "[Selfest] (1)."

APPENDIX 4.C: DESCRIPTION OF THE PROCEDURE IN AMOS

As the typical way to specify a model in AMOS consists of using the graphical interface, the estimation and comparison of latent means is described verbally although AMOS also allows running a syntax code.

At the first step, a multigroup model structure has to be specified (here I assume that the reader is familiar with setting up a baseline CFA model). Incorporation of the mean structure is achieved by clicking on "Analysis properties," then "Estimation." In the opening mask, click on "Estimate means and intercepts."

Via "Analyze"/"Multi-Group Analysis," the models that AMOS is going to estimate are visualized in columns. Each column contains a mark referring to the specific parameter matrix that has to be constrained to be equal. Per default, the first model is the unconstrained model. Column 1 refers to equal measurement weights (metric invariance), column 2 to equal intercepts (scalar invariance), and column 3 refers to the test of equal means. The further columns refer to tests that may or may not be of interest (e.g., equal residuals).

The default approach to identify the mean structure in AMOS is the reference-group approach (i.e., the latent means of the groups are fixed to zero and all intercepts are estimated). If the user intends to apply the marker approach, the intercept of the marker has to be fixed to zero (in the "Manage Models" box), and the latent means (which are zero by default) have to be labeled and, hence, freely estimated. If the reference-group method is applied instead, the mean of the second group has to be freed when testing for scalar invariance as otherwise, the mean structure is not identified. When finally testing for mean invariance, the mean of the second group is again fixed to zero.

Running the model conducts all the invariance tests marked in the "Multi-Group Analysis" input panel. The output delivers test statistics and fit indexes for the models as well as the chi-square difference tests and the differences in some fit indexes (Arbuckle, 1999).

5

Biased Latent Variable Mean Comparisons due to Measurement Noninvariance: A Simulation Study

Alain De Beuckelaer
Ghent University and Radboud University Nijmegen

Gilbert Swinnen
Hasselt University

5.1 INTRODUCTION

Making valid comparisons of latent variable (LV) mean scores* across groups is anything but a trivial task as it relies on stringent measurement invariance conditions. Many authors (e.g., Little, 1997; Meredith, 1993; Van de Vijver & Leung, 1997) have firmly stated that in order for such comparisons to be valid, *all* factor loadings as well as *all* indicator intercepts need to be invariant across groups (i.e., they are required to exhibit *scalar* invariance, also referred to as *full score* invariance across groups; Van de Vijver & Leung, 1997, p. 144).

In contrast, some authors have promoted the use of less stringent measurement invariance conditions. For instance, according to Alwin and Jackson (1981) the equality of *all* factor loadings (i.e., an invariance condition referred to as "metric invariance" across groups) would be a sufficient

* In this study, we deal only with the comparison of LV means across groups. Cross-group comparisons of structural relationships between observed or LVs are not considered. Such comparisons require only the factor loadings of LV indicators to be identical across the groups (i.e., metric invariance across groups) involved in the comparison (see, for instance, De Beuckelaer, Lievens, & Swinnen, 2007; Van de Vijver & Leung, 1997).

condition. Still others (Byrne, 1989; Byrne, Shavelson, & Muthén, 1989; Marsh & Hocevar, 1985; Muthén & Christofferson, 1981; Reise, Widaman, & Pugh, 1993) have argued that only a subset of all factor loadings (i.e., "partial metric invariance" across groups) would be a sufficient condition. The willingness to accept less stringent measurement invariance conditions (when comparing LV mean scores) may be caused by a growing belief that (survey) measurement instruments can hardly ever be totally invariant across groups (e.g., Byrne & Watkins, 2003; Horn, McArdle, & Mason, 1983). As a matter of fact, many large-scale international studies (e.g., Davidov, 2008; Davidov, Schmidt, & Schwartz, 2008; De Beuckelaer, Lievens, & Swinnen, 2007) have shown that survey instruments typically do not exhibit scalar invariance across a large number of nations—a group delimiter that is very frequently used in cross-cultural comparative research (e.g., Schaffer & Riordan, 2003).

A major point of concern is that much supportive evidence exists to support the claim that many researchers doing cross-cultural comparative research fail to test formally for possible sources of noninvariance of measurement parameters across groups (for instance, see Cheung & Rensvold, 1999; He, Merz, & Alden, 2008; Schaffer & Riordan, 2003; Vandenberg & Lance, 2000; Williams, Edwards, & Vandenberg, 2003). As such, many researchers run a high risk of drawing erroneous conclusions from a cross-group comparison of LV mean scores. For this reason it makes sense to examine the consequences of *falsely* assuming that the measurement instrument used exhibits a high level of measurement invariance, namely, scalar invariance across groups.

As argued by Vandenberg (2002), there is a growing need for research to help understand the sensitivity of the analytical procedures when making cross-cultural comparisons (e.g., multigroup mean and covariance structure (i.e., multigroup MACS) analysis, and the extent to which less stringent measurement invariance conditions (if unnoticed) can affect LV mean comparisons across groups. One way to adequately explore the extent to which the requirement of scalar invariance can be relaxed (without threatening the validity of cross-group comparisons) is to make use of carefully designed simulation research. Such simulation research may (at least potentially) provide valuable empirical evidence to justify the adoption of less stringent measurement invariance conditions. Except for an older study by Kaplan and George (1995) that did not include invariance conditions relating to indicator intercepts, we did not find any published simulation study that enables us to infer to what degree the measurement invariance conditions across groups can be relaxed without running the risk of drawing erroneous conclusions from cross-group comparisons of LV mean scores.

In this chapter, we will try to fill this gap in the literature by presenting a simulation study that investigates the extent to which noninvariance of factor loadings and indicator intercepts may lead to false statistical conclusions in terms of (the reported significance of) LV mean differences across groups. The next sections will elaborate on the method of research and the analysis strategy, the presentation of some detailed results, and the general conclusions.

5.2 METHOD

In this simulation study, Satorra and Bentler's scaled chi-square statistic* was used because of its superior performance in earlier simulation studies (Chou & Bentler, 1995; Curran, West, & Finch, 1996; Hu, Bentler, & Kano, 1992; Olsson, Finch, & Curran, 1995). The design characteristics of this simulation study resemble, at least to some extent, the design characteristics of the simulation study by Kaplan and George (1995). As will be explained in the next paragraphs however, there are also some important differences.

5.2.1 Experimental Design Factors Included

In this simulation study, noninvariance conditions were represented by just one LV indicator (i.e., always the second LV indicator) with a noninvariant factor loading applied to the LV indicator and/or a noninvariant indicator intercept.

The following design factors were used in the simulation study:

- Number of indicators for the LV (design factor 0)
- Type of distribution of the indicators (design factor 1)
- Sample size in the different groups (design factor 2)

* More precisely, it is the mean- and variance-adjusted chi-square statistic with robust standard errors (see Muthén & Muthén, 1999), which is used in this simulation study.

- LV mean difference between groups at population level (design factor 3)
- Noninvariance of factor loadings and indicator intercepts (design factor 4 and design factor 5, respectively)

The simulation was set up using a full-factorial experimental design so that all possible combinations are represented in the simulation study.

We make a distinction between two groups of design factors: "side design factors" and (measurement) "noninvariance design factors." Side design factors relate to characteristics of the data that are not related to the measurement (non)invariance of the data across groups. They include (see Table 5.1):

- A fixed number of two groups to be involved in the LV mean comparison
- The number of indicators used to measure the LV under study (either 3 or 4)
- The statistical or empirical distribution underlying LV indicator scores (standard normal distribution)
- Discrete 5-point response scales showing either a unimodal left-skewed distribution or a symmetric bimodal distribution*
- The size of the sample in the two groups involved in the LV mean comparison.

Next, measurement noninvariance design factors determine the degree of measurement noninvariance of the noninvariant indicator (i.e., always the second indicator of the LV). Specifications regarding the levels of individual design factors are presented in Table 5.1. This table contains essential information about the simulations conducted. As the Results section often makes reference to abbreviations indicating simulated conditions that are specified in Table 5.1 (see Section 5.2), a technically interested reader may benefit greatly from copying this table prior to examining in-depth the results discussed in that section. By doing so, technical details concerning the nature of the simulated experimental

* Especially because of these scales, the present simulation study is to be conceived as more realistic than the study by Kaplan and George (1995).

TABLE 5.1

Values Specified for the Design Factors

Design Factors	Specification of Levels/Values Assigned	Further Remarks
Side design factors		
Number of groups	Always two groups to be compared	
F0: Number of indicators for the LV (i.e., design factor 0, shortly F0)	3 (F0 = 1) or 4 (F0 = 2)	
F1: Distribution of indicators (i.e., design factor 1, shortly F1)	*Continuous data following a standard normal distribution* (F1 = 1) as well as two discrete response scales with five ordinally ordered response categories following either a *unimodal, left-skewed distribution* (F1 = 2) or a *symmetric bimodal distribution* (F1 = 3); thresholds have been specified such that the distribution (in % of cases) across category points is as follows: unimodal, left-skewed: 8% [1]; 12% [2] 15% [3]; 40% [4]; 25% [5], and symmetric bimodal: 15% [1 and 5], 30% [2 and 4], 10% [3].	The study by Kaplan and George (1995) made use of the standard normal distribution only (also replicated in our study if F1 = 1); the two empirical distributions (e.g., unimodal, left-skewed [F1 = 2] and bimodal symmetrical [F1 = 3] based on five-ordered response categories) as used in our simulation study are often encountered in applied research making use of Likert-type of scales.
F2: Sample sizes (i.e., design factor 2, shortly F2)	Group sample size varies between 200 and 750; $F_2 = 1$: $N_1 = N_2 = 200$; $F_2 = 2$: $N_1 = N_2 = 300$; $F_2 = 3$: $N_1 = N_2 = 400$; $F_2 = 4$: $N_1 = N_2 = 500$; $F_2 = 5$: $N_1 = N_2 = 750$; $F_2 = 6$: $N_1 = 200$, $N_2 = 400$ (N_i means sample size in group i; $i = 1,2$; there are always two groups to be compared)	Except for one condition (i.e., (F2 = 6) all experimental conditions are balanced (i.e., having an equal number of observations in both groups).

(*Continued*)

TABLE 5.1 (Continued)

Values Specified for the Design Factors

Design Factors	Specification of Levels/Values Assigned	Further Remarks
Side design factors		
F3: Latent variable mean difference (i.e., design factor 3, shortly F3)	The LV mean in group 1 (G1) is always 0.00; the LV mean in group 2 (G2) is –0.30 (F3 = 1); –0.15 (F3 = 2); 0.00 (F3 = 3); 0.15 (F3 = 4); and 0.30 (F3 = 5); conditions 4 and 5 (i.e., F3 = 4 and F3 = 5) represent positive discrepancy cases (i.e., conditions in which the LV mean in the second group is larger than the LV mean in the first group). In negative discrepancy cases (F3 = 1 and F3 = 2), the reverse condition applies; an absolute difference of 0.15 (F3 = 2 and F3 = 4) may be considered to be small, whereas an absolute difference of 0.30 (F3 = 1 and F3 = 5) may be considered to be large (adequate empirical evidence for the use of the qualifiers small and large can be provided by the first author using detailed descriptive results of correct statistical conclusions obtained in the simulation study; see Results section).	Condition 3 (F3 = 3) serves as a means to assess the test's actual control over the type I error rate (i.e., falsely concluding that LV means are different); all other conditions help determine the test's statistical power.

Noninvariance design factors		
F4: Noninvariance of factor loadings across groups (i.e., design factor 4, shortly F4)	In group 1 (G1) the factor loadings are always fixed as follows: $\lambda_1 = 0.7$; $\lambda_2 = 0.6$; $\lambda_3 = 0.5$ (in 3-indicator conditions; see F0) or $\lambda_1 = 0.7$; $\lambda_2 = \lambda_3 = 0.6$; $\lambda_4 = 0.5$ (in 4-indicator conditions; see F0); in group 2 (G2) the factor loading of the second indicator (i.e., λ_2) varies as follows: F4 = 1: $\lambda_2 = 0.4$ (indicator reliability = 0.24); F4 = 2: $\lambda_2 = 0.6$ (indicator reliability = 0.41); F4 = 3: $\lambda_2 = 0.8$ (indicator reliability = 0.56) The factor loadings of all other indicators are invariant across both groups.	Either the second indicator (i.e., λ_2) and/or its intercept are noninvariant across groups in noninvariance conditions. Condition 2 (i.e., F4 = 2) represents a condition in which no violation of invariance (across groups) occurs, at least not as far as factor loadings are concerned
F5: Noninvariance of indicator intercepts across groups (i.e., design factor 5, shortly F5)	The four experimental conditions are as follows: F5 = 1: Indicator 2 has an intercept in G2, which is identical to the intercept of indicator 2 in G1; F5 = 2: Indicator 2 has an intercept in G2, which is 0.15 higher than the intercept of indicator 2 in G1; F5 = 3: Indicator 2 has an intercept in G2, which is 0.30 higher than the intercept of indicator 2 in G1; F5 = 4: Indicator 2 has an intercept in G2, which is 0.45 higher than the intercept of indicator 2 in G1 The indicator intercepts of all other indicators are invariant across both groups.	Only the intercept of the second indicator may but does not have to be noninvariant. Condition 1 (i.e., F5 = 1) represents a condition in which no violation of invariance (across groups) occurs, at least not as far as indicator intercepts are concerned.

Notes: The notation $Fx = k$ is used to refer to level number k for design factor x (e.g., F1 = 1); In all replications the variance of the LV is always fixed to one.

conditions as displayed in Table 5.1 are readily available to the reader at all times.

5.2.1.1 Noninvariance and Invariance Conditions

As explained before, (measurement) noninvariance is caused by only one indicator, namely, the second LV indicator out of three or four indicators. Depending on the particular condition, the second LV indicator may exhibit noninvariance due to a noninvariant factor loading across groups (F4 = 1 or F4 = 3 [i.e., level 1 or level 3 is specified for design factor 4]; see F4 in Table 5.1) and/or a noninvariant indicator intercept across groups (F5 = 2, 3, or 4; see F5 in Table 5.1). Alternatively, the second indicator may exhibit measurement invariance (i.e., if F4 = 2 and F5 = 1; see F4 and F5 in Table 5.1). Further on in this chapter we will use the notation "λ_2" and "Int_2" to refer to the factor loading and the indicator intercept of the second LV indicator, respectively. Whenever we refer to a group, we will add a suffix labeled "G*i*" ($i = 1$ or 2).

The settings for factor loadings used in our study resemble the settings specified by Kaplan and George (1995). As shown in Table 5.1, indicator reliabilities ranged between 0.24 (with a factor loading equal to 0.4) and 0.56 (with a factor loading equal to 0.8).* Differences in the indicator intercepts across groups varied between 0.00 and 0.45. The latter value of the indicator intercept represents a distance of nearly one-tenth of the length of the total scale consisting of five response categories (see Table 5.1).

One may reasonably expect that differences in indicator intercepts across groups are more harmful than differences in factor loadings when (estimated) LV mean scores are to be compared across groups. Differences in indicator intercepts will bias estimated LV mean scores equally for each observation (or person), whereas the bias resulting from differences in factor loadings really depends on the observation's (or person's) score on the underlying construct.

As mentioned before, we specified (corresponding) measurement invariance conditions in addition to noninvariance conditions. The major advantage of doing so is that measurement invariance conditions may serve as a natural benchmark (condition) against which the

---

* The reliability of the *i*th LV indicator is calculated as follows: 1 – (error variance / [λ_i^2 + error variance]). The error variance is always fixed to 0.51 in the simulation study.

(statistical) performance of the LV mean difference test may be evaluated in noninvariance conditions. Further details concerning exactly how this will be done are provided in the Analysis section.

5.2.1.2 Asymmetrical Structure of the Simulation Design

The specific noninvariance conditions, as specified in Table 5.1, demonstrate that the experimental design used has a structure that is asymmetrical. The factor loading of the (possibly noninvariant) second LV indicator is specified to be *smaller* than, equal to, or *larger* than the corresponding factor loading in group one. In contrast, the indicator intercept of this LV indicator in the second group (G2) is specified to be either equal to or *larger* than the corresponding indicator intercept in group one. As the smaller than condition is missing here, the asymmetric structure is entirely due to the experimental settings specified for the intercept of the (possibly noninvariant) second indicator of the LV.

Because of this asymmetry, the effect of unequal indicator intercepts across groups on the estimated size of the (absolute) difference in LV means across groups were different for positive and negative discrepancy cases (i.e., conditions in which the LV mean in group 2 [G2] is higher [*positive* discrepancy] or lower [*negative* discrepancy] compared to the LV mean in group 1 [G1]). In positive discrepancy cases (i.e., $\mu_{LV,G2} > \mu_{LV,G1}$), unequal indicator intercepts increase the estimated discrepancy between LV means. In negative discrepancy cases (i.e., $\mu_{LV,G2} < \mu_{LV,G1}$), the estimated discrepancy between LV means decreases due to the inequality of indicator intercepts across groups. Therefore, the inclusion of negative indicator intercepts in the simulation design (in addition to positive indicator intercepts) would only lead to duplicate information as some conditions with a positive discrepancy between LV means would be identical to some other conditions with a negative discrepancy between LV means.

5.2.2 Data Generation and Analysis Strategy

5.2.2.1 Data Generation

Multiple data files (i.e., 50) were generated for each experimental condition. Several computer programs were written to run the simulations. These computer programs took care of the data preparation and data extraction tasks. The actual parameter estimations were provided by a dedicated software program, namely, Mplus (Muthén & Muthén, 1999). A more detailed description of all programs used and their functionality in the simulation process is available from the first author.

5.2.2.2 Data Analysis Strategy

The results from the simulation study were analyzed in two consecutive steps. These two steps are explained below.

Step 1: Correct and Incorrect Statistical Conclusions

Using the simulated data files, LV means were estimated for both groups. The estimation was carried out under the (possibly false) assumption that scalar invariance holds for all indicators across groups (i.e., imposing constraints regarding the equality of factor loadings and indicator intercepts across groups; i.e., imposing the scalar invariance model across groups onto the data).

The robust maximum likelihood procedure, as implemented in the software Mplus (Muthén & Muthén 1999), was used to estimate the model parameters. To test whether the LV mean in G2 was identical to the LV mean in G1 (the latter one is fixed to zero in all simulations; see Table 5.1), a simple z-statistic (i.e., the estimated LV mean in the second group divided by its standard error) was used. Provided that the estimated LV mean in G2 is zero (i.e., that the null-hypothesis holds), the z-statistic follows a standard normal distribution, asymptotically. The correctness of the LV mean difference test (i.e., reject or don't reject the null-hypothesis) was then assessed using information about the true difference (if not zero) in the LV means (see Table 5.1, design factor 3). For each of the 50 replications of all experimental conditions the correctness of the statistical conclusion was flagged by a "not correct" [0]/"correct" [1] indicator. Incorrect decisions in the opposite direction (e.g., finding a significant positive discrepancy when the actual difference between LV means was negative) were not produced in this simulation study.

Next, the influence of the individual design parameters (see Table 5.1) on the *correctness* of statistical conclusions regarding the LV mean difference test across groups was assessed. Previous research (i.e., Kaplan & George, 1995) has shown that the effect of the difference between LV means at population level (i.e., design factor 3) is dominant when compared to other effects. This is logical as the probability of finding a significant difference between LV means in two independent samples is directly related to the size of the difference between LV means at population level. This effect is, however, not relevant for the research problem at hand. The main research question is to evaluate the extent to which measurement noninvariance conditions (i.e., design factor 4 and 5) and certain side conditions (such as number of indicators, distribution of indicators, and sample sizes) bias LV mean comparisons across groups. Therefore, the LV mean difference at population level may be regarded as an extraneous factor. Consequently, the effects of all other design parameters were assessed separately for various levels of the LV mean difference at population level.

The design parameters were indicated by means of binary variables (i.e., 0/1 variables). The following notation was used: F*i*_D*j* with *i* representing the number identifying the design factor and *j* representing the number identifying the level specified for that design factor (see Table 5.1). So, F5_D1 means that the first level applies to design factor 5 (i.e. indicator intercept of indicator 2 is identical in G2 and G1; see Table 5.1).

We made use of the classification and regression tree (C&RTree) technique by Breiman, Friedman, Olshen, and Stone (1984) to identify the impact of the design parameters (i.e., levels of design factors) on the correctness of the statistical conclusion regarding the LV mean difference between groups. In these C&RTree analyses, the particular values of design parameters (as represented by a series of binary F*i*_D*j* variables; see above) serve as independent variables, while the binary indicator showing the correctness of the LV mean difference test across groups (i.e., not correct [0]/correct [1]) acts as the dependent variable. By optimizing a statistical criterion (i.e., the statistical significance of difference in percentage correct statistical conclusions), the C&RTree technique successively splits the entire sample into (sub)samples until at least one convergence criterion is reached. Just as in our study, a convergence or stop criterion is reached if statistical significance of the next candidate sample-split drops below a minimum level or, alternatively, the number of observations (or, in our study, replications of simulated conditions) in the sample to be split has dropped below a minimum value. Sample-splits can be made using a particular main effect (e.g., F2_D5, i.e., replications for which design factor 2 has value 5 versus replications for which design factor 2 has values other than 5; for details regarding the design factors see Table 5.1), or a particular interaction effect (e.g., F2_D5 * F1_D3, i.e., replications for which design factor 2 has value 5 and design factor 1 has value 3 versus replications for which other combinations of the design factors 2 and 1 apply).

The results of a C&RTree analysis are graphically depicted in a tree-based structure, which is referred to as a C&RTree. An example of a C&RTree is provided in Figure 5.1.

Provided that none of the convergence criteria are met, a first sample-split is made based on one main effect or one interaction effect between (levels of) the design factors. The first sample-split in Figure 5.1 differentiates between replications using very large datasets (i.e., 5th level of design factor 5 applies [F2_D5 = 1]; see Table 5.1), and replications using smaller data sets (F2_D5 = 0). So, a main effect (F2_D5 = 0 or 1) is used to split the overall sample (with 48% correct statistical conclusions) into two (sub) samples with 31% (F2_D5 = 0) and 57% (F2_D5 = 1) correct statistical conclusions regarding the LV mean difference test, respectively. Among all candidate sample-splits (i.e., all main and interaction effects of levels of design parameters), the main effect F2_D5 = 0 or 1 leads to the largest possible difference between the percentage of correct statistical conclusions as obtained for both subsamples.

Next, a C&RTree analysis will determine whether or not further sample-splits can be made. To this end, some statistical evaluations are made for each of the two (sub)samples resulting from the first sample-split. In fact, for each subsample one statistical evaluation is made for all levels (or combinations of levels) of the design factors that have not been used in the first sample-split (or, in more general terms, higher up in the C&RTree). As far as the example is concerned (see Figure 5.1), this means that the main effect

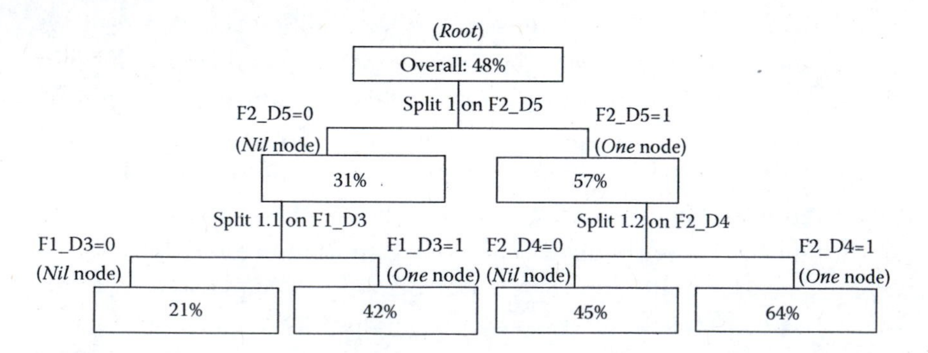

FIGURE 5.1
Percentage correct statistical conclusions (4-indicator cases; only large negative discrepancy cases [i.e., F3 = 1]).

F2_D5 = 0 or 1 cannot be used anymore as a splitting variable after it has been used as the variable determining the very first sample split. Provided none of the convergence criteria are met, each (sub)sample emerging from the first sample-split may be split again in two new (sub)samples, producing up to four different (sub)samples. In Figure 5.1 further sample-splits are made using the following two main effects: F1_D3 = 0 or 1, and F2_D4 = 0 or 1. Once again, these sample-splits lead to the largest possible difference between the percentages of correct statistical conclusions as obtained for both subsamples. This process of splitting (sub)samples continues until no further sample-splits can be made (i.e., when at least one of the convergence criteria is met).

In order to correctly interpret the results of C&RTree analyses, one may therefore rely on the following two basic principles:

Principle #1: The importance of the individual design parameters (i.e., levels of the design factors) in terms of predicting the correctness of the LV mean difference test is reflected by the sequence in which these sample-splits are made. In other words, sample-splits that are positioned lower down the C&RTree are, from a statistical point of view, somewhat less important than sample-splits that are positioned higher up the C&RTree. Principle #2: All design parameters that have not been used anywhere in the C&RTree are, from a statistical point of view, of a lesser importance (i.e., they do not help very much in discriminating in terms of percentage of correct statistical conclusions regarding the LV mean difference test).

Step 2: Robust and Nonrobust Conditions

So far, the unit of analysis has been a replication of an experimental condition (i.e., 50 replications per experimental condition). To assess the robustness of the experimental conditions against violations of the scalar invariance assumption across groups (i.e., Step 2), aggregated data are needed. In particular, the data of all replications need to be aggregated for every experimental condition.

The analysis strategy is to use the total number of correct statistical conclusions of invariance conditions as a reference against which the robustness of all (related*) noninvariance conditions is evaluated. Based on the

---

* Related noninvariance conditions are characterised by an identical LV mean difference between both groups and a noninvariant indicator having an unequal factor loading and/or indicator intercept across groups.

binomial distribution, a 99% confidence interval* is specified around the number of correct statistical conclusions of invariance conditions. If the number of correct statistical conclusions of a related noninvariance condition falls within this interval, the noninvariance condition is considered to be robust against violations of the scalar invariance assumption across groups. Otherwise, it is not considered to be robust. Based on such an analysis, all noninvariance conditions are flagged with a "not-robust" [0]/"robust" [1] indicator. In summary, the idea is to examine the decrease (or increase) in the number of correct statistical conclusions of noninvariance conditions using the number of correct statistical conclusions of invariance conditions as a benchmark (or reference condition).

C&RTree analyses are also used in this second step to determine the influence of the individual design parameters on the robustness of the experimental condition against violations of the scalar invariance assumption across groups. So, instead of using the statistical correctness of the LV mean difference test (in each replication of an experimental condition), the robustness of the experimental condition (i.e., across all replications of that experimental condition) is used as the dependent or criterion variable in these C&RTree analyses. As the unit of analysis is an experimental condition rather than a replication (of a particular experimental condition), a relatively small number of observations is available for these C&RTree analyses.

5.3 RESULTS

Step 1: Correct and Incorrect Statistical Conclusions

5.3.1 Descriptive Results

The percentage of correct conclusions regarding the LV mean difference test varies around 66% across all simulated conditions, regardless of the

* The specification of a confidence interval (CI) is always a somewhat arbitrary decision. Changing from a 99% CI to a 95% CI would not have had a substantial impact on the decisions regarding robustness/nonrobustness of the noninvariance condition (i.e., on average across all noninvariance conditions, less than one replication [i.e., 0.80; SD = 0.60] would have been classified differently).

TABLE 5.2

Percentage of Correct Conclusions Regarding the LV Mean Difference Test

Percentage of Correct Statistical Conclusions	Negative Discrepancy Cases		No Discrepancy Cases	Positive Discrepancy Cases	
	LV Mean in Group 2 (G2)				
	= –0.30 (F3 = 1)	= –0.15 (F3 = 2)	= 0.00 (F3 = 3)	= 0.15 (F3 = 4)	= 0.30 (F3 = 5)
3 indicators Overall: 65.2%	62.5%	32.9%	55.5%	79.4%	95.5%
4 indicators Overall: 67.3%	69.5% [+]	28.7% [–]	67.3% [+]	76.1% [–]	95.0%

Note: A plus or minus sign between square brackets indicates the direction of significant increases [+] or decreases [–] in terms of the percentage of correct statistical conclusions (when comparing 4-indicator conditions to 3-indicator conditions).

number of indicators used in the LV indicator model (i.e., 3 or 4 indicators). This is shown in Table 5.2. The table also shows percentages of correct statistical conclusions tabulated for different levels of the LV mean difference at population level (i.e., the different levels for F3).

Table 5.2 shows that the percentage of correct statistical conclusions increases with an increasing positive difference in LV means. This finding is in line with our expectations as the asymmetrical structure of the experimental design (in particular the larger indicator intercept in G2 in noninvariance conditions including one unequal indicator intercept across groups) artificially increases the estimate of the LV mean in G2. The artificial increase works in favor of a rejection of the null-hypothesis in positive discrepancy cases (see Table 5.2) in which the LV mean at population level is higher in G2 than in G1. However, in negative discrepancy cases in which the LV mean at population level is lower in G2 than in G1, the (negative) difference in the LV means across both groups is underestimated (i.e., pushed up toward zero, the LV mean of G1) because of a larger indicator intercept of one LV indicator in G2. This is particularly true in those noninvariance conditions that include one unequal indicator intercept across groups (see F5 in Table 5.1).

When mutually comparing 4-indicator conditions with 3-indicator conditions, significantly different percentages of correct statistical conclusions were obtained (see plus or minus signs indicated between square brackets in Table 5.2). Taking into account the large number of (simulated) replications included in each cell (*N*/cell = 10,800) in Table 5.2, significant differences in the percentage of correct statistical conclusions should not come as a surprise. A further inspection of the sign of the significant differences across 4- and 3-indicator conditions shows that there is no winner. The 4-indicator conditions report higher percentages of correct statistical conclusions for F3 = 1 and F3 = 3, whereas the 3-indicator conditions report higher percentages for F3 = 2 and F3 = 4. More detailed tables showing aggregated results for different noninvariance conditions as well as scalar invariance conditions may be obtained from the first author.*

5.3.2 Inferential Results

As expected, the LV mean difference at population level (i.e., design factor 3) turned out to be the most influential design factor determining the correctness of the statistical conclusion regarding the LV mean difference test. In the C&RTree analyses for both 3- and 4-indicator conditions (not listed in Appendix 5.A to save book space), all sample-splits involved different levels of design factor 3.

Inferential results for large negative discrepancy cases: In large negative discrepancy cases (i.e., F3 = 1), the noninvariant factor loading (i.e., design factor 4) was selected as the first variable to split all (simulated) replications in two subsamples. This is shown in the C&RTrees CT_01 (3-indicator condition) and CT_02 (4-indicator condition) in Appendix 5.A. This sample-split indicated that a *factor loading* of 0.4 for the noninvariant indicator in G2 (versus 0.6 in G1) substantially lowered the probability of making correct conclusions regarding the LV mean difference test. Further sample-splits (in both subsamples) were based on the noninvariant indicator intercept (i.e., design factor 5). Furthermore, the analyses showed that the larger the discrepancy in the noninvariant indicator *intercept*, the

* These additional tables were not included in this chapter to save space. These tables do, however, show that the test of equality of LV means in both groups does provide reasonable control over the type I error rate (i.e., as assessed in scalar invariance conditions). As type I error rates occur when one *falsely* rejects the hypothesis of equal LV means at population level (i.e., the null-hypothesis), the test's control over the type I error rate is evaluated by examining statistical results obtained in "no discrepancy conditions" (i.e., those conditions in which the null-hypothesis truly holds at population level). In addition, such tables provide useful information on the power of the statistical test (i.e., as assessed in noninvariance conditions).

lower the probability of drawing the correct statistical conclusion based on the difference in LV means (i.e., as the noninvariant indicator intercept is opposite to the direction of the difference between LV means at population level). In summary, the results showed that in large negative discrepancy cases, both a noninvariant factor loading and a noninvariant indicator intercept were factors that had a strong influence on the correctness of the statistical conclusion regarding the LV mean difference test.

Inferential results for small negative discrepancy cases: In small negative discrepancy cases (i.e., F3 = 2), the sample of simulated replications was first split using the size of differences in the noninvariant indicator intercept (i.e., design factor 5) as a variable on which to split the sample. This is shown in the C&RTrees CT_03 and CT_04 in Appendix 5.A. Further down in both trees, more splits were made using other levels of design factor 5 as splitting variables. The implication is (once again) that a larger noninvariant indicator intercept has a strong negative impact on the percentage of correct statistical conclusions in negative discrepancy cases. Further inspection of C&RTrees CT_03 and CT_04 revealed that additional sample-splits were made using the degree of noninvariance of the factor loading as a variable on which to split the sample (e.g., F4_D1 and F4_D3). These findings support the conclusion that noninvariance conditions (i.e., design factors 4 and 5) have a strong impact on the percentage of correct statistical conclusions.

Inferential results for no discrepancy cases: In the no difference cases (i.e., F3 = 3) successive splits were made using various levels of design factor 5 as splitting variables. This is shown in C&RTrees CT_05 and CT_06. The smaller the difference in the noninvariant indicator intercept, the higher the probability of drawing the right statistical conclusion with respect to the difference in LV means across groups. Since noninvariant indicator intercepts exert an upward bias on the estimated LV mean in G2, this will be reflected on the LV mean difference between G2 and G1. As a consequence, the probability of rejecting the hypothesis of equal LV means at population level (i.e., in this case, the correct statistical conclusion) decreases.

Inferential results for small positive discrepancy cases: In small positive discrepancy cases (i.e., F3 = 4), the difference in the noninvariant indicator intercept was successively used as the design factor on which sample-splits were made (see C&RTrees CT_07 and CT_08 in Appendix 5.A). Larger differences in the noninvariant indicator intercept enlarge the (estimated) difference between LV means at population level. As a result, the probability of drawing the correct statistical conclusion (namely, a significant difference between the LV means in both groups) increased artificially because of the upward bias on the LV mean in G2 caused by the noninvariant indicator intercept.

Inferential results for large positive discrepancy cases: In large positive discrepancy cases (i.e., F3 = 5), the percentage of correct statistical conclusions regarding the LV mean difference test turned out to be very high (i.e., around 95% in both 3- and 4-indicator conditions). The C&RTrees CT_09 and CT_10 (see Appendix 5.A) showed that the sample was first split using the first level of design factor 4 (i.e., a noninvariant factor loading of 0.4 in G2 versus a factor loading of 0.6 in G1) as the variable on which to split the sample. The small difference in the percentage of correct statistical conclusions reported for both subsamples (as well as the size of the calculated measure of improvement) showed that this sample-split was only marginally relevant. In conclusion, the difference in LV means at population level (+0.30) was large enough to ensure a very high proportion of correct statistical conclusions (i.e., close to 95%). Obviously, the bias caused by a noninvariant indicator intercept (as present in many simulated conditions) was to a large extent responsible for this high percentage in correct statistical conclusions.

Summary of inferential results on statistical correctness: Overall, the C&RT analyses showed that measurement noninvariance exerted a strong influence on the percentage of correct statistical conclusions regarding the LV mean difference test. In particular, a difference in the noninvariant indicator intercept as large as (approximately) one-tenth of the total length of the scale (a difference of 0.45 on a 5-point scale), or even smaller, was found to have a strong effect on the correctness of the outcome of the LV mean difference test. The effect could either be positive (in positive discrepancy cases [i.e., F3 = 4 and F3 = 5]) or negative (in negative discrepancy cases [i.e., F3 = 1 and F3 = 2] and the no difference cases [F3 = 3]). Next, a noninvariant factor loading showing a difference of 0.2 (factor loading in G1 is 0.6; factor loading in G2 is 0.4) was also found to have a substantial effect on the correctness of the outcome of the LV mean difference test. These findings were largely consistent across 3- and 4-indicator conditions.

Step 2: Robust and Nonrobust Conditions

5.3.3 Descriptive Results

Robustness is only a relevant concept in noninvariance conditions. Of all noninvariance conditions, (only) about 35% was found to be robust. This conclusion applies to both the 3- and 4-indicator conditions. The percentage of robust noninvariance conditions was relatively high in large positive discrepancy cases (i.e., F3 = 5) as this percentage varied between 65% and 75%. In all other cases the percentage of robust noninvariance conditions was much smaller (see Table 5.3). When comparing the percentage of robust conditions across 3- and 4-indicator conditions, no significant differences were found. As a consequence, we had to conclude—once more—that neither of the two LV indicator models outperformed the other and that the number of indicators (at least when 3 and 4 indicators are compared) does not have an effect of the percentage of correct conclusions of the LV mean difference test.

5.3.4 Inferential Results

In an overall C&RT analysis (i.e., across all levels of design factor 3) for both 3- and 4-indicator conditions (C&RTrees are not included in Appendix 5.A), design factor 3 popped up as the first design factor on which to split the sample. Large positive discrepancy cases (i.e., F3 = 5) were separated

TABLE 5.3

Percentage of Robust Noninvariance Conditions

	Negative Discrepancy Cases		No Discrepancy Cases	Positive Discrepancy Cases	
	LV Mean in Group 2 (G2)				
Percentage of Robust Cases	**= −0.30 (F3 = 1)**	**= −0.15 (F3 = 2)**	**= 0.00 (F3 = 3)**	**= +0.15 (F3 = 4)**	**= +0.30 (F3 = 5)**
$K = 3$ indicators Overall: 35.5%	19.7%	39.4%	30.3%	15.2%	72.7%
$K = 4$ indicators Overall: 34.9%	28.3%	26.3%	34.9%	18.7%	66.2%

Note: The percentage of robust noninvariance conditions is not significantly different across 3- and 4-indicator conditions.

from all other conditions (i.e., F3 different from 5) in the first sample-split. Consistent with the results presented in Table 5.3, the percentage of robust noninvariance conditions were relatively large in conditions representing large positive discrepancy cases. Further down in the C&RTrees, subsamples were formed based on the degree of noninvariance of the indicator intercept (i.e., design factor 5). Larger differences in the noninvariant indicator intercept decreased the probability that the noninvariance condition was robust. In the next paragraphs C&RTrees will be presented for each level of design factor 3.

Inferential results for large negative discrepancy cases: As far as large negative discrepancy cases (i.e., F3 = 1) are concerned, C&RTrees RT_01 and RT_02 in Appendix 5.A reveal that the first important sample-split was made using the third level of design factor 4 (i.e., a noninvariant factor loading equal to 0.8 in G2 versus 0.6 in G1) as the variable on which to split the sample. Actually, in C&RTree RT_01 the very first sample-split was made using an interaction effect as the splitting variable (i.e., interaction effect: F4 = 3 and F5 = 2). This sample-split may be considered to be relatively unimportant because of the limited number of observations in the right branch of the tree ($N = 18$, a detail that is not listed in Appendix 5.A). In C&RTree RT_02, the very first sample-split was made using the third level of design factor 4 (i.e., F4 = 3) as the splitting variable. In the same tree, further sample-splits were made using various degrees of noninvariance of the indicator intercept as splitting variables. C&RTree RT_02 clearly shows that a large noninvariant factor loading combined with a large noninvariant indicator intercept may lead to a very small percentage of robust cases (i.e., 16.7%). C&RTree RT_01 shows different sample-splits, but they all turned out to be relatively unimportant as indicated by the small score obtained for the measure of improvement (a detail that is not listed in Appendix 5.A).

Inferential results for small negative discrepancy cases: In small negative discrepancy cases (i.e., F3 = 2), the first sample-split distinguished between conditions with very small sample sizes ($N = 200$ per group) and all other conditions (see C&RTree RT_03 and RT_04 in Appendix 5.A). Small sample sizes seem to have a positive effect on the robustness of the noninvariance condition. Further down the C&RTrees (C&RT RT_03 and RT_04), the sample was split using a pair of interaction effects between the noninvariant measurement parameters as splitting variables (i.e., the interaction effects: F4 = 1 & F5 = 4 and F4 = 3 & F5 = 2 in 3-indicator conditions, and the interaction effect: F4 = 3 & F5 = 2 in 4-indicator conditions). Apparently, a smaller noninvariant factor loading (in G2 when compared to G1) can partially compensate for the decrease in robustness due to a larger noninvariant indicator intercept (in G2 when compared to G1). Still further down the same C&RTrees, most sample-splits were made using various levels of the noninvariant indicator intercept or the noninvariant factor loading as splitting variables.

Inferential results for no discrepancy cases: In no difference cases (F3 = 3), successive sample-splits were made using various degrees of noninvariance of the indicator intercept as splitting variables (see C&RTrees RT_05 and RT_06). The results actually show that the larger the difference in the noninvariant indicator intercepts becomes, the smaller the probability that the noninvariance condition is robust against violations of the scalar invariance assumption (across groups).

Inferential results for small positive discrepancy cases: In small positive discrepancy cases (i.e., F3 = 4), various levels of noninvariance of the indicator intercept were successively chosen as splitting variables (see C&RTrees RT_07 and RT_08). The results may be interpreted as follows: the higher the noninvariance of the indicator intercepts, the smaller the probability that the noninvariance condition is robust against violations of the scalar invariance assumption (across groups).

Inferential results for large positive discrepancy cases: In large positive discrepancy cases (i.e., F3 = 5), the first pair of sample-splits were made using different sample sizes per group (i.e., F2) as splitting variables (see C&RTrees RT_09 and RT_10). In contrast to small negative discrepancy cases, the first sample-split in C&RTrees RT_09 and RT_10 shows a negative rather than a positive impact of a small sample size per group (i.e., $N = 200$ in both groups) on the percentage of robust noninvariance conditions. Further sample-splits were made using the degree of noninvariance of the factor loading (i.e., F4) as the splitting variable. A substantially smaller percentage of robust noninvariance conditions were reported in conditions with a noninvariant factor loading equal to 0.4 in the G2 (and a corresponding factor loading of 0.6 in G1).

Summary of inferential results on robustness: Our inferential analyses have shown that violations of the scalar invariance assumption across groups may have a very strong impact on the robustness of (simulated) noninvariance conditions. The extent to which noninvariance conditions are nonrobust depends on which measurement parameters (i.e., factor loading and/or indicator intercept) fail to exhibit measurement noninvariance across groups. The influence of a noninvariant intercept is dominant when compared to a noninvariant factor loading in negative discrepancy cases and in small positive discrepancy cases. In large positive discrepancy cases, the effect of a noninvariant factor loading is more significant than in all other noninvariance conditions. In negative discrepancy cases, a smaller noninvariant factor loading (in G2) may partially compensate for the negative effect of a larger noninvariant indicator intercept on the robustness of the noninvariance condition (for instance, when sample size per group is small [i.e., F2 = 2]). The robustness of the noninvariance condition is also influenced by the size of the sample size in each group. This is true for small negative discrepancy cases and large positive discrepancy cases. The distribution of indicators does not affect the robustness of noninvariance conditions.

5.4 CONCLUSIONS

Our simulation study has shown that a noninvariant LV indicator (if not noticed by the researcher) may have a very strong impact on the percentage of correct statistical conclusions of a LV mean difference test. Of all simulated replications about 65% resulted in a correct (statistical) outcome for the LV mean difference test.

A difference in the noninvariant indicator intercept as large as (about) one-tenth of the total length of the scale (a difference of 0.45 on a 5-point scale)—or even smaller—strongly reduced the probability of drawing correct statistical conclusions based on a LV mean difference test. The same is true for a 0.2 difference in a noninvariant factor loading. In our study, neither sample size (per group) nor the underlying distribution of the LV indicator(s) was found to exert a substantial influence on the correctness of the LV mean difference test. This finding is important as it shows that treating ordinal data as if they were metric does not seem to be problematic. All of these conclusions apply equally well to 3- and 4-indicator conditions (i.e., conditions in which the LV is measured by 3 or 4 indicator variables, respectively). Obviously, these conclusions are contingent on the choices made with respect to the design parameters in our study (e.g., only 5-point Likert-type of scales with a left-skewed distribution or a symmetric bimodal distribution; sample sizes exceeding 200 observations per group). However, these conditions are very common in survey research and thus reflect realistic conditions.

The main research question in this simulation study was to evaluate the extent to which noninvariance conditions are robust against violations of the scalar invariance assumption (across groups). Of all simulated noninvariance conditions, only about 35% turned out to be robust. The low overall percentage of robust noninvariance conditions shows that noninvariant measurement parameters (of one indicator across groups) have a very strong impact on the robustness of noninvariance conditions. In this simulation study, robust noninvariance conditions were rather exceptional.

Apart from a difference in LV means (at population level), the major determinant of the robustness of noninvariance conditions turned out to be the degree of noninvariance of the indicator intercept. This is true for all simulated noninvariance conditions, except for noninvariance conditions with a large *positive* discrepancy between LV means (i.e., the notion of *positive* and *negative* discrepancy is explained in detail in Table 5.1).

The effect of the noninvariant factor loading was somewhat more important in large positive discrepancy cases. In these cases, the percentage of robust noninvariance conditions was rather high (about 70%). The combination of: (1) a large difference in LV means at population level and (2) the positive bias due to a noninvariant indicator intercept was responsible for a small difference in the percentage of correct statistical conclusions between noninvariance conditions and their corresponding scalar invariance condition. As a consequence, a high percentage of robust noninvariance conditions were obtained.

A smaller factor loading (in group 2) could partially compensate for the bias due to a larger indicator intercept (in the same group). In addition to the effect of noninvariant measurement parameters, there was also an effect of sample size per group on the robustness of the noninvariance condition. This effect was found in small negative discrepancy cases and large positive discrepancy cases. The distribution of the indicators did not exert an influence on the robustness of noninvariance conditions. All conclusions regarding the design factors determining the robustness of noninvariance conditions were consistent across 3- and 4-indicator cases.

Overall, this simulation study has shown that noninvariant measurement parameters form a serious threat to the correctness of a LV mean difference test between two groups (when making a *false* assumption that all indicators exhibit scalar invariance across groups). A noninvariant factor loading, and in particular a noninvariant indicator intercept, have a strong impact on the percentage of correct statistical conclusions regarding the LV mean difference test. The degree of noninvariance (as simulated in this study) was severe enough to seriously affect the robustness of the LV mean difference test against violations of the scalar invariance assumption (across groups). Furthermore, it does not seem to matter very much if one uses three or four indicators to measure the underlying (one-dimensional) LV. The results were highly consistent across 3- and 4-indicator conditions.

For these reasons, the general advice for researchers is to conduct formal tests on measurement invariance of construct indicators (e.g., running multigroup mean and covariance structure analyses) *prior* to conducting any LV mean comparisons across groups. It is crucial that indicators that do not exhibit measurement invariance across groups are either removed from the measurement model or, alternatively, adequate corrections are made to correct for the bias of (a) noninvariant LV indicator(s). Provided that two indicators of the same construct exhibit scalar invariance, such technical corrections are possible. This has been demonstrated by Steenkamp and Baumgartner (1998), and Scholderer, Grunert, and Brunsø (2005).

Even though such technical corrections (see Scholderer et al., 2005; Steenkamp & Baumgartner, 1998) have been introduced one never knows exactly what one is controlling for. For this reason, we recommend (whenever possible) to identify the causes of measurement noninvariance *prior* to making statistical corrections to the LV mean difference test. For instance, response styles such as acquiescence response style or extreme response style are generally known to form a serious threat to measurement (scalar) invariance of indicators across groups (Weijters, 2006).

A good overview of how response styles can be measured (and corrected for) in survey research is provided in Baumgartner and Steenkamp (2006). An even more recent paper by Weijters, Schillewaert, and Geuens (2008) introduces a sound but sophisticated approach to correct for different types of response styles. Their approach is based on the inclusion of a separate, heterogeneous set of response style indicators drawn from a wide universe of multi-item survey measures. This approach enables a valid and reliable assessment of response styles (i.e., due to the heterogeneity of response style indicators), while avoiding a possible confound between questionnaire *content* and response *style* of the respondent (i.e., as response style indicators are not used for substantive purposes; see De Beuckelaer, Weijters, & Rutten, 2010).

ACKNOWLEDGMENTS

We would like to thank Albert Satorra, Steffen Kühnel, and Gerrit K. Janssens for their valuable comments on an earlier version of this chapter. In addition, we are also indebted to the critical reviewers Eldad Davidov and Holger Steinmetz, who provided us with valuable suggestions on how to improve this chapter.

REFERENCES

Alwin, D. F., & Jackson, D. J. (1981). Applications of simultaneous factor analysis to issues of factorial invariance. In D. J. Jackson & E. F. Borgatta (Eds.), *Factor analysis and measurement in sociological research* (pp. 249–279). Beverly Hills, CA: Sage.

Baumgartner, H., & Steenkamp, J.-B. E. M. (2006). Response biases in marketing research. In R. Grover & M. Vriens (Eds.), *The handbook of marketing research: Uses, misuses, and future advances* (pp. 95–109). Thousand Oaks, CA: Sage.

Breiman, L., Friedman, J. H., Olshen, R. A., & Stone, P. J. (1984). *Classification and regression trees.* Belmont, CA: Wadsworth.

Byrne, B. M. (1989). *A primer of LISREL: Basic applications and programming for confirmatory factor analytic models.* New York, NY: Springer-Verlag.

Byrne, B. M., Shavelson, R. J., & Muthén, B. (1989). Testing for the equivalence of factor covariance and mean structures: The issue of partial measurement invariance. *Psychological Bulletin, 105,* 456–466.

Byrne, B. M., & Watkins, D. (2003). The issue of measurement invariance revisited. *Journal of Cross-Cultural Psychology, 34,* 155–175.

Cheung, G. W., & Rensvold, R. B. (1999). Testing factorial invariance across groups. A reconceptualization and proposed new method. *Journal of Management, 25,* 1–27.

Chou, C.-P., & Bentler, P. M. (1995). Estimates and tests in structural equation modeling. In Hoyle, R.H. (Ed.), *Structural equation modeling: Concepts, issues and applications* (pp. 37–55). Newbury Park, CA: Sage.

Curran, P. J., West, S. G., & Finch, J. F. (1996). The robustness of test statistics to nonnormality and specification error in confirmatory factor analysis. *Psychological Methods, 1,* 16–29.

Davidov, E. (2008). A cross-country and cross-time comparison of the human values measurements with the second round of the European Social Survey. *Survey Research Methods, 2,* 33–46.

Davidov, E., Schmidt, P., & Schwartz, S. (2008). Bringing values back in: The adequacy of the European Social Survey to measure values in 20 countries. *Public Opinion Quarterly, 72,* 420–445.

De Beuckelaer, A., Lievens, F., & Swinnen, G. (2007). Measurement equivalence in the conduct of a global organizational survey across six cultural regions. *Journal of Occupational and Organizational Psychology, 80,* 575–600.

De Beuckelaer, A., Weijters, B., & Rutten, A. (2010). Using ad hoc measures for response styles. A cautionary note. *Quality and Quantity, 44,* 761–775.

He, Y., Merz, M. A., & Alden, D. L. (2008). Diffusion of measurement invariance assessment in cross-national empirical marketing research: Perspectives from the literature and a survey of researchers. *Journal of International Marketing, 16,* 64–83.

Horn, J. L., McArdle, J. J., and Mason, R. (1983). When is invariance not invariant: A practical scientist's look at the ethereal concept of factor invariance. *Southern Psychologist, 1,* 179–188.

Hu, L., Bentler, P. M., & Kano, Y. (1992). Can test statistics in covariance structure analysis be trusted? *Psychological Bulletin, 112,* 351–362.

Kaplan, D., & George, R. (1995). A study of the power associated with testing factor mean differences under violations of factorial invariance. *Structural Equation Modeling: An Interdisciplinary Journal, 2,* 101–118.

Little, T. D. (1997). Mean and covariance structures (MACS) analyses of cross-cultural data: Practical and theoretical issues. *Multivariate Behavioral Research, 32,* 53–76.

Marsh, H. W., & Hocevar, D. (1985). Application of confirmatory factor analysis to the study of self-concept: First- and higher order factor models and their invariance across groups. *Psychological Bulletin, 97,* 562–582.

Meredith, W. (1993). Measurement invariance, factor analysis and factorial invariance. *Psychometrika, 58,* 525–543.

Muthén, B. O., & Christoffersson, A. (1981). Simultaneous factor analysis of dichotomous variables in several groups. *Psychometrika, 46,* 407–419.

Muthén, L. K., & Muthén, B. O. (1999). *Mplus, the comprehensive modeling program for applied researchers. User's guide* (2nd printing). Los Angeles, CA: Muthén and Muthén.

Olsson, U. H., Finch, J. F., & Curran, P. J. (1995). The performance of ML, GLS, and WLS estimation in structural equation modeling under conditions of misspecification and nonnormality. *Structural Equation Modeling: An Interdisciplinary Journal, 7,* 557–595.

Reise, S., Widaman, K. F., & Pugh, R. H. (1993). Confirmatory factor analysis and item response theory: Two approaches for exploring measurement invariance. *Psychological Bulletin, 114,* 552–566.

Schaffer, B. S., & Riordan, C. H. (2003). A review of cross-cultural methodologies for organizational research: A best-practices approach. *Organizational Research Methods, 6,* 169–216.

Scholderer, J., Grunert, K. G., & Brunsø, K. (2005). A procedure for eliminating additive bias from cross-cultural survey data. *Journal of Business Research, 58,* 72–78.

Steenkamp, J-B. E. M., & Baumgartner, H. (1998). Assessing measurement invariance in cross-national consumer research. *Journal of Consumer Research, 25,* 78–90.

Vandenberg, R. J. (2002). Toward a further understanding of and improvement in measurement invariance methods and procedures. *Organizational Research Methods, 5,* 139–158.

Vandenberg, R. J., & Lance, C. E. (2000). A review and synthesis of the measurement invariance literature: Suggestions, practices, and recommendations for organisational research. *Organizational Research Methods, 3,* 4–70.

Van de Vijver, F. J. R., & Leung, K. (1997). *Methods and data analysis for cross-cultural research.* London: Sage.

Weijters, B. (2006). *Response styles in consumer research.* PhD Dissertation, Vlerick Leuven Gent Management School, Ghent, Belgium.

Weijters, B., Schillewaert, N., & Geuens, M. (2008). Assessing response styles across modes of data collection. *Journal of the Academy of Marketing Science, 36,* 409–422.

Williams, L. J., Edwards, J. R., & Vandenberg, R. J. (2003). Recent advances in causal modelling methods for organizational and management research. *Journal of Management, 29,* 903–993.

APPENDIX 5.A: CLASSIFICATION AND REGRESSION TREES (C&RTREES)

Percentage of correct statistical conclusions(latent variable [LV] mean difference test)
ILLUSTRATIVE EXAMPLE of a C&RTree (see also Figure 5.A.1)
Example_C&RTree (4 indicators; *N*=198) {[Overall: 22.3%];
[Split 1=F4_D3 [upper=root]: nil=7.9%; one=63.9%];
[Split 1.1=F5_D2 [upper=nil]: nil=1.1%; one=25.0%];
[Split 1.2=F5_D4 [upper=one]: nil=79.6%; one=16.7%];
[Split 1.1.1=F2_D1 [upper=nil]: nil=0.0%; one=6.7];
[Split 1.1.2=F4_D1 [upper=one]: nil=50.0%; one=0.0%];
[Split 1.2.1=F4_D3*F5_D3 [upper=nil]: nil=88.9%; one=61.1%]}

Notes: This example C&RTree is identical to RT_02 (see below); clarification of the notation used: F4_D3=1 means the factor loading of indicator 1, i.e. λ_2, equals 0.8 in Group 2 (see F4 in Table 5.1); F5_D2=1 means the intercept of indicator 2 is 0.15 higher for Group 2 (see F5 in Table 5.1); F5_D4 means the intercept of indicator 2 is 0.45 higher for Group 2 (see F5 in Table 5.1).

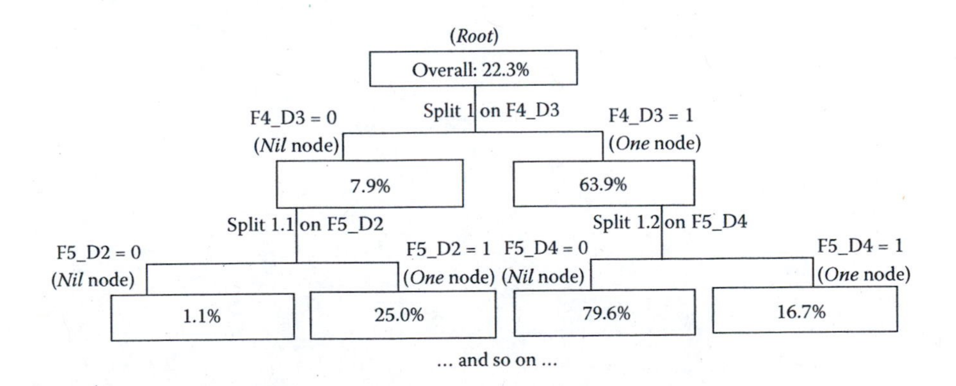

FIGURE 5.A.1
Percentage robust noninvariance conditions (F3 = 1; 4 indicators).

CT_01 (F3=1; 3 indicators; *N*=10,800):
{[Overall: 62.5%];
[Split 1=F4_D1 [upper=root]: nil=73.3%; one=40.9%];
[Split 1.1=F5_D4 [upper=nil]: nil=81.8%; one=47.9%];
[Split 1.2=F4_D4 [upper=one]: nil=47.0%; one=22.3%];
[Split 1.1.1=F5_D3 [upper=nil]: nil=89.5%; one=66.5%];
[Split 1.1.2=F4_D3*F5_D4 [upper=one]: nil=33.1%; one=62.7%];
[Split 1.2.1=F5_D3 [upper=nil]: nil=58.9%; one=23.2%];
[Split 1.1.1.1=F4_D3*F5_D3 [upper=one]: nil=53.6%; one=79.4%];
[Split 1.2.1.1=F5_D2 [upper=nil]: nil=71.5%; one=46.3%]}

CT_02 (F3=1; 4 indicators; *N*=10,800):
{[Overall: 69.5%];
[Split 1=F4_D1 [upper=root]: nil=81.6%; one=45.1%];
[Split 1.1=F5_D4 [upper=nil]: nil=87.3%; one=64.6%];
[Split 1.2=F4_D1*F5_D4 [upper=one]: nil=52.8%; one=21.9%];
[Split 1.1.1=F5_D3 [upper=nil]: nil=92.6%; one=76.7%];
[Split 1.2.1=F4_D1*F5_D3 [upper=nil]: nil=62.6%; one=33.2%];
[Split 1.1.1.1=F4_D3*F5_D3 [upper=one]: nil=64.1%; one=89.3%];
[Split 1.2.1.1=F5_D2 [upper=nil]: nil=73.3%; one=51.9%]}

CT_03 (F3=2; 3 indicators; *N*=10,800)
{[Overall: 32.9%];
[Split 1=F5_D3 [upper=root]: nil=37.5%; one=19.1%];
[Split 1.1=F5_D2 [upper=nil]: nil=43.3%; one=33.2%];
[Split 1.1.1=F5_D4 [upper=nil]: nil=51.7%; one=35.0%];
[Split 1.1.2=F5_D2 [upper=one]: nil=20.2%; one=37.0%];
[Split 1.1.1.1=F4_D3 [upper=nil]: nil=43.2%; one=68.9%];
[Split 1.1.1.2=F4_D1*F5D4 [upper=one]: nil=29.6%; one=45.8%]}

CT_04 (F3=2; 4 indicators; *N*=10,800)
{[Overall: 28.7%];
[Split 1=F5_D4 [upper=root]: nil=33.0%; one=15.8%];
[Split 1.1=F5_D3 [upper=nil]: nil=41.2%; one=16.5%];
[Split 1.2=F4_D3 [upper=one]: nil=17.8%; one=11.7%];
[Split 1.1.1=F4_D3 [upper=nil]: nil=33.5%; one=56.6%];
[Split 1.1.2=F4_D3 [upper=one]: nil=12.1%; one=25.2%];
[Split 1.1.1.1=F5_D2 [upper=nil]: nil=43.8%; one=23.2%];
[Split 1.1.1.2=F4_D3*F5_D2 [upper=one]: nil=12.1%; one=25.2%]}
[Split 1.1.1.1.1=F4_D1 [upper=nil]: nil=53.0%; one=34.6%];
[Split 1.1.1.1.2=F4_D1 [upper=one]: nil=28.9%; one=17.6%]}

CT_05 (F3=3; 3 indicators; *N*=10,800) {[Overall: 55.5%]; [Split 1=F5_D4 [upper=root]: nil=67.6%; one=19.2%]; [Split 1.1=F5_D3 [upper=nil]: nil=80.7%; one=41.2%]; [Split 1.1.1=F5_D2 [upper=nil]: nil=87.7%; one=73.7%]}	CT_06 (F3=3; 4 indicators; *N*=10,800) {[Overall: 67.3%]; [Split 1=F5_D4 [upper=root]: nil=76.4%; one=39.7%]; [Split 1.1=F5_D3 [upper=nil]: nil=85.3%; one=58.6%]; [Split 1.1.1=F5_D2 [upper=nil]: nil=90.0%; one=80.7%]}
CT_07 (F3=4; 3 indicators; *N*=10,800) {[Overall: 79.4%]; [Split 1=F5_D4 [upper=root]: nil=73.6%; one=97.0%]; [Split 1.1=F5_D3 [upper=nil]: nil=64.7%; one=91.5%]; [Split 1.1.1=F5_D2 [upper=nil]: nil=50.0%; one=79.3%]; [Split 1.1.1.1=F4_D3 [upper=nil]: nil=42.8%; one=64.4%]}	CT_08 (F3=4; 4 indicators; *N*=10,800) {[Overall: 76.1%]; [Split 1=F5_D4 [upper=root]: nil=70.3%; one=93.6%]; [Split 1.1=F5_D3 [upper=nil]: nil=62.0%; one=86.8%]; [Split 1.2=F4_D1*F5D4 [upper=one]: nil=96.9%; one=87.0%]; [Split 1.1.1=F5_D2 [upper=nil]: nil=51.1%; one=72.9%]; [Split 1.1.1.1=F4_D1 [upper=nil]: nil=59.5%; one=34.2%]; [Split 1.1.1.2=F4_D1*F5_D2 [upper=one]: nil=79.6%; one=59.4%]}
CT_09 (F3=5; 3 indicators; *N*=10,800) {[Overall: 95.5%]; [Split 1=F4_D1 [upper=root]: nil=97.8%; one=90.7%]}	CT_10 (F3=5; 4 indicators; *N*=10,800) {[Overall: 95.0%]; [Split 1=F4_D1 [upper=root]: nil=97.9%; one=89.1%]}

Notes: % indicate percentage of correct statistical conclusions (LV mean difference test); *nil* and *one* indicate the nodes of the tree where the condition (e.g., F5_D1) equals zero and one, respectively.

Percentage of robust noninvariance conditions	
RT_01 (F3=1; 3 indicators; *N*=198) {[Overall: 19.7%]; [Split 1=F4_D3*F5_D2 [upper=root]: nil=12.8%; one=88.9%%]; [Split 1.1=F4_D3 [upper=nil]: nil=4.8%; one=31.5%]; [Split 1.1.1=F2_D1 [upper=nil]: nil=1.9%; one=19.0%]; [Split 1.1.2=F4_D3*F5_D4 [upper=one]: nil=47.2%; one=0.0%]; [Split 1.1.1.1=F5_D2 [upper=nil]: nil=0.0%; one=6.7%]; [Split 1.1.2.1=F4_D3*F5_D3 [upper=nil]: nil=72.2%; one=22.2%]}	RT_02 (F3=1; 4 indicators; *N*=198) {[Overall: 22.3%]; [Split 1=F4_D3 [upper=root]: nil=7.9%; one=63.9%]; [Split 1.1=F5_D2 [upper=nil]: nil=1.1%; one=25.0%]; [Split 1.2=F5_D4 [upper=one]: nil=79.6%; one=16.7%]; [Split 1.1.1=F2_D1 [upper=nil]: nil=0.0%; one=6.7]; [Split 1.1.2=F4_D1 [upper=one]: nil=50.0%; one=0.0%]; [Split 1.2.1=F4_D3*F5_D3 [upper=nil]: nil=88.9%; one=61.1%]}
RT_03 (F3=2; 3 indicators; *N*=198) {[Overall: 39.4%]; [Split 1=F2_D1 [upper=root]: nil=31.5%; one=78.8%]; [Split 1.1=F4_D1*F5_D4 [upper=nil]: nil=26.0%; one=86.7%]; [Split 1.1.1=F4_D3*F5_d2 [upper=nil]: nil=22.2%; one=60.0%]; [Split 1.1.1.1=F5_D3 [upper=nil]: nil=28.9%; one=8.9%]; [Split 1.1.1.1.1=F5_D2 [upper=nil]: nil=40.0%; one=6.7%]; [Split 1.1.1.1.2=F4_D1 [upper=one]: nil=3.3%; one=20.0%]}	RT_04 (F3=2; 4 indicators; *N*=198) {[Overall: 26.3%]; [Split 1=F2_D1 [upper=root]: nil=19.4%; one=60.6%]; [Split 1.1=F4_D3*F5_D2 [upper=nil]: nil=14.0%; one=73.3%]; [Split 1.1.1=F4_D3 [upper=nil]: nil=8.6%; one=26.7%]; [Split 1.1.1.1=F5_D3 [upper=nil]: nil=12.0%; one=0.0%]; [Split 1.1.1.2=F4_D3*F5_D4 [upper=one]: nil=40.0%; one=0.0%]; [Split 1.1.1.1.1=F2_D3 [upper=nil]: nil=8.3%; one=26.7%]}

RT_05 (F3=3; 3 indicators; *N*=198) {[Overall: 30.3%]; [Split 1=F5_D4 [upper=root]: nil=41.7%; one=0.0%]; [Split 1.1=F5_D3 [upper=nil]: nil=66.7%; one=0.0%]; [Split 1.1.1=F2_D4 [upper=nil]: nil=74.7%; one=26.7%]; [Split 1.1.1.1=F2_D3 [upper=nil]: nil=68.3%; one=100%]; [Split 1.1.1.1.1=F5_D2 [upper=nil]: nil=87.5%; one=55.6%]}	RT_06 (F3=3; 4 indicators; *N*=198) {[Overall: 34.9%]; [Split 1=F5_D4 [upper=root]: nil=47.9%; one=0.0%]; [Split 1.1=F5_D3 [upper=nil]: nil=71.1%; one=9.3%]; [Split 1.1.1=F5_D2 [upper=nil]: nil=94.4%; one=55.6%]; [Split 1.1.2=F1_D2 [upper=one]: nil=2.8%; one=22.2%]; [Split 1.1.1.1=F1_D3 [upper=one]: nil=47.2%; one=72.2]}
RT_07 (F3=4; 3 indicators; *N*=198) {[Overall: 15.1%]; [Split 1=F5_D4 [upper=root]: nil=20.8%; one=0.0%]; [Split 1.1=F5_D3 [upper=nil]: nil=33.3%; one=0.0%]; [Split 1.1.1=F5_D2 [upper=nil]: nil=55.6%; one=18.5%]; [Split 1.1.1.1=F4_D1 [upper=one]: nil=8.3%; one=38.9%]; [Split 1.1.1.1.1=F4_D3*F5_D2 [upper=nil]: nil=16.7%; one=0.0%]}	RT_08 (F3=4; 4 indicators; *N*=198) {[Overall: 18.7%]; [Split 1=F4_D1*F5_D2 [upper=root]: nil=12.2%; one=83.3%]; [Split 1.1=F5_D4 [upper=nil]: nil=17.5%; one=0.0%]; [Split 1.1.1=F5_D3 [upper=nil]: nil=30.6%; one=0.0%]; [Split 1.1.1.1=F5_D2 [upper=nil]: nil=50.0%; one=11.1%]; [Split 1.1.1.1.1=F4_D3 [upper=one]: nil=22.2%; one=0.0%]}
RT_09 (F3=5; 3 indicators; *N*=198) {[Overall: 72.7%]; [Split 1=F2_D1 [upper=root]: nil=82.4%; one=24.2%]; [Split 1.1=F2_D6 [upper=nil]: nil=89.9%; one=60.6%]; [Split 1.1.1=F4_D1 [upper=nil]: nil=95.2%; one=75.0%]; [Split 1.1.1.1=F5_D2 [upper=nil]: nil=93.3%; one=100.0%]; [Split 1.1.1.1.1=F5_D4 [upper=nil]: nil=88.9%; one=100.0%]}	RT_10 (F3=5; 4 indicators; *N*=198) {[Overall: 66.2%]; [Split 1=F2_D1 [upper=root]: nil=73.3%; one=30.3%]; [Split 1.1=F2_D2 [upper=nil]: nil=79.6%; one=48.5%]; [Split 1.1.1=F2_D6 [upper=nil]: nil=85.9%; one=60.6%]; [Split 1.1.1.1=F4_D1 [upper=nil]: nil=95.2%; one=69.4%]; [Split 1.1.1.1.1=F4_D3 [upper=nil]: nil=100.0%; one=91.7%]}

Notes: % indicate percentage of robust noninvariance conditions; *nil* and *one* indicate the nodes of the tree where the condition (e.g., F5_D1) equals zero and one, respectively.

6

Testing the Invariance of Values in the Benelux Countries with the European Social Survey: Accounting for Ordinality

Eldad Davidov
University of Zurich

Georg Datler
University of Zurich

Peter Schmidt
University of Marburg

Shalom H. Schwartz
Hebrew University of Jerusalem

6.1 INTRODUCTION

The increasing importance of comparative studies across countries and over time has encouraged the collection of survey data in diverse contexts and time points in recent decades (e.g., the European Social Survey [ESS], the International Social Survey Program, the European Value Study, or the World Value Survey). These surveys share the goals of collecting comparable responses from large, national representative samples and of gathering data at multiple points in time to permit the study of differences and similarities among cultures and change over time. However, the methodological literature has emphasized that comparisons between groups and/or time points are not legitimate without first assessing whether the concepts used (e.g., human values) are indeed comparable across countries or over time (e.g., Billiet, 2003; Cheung & Rensvold, 2002; De Beuckelaer, 2005; Steenkamp & Baumgartner, 1998; Vandenberg, 2002; Vandenberg & Lance, 2000).

Several techniques have been developed to assess the comparability of concepts. Two of the most common techniques are multiple-group confirmatory factor analysis (MGCFA; Bollen, 1989; Jöreskog, 1971) and means and covariance structure analysis (MACS; Sörbom, 1974, 1978). These techniques can test for configural, metric, and scalar invariance (see e.g., Chapters 2–4, 7, and 9 in this book). Configural invariance indicates that the same indicators measure the same theoretical constructs across groups or time points. Metric invariance is more restrictive; it indicates that respondents interpret the intervals on the response scale in a similar way across groups. Metric invariance with continuous latent variables indicators means that the loadings of the indicators on the factors are equal across groups and/or time points. This implies that the constructs tap the same content across the groups. The most restrictive level of invariance with continuous latent variables indicators, scalar invariance, requires that the intercepts of each item be the same across groups and/or time points. This means that respondents in different contexts use the same scale origin. As other chapters in this book explain (e.g., Chapters 4, 5, 7, and 9), metric invariance permits the comparison of correlates across countries and/or time. Scalar invariance also permits the comparison of latent variable means. The scalar invariance model constrains the means of the latent variables to zero in one group (referred to as the reference group) and estimates them in the other groups.

A differentiation can also be made between full and partial invariance. A partial metric invariance model constrains the factor loadings of at least two indicators of a construct to be equal across groups. A partial scalar invariance model constrains the factor loadings *and* intercepts of at least two indicators to be equal across groups (Byrne, Shavelson, & Muthén, 1989; Steenkamp & Baumgartner, 1998). If the factor loadings of *all* indicators are constrained to be equal across groups, we term the model full metric invariance. If the intercepts *and* factor loadings of *all* indicators are constrained to be equal across groups, one terms the model full scalar invariance.

Multigroup confirmatory factor analysis (MGCFA) is designed for continuous and normally distributed data. Nevertheless, it is often applied to Likert-type scales where researchers typically assume continuity and a normal distribution underlying the scales used. However, Lubke and

Muthén (2004) have criticized the analysis of Likert-type scales under the assumption of multivariate normality. If Likert-type data are analyzed assuming that multivariate normality holds, different factor structures may be found in different groups even if these factor structures are actually invariant across groups (however, they find that the estimates of latent mean differences are rather robust). They propose, instead, fitting a model for ordinal indicators.

The structural equation modeling software programs LISREL (Jöreskog & Sörbom, 1996) and Mplus (Muthén & Muthén, 2007) use two different strategies to identify a model that is fitted to ordinal data. They both include threshold parameters and polychoric correlations between the measurements. The major difference between the two programs is that the LISREL program assumes that the thresholds are equal across groups whereas the Mplus program allows the actual testing of whether this is so. Based on this difference we have chosen to apply the Mplus approach to the data presented in this chapter.

Several simulation studies have shown that MGCFA works well when testing for cross-cultural invariance even when the data are ordinal rather than continuous or normally distributed (Welkenhuysen-Gybels & Billiet, 2002; Welkenhuysen-Gybels, 2004; De Beuckelaer's Chapter 5 in this book).* The current chapter is, to the best of our knowledge, the first to compare the results of an invariance test using MGCFA for ordinal data with the outcomes of an MGCFA that assumes continuous indicators using actual survey data on basic human values available from the ESS.

The following section first describes the theory of human values that we will assess. Then we provide a description of the method that is utilized for measuring values in the ESS. In the empirical part of the chapter, the results of measurement invariance testing using MGCFA under the assumption of normality reported by Davidov and Schmidt (2007) are summarized. This is followed by a presentation of the procedure for testing invariance designed for ordinal indicators and the results of applying this method to the same data. We conclude with summarizing remarks and considerations.

---

* These studies report simulations that examine whether assuming normality and continuity of measurement scales when using ordinal categorical scales yields different conclusions *in a cross-cultural invariance test*. Comparisons of several estimation methods based on different assumptions *for other types of models* have also been conducted. They generally conclude that the maximum likelihood parameter estimates and standard errors are rather robust for small violations of normality (see e.g., Coenders & Saris, 1995; Coenders, Satorra, & Saris, 1997).

6.2 THEORY

Values have played an increasingly important role in the social sciences in recent decades. However, the absence of a widely accepted theory for conceptualizing values and of valid scales to measure them have limited researchers' ability to conduct empirical studies using the value concept. This changed with the introduction of the Schwartz (1992) value theory. This theory specifies 10 basic values that form four higher-order value dimensions that people around the world apparently recognize (Schwartz, 1992, 1994, 2005). Starting with its first round in 2002–2003, the ESS included an instrument to measure the 10 values in the theory.

The theory defines values as *desirable, trans-situational goals, varying in importance, that serve as guiding principles in people's lives.* It proposes 10 motivationally distinct human values: power, achievement, hedonism, stimulation, self-direction, universalism, benevolence, tradition, conformity, and security. Table 6.1 presents the motivational goal that each value expresses. For example, the core motivational goal of power values is social status and prestige, control or dominance over people and resources.

The theory also postulates dynamic relations of interdependence among the values. Values are compatible if the motivational goals they express can be pursued simultaneously (e.g., conformity and tradition). Such values will correlate positively with each other. Values are incompatible if pursuing the motivational goal of one value conflicts with pursuing the goal of the other (e.g., security and stimulation). Such values will correlate negatively. Values are neither compatible nor incompatible if pursuing the motivational goal of one does not affect the other (e.g., benevolence and self-direction). Such values will typically show nonsignificant correlations.

Figure 6.1 portrays the full set of dynamic relations among the 10 values. Values with compatible motivational goals are close to each other within the circle; those values with incompatible goals are further apart. For example, the values power and universalism are far apart from each other within the circle. This reflects the theoretical idea that pursuing the goals of universalism values tends to oppose pursuing the goals of power values. Devoting oneself to the welfare of *all* people is largely incompatible with seeking control and dominance for oneself over other people and resources. In contrast, universalism and benevolence are adjacent to each other in Figure 6.1 because their goals are compatible: It is possible to

TABLE 6.1

Definitions of the Motivational Types of Values in Terms of their Core Goal

POWER: Social status and prestige, control or dominance over people and resources
ACHIEVEMENT: Personal success through demonstrating competence according to social standards
HEDONISM: Pleasure and sensuous gratification for oneself
STIMULATION: Excitement, novelty, and challenge in life
SELF-DIRECTION: Independent thought and action—choosing, creating, exploring
UNIVERSALISM: Understanding, appreciation, tolerance, and protection for the welfare of all people and for nature
BENEVOLENCE: Preservation and enhancement of the welfare of people with whom one is in frequent personal contact
TRADITION: Respect, commitment, and acceptance of the customs and ideas that traditional culture or religion provide the self
CONFORMITY: Restraint of actions, inclinations, and impulses likely to upset or harm others and violate social expectations or norms
SECURITY: Safety, harmony, and stability of society, of relationships, and of self

Source: Adapted from Sagiv, L., and Schwartz, S. H. *Journal of Personality and Social Psychology, 69*, 437–448, 1995.

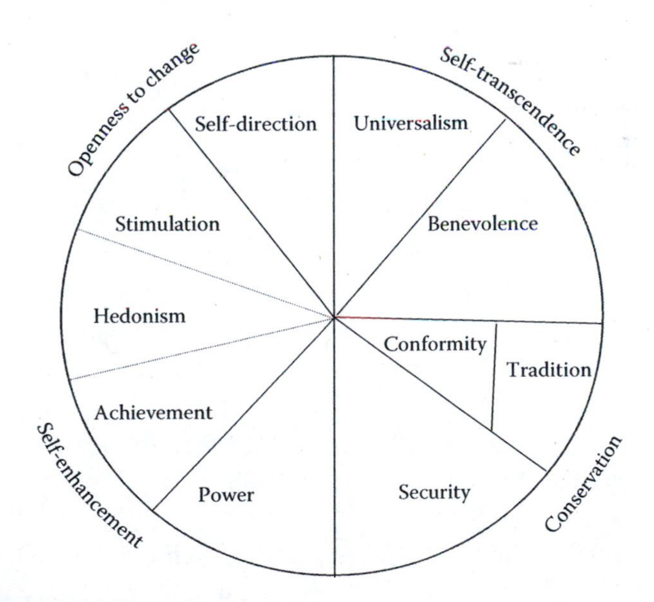

FIGURE 6.1
The dynamic relations between the values.

devote oneself to the welfare of all and also to seek to enhance the welfare of those with whom one is close.

The theory distinguishes 10 value factors, but one may not always be able to discriminate all 10 values empirically. This may occur, for example, if there are practical measurement restrictions such as very few items to measure each value and poor discriminant validity between values with related motivational goals (Campbell & Fiske, 1959; Knoppen & Saris, 2009). Instead, pairs of adjacent values (e.g., universalism and benevolence) may be captured as a single value (e.g., a unified universalism–benevolence value).

The compatibilities and oppositions among the values may be summarized using the higher order factors and dimensions shown in Figure 6.1. One dimension contrasts self-enhancement and self-transcendence values. This dimension contrasts power and achievement values (that emphasize one's pursuit of success and dominance) to universalism and benevolence values (that involve concern for the welfare and interests of other people). The second dimension contrasts openness to change and conservation values. It opposes self-direction and stimulation values (that emphasize independence and readiness for new experiences) to conservation values (that emphasize self-restriction, order, and resistance to change). For a more detailed discussion see, for example, Schwartz, 1992, 1994.

6.3 THE ESS MEASUREMENT OF THE TEN BASIC HUMAN VALUES

A shortened version of the original 40-item portrait value questionnaire (PVQ) to measure values (Schwartz et al., 2001; Schwartz, 2005) was developed for the ESS. Due to time and budgetary constraints, the ESS instrument includes only 21 questions to measure the 10 values. Two items were chosen for each value (three for universalism) with the objective of providing maximum coverage of the conceptual breadth of the value rather than to maximize internal indicator reliability and high discriminant validity.

The ESS scale describes 21 different people, gender-matched with the respondent. Each description portrays a person in terms of what is important to him or her, thereby pointing to one of the 10 values. For example: "Thinking up new ideas and being creative is important to him—he likes to do things in his own original way" describes a person for whom self-direction is important. Regarding each description of a person, respondents are asked to answer: "How much like you is this person?" Responses are recorded on a Likert-type rating scale ranging from 1 (*not like me at all*) to 6 (*very much like me*). Respondents' own values are inferred from their self-reported similarity to people described implicitly in terms of particular values. Table 6.2 presents the 10 values as they appear in the ESS scale. Two items measure each value with the exception of universalism, which is measured by three items because of its very broad content.

6.4 EMPIRICAL ANALYSES

Three countries are included in the analysis: Belgium ($N = 1778$), Luxemburg ($N = 1635$), and the Netherlands ($N = 1881$; total $N = 5294$). Details on the data collection techniques that were used in each country are documented on the Web site http://www.europeansocialsurvey.org. The data used in the analyses are from the second round (2004–2005) of the European Social Survey (ESS) and were downloaded from the Web site http://ess.nsd.uib.no

6.4.1 Previous Findings

The first studies to assess invariance of the measurement of values across ESS countries applied MGCFA (Davidov, 2008; Davidov & Schmidt, 2007; Davidov, Schmidt, & Schwartz, 2008). In these studies, seven distinct values, rather than the 10 values postulated by the theory, were identified in most of the ESS countries. Three pairs from the original 10 values had to be unified: power with achievement, conformity with tradition, and universalism with benevolence. These pairs of values had very high intercorrelations and could not be modeled separately. Two reasons have been proposed for this finding. First, the use of 21 instead of the original 40 PVQ questions to measure values does not provide a sufficient number of questions to measure each value separately in a confirmatory factor analysis (CFA; Davidov, Schmidt, & Schwartz, 2008). Second, high correlations among some values attest to a lack of discriminant validity (Knoppen & Saris, 2009), requiring them to be unified.

TABLE 6.2

The ESS Human Values Scale in the Second Round (Male Version)

Value	Item # (Numbered and Labeled as in the ESS Questionnaire)
Self-direction (SD)	1. Thinking up new ideas and being creative is important to him. He likes to do things in his own original way (ipcrtiv).
	11. It is important for him to make his own decisions about what he does. He likes to be free to plan and not depend on others (impfree).
Universalism (UN)	3. He thinks it is important that every person in the world be treated equally. He believes everyone should have equal opportunities in life (ipeqopt).
	8. It is important for him to listen to people who are different from him. Even when he disagrees with them, he still wants to understand them (ipudrst).
	19. He strongly believes that people should care for nature. Looking after the environment is important to him (impenv).
Benevolence (BE)	12. It is very important for him to help the people around him. He wants to care for their well-being (iphlppl).
	18. It is important for him to be loyal to his friends. He wants to devote himself to people close to him (iplylfr).
Tradition (TR)	9. It is important for him to be humble and modest. He tries not to draw attention to himself (ipmodst).
	20. Tradition is important to him. He tries to follow the customs handed down by his religion or his family (imptrad).
Conformity (CO)	7. He believes that people should do what they're told. He thinks people should follow rules at all times, even when no one is watching (ipfrule).
	16. It is important for him to always behave properly. He wants to avoid doing anything people would say is wrong (ipbhprp).
Security (SEC)	5. It is important for him to live in secure surroundings. He avoids anything that might endanger his safety (impsafe).
	14. It is important for him that the government insures his safety against all threats. He wants the state to be strong so it can defend its citizens (ipstrgv).
Power (PO)	2. It is important for him to be rich. He wants to have a lot of money and expensive things (imprich).
	17. It is important for him to get respect from others. He wants people to do what he says (iprspot).
Achievement (AC)	4. It is important for him to show his abilities. He wants people to admire what he does (ipshabt).
	13. Being very successful is important to him. He hopes people will recognize his achievements (ipsuces).

TABLE 6.2 (CONTINUED)

The ESS Human Values Scale in the Second Round (Male Version)

Value	Item # (Numbered and Labeled as in the ESS Questionnaire)
Hedonism (HE)	10. Having a good time is important to him. He likes to "spoil" himself (ipgdtim).
	21. He seeks every chance he can to have fun. It is important for him to do things that give him pleasure (impfun).
Stimulation (ST)	6. He likes surprises and is always looking for new things to do. He thinks it is important to do lots of different things in life (impdiff).
	15. He looks for adventures and likes to take risks. He wants to have an exciting life (ipadvnt).

Source: Adapted from Davidov, E. *Survey Research Methods*, 2(1), 33–46, 2008.

The three pairs of values that had to be unified are adjacent in the circular theoretical structure portrayed in Figure 6.1. The need to unify them, therefore, does not contradict the theory of the circular value structure. In addition, five additional paths (cross loadings) were introduced in the MGCFA to improve the solution. Each addition was a path from one of the unified value factors to a distant value indicator: (1) from the universalism–benevolence factor to the item "important to be rich," (2) from the universalism–benevolence factor to the item "important to have adventures," (3) from the conformity–tradition factor to the item "important to get respect from others," (4) from the power–achievement factor to the item "important to be modest," and (5) from the conformity–tradition factor to the item "important to be rich" (Davidov et al., 2008).* Figure 6.2 depicts the best fitting model from this study that was calculated using the structural equation modeling software Amos (Arbuckle, 2005).

* The negative cross loadings indicate that the association (covariance) between the opposing latent value constructs did not capture all of the opposition for these items. The positive cross loadings indicate that these associations overestimated the opposition for two items. The need for these cross loadings may be due to the reduction from 10 original values to 7. Without introducing them, the model fit was not acceptable. From a measurement point of view, cross loadings are not elegant. Cross loadings contaminate correlations between factors, a problem if one is interested in the correlations. However, our main interest was not to evaluate the strengths of relationships between values but to examine whether measurement properties, such as factor loadings and intercepts, are invariant across countries.

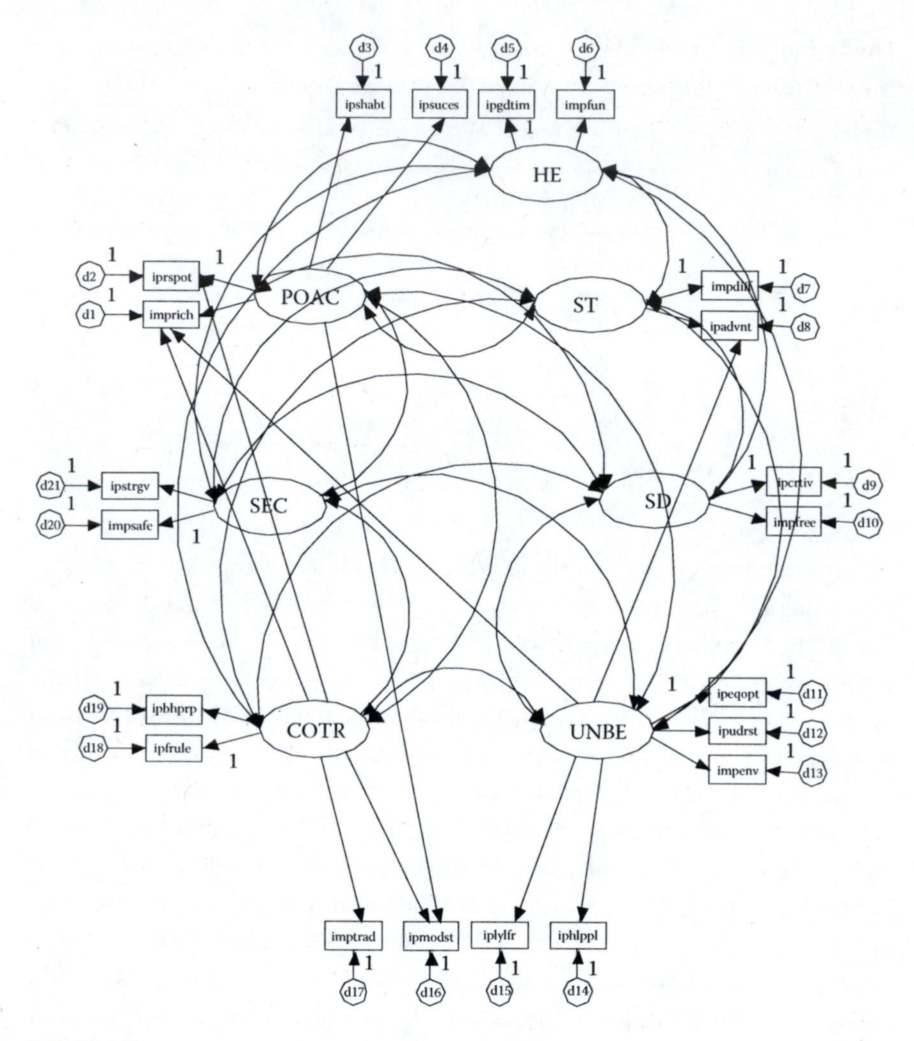

FIGURE 6.2
The CFA model. All values are allowed to correlate with each other. The large circles represent the values. For example, HE represents the value hedonism, and UNBE represents the unified value universalism–benevolence. The small circles represent measurement errors. The rectangles stand for the indicators measuring the values. For item and value abbreviations see Table 6.2.

Davidov and Schmidt (2007) tested for invariance of the value measurements across three countries: Belgium, Luxembourg, and the Netherlands. They used the model just described (that differentiates between seven values) in their application of MGCFA to data from the second round of the ESS. In their analysis they assumed continuity and normality of the value scales.

They reported that configural and metric invariance was found across the three countries for the seven values. However, analysis of the data did not support scalar invariance for all seven values. Rather, only stimulation values, self-direction values, and the unified universalism–benevolence value displayed scalar invariance. Thus, latent mean comparisons between the three countries are legitimate only for these three values (Steenkamp & Baumgartner, 1998).

In the present analysis we assess the invariance of the value scales when fitting the model for ordinal indicators using MGCFA. To do this, we employ the same value data for Belgium, Luxembourg, and the Netherlands available from the second round of the ESS. Finally, we compare the results of this test with the findings of Davidov and Schmidt (2007).

6.4.2 Testing for Invariance While Accounting for Ordinality of the Data

Muthén, du Toit, and Spisic (1997) and Muthén and Muthén (1998, pp. 357–358) propose a theoretically more appropriate method for ordinal (ordered-categorical) scales. Their proposed method fits a CFA model to polychoric correlations using robust weighted least squares (robust WLS: see also Flora & Curran, 2004). This approach is based on the work of Satorra and colleagues (Chou, Bentler, & Satorra, 1991; Satorra, 1992; Satorra & Bentler, 1990). This estimator is available in the software program Mplus. In the present analysis we use Mplus version 3.0 (Muthén & Muthén, 2007) and robust WLS to assess the invariance of the value measurements, following procedural guidelines suggested by Millsap and Yun-Tein (2004) and Temme (2006).

Figure 6.3 displays the path diagram of a single factor CFA for the ordinal case compared to the continuous case. In contrast to continuous indicators, CFA (and MGCFA) for ordinal data (such as Likert-type scales) assumes that the observed items (y's in Figure 6.3) are not directly influenced by their corresponding latent factor but indirectly via a continuous latent response variable (y^* in Figure 6.3; Temme, 2006). The main difference resulting from this specification is that we have to estimate item-specific threshold parameters (ν in Figure 6.3). These threshold parameters (ν in Figure 6.3) partition the continuous normally distributed latent response variable into several categories. With six response categories for each item in our case

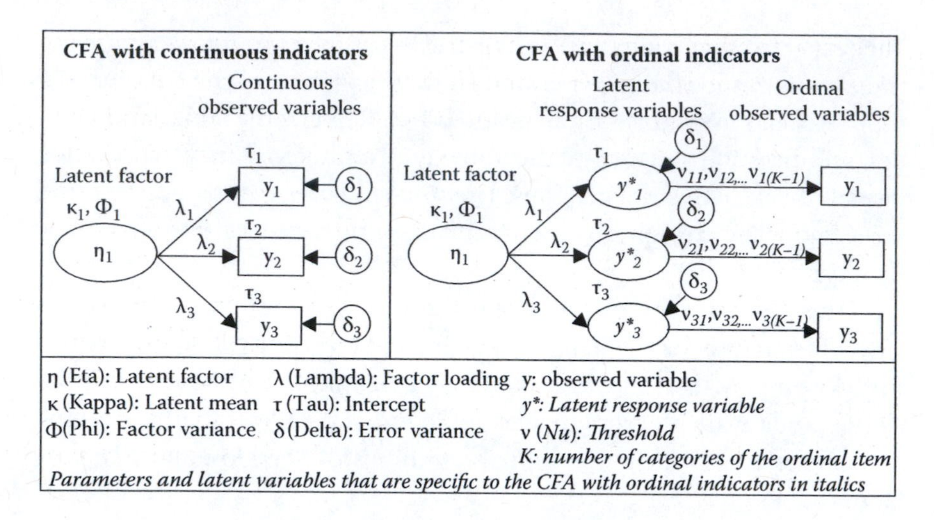

FIGURE 6.3
CFA with ordinal indicators compared to CFA with continuous indicators.

there are five thresholds.* If the value for the continuous latent response variable exceeds a threshold, the observed value of the item changes to the next category. The ordinal CFA model, just like the continuous CFA model, contains factor loadings (λ in Figure 6.3) and intercepts (τ in Figure 6.3). Whereas in the continuous case factor loadings and intercepts are parameters of the observed indicators, in the ordinal case factor loadings and intercepts are parameters of the latent response variable (for further details, see Millsap & Yun-Tein, 2004; Muthén & Asparouhov, 2002).

In testing for invariance with continuous MGCFA, the distinction between metric invariance and scalar invariance is well established. In the continuous case it is *only the factor loadings* that determine the slopes of the item response curves. The intercepts only influence the starting points of the item response curves but not their slopes. Therefore, it is sufficient to constrain the factor loadings to be equal to guarantee metric invariance and to compare structural associations of the latent variables across groups. Latent mean comparison requires equality of intercepts (scalar invariance) in addition.

In the *ordinal* CFA (see Figure 6.3), in contrast, the item probability curves (i.e., the scores of the ordinal indicators) are jointly influenced by the factor loadings (λ's), the intercepts (τ's), and the thresholds (ν's).

---

* A threshold captures transitions from one category to another. Thus, if there are *K* response categories for an indicator, there are *K*–1 threshold parameters for the latent response variable.

Thus, guaranteeing only that factor loadings are equal across groups is not enough to ensure that the item response curves are comparable in the ordinal case. Comparison of group means is still not permissible. Establishing measurement invariance in the ordinal case requires constraining factor loadings, thresholds, and intercepts simultaneously. Thus, a distinction between metric and scalar invariance is not substantively meaningful in the ordinal case because there is only one step in the measurement invariance test, the step that constrains all parameters to be equal.

Identifying the measurement invariance model for the ordinal case requires a somewhat different set of constraints than those required in the continuous case (Millsap & Yun-Tein, 2004; Temme, 2006). The reason is that it is not possible to estimate the thresholds and the intercept at the same time. The programs LISREL and Mplus employ different strategies to deal with this issue.

The LISREL program (Jöreskog & Sörbom, 1996) constrains all the threshold parameters to be equal across groups. This allows testing the equality of the intercepts and factor loadings. However, there is no reason to believe that thresholds are equal. The equality of thresholds is an empirical question that can only be answered in an empirical test. The Mplus program (Muthén & Muthén, 2007) permits testing the equality of threshold parameters but constrains, as a default, all the intercepts to be zero (for identification purposes). Estimating the thresholds and constraining the intercepts is more informative than the other way around. In fact, the intercept parameter is equal to a constant shift in all the thresholds of an indicator.* If intercepts are found to be different across groups, one does not know whether this is due to differences in the full set of thresholds across groups or only some of the thresholds differ across groups. By contrast, testing for the equality of thresholds may allow certain thresholds to differ across groups. Thus, the flexibility of Mplus makes it preferable to LISREL for testing invariance in the ordinal case (Millsap & Yun-Tein, 2004).

The minimum number of constraints required to identify the model in the ordinal case depends on the number of categories of the observed variables and the model structure. Two model structures can be considered, a congeneric model and a noncongeneric model (Millsap & Yun-Tein, 2004). In a congeneric model there are no cross loadings and each item loads only

* In principle, the equality constraint of the intercepts may be released in Mplus by introducing a perfectly measured factor behind the latent response variable (Muthén & Asparouhov, 2002, p. 15).

on one factor. In a noncongeneric model one or more items may load on more than one factor. Accordingly, in the congeneric model one has to set at least one threshold for each indicator to be equal across groups. In addition, a second threshold of the reference indicator of each latent variable is also constrained to be equal across groups. In the noncongeneric model, one has to constrain at least two thresholds to be equal for all indicators. In this model all intercepts have also to be constrained to zero. Our model includes five cross loadings and is thus noncongeneric. In addition, as in the continuous case, the factor loading of one reference indicator is set to 1.*

We adopted a top-down strategy. We started with the most restrictive model that imposes equality constraints across groups on the thresholds, intercepts, and factor loadings. Then we gradually released some of the equality constraints on the thresholds for the indicators whose constructs did not pass the scalar invariance test in the continuous model. To decide whether the data support a model, we followed the cutoff criteria suggested by Hu and Bentler (1999) and Marsh, Hau, and Wen (2004). They suggest a minimum value of 0.90–0.95 for the comparative fit index (CFI), and a maximum value of 0.05–0.08 for the root mean square error of approximation (RMSEA) fit measure. To compare models, we used the criteria proposed by Chen (2007) who suggested assessing differences between models by looking at differences in the fit measures CFI and RMSEA. If both the decrease in the CFI and the increase in the RMSEA in a more restrictive model are smaller than 0.01, then the more restrictive model can be considered as acceptable. We do not use the chi-square difference test and the *p*-value to distinguish between models because even small misspecifications may lead to model rejection with large sample sizes (Cheung & Rensvold, 2002).†

6.4.3 Results

Table 6.3 summarizes the global fit measures of the models—chi-square, degrees of freedom (df), *p*-value, RMSEA, p of close fit (PCLOSE), and CFI.

* Two parameterizations are possible for running the model: Theta and Delta (Muthén & Muthén, 2007). The Theta parameterization includes residual variances for the continuous latent response variables (see Muthén & Muthén, 2007, pp. 485–486). This has the advantage of also permitting a test of the invariance of the residual variances (Millsap & Yun-Tein, 2004, Muthén & Asparouhov, 2002). We applied both the Theta and Delta parameterizations and obtained essentially the same results. See Appendix 6.A for the final model.

† Before testing for measurement invariance, we examined the level of skewness and kurtosis of the values across the countries. Skewness (both left and right, depending on the item) was significant for all 21 items in the three countries. Kurtosis was significant for 20 items.

TABLE 6.3

Global Fit Measures in the Different Models[a]

	MGCFA Under Assumption of Normality—the Continuous Case	MGCFA Using Robust WLS—the Ordinal Case
Model 1: Full measurement invariance (scalar in the continuous case) of seven values		
Chi-square	4165	3888[b]
df	555	355[b]
p-value	0.000	0.000[b]
RMSEA	0.035	0.077
PCLOSE	1.000	—[c]
CFI	0.849	0.855
Model 2: Full measurement invariance (scalar in the continuous case) of three values (UNBE, ST, and SD)		
Chi-square	2926	2492[b]
df	539	310[b]
p-value	0.000	0.000[b]
RMSEA	0.029	0.065
PCLOSE	1.000	—[c]
CFI	0.900	0.911

[a] df = degrees of freedom; RMSEA = root mean square error of approximation; PCLOSE = probability of close fit; CFI = comparative fit index; For details see, for example, Arbuckle, J. L., *Amos 6.0 User's* Guide, SPSS, Chicago, IL, 2005 and Muthén, L. K., and Muthén, B. O., *Mplus User's Guide*, Muthén & Muthén, Los Angeles, CA, 2007.

[b] With WLSMV estimation (which corresponds to robust WLS), chi-square values are mean and variance adjusted and degrees of freedom are estimated rather than derived from the model structure. Chi-square and the number of degrees of freedom are thus not meaningful themselves but rather adjusted in order to provide correct *p*-values.

[c] PCLOSE is not provided by Mplus for multiple group analyses.

Column 1 presents the fit measures using MGCFA under the assumption of multivariate normality (based on Davidov & Schmidt, 2007). We name this model "the continuous case" model. Column 2 presents the fit measures after accounting for ordinality of the outcomes. We name this model "the ordinal case" model. Table 6.3 clearly shows that the most restrictive (invariant) model (Model 1), for seven values, is rejected by the data in both the continuous and ordinal case. Whereas the RMSEA displays satisfactory levels, the CFI does not achieve the minimum criterion for an acceptable fit.

Model 2 constrains invariance for only the three values that Davidov and Schmidt (2007) reported as showing scalar invariance: stimulation

(ST), self-direction (SD), and the unified value universalism–benevolence (UNBE). The measurement of the four other values hedonism (HE), security (SEC), and the unified values conformity–tradition (COTR) and power–achievement (POAC) is allowed to vary across countries. As shown, the data supported this model both in the continuous and in the ordinal case. In other words, it is legitimate to compare the means of these three values across countries.

One technical point is worth noting for the two ordinal models: In an ordinal model, the minimum number of necessary threshold constraints also depends on the constraints already in place for the factor loadings (Millsap & Yun-Tein, 2004, p. 490). When we released the threshold constraints on the four noninvariant factors but still constrained the factor loadings to be equal across groups, it was not necessary anymore to set two thresholds of *all indicators* to be equal across groups (as suggested by Millsap & Yun-Tein, 2004). It was sufficient to set two thresholds of only *one indicator per factor* (instead of two thresholds of all indicators) for the four noninvariant factors to be equal across groups to identify the model (see Appendix 6.A).

Table 6.4 displays the means of the values in Luxembourg and the Netherlands. The mean values in Belgium are constrained to zero as Belgium is the reference group (for other identification methods to estimate latent means see Little, Slegers, & Card, 2006, and Chapter 3 in this book). There are several significant differences in the means across countries. In the continuous case (Davidov & Schmidt, 2007), people

TABLE 6.4

Mean Differences of the Values for Luxembourg and the Netherlands (Compared with Belgium, the Reference Group)

	Luxembourg		The Netherlands	
	MGCFA Under Assumption of Normality	MGCFA Using Robust WLS	MGCFA Under Assumption of Normality	MGCFA Using Robust WLS
Universalism–benevolence	0.00	0.09*	−0.12**	−0.18**
Stimulation	0.08*	0.16**	−0.02	−0.03
Self-direction	−0.01	0.05	0.06	0.05

*$p < .05$; **$p < .01$.

in Luxembourg rate stimulation values as more important (0.08) than people in the other countries do and people in the Netherlands rate universalism–benevolence values as less important (–0.12) than the others do. The remaining value ratings do not differ across the three countries. Accounting for ordinality leads to similar conclusions in most cases, but mean differences are more pronounced. The higher rating of stimulation in Luxembourg is 0.16 and the lower rating of universalism–benevolence in the Netherlands is –0.18. In addition, the rating of universalism–benevolence is higher in Luxembourg (0.09) than in Belgium (0.00 as the reference group). However, under the assumption of multivariate normality the latter difference was not significant.

From the analyses that account for ordinality we can conclude that self-direction values are equally important in all three countries. Stimulation values are equally important in Belgium and the Netherlands, but more important in Luxembourg, and the unified value universalism–benevolence is more important in Luxembourg than in either of the other countries. However, from a substantive point of view, these differences are rather small, reflecting cultural similarities across the Benelux countries. We cannot compare means for the other four values because they do not exhibit the necessary level of invariance across countries.

6.5 CONCLUSIONS

In this chapter we tested the comparability of the human values measurement across Belgium, the Netherlands, and Luxembourg using data from the second round (2004–2005) of the ESS. A previous study (Davidov & Schmidt, 2007) established metric invariance across these countries for seven values and scalar invariance for three values, stimulation, self-direction, and the unified value universalism–benevolence. That study applied MGCFA and assumed a continuous scale with normally distributed responses. However, Lubke and Muthén (2004) have argued that MGCFA is not appropriate in testing for invariance of Likert-type scales. We addressed this criticism by fitting a model for ordinal (ordered-categorical) outcomes to test for invariance.

Previous studies (Welkenhuysen-Gybels, 2004; Welkenhuysen-Gybels & Billiet, 2002; Chapter 5 in this book) have demonstrated, based on simulation studies, that assuming normality and continuity in the case of Likert-type scales generally does not lead to erroneous conclusions and works well for invariance tests across groups.* This chapter assessed whether this conclusion holds with actual survey data on human values as measured in the ESS.

The conclusions with respect to the invariance of the scales were very similar for the model that assumed multivariate normality and the one which accounted for ordinality. The model for ordinal indicators, like the model assuming multivariate normality and continuity, showed that invariance is present for only three of the seven values—stimulation, self-direction, and the unified value universalism–benevolence. Thus, both models justified comparison across the three countries of the means of these three values. Mean comparisons with the two models yielded fairly similar results. Notably, the mean differences were somewhat more pronounced with the ordinal model and, moreover, only the ordinal model revealed that the mean importance of the unified universalism–benevolence value was significantly higher in Luxembourg. In sum, our results are largely in accordance with simulation studies and justify using MGCFA for Likert scales in the analysis of cross-cultural and longitudinal data. The results also suggest that an ordinal MGCFA for such scales is more powerful to compare latent means.

REFERENCES

Arbuckle, J. L. (2005). *Amos 6.0 user's guide*. Chicago, IL: SPSS.

Billiet, J. (2003). Cross-cultural equivalence with structural equation modeling. In J. A. Harkness, F. J. R. Van de Vijver, & P. P. Mohler (Eds.), *Cross-cultural survey methods* (pp. 247–264). New York, NY: John Wiley.

Bollen, K. A. (1989). *Structural equations with latent variables*. New York, NY: Wiley.

Byrne, B. M., Shavelson, R. J., & Muthén, B. (1989). Testing for the equivalence of factor covariance and mean' structures: The issue of partial measurement invariance. *Psychological Bulletin, 105*, 456–466.

Campbell, D. T., & Fiske, D. W. (1959). Convergent and discriminant validation by the multitrait multimethod matrices. *Psychological Bulletin, 56*, 81–105.

Chen, F. F. (2007). Sensitivity of goodness of fit indices to lack of measurement invariance. *Structural Equation Modeling, 14*, 464–504.

* Though the power of MGCFA is lower than proportional odds modeling (see Welkenhuysen-Gybels & Billiet, 2002, p. 216).

Cheung, G. W., & Rensvold, R. B. (2002). Evaluating goodness-of-fit indexes for testing measurement invariance. *Structural Equation Modeling, 9*, 233–255.

Chou, C.-P., Bentler, P. M., & Satorra, A. (1991). Scaled test statistics and robust standard errors for non-normal data in covariance structure analysis: A Monte Carlo study. *British Journal of Mathematical and Statistical Psychology, 44*, 347–357.

Coenders, G., & Saris, W. E. (1995). Categorization and measurement quality. The choice between Pearson and polychoric Correlations. In W. E. Saris & Á. Münnich (Eds.), *The multitrait-multimethod approach to evaluate measurement instruments* (pp. 125–144). Budapest, Hungary: Eötvös University Press.

Coenders, G., Satorra, A., & Saris, W. E. (1997). Alternative approaches to structural modeling of ordinal data. A Monte Carlo study. *Structural Equation Modeling, 4*, 261–282.

Davidov, E. (2008). A cross-country and cross-time comparison of the human values measurements with the second round of the European Social Survey. *Survey Research Methods, 2*(1), 33–46.

Davidov, E., & Schmidt, P. (2007). Are values in the Benelux comparable? In G. Loosveldt, M. Swyngedouw, & B. Cambré (Eds.), *Measuring meaningful data in social research* (pp. 373–386). Leuven, Belgium: Acco.

Davidov, E., Schmidt, P., & Schwartz, S. H. (2008). Bringing values back in: Testing the adequacy of the European Social Survey to measure values in 20 Countries. *Public Opinion Quarterly, 72*, 420–445.

De Beuckelaer, A. (2005). *Measurement invariance issues in international management research*. Unpublished doctoral dissertation, Hasselt University, Diepenbeek, Belgium.

Flora, D. B., & Curran, P. J. (2004). An empirical evaluation of alternative methods of estimation for confirmatory factor analysis with ordinal data. *Psychological Methods, 9*, 466–491.

Hu, L., & Bentler, P. M. (1999). Cutoff criteria for fit indexes in covariance structure analysis: Conventional criteria versus new alternatives. *Structural Equation Modeling, 6*, 1–55.

Jöreskog, K. G. (1971). Simultaneous factor analysis in several populations. *Psychometrika, 36*, 409–426.

Jöreskog, K. G., & Sörbom, D. (1996). *LISREL 8 user's reference guide*. Chicago, IL: Scientific Software International.

Knoppen, D., & Saris, W. (2009). Do we have to combine values in the Schwartz's Human Values Scale? A comment on the Davidov studies. *Survey Research Methods, 3*, 91–103.

Little, T. D., Slegers, D. W., & Card, N. A. (2006). A non-arbitrary method of identifying and scaling latent variables in SEM and MACS models. *Structural Equation Modeling, 13*, 59–72.

Lubke, G. H., & Muthén, B. O. (2004). Applying multigroup confirmatory factor models for continuous outcomes to Likert scale data complicates meaningful group comparisons. *Structural Equation Modeling, 11*, 514–534.

Marsh, H. W., Hau, K.-T., & Wen, Z. (2004). In search of golden rules: Comment on hypothesis-testing approaches to setting cutoff values for fit indexes and dangers in overgeneralizing Hu and Bentler's (1999) findings. *Structural Equation Modeling, 11*, 320–341.

Millsap, R. E., & Yun-Tein, J. (2004). Assessing factorial invariance in ordered-categorical measures. *Multivariate Behavioral Research, 39*, 479–515.

Muthén, B. O., & Asparouhov, T. (2002). *Latent variable analysis with categorical outcomes: Multiple-group and growth modeling in Mplus* (Mplus Web Notes, No. 4). Retrieved from http://www.statmodel.com/examples/webnote.shtml

Muthén, B. O., du Toit, S. H. C., & Spisic, D. (1997). *Robust inference using weighted least squares and quadratic estimating equations in latent variable modeling with categorical and continuous outcomes.* Unpublished technical report. Retrieved from http://www.gseis.ucla.edu/faculty/muthen/articles/Article_075.pdf

Muthén, L. K., & Muthén, B. O. (1998). *Mplus user's guide.* Los Angeles, CA: Author.

Muthén, L. K., & Muthén, B. O. (2007). *Mplus user's guide.* Los Angeles, CA: Author.

Sagiv, L., & Schwartz, S. H. (1995). Value priorities and readiness for out-group social contact. *Journal of Personality and Social Psychology, 69,* 437–448.

Satorra, A. (1992). Asymptotic robust inferences in the analysis of mean and covariance structures. In P. Marsden (Ed.), *Sociological methodology 1992.* Washington, DC: American Sociological Association.

Satorra, A., & Bentler, P. M. (1990). Model conditions for asymptotic robustness in the analysis of linear relations. *Computational Statistics and Data Analysis, 10,* 235–249.

Schwartz, S. H. (1992). Universals in the content and structure of values: Theoretical advances and empirical tests in 20 countries. *Advances in Experimental Social Psychology, 25,* 1–65.

Schwartz, S. H. (1994). Are there universal aspects in the content and structure of values? *Journal of Social Issues, 50,* 19–45.

Schwartz, S. H. (2005). Basic human values: Their content and structure across countries. In A. Tamayo & J. B. Porto (Eds.), *Valores e Comportamento nas Organizações* [Values and behavior in organizations] (pp. 21–55). Petrópolis, Brazil: Vozes.

Schwartz, S. H., Melech, G., Lehmann A., Burgess, S., Harris, M., & Owens, V. (2001). Extending the cross-cultural validity of the theory of basic human values with a different method of measurement. *Journal of Cross Cultural Psychology, 32,* 519–542.

Sörbom, D. (1974). A general method for studying differences in factor means and factor structure between groups. *British Journal of Mathematical and Statistical Psychology, 27,* 229–239.

Sörbom, D. (1978). An alternative to the methodology for analysis of covariance. *Psychometrika, 43,* 381–396.

Steenkamp, J.-B. E. M., & Baumgartner, H. (1998). Assessing measurement invariance in cross national consumer research. *Journal of Consumer Research, 25,* 78–90.

Temme, D. (2006). Assessing measurement invariance of ordinal indicators in cross-national research. In S. Diehl & R. Terlutter (Eds.), *International advertising and communication. Current insights and empirical findings* (pp. 455–472). Wiesbaden, Germany: GWV.

Vandenberg, R. J. (2002). Towards a further understanding of and improvement in measurement invariance methods and procedures. *Organizational Research Methods, 5,* 139–158.

Vandenberg, R. J., & Lance, C. E. (2000). A review and synthesis of the measurement invariance literature: Suggestions, practices and recommendations for organizational research. *Organizational Research Methods, 3,* 4–69.

Welkenhuysen-Gybels, J., & Billiet, J. (2002). A comparison of techniques for detecting cross-cultural inequivalence at the item level. *Quality & Quantity, 36,* 197–218.

Welkenhuysen-Gybels, J. (2004). The performance of some observed and unobserved conditional invariance techniques for the detection of differential item functioning. *Quality & Quantity, 38,* 681–702.

APPENDIX 6.A: MPLUS SYNTAX FOR THE FINAL MODEL WITH INVARIANCE OF THREE VALUES

```
1   title: MGCFA Values ESS Round 2 - Belgium, Luxembourg, Netherlands;
2   data: file is benelux_values.dat;
3   variable: names are ipcrtiv imprich ipeqopt ipshabt impsafe impdiff ipfrule ipudrst
4   ipmodst ipgdtim impfree iphlppl ipsuces ipstrgv ipadvnt ipbhprp iprspot iplylfr
5   impenv imptrad impfun country;
6   categorical are all;
7   grouping is country (1=BE 2=LU 3=NL);
8   missing = all (7-9);
9   Analysis: PARAM = THETA;
10  Model:
11  SD by impfree* ipcrtiv@1;
12  UNBE by ipeqopt* ipudrst@1 impenv iphlppl iplylfr ipadvnt imprich;
13  COTR by ipmodst* imptrad* ipfrule@1 ipbhprp iprspot imprich;
14  SEC by impsafe@1 ipstrgv;
15  POAC by imprich* iprspot* ipshabt@1 ipsuces ipmodst;
16  HE by ipgdtim@1 impfun;
17  ST by impdiff@1 ipadvnt;
18  Model LU:
19  [ipfrule$3* ipfrule$4* ipfrule$5*];
20  [ipbhprp$1* ipbhprp$2* ipbhprp$3* ipbhprp$4* ipbhprp$5*];
21  [imptrad$1* imptrad$2* imptrad$3* imptrad$4* imptrad$5*];
22  [ipmodst$1* ipmodst$2* ipmodst$3* ipmodst$4* ipmodst$5*];
23  [ipstrgv$1* ipstrgv$2* ipstrgv$3* ipstrgv$4* ipstrgv$5*];
24  [impsafe$3* impsafe$4* impsafe$5*];
25  [ipshabt$3* ipshabt$4* ipshabt$5*];
26  [ipsuces$1* ipsuces$2* ipsuces$3* ipsuces$4* ipsuces$5*];
27  [iprspot$1* iprspot$2* iprspot$3* iprspot$4* iprspot$5*];
28  [imprich$1* imprich$2* imprich$3* imprich$4* imprich$5*];
29  [ipgdtim$1* ipgdtim$2* ipgdtim$3* ipgdtim$4* ipgdtim$5*];
30  [impfun$3* impfun$4* impfun$5*];
31  Model NL:
32  [ipfrule$3* ipfrule$4* ipfrule$5*];
```

(Continued)

```
33   [ipbhprp$1* ipbhprp$2* ipbhprp$3* ipbhprp$4* ipbhprp$5*];
34   [imptrad$1* imptrad$2* imptrad$3* imptrad$4* imptrad$5*];
35   [ipmodst$1* ipmodst$2* ipmodst$3* ipmodst$4* ipmodst$5*];
36   [ipstrgv$1* ipstrgv$2* ipstrgv$3* ipstrgv$4* ipstrgv$5*];
37   [impsafe$3* impsafe$4* impsafe$5*];
38   [ipshabt$3* ipshabt$4* ipshabt$5*];
39   [ipsuces$1* ipsuces$2* ipsuces$3* ipsuces$4* ipsuces$5*];
40   [iprspot$1* iprspot$2* iprspot$3* iprspot$4* iprspot$5*];
41   [imprich$1* imprich$2* imprich$3* imprich$4* imprich$5*];
42   [ipgdtim$1* ipgdtim$2* ipgdtim$3* ipgdtim$4* ipgdtim$5*];
43   [impfun$3* impfun$4* impfun$5*];
44   output: stand; res;
```

Explanation

The syntax in Mplus only needs to specify deviations from the Mplus default. The Mplus default for MGCFAs with ordinal data is:

Parameterization:	DELTA
Estimation:	WLSMV
Constraints:	First factor loading on each "by" statement set to 1, all intercepts set to 0, all factor loadings and thresholds constrained equal across groups
Lines 1–6	Data source, variable names, definition as categorical
Line 7	Multiple groups
Line 8	Indication of which categories represent missing values for all variables
Line 9	Theta parameterization
Lines 10–17	Model for all groups, "*" specifies that a parameter should be estimated, "@" fixes a parameter. "SD by impfree* ipcrtiv@1"; overrides the Mplus default to constrain the first factor loading to 1 and takes the second instead.
Lines 18–30	Threshold parameters for the four factors that are not invariant across groups are set free in the group "Luxembourg." Thresholds that are not mentioned explicitly remain constrained across groups automatically (the same applies to the factor loadings), e.g.,

	"[ipfrule$3* ipfrule$4* ipfrule$5*];" sets the last three thresholds of the item ipfrule free and leaves the first two constrained
Lines 32–43	Threshold parameters for the four factors that are not invariant across groups are set free in the group "Netherlands."
Line 44	Request of standardized estimates and residual statistics in the output

7

Religious Involvement: Its Relation to Values and Social Attitudes

Bart Meuleman
University of Leuven

Jaak Billiet
University of Leuven

7.1 INTRODUCTION

Although we have witnessed a clear tendency toward secularization during the last decades (Dobbelaere, 1993; Norris & Inglehart, 2004), religion continues to play an important role in contemporary European societies (Stark & Finke, 2000). A vast body of research has shown that, even today, religious outlooks continue to structure the individual's values, attitudes, and behavior (see Ervasti, 2008). At the same time, the degree to which individuals participate in religious life is not evenly spread across the population, but instead depends on the individual's social-structural position in society. In this sense, religiosity can be seen as an important intermediary variable between social structure, on the one hand, and attitude patterns, on the other.

In this study, we focus on this interplay between religious involvement, value orientations, social attitudes, and social structural variables. The social attitudes studied here are perceived ethnic threat, social trust, and political trust. Does religious involvement have a favorable influence on the development of such attitudes that are conducive to social integration? Previous research has shown that the relationship between religious involvement and these social attitudes is not the same in all countries and thus depends on the broader cultural context (Billiet, 1998; Billiet et al., 2003; Cambré, 2002).

Research has also revealed that some value orientations, such as self-transcendence and conservation, are related to religious involvement and at the same time have an influence on social attitudes such as ethnic threat (Davidov, Meuleman, Billiet, & Schmidt, 2008a; Roccas, 2005). It is therefore important to take these values into consideration if one wants to evaluate the impact of religious involvement on the social attitudes in question.

In this chapter we use European Social Survey (ESS) data to test the aforementioned relations within a complete explanatory model in more than 20 European countries. This allows us to find out whether there are country differences in the relationships between social structure, religious involvement, value priorities, and social attitudes. The focus of the present paper is on both the methodological and the substantive, as we provide an illustration of how a structural equation modeling approach can be useful in cross-national research. We present a multigroup structural equation model in which the measurement part and the structural part are tested simultaneously, and in which serious attention is paid to the cross-national equivalence of the measures.

The explanation of the observed differences between countries by means of relevant context variables, although a logical continuation of our analysis, is not elaborated in this chapter. This is for several reasons. A rather straightforward completion of the chapter with the estimation of context effects might possibly extend the structural equation model to include a multilevel component. However, a simulation study based on ESS data showed that a multilevel structural equation model involving only 25 countries provides very unreliable and unstable estimates of the context effects (Meuleman & Billiet, 2009). Trying to develop relevant and valid contextual variables would lead us into a completely new kind of research. Giving this issue the attention it deserves would have enlarged the chapter substantially. We therefore decided to focus on equivalent measurements at the microlevel and on the simultaneous estimation of measurement and structural models in a multi-country situation.

This chapter starts with a theoretical overview of the substantive research questions. After the data and methods section, in which the measurements are discussed, formal tests for cross-country measurement equivalence of the latent variables receives serious attention. After an overview of the substantive findings, some methodological problems are discussed. As already mentioned, the focus is on the testing of a simultaneous model with a measurement part and a structural part within a multigroup context.

7.2 THEORETICAL MODEL: RELIGIOUS INVOLVEMENT, SOCIAL ATTITUDES, VALUES, AND SOCIODEMOGRAPHIC VARIABLES

Does religious commitment affect social attitudes that are favorable to social integration? From a social capital point of view, social integration is understood as the maintenance of orientations and attitudes that are favorable to the justification and functioning of a pluralistic, democratic political system. Social capital refers to aspects of social relationships or structures that facilitate the purposeful cooperation of individuals within these relationships. These aspects include mutual obligations and expectations, the availability of information, purposeful social organizations, norms of reciprocity, civic commitment, and social confidence (Coleman, 1988, 1990; Putnam, 1993).

What do we know from previous studies? An empirical study in Belgium showed that involvement in religious-ideological associations had a significant effect on several indicators of social integration (Billiet, 1998). These indicators were: distrust in others and in the future, feelings of being threatened by immigrants, racist views concerning newcomers in society, utilitarian individualism, political alienation, and the lack of political interest and participation. All these indicators were measured on the individual level of social attitudes (Brehm & Rahn, 1997). As was expected, church involvement and active participation in voluntary associations were negatively correlated with these indicators of social disintegration. Those deeply involved in the Catholic Church* or who participated actively in voluntary organizations were less likely to score high on the indicators of social disintegration than marginal Catholics and people with no philosophy of life. The effect of religious-philosophical involvement, however, was not very strong (Billiet, 1998).

Research in a cross-country context, however, does not univocally support the claim that religious involvement stimulates attitudes that are conducive to social (dis)integration. It was found that the relationship between religious involvement and ethnocentrism varies considerably across societies, religions, and the kinds of immigrants referred to (Eisinga, Felling, & Peters, 1990). Using the Religious and Moral Pluralism (RAMP, 1998)

* This was also the case, however, for a-religious humanists ("free thinkers").

dataset and the 1995 dataset of the International Social Survey Program (ISSP), Cambré (2002) systematically investigated the (net) relationship between church involvement and ethnocentrism in 13 Western European countries. In general, the non-church members were less likely than members to harbor negative attitudes toward immigrants. However, among church members the relationship between the degree of involvement and ethnocentrism varied from country to country and from denomination to denomination. Because attempts to explain these differences by variations in the characteristics of the particular religious systems failed, Cambré concluded that the characteristics of the different social systems (at the national level) and their interaction with the characteristics of the different religious systems might be more important. Because of the small number of countries included in the analysis, however, this claim could not be tested empirically.

Scheepers, Gijsberts, and Hello (2000) also used the RAMP dataset in order to analyze the relationship between religious involvement and ethnic prejudice from a comparative perspective. Surprisingly, these researchers came to findings that are in contradiction with the conclusions of Cambré (2002). According to the study of Scheepers et al. (2000), the more frequently people attend church, the more prejudiced they are, and this relationship holds for all 11 countries in RAMP. The fact that this finding is so incompatible with the findings of Cambré, who used the same data, calls for a careful investigation of the parameters measurements that were used. The most striking difference between these studies concerns the operationalization of ethnocentrism. Cambré systematically tested the measurement equivalence of all six indicators that were used in RAMP in order to measure ethnocentrism. He found that there were serious problems in the wording and translation from the source questionnaire concerning the three positively worded ethnocentric items (Cambré, Welkenhuysen-Gybels, & Billiet, 2002). The mixed and even contradictory findings concerning the relationship between ethnocentrism and religious involvement is one of the reasons to pay serious attention to the equivalent measurement of the latent attitudinal variables and values in the present study.

To study the interplay between religious involvement, the value priorities and the social attitudes that are either supportive (political and social trust) or destructive (ethnic threat) for social integration, we propose the theoretical model depicted in Figure 7.1. This model shows religious involvement as a key mediator between social-structural

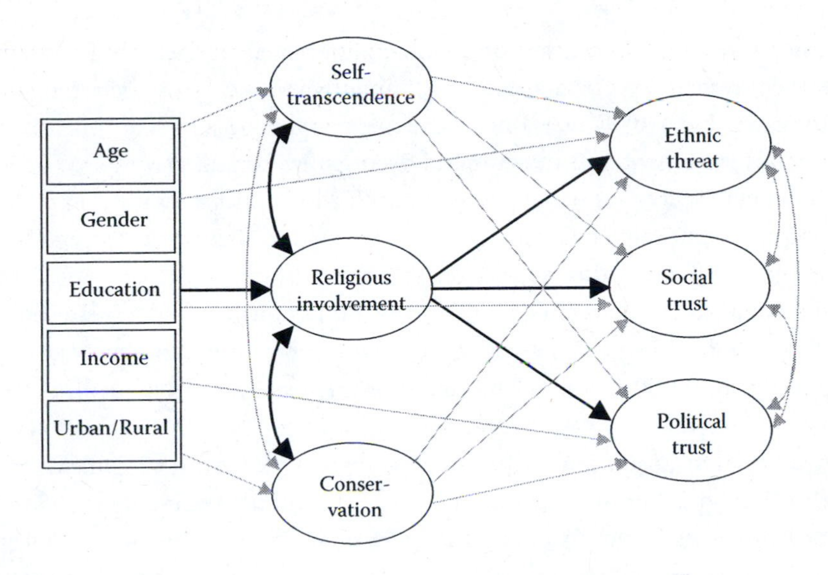

FIGURE 7.1
Theoretical model.

variables, values, and attitudes. Our primary interest goes to three parts of the model: (1) the effect of sociodemographic variables on religious involvement, (2) the correlation between religious involvement and value priorities, and (3) the (net) effect of religious involvement on social attitudes.

7.2.1 Religious Involvement and Social Attitudes

Let us start with the third step, the relation between religious involvement and the social attitudes: ethnic threat, social trust, and political trust. It has been argued that there is no clear relationship between religious orientation and ethnic prejudice and that researchers must take particular religious and social norms into account (Griffin, Elmer, & Gorsuch, 1987). Why can we expect differences in this relationship? It is known that anomie (or social disintegration) is one of the strongest predictors for negative feelings toward immigrants (Scheepers, Felling, & Peters, 1992). Those who are more involved in churches or religious denominations are less opposed to immigrants because they are more active in organizational networks, and consequently less subjected to anomie (Carr & Hauser, 1976; Kanagy, Fern, Willits, & Crider, 1990). It has also been argued that preaching with a strong accent on tolerance, charity, and social justice on the basis of Christian principles might make those who are more strongly integrated in their local church more concerned with the social and humanistic aspects of their religion (Eisinga et al., 1990). This is one side of the story, but there is another side. Church involvement and integration into organizational networks go hand in hand with increased social control, and so with conformist ideas and traditionalism. Christians who are strongly oriented to their local community develop "localistic" attitudes and a high degree of solidarity and consensus about values and norms (Roof, 1974). This can potentially make them intolerant of people from other social groups who might want to penetrate the tight local network or who would question the existing values and norms. Localistic orientations can potentially give rise to social identification with the national in-group and at the same time to social contra-identification with other social groups (Lehman, 1986). The latter arguments, however, are mainly derived from studies among local churches in the United States. Theories that predict a moderating effect of religious involvement on negative feelings toward immigrants apply more often to European countries in which the mainstream churches are related to social movements and in which the message of social justice and care for foreigners is dominant. We therefore expect that religious involvement will temper negative attitudes toward immigrants, but this effect is not necessarily equal in all countries.

The central role of social trust in social capital has long been emphasized by social and political theorists (Newton, 2001). Social psychologists claim that social trust is an integral part of a broader syndrome of personality characteristics that includes optimism and belief in the possibility of cooperation with others, while distrust is an integral part of the misanthropic personality, which involves pessimism and cynicism about the possibilities for social and political cooperation (Rosenberg, 1956).

Why do we expect a positive relationship between generalized (social) trust and religious involvement? Two theoretical hypotheses predict it, the religious belief hypothesis and the religious network hypothesis. According to the *religious belief hypothesis*, social trust has an important foundation in moral beliefs and views of human nature (Uslaner, 2002). Generalized trust is founded on the perception that most people are part of the same moral community. Theologies that advance inclusive doctrines of common grace, human potential, and goodness will encourage their adherents to be trusting. These views are most likely to be endorsed by majority religious traditions that are well integrated into the wider society, such as mainline Protestantism and Catholicism (Traunmüller, 2009, p. 358). However, religious involvement may also lead to distrust of other people in the case of rigid religious groups whose view of human nature is pervaded by ideas of sinfulness, and whose identity is based on strong symbolic boundaries between members of the religious in-group and the rest of society (Welch, Sikkink, Sartain, & Bond, 2004). It is most likely that religious involvement will be positively related to social trust, since a large majority of the religious persons in the ESS samples belong to mainline Christian churches. The *religious network hypothesis* (Traunmüller, 2009, p. 350) states that religiously involved people are more strongly embedded in interactive networks of social ties characterized by their value orientation. It is assumed that cooperative ties of this kind, based on values, are eminently suited to fulfilling the functions of (bridging) social capital, not in the least because they can provide individuals with a buffer against the atomization and social disintegration of society as a whole (Hooghe, Reeskens, Stolle, & Trappers, 2009; Strømsnes, 2008). This view relates to the ideas and findings of Putnam, who maintains that members of associations have greater trust in others and participate more in political life (Putnam, 1995). This also holds for religious participation, as is demonstrated in numerous studies (Parry, Moyser, & Day, 1992; Putnam, 2000, pp. 65–79; Verba, Scholzman, & Brady, 1995).

Trust in political institutions is a crucial aspect of the attitude toward politics and is considered vital to the long-term viability of a democracy. It is the opposite of political cynicism (Almond & Verba, 1965). The relationship between religious involvement and trust in politics is less developed than is the case with generalized trust. The theoretical expectations concerning this relationship are based on the *social network hypothesis* (see above). Religious persons are less cynical about the government and political institutions because they are more devoted to social norms than nonreligious persons (Kitchelt, 1994). We expect a positive relationship between trust in politics and religious involvement.

7.2.2 Religious Involvement and Value Orientations

The present study on religious involvement and social attitudes includes two crucial value orientations in the theoretical model: *self-transcendence* and *conservation*. In the context of previous theoretical reflections on the relationships between religious involvement and social attitudes, these value orientations are crucial in terms of whether positive or negative relationships were to be expected. The direction of the relationships between religious involvement and social attitudes is contingent upon the kinds of values and norms that are endorsed within the networks that religious persons take part in. In the model that has been specified in Figure 7.1, the values are not included as control variables since this might lower or even neutralize the direct effects of religious involvement on the social attitudes. The value orientations are simply included as covariates in order to find out what values covary with religious involvement and how. This might help the reader to understand the relationship between religious involvement and the social attitudes.

Citizens who endorse the value orientations related to self-transcendence are more ready to treat others equally, take care of nature, try to understand people with different views, and help other people. This tendency to transcend selfish interests obviously facilitates social integration. On the other hand, individuals who give priority to conservation values, such as respect for tradition and conformity to social norms, are expected to have more negative attitudes toward immigration. It is known that these value types are related to religious involvement (Norris & Inglehart, 2004). The link between religious involvement and value priorities takes place through at least two mechanisms that operate in the opposite causal direction. On the one hand, certain value patterns may stimulate involvement in religious life. And yet at the same time, membership in religious communities probably also entails an aspect of socialization of values (Schwartz & Huismans, 1995).

7.2.3 Religious Involvement and Sociodemographic Variables

Although the focus is on the relations between religious involvement, values and social attitudes, several sociodemographic variables are also included in the model as predictors for religious involvement and as control variables for the relations between religious involvement and social attitudes. Among the relevant social background variables, age seemed to have the strongest effect on religious involvement in previous research (Billiet et al., 2003). The younger generations are less religious than older generations. In this study, age expressed in years is used as an independent variable. It is generally acknowledged that women are more religious than men and there is a large amount of empirical evidence for this (Flere, 2007). Evidence with respect to the effects of education on religious involvement is mixed. In some studies, the lower educated turned out to be less religious than the higher educated, but this is not always the case. Furthermore, the education effect often disappears after controls for the other background variables are introduced (Billiet et al., 2003). We also anticipate an effect of income (as a proxy for social class position). According to social deprivation theory, it is most likely that poor people will be more religious than rich people because of the comfort function of religion for people who suffer (Glock, Ringer, & Babbie, 1967). Wealthy people are more likely to be less religious since, because of the opportunities they have, they are more subjected to individualization. Finally, in line with secularization theory, the urban environment in which the respondent lives also seems to be related to religious involvement (Billiet et al., 2003; Dobbelaere, 2002, pp. 142–143). People living in an urban environment are less subjected to social control and are much more challenged by a culturally diverse environment.

7.3 DATA AND METHODS

Round 2 of the ESS is used for the multigroup structural equation modeling (MGSEM) analysis in this chapter. With the exception of a small number of countries, a majority of the countries participating in Round 2 completed their fieldwork during the last semester of 2004 and the first half of 2005. The following 25 countries participated in Round 2: Austria (AT), Belgium (BE), Czech Republic (CZ), Denmark (DK), Estonia (EE), Finland (FI), France (FR), Germany (DE), Greece (GR), Hungary (HU), Iceland (IS), Ireland (IE), Luxembourg (LU), Netherlands (NL), Norway (NO), Poland (PL), Portugal (PT), Slovakia (SK), Slovenia (SI), Spain (ES), Sweden (SE), Switzerland (CH), Turkey (TR), the United Kingdom (UK), and Ukraine (UA). All samples are random samples based on different sampling designs, but design weights are included in the datasets in order to be able to adjust for design effects.

7.3.1 Measurement of Religious Involvement

The ESS Round 2 questionnaire contains several questions about religion. These items include whether the respondent currently belongs or in the past has belonged to a religious group or denomination (yes/no). Other items relate to the degree of religious involvement, and to the frequency of praying and of participation in religious services (see Table 7.1 for the exact wording of the questions). We hypothesize the latter three items to measure a single

TABLE 7.1

Wording of the Questions for Religious Involvement and Social Attitudes

Religious involvement	C13	Regardless of whether you belong to a particular religion, how religious would you say you are? (0 = not at all to 10 = very religious)
	C14	Apart from special occasions such as weddings and funerals, about how often do you attend religious services currently? (1 = every day to 7 = never)
	C15[a]	Apart from when you are at religious services, how often, if at all, do you pray? (1 = every day to 7 = never)
Ethnic threat	B38	Would you say it is generally bad or good for [*country's*] economy that people come to live here from other countries? (0 = bad for the economy to 10 = good for the economy)
	B39	Would you say that [*country's*] cultural life is generally undermined or enriched by people coming to live here from other countries? (0 = cultural life undermined to 10 = cultural life enriched)
	B40	Is [*country*] made a worse or a better place to live by people coming to live here from other countries? (0 = worse place to live to 10 = better place to live)
Political trust		Please tell me on a score of 0 to 10 how much you personally trust each of the institutions I read out. (0 = no trust at all to 10 = complete trust)
	B4	Country's Parliament
	B7	Politicians
	B8	Political parties
Social trust	A8	Generally speaking, would you say that most people can be trusted, or rather that you cannot be too careful in dealing with people? (0 = you cannot be too careful to 10 = most people can be trusted)
	A9	Do you think that most people would try to take advantage of you if they got the chance, or would they try to be fair? (0 = take advantage to 10 = be fair)
	A10	Would you say that most of the time people try to be helpful or that they are mostly looking out for themselves? (0 = looking out for themselves to 10 = try to be helpful)

[a] Country specific data from the UK, FI, and HU are used for the indicators of religious involvement.

latent construct, namely, religious involvement.* We will further examine whether this concept is measured in a cross-culturally equivalent way.

7.3.2 Measurement of the Social Attitudes

ESS Round 2 includes six items on attitudes toward immigration, covering two different concepts, namely, the acceptance of new immigration and perceived ethnic threat. In this study the latter concept (ethnic threat) will be used, since the meaning of this concept is most closely related to the measurement of ethnocentrism used in previous studies (Cambré, 2002; Scheepers et al., 2000). This concept relates to how respondents evaluate the consequences of immigration for the country's economy, cultural life, and living conditions in general. Higher scores on the ethnic threat scale refer to stronger perceptions of threat, and thus more negative attitudes toward ethnic groups.

In the core module of ESS, social trust was measured by the so-called Rosenberg scale (Rosenberg, 1956), which consists of three items relating to whether the respondent believes people in general to be trustful, fair, and helpful. Political trust was measured by a set of six items. In this paper, we only use three items that deal with political institutions and actors at the country level and not with supranational entities such as the European Union and the United Nations. The respondent's subjective feeling of trust in politics is measured by items concerning the national parliament, the politicians, and the political parties.

7.3.3 Measurement of Basic Human Values

Schwartz (1992) postulated a theory that describes 10 basic types of human values that are distinguished by their motivational goals. In several studies, the structural relations among the 10 values are graphically presented in a circular continuum. Adjacent value types share some motivational emphases and are therefore compatible, while values that are further away are often more conflicting or even diametrically opposed. Universalism and benevolence, for example, share the quality of transcendence of selfish interests, while

* This operationalization of religious involvement does not admit a distinction between people who adhere strongly to a nonreligious way of life, people who only marginally relate to their religion, and people who belong to a religion but vary in terms of degree of involvement, in both the past and in present situations. There is only a differentiation going from actually not involved to strongly involved in the present situation.

the opposite value type, achievement, focuses on personal success (Schwartz, 1994). One of the most appealing features of Schwartz's theory is the integration of basic value types into a broader value system with two broader value dimensions: self-transcendence versus self-enhancement, and openness to change versus conservation. In this study, two broader value scales are used in line with the analysis carried out by Davidov (2008) and Davidov, Schmidt, and Schwartz (2008b). Instead of working with single value types, we measure the two higher-order dimensions—self-transcendence and conservation—directly by the items. This is shown in the overview below. In ESS Round 2, value priorities are measured by means of a shorter version of the Portrait Values Questionnaire (PVQ; Schwartz et al., 2001). The PVQ items are verbal portraits of 21 different people, gender-matched with the respondent. Each portrait describes a person's goals, aspirations, and wishes that point implicitly to the importance of a value. For each portrait, the respondents were asked to tell how strong the similarities are between themselves and the person described, using a 6-point Likert scales (1 = "very much like me" to 6 = "not like me at all"). As already explained, the relevant value dimensions in this study are self-transcendence and universalism. The wording of the questions for the value scales (male version) are given in Table 7.2.

Self-transcendence represents two values: universalism, measured by three indicators and benevolence, measured by two. Citizens who endorse these values are more ready to treat others equally, take care of nature, try to understand people with different views, and help other people. Conservation reflects three other values: tradition, conformity, and security, each measured by two indicators. We utilize the six indicators to measure conservation directly.

7.3.4 Sociodemographic Characteristics

The social sociodemographic variables have already been introduced in the theoretical part. The operationalization of age and gender do not need further consideration. Education is measured here as an ordinal variable ranging from 0 (not completed primary education) to 6 (second stage of tertiary). Income is operationalized here as the monthly net household income subdivided into 12 classes. Urbanization environment is measured by asking what phrase describes best the area in which the respondent lives (a big city, a suburb of a big city, a country village, the countryside). In the analysis, the variable ranges from 0 (countryside) to 5 (big city).

TABLE 7.2

Wording of the Questions for the Value Items

Dimension	Value	Item # (According to its Order in the ESS Questionnaire) and Wording (Male Version)
Self-transcendence	Universalism	3. He thinks it is important that every person in the world be treated equally. He believes everyone should have equal opportunities in life.
		8. It is important to him to listen to people who are different from him. Even when he disagrees with them, he still wants to understand them.
		19. He strongly believes that people should care for nature. Looking after the environment is important to him.
	Benevolence	12. It is very important to him to help the people around him. He wants to care for their well-being.
		18. It is important to him to be loyal to his friends. He wants to devote himself to people close to him.
Conservation	Tradition	9. It is important to him to be humble and modest. He tries not to draw attention to himself.
		20. Tradition is important to him. He tries to follow the customs handed down by his religion or his family.
	Conformity	7. He believes that people should do what they're told. He thinks people should follow rules at all times, even when no one is watching.
		16. It is important to him always to behave properly. He wants to avoid doing anything people would say is wrong.
	Security	5. It is important to him to live in secure surroundings. He avoids anything that might endanger his safety.
		14. It is important to him that the government ensures his safety against all threats. He wants the state to be strong so it can defend its citizens.

7.4 CROSS-CULTURAL EQUIVALENCE OF THE MEASUREMENT SCALES

Before analyzing the data, it is necessary to investigate whether the concepts measured have the same meaning in the different countries under study. One cannot be sure whether the measurement scales operate in exactly the same way in different countries, especially since our study contains countries with very diverse religious backgrounds. The observed differences may be due to cross-cultural differences in the interpretation of items rather than to substantive differences in terms of the concepts that we intended to measure. Thus, before meaningful comparisons can be made across countries, the cross-cultural equivalence of the measures needs to be tested for (Horn & McArdle, 1992; Vandenberg & Lance, 2000).

7.4.1 The Multigroup Confirmatory Factor Analysis (MGCFA) Approach to Equivalence

To test for measurement equivalence, we use MGCFA (Billiet, 2003; Steenkamp & Baumgartner, 1998). In this approach, the observed indicators x_j are modeled as linear functions of a latent variable ξ. The τ_i, λ_i, and δ_i refer, respectively, to the intercept, the slope (i.e., factor loading) and the error term in these functions. The superscript (g) indicates the group (in our case: country) under study.

$$x_j^{(g)} = \tau_j^{(g)} + \lambda_j^{(g)}\xi^{(g)} + \delta_j^{(g)} \tag{7.1}$$

The extent to which scores can be compared across cultures depends on the level of measurement equivalence. When measurement models in the different countries have the same factor structure, the scale is said to be *configural invariant*. However, this basal level of measurement does not allow any comparison of scores. If the factor loadings (λ's) of the items on the underlying trait they purportedly measure are found to be invariant across countries, *metric equivalence* is obtained. This level of measurement equivalence implies that the scale intervals for the latent trait are equal across groups. Consequently, statistics that are based on difference scores, such as regression coefficients or covariances, may be compared cross-nationally. If the intercepts (τ's) of the functions that describe the relations between items and latent factors are also invariant, *scalar equivalence* is obtained and full score comparability is guaranteed. It then becomes possible to compare the latent means between groups (Steenkamp & Baumgartner, 1998).

Byrne, Shavelson, and Muthén (1989) argued that full equivalence (i.e., invariance of the parameters for all items), is not necessary in order for substantive analyses to be meaningful. Provided that at least two items

TABLE 7.3

Equivalence Tests for Religious Involvement

Model Specifications		χ^2	df	RMSEA	CFI	$\Delta\chi^2$
M0	Full scalar invariance	1832.44	96	0.098	0.981	—
M1	$\lambda_{c14}{}^{TR}$ free	1057.16	95	0.073	0.990	775.28
M2	$\tau_{c13}{}^{IE}$ free	951.82	94	0.069	0.991	105.34
M3	$\tau_{c15}{}^{TR}$ free	834.65	93	0.065	0.992	117.17
M4	$\tau_{c13}{}^{BE}$ free	738.83	92	0.061	0.993	95.83
M5	$\tau_{c14}{}^{IS}$ free	639.83	91	0.056	0.994	99.00
M6	$\tau_{c14}{}^{PL}$ free	593.93	90	0.054	0.995	45.89
M7	$\tau_{c13}{}^{NL}$ free	549.65	89	0.052	0.995	44.28
M8	$\tau_{c14}{}^{GB}$ free	513.56	88	0.050	0.995	36.09
M9	$\tau_{c14}{}^{FI}$ free	479.46	87	0.049	0.996	34.10

per latent construct; namely, the item that is fixed at unity to identify the model and one other item, are equivalent, cross-national comparisons that can be made in a valid way. Thus, *partial equivalence* requires cross-country invariance of some, but not necessarily all, of the salient loadings. This idea is also supported by Steenkamp and Baumgartner (1998).

7.4.2 Is the Measurement of Religious Involvement Equivalent Over all Countries of ESS Round 2?

Since we are interested in comparing country means of religious involvement, we need (partial) scalar equivalence for this measurement scale.* To test this level of measurement equivalence, we use a top-down approach, starting from the most restrictive model with all intercepts and slopes constrained to be invariant across countries. Subsequent steps assess whether the model fit can be improved substantially by freeing some of the constrained parameters.† Table 7.3 gives an overview of the model fitting procedure. The completely invariant model has a bad overall model fit, as the root mean square error of approximation (RMSEA) is substantially larger

* The equivalence of the error covariances over the countries has neither been specified nor tested in any of the models.

† All models are estimated with LISREL 8.7 (Jöreskog & Sörbom, 1993). Because the three items are measured on ordinal scales, we decided to use a weighted least squares (WLS) estimation procedure in which polychoric correlations and asymptotic covariance matrices are used as input rather than regular covariance matrices (Jöreskog, 1990).

than what is generally considered to be acceptable (Byrne, 1998). This lack of fit is for a large part caused by untenable equivalence constraints on factor loadings and intercepts. The model could be improved seriously by dropping 10 of these cross-country equality constraints. After these modifications, no further possibilities remained for substantial model improvement. The final model fits the data well, as the RMSEA is lower than 0.05.

Since some equivalence constraints were found to be untenable, full measurement equivalence could not be established. As already mentioned, however, the absence of full invariance does not necessarily mean that it is impossible to make valid cross-cultural comparisons. Provided that C13 and C15 are chosen as the two items calibrating the scale, partial scalar equivalence—a necessary condition for country mean comparisons—is present for all countries except Belgium, Ireland, the Netherlands, and Turkey. These are the countries with deviating intercepts or loadings for one of the two calibration items (C13 and C15). Furthermore, our analysis makes clear that only one deviating factor loading is present. By consequence, partial metric equivalence is present for all countries, and regression coefficients can be meaningfully compared over all countries.

The estimated (unstandardized) slope parameters (factor loadings) and intercepts are given in Table 7.4. The deviating parameters for Turkey reveal that religious involvement is conceived very differently in Turkey than in

TABLE 7.4

Parameter Estimates for the Final Model

	Slope Parameters			Intercepts		
	c13[a]	c14	c15	c13	c14	c15
	rlgdgr	rlgatnd	Pray	rlgdgr	rlgatnd	pray
Common	1.000	−0.945	−1.076	0.107	−0.131	−0.070
BE				0.582		
FI					0.102	
GB					0.146	
IE				−0.398		
IS					0.424	
NL				0.416		
PL					−0.392	
TR		−0.256				−0.604

[a]Parameter fixed to unity to identify the model.

the other ESS countries. This can be explained by the fact that Turkey is the only country where the population consists predominantly of Muslims. First of all, the low factor loading for C14 indicates that attending religious services is hardly related to religious involvement in Turkey. In Islam, it is not customary for females to attend religious services, but this does not prevent them from being religiously involved. Second, frequency of praying (C15) has a very different meaning in Turkey. The higher intercept means that, given their level of religious involvement, Turks pray more often than in other countries. But at the same time, the lower factor loading suggests that praying is less of a determinant than in other countries in terms of whether someone is religiously involved.

7.4.3 Equivalence of the Social Attitudes and Values

In a similar way, measurement was assessed for the scales indicating social attitudes and value priorities. Because, for these variables, our goal is to compare relations (with religious involvement) rather than means between the countries, metric equivalence (i.e., the equality of factor loadings) is sufficient. To save space, these tests are not discussed in detail here. Instead, only the conclusions are given.* For ethnic threat, social trust, and political trust, partial metric equivalence for all countries was obtained, so that meaningful comparisons of regression coefficients and covariances are possible. The cross-cultural comparability for the two higher order values (self-transcendence and conservation) is somewhat more problematic. The measurements of self-transcendence in Finland and of conservation in Ukraine were found not to be even partially metrically equivalent. Concretely, this implies that cross-cultural comparisons on the value scales for these two countries could be problematic.

7.5 FINDINGS

Before focussing on the actual explanation models, we will demonstrate the religious diversity in Europe by comparing the mean scores on religious involvement in the 25 countries that take part in ESS Round 2. Then,

* Detailed results can be obtained from the authors.

we will explore the extent to which the effects of social-structural predictors of religious involvement are of the same order or in the same direction in all the countries. Finally, we will formulate conclusions on the role that individual religious involvement plays in the formation of attitudes and values that are supportive of social integration. For this purpose, we will look at the relations between religious involvement and each of the social attitudes and values.

7.5.1 The Religious Diversity in Europe

Given the indicators that are included in the ESS core module, one can explore the religious diversity in Europe in different ways. The first approach uses the question about belonging to a religion or a denomination. This is a subjective question that elicits the respondents' current self-definition, independent of formal ties to a religion or whatever religious feelings the individual may have. The response category "not-belonging" was derived directly from the question above about currently belonging. If one considers the percentage of citizens not belonging to a religious denomination as an indicator of the secularization* of society, then we may conclude that the most secularized countries—those with more than 50% of their citizens claiming not to belong to a religion—are the Netherlands, Belgium, Czech Republic, Estonia, and Sweden. There is no clear geopolitical pattern among this group of five. It includes two countries from the former Eastern bloc, two Western European countries, and one Scandinavian. At the opposite extreme are eight countries where not only do the majority of the citizens belong to a religion, but they also regularly take part in religious services. These are Poland, Greece, Portugal, Ukraine, Turkey, Slovenia, Austria, and Slovak Republic. Most of these are countries in which Catholicism is the dominant religion. The three exceptions include two countries (Greece and Ukraine) in which Eastern Orthodoxy is the dominant religion, and one in which the vast majority of the population is Muslim.

The ESS makes it possible not only to consider current belonging but also past belonging. Here, a distinction can be made between first generation

---

* Secularization is conceived of here as a process at the individual level, which is measured by the decline in individual participation in religious associations and services. This is only one aspect of the concept of secularization (Dobbelaere, 2002).

not-belonging (i.e., persons who belonged to a religious group in the past, but not anymore) and second generation not-belonging (i.e., those who have never belonged to any religious denomination). Drawing this distinction may better enable us to understand past developments in the direction of a secularized society. Countries with high second/first generation belonging ratios are countries in which secularization is much further developed (Estland, Czech Republic, and Sweden) than in countries in which the ratio is much lower. In Turkey, Poland, and Greece, secularization at the individual level has not yet really started according to this indicator.

Finally, a third way of looking at the religious diversity in Europe is based on the latent variable "religious involvement." In a previous section of this chapter, we extensively explained this construct, which was shown to be measured in a partial scalar equivalent way. With the exception of Turkey, Ireland, Belgium, and the Netherlands (indicated with *), the latent mean scores on religious involvement can be meaningfully compared. The lowest latent mean score for religious involvement is obtained in the Czech Republic (–1.08). At the other end of the scale, we find Ireland (0.79). Greece (0.72), Turkey (0.69), and Poland (0.57) with high levels of religious involvement. We may presumably have a biased view of Ireland, and especially of Turkey, because of the lack of complete measurement equivalence. The level is underestimated in Turkey because of the "participation in public religious services" factor, which is not measured correctly for women.

The next step in this study consists of investigating the interplay between social background, religious involvement, value priorities, and social attitudes. For this purpose, a multigroup structural equation model including all these variables was estimated for the countries in this study (the structure of this model is depicted in Figure 7.1). Unfortunately, three countries had to be dropped due to estimating problems (namely, non-positive definite input matrices, see Wothke, 1993) leading to non-convergence or unreliable estimates due to extremely large standard errors. The resulting model with 22 countries had a good fit (chi-square = 38,583.78 df = 6932; RMSEA = 0.048; CFI = 0.940).

7.5.2 What Sociodemographic Variables Still Explain the Variance in Religious Involvement?

Our second question deals with the explanatory power of social background variables. The reason why we are interested in this is that it is

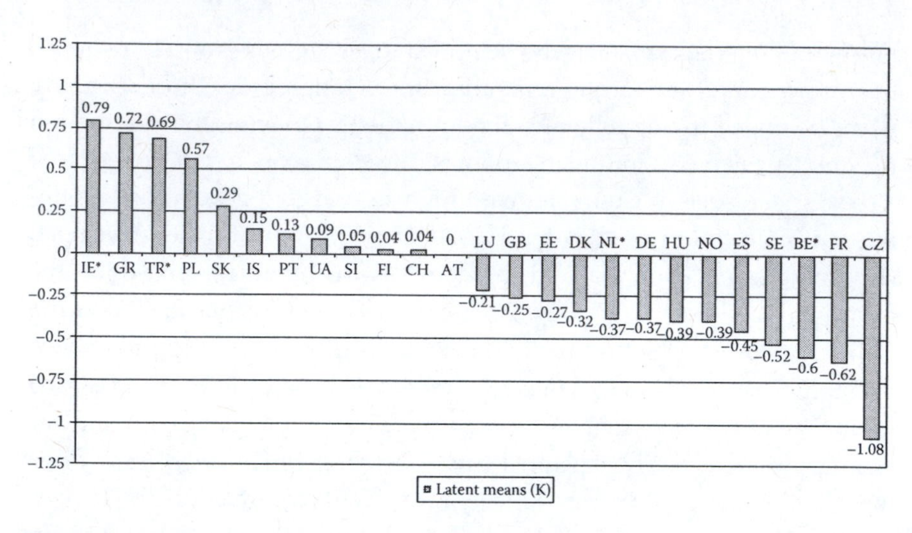

FIGURE 7.2
Latent means of religious involvement in ESS Round 2.

often claimed that the increasing individualization of society goes hand in hand with the decreasing predictive power of social structural variables for variations in social participation, including religious involvement (Ester, Halman, & De Moor, 1993). This is the so-called privatization aspect of the individualization of society, which means that values and political attitudes are becoming more and more a matter of private choice, and thus are less predictable on the basis of the individual's social background. In every domain of life, the authority of traditional institutions is being replaced by individual autonomy (Beck & Beck-Gernsheim, 1996, pp. 24–25). However, it is often shown in studies over time that the effect of some background variables is indeed declining somewhat, but also that other background variables still play a crucial role, for example, the individual's level of education (Vandecasteele & Billiet, 2004). What do we find in the ESS? The ESS in fact does not provide us with data collected over a long period of time, though it was collected over a large number of countries, which thus makes it possible to compare those 25 countries with one another. We still expect to find the effects of the major background variables that traditionally predict religious involvement. Moreover, we also hypothesize that the explanatory power will differ according to the level of religious involvement in the different countries. Since secularization at the individual level theoretically goes hand in hand with individualization, one may expect the social background variables to have lower explanatory power in countries with low mean scores on religious involvement. We recall that the effects of the parameters relating to the social background variables on religious involvement are still estimated in simultaneous measurement and structural models.

Table 7.5 shows for each country of ESS Round 2 the parameters of the regression models, with religious involvement as a dependent variable and the social background variables as predictors. Table 7.5 contains both unstandardized and standardized regression parameters. Because the metric equivalence of the scales has been demonstrated, the unstandardized parameters can be used to compare the strength of the effects between countries (row comparisons; Kim & Ferree, 1981). Cross-country comparisons of standardized parameters are not allowed, because this would additionally presuppose equality of the variances of the latent variables, an assumption we have not tested. However, the standardized parameters are useful for comparing the strength of the effects of each predictor on religious involvement within each country (column comparisons).

Gender is still an important predictor for religious involvement in all countries but Ireland, and this effect is nearly always positive, which means that women are more religiously involved than men (the reference category). The largest effects are found in Ukraine, Greece, and Portugal. Turkey is clearly an exception, since in that country women are found to be religiously less involved than men. As was already mentioned, this finding is an artifact of our measurement instrument, which was shown not to be cross-culturally equivalent. If one looks carefully at the separate indicators, then one can find out that the women in Turkey feel more religious than the men, and that the women pray more, but that they do not attend public religious services as much, because these services are mostly reserved for men.

As expected, *age* has positive effects on religious involvement in most countries (except the United Kingdom, Norway, Sweden, and Slovenia, where the age-effect is insignificant). The older the sampled persons are, the more religiously involved they are. The largest effects are found in highly religious countries such as Ireland, Turkey, Poland, Greece, and Portugal.

The effect of the level of education on religious involvement is less clear. Education has a significant effect in six countries only. In five of these countries (Switzerland, Germany, France, Luxemburg, and Poland), the

TABLE 7.5

Multiple Regression of Background Variables on Religious Involvement: Unstandardized and Standardized (Between Brackets) Parameters

	Gender			Age			Education			Income			Urban			R^2
AT	0.10	(0.12)	***	0.16	(0.20)	***	0.00	(−0.01)		−0.04	(−0.05)	*	−0.18	(−0.22)	***	0.12
BE	0.11	(0.13)	**	0.23	(0.27)	***	0.00	(0.00)		−0.10	(−0.12)	***	0.07	(0.09)	***	0.14
CH	0.10	(0.12)	**	0.19	(0.23)	***	−0.12	(−0.15)	***	−0.04	(−0.05)	*	−0.06	(−0.08)	***	0.11
CZ	0.10	(0.12)	***	0.10	(0.11)	***	−0.04	(−0.04)		−0.10	(−0.11)	***	−0.10	(−0.11)	***	0.07
DE	0.23	(0.27)	***	0.22	(0.26)	***	−0.07	(−0.09)	**	0.08	(0.10)	***	−0.04	(−0.04)	*	0.13
DK	0.11	(0.15)	***	0.12	(0.15)	***	0.02	(0.02)		−0.09	(−0.11)	***	−0.03	(−0.04)		0.08
EE	0.18	(0.22)	***	0.10	(0.13)	*	0.01	(0.02)		−0.08	(−0.10)	**	0.15	(0.19)	***	0.14
ES	0.11	(0.13)	*	0.17	(0.20)	***	−0.01	(−0.01)		−0.12	(−0.14)	***	0.02	(0.03)		0.13
FI	0.23	(0.29)	***	0.16	(0.20)	***	0.05	(0.06)		−0.08	(−0.11)	***	−0.06	(−0.07)	***	0.19
FR	0.11	(0.13)	**	0.17	(0.20)	***	−0.10	(−0.12)	***	−0.07	(−0.08)	***	0.02	(0.02)		0.13
GB	0.15	(0.17)	***	0.06	(0.07)		0.13	(0.16)	***	−0.17	(−0.20)	***	0.03	(0.03)		0.09
GR	0.26	(0.35)	**	0.27	(0.36)	**	−0.03	(−0.04)		−0.08	(−0.11)	***	−0.10	(−0.13)	***	0.27
IE	0.00	(0.00)		0.40	(0.49)	***	−0.05	(−0.07)		−0.05	(−0.07)	*	−0.12	(−0.15)	***	0.33
LU	0.15	(0.18)	***	0.20	(0.24)	***	−0.06	(−0.07)	**	−0.09	(−0.10)	***	−0.03	(−0.04)		0.12
NL	0.06	(0.07)	*	0.15	(0.18)	***	−0.01	(−0.02)		−0.06	(−0.07)	**	−0.11	(−0.13)	***	0.07
NO	0.10	(0.12)	***	0.08	(0.09)		0.04	(0.05)		−0.08	(−0.10)	***	0.01	(0.01)		0.04
PL	0.17	(0.21)	***	0.21	(0.26)	***	−0.10	(−0.13)	***	−0.02	(−0.03)		−0.13	(−0.16)	***	0.17
PT	0.25	(0.31)	***	0.27	(0.32)	***	0.01	(0.01)		−0.07	(−0.09)	*	−0.07	(−0.09)	***	0.25
SE	0.13	(0.16)	*	0.07	(0.09)		0.09	(0.11)		−0.10	(−0.12)	***	0.03	(0.03)		0.06
SI	0.23	(0.28)	*	0.17	(0.21)		−0.05	(−0.06)		−0.02	(−0.03)		−0.10	(−0.13)	***	0.09
TR	−0.16	(−0.25)	**	0.28	(0.43)	***	0.09	(0.14)		−0.04	(−0.06)		−0.03	(−0.04)		0.27
UA	0.34	(0.41)	***	0.26	(0.32)	**	−0.04	(−0.05)		0.04	(0.05)		0.01	(0.01)		0.17

*$p < .05$; **$p < .01$; ***$p < .001$.

effect of education is negative, which means that higher levels of religious involvement are found among the less educated. Nevertheless, in the United Kingdom, the relation between education and religious involvement is the opposite. Almost in all countries (19 out of 22), a higher income is found to coincide with lower levels of religiosity. Germany, where people in higher income categories are found to be more religious, is a clear exception to this pattern. However, this positive income effect is spurious and therefore misleading. As a result of specific historical conditions (Froese & Pfaff, 2005), the poorer Eastern Germany is far more secularized than the richer Western Germany (see Section 7.5.4 for further elaboration of this point). If we look at Eastern and Western Germany separately, the positive relation between income and religion disappears. In Poland and Ukraine, finally, significant income-effects are absent.

The effect of the *urbanization level* goes in the expected direction in 11 countries. Sampled persons who are living in rural areas are more religious than those living in more urban regions, but, contrary to expectations, this is not the case in Belgium and Estonia. One should realize that these are the net effects established after controlling for income. Only after a more advanced analysis of the religious situation can these two countries help us to explain these findings.

Is the *explanatory power* of the social background variables on religious involvement decreasing, as is to be expected according to the theory of individualization? It is impossible to answer this question, since we have no comparable longitudinal data. It is however possible to examine the variation in predictive power between countries (see last column of Table 7.5).

First of all, the proportion of explained variance is rather low. It is never more than 33%, and in most cases it is even below 15%. The countries in which the explanatory power of the regression models is highest are Ireland, Turkey, Greece, and Portugal. At the other end of the range, we find countries with very low proportions of explanatory power, namely, Sweden, Norway, Denmark, the Czech Republic, the Netherlands, and Hungary.*

* We should be cautious of comparing the proportion of explained variance across countries. After all, R^2 is a standardized measure and therefore assumes equivalence of the variances of latent concepts over countries. Variance equivalence was not tested in this study (we would like to thank Eldad Davidov for his comment on this).

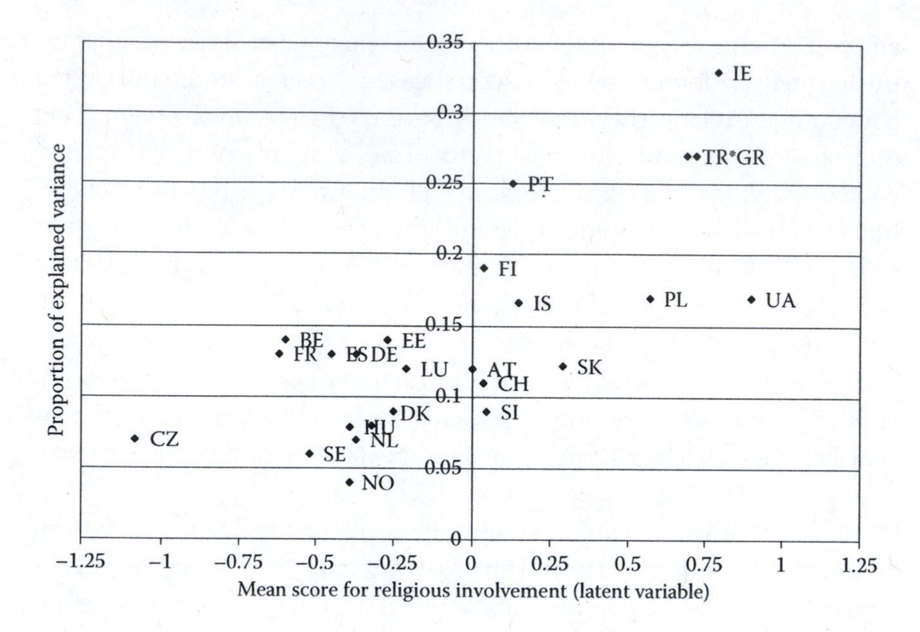

FIGURE 7.3
Correlation of mean latent scores for religious involvement, with the proportion of explained variance in regression models with social background variables.

Figure 7.3 displays the relation between the degree of religious involvement and the proportion of explained variance. The country means of religious involvement are the latent variable means, with Austria as the reference country (mean = 0) and the other country means being expressed as deviations from the reference. A linear model gives a rather good description of these data points at the country level. Generally speaking, the greater the religious involvement, the greater the proportion of explained variance (Pearson correlation = 0.737).

7.5.3 Religious Involvement, Values, and Sociopolitical Attitudes

The remaining question in this chapter deals with the relationships between religious involvement and two values on the one hand, and the direct effects of religious involvement on three social attitudes that are relevant for the integration of the citizens into a democratic society on the other. The meaning of these variables has already been discussed in the measurement section. The attitudes relate to feelings of being threatened by newcomers, trust in other people, and trust in political institutions. The two value orientations also have clear social implications. As already explained, citizens who endorse the items that measure self-transcendence are more ready to treat others equally, to take care of nature, to try to understand people with different views, and to help other people. Conservation, on the other hand, relates to attitudes such as modesty, respect for tradition and established customs, and behaving according to rules and norms. How is religious involvement related to these attitudes and values? Because (partial) metric equivalence was shown for the measurement scales, it is possible to assess whether cross-national differences in the strength of these relationships exist. In this study, we first explore the relations between religious involvement and the two values and second, we discuss the effects of religious involvement on the social attitudes.

The covariances (for cross-country comparison) and correlations (to compare effect sizes across variables) between religious involvement and the two values are reported in Table 7.6. All of the parameters but one are significantly larger than zero. The exception is Ukraine, where the covariance with self-transcendence values not significantly different from 0. The overall pattern of positive correlations between religiosity and the value scales means that, on average, religiously involved persons give greater priority both to self-transcendence and to conservation values. Notwithstanding the wide variety of countries in this study and the very diverse religious backgrounds of these countries, the covariances are remarkably similar, a fact that is indicative of the cross-cultural robustness of these findings.

In 16 countries, *social trust* is significantly related to religious involvement (Table 7.7). This relation is positive most of the time, and negative in only one case, namely, Greece. This means that in most of the countries, people who are more religiously involved tend to be somewhat more likely to trust other persons. This effect, generally speaking, is not very strong, though it is strongest in Ireland. *Trust in political institutions* is related to religious involvement in all countries except for Portugal. The effect of religious involvement on political trust is always positive. This means that, in general, higher levels of political trust are found among people who are religiously involved.

In three countries we do not find a significant relation between religious involvement and ethnic threat. These countries are Poland, Portugal, and Turkey. In the other countries, the effect of religious involvement on ethnic threat is predominantly negative: Involvement in religious communities

TABLE 7.6

Covariance and Correlation Coefficients Per Country for the Religious Involvement and Human Value Scales (ESS Round[2])

	Self-Transcendence			Conservation		
AT	0.11	(0.21)	***	0.20	(0.35)	***
BE	0.11	(0.21)	***	0.21	(0.39)	***
CH	0.13	(0.26)	***	0.18	(0.35)	***
CZ	0.12	(0.19)	***	0.21	(0.31)	***
DE	0.06	(0.13)	***	0.15	(0.27)	***
DK	0.09	(0.20)	***	0.17	(0.31)	***
EE	0.12	(0.23)	***	0.20	(0.38)	***
ES	0.06	(0.11)	***	0.20	(0.32)	***
FI	0.14[a]	(0.26)	***	0.22	(0.40)	***
FR	0.12	(0.22)	***	0.24	(0.40)	***
UK	0.14	(0.24)	***	0.21	(0.36)	***
GR	0.06	(0.12)	***	0.08	(0.14)	***
IE	0.14	(0.24)	***	0.25	(0.37)	***
LU	0.08	(0.15)	***	0.20	(0.35)	***
NL	0.12	(0.23)	***	0.23	(0.35)	***
NO	0.09	(0.17)	***	0.17	(0.31)	***
PL	0.08	(0.14)	***	0.18	(0.30)	***
PT	0.09	(0.16)	***	0.14	(0.25)	***
SE	0.10	(0.20)	***	0.17	(0.32)	***
SI	0.05	(0.09)	**	0.10	(0.16)	***
TR	0.03	(0.06)	*	0.10	(0.20)	***
UA	0.00	(−0.01)		0.05[a]	(0.07)	*

*$p < .05$; **$p < .01$; ***$p < .001$.
[a]Not a partially metric equivalent.

seems to temper negative feelings toward immigrants, irrespective of the specific religious background.

Again, Greece is an exception, since a positive effect is found in that country. The higher the scores for religious involvement, the more Greeks feel threatened by the presence of newcomers. The strongest negative effect of religion in this case is in the United Kingdom, where the more religious feel less threatened by immigrants. Thus the study shows that the effects of religious involvement are the strongest in these two countries, albeit in opposite directions relating to ethnic threat.

As was theoretically expected, religion seems to play a positive role, stimulating social attitudes that support social integration. In the vast majority

TABLE 7.7

Unstandardized and Standardized Regression Coefficients per Country, with Religious Involvement as Independent Variable and Each Attitude as Dependent Variable (ESS Round[2])

	Social Trust			Political Trust			Ethnic Threat		
AT	0.13	(0.14)	***	0.16	(0.15)	***	−0.14	(−0.14)	***
BE	0.06	(0.08)	*	0.14	(0.13)	***	−0.16	(−0.18)	***
CH	0.08	(0.10)	**	0.10	(0.09)	**	−0.16	(−0.17)	***
CZ	−0.01	(−0.01)		0.06	(0.05)	*	−0.10	(−0.11)	***
DE	0.13	(0.14)	***	0.27	(0.24)	***	−0.09	(−0.10)	***
DK	−0.01	(−0.01)		0.15	(0.12)	***	−0.22	(−0.21)	***
EE	0.13	(0.14)	***	0.08	(0.07)	*	−0.18	(−0.18)	***
ES	0.20	(0.22)	***	0.16	(0.14)	***	−0.16	(−0.17)	***
FI	0.08	(0.08)	*	0.11	(0.10)	**	−0.10	(−0.10)	**
FR	0.08	(0.10)	*	0.26	(0.25)	***	−0.18	(−0.18)	***
UK	0.15	(0.17)	***	0.31	(0.28)	***	−0.31	(−0.32)	***
GR	−0.09	(−0.08)	**	0.13	(0.11)	***	0.26	(0.23)	***
IE	0.31	(0.33)	***	0.29	(0.26)	***	−0.16	(−0.15)	*
LU	−0.02	(−0.02)		0.13	(0.12)	***	−0.21	(−0.23)	***
NL	0.11	(0.12)	***	0.16	(0.16)	***	−0.09	(−0.10)	***
NO	0.06	(0.07)	*	0.20	(0.18)	***	−0.05	(−0.05)	*
PL	0.16	(0.18)	***	0.15	(0.12)	***	−0.04	(−0.04)	
PT	0.05	(0.06)		0.04	(0.03)		−0.01	(−0.01)	
SE	0.10	(0.10)	*	0.17	(0.15)	***	−0.20	(−0.21)	***
SI	0.23	(0.24)	***	0.21	(0.18)	***	−0.20	(−0.21)	***
TR	0.36	(0.29)		0.93	(0.62)	*	0.00	(0.00)	
UA	0.03	(0.03)		0.08	(0.07)	*	−0.08	(−0.08)	**

*$p < .05$; **$p < .01$; ***$p < .001$.

of the countries, we found firm positive effects on social and political trust, and a marked negative effect on ethnic threat. Only in Greece did we find effects in the opposite direction. In the Czech Republic, Portugal, and Turkey, weak or even no effects were found. Trying to understand the variation in relations is a real challenge for further in-depth research.

7.5.4 One or Two Religious Germanies?*

In making country comparisons, we treat the countries as homogeneous entities. For some countries at least, ignoring regional variation within the

* We would like to thank Hermann Dülmer for suggesting to us a regional treatment of Germany.

country can be problematic. Germany is perhaps the clearest illustration of this. Specific historical conditions—in the German Reich (1871–1945), as well as in the DDR period—caused a dramatic decline in religiosity in Eastern Germany, leading to "the emergence of the most secularized society in the world today" (Froese & Pfaff, 2005, p. 397). To give a more accurate picture of religious Germany, we briefly present some additional analysis for East and West Germany separately.*

Despite the very different historical conditions, we found that full scalar equivalence holds for the religious involvement scale in both East and West Germany. However, the average degree of religious involvement turns out to differ enormously between the two regions. The latent country mean score for Germany as a whole is −0.47 (see Section 7.5.1 of this chapter). If we consider East Germany separately, however, a latent mean score of −0.99 is found. This makes East Germany the second most secularized country in Europe, after the Czech Republic. West Germany, on the other hand, is situated somewhere in the middle of the country ranking, with a latent mean score of −0.121.

Religion also relates quite differently to some of the background variables and values studied in this paper. In West Germany—as in all other European countries—religion is positively related to conservation values. In East Germany, this relation is not statistically significant. West Germans living in urbanized areas are found to be less religious, while urbanization does not influence religious involvement in East Germany. The link between religion and social attitudes is virtually identical across the German regions.

7.6 CONCLUSIONS

The major aim of this study was to demonstrate how MGSEM can be useful in comparative research by simultaneously testing measurement and structural models. The study was descriptive and is simply an initial impetus for further reflection and in-depth analysis in each of the countries in order to understand the differences. More elaborated explanatory

* Due to lack of space, it is not possible to present these analyses in great detail. However, full results can be obtained from the first author.

models are also necessary and possible. It has been our intention to show that comparative analysis requires a number of preparatory steps. Attention was given to the operationalization of the concepts, and especially to preparatory research in which the cross-cultural measurement validity was tested. It is crucial for this kind of research that the measured concepts are equivalent over countries and that exceptions are documented. This chapter contains an extensive equivalence test of the indicators for the central concept of religious involvement, and it briefly summarizes the results of similar tests for two human values and three social attitudes. We have found that, except for the value scales in two countries, all concepts are measured in an at least a partially metric equivalent way. This was sufficient for the regression parameters and the correlations to be comparable in a meaningful way. We were somewhat stricter for our main variable, religious involvement, since we were also interested in the latent means. Because of this (partial) scalar equivalence was necessary.

During the equivalence tests, we found that the set of items that we developed for the ESS core is not really suitable for non-Christian religions such as Islam. One of the reasons for this was exposed: The indicator of participation in public religious service does not function for Muslim women. For the purposes of future research in Europe, an alternative indicator must be found. Moreover, it is possible that the question about religious belonging does not function so well for non-Christian religions and for countries in which an official State Church exists, of which every citizen, in principle, is assumed to be a member. Concepts such as membership and belonging are somewhat problematic and their interpretation can vary from country to country. However, in general we have found only minor problems in the European countries.

The predictive power of social background variables that traditionally explain the variance was shown to be related to the average level of religious involvement in a country. In less religious countries, the background variables were less successful in explaining religious involvement. This is in line with individualization theory.

Finally, in the analysis of the relations between church involvement on the one hand, and the social and political attitudes and values on the other hand, we found that at the individual level religious involvement is weakly to moderately related to each of the social–political attitudes and values in our study. However, the picture varies according to the particular variable, and the relations are not statistically significant in every country. Political trust, conservation, and self-transcendence are related to religious involvement in nearly all countries. For these variables, the relations are in the same direction most of the time. Concerning the social attitudes, we observe some remarkable differences in the relations with religious involvement. It was already known from previous research that religious involvement functions differently according to religious denomination and country (Cambré, 2002). This has now been confirmed. Greece, for example, shows opposite relations, and it is a challenge to find out whether this finding is substantial, and how it can be explained by historical and contemporary country characteristics.

This study provides an example of how MGSEM can be used in comparative social research. This approach has several important advantages. Perhaps most importantly, it offers a straightforward environment to test whether measurements are cross-culturally equivalent. If metric equivalence is present, MGSEM can be used to perform statistical tests for the cross-cultural equality of effect sizes (by imposing constraints over countries). Researchers can even attempt to find clusters of countries with equal effect sizes (for an example of this cluster approach, see Davidov et al., 2008a). This was not done here, because the number of possible comparisons was too large to include them in this study. Another interesting feature of MGSEM is the estimation of more complex path models with direct and indirect effects, a feature that is very useful when analyzing a variable, such as religious involvement, which takes an intermediary position. Another advantage is that MGSEM, contrary to multilevel modelling, does not require a minimum number of countries to guarantee an accurate estimate—even with as little as two countries, meaningful comparisons can be made. At the same time, the MGSEM approach naturally has some drawbacks. First, it is far from straightforward as to how context-level variables could be added in the analysis, although one could think of a two-step approach in which certain parameters of the MGSEM model (e.g., means or effects) are regressed on context-level variables (cf. Achen, 2005). And secondly, MGSEM, at least when polychoric correlations are used, is computationally quite demanding, which puts a limit on the complexity of the model. Including too many variables in the model can lead to very long runtimes and/or estimation difficulties.

REFERENCES

Achen, C. H. (2005). Two-step hierarchical estimation: Beyond regression analysis. *Political Analysis, 13*(4), 447–456.

Almond, G. A., & Verba, S. (1965). *The civic culture. Political attitudes and democracy in five nations.* Princeton, NJ: Princeton University Press.

Beck, U., & Beck-Gernsheim, E. (1996). Individualisation and precarious freedoms: Perspectives and controversies of a subject-oriented sociology. In P. Heelas, S. Lash, & P. Morris (Eds.), *Detraditionalization* (pp. 23–48). Cambridge: Blackwell.

Billiet, J. (1998). Social capital, religious-philosophical involvement and social integration in Belgium: An empirical investigation. In R. Laermans, B. Wilson, & J. Billiet (Eds.), *Secularization and social integration* (pp. 233–252). Leuven, Belgium: Leuven University Press.

Billiet, J. (2003). Cross-cultural equivalence with structural equation modeling. In J. Harkness, F. Van de Vijver, & P. Mohler (Eds.), *Cross-cultural survey methods* (pp. 247–264). Hoboken, NJ: John Wiley & Sons.

Billiet, J., Dobbelaere, K., Riis, O., Vilaça H., Voyé, L., & Welkenhuysen-Gybels, J. (2003). Church commitment and some consequences in Western and Central Europe. *Research in the Social Scientific Study of Religion, 14*, 129–160.

Brehm, J., & Rahn, W. (1997). Individual level evidence for the causes and consequences of social capital. *American Journal of Political Science, 41*, 999–1023.

Byrne, B. (1998). *Structural equation modeling with LISREL, PRELIS and SIMPLIS: Basic concepts, applications and programming.* Mahwah, NJ: Lawrence Erlbaum.

Byrne, B. M., Shavelson, R. J., & Muthén, B. (1989). Testing for the equivalence of factor covariance and mean structures: The issue of partial measurement invariance. *Psychological Bulletin, 105*, 456–466.

Cambre, B. (2002). *De relatie tussen religiositeit en etnocentrisme. Een contextuele benadering met cross-culturele data.* [The relationship between religiosity and ethnocentrism. A contextual approach with cross-cultural data.] PhD Dissertation, University of Leuven.

Cambré, B., Welkenhuysen-Gybels, J., & Billiet, J. (2002). Is it content or style? An evaluation of two competitive measurement models applies to a balanced set of ethnocentrism items. *International Journal of Comparative Sociology, 43*(1), 1–20.

Carr, L. G., & Hauser, J. (1976). Anomie and religiosity: An empirical re-examination. *Journal of the Scientific Study of Religion, 15*, 69–74.

Coleman, J. (1988). Social capital in the creation of human capital. *American Journal of Sociology, 94*(Suppl.), S95–S210.

Coleman, J. (1990). *Foundations of social theory.* Cambridge, MA: Harvard University Press.

Davidov, E. (2008). A cross-country and cross-time comparison of the human values measurements with the second round of the European Social Survey. *Survey Research Methods, 2*, 33–46.

Davidov, E., Meuleman, B., Billiet, J., and Schmidt, P. (2008a). Values and support for immigration: A cross-country comparison. *European Sociological Review, 24*(5), 583–599.

Davidov, E., Schmidt, P., & Schwartz, S. (2008b). Bringing values back in: The adequacy of the European Social Survey to measure values in 20 countries. *Public Opinion Quarterly, 72*(3), 420–445.

Dobbelaere, K. (1993). Church involvement and secularization: Making sense of the European case. In E. Barker, J. A. Beckford, & K. Dobbelaere (Eds.), *Secularization, rationalism and sectarianism* (pp. 19–36). Oxford: Clarendon Press.

Dobbelaere, K. (2002). *Secularization: An analysis at three levels.* Brussels, Belgium: Peter Lang.

Eisinga, R., Felling, A., & Peters, J. (1990). Religious belief, church involvement and ethnocentrism in the Netherlands. *Journal for the Scientific Study of Religion, 29*, 54–56.

Ervasti, H. (2008). The meaning and implications of religiosity. In H. Ervasti, T. Fridberg, M. Hjerm, & K. Ringdal (Eds.), *Nordic social attitudes in a European perspective* (pp. 231–248). Chelterham: Edward Elgar Publishing.

Ester, P., Halman, L., & De Moor, R. (1993). *The individualizing society. Value change in Europe and North America.* Tilburg, The Netherlands: Tilburg University Press.

Flere, S. (2007). Gender and religious orientation. *Social Compass, 54*(2), 239–254.

Froese, P., & Pfaff, S. (2005). Explaining a religious anomaly: A historical analysis of secularization in Eastern Germany. *Journal for the Scientific Study of Religion, 44*(4), 397–422.

Glock, Ch. Y., Ringer, B. B., & Babbie, E. (1967). *To comfort and to challenge; A dilemma of the contemporary church.* Berkeley, CA: University of California Press.

Griffin, G., Elmer, A., & Gorsuch, R. L. (1987). A cross-cultural investigation of religious orientation, social norms, and prejudice. *Journal of the Scientific Study of Religion, 26*(3), 358–365.

Hooghe, M., Reeskens, T., Stolle, D., & Trappers, A. (2009). Ethnic diversity and generalized trust in Europe: A cross-national multilevel study. *Comparative Political Studies, 42*(2), 198–223.

Horn, J. L., & McArdle, J. J. (1992). A practical and theoretical guide to measurement invariance in aging research. *Experimental Aging Research, 18*(3), 117–144.

Jöreskog, K. G. (1990). New developments in LISREL: Analysis of ordinal variables using polychoric correlations and weighted least squares. *Quality and Quantity, 24*(4), 387–404.

Jöreskog, K. G., & Sörbom, D. (1993). *LISREL 8 user's reference guide.* Mooresville, IN: Scientific Software.

Kanagy, C., Fern, L., Willits, K., and Crider, D. M. (1990). Anomie and religiosity: Data from a panel study of middle-aged subjects. *Journal of the Scientific Study of Religion, 13*, 35–47.

Kim, J. O., & Ferree, G. D. (1981). Standardization in causal analysis. *Sociological Methods and Research, 10*, 187–210.

Kitchelt, H. (1994). *The transformation of European social democracy.* Cambridge: Cambridge University Press.

Lehman, E. C. (1986). The local/cosmopolitan dichotomy and acceptance of women clergy. A replication and extension of Roof. *Journal for the Scientific Study of Religion, 25*(4), 461–482.

Meuleman, B., & Billiet, J. (2009). A Monte Carlo sample size study: How many countries are needed for accurate multilevel SEM? *Survey Research Methods, 3*(1), 45–58.

Newton, K. (2001). Trust, social capital, civil society, and democracy. *International Political Science Review, 22*(2), 201–214.

Norris, P., & Inglehart, R. (Ed.). (2004). *Sacred and secular. Religion and politics worldwide.* Cambridge: Cambridge University Press.

Parry, G., Moyser, G., & Day, N. (1992). *Political participation and democracy in Britain*. Cambridge: Cambridge University Press.

Putnam, R. D. (1993). *Making democracy work: Civic traditions in Italy*. Princeton, NJ: Princeton University Press.

Putnam, R. D. (1995). Bowling alone: America's declining social capital. *Journal of Democracy, 6*, 65–78.

Putnam, R. D. (2000). *Bowling alone. The collapse and revival of American commitment*. New York, NY: Simon and Schuster.

Roccas, S. (2005). Religion and value systems. *Journal of Social Issues, 61*(4), 747–759.

Roof, W. C. (1974). Religious orthodoxy and minority prejudice. Causal relationship or reflection of localistic world view? *American Journal of Sociology, 80*(4), 643–664.

Rosenberg, M. (1956). Misanthropy and political ideology. *American Sociological Review, 61*(6), 690–696.

Scheepers, P., Felling, A., & Peters, J. (1992). Anomie, authoritarianism and ethnocentrism: Update of a classic theme and an empirical test. *Politics and the Individual, 1*(1), 29–42.

Scheepers, P., Gijsberts, M., & Hello, E. (2000). Religiosity and prejudice against ethnic minorities in Europe: Cross-national tests on a controversial relationship. *Review of Religious Research, 43*(3), 242–265.

Schwartz, S. H. (1992). Universals in the content and structure of values: Theoretical advances and empirical tests in 20 countries. In P. Zanna (Ed.), *Advances in experimental social psychology* (Vol. 25, pp. 1–65). San Diego, CA: Academic Press.

Schwartz, S. H. (1994). Are there universal aspects in the structure and contents of human values? *Journal of Social Issues, 50*(4), 19–45.

Schwartz, S. H., & Huismans, E. (1995). Value priorities and religiosity in four western religions. *Social Psychology Quarterly, 58*(2), 88–107.

Schwartz, S. H., Melech, G., Lehmann, A., Burgess, S., Harris, M., & Owens, V. (2001). Extending the cross-cultural validity of the theory of basic human values with a different method of measurement. *Journal of Cross-Cultural Psychology, 32*(5), 519–542.

Stark, R., & Finke, R. (2000). *Acts of faith: Explaining the human side of religion*. Berkeley, CA: University of California Press.

Steenkamp, J. E., & Baumgartner, H. (1998). Assessing measurement invariance in cross-national consumer research. *Journal of Consumer Research, 25*, 78–90.

Strømsnes, K. (2008). The importance of church attendance and membership of religious voluntary organizations for the formation of social capital. *Social Compass, 55*(4), 478–496.

Traunmüller, R. (2009). Individual religiosity, religious context, and the creation of social trust in Germany. *Schmollers Jahrbuch, 129*, 357–365.

Uslaner, E. M. (2002). *The moral foundations of trust*. Cambridge: Cambridge University Press.

Vandecasteele, L., & Billiet, J. (2004). Privatization in the family sphere: Longitudinal and comparative analysis in four European countries. In W. Arts & L. Halman (Eds.), *European values at the turn of the millennium* (pp. 205–229). Leiden, The Netherlands: Brill.

Vandenberg, R. J., & Lance, C. E. (2000). A review and synthesis of the measurement invariance literature: Suggestions, practices, and recommendations for organizational research. *Organizational Research Methods, 3*, 4–70.

Verba, S., Scholzman, K. L., & Brady, H. E. (1995). *Voice and equality: Civic voluntarism in American politics*. Cambridge, MA: Harvard University Press.

Welch, M. R., Sikkink, D., Sartain, E., & Bond, C. (2004). Trust in God and trust in man: The ambivalent role of religion in shaping dimensions of social trust. *Journal for the Scientific Study of Religion, 34*(3), 317–343.

Wothke, W. (1993). Nonpositive definite matrices in structural modeling. In K. A. Bollen & J. S. Long (Eds.), *Testing structural equation models* (pp. 256–293). Newbury Park, CA: Sage.

8

Causes of Generalized Social Trust

William M. van der Veld
Radboud Universiteit Nijmegen

Willem E. Saris
ESADE, Universitat Ramon Llull and Universitat Pompeu Fabra

8.1 INTRODUCTION

What do the following studies have in common: Adam (2008), Delhey and Newton (2005), Herreros and Criado (2008), Inglehart (1999), Kaase (1999), Kaasa and Parts (2008), Knack and Keefer (1997), Letki and Evans (2008), Paxton (2002), Rothstein and Uslaner (2005), and Zmerli and Newton (2008)? In all these studies it is assumed that the measure of generalized social trust (GST) is meaningfully comparable across countries. In addition, it is also assumed that the endogenous and exogenous variables in those studies are measured without error. If any of these assumptions do not hold then conclusions from these studies will be questionable, to say the least. Because measurement without error is very unlikely, one should correct for measurement error. Correction for measurement error can be done in various ways. In this chapter we will discuss how this can be done using estimates from a multitrait multimethod (MTMM) experiment. Correction for measurement error is a necessary step in any comparative study, it does not, however, ensure equivalence of the measures. In order to test whether survey measures are equivalent we have to assess the measurement invariance (Meredith, 1993).

The common procedure to test for invariance of measures is by means of a multigroup confirmatory factor analysis (MGCFA). Testing in structural equation modeling (SEM) has become rather difficult to comprehend with the introduction of so many goodness-of-fit measures (Marsh, Hau, & Wen, 2004). How should we evaluate structural equation models, and what to do if a model is rejected? Where should we begin to improve the model? Usually, there are many possibilities for improvement and each one will have an effect on the set of countries that can be meaningfully compared. Because of the many possibilities, we will suggest an analytic strategy that can guide this process. The strategy requires that JRule (Van der Veld, Saris, & Satorra, 2008) is used to evaluate the MGCFA model. JRule is primarily developed to detect misspecifications in SEM models. Standard procedures to evaluate model fit are affected by the power of the test and this is not limited to the CHI2 alone, but holds true for other goodness-of-fit measures too (Saris, Satorra, & Van der Veld, 2009). JRule can detect misspecifications taking into account the power of the test, which is not possible with any other SEM software. To be clear, JRule does not perform a global model evaluation, but it judges whether constrained parameters are constrained to the correct values. We will explain this procedure in Section 8.2.4.

It is not only the standard model evaluation procedure that we suggest to change. The standard model (Meredith, 1993) that is used to assess the cross-national equivalence is flawed too. The reason that the standard model is flawed is because the unique factors in the common factor model are confounded with random measurement error and also that the common (substantive) factor is confounded with systematic measurement error. Therefore the invariance restrictions will lead to wrong conclusions if both random and systematic measurement error components are not the same across countries. We suggest making a distinction between the unique components in the indicators and the random errors in the indicators, as well as between the systematic error component in the indicators and the common factor. The same was also suggested by Saris and Gallhofer (2007) and by Millsap and Meredith (2007), the latter two authors did, however, not elaborate on this, nor did they empirically make this distinction.

It is the goal of this chapter to apply these methodological innovations to test the cross-national equivalence of GST in the European Social Survey (ESS) and also to test the causes of GST. Reeskens and Hooghe (2008) have already discussed the cross-national equivalence of generalized trust in the ESS and found that the measure of GST should not be used in comparative studies. We hope to arrive at more promising conclusions using our improved methodology. Delhey and Newton (2003) have already discussed the causes of social trust and found that at the individual level there were large cross-national differences. We believe that their conclusions are odd. Therefore, we will test whether the same causes are at work in all countries and whether the effect of each cause is more or less the same in all countries. We therefore question previous findings and expect that the causes of GST are the same across all countries and that the effect of each cause is also more or less the same.

The structure of this chapter is as follows, we will first introduce the procedures to test for configural, metric, and scalar invariance. After that we will introduce how we correct for random and systematic measurement error in these invariance tests. Next we will suggest an analytical strategy for the assessment of measurement invariance. This is followed by an introduction to a new procedure to evaluate structural equation models: *the detection of misspecifications using JRule*. Finally, we will apply these methodological improvements and test whether the ESS measure of GST can be meaningfully used in comparative research and if so, whether the causes of GST are the same across the set of countries we analyze.

8.2 INNOVATIONS

8.2.1 The Standard Procedure for Measurement Invariance Tests

The standard test has been explained elsewhere in the book, so we will skip most of the details. Tests of measurement invariance put restrictions on the measurement model. The basic measurement model is presented below. The superscript is used to indicate different countries; that is, to indicate that this is a multigroup model:

$$\mathbf{y}^{(n)} = \tau^{(n)} + \Lambda^{(n)}\mathbf{f}^{(n)} + \delta^{(n)}. \tag{8.1}$$

In this model $\mathbf{y}$ is the vector of observed variables, τ is a vector of intercepts of the observed variables, $\mathbf{f}$ is a vector of latent variables, δ is a vector of disturbance terms of the observed variables, and Λ is the matrix of relationships between the observed and latent variables (i.e., the loadings).

It is assumed that the mean of all disturbance terms δ is zero and that the covariance among the disturbance terms δ as well as between the between the disturbance terms and the common factors (f) are zero. If these assumptions hold, then the expected value of **y** can be expressed as:

$$\mu_y^{(n)} = \tau^{(n)} + \Lambda^{(n)}\mu_f^{(n)}. \tag{8.2}$$

If constraints are implied on Model 8.1, we obtain different forms of measurement invariance. The following two sets of equations are important restrictions:

$$\Lambda^{(1)} = \Lambda^{(2)} = \Lambda^{(3)} = \ldots = \Lambda^{(n)}, \tag{8.3}$$

$$\tau^{(1)} = \tau^{(2)} = \tau^{(3)} = \ldots = \tau^{(n)}. \tag{8.4}$$

Meredith (1993) has pointed out that there are three forms of invariance that are important for cross-national comparative research: (1) *Configural invariance,* which implies that the measurement model, Equation 8.1, holds across all countries; (2) *Metric invariance,* which implies that configural invariance holds, as well as Equation 8.3; (3) *Scalar invariance* implies that metric invariance holds as well as Equation 8.4. If configural invariance holds it implies that the measurement instrument is the same across countries, however, comparisons of the measures are still not meaningful. If metric invariance holds, comparisons of relationships between unstandardized measures become meaningful, and if scalar invariance holds it also becomes meaningful to compare the means of the measures.

8.2.2 Correction for Measurement Error in Measurement Invariance Testing

It is a well-known fact that the disturbance terms (δ) in the common factor model contain both item specific factors as well as random measurement error (Heise & Bohrnstedt, 1970, p. 107; Van der Veld & Saris, 2004). This fact is commonly ignored in factor analysis and also in invariance testing, except for Millsap and Meredith (2007) and Saris and Gallhofer (2007), as a result the wrong parameters are estimated and tested. In order to solve this issue, we should separate the random error component from the unique component. The model that enables us to do this is explained in Saris and Gallhofer (2007) and Van der Veld (2006). They make a distinction between two response processes as a result of a stimulus (i.e., the survey item). The first process results in an attitude/opinion or a trait/state (e.g., Steyer & Schmitt, 1990), while the second process results in a response. The processes are represented by respectively Equation 8.5a and b:

$$\mathbf{s}^{(n)} = \tau_s^{(n)} + \mathbf{C}^{(n)}\mathbf{f}^{(n)} + \mathbf{u}^{(n)}, \tag{8.5a}$$

$$\mathbf{y}^{(n)} = \tau_y^{(n)} + \mathbf{Q}^{(n)}\mathbf{s}^{(n)} + \mathbf{e}^{(n)}. \tag{8.5b}$$

In Equation 8.5a, **f** is a vector of common factors and **s** is a vector of item specific vectors, **u** is a vector of unique components, and τ_s is a vector of intercepts of the item specific factors. The distinction, *common factor* versus *item specific factors*, was also made by Saris and Gallhofer (2007), following the footsteps of Filmer Northrop (1969, p. 82) and Hubert Blalock (1968). They refer to the common factor as a measure of a concept-by-postulation and to the item specific factor as a measure of a concept-by-intuition. Examples of concepts-by-intuition are judgments, for example, *do you like the house you live in*, or feelings, for example, *taking all things together, how happy would you say you are*. Thus, concepts-by-intuition are measured with single survey items and their meaning is obvious from formulation. Examples of concepts-by-postulation might include GST, or perceived control over one's life. A single survey item cannot present GST or perceived control, but several concepts-by-intuition can form a concept-by-postulation. The difference between a concept-by-postulation (f) and a concept-by-intuition (s) is defined by the model (Equation 8.5a) as the unique component (u). The matrix **C** is a matrix with consistency coefficients, representing the agreement between a concept-by-postulation (f) and a concept-by-intuition (s). We have called these parameters consistency coefficients following Saris and Gallhofer (2007), however, Heise and Bohrnstedt (1970, p. 107) have referred to these parameters as validity coefficients. The reasoning behind the latter definition is that the larger the coefficient, the better that item specific factor (s) represents the concept-by-postulation (f). We, however, prefer the term consistency coefficient in order to make a distinction with the indicator validity coefficients in MTMM models, which we will refer to later in this chapter.

In Equation 8.5b, **y** is a vector of observed variables, **e** is a vector of random measurement error components, and τ_y is a vector of intercepts of the observed variables. Furthermore, **Q** is a matrix of quality coefficients, indicating the quality of each observed y.

In this model, Equations 8.5a and 8.5b, it is assumed that the random error components (e) are unrelated among themselves as well as with the unique components (u), the item specific factors (s), and the common factors (f). The unique component (u) is also uncorrelated among themselves, and uncorrelated with the common factors (f). Furthermore, the unique components (u) and random error components (e) have a mean of zero.

Next to random measurement error (e), there could also be systematic measurement error (m) as a result of using the same measurement procedure for indicators in the model (Andrews, 1984; Saris & Andrews, 1991; Scherpenzeel & Saris, 1997). This will result in common variance between the indicators due to the common measurement procedure. To put it differently, part of the variance of the common factor (f) could actually be the result of the respondents' systematic reactions to a common measurement procedure. In order to correct for this we will introduce a common method factor in Equation 8.5b.

$$\mathbf{s}^{(n)} = \tau_s^{(n)} + \mathbf{C}^{(n)}\mathbf{f}^{(n)} + \mathbf{u}^{(n)}, \qquad (8.6a)$$

$$\mathbf{y}^{(n)} = \tau_y^{(n)} + \mathbf{Q}^{(n)}\mathbf{s}^{(n)} + \mathbf{I}^{(n)}\mathbf{m}^{(n)} + \mathbf{e}^{(n)}. \qquad (8.6b)$$

Where **m** is a vector of common method factors that causes the common variance due to the measurement procedure. The matrix **I** contains the invalidity coefficients, which are called this way, because they represent the effect of the common method factor (m) on the indicators. We make the same assumptions as for Equations 8.5a and 8.5b. In addition, we assume that the common method factors (m) are not correlated with the common factors (f), nor with the item specific factors (s). Furthermore, we assume that the unique component (u) and the random error components (e) are also uncorrelated with the common method factors (m). If these assumptions hold, then the expected value of **y** can be expressed as:

$$\mu_y^{(n)} = \tau_y^{(n)} + \mathbf{Q}^{(n)}[\tau_s^{(n)} + \mathbf{C}\mu_F^{(n)}] + \mathbf{I}\mu_m^{(n)}. \qquad (8.7)$$

Where μ_f is a vector with the means of the common factors (f) and μ_m is a vector of means of the method factors (m). All other parameters were introduced and explained previously.

It is not easy to visualize the path model implied by Equations 8.6a, b, and 8.7. In order to clarify the model we have inserted a path model (Figure 8.1) in agreement with these equations for three observed variables that measure a common construct. This path model illustrates that the covariance between the observed variables is explained by a common substantive factor f and a method factor m (systematic error). The variances of the item specific factors are explained by the common factor and the unique components. The variances of the observed variables are explained by the item specific factors, the method factor, and a random error component. The mean structure is presented using arrows with the dotted lines. Finally, the model contains several elements with newly developed names, for example, consistency coefficient, quality coefficient, item specific factor, and also names that are sometimes used in a different context, for example, unique component. Unfortunately there is no common agreed name for most of the elements in this model, except that

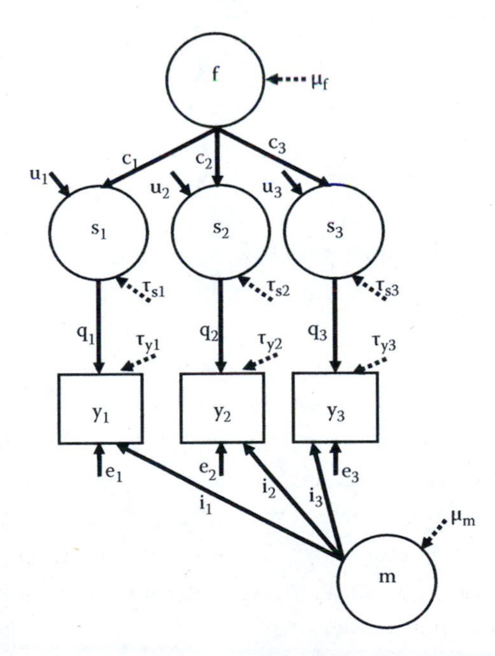

FIGURE 8.1
Path model of the model represented by Equations 8.6a and b.

f is clearly a common factor, and the y's are clearly indicators. Most problematic in this respect is probably the item specific factor (s). Its name is derived from the fact that those factors only load on a single indicator and are therefore specific for the item that measures this indicator.

8.2.2.1 The New Metric Invariance Test

The constraints to test for metric and scalar measurement invariance are on different parameters compared to the standard procedure. Metric invariance is assessed by testing:

$$\mathbf{C}^{(1)} = \mathbf{C}^{(2)} = \mathbf{C}^{(3)} = \ldots = \mathbf{C}^{(n)}. \tag{8.8}$$

For the reader it will not be immediately clear that this is a test of metric invariance. The essence of a test for metric invariance is that the common factor is expressed on the same scale (i.e., in the same metric) cross-nationally. In any factor model the scales of the latent variables are undefined. The common way to provide a scale for the latent variables is by fixing the loading of one of the indicators to 1 (unit loading identification). The result is that the latent variable is expressed on the same scale as the response scale that was used to measure that indicator. This principle ensures that our metric invariance test, Equation 8.8, is truly a test of metric invariance. We will deal with identification later, but we have to introduce this topic here, less detailed though, to illustrate that this is true. The scales for the item specific factors (s) are defined by fixing the quality coefficients to 1. By doing that, the item specific factors are expressed in the same metric as the observed variables. Furthermore, the scale of the common factor is defined by fixing one of the consistency coefficients to 1. So, now the metric of the common factor is the same as the metric of the observed variable for which both the quality and consistency coefficient are 1. If Equation 8.8 holds, then the metric of the common factor is the same across all countries. Under the condition that, of course, the indicators are observed with the same response scale in all countries.

The meaning of this constraint follows from the interpretation of the consistency coefficient, which is the agreement between what we intended to measure (f) and what we measured (s) after correction for measurement error. To put it differently, the consistency coefficient indicates how well the item is *understood*, in the light of what we intended to measure with the item. If the item is *understood* in the same way as the intended measure (f), then the consistency coefficient is perfect (i.e., 1). Hence, cross-national equality constraints on the consistency coefficients imply that the item is *understood* in the same way (i.e., *conveys the same meaning*; Kumata & Schramm, 1956), across countries.

If this constraint, Equation 8.8, also results in metric invariance, what then is the difference with the standard test? If we express the standard test for metric invariance (Equation 8.3) in terms of the parameters from Equations 8.6a and b, the test would look as follows: $(\mathbf{QC})^{(1)} = (\mathbf{QC})^{(2)} = \ldots = (\mathbf{QC})^{(n)}$. Thus in the commonly used procedure it is assumed that the product of the measurement quality (q) and the consistency (c) is the same across countries. That is an assumption that is not warranted. Several studies have shown that the quality of measures varies across Europe, for example, Scherpenzeel (1995b) for life satisfaction, and Saris and Gallhofer (2003) for a variety of measures in the ESS. Given the evidence that the quality is in general not equal across countries, we should impose equality only on the consistency coefficients. This is exactly what is done in the test (Equation 8.8) we propose.

8.2.2.2 The New Scalar Invariance Test

For the test of scalar invariance there are similar issues, which leads to the following model restriction for the scalar invariance test (in addition to the metric invariance constraint):

$$\tau_s^{(1)} = \tau_s^{(2)} = \tau_s^{(3)} = \ldots = \tau_s^{(n)}. \qquad (8.9)$$

If this equality holds then the common factor has the same zero point across all countries, and thus it becomes meaningful to compare latent scores across countries. If we express the standard test for scalar invariance (Equation 8.4) in terms of the parameters from Equations 8.6a and b, the test would look like: $(\tau_y + \mathbf{Q}\tau_s)^{(1)} = (\tau_y + \mathbf{Q}\tau_s)^{(2)} = \ldots\ldots = (\tau_y + \mathbf{Q}\tau_s)^{(n)}$.

In this equation the intercepts of the indicators (τ_y) and the measurement quality (q) can vary across countries due to the measurement procedure. Cross-national variation in the quality was already discussed in the metric invariance test. Cross-national variation of the intercept of the indicators (τ_y) has the same roots. An intercept commonly changes with the addition of extra predictors. In Equation 8.6b there is an extra predictor (compared to Equation 8.1) for the indicator, namely the method factor (m). If the method factor has a mean different from zero and if this mean varies cross-nationally, than the intercept of the indicator (τ_y) will also vary. For this reason we suggest testing the restriction of Equation 8.9 and not the restriction specified in Equation 8.4.

8.2.3 Strategy for Measurement Invariance Testing

There are two general approaches to testing for invariance, the top-down approach and the bottom-up approach. The top-down approach starts with the most constrained model, in our case this is the model with equal loadings and equal intercepts. In addition to the measurement invariance constraints, the factor model itself also constraints cross-loadings and correlated error terms at zero. All the constraints are tested. If the model fits, according to some criterion, there is no problem. However, if the model is rejected *according to some criterion*, improvements can be made to the model by releasing constraints. The big question is: Where to start? The number of constraints is very large. For example in a simple single factor model with 4 indicators scalar invariance across 20 countries results in 280 constrained parameters. Which ones should we release? Do we first introduce correlated errors and cross-loadings, or do we first release the measurement invariance constraints. Therefore, a good reason not to start with the most constrained model is that one immediately starts with a huge number of constrained parameters that can all potentially be incorrect. Another reason not to start with the most constrained model is that measurement invariance constraints can cause residual covariances between the items in some countries. These residuals might be significant and one therefore might want to introduce (estimate) those correlated errors, but that would be a mistake because they are artifact of the measurement invariance constraints.

A better approach is the bottom-up approach, where one starts with the least constrained model (i.e., configural invariance), and then proceeds by introducing more constraints to the model. The advantage of the bottom-up approach is that the problems one faces in each step are more manageable compared to the top-down approach. The bottom-up procedure will be discussed in the following three paragraphs dealing with the different forms of invariance testing. However, note that nothing is mentioned about which goodness-of-fit measures are used. Instead we will use the phrase *according to some criterion*. We will come back to this issue in Section 8.2.4.

8.2.3.1 The Configural Invariance Test

The test for configural invariance is, in essence, a test to check whether the indicators measure the latent variable(s) they are intended to measure. It is imperative that there is a test for configural invariance; we will introduce constraints in the model during the phase of testing for metric and scalar invariance. When those models show a lack of fit, we want to be able to uniquely attribute this to the extra constraints imposed on the model by metric and scalar invariance. That is not possible if the less constrained model is not tested; hence, a test for configural invariance is imperative.

In the social sciences, measurement instruments often only have one, two, or three indicators. Such measurement instruments cannot be tested; the one and the two indicator model are not identified (without restrictions) and the three indicator model is just identified. So, only in case an instrument has four or more indicators, is it possible to test the instrument exhibiting configural invariance. When a measurement instrument only has two or three indicators it is possible to do a test, but requires the measurement model to be extended by: (1) one or more other measurement instruments, (2) causes (predictors) and/or consequences of the construct, (3) extra within country restrictions, or (4) any combination of these.

What constraints are tested for configural invariance? By definition we test whether the indicators measure the latent variable(s) they should measure. For a model with several latent variables and a set of predictors this implies that we test whether the following constraints hold: (1) the correlations between the unique factors are zero, (2) all cross-loadings are zero unless the theory dictates otherwise, and (3) the predictors have no direct (thus zero) effect on the indicators. If the test indicates that the model is misspecified *according to some criterion*, the misspecified parameter(s) should be estimated, because ignoring these misspecifications could lead to biased parameter estimates. Obviously we would like to understand precisely why this misspecification occurs, but such post hoc reasoning will only be helpful for future research. For the study at hand, one should estimate the misspecified parameter or any equivalent solution to the misspecification.

After the model is judged acceptable *according to some criterion*, it is time to select the reference country for the metric (and scalar) invariance test. The test for metric invariance assesses whether the consistency coefficients are equal to each other (Equation 8.9). It is therefore necessary to have a reference country for which the consistency coefficient of each indicator is not too extreme compared to the other countries. In order to find this reference country, one should make a table with a country on each row and the consistency estimates of the indicators in the columns. By sorting the table one can easily find a country that is somewhere in the middle and that has no extreme estimates. This should be the reference country for the metric invariance test. The reason for following this procedure is one needs to compare as many countries as are available. If a country, with high or low factor loadings compared to the average, is selected as the reference country it is *more likely* that that country is not invariant. If a noninvariant country is selected, it will result in a smaller set of comparable countries, compared to the procedure we suggested. The reason for this is that one cannot free parameters of the reference country to become noninvariant because those parameters are already free. Obviously, this procedure is not flawless, there are specific configurations of countries that would result in the opposite that this procedure tries to accomplish. For example, a configuration with one country at the average and two large groups of countries at the extremes, could lead to a smaller set of comparable countries if the *average* country is selected.

Apart from choosing a reference country, one should also decide on a referent indicator; that is, an indicator used to define the scale for the latent variable and therefore drops out of the test for metric and scalar invariance. In principle the choice of a reference indicator should be made for an indicator that is known to be invariant; but this is something we cannot know. Another strategy would be to use an indicator that has the highest face validity for the concept that we wish to measure. This is our preferred choice, but it should be supported by an analysis to see whether that loading of that indicator indeed shows little variation across countries. The choice of a noninvariant reference indicator can be quite problematic as Johnson, Meade, and DuVernet (2009), Rensvold and Cheung (2001), and Yoon and Millsap (2007) have pointed out.

8.2.3.2 The Metric Invariance Test

This test will reveal which loadings are noninvariant across countries. If noninvariant loadings are present, one faces the problem of where to start releasing the constraints. In principle one should start with the indicators that are most deviant. These indicators are easily found in the table that was created to select the reference country. Model adjustments should be made one at a time until an acceptable model is obtained *according to some criterion*. If model adjustments are necessary, it *could* result in partial metric invariance as described by Byrne, Shavelson, and Muthén (1989). Partial metric invariance means that at least one metric invariant indicator per factor remain, plus the referent indicator that is also assumed invariant. If there is partial invariance then composite scores or sum scores, which are often used in research, should not be used since they will bias substantive conclusions (Saris & Gallhofer, 2007, Chapter 16). On the other hand, Byrne et al. (1989) have pointed out that when the sources of noninvariance are explicitly modeled, then only one invariant indicator is enough for meaningful cross-national comparisons within the context of SE modeling. A final strategic note on metric invariance testing is that one should not introduce correlated unique components or correlated random error components, because they should have been detected during the configural invariance testing. If they are found during the metric invariance testing, they should be the result of the restrictions on the parameters implied by metric invariance.

8.2.3.3 The Scalar Invariance Test

If the test for metric invariance resulted in indicators that lack metric invariance it will make no sense to include those noninvariant indicators in the test for scalar invariance. The reason is that metric invariance is a requirement for scalar invariance. As a consequence, indicators that were found to lack metric invariance should not be included in the constraints for the scalar invariance test. Therefore, for the nonmetric-invariant indicators, the τ_s should be estimated without constraints. The test of the scalar invariance will indicate those indicators for which countries are not scalar invariant *according to some criterion*. If problematic indicators are present, one faces the problem where to start releasing the scalar invariance constraints. In this case we do not have a list of unconstrained estimates of the intercepts (τ_s) of the true scores, as we did have for the consistency coefficients in the metric invariance test. The reason is that one cannot estimate all these intercepts without restrictions.* Therefore

* It is possible to estimate the intercepts τ_s if the mean of the latent variable (f) is fixed to zero as well as the intercepts τ_y of the indicators, but in that case the intercepts will be equal to the observed means. In that case we could search for the intercept that is most deviant from the estimate; nevertheless, the procedure suggested in the text does exactly that (i.e., inspect the residuals of the means).

we suggest a different approach, which is to look at the residuals of the means of the observed variables. In principle one should start to free that intercept (τ_s), which has the largest difference from the reference value. Model adjustments should be made one at a time until an acceptable model is obtained *according to some criterion.* If such model adjustments are necessary, it could result in partial scalar invariance as described by Byrne et al. (1989). Partial scalar invariance means that at least two scalar invariant indicators per factor remain. Again, one should be careful with the construction of composite scores if there is partial invariance (Saris & Gallhofer, 2007, Chapter 16).

8.2.4 An Alternative Model Evaluation Procedure

8.2.4.1 The Detection of Misspecifications

So far we have used the phrase *accep*table *to some criterion* several times without specifying what that criterion is. For these generally complex models it is not clear what criterion to use, commonly a mixture of goodness-of-fit indices are used with the cutoff criteria suggested by Hu and Bentler (1999). Recent studies have, however, shown that fit indices with fixed critical values (e.g., the root mean square error of approximation [RMSEA], goodness-of-fit index [GFI]) don't work as they should, because it is not possible to control for type I and type II errors (Barrett, 2007; Marsh et al., 2004; Saris et al., 2009). This means that correct theories are rejected and incorrect theories are accepted in unknown rates. An alternative procedure, *the detection of misspecifications*, has recently been suggested by Saris et al. (2009). The procedure is build upon the idea that models are simplifications of reality and are therefore always misspecified to some extent (Browne & Cudeck, 1993; MacCallum, Browne, & Sugawara, 1996). This is normally problematic when the power of the test is large, the model will be rejected because of irrelevant misspecification and one can detect even the smallest misspecification. However, in our procedure we can control what magnitude of misspecification should be detected with high power.

The traditional procedure to detect misspecifications is by use of the modification index (MI) together with the expected parameter change (EPC) to judge whether the constrained parameter is a misspecification (Kaplan, 1989; Saris, Satorra, & Sörbom, 1987). However, the MI is sensitive to the power of the test (Saris et al., 2009), therefore one should take the power of the MI-test into account. The power of the MI-test to detect a misspecification of size delta or larger for any constrained parameter can be derived if the noncentrality parameter (ncp) for the MI-test is known. The ncp can be computed with the following formula:

$$\text{ncp} = (\text{MI}/\text{EPC}^2)\ \delta^2. \quad (8.10)$$

In this equation the MI is the modification index and the EPC is the expected parameter change, which both can be found in the output that SEM software produce (for more details see Saris et al., 2009). Furthermore, δ (delta) is the size (magnitude) of the misspecification we would like to detect with high power. Its value can be chosen by the researcher and may vary across disciplines and the state of the theory under investigation. However, guidelines exist as to which magnitude of misspecifications are important for detection under general conditions. These suggestions will be discussed later. The power of the test, for which we want to control in the end, can be obtained from the tables of the noncentral χ^2 distribution.

Whether or not a constrained parameter is a misspecification can be judged from the combination of the power, which is high or low, and the MI, which is significant or not. The decision rules are presented in Table 8.1. There is a misspecification when the power to detect a misspecification of delta is low and the MI is significant. There could also be a misspecification when the power is high and the MI is significant. In that case, the MI could be significant due to the high power or because there is a large misspecification. Thus, in this instance if the EPC is larger than delta, we decide that there is a misspecification. Other combinations are also possible and indicate either no misspecification or a lack of

TABLE 8.1

The Judgment Rules

JR	MI	Power	Evaluation
1	MI = not significant	power = high	No misspecification
2	MI = significant	power = low	Misspecification present
3	MI = significant	power = high	Use EPC
4	MI = not significant	power = low	No decision

power to detect a misspecification. One can imagine that this procedure is quite laborious; for each constrained parameter we have to compute the power of the test and then decide on a misspecification using the judgment rules in Table 8.1. For a simple multigroup factor model with four indicators, 20 countries, and the scalar invariance constraints, there are already 280 constraints. Therefore a software program called JRule* has been developed by Van der Veld et al. (2008) that automates the whole procedure.

8.2.4.2 Using JRule in Cross-National Analysis

JRule reads the output of either LISREL (Jöreskog & Sörbom, 1996) or Mplus (Muthén & Muthén, 1998–2007) and collects model information (MI & EPC) necessary to make a judgment about whether the constrained parameters in the model are misspecified or not, or whether there is no statistical basis to make a sound judgment. In Figure 8.2 a screenshot of JRule is presented. The program is fairly simple to use. The user only has to select a SEM-output file and then press the button "Compute Judgment

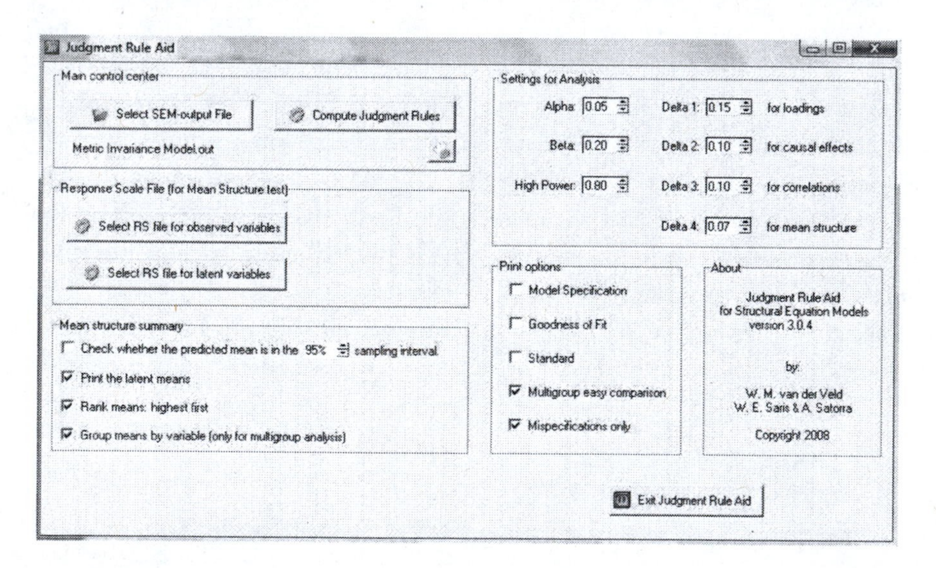

FIGURE 8.2
Screenshot of JRule.

* JRule is currently freeware and can be obtained by sending a request to the first author of this chapter via e-mail (w.vanderveld@socsci.ru.nl).

Rules." JRule will then compute all judgment rules for the constrained parameters and present them in a text file, readable with any text editor. One can furthermore see that the user can specify the levels of α and β for the test. In addition, the user can specify the magnitude of the misspecification that he likes to detect, or better, that he does not want to ignore.

A special feature—multigroup easy comparison—makes the evaluation of multigroup models a lot easier than it would be when the standard SEM output is used to make an evaluation. The reason for this is that SEM programs commonly produce output group by group, instead of parameter by parameter. In the case of measurement invariance testing, the interest is especially in detecting whether there are countries that are deviant. Already in simple models one gets lost in the amount of output, because it is not structured efficiently for this purpose. The output that JRule produces is organized in such a way that it becomes very easy to compare the same constrained parameter across all countries. Figure 8.3 shows a fragment of such an output. An overview is presented

Relation	Between	G1	G2	G3	G4	G5	G6	G7	G8	G9	G10
X1	X1	–	–	–	–	–	–	–	–	–	–
X2	X1	4	2	2	4	1	4	2	1	4	4
X3	X1	2	3	3	1	3	4	4	3	3	2
X4	X1	1	1	3	1	3	1	1	1	3	1
X5	X1	3	1	3	1	3	1	1	1	1	1
X2	X2	–	–	–	–	–	–	–	–	–	–
X3	X2	2	1	1	1	3	4	4	3	3	4
X4	X2	1	1	1	1	1	1	1	1	3	1
X5	X2	3	1	1	1	3	1	1	3	1	1

FIGURE 8.3
Fragment from a JRule output with multigroup easy comparison, indicating the misspecified correlated errors. G1, G2, and G3 refer to the groups or countries in the analysis. JRule presents a table in the output that makes the link between the names the user has given to the groups and G1, G2, and so on, explicit. These short names, G1, G2, and so on, are used to enable a more comprehensible layout of the results. The numbers in the table are judgment rules, which must be interpreted using Table 8.1.

in Figure 8.3 for the misspecifications in a part of the variance-covariance matrix of random error components. So, this overview indicates whether and where there are misspecified correlated errors. On each row, one can find the judgment rules for a single parameter for all countries in the analysis. Here the countries are indicated with G1–G10. So, one can see that the parameter "X2 with X1" is misspecified (JR = 2) in G2, G3, G7, in addition, for six countries one lacks statistical information (JR = 4) to make a sound judgment on whether that parameter is misspecified. It is clear that organizing the output in this way makes it a lot easier to see what parameters are misspecified in which countries, and also whether a certain parameter is misspecified in many countries or only incidentally. In addition, JRule also provides the opportunity to print only the misspecified parameters, which makes it even easier to evaluate if something is wrong.

8.3 THE CROSS-NATIONAL COMPARABILITY OF GST

8.3.1 Theoretical Context

GST is a central variable in the social sciences because it is assumed to be fundamental for a healthy society (Fukuyama, 1995; Putnam, 1993). Nevertheless it is not clear how because *trust appears to work somewhat mysteriously* (Uslaner, 2000, p. 569). That is, it is not clear why some people are more trusting than others, or why citizens in some countries are more trusting than in other countries. We are interested in explaining GST. There are two categories of explanations: country level explanations and individual level explanations. We focus on the individual level explanations. Delhey and Newton (2003) mention five individual level theories that they have named: personality theory, success and well-being theory, voluntary organization theory, social network theory, and community theory. In the personality theory it is assumed that attitudes are formed in early childhood and personality features that determines trust in others (Erikson, 1950). In the success and well-being theory it is assumed that those who have more success in life (i.e., those who are better off), will be more trusting of others (Putnam, 2000). The social network theory suggests that direct participation in the social networks of everyday life (e.g., friends, family, and colleagues), will promote trust in others. The community theory suggests that trust in others is fostered by features of the local context in which people live. This is in contrast to what Delhey and Newton (2003) named societal theory, which is concerned with country level variables such as gross domestic product (GDP) or democratic level that we ignore in our study. Finally, the voluntary organizations theory suggests that it is participation in formal organizations that promotes trust in others. This theory is one of the more popular explanations. It has been put forward by Putnam (1993), who, following Alexis de Tocqueville and John Stuart Mill, argues that participation in civic organizations leads people to trust each other. There is, however, no consistent evidence for this idea (Delhey & Newton, 2005; Gesthuizen, Scheepers, Van der Veld, & Völker, in press; Saris & Gallhofer, 2007, Chapter 15; Torcal & Montero, 1999) and it has also been criticized on theoretical grounds (Levi, 1996; Newton, 1997). We agree with these critics and therefore will not further develop this idea here. Finally, there are three often used demographic variables (gender, age, and education) that also have an effect on GST, but the theoretical justifications are not well-founded.

In their study that tests the five theories, Delhey and Newton (2003) find some results hard to explain. The most eye-catching result is that the relative importance of these theories differs across countries. This implies that people living in these countries trust for different reasons. This is hard to believe. People are people so why should it be that in country A happy people trust others more, while in country B more social active people trust others more. One would expect that the same causes, with more or less the same effect, are at work in country A as well as in country B. After all we are dealing with the same causal mechanisms. The fact that Delhey and Newton (2003), as well as other scholars (e.g., Kaasa & Parts, 2008; Zmerli & Newton, 2008) find these inconsistent results might be that they do not correct for measurement error. For example, it is more than likely that instruments used to measure the causes (and consequence, i.e., GST) differ in quality across countries. If the true effects of the causes are the same across countries, then we will find that the estimated effects will be different, due to attenuation for measurement error.

Uslaner (2000) provides another explanation for GST that does not fit into any of the previously mentioned theories. He argues that the trust in others is explained by how religious one is. Uslaner (2000) finds that Christian fundamentalists are substantially less likely than other believers to say that they trust other people. The rationale behind this is based upon the perception that Christian fundamentalists do take part in civic life, but only with their own kind. As a result they trust those who are similar, but not the general others. We will refer to this theory as the Orthodoxy theory.

The aim of this last part of the chapter is to test these theories in the causes of GST. We will do this using the procedures we suggested in this chapter, by correcting our measures for measurement error and using a different model evaluation procedure.

8.3.2 Data

The data for the analysis are collected by the ESS, and we use Round 1 data. The ESS is built upon the belief that cross-national comparative research requires more than just having respondents completing the same questionnaire in different countries. The procedures, used in the ESS, to ensure cross-national equivalence are pretty elaborate and involve, among others, the control of sampling designs, questionnaire design, translation procedures, data entry, and MTMM experiments for quality control. The whole survey process is being controlled as much as possible in every participating country. GST is measured in the ESS with three survey questions. The formulations are presented in Table 8.2.

In order to test the theories (personality theory, success and well-being theory, social network theory, community theory, and Orthodoxy theory)

TABLE 8.2

The Formulation of the Indicators of GST[a]

Names	Formulation of Survey Items
Trust	Using this card, generally speaking, would you say that most people can be trusted, or that you can't be too careful in dealing with people? Please tell me on a score of 0–10, where 0 means you can't be too careful and 10 means that most people can be trusted.
Fair	Do you think that most people would try to take advantage of you if they got a chance or would they try to be fair?
Help	Would you say that most of the time people try to be helpful or are they mostly looking out for themselves?

[a] Measured on an 11-point scale running from 0 to 10 with item specific endpoint labels.

we need indicators for these theories. There is, however, little agreement about which variables are important and even less how they should be measured. In addition we are limited in our possibilities to what is available in the ESS. We have used one measure for most theories, and selected those indicators that closely resembled the indicators used in the study by Delhey and Newton (2003).

The ESS, Round 1, does not provide any indicators for the personality theory, so we ignore this theory in our analysis. The success and well-being theory was tested with two measures: an objective and a subjective one. The subjective indicator is an item about how happy one is (Happy) and the objective indicator is an item about whether people find it difficult to make ends meet (MeetEnd). The social network theory is tested using a measure that asks for frequency with which one meets with friends, relatives, or work colleagues (Social). The community theory was tested with two measures: an objective and a subjective one. The subjective measure is whether one feels safe at night in the neighborhood (FlSafe) and the objective measure is about the size of the city where one lives (Urban). The Orthodoxy theory was tested with a measure about how important religion is in one's life (Religs). The formulations of these measures are presented in Table 8.3. We have skipped the formulation of the measures for gender and age, since they are standard measures.

8.3.3 Model Identification

The model we test is presented in Figure 8.4. This model is not identified without restrictions. In order to define the scales for the item specific factors (s), all quality coefficients were fixed to 1. Differences in the quality are still possible because the random error components (e) are not constrained. The scale for GST is defined by fixing the consistency coefficient of TRUST to 1. Furthermore, the scale for the systematic measurement error factor (m) is defined by fixing all invalidity coefficients to 1. The result is that the method factor (m) has the same effect within a country on the different items, but can have a different effect in each country because the variance of the method factor (m) can differ across countries. Corten et al. (2002) have studied what specification of the effect of the method factor works best. They found that a specification where the method factor had an additive scale dependent effect fitted the data best. We have used that specific specification.

TABLE 8.3

The Formulation of the Predictors of GST

Names	Formulation of Survey Items
Happy[a]	Taking all things together, how happy would you say you are?
MeetEnd	How do you feel about your household's income currently? (1) Living comfortably on present income, (2) coping on present income, (3) finding it difficult on present income, and (4) finding it very difficult on present income.
Social[b]	How often do you meet socially with friends, relatives, or work colleagues?
FlSafe	How safe do you—or would you—feel walking alone in this area after dark? (1) Very unsafe, (2) Unsafe, (3) Safe, and (4) Very safe.
Religs[c]	How important is religion in your life?
Urban	Which phrase on this card best describes the area where you live? (1) A big city, (2) the suburbs or outskirts of a big city, (3) a town or a small city, (4) a country village, and (5) a farm or home in the countryside.
Educ[d]	What is the highest level of education you have achieved?

[a] Measured on an 11-point scale with endpoint labels (0 = Extremely unhappy, 10 = Extremely happy).

[b] Measured on a 7-point fully labeled scale with subjective frequencies (never … everyday).

[c] Measured on an 11-point scale with endpoint labels (0 = Extremely unimportant, 10 = Extremely important).

[d] Measured with country specific scales, lower values mean lower education. Basically incomparable values due to differences in educational systems.

Defining the scales for the latent variables, however, does not make the model identified. There is still an identification problem in the measurement part of the model. This problem is found in the random error component (e) and method factor (m) variance. There are no equality restrictions possible to make this model identified. There are nevertheless two solutions to this problem. A first possibility is to extend the model and data collection design following the MTMM approach (Saris & Andrews, 1991; Scherpenzeel, 1995a). That would, however, make the specification, testing, and estimation of the model very complex. A second, more simple solution is to fix the values of the random error components and method factor variances to a reasonable value. In that case we do not have to estimate those coefficients, which makes the model identified. But what are reasonable values for the random and systematic error components? We can obtain reasonable values in two ways. A first possibility is to predict the random and systematic error components using the Survey Quality Predictor (Saris & Gallhofer, 2007; Saris, Van der Veld, & Gallhofer, 2004). Unfortunately that procedure

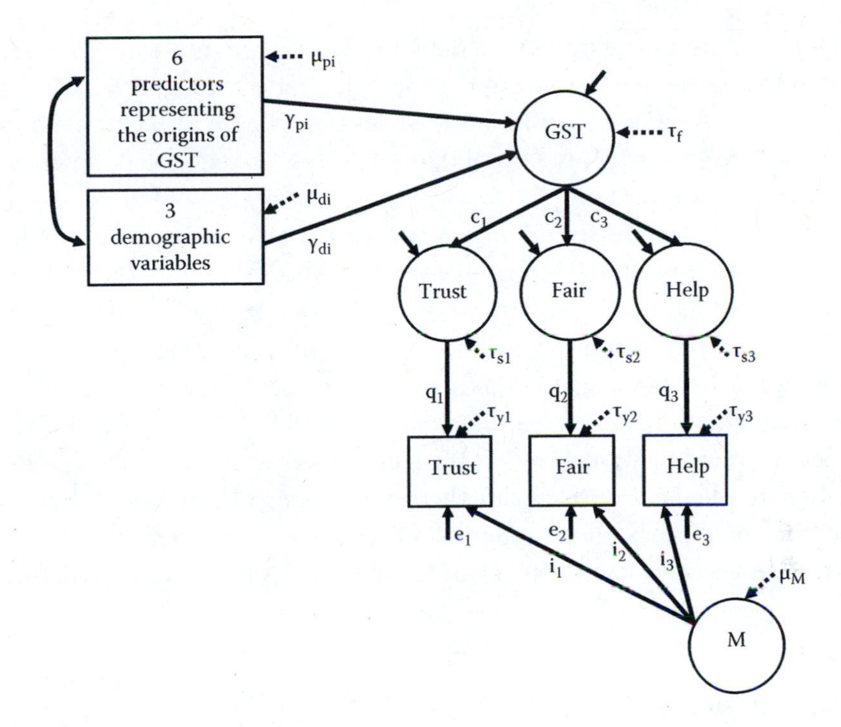

FIGURE 8.4
Path model to test theory of the causes of GST. The means of the predictors is indicated by μ_{pi}, where the subscript pi refers to different predictors in the model. The regression effects of the predictors are indicated with γ_{pi}. In the model it looks as if there is only one regression effect, but in fact there is one for each predictor. The means of the demographic variables is indicated by μ_{di}, where the subscript di refers to the different demographical variables in the model. For the regression effects of the demographic variables (γ_{di}) it's the same story as for the predictors. In addition, demographic variables are in a sense also predictors, but because there is no theory we have made this distinction.

only works for Dutch, English, and German questionnaires currently. The second possibility, and our choice, would be to estimate the random (e) and systematic error (m) components in a different context and then introduce these estimates as fixed values in the model (Figure 8.4). This is possible because the items Trust, Fair, and Help have been collected as part of a MTMM experiment in the ESS. This design enables us to estimate the random and systematic error components using the MTMM approach.

After these restrictions, the model is identified and a test can be performed for configural and metric invariance. A test for scalar invariance is, however, not possible, because the means of the method factors are not identified. We need extra restrictions to identify the model. Our solution is to assume that the method factor means have the same value in all countries. Because the actual value is irrelevant, we have fixed the method factor means to zero. This assumption might not be warranted, however, there is no easy alternative.*

Even after all these restrictions, a test for scalar invariance cannot be performed because the intercepts of the item specific factors (τ_s) and the intercepts of the observed variables (τ_y) cannot be simultaneously estimated. We need another restriction to identify the model. Byrne and Stewart (2006) have suggested fixing the intercepts of the first-order factors, in our case the item specific factors (s), to 0. But their model is slightly different from our model in that their model has multiple indicators for each first-order factor. In our case there is only one indicator for each first-order factor. It is, therefore, arbitrary whether we would fix the intercepts of the item specific factors (s) or of the observed variables (indictors) to zero. We have chosen the latter option.

8.3.3.1 The Estimation of Random and Systematic Error Variance (Quality and Invalidity)

In order to obtain the estimates for the random error and method variances for all countries we first estimated an MTMM model for each country. We will not discuss this model in any detail, except that the model that we estimated was the classic MTMM model as used by Andrews (1984) and described by Batista-Foguet and Coenders (2000), but using a multigroup design called SB-MTMM (Saris, Satorra, & Coenders, 2004) to minimize response burden. The first round of the ESS contains SB-MTMM experiments for Trust, Fair, and Help, which we have used to estimate the parameters of interest. We used the full information maximum likelihood procedure available in LISREL 8.8 (Jöreskog & Sörbom, 1996) to estimate our model and account for missing data.† The results of the analysis are presented in Table 8.4. The second to the fourth column contain the

* It should be possible to estimate the latent means of the common method factors in the context of measurement invariance testing, using an MTMM or split ballot MTMM design. However, the models that have to be specified will be very complex, making this an unattractive solution.

† Most missing data were missing by design, because of the split ballot nature of the MTMM experiments. Only a small percentage of the data were not missing by design and we assumed they were missing at random.

TABLE 8.4

Estimates of the Variance of Random and Systematic Error Components per Country[a]

	Random Error Variance			Systematic Error Variance
Country[b]	**Trust**	**Fair**	**Help**	**Method**
Sweden	1.44	1.53	1.83	0.01[FI]
Austria	1.32	1.24	1.17	0.01[FI]
Belgium	1.29	1.75	1.24	0.24[ns]
Switzerland	1.69	1.21	1.71	0.01[FI]
Czech Republic	1.48	1.37	1.40	0.61
Germany	1.99	1.84	1.91	0.01[FI]
Denmark	0.86	0.90	1.62	0.01[FI]
Spain	0.93	1.31	2.03	0.24[ns]
Finland	1.30	1.27	1.73	0.41[ns]
Great Britain	1.46	1.28	1.70	0.01[FI]
Greece	0.89	0.95	1.28	0.01[FI]
Ireland	1.61	1.28	1.64	0.01[FI]
Israel	2.27	1.69	2.62	0.44[ns]
Italy	1.66	2.14	2.28	0.50
Netherlands	1.10	1.13	1.20	0.01[FI]
Norway	0.86	0.67	2.26	0.01[FI]
Poland	1.76	2.15	2.72	0.63
Portugal	0.78	0.92	0.96	0.01[FI]
Slovenia	2.65	2.32	2.09	0.55[ns]

[a] All estimates are significant at $\alpha = 0.05$, unless stated otherwise. ns denotes that the estimate is not significant. FI denotes that the parameter is fixed to 0.01. This was necessary if the estimated variance was negative, in all instances where this happened the estimate was not significant.

[b] Nineteen countries are presented, while there are 22 countries that participated in the first round of the ESS. The difference is due to the fact that in France, Hungary, and Luxembourg, no MTMM experiments were conducted or conducted poorly.

estimates of the random error components. One can see that the estimates are significantly different from zero, while zero would indicate a measure without random measurement error. In addition, the random error components vary across different items as well as across countries. The latter result justifies that we make a distinction between the unique components and random error components as we did in Equation 8.6a and b. Column 5 presents the systematic error components, the method factor variances. In this specific case the systematic error components are not significant in most countries, this is indicated by either *ns* or FI in Table 8.4. There is a good reason why the systematic error components are not significant in most countries. The main reason is that this scale was tested in the ESS pilot study for Round 1 and the results showed that the method effects (i.e., systematic measurement error) were not significant for this scale. A more theoretical reason is that the response scales are item specific and thus reduce the common variance due to a systematic reaction within respondents on the response format. This format is in sharp contrast to response scale formats such as agree–disagree, or never–often. Saris, Revilla, Krosnick, and Shaeffer (2010) have studied these differences and found that item specific response scales perform much better (i.e., little systematic measurement error, compared to agree–disagree scales).

The values of the random error components in Table 8.4 are the ones that we have introduced as fixed values in the complete model as depicted in Figure 8.4. For the systematic error components we have chosen a much simpler solution. For most countries we do not find significant systematic measurement errors, therefore we will ignore the method factor in the tests for measurement invariance.

8.3.4 Two Unfortunate Facts

Our aim is to make a cross-national comparison of several theories that explain GST. This would require that (1) the measures of all variables in our model show scalar measurement invariance and (2) that we can correct all our measures for measurement error. This is possible for the endogenous variable GST, but not for the exogenous variables. It is not absolutely necessary that the exogenous variables are scalar invariant. If they are not, we could still determine what theory is the most important theory within each country, and those results can be compared cross-nationally. In contrast we cannot say, in the case of the absence of scalar invariance that success and well-being has twice as much explanatory power in the UK compared to Italy. However, we would be happy when we can compare the importance of each theory within countries. That, however, is not possible either. The reason is that in path (and regression) analysis it is assumed that the exogenous variables are observed without measurement error. If this is not the case, and that's very likely, then the estimates of the path-coefficients are biased. An alternative would be that we correct for measurement error in a similar way as we did for GST. Unfortunately, this is not possible with the data that we have. We do not have MTMM data available in the ESS for the exogenous variables. Another alternative would be to use the multiple indicators approach (Ganzeboom, 2009) for each exogenous variable. That is also no option, because we lack multiple indicators. The bitter conclusion is then the we can estimate all the paths, but we cannot—with any confidence—interpret the results due to the distorting effect of measurement error. The question that pops up is then whether we should have introduced the theory about the causes of GST. We do have two reasons to introduce such a theory. First, in the common approach (which was referenced at the beginning of this chapter) the consequences of the presence of measurement error as well as the comparability of the measures are ignored. We explicitly want to illustrate that one should not ignore these issues by confronting the reader with a theoretical context first and then stress the requirements necessary to perform a test on the theories. Second, there is another use for the exogenous variables. We can use them to over identify the model so that we have a test of configural invariance. This is an important test, as discussed in Section 8.2.3, because the measurement model for GST is exactly identified after introduction of the quality and invalidity coefficients in the model as fixed parameters (see Section 8.3.3). Thus, by including exogenous variables in the model we obtain a test for configural invariance. It is for these reasons that we decided to include a section on the theoretical context (i.e., the causes of GST). We will provide the results; that is, the effects from the exogenous variables on GST and interpret them. However, because we cannot deny the possibility that there is measurement error in the predictors leading to biased substantive conclusion, the conclusions should be taken with a grain of salt.

8.3.5 Model Estimation

The model parameters are estimated with the robust maximum likelihood estimation procedure (Satorra & Bentler, 1994) in LISREL 8.8 (Jöreskog & Sörbom, 1996), using the asymptotic covariance matrix to correct for nonnormality in the observed data. Missing values were dealt with using listwise deletion. Full information maximum likelihood (FIML) shows a superior performance (Enders & Bandalos, 2001) compared to listwise deletion, however FIML is incompatible with robust ML. Listwise deletion produces unbiased estimates under MCAR conditions and is not efficient under MCAR/MAR because cases are deleted that do have observed values on some variables. We can live with this loss of efficiency because the number of cases remains sufficient for our analysis. Furthermore, we have used the design weight, present in the ESS data, to correct for cross-national differences in the sampling procedures.

Finally, all models are evaluated using the procedure suggested by Saris et al. (2009) as implemented in JRule (Van der Veld et al., 2008). For the evaluation (i.e., the computation of the judgment rules), we have used the following settings: $\alpha = 0.05$, high power = 0.80, $\delta_1 = 0.30$, $\delta_2 = 0.15$, $\delta_3 = 0.15$, and $\delta_4 = 0.07$.

8.3.5.1 Results for Configural Invariance

For the test of configural invariance we can ignore the mean structure, thus all variables are expressed in deviation scores for this analysis. We estimated the model for all 19 countries and then analyzed the output with JRule. This resulted in the detection of 39 misspecifications. Given the total number of constraints in the model, 1634 (86 constraints × 19 countries), 39 misspecifications is only a small percentage (2%). Only by chance alone one can expect a small percentage of misspecifications. The exact percentage is difficult to give because some misspecifications are tied to each other (i.e., they represent equivalent models). In other words, not all misspecifications are independent (Saris, 2009). Nevertheless, we should judge every misspecification, but that does not mean we have to solve all misspecifications to have an acceptable model.

For Belgium, Germany, and Sweden we estimated a direct effect from the predictors to the item specific factors (s) to solve some misspecifications (see footnotes in Table 8.5 for details). We also included a correlation between the unique components (u) of TRUST and FAIR in Israel and Portugal. After these respecifications, the model was estimated again and 24 misspecifications remained. In our view they were not serious enough and we ignored them in further analysis.

The important model estimates are presented in Table 8.5. The 5th and the 6th column contain the unstandardized estimates of the consistency coefficients. One can see that there is some variation across countries, which might lead to problematic issues when they are assumed equal for the metric invariance test. The average size of the consistency of Fair is 1.02 and for Help it is 0.79, for Trust it is 1 because that was the indicator used to define the latent scale of GST.

8.3.5.2 Results for Metric Invariance

In agreement with the suggested strategy (see Section 8.2.3) we have selected Sweden as the reference country. The metric test involves the constraint as defined in Equation 8.9. In this test the means play no role, so again all

TABLE 8.5

Results of the Configural Invariance Test[a]

Group	Country	Consistency Coefficients		
		Trust	Fair	Help
1[b]	Sweden	1.00	1.04	0.82
2	Austria	1.00	1.11	0.92
3[b]	Belgium	1.00	0.95	0.79
4[b]	Switzerland	1.00	0.96	0.68
5	Czech Republic	1.00	0.95	0.77
6[b]	Germany	1.00	1.19	0.90
7	Denmark	1.00	0.91	0.71
8	Spain	1.00	0.91	0.71
9	Finland	1.00	0.98	0.86
10	Great Britain	1.00	1.09	0.87
11	Greece	1.00	1.03	0.85
12	Ireland	1.00	1.09	0.82
13[c]	Israel	1.00	1.02	0.70
14	Italy	1.00	1.14	0.90
15	Netherlands	1.00	0.90	0.68
16	Norway	1.00	0.98	0.67
17	Poland	1.00	1.05	0.80
18[c]	Portugal	1.00	0.99	0.62
19	Slovenia	1.00	1.09	0.87

[a] The presented figures are the unstandardized estimates. All estimates are significant at alpha = 0.05. The consistency of TRUST is fixed to 1 to define the latent scale of GST.

[b] In these countries we estimated an extra direct effect: Education on TRUST (Belgium, Sweden), FeelSafe on TRUST (Germany).

[c] In these countries we estimated an extra correlated unique component: HELP with TRUST.

observed variables are expressed as deviation scores. All metric invariance constraints are tested with a delta2 of 0.15 and high power is 0.8 or larger. This resulted in the detection of two misspecifications for the metric invariance constraints. For the consistency of TRUST there is a misspecification in Norway (Cntry = 16), but it is not possible to estimate this parameter because it is the reference indicator. In principle, one should select another indicator as the reference indicator (Steenkamp & Baumgartner, 1998), however, this would only make sense if there is an indicator that is fully metric invariant; which is not the case. For the consistency of HELP there is a misspecification in Portugal (Cntry = 18). This misspecification was solved by estimating that consistency coefficient not constrained to other consistency coefficients.

8.3.5.3 Result for Scalar Invariance

The test involves the constraint as defined in Equation 8.10. Here we also test the mean-structure, therefore the means of the observed variables are added to the model. The default procedure in the estimation of latent means is to fix the mean of the latent variables in the reference country to zero so that the latent means in the other countries are estimated relative to zero. We have, however, chosen to fix the latent mean of GST in the reference country (Sweden) to the weighted mean of the indicators so that the estimated latent means can be more easily related to the scale on which the variables are measured. Finally, all scalar invariance constraints are tested with a delta4 of 0.07 and high power is 0.8 or larger.

The test for metric invariance resulted in one country, Portugal (Cntry = 18), with a noninvariant consistency coefficient. In agreement with our own suggestion (see Section 8.2.3) we have excluded, for Portugal, the intercept of HELP from the equality constraints. We estimated the model for all 19 countries and then analyzed the output with JRule, resulting in the detection of three misspecifications. Two for the intercept of TRUST in Belgium and Germany, and one for the intercept of Help in Ireland. The misspecification in Germany was rather large and we released the constraint on the intercept of TRUST in Germany. This resulted in a model with two misspecifications (i.e., in Belgium and Ireland). However, solving these misspecification and reestimating the model again did not lead to changes in the other parameters, so we choose to accept those misspecifications.

8.3.6 Conclusion

The analysis of measurement invariance of GST indicates that the instrument available in the ESS is both partial metric and partial scalar invariant. This is very good news for studies (see again references at the beginning of this chapter) that assumed that the ESS measure of GST is comparable. In those studies however, the variable GST was created as composite score, and for composite scores it is imperative that GST shows full metric and scalar invariance (Saris & Gallhofer, 2007, Chapter 16). That is not the case here, but the number of noninvariant parameters is so small (3 in total) that it is unlikely to have a significant effect on the comparability if composite scores are used. However, it is easier to continue analyzing the data in the framework of SEM, treating GST as a latent variable. Because in that framework it is possible to correct for misspecifications (e.g., noninvariant parameters), these misspecifications do not bias parameter estimates. Note that this is not the same as saying that the parameter estimates are unbiased after misspecifications are solved, which can only be true if other model assumptions (e.g., error-free observations) are not violated.

Now that we established that the measure of GST is partial metric and partial scalar invariant we can make cross-national comparisons in two ways. We can make a ranking of the level of GST, the latent variable, in the 19 countries. We can also study, in principle, the causes of GST cross-nationally. Table 8.6 ranks the countries in our analysis on their level of

TABLE 8.6

The Estimates of the Latent Means of GST[a]

Country	Mean GST
Denmark	6.81[b]
Norway	6.51[b]
Finland	6.34[b]
Sweden	5.97[b]
Switzerland	5.71[b]
Netherlands	5.70[b]
Ireland	5.69[b]
Germany	5.30[b]
Great Britain	5.27[b]
Austria	5.27[b]
Belgium	5.02[b]
Israel	4.91[b]
Spain	4.83[b]
Portugal	4.60[b]
Czech Republic	4.49[b]
Italy	4.36[b]
Slovenia	4.29[b]
Poland	3.83[b]
Greece	3.43[b]

[a] Countries are sorted in descending order of the means.

[b] Significant at $\alpha = 0.05$

GST. The results are more or less in line with earlier studies on data from the World Values Studies (WVS) by Van Deth (2001), Norris (2002), and Inglehart (1999), the European Values Studies (EVS) by Adam (2008), the Euromodule survey by Delhey and Newton (2005), and the ESS by Reeskens and Hooghe (2008) and Zmerli and Newton (2008). However, note that studies based on the WVS only use a single question to measure GST and therefore produce very different levels of trust. Nevertheless, the rank-order of the countries is rather similar.

While ranking the countries on their mean levels could be an interesting exercise to describe where countries are, it does not explain much. Our initial interest was more in exploring the causes (and level) of GST. Previous studies have resulted in mixed conclusions, as described in detail by Newton (2004). He mentions that there is no single theory that holds across most countries; that is, some theories work in some countries but not in others. It is our belief that such conclusions are not warranted, because the predictors in those studies contained, most certainly, measurement error. This is also the reason why we dare not draw any conclusion from our model in this respect. Despite that, we have presented the results in Table 8.7.

Table 8.7 holds the figures that provide an answer to which (individual level) theories explain GST. Even though we have our methodological reservations, we will interpret some of the results, but conclusion should be taken with a *grain of salt*. The standardized estimates in Table 8.7 reveal that the effect of each predictor on GST is pretty consistent across the countries. The variable Happy (success and well-being theory) explains most of GST. Then there are several variables that explain GST a bit less well (in order of importance): the subjective experience of the neighborhood (FlSafe), whether people find it difficult to make ends meet (MeetEnd), and the frequency of social contacts (Social). The following two variables do not contribute at all to GST the size of the community (Urban) and Religiosity (Religs). The effect of Gndr is at average very small, with three eye-catching exceptions, Sweden, Norway, and Denmark. One would like to speculate—but we don't—why these countries are so deviant, because they are geographically and politically close to each other. Finally, the variable education explains on average 1.6% of the variance in GST, which makes this a relatively important variable in comparison with the others. This finding is in contrast to what Delhey and Newton (2003) found, who reported to their own surprise no effect of education. A

TABLE 8.7

The Completely Standardized Total Effect of the Predictors on GST[a]

Country	Happy	FlSafe	MeetEnd	Social	Religs	Urban	Educ	Age	Gndr	R^2
Sweden	.21[b]	.21[b]	–.09[b]	.08[b]	.08[b]	.01	.08[b]	.12[b]	.16[b]	16%
Austria	.22[b]	.13[b]	–.11[b]	.03	.02	–.02	.07[b]	–.04[b]	.03	13%
Belgium	.16[b]	.12[b]	–.19[b]	.10[b]	.08[b]	–.03	.15[b]	.02	.02	17%
Switzerland	.24[b]	.16[b]	–.13[b]	.11[b]	.03	–.01	.13[b]	.13[b]	.05	16%
Czech Rep.	.21[b]	.15[b]	–.04	.05	.02	.02	.15[b]	.03	.05[b]	12%
Germany	.23[b]	.09[b]	–.11[b]	.10[b]	.06	.03	.07[b]	.09[b]	.06[b]	13%
Denmark	.21[b]	.12[b]	–.08[b]	.02	.02	.04	.20[b]	.10[b]	.18[b]	15%
Spain	.14[b]	.14[b]	–.12[b]	.01	.01	.03	.12[b]	.05	.00	8%
Finland	.26[b]	.19[b]	–.13[b]	.06	.10[b]	.08[b]	.03	.06	.09[b]	17%
Great Britain	.21[b]	.19[b]	–.03	.05	.07[b]	–.03	.11[b]	.19[b]	.03	15%
Greece	.18[b]	.14[b]	–.02	.02	–.07[b]	.04	.09[b]	.02	.05[b]	9%
Ireland	.21[b]	.12[b]	–.07[b]	.06[b]	.03	.00	.12[b]	.15[b]	.04	12%
Israel	.21[b]	.03	–.10[b]	.12[b]	.03	–.03	.15[b]	.13[b]	.07[b]	13%
Italy	.18[b]	.13[b]	–.12[b]	.07[b]	.00	–.04[b]	.15[b]	.07[b]	.07[b]	14%
Netherlands	.17[b]	.15[b]	–.09[b]	.03	.04	–.06[b]	.15[b]	.04	.08[b]	12%
Norway	.23[b]	.16[b]	–.06[b]	.12[b]	–.04	–.05	.17[b]	.20[b]	.20[b]	18%
Poland	.27[b]	.11[b]	–.04	.10[b]	.08[b]	.10[b]	.11[b]	–.01	.07[b]	16%
Portugal	.17[b]	.19[b]	.05	.11[b]	–.06[b]	–.07[b]	.15[b]	.18[b]	.04	11%
Slovenia	.21[b]	.08[b]	–.09[b]	.08[b]	.04	–.02[b]	.12[b]	.08[b]	.00	11%

[a] All estimates are within group completely standardized estimates.
[b] Significant at $\alpha = .05$.

very tentative overall conclusion would be that in contrast to Delhey and Newton (2003), we find rather consistent cross-national results. That is, Happy is always the most important cause. In addition, the standardized effect of all predictors are more or less the same cross-nationally. However, these conclusions are very tentative for the reasons we mentioned earlier.

8.4 CONCLUSIONS

The reader might have the feeling that this chapter does not live up to the expectation set at the start of this chapter. We aimed at carrying out a cross-national analysis for the causes of GST while also introducing two innovations (i.e. model testing and correction for random and systematic measurement error in measurement invariance tests). The disappointment lays—for some part—in the fact that in the end we did not correct for systematic measurement error in the indicators of GST and we also did not draw *real* conclusions from the causal analysis. Hence, did we choose the wrong topic to illustrate our innovations? Certainly not! Generalized social trust is believed to be at the heart of a healthy society (Putnam, 1993; Uslaner, 1999; Uslaner, 2000), which justifies our choice. The fact that we did not correct for systematic measurement error in the end was related to the fact that for all but three countries the method factor variance, due to the measurement procedure, was not significant. This result was expected, because MTMM experiments in the ESS pilot study indicated that the response scales and formulation of the items to measure GST produced little if any method factor variance (Saris & Gallhofer, 2003). That was also the reason they were included in the main ESS questionnaire. In addition, the—more or less—absence of systematic measurement error allowed us to simplify the presentation and discussion of the models. Another part of the disappointment is grounded in our reluctance to seriously interpret the results of the causal analysis. The reason is simply that an important assumption of the model (i.e., exogenous variables are observed without measurement error) was violated. This assumption is quite often ignored in research. The negative consequences of this neglect will be illustrated with a simple example.

In Figures 8.5 and 8.6, a regression model is presented with three observed variables ($y1$,$x1$,$x2$). The observed correlations between these

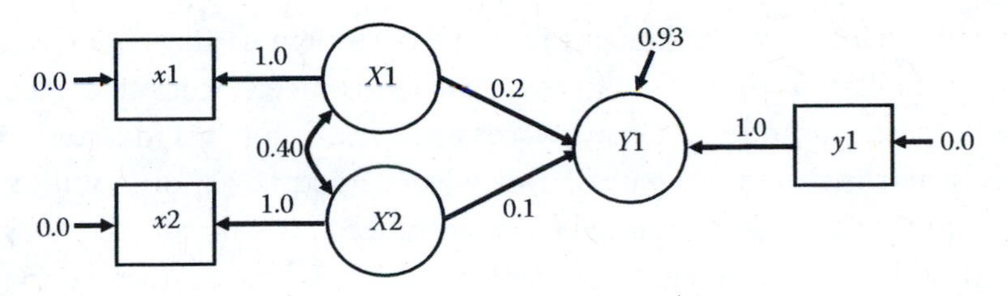

FIGURE 8.5
Regression estimates when *x*1 and *x*2 are assumed to be observed without measurement error.

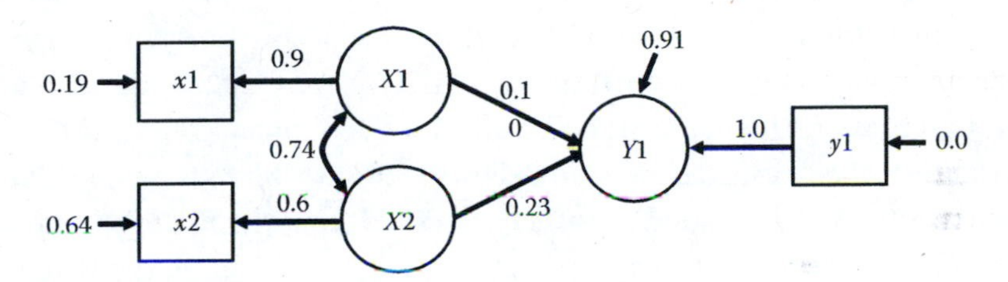

FIGURE 8.6
Regression estimates taking into account that *x*1 and *x*2 are observed with measurement error. Reliability of *x*1 is 0.81 and of *x*2 is 0.36 (i.e., the square of the factor loadings).

variables are: 0.24, 0.18, and 0.40. For the sake of simplicity we let *y*1 be observed without errors, but *x*1 and *x*2 both contain random measurement error. The regression estimates, ignoring the presence of measurement error, are presented in Figure 8.5. One can see that *x*1 is the most important predictor with a standardized effect of 0.20 on *y*1. However, due to the presence of measurement error things can change dramatically. Let the measure of *x*1 have a reliability of 0.81, and the measure of *x*2 a reliability of 0.36. The latter reliability is not particularly good, but it is also not uncommon to have indicators with a loading of 0.6, which actually is a reliability of 0.36. Figure 8.6 presents the same model as before, but now corrected for measurement error. It is immediately clear that the substantive conclusions are very different. It is now variable *x*2 that is the most important predictor with an effect of 0.23. Because we realize that something similar could occur in our analysis of GST, we did not dare draw substantive conclusions. Nevertheless, it was very tempting given that the results are in line with our expectations that *the same causal theories are at work across countries and that each theory has approximately the same importance across countries.*

In this chapter we concluded that the instrument to measure GST, as used in the ESS, is partial scalar invariant. This means that we can compare both means and relationships cross-nationally for this measure with other scalar invariant measures. This is very good news for studies that assumed that GST is comparable across the ESS. Reeskens and Hooghe (2008) arrived, however, at a different conclusion. That is, they seriously questioned the scalar invariance of this instrument. This is strange because their conclusion is based on the same data. The answer to why the conclusions are so different are related to our innovations. We correct for random (and systematic) measurement error in the indicators of the instrument, they don't. Hence, their metric and scalar invariance tests are concerned with different parameters. We evaluate our models through the detection of misspecifications, taking into account the power of the test, they evaluate their models with the RMSEA, the NNFI, and the MI. We have illustrated in Saris et al. (2009) that the RMSEA and the MI are sensitive to the power. When the power is very high, the RMSEA and the MI tend to over-reject models. We have seen in our analysis (unreported findings of this study) that the inclusion of a mean structure in the model increases the power of the test considerably, which can explain why Reeskens and Hooghe (2008) were forced to reject the scalar invariance of GST.

Finally, we should say something about the alternative test procedure because it is closely linked to our successful attempt to illustrate the partial scalar invariance of GST. Our procedure to evaluate structural equation models has two distinct features. First of all, the procedure takes the power of the test into account. Second, the procedure allows—in a sense—for nonexact testing (i.e., the test ignores, in principle, misspecifications that are smaller than delta). This way, a distinction can be made between relevant and irrelevant misspecifications. What relevant and irrelevant is, is not easy to define but by and large one could say that misspecifications that do not alter the substantive conclusions are irrelevant. As a rule of thumb 0.10 is considered a relevant misspecification for correlations and effects, and 0.40 for factor loadings (Saris et al., 2009). For the correlations between random error terms (e) we consider a misspecification of 0.10 as relevant, although, given the random nature of these errors we believe such misspecifications cannot be present. For correlations between unique components (u) we consider a misspecification of 0.15 as relevant. The reason that we allow for a larger misspecification in this case (compared to the rule of thumb-value 0.10) is that we correct for the presence of measurement error. If we correct a correlation of 0.10 for attenuation using the average the quality of single item measure, which is 0.8 (Saris & Gallhofer, 2007; Scherpenzeel, 1995b), we obtain a corrected correlation of 0.15 (= 0.10/0.8 × 0.8). We have used the same value (0.15) for regression effects from the predictors (x) on the item specific factors (s). For the metric and scalar invariance tests we test for the equality factor loadings and on intercepts. For such equality constraints there are no rules of thumb. In spite of a lack of rules, we have come up with a set of values for delta that we believe are relevant misspecifications. In order to determine what a relevant misspecification for the equality constraints on the factor loadings and intercepts is, we used the results from the study by De Beuckelaer and Swinnen (Chapter 5). They found that the probability of drawing an incorrect conclusion that two countries have different (or the same) latent means increases strongly under the following two conditions. First, if factor loadings deviate more than 30% from the population value, and second if intercepts deviate more than 10% of the length of the response scale from the population value. Because their analysis was on standardized variables, these percentages correspond to relevant misspecifications of 0.30 and 0.10. However, in order to be on the safe side, we decided to test for misspecifications that were only half the magnitude that would follow from the study by De Beuckelaer and Swinnen. Hence, we considered 0.15 (or larger) a relevant misspecification for factor loadings that are constrained to equality, and 0.07 (or larger) a misspecification for intercepts that are restricted to be the same. Please note that the values for relevant misspecifications (deltas) are standardized values, but normally, we analyze unstandardized variables. These standardized deltas will, however, be unstandardized in JRule using the scales and variances of the variables in the model.*

* We would like to thank Peter Schmidt, Fons van de Vijver, and William Burk for their valuable suggestions on how to improve this chapter.

REFERENCES

Adam, F. (2008). Mapping social capital across Europe: Findings, trends and methodological shortcomings of cross-national surveys. *Social Science Information, 47*(2), 159–186.

Andrews, F. M. (1984). Construct validity and error components of survey measures: A structural modeling approach. *Public Opinion Quarterly, 48*(2), 409–442.

Barrett, P. (2007). Structural equation modelling: Adjudging model fit. *Personality and Individual Differences, 42*(5), 815–824.

Batista-Foguet, J. M., & Coenders, G. (2000). Modelos de Ecuaciones Estructurales. Madrid, Spain: La Muralla.

Blalock, H. M., Jr. (1968). The measurement problem: A gap between languages of theory and research. In H. M. Blalock & A. B. Blalock (Eds.), *Methodology in the social sciences*. 5–27. London: Sage.

Browne, M. W., & Cudeck, R. (1993). Alternative ways of assessing model fit. In K. Bollen & J. S. Scott (Eds.), *Testing structural equation models* (pp. 136–162). London: Sage.

Byrne, B. M., Shavelson, R. J., & Muthén, B. (1989). Testing for the equivalence of factor covariance and mean structures: The issue of partial measurement invariance. *Psychological Bulletin, 105*(3), 456–466.

Byrne, B. M., & Stewart, S. M. (2006). The MACS approach to testing for multigroup invariance of a second-order structure: A walk through the process. *Structural Equation Modeling: A Multidisciplinary Journal, 13*(2), 287–321.

Corten, I. W., Saris, W. E., Coenders, G., Van der Veld, W. M., Aalberts, C. E., & Kornelis, C. (2002). Fit of different models for multitrait–multimethod experiments. *Structural Equation Modeling: A Multidisciplinary Journal, 9*(2), 213–232.

Delhey, J., & Newton, K. (2003). Who trusts? The causes of social trust in seven societies. *European Societies, 5*(2), 93–137.

Delhey, J., & Newton, K. (2005). Predicting cross-national levels of social trust: Global pattern or nordic exceptionalism? *European Sociological Review, 21*(4), 311–327.

Enders, C. K., & Bandalos, D. L. (2001). The relative performance of full information maximum likelihood estimation for missing data in structural equation models. *Structural Equation Modeling: A Multidisciplinary Journal, 8*(3), 430–457.

Erikson, E. H. (1950). *Childhood and society*. New York, NY: Norton.

Fukuyama, F. (1995). *Trust: The social virtues and the creation of prosperity*. New York, NY: The Free Press.

Ganzeboom, H. B. G. (2009). Multiple indicator measurement of social background. *Keynote presented at the 3rd conference of the European Survey Research Association*, Warsaw, Poland.

Gesthuizen, M., Scheepers, P., Van der Veld, W. M., & Völker, B. (in press). Structural aspects of social capital: Tests for cross-national equivalence in Europe. *Quality and Quantity*.

Heise, D. R., & Bohrnstedt, G. W. (1970). Validity, invalidity, and reliability. *Sociological Methodology, 2*, 104–129.

Herreros, F., & Criado, H. (2008). The state and the development of social trust. *International Political Science Review, 29*(1), 53–71.

Hu, L.-T., & Bentler, P. M. (1999). Cutoff criteria for fit indexes in covariance structure analysis: Conventional criteria versus new alternatives. *Structural Equation Modeling: A Multidisciplinary Journal, 6*(1), 1–55.

Inglehart, R. (1999). Trust, well-being, and democracy. In M. E. Warren (Ed.), *Democracy and trust* (pp. 88–121). Cambridge: Cambridge University Press.

Johnson, E. C., Meade, A. W., & DuVernet, A. M. (2009). The role of referent indicators in tests of measurement invariance. *Structural Equation Modeling: A Multidisciplinary Journal, 16*(4), 642–657.

Jöreskog, K. G., & Sörbom, D. (1996). *LISREL® 8 user's reference guide*. Chicago, IL: Scientific Software International.

Kaasa, A., & Parts, E. (2008). Individual-level determinants of social capital in Europe. Differences between country groups. *Acta Sociologica, 51*(2), 145–168.

Kaase, M. (1999). Interpersonal trust, political trust and non-institutionalised political participation in Western Europe. *West European Politics, 22*(3), 1–21.

Kaplan, D. (1989). Model modification in covariance structure analysis: Application of the expected parameter change statistic. *Multivariate Behavioral Research, 24*(3), 285–305.

Knack, S., & Keefer, P. (1997). Does social capital have an economic payoff? A cross-country investigation. *The Quarterly Journal of Economics, 112*(4), 1251–1288.

Kumata, H., & Schramm, W. (1956). A pilot study of cross-cultural meaning. *Public Opinion Quarterly, 20*(1), 229–238.

Letki, N., & Evans, G. (2008). Endogenizing social trust: Democratization in East-Central Europe. *British Journal of Political Science, 35*, 515–529.

Levi, M. (1996). Social and unsocial capital: A review essay of Robert Putnam's making democracy work. *Politics and Society, 24*(1), 45–55.

MacCallum, R. C., Browne, M. W., & Sugawara, H. M. (1996). Power analysis and determination of sample size for covariance structure modeling. *Psychological Methods, 1*(2), 130–149.

Marsh, H. W., Hau, K.-T., & Wen, Z. (2004). In search of golden rules: Comment on hypothesis-testing approaches to setting cutoff values for fit indexes and dangers in overgeneralizing Hu and Bentler's (1999) findings. *Structural Equation Modeling: A Multidisciplinary Journal, 11*(3), 320–341.

Meredith, W. (1993). Measurement invariance, factor analysis, and factorial invariance. *Psychometrika, 58*(4), 525–543.

Millsap, R. E., & Meredith, W. (2007). Factorial invariance: Historical perspectives and new problems. In R. Cudeck & R. C. MacCallum (Eds.), *Factor analysis at 100: Historical developments and future directions* (pp. 130–152). Mahwah, NJ: Lawrence Erlbaum.

Muthén, L. K., & Muthén, B. O. (1998–2007). *Mplus user's guide.* 5th ed.). Los Angeles, CA: Author.

Newton, K. (1997). Social capital and democracy. *American Behavioral Scientist, 40*(5), 575–586.

Newton, K. (2004). Social trust: Individual and cross-national approaches. *Portuguese Journal of Social Science, 3*(1), 15–35.

Norris, P. (2002). Making democracies work: Social capital and civic engagement in 47 societies. Paper presented at the *Midwest Political Science Association 60th annual meeting,* Chicago, IL.

Northrop, F. S.C. (1969). *The logic of the sciences and the humanities.* Cleveland, OH: World Publishing Company.

Paxton, P. (2002). Social capital and democracy: An interdependent relationship. *American Sociological Review, 67*(2), 254–277.

Putnam, R. D. (1993). *Making democracy work: Civic traditions in modern Italy*. Princeton, NJ: Princeton University Press.

Putnam, R. D. (2000). *Bowling alone: The collapse and revival of American community*. New York, NY: Simon & Schuster.

Reeskens, T., & Hooghe, M. (2008). Cross-cultural measurement equivalence of generalized trust. Evidence from the European Social Survey (2002 and 2004). *Social Indicators Research, 85*(3), 515–532.

Rensvold, R. B., & Cheung, G. W. (2001). Testing for metric invariance using structural equation models. Solving the standardization problem. In C. A. Schriesheim & L. L. Neider (Eds.), *Equivalence in measurement* (pp. 25–50). Greenwich, CT: Information Age Publishing.

Rothstein, B., & Uslaner, E. M. (2005). All for all: Equality and social trust. *LSE Health and Social Care Discussion Paper No. 15*. SSRN: http://ssrn.com/abstract = 824506

Saris, W. E. (2009). Some important considerations while testing for misspecifications in SEM. *Study presented at the 3rd conference of the European Survey Research Association*, Warsaw, Poland.

Saris, W. E., & Andrews, F. M. (1991). Evaluation of measurement instruments using a structural modeling approach. In P. P. Biemer, R. M. Groves, L. E. Lyberg, N. A. Mathiowetz, & S. Sudman (Eds.), *Measurement errors in surveys* (pp. 575–599). New York, NY: John Wiley.

Saris, W. E., & Gallhofer, I. N. (2003). *Report on the MTMM experiments in the pilot studies and proposals for round 1 of the ESS*. London: Central Coordinating Team of the European Social Survey.

Saris, W. E., & Gallhofer, I. N. (2007). *Design, evaluation and analysis of questionnaires for survey research*. Hoboken, NJ: John Wiley.

Saris, W. E., Revilla, M., Krosnick, J. A., & Shaeffer, E. M. (2010). Comparing questions with agree/disagree response options to questions with item-specific response options. *Survey Research Methods, 4(1)*, 61–79.

Saris, W. E., Satorra, A., & Coenders, G. (2004). A new approach to evaluating the quality of measurement instruments: The split-ballot MTMM design. *Sociological Methodology, 34*, 311–347.

Saris, W. E., Satorra, A., & Sörbom, D. (1987). The detection and correction of specifications errors in structural equation models. *Sociological Methodology, 17*, 105–129.

Saris, W. E., Satorra, A., & Van der Veld, W. M. (2009). Testing structural equation models or detection of misspecifications? *Structural Equation Modeling: A Multidisciplinary Journal, 16*(4), 561–582.

Saris W. E., Van der Veld, W. M., & Gallhofer, I. N. (2004). Development and improvement of questionnaires using predictions of reliability and validity. In S. Presser, J. M. Rothgeb, M. P. Couper, J. T. Lessler, E. Martin, J. Martin, & E. Singer (Eds.), *Methods for testing and evaluating survey questionnaires* (pp. 275–298). New York, NY: John Wiley.

Satorra, A., & Bentler, P. M. (1994). Corrections to test statistics and standard errors in covariance structure analysis. In A. Von Eye & C. Clogg (Eds.), *Latent variables analysis: Applications for developmental research* (pp. 399–419). Thousand Oaks, CA: Sage.

Scherpenzeel, A. C. (1995a). *A question of quality. Evaluating survey questions by multitrait-multimethod studies*. Dissertation. Koninklijke PTT Nederland NV, KPN Research.

Scherpenzeel, A. C. (1995b). Life satisfaction in The Netherlands. In W. E. Saris, R. Veenhoven, A. C. Scherpenzeel, & B. Bunting (Eds.), *A comparative study of satisfaction with life in Europe*. Budapest, Hungary: Eötvös University Press.

Scherpenzeel, A. C., & Saris, W. E. (1997). The validity and reliability of survey questions: A meta-analysis of MTMM studies. *Sociological Methods and Research, 25*(3), 341–383.

Steenkamp, J.-B. E. M., & Baumgartner, H. (1998). Assessing measurement equivalence in cross-national consumer research. *Journal of Consumer Research, 25*(1), 78–90.

Steyer, R., & Schmitt, M. J. (1990). Latent state-trait models in attitude research. *Quality and Quantity, 24*(4), 427–445.

Torcal, M., & Montero, J. R. (1999). Facets of social capital in new democracies. In J. Van Deth, M. Maraffi, K. Newton, & P. Whiteley (Eds.), *Social capital and European democracy* (pp. 167–191). London: Routledge.

Uslaner, E. M. (1999). Democracy and social capital. In M. Warren (Ed.), *Democracy and trust* (pp. 121–150). Cambridge: Cambridge University Press.

Uslaner, E. M. (2000). Producing and consuming trust. *Political Science Quarterly, 115*(4), 569–590.

Van der Veld, W. M. (2006). *The survey response dissected. A new theory about the survey response process*. Dissertation, University of Amsterdam: Amsterdam School for Communications Research (ASCoR).

Van der Veld, W. M., & Saris, W. E. (2004). Separation of reliability, validity, stability, and opinion crystallization. In W. E. Saris & P. M. Sniderman (Eds.), *Studies in public opinion: Attitudes, nonattitudes, measurement error, and change*. Princeton, NJ: Princeton University Press.

Van der Veld, W. M., Saris, W. E., & Satorra, A. (2008). *JRule 3.0: User's guide*. Retrieved from http://www.vanderveld.nl

Van Deth, J. W. (2001). The proof of the pudding: Social capital, democracy, and citizenship. *Paper prepared for delivery at the EURESCO conference on Social Capital: Interdisciplinary Perspectives*. Exeter, UK.

Yoon, M., & Millsap, R. E. (2007). Detecting violations of factorial invariance using data-based specification searches: A Monte Carlo study. *Structural Equation Modeling: A Multidisciplinary Journal, 14*(3), 435–463.

Zmerli, S., & Newton, K. (2008). Social trust and attitudes toward democracy. *Public Opinion Quarterly, 72*(4), 706–724.

9

Measurement Equivalence of the Dispositional Resistance to Change Scale

Shaul Oreg, University of Haifa; *Mahmut Bayazıt,* Sabanci University; *Maria Vakola,* Athens University of Economics and Business; *Luis Arciniega,* ITAM (Instituto Tecnologico Autonomo De Mexico); *Achilles Armenakis,* Auburn University; *Rasa Barkauskiene,* Vilnius University; *Nikos Bozionelos,* University of Durham; *Yuka Fujimoto,* Deakin University; *Luis González,* University of Salamana; *Jian Han,* China Europe International Business School and Peking University; *Martina Hřebíčková,* Academy of Science of the Czech Republic; *Nerina Jimmieson,* University of Queensland; *Jana Kordačová,* Slovak Academy of Sciences; *Hitoshi Mitsuhashi,* University of Tsukuba; *Boris Mlačić,* Institute of Social Sciences Ivo Pilar in Zagreb; *Ivana Ferić,* Institute of Social Sciences Ivo Pilar in Zagreb; *Marina Kotrla Topić,* Institute of Social Sciences Ivo Pilar in Zagreb; *Sandra Ohly,* Johann Wolfgang Goethe-Universität Frankfurt; *Per Øystein Saksvik,* Norwegian University of Science and Technology; *Hilde Hetland,* University of Bergen; *Ingvild Berg Saksvik,* University of Bergen; *and Karen van Dam,* Tilburg University

9.1 INTRODUCTION

Individuals differ in their typical responses to change situations. Whereas some people readily accept them, others tend to resist. These differences in the typical reaction to change have been conceptualized as a personality trait, namely, dispositional resistance to change (Oreg, 2003). The resistance to change trait and its measurement scale (henceforth the RTC scale) were established through a series of studies in which the scale's structural, construct, concurrent, and predictive validities were demonstrated. The more dispositionally resistant to change an individual is, the more likely will he or she exhibit negative attitudes toward specific changes, and the less likely to voluntarily initiate changes (e.g., Nov & Ye, 2008; Oreg, 2006; Oreg, Nevo, Metzer, Leder, & Castro, 2009). The trait is related to, yet both conceptually and empirically distinct from other traits (see Oreg, 2003), such as sensation seeking (Zuckerman, 1994), intolerance for ambiguity (Budner, 1962), risk aversion (Slovic, 1972), dogmatism (Rokeach, 1960), and openness to experience (Digman, 1990).

The trait comprises four dimensions: *Routine seeking* involves the extent to which one enjoys and seeks out stable and routine environments; *emotional reaction* reflects the extent to which individuals feel stressed and uncomfortable in response to imposed change; *short-term focus* also derives from affective sources and involves the degree to which individuals are preoccupied with the short-term inconveniences versus the potential long-term benefits of the change; finally, *cognitive rigidity* represents a form of stubbornness and an unwillingness to consider alternative ideas and perspectives. While different dimensions become salient in different contexts, the composite RTC score has been shown to predict individuals' reactions to change in a variety of contexts under both voluntary and imposed conditions (Nov & Ye, 2008; Oreg, 2003, Studies 5–7, 2006).

Most of the data with which the scale has been validated were collected in the United States and Israel. This raised concern about the generalizability of the trait and its measurement scale to other cultural settings. Before a construct is applied to new contexts that vary from that within which it has been validated, one must first verify that the construct maintains its meaning and dimensionality. The dispositional resistance to change construct has been recently validated with samples from 17 countries, using multigroup confirmatory factor analysis (MGCFA; Oreg et al., 2008). However, as we describe below, MGCFA relies on certain assumptions that are not always met, and that are not required by other techniques, such as multidimensional scaling (Borg & Groenen, 2005). Furthermore, multidimensional scaling provides another means of testing construct dimensionality that complements the results of MGCFA. Therefore, in the present chapter we supplement the MGCFA analysis with a multidimensional scaling technique and compare results of the two methods.

9.1.1 Scale Validation Across Cultures

Individuals within a given culture share certain aspects of their cognitive, affective, and behavioral orientations, which vary across cultures (e.g., Hofstede, 1980). Accordingly, constructs with a given meaning in one culture, even if appropriately translated linguistically, may undertake quite a different meaning in a different culture. Therefore, before researchers and practitioners from one culture adopt a construct that has been conceptualized in another culture, they must first verify that the construct and its measurement scale are indeed equivalent across the two cultures (e.g., Cheung, Leung, & Au, 2006; Church & Lonner, 1998; Ghorpade, Hattrup, & Lackritz, 1999; Liu, Borg, & Spector, 2004). From a methodological perspective, what should be sought is evidence for the scale's *measurement equivalence* (e.g., Liu et al., 2004; Vandenberg & Lance, 2000). Measurement equivalence not only indicates that an instrument takes on the necessary psychometric characteristics across cultures, but more importantly it provides evidence that the instrument taps the same psychological meanings (Ghorpade et al., 1999).

To date, the most common means of establishing such measurement equivalence is through the use of a MGCFA (Jöreskog, 1971), which tests the homogeneity of correlation matrices across samples (Cheung et al., 2006). While a variety of methods for testing measurement equivalence (also known as measurement *invariance*) have been proposed, there is general agreement that MGCFA constitutes "the most powerful and versatile approach to testing for cross-national measurement invariance" (Steenkamp & Baumgartner, 1998, p. 78). Nevertheless, like any analytic technique, MGCFA has its limitations, among which is that it is based on assumptions of multivariate normality of the items and a linear relationship between items and factors (Bauer, 2005; Cohen, 2008). Such requirements, however, are often not met. Because normality and linearity are typically assumed, and not tested, it is difficult to estimate the prevalence and severity of nonnormality and nonlinearity. Nevertheless, tests related to the linearity assumption suggest that even apparently mild cases of nonlinearity (i.e., small quadratic effects) can substantially restrict the validity of standard measurement equivalence tests (Bauer, 2005).

Thus, in the present chapter we supplement the MGCFA with a multidimensional scaling technique, which is a less demanding and more parsimonious nonmetric alternative (Cohen, 2008). Specifically, we use a smallest space analysis (SSA; Guttman, 1968; Shye, Elizur, & Hoffman, 1994). Like in all multidimensional scaling techniques, SSA items are mapped onto a geometric space (e.g., a two-dimensional plane), whereby the distance between item representations on this space represents the conceptual similarity between items (Borg & Groenen, 2005; Shye et al., 1994). The typical index used for representing item similarity is the interitem correlation coefficient. When considering the pattern of correlations between an item and all other items, the stronger the correlation between scale items, the closer will their geometric representation be. The graphical representation offered by SSA provides a vivid demonstration of the relationships among items, which is often more readily and intuitively interpretable than the results of MGCFAs.

Although its primary use is for examining relationships among construct dimensions, SSA can also be used for assessing the number of dimensions (called *elements* in SSA terminology; Shye et al., 1994) that exist within a construct. The geometric representation of scale items provides information on scale structure. When a theory already exists about the scale's structure, confirmatory SSA can be used to test one's theory (Shye et al., 1994). Assuming items designed to tap the same conceptual dimension—within the overarching construct measured—are perceived as more similar to one another than items measuring different dimensions, scale dimensionality will appear in the form of distinct clusters of item representations (i.e., dots) on the geometric space. With any given data set, the degree to which scale item clusterings correspond with the conceptual dimensionality of the construct measured represents the degree to which the scale's structure is confirmed. The order and pattern of clusters within the overall geometric space provides additional information on the interrelationships between construct dimensions. Confirmatory SSA provides measures, such as the Separation Index, which serve as fit indexes and represent the degree to which SSA item mappings conform with one's apriori model. A comparison of confirmatory SSA results across multiple samples can be used to test the equivalence of the scale's structure across samples.

Contrary to MGCFA, however, SSA does not directly test the degree to which the observed variables correspond with their underlying latent constructs. Furthermore, SSA does not test the cross-sample equivalence of the relationships among observed variables. Rather, it allows one to infer about the existence of latent constructs, and their comparability across samples, from the graphically presented patterns of relationships among observed variables in each sample. MGCFA and SSA thus offer complementary approaches to establishing and validating the structure of a construct across samples.

In this chapter, MGCFA and confirmatory SSA will be used on the same data, as complementary tests of the RTC scale structure. Only very few studies have used both confirmatory factor analytic and multidimensional scaling techniques to test construct dimensionality (see examples in Boehnke, Schwartz, Stromberg, & Sagiv, 1998; Davison, 1981; Silverstein, 1987), and to the best of our knowledge the present study is the first to apply both MGCFA and confirmatory SSA for testing the measurement equivalence of a scale. We begin by reviewing our data and findings from the confirmatory factor analyses conducted in Oreg et al. (2008). We will then continue by describing the SSAs, and will conclude, in the Discussion section, by integrating the insights obtained from both analyses.

9.2 METHOD

9.2.1 Participants

To ensure sample comparability (Steenkamp & Baumgartner, 1998), we used samples of undergraduates, thus matching samples on level of education and age. A total of 4201 undergraduate students from 17 countries participated in the study for course credit or as part of the course requirements. Table 9.1 provides descriptive statistics of the samples' characteristics.

The countries sampled for the present study, listed in alphabetical order, are Australia, China, Croatia, the Czech Republic, Germany, Greece, Israel, Japan, Lithuania, Mexico, the Netherlands, Norway, Slovakia, Spain, Turkey, the United Kingdom, and the United States. The

TABLE 9.1

Descriptive Statistics on Samples' Demographics

Country	Town	*N*	Language	Religion (Majority)	% Female	Mean Age (SD in Parentheses)
Australia	Burwood and St Lucia	251	English	30% atheist	67	21.09 (3.61)
China	Beijing	194	Chinese	—[a]	56	20.72 (1.09)
Croatia	Zagreb	246	Croatian	81% Roman Catholic	83	21.43 (1.79)
Czech Republic	Brno	224	Czech	50% Roman Catholic	78	22.49 (2.10)
Germany	Braunschweig	206	German	51% Protestant	49	23.03 (4.35)
Greece	Athens	386	Greek	87% Greek Orthodox	60	20.97 (2.31)
Israel	Haifa	241	Hebrew	83% Jewish	82	24.35 (3.21)
Japan	Tsukuba	337	Japanese	—	23	19.71 (1.62)
Lithuania	Vilnius	212	Lithuanian	96% Catholic	77	20.31 (1.67)
Mexico	Mexico City	265	Spanish	82% Catholic	51	20.62 (2.19)
Netherlands	Tilburg	205	Dutch	—	80	20.22 (3.45)
Norway	Bergen	266	Norwegian	67% Christian	74	23.24 (4.40)

Slovakia	Bratislava	171	Slovakian	50% Catholic	54	21.40 (1.10)
Spain	Salamanca	288	Spanish	—	59	21.90 (1.55)
Turkey	Istanbul	241	Turkish	98% Muslim	39	21.04 (1.52)
United Kingdom	Durham	204	English	95% Christian	45	19.22 (1.83)
United States	Auburn, AL	264	English	49% Christian	50	21.19 (2.38)
Total		4201			60.41	21.35 (2.37)

Source: Oreg, S., Bayazit, M., Vakola, M., Arciniega, L., Armenakis, A. A., Barkauskiene, R., . . . van Dam, K., *Journal of Applied Psychology*, 93(4), 935–944, 2008.

[a] In some countries it was deemed inappropriate to collect data on respondents' religion in the context of this study. This information is therefore missing for these countries.

mean sample size was 241 ranging from 171 to 386. With the exception of China and Slovakia, for which sample sizes were 194 and 171, respectively, all samples included more than 200 respondents, thus increasing the likelihood of obtaining stable results in the confirmatory factor analytic procedures (Kline, 1998).

9.2.2 Measures and Procedure

The RTC scale was translated to the native language of each participating country through a translation-back-translation process (e.g., Schaffer & Riordan, 2003). The translation was conducted by two individuals, fluent in both English and the country's native language. Differences between the original and back-translated versions were discussed by the two translators until agreement was reached concerning the most appropriate translation.

Participants filled out the RTC scale and answered questions about their demographics. The RTC scale consists of 17 statements concerning one's typical orientation toward, and reaction to, change (see first column of Table 9.2). Response options range from 1 ("Strongly disagree") to 6 ("Strongly agree"). The reliability (Chronbach's alpha) of the scale in each country is presented in the third column of Table 9.3.

9.2.3 Analyses

MGCFA. The MGCFA procedure was conducted using the AMOS software (version 7.0; Arbuckle, 2006). Tests of measurement equivalence in cross-cultural research typically follow a three-step series of tests, involving nested constraints that are placed on parameters across samples (e.g., Grouzet et al., 2005; Meredith, 1993; Steenkamp & Baumgartner, 1998). As we elaborate below, these are called tests of *configural*, *metric*, and *scalar* invariance. Configural and metric invariance are conducted to establish that a construct holds the same psychological meaning across samples. Following the establishment of configural and metric invariance, scalar invariance is required when one wishes to compare sample score means. In practice, such comparisons are frequently conducted in the process of scale validation. However, in computing the score mean of individuals from a given culture, one is in essence aggregating from an individual-level construct to the culture level, and while the meaning of the individual-level construct

TABLE 9.2

RTC Items and Mean CFA Factor-Loading across the 17 Samples

Item	Factor	Mean Standardized Loading	Loading SD
1. I generally consider changes to be a negative thing.	Routine seeking	0.54	0.14
2. I'll take a routine day over a day full of unexpected events any time.		0.64	0.10
3. I like to do the same old things rather than try new and different ones.		0.70	0.08
4. Whenever my life forms a stable routine, I look for ways to change it.[a]		0.44	0.11
5. I'd rather be bored than surprised.		0.50	0.09
6. If I were to be informed that there's going to be a significant change regarding the way things are done at school, I would probably feel stressed.[b]	Emotional reaction	0.64	0.08
7. When I am informed of a change of plans, I tense up a bit.		0.72	0.08
8. When things don't go according to plans, it stresses me out.		0.64	0.08
9. If one of my professors changed the grading criteria, it would probably make me feel uncomfortable even if I thought I'd do just as well without having to do any extra work.[b]		0.54	0.10
10. Changing plans seems like a real hassle to me.	Short-term focus	0.62	0.11
11. Often, I feel a bit uncomfortable even about changes that may potentially improve my life.		0.72	0.09
12. When someone pressures me to change something, I tend to resist it even if I think the change may ultimately benefit me.		0.49	0.10
13. I sometimes find myself avoiding changes that I know will be good for me.		0.50	0.09

(*Continued*)

TABLE 9.2 (Continued)

RTC Items and Mean CFA Factor-Loading across the 17 Samples

Item	Factor	Mean Standardized Loading	Loading SD
14. I often change my mind.[a]	Cognitive rigidity	0.48	0.17
15. I don't change my mind easily.		0.63	0.11
16. Once I've come to a conclusion, I'm not likely to change my mind.		0.68	0.08
17. My views are very consistent over time.		0.64	0.13

Source: Oreg, S., Bayazit, M., Vakola, M., Arciniega, L., Armenakis, A. A., Barkauskiene, R., . . . van Dam, K., *Journal of Applied Psychology*, 93(4), 935–944, 2008. © 2008 by the American Psychological Association. Reproduced with permission.

[a] These items are reverse-coded.

[b] When used in a job setting, these items are rephrased to fit the organization al context.

being validated is typically well established, this is often not the case for the aggregate-level construct. To be interpretable, comparisons of sample score means require that the aggregate level construct be first conceptually established and empirically validated. In the case of dispositional resistance to change, one should first be clear on what resistance to change means at the country level, before comparing country-level resistance to change scores. For this, separate theoretical and empirical work, aimed at establishing the country-level resistance to change concept, should first be conducted. Because our focus in the present study was on establishing the measurement equivalence of the individual-level construct, we restrict our analyses to the first two tests: configural and metric invariance.

Configural invariance constitutes the most basic test of measurement equivalence and involves an examination of the configuration of relationships between items and latent variables across samples. Each of the scale items is required to show the same pattern of zero and nonzero loadings on the latent factors in each of the samples. In our case, this step would involve a test of the extent to which the same four-factor RTC structure is supported in all samples.

Replicating a construct's structure by demonstrating configural invariance, however, provides only preliminary evidence that the construct shares its meaning across samples. A much stronger case is made if item

TABLE 9.3

Coefficient Alphas, Descriptive Statistics and Fit Indexes for the 17 Samples

Country	N	RTC α Chronbach	RTC Mean	RTC SD	$\chi^2_{(107)}$	RMSEA[a]	CFI[b]	GFI[c]
Australia	251	0.82	3.09	0.57	172.56	0.050	0.93	0.93
China	194	0.85	3.14	0.62	170.07	0.055	0.94	0.91
Croatia	246	0.84	3.01	0.61	159.88	0.045	0.97	0.93
Czech Republic	224	0.84	3.13	0.56	184.24	0.057	0.92	0.91
Germany	206	0.77	3.12	0.48	131.36	0.033	0.97	0.93
Greece	386	0.72	3.03	0.50	227.29	0.054	0.93	0.94
Israel	241	0.85	3.15	0.59	193.42	0.058	0.93	0.92
Japan	337	0.75	3.22	0.52	199.46	0.051	0.91	0.93
Lithuania	212	0.77	2.86	0.51	171.39	0.053	0.92	0.91
Mexico	265	0.79	2.79	0.58	216.74	0.062	0.92	0.90
Netherlands	205	0.85	3.17	0.52	177.59	0.058	0.94	0.91
Norway	266	0.84	2.91	0.56	218.21	0.063	0.92	0.91
Slovakia	171	0.79	3.27	0.51	184.28	0.065	0.90	0.89
Spain	288	0.81	3.01	0.58	165.97	0.044	0.95	0.94
Turkey	241	0.77	3.03	0.54	188.86	0.056	0.90	0.91
United Kingdom	204	0.78	3.02	0.51	190.22	0.062	0.90	0.90
United States	264	0.83	3.05	0.54	160.90	0.044	0.95	0.94
Mean	247.12	0.80	3.06	0.55	183.08	0.050	0.93	0.92

Source: Oreg, S., Bayazit, M., Vakola, M., Arciniega, L., Armenakis, A. A., Barkauskiene, R., . . . van Dam, K., *Journal of Applied Psychology*, 93(4), 935–944, 2008. © 2008 by the American Psychological Association. Reproduced with permission.

[a] Root-Mean-Square Error of Approximation.
[b] Comparative Fit Index.
[c] Goodness-of-Fit Index.

loadings are of the same magnitude across samples (Meredith, 1993; Vandenberg & Lance, 2000). This indicates that members of the different samples calibrate the measure, and thus interpret the construct, in the same way. This form of invariance is called *metric invariance* and involves a model identical to that tested for configural invariance with the added constraint of having the same factor loadings across samples.

In line with Coovert and Craiger's (2000) recommendations, we included the two indexes considered most important for determining model fit: the root mean square error of approximation (RMSEA) and the comparative fit index (CFI). We also looked at the goodness-of-fit index (GFI), which is commonly considered in CFAs. The CFI and GFI values range from 0 to 1.00, where values greater than 0.95 indicate good fit (Hu & Bentler, 1999) and values greater than 0.90 are considered satisfactory (Hoyle, 1995). For RMSEA values of 0.05 or less indicates a close fit, and values of up to 0.08 represent reasonable errors of approximation (Browne & Cudeck, 1993).

As evidence for metric invariance, beyond having a satisfactory fit, the fit of the *metric* model should not be significantly poorer than that of the *configural* model. Although traditionally only the chi-square difference test has been used, it is well acknowledged that a statistically significant chi-square is often obtained even when there are only minor differences between groups' factor patterns (Vandenberg & Lance, 2000). Thus, as in the case of establishing model fit, differences between models should be established through the use of fit indices beyond the chi-square (Bollen, 1989; Vandenberg & Lance, 2000). In particular, use of the differences between indexes such as the RMSEAs and CFIs of both models has been recommended (Cheung & Rensvold, 2002). For the ΔCFI, an absolute value of 0.01 or smaller indicates that the invariance hypothesis should not be rejected. Values over 0.02 indicate a lack of invariance, and values between 0.01 and 0.02 suggest that some differences may exist between models (Cheung & Rensvold, 2002). No critical values have been indicated in the literature for the RMSEA.

However, it should be noted that full measurement invariance is quite rare, with some researchers arguing that it is particularly unlikely when testing forms of invariance beyond configural invariance (Horn, 1991; Steenkamp & Baumgartner, 1998). Therefore, for many constructs, and in particular when testing invariance across a large variety of samples, it may be that only *partial measurement invariance* exists (Byrne, Shavelson, & Muthén, 1989; Steenkamp & Baumgartner, 1998). A test of partial metric invariance would require relaxing some of the item loading constraints. While all of the items would still be required to load on the same factors in each of the samples, the requirement that the loadings be of the same magnitude across samples may be dropped for some. The choice of constraints to be relaxed, however, should be based on substantive criteria rather than on sample-specific empirical data.

9.2.4 Confirmatory Smallest Space Analysis

We conducted the confirmatory SSA using Shye's (1997) Faceted SSA computer program. As noted above, SSA translates item similarity indexes (e.g., correlation coefficients) into an m-dimensional geometric space. The specific location of a data point on the geometric space is arbitrary and what matters is only a point's position relative to the other points. The most frequently used, and most easily interpretable, translation is into a two-dimensional plane. The starting point for the analysis is the conversion of the item correlation matrix into linear distances, such that larger correlations are represented by shorter distances. This is done after first reversing the scoring of any negatively worded items. The correlation coefficient used is the regression-free monotonicity coefficient (Guttman, 1968). The degree of fit between the correlation matrix and the spatial representation established is indicated by the *alienation coefficient*, which is a type of *stress* index, used in multidimensional scaling techniques. The alienation coefficient takes on values between 0 and 1, with 0 representing perfect fit. The degree of fit indicated by a given alienation coefficient depends on the number of scale items, with greater leniency applied for scales with a greater number of items. Overall, small alienation coefficients indicate that the data can be faithfully represented in the m-dimensional space chosen. Although Guttman's (1968) original rule of thumb for evaluating fit indicated a coefficient equal to or smaller than 0.15, satisfactory fit has been said to exist with values up to 0.20 (Borg & Lingoes, 1987) or even 0.25 (Ben-Shalom & Horenczyk, 2003).

The alienation coefficient, however, does not provide information on the degree to which the spatial representation fits with the hypothesized dimensionality of the construct. Such information is provided in confirmatory SSA through the *separation index* (Shye et al., 1994). The separation index indicates the degree to which items are spatially represented in regions in accordance with theoretical predictions. Items of the same subscale are expected to be represented within the same region, and items from different subscales are expected to be represented in distinct regions. The separation index represents the average deviation of items from their expected region (Borg & Shye, 1995). It is calculated using the equation: $SI = 1 - (L/N)$ where L is the sum of the deviations and N is a normalizing function computed on the basis of a random distribution of points in space (Borg & Shye, 1995). The separation index therefore ranges from 0 to 1, with 1 indicating that all items fall within their expected region. Acceptable separation index values have not been previously designated. In the present analysis we will consider values of 0.90 or above to indicate satisfactory fit.

9.3 RESULTS

As can be seen in column three of Table 9.3, all reliability coefficients alpha achieved a satisfactory level of 0.70 or above. The mean alpha was 0.80, with coefficients ranging from 0.72 to 0.85. As a first step in establishing measurement equivalence, a separate CFA was run for each sample. The expected structure in our model was of a four-factor solution, with intercorrelations among factors (see Figure 9.1; additional structures, including one with a higher-order RTC latent variable, were tested in Oreg et al., 2008). In each of the 17 CFAs, all of the items significantly loaded ($p < .05$) on their expected factor (see Table 9.2). Furthermore, as can be seen in Table 9.3, the four-factor RTC scale presented at least satisfactory fit across all countries, with the exception of Slovakia, in which the GFI was just below 0.90. The RMSEAs ranged from 0.033 to 0.065, CFIs ranged from 0.90 to 0.97, and GFIs ranged from 0.89 to 0.94. The mean RMSEA, CFI, and GFI values across the 17 samples, were 0.050, 0.93, and 0.92, respectively.

In line with Oreg's (2003) findings, there were significant correlations among RTC subscales (Table 9.4), with the highest correlation being between emotional reaction and short-term focus, and the lowest were those involving cognitive rigidity. The high correlation between emotional reaction and short-term focus has been previously explained on the basis that both dimensions are affective in nature. Following Oreg (2003), we compared the four-factor model with a three-factor model, whereby items of emotional reaction and short-term focus were all set to load on a single affective factor. The three-factor model presented poorer fit on all three fit indexes in all samples with the exception of Lithuania in which the two models presented virtually equal fit. With this exception of Lithuania, the chi-squared tests comparing the three-and four-factor models in each of the samples indicated that the fit of the four-factor model was significantly ($p < .01$) better.*

9.3.1 MGCFA

After testing model fit in each country separately, we proceeded with the four-factor model to test the configural and metric invariance of the

* Additional analyses were conducted, comparing the interrelated four-factor model to a model with a higher-order, overarching, latent variable. Results of these additional analyses are reported in Oreg et al. (2008).

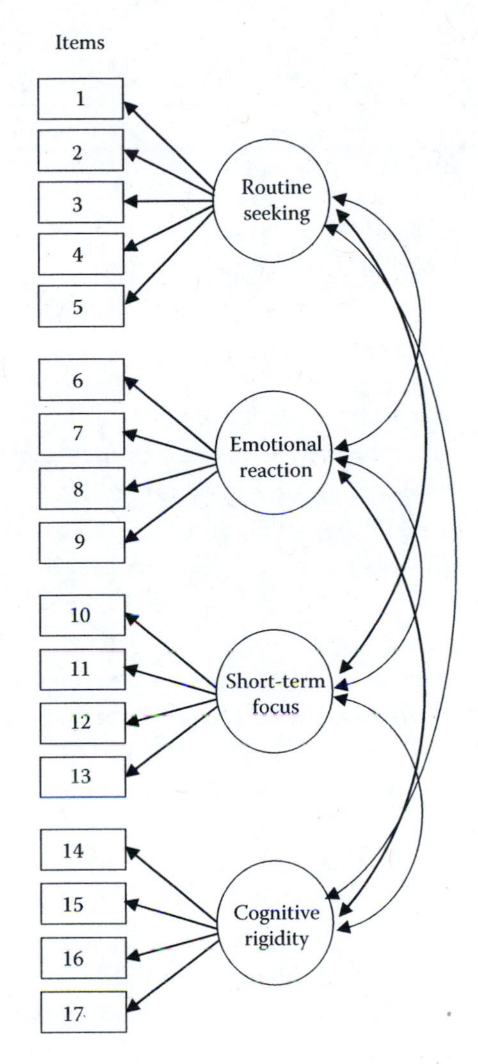

FIGURE 9.1
RTC's four-factor model with intercorrelated factors.

scale across the 17 samples. In the configural invariance model all items yielded a significant loading on their corresponding factor in all 17 countries. Furthermore, the model presented a satisfactory fit (RMSEA = 0.013, CFI = 0.928, GFI = 0.919), indicating that the pattern of item loadings is consistent across samples. Similar results were obtained for the metric invariance model. All items loaded on their corresponding factors and model fit was satisfactory (RMSEA = 0.014, CFI = 0.915, GFI = 0.909), suggesting that the magnitude of item loadings was consistent across samples.

TABLE 9.4

Mean Correlations among RTC Subscales across Samples[a]

Subscale	1	2	3
1. Routine seeking			
2. Emotional reaction	0.49		
3. Short-term focus	0.61	0.77	
4. Cognitive rigidity	0.23	0.16	0.21

[a] Correlations (estimated) among RTC subscales were derived within the CFAs.

Stronger evidence for metric invariance is established by comparing the extent to which the fit of the metric model is poorer than that of the configural model. We therefore ran the chi-square difference test and looked at the differences in RMSEAs, CFIs, and GFIs across models. The chi-square difference test was significant ($\Delta\chi^2_{(195).} = 446$, $p < .01$). However, as noted above, considering that the chi-square difference test suffers from the same problems as the chi-square test for determining model fit, this should not be considered as evidence for the lack of invariance. Calculated from the fit indexes of the two models (configural and metric), the differences in the fit indexes were 0.001, 0.013, and 0.010 for the ΔRMSEA, ΔCFI, and ΔGFI, respectively. Although the ΔRMSEA and ΔGFI meet the 0.01 threshold and indicate a negligible difference between the fit of the two models, the ΔCFI suggests that some of the constraints on item loadings may not be justified. Therefore, even though the fully constrained metric model yielded satisfactory fit, we wanted to gain additional insights as to why its fit was somewhat poorer than the fit of the configural invariance model. We therefore turned to consider the possibility of partial metric invariance by relaxing some of the loading constraints.

While previous research with the RTC scale provides little basis for determining which of the RTC items would hold a more consistent meaning across cultures, differences in responses of participants from different cultures might be expected for the scale's two negatively worded items (i.e., 4 and 14). Previous research on the use of personality scales across cultures indicates that negatively worded items often yield different responses and have a differential effect across cultures (e.g., Lai & Yue, 2000; Schmitt & Allik, 2005). Thus, despite the fact that items 4 and 14 loaded significantly on their expected factors in all 17 samples, the magnitude of their loadings may not be invariant across samples. We therefore relaxed the loading constraints for these two items and retested the metric invariance. As expected, model fit improved: RMSEA = 0.013, CFI = 0.919, GFI = 0.911. Although the chi-square difference test was still significant, the differences in fit indexes between the configural model and this metric model were now 0.001, 0.009, and 0.008 for the RMSEA, CFI, and GFI, respectively, thus meeting Cheung and Rensvold's (2002) criteria for invariance.

9.3.2 Confirmatory SSA

We used the FSSA (Faceted Smallest Space Analysis; Shye, 1997) software to plot the SSA maps in each of the 17 samples (see Figure 9.2). The alienation coefficients for each of the samples are listed in the second column of Table 9.5. As can be seen, all of the coefficients fall below the 0.25 cut-off point, yet seven of them (Australia, China, Israel, Japan, Lithuania, Turkey, and the United States) are larger than the more conservative (Borg & Lingoes, 1987) 0.20 threshold, indicating marginal fit of the spatial representation to the data in these samples. This does not provide information about the scale's structure, but rather, indicates that to more accurately portray a geometric representation of the entire set of interitem relationships, more than two dimensions may be required.

After determining the spatial representation of scale items, FSSA estimates the best possible partitions among hypothesized regions. This part of the analysis pertains to the fit between hypothesized scale structure and the observed positioning of the scale items. It is comparable with the tests of configural invariance established in MGCFA. We used FSSA's angular partition, in which straight lines originating at a single center (this center can be outside the scope of the SSA plot) are drawn for partitioning items (see Figure 9.2). Given that the particular pattern of relationships among RTC dimensions has not been previously formulated (other than the existence of relationships, Oreg, 2003; Oreg et al., 2008), we had no conceptual basis for choosing the angular partitioning method over other available partitionings (i.e., axial and radial). We chose angular partitioning because it appears to be the most frequently used in published work and is therefore the more familiar among partitioning approaches. However, it is noteworthy that equivalent patterns of results were obtained using axial and radial partitioning (for more information on these partitioning approaches see Shye et al., 1994).

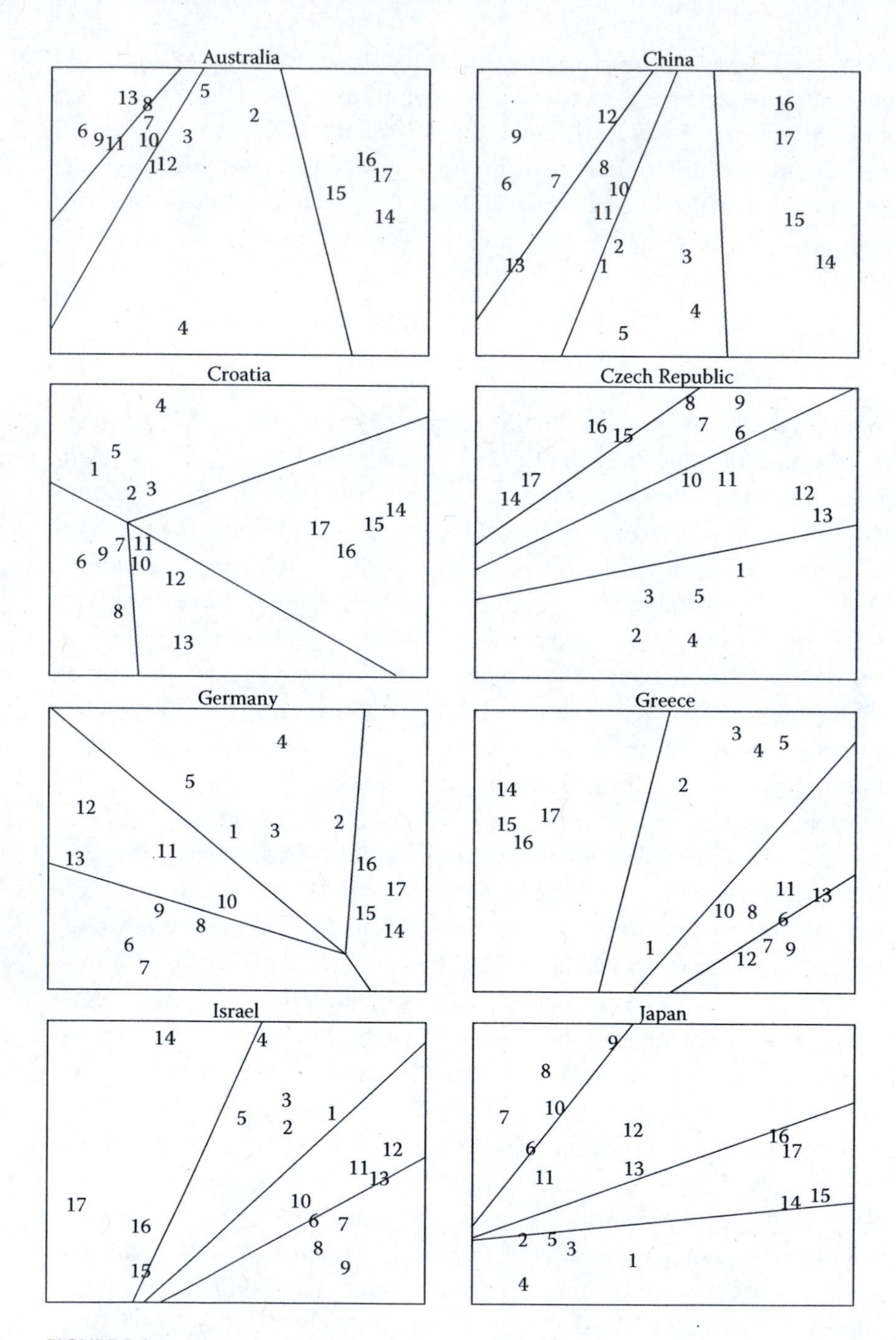

FIGURE 9.2
SSA maps, with angular partition lines, for the 17 samples.

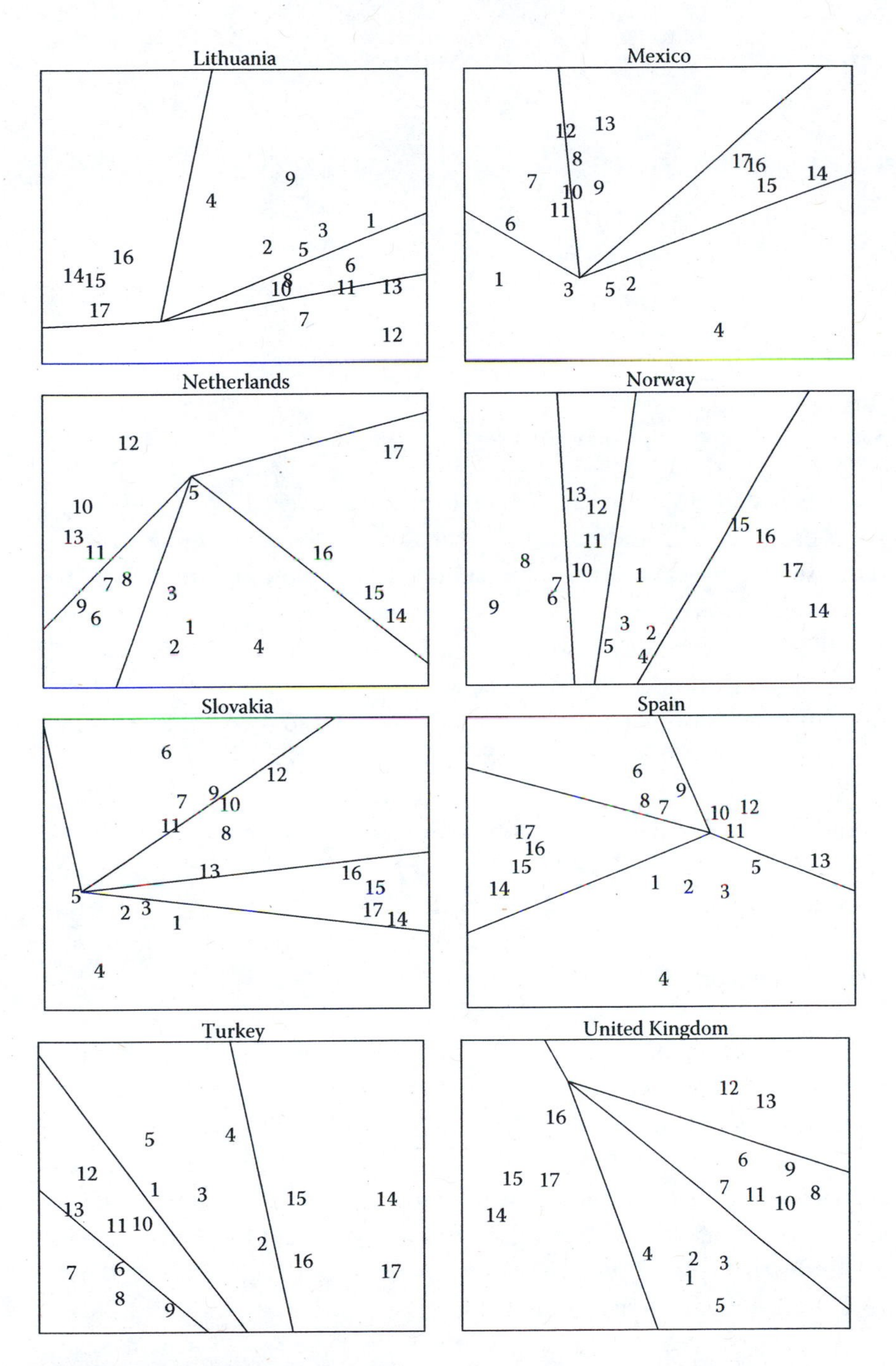

FIGURE 9.2 (Continued)
SSA maps, with angular partition lines, for the 17 samples.

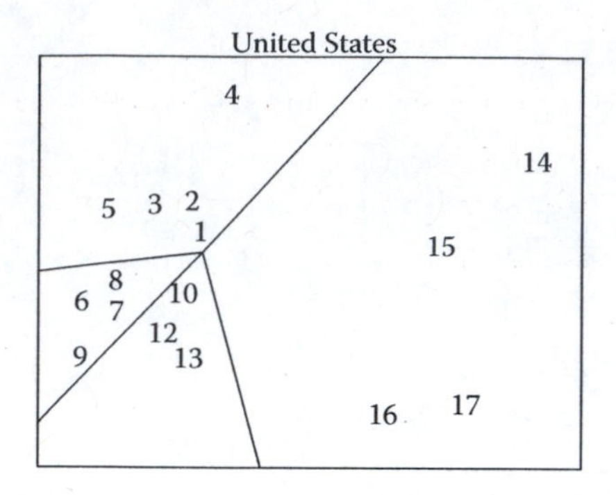

FIGURE 9.2 (Continued)
SSA maps, with angular partition lines, for the 17 samples.

Unlike MGCFA, which provides indexes of overall fit of the model across samples, the approach to establishing fit across samples in FSSA is by separately examining each sample's SSA plot, and searching for consistent patterns across plots. The number of deviant items and separation indexes provide an objective indication to the degree of fit in each plot, yet they do not substitute visually examining the overall patterns of item distributions on the maps. Columns 3 and 4 of Table 9.5 show the number of deviant items and separation indexes, respectively. As Table 9.5 and Figure 9.2 show, in nine of the samples, item representation perfectly matched the hypothesized four-region partitioning. In the remaining eight samples (Australia, China, Greece, Japan, Lithuania, Mexico, Slovakia, and the United Kingdom) there were either three or four deviant items in each, yet except for Lithuania (0.79) and the United Kingdom (0.88), the separation indexes were still high (i.e., 0.90 or above).

An examination of the SSA plots reveals that in 15 of the SSA maps (the remaining two are those of Australia and Lithuania), there are distinct regions for the routine seeking items (items 1–5) and the cognitive rigidity dimension (items 14–17). Where deviant items existed, this was only across the two affect-related dimensions of emotional reaction (items 6–9) and short-term focus (items 10–13). In other words, except for the Australian and Lithuanian maps, items in each map are clustered into three regions—routine seeking, affective-related response, and cognitive rigidity—each situated within a separate section of the map. The maps of Australia and Lithuania included points that deviated into regions beyond the two affective ones, and do not appear to indicate a consistent pattern. Thus, whereas

TABLE 9.5

SSA Alienation Coefficients and Fit Indexes for the 17 Samples

		Four-Factor Solution		Three-Factor Solution	
Country	Alienation Coefficient	# of Deviant Items	Separation Index	# of Deviant Items	Separation Index
Australia	0.21	3	0.90	1	0.95
China	0.24	3	0.95	0	1
Croatia	0.15	0	1	0	1
Czech Republic	0.19	0	1	0	1
Germany	0.20	0	1	0	1
Greece	0.19	3	0.94	0	1
Israel	0.21	0	1	0	1
Japan	0.21	3	0.97	0	1
Lithuania	0.23	4	0.79	2	0.95
Mexico	0.20	3	0.92	0	1
Netherlands	0.16	0	1	0	1
Norway	0.14	0	1	0	1
Slovakia	0.19	4	0.95	0	1
Spain	0.19	0	1	0	1
Turkey	0.23	0	1	0	1
United Kingdom	0.21	4	0.88	0	1
United States	0.18	0	1	0	1
Mean	0.19	1.59	0.96	0.18	0.99

a four-region map obtains full support in nine of the samples, and partial support in the remaining eight, a three-region map obtains full support in 15 of the samples, and partial support in the remaining two.

To illustrate, in another set of SSAs, this time with three regions hypothesized, corresponding to the three-factor alternative CFA models tested above, model fit was perfect in the 15 samples (i.e., separation index was zero), and the separation index increased to 0.95 in both Australia and Lithuania (see Columns 5 and 6 in Table 9.5). An examination of the specific items that tended to deviate from their hypothesized region indicated items 8 ("When things don't go according to plans, it stresses me out") and 12 ("When someone pressures me to change something, I tend to resist it even if I think the change may ultimately benefit me"), each of which deviated in four maps. Both points deviated in the maps of China, Greece, and Mexico, and in addition, item 12 deviated in Australia and item 8 in Slovakia.

In addition, the MGCFA findings above concerning the negatively worded items (i.e., items 4 and 14) warranted a closer examination of these items in each of the SSA plots. Although both items tended to appear within their hypothesized cluster, item 4 appeared separate from the other items in 12 of the samples. It was clearly distinct in Australia, Lithuania, Mexico, Slovakia, Spain, and the United States, and while not as conspicuous, still separate from the other subscale items in Croatia, Germany, Israel, Japan, the Netherlands, and Turkey. Even when item 4 was not separated from the other items in its subscale, it still tended to be situated at the margins of the SSA map (see, for example, the maps of China and the Czech Republic). Item 14 was clearly separate from the other items in Israel and the United States. In 12 of the maps it was the item nearest the border of the SSA map, indicating its relative distinctiveness from the majority of items on the map.

9.4 DISCUSSION

In this study we tested whether the dispositional resistance to change construct takes on equivalent meanings across samples from different countries, using two distinct sets of analyses. Using the same data reported in Oreg et al. (2008), we complemented the previously applied factor analytic procedures with confirmatory SSA. To the best of our knowledge, this is the first study to compare results from a MGCFA, with those of a confirmatory SSA. The two methods contribute incrementally to our understanding of the data. As we elaborate below, alongside an overlap in the conclusions yielded by the two methods, each highlights some distinct aspects of the data, which together provide greater insights into the measure used and its underlying construct.

With few exceptions, the confirmatory factor analyses indicated the cross-national validity of dispositional resistance to change. A replication of the scale's structure was achieved in all 17 samples, and evidence for partial metric invariance using MGCFA was achieved. With the exception of the two negatively worded items, all of the items had invariant loadings across countries. The confirmatory SSA provided further support for the scale's structure. The four-region solution achieved perfect fit in nine of the samples, and good fit in 15 of the 17 samples. As hypothesized, items from each of the four construct dimensions (i.e., routine seeking, emotional reaction, short-term focus, and cognitive rigidity) were typically clustered in distinct regions of the SSA maps.

Corresponding with the high correlation between the emotional reaction and short-term focus dimensions, as indicated in the CFAs (see Table 9.4), item clusters of these two dimensions were always adjacent, and in almost all cases where deviant items existed, these were the two regions between which deviations occurred. Because decreasing the number of hypothesized regions in confirmatory SSA is likely, by the very nature of this analysis, to increase model fit, it is no surprise that a better fit is achieved for the three-region models. Although this better fit might suggest that the three-region solution is more parsimonious and robust, it should not be interpreted as indication that it is superior to the four-factor solution. The combined results of the CFAs and the FSSAs indicate that the distinction between the emotional reaction and short-term focus is still meaningful. Furthermore, differential findings were obtained for the two subscales in a number of studies in which the RTC scale was used to predict individuals' responses to specific changes (e.g., Oreg, 2003, Studies 5–7). Thus, at this point, we recommend maintaining the distinction between the two subscales.

Beyond the examination of the construct's overall structure, the SSA allowed for a direct examination of specific items and their position with respect to the other scale items. First, an examination of the negatively worded items supported the conclusions of the MGCFA concerning the irregularity of these items. The two items, and in particular item 4, although still situated within their hypothesized cluster, tended to stray somewhat from the remaining items and often appeared near the margins of the SSA maps. This corresponds with the notion that negatively worded items are often perceived as somewhat distinct from the remaining scale items. Overall, the two analyses independently raise concern about the appropriateness of using negatively worded items when importing such personality scales from one cultural context to another.

Second, an examination of the deviating items indicated that in half of the eight SSA maps in which deviations occurred, items 8 and 12 were involved. Item 8 is part of the emotional reaction subscale. Considering its particular content, which pertains to individuals' experience of stress when changing plans, it makes sense that this item could stray into the adjacent *short-term focus* region because changing plans is generally most inconvenient in the short-term, with potential benefits for the long-term. In contrast, item 12, which is part of the short-term focus subscale, strays into the *emotional reaction* region. While it does not explicitly include reference to an emotional reaction, one could imagine how resisting a potentially beneficial change would be driven by emotional factors. Furthermore, the reference in this item to an external pressure to change may be particularly likely to yield an emotional response (see, for example, the theory of psychological reactance; Brehm, 1966). Clearly, these post hoc explanations are only tentative, and one should bear in mind that these two items did *not* deviate from their hypothesized clusters in 13 of the 17 samples. Aside from these deviations, there was little consistency in the items that deviated, and furthermore, we could not identify a common denominator among the countries in which deviations occurred.

Despite the overall support of the SSAs for the scale's structure, support for the four-region solution was somewhat poorer in the United Kingdom and Lithuanian samples. The separation index in the United Kingdom was 0.88, which was only slightly lower than our predetermined 0.90 cutoff point. The separation was substantially lower in the Lithuanian sample (i.e., 0.79). Indeed, the Lithuanian sample is the only sample in which the four-factor CFA model did not present superior fit over the three-factor CFA. We have no theoretical explanation as to why the three-region/factor solution would be more appropriate specifically in Lithuania.

Another sample in which some irregularities existed was the Australian sample. Although the four-region separation index was 0.90, deviations in this sample were not restricted to deviations between the two affect-related subscales. An examination of the Australian SSA plot reveals that item 4 deviates substantially from all other scale items and is a clear outlier. In SSA, such a deviation can distort the pattern of relationships mapped among the remaining scale items. We therefore ran a separate SSA, excluding item 4. Items were now all clustered in accordance with their hypothesized subscale, with no deviant items (i.e., the separation index was 1).

Overall, our results suggest that the construct of dispositional resistance to change carries equivalent meanings across nations and that its measurement scale can be reliably and validly used in the countries sampled for this study. Both sets of analyses suggest that caution should be taken when interpreting individuals' responses to the two negatively worded items.

Furthermore, in both sets of analyses data from the United Kingdom appear to yield a somewhat poorer fit compared with the majority of our samples. In the CFAs, although the fit was still satisfactory, fit indexes for the UK data were at the lower end of the overall values obtained, with an RMSEA of 0.062 and a CFI and GFI of 0.90. Correspondingly, in the FSSA the UK data had the second lowest separation index of 0.88. Given that the fit was still reasonable, and that we have no theoretical explanation for why the United Kingdom should stand out from the remaining samples, we attribute this finding to random error and recommend collecting additional data from the United Kingdom before any definitive conclusions are drawn.

However, alongside these overlapping indications from both analytic procedures, there were some samples that stood out in one method, but not so much in the other. For example, Slovakia yielded the poorest fit in the CFAs, with an RMSEA of 0.065, a CFI of 0.90, and a GFI of 0.89, but was in the middle range of fit according to the FSSA. Contrarily, the Lithuanian and Australian data yielded poorer fit in the FSSA, while yielding relatively high fit indexes in the CFAs. An explanation for the particular deviance of the Slovakian sample in the CFAs may have to do with the normality or linearity of the data, which would have influenced CFA results, but not those of the FSSA, which does not presume normality or linearity. On the other hand, the poorer fit of the Lithuanian and Australian samples in the FSSA appears to be related to extreme deviations of particular items, such as item 9 in Lithuania and item 4 in Australia. These deviations appear to have substantially skewed results in the FSSAs, yet did not show a strong trace in the CFAs. Such differences in findings across the two methods highlight the complementary value of implementing both, with each drawing attention to different aspects of the data.

Two limitations of the present study are worth noting. First, because we could not collect data from random samples, we used a matched-sample design to increase sample comparability. While such comparability is essential for cross-cultural validation studies, the price, in this case, was that our samples were not representative of their national cultures. Moreover, matching on a given variable may inadvertently result in an unmatching on other variables (Meehl, 1970), thus raising further doubts about the generalizability of one's findings. However, some evidence for the external validity of our findings lies in the fact that Oreg's (2003) findings with U.S. undergraduates were equivalent to those found for U.S. employees.

A related limitation has to do with the sampling of cultures in our study. The cultures we sampled do not represent all existing national cultures around the globe. While our results indicate measurement equivalence across the 17 countries sampled, it is yet to be determined whether such equivalence exists across additional countries. In particular, none of our samples were from Africa or South America. Additional data from countries in these continents would be necessary to more confidently argue for a universally shared meaning of the dispositional resistance to change construct.

Our findings suggest that dispositional resistance to change shares its meaning, as an individual-level construct, across cultures. Thus, the RTC scale can be used to compare individuals within a given culture, across a large variety of cultures. This is distinct from being able to compare cultures in their aggregate level of dispositional resistance. Measurement equivalence at the individual level is a necessary, yet insufficient, criterion for making comparisons between units at a higher level (van de Vijver & Poortinga, 2002). This is because differences between individuals across cultures are not necessarily equivalent in meaning to differences between cultures (Cheung et al., 2006). As noted above, the extent to which resistance to change can be viewed as a culture-level construct requires a separate validation process, which would explore, both theoretically and empirically, the meaningfulness of resistance to change as a cultural dimension. Such a validation process should include an explicit discussion of what it means for a culture to be change-resistant, as is done in discussions of other culture-level constructs, such as uncertainty avoidance (Hofstede, 1980). This discussion may or may not be similar to the discussion of individual differences in resistance. From an empirical perspective, data would need to be collected from a large number of cultures to permit the necessary statistical analyses. Furthermore, correlations between culture-level resistance and other culture-level variables would have to be tested to establish construct validity.

We believe the primary contribution of this study to be in combining two alternative statistical techniques for the cross-national validation of a construct. Each of the methods we used was based on a separate set of assumptions, and each offered a separate set of advantages. Among the advantages of MGCFA is its simultaneous test of item loadings across the various data samples. This provides for a powerful test of the degree to which scale items take on equivalent meanings across samples.

The key advantages of using confirmatory SSA are twofold. First, unlike factor analytic techniques, SSA makes fewer assumptions about the data. It does not assume multivariate normality of the items or a linear relationship between them. Thus, results with SSA can be generalized even to contexts where the data may not conform to these assumptions. Second, the geometric representation of items allows for a direct and explicit examination of the complete pattern of relationships among items and dimensions. The SSA maps offer a clear visual depiction of these relationships, which when combined with information from CFAs, provide for a more complete and concrete understanding of a scale's structure. Results from the two analyses serve to validate one another and together provide strong support for the RTC scale's structure across cultural contexts. We recommend that future work take on similar procedures, employing distinct analytic techniques, for the validation of other constructs as well.*

REFERENCES

Arbuckle, J. L. (2006). *Amos (Version 7.0).* Chicago, IL: SPSS.

Bauer, D. J. (2005). The role of nonlinear factor-to-indicator relationships in tests of measurement equivalence. *Psychological Methods, 10*(3), 305.

Ben-Shalom, U., & Horenczyk, G. (2003). Acculturation orientations: A facet theory perspective on the bidimensional model. *Journal of Cross-Cultural Psychology, 34*(2), 176.

Boehnke, K., Schwartz, S., Stromberg, C., & Sagiv, L. (1998). The structure and dynamics of worry: Theory, measurement, and cross-national replications. *Journal of Personality, 66*(5), 745–782.

* The authors wish to thank Shmuel Shye, Adi Amit, and Liat Levontin for their assistance in running the FSSA software. We also thank Shalom Schwartz and Holger Steinmetz for helpful comments on a previous version of this manuscript. A number of paragraphs in this article are © 2008 by the American Psychological Association and reproduced with permission. The use of this information does not imply endorsement by the publisher.

The Czech participation was supported by grant IAA700250702 from the Grant Agency of the Academy of Sciences of the Czech Republic and is related to research plan AV0Z0250504 of the Institute of Psychology, Academy of Sciences of the Czech Republic. Funds for the Croatian participation have been provided by Grant 194-1941558-1530 from the Ministry of Science, Education, and Sports in Croatia. Slovak participation was supported by grant no. 2/6185/26 approved by the Scientific Grant Agency of the Ministry of Education of the Slovak Republic and the Slovak Academy of Sciences, VEGA. Data collection in China was supported by the Chinese National Science Foundation.

Bollen, K. A. (1989). A new incremental fit index for general structural equation models. *Sociological Methods and Research, 17*, 303–316.

Borg, I., & Groenen, P. J. F. (2005). *Modern multidimensional scaling: Theory and applications* (2nd ed.). New York, NY: Springer.

Borg, I., & Lingoes, J. C. (1987). *Multidimensional similarity structure analysis*. New York, NY: Springer.

Borg, I., & Shye, S. (1995). *Facet theory: Form and content*. Thousand Oaks, CA: Sage.

Brehm, J. W. (1966). *A theory of psychological reactance*. New York, NY: Academic Press.

Browne, M. W., & Cudeck, R. (1993). Alternative ways of assessing model fit. In K. A. Bollen & J. S. Long (Eds.), *Testing structural equation models* (pp. 136–162). Newbury Park, CA: Sage.

Budner, S. (1962). Intolerance of ambiguity as a personality variable. *Journal of Personality, 30*, 29–50.

Byrne, B. M., Shavelson, R. J., & Muthén, B. (1989). Testing for the equivalence of factor covariance and mean structures: The issue of partial measurement invariance. *Psychological Bulletin, 105*, 456–466.

Cheung, G. W., & Rensvold, R. B. (2002). Evaluating goodness-of-fit indexes for testing measurement invariance. *Structural Equation Modeling, 9*, 233–255.

Cheung, M. W. L., Leung, K., & Au, K. (2006). Evaluating multilevel models in cross-cultural research: An illustration with social axioms. *Journal of Cross Cultural Psychology, 37*, 522–541.

Church, A. T., & Lonner, W. J. (1998). The cross-cultural perspective in the study of personality: Rationale and current research. *Journal of Cross Cultural Psychology, 29*, 32–62.

Cohen, A. (2008). The underlying structure of the Beck Depression Inventory II: A multidimensional scaling approach. *Journal of Research in Personality, 42*(3), 779–786.

Coovert, M., & Craiger, P. (2000). An expert system for integrating multiple fit indices for structural equation models. *New Review of Applied Expert Systems and Emerging Technologies, 6*, 39–56.

Davison, M. L. (1981, August). *Multidimensional scaling vs. factor analysis of tests and items*. Paper presented at the Annual meeting of the American Psychological Association, Los Angeles, CA.

Digman, J. M. (1990). Personality structure: Emergence of the five-factor model. *Annual Review of Psychology, 41*, 417–440.

Ghorpade, J., Hattrup, K., & Lackritz, J. R. (1999). The use of personality measures in cross-cultural research: A test of three personality scales across two countries. *Journal of Applied Psychology, 84*, 670–679.

Grouzet, F. M. E., Kasser, T., Ahuvia, A., Dols, J. M. F., Kim, Y., Lau, S., . . . Sheldon, K. M. (2005). The structure of goal contents across 15 cultures. *Journal of Personality and Social Psychology, 89*, 800–816.

Guttman, L. A. (1968). A general nonmetric technique for finding the smallest coordinate space for a configuration of points. *Psychometrika, 33*, 469–506.

Hofstede, G. (1980). *Culture's consequences, international differences in work-related values*. Beverly Hills, CA: Sage.

Horn, J. L. (1991). Comments on issues in factorial invariance. In L. M. Collins & J. L. Horn (Eds.), *Best methods for the analysis of change: Recent advances, unanswered questions, future directions* (Vol. 1, pp. 14–125). Washington, DC: American Psychological Association.

Hoyle, R. H. (1995). The structural equation modeling approach: Basic concepts and fundamental issues. In R. H. Hoyle (Ed.), *Structural equation modeling: Concepts, issues, and applications* (pp. 1–15). Thousand Oaks, CA: Sage.

Hu, L. T., & Bentler, P. M. (1999). Cutoff criteria for fit indexes in covariance structure analysis: Conventional criteria versus new alternatives. *Structural Equation Modeling, 6*(1), 1–55.

Jöreskog, K. G. (1971). Simultaneous factor analysis in several populations. *Psychometrika, 36*(4), 409–426.

Kline, R. B. (1998). *Principles and practice of structural equation modeling.* New York, NY: Guilford Press.

Lai, J. C. L., & Yue, X. (2000). Measuring optimism in Hong Kong and mainland Chinese with the revised Life Orientation Test. *Personality and Individual Differences, 28*, 781–796.

Liu, C., Borg, I., & Spector, P. E. (2004). Measurement equivalence of the German job satisfaction survey used in a multinational organization: Implications of Schwartz's culture model. *Journal of Applied Psychology, 89*, 1070–1082.

Meehl, P. E. (1970). Nuisance variables and the ex post facto design. In M. Radner & S. Winokur (Eds.), *Minnesota studies in the philosophy of science: Vol. 4. Analyses of theories and methods of physics and psychology* (pp. 373–402). Minneapolis, MN: University of Minnesota Press.

Meredith, W. (1993). Measurement invariance, factor analysis and factorial invariance. *Psychometrika, 58*, 525–543.

Nov, O., & Ye, C. (2008). Users' personality and perceived ease of use of digital libraries: The case for resistance to change. *Journal of the American Society for Information Science and Technology, 59*(5), 845–851.

Oreg, S. (2003). Resistance to change: Developing an individual differences measure. *Journal of Applied Psychology, 88*, 680–693.

Oreg, S. (2006). Personality, context, and resistance to organizational change. *European Journal of Work and Organizational Psychology, 15*, 73–101.

Oreg, S., Bayazit, M., Vakola, M., Arciniega, L., Armenakis, A. A., Barkauskiene, R., . . . van Dam, K. (2008). Dispositional resistance to change: Measurement equivalence and the link to personal values across 17 nations. *Journal of Applied Psychology, 93*(4), 935–944.

Oreg, S., Nevo, O., Metzer, H., Leder, N., & Castro, D. (2009). Dispositional resistance to change and occupational interests and choices. *Journal of Career Assessment, 17(3)*, 312–323.

Rokeach, M. (1960). *The open and closed mind.* New York, NY: Basic Books.

Schaffer, B. S., & Riordan, C. M. (2003). A review of cross-cultural methodologies for organizational research: A best-practices approach. *Organizational Research Methods, 6*, 169–215.

Schmitt, D. P., & Allik, J. (2005). Simultaneous administration of the Rosenberg self-esteem scale in 53 nations: Exploring the universal and culture-specific features of global self-esteem. *Journal of Personality and Social Psychology, 89*, 623–642.

Shye, S. (1997). *FSSAWIN (Version 1.0).* Jerusalem, Israel: Lous Guttman Israel Institute of Applied Social Research.

Shye, S., Elizur, D., & Hoffman, M. (1994). *Introduction to facet theory: Content design and intrinsic data analysis in behavioral research:* Thousand Oaks, CA: Sage.

Silverstein, A. B. (1987). Multidimensional scaling vs. factor analysis of Wechsler's intelligence scales. *Journal of Clinical Psychology, 43*(3), 381–386.

Slovic, P. (1972). Information processing, situation specificity, and the generality of risk taking behavior. *Journal of Personality and Social Psychology, 22*, 128–134.

Steenkamp, J. B. E. M., & Baumgartner, H. (1998). Assessing measurement invariance in cross-national consumer research. *Journal of Consumer Research, 25*, 78–90.

Vandenberg, R. J., & Lance, C. E. (2000). A review and synthesis of the measurement invariance literature: Suggestions, practices, and recommendations for organizational research. *Organizational Research Methods, 3*, 4–69.

van de Vijver, F. J. R., & Poortinga, Y. H. (2002). Structural equivalence in multilevel research. *Journal of Cross Cultural Psychology, 33*, 141–156.

Zuckerman, M. (1994). *Behavioral expressions and biosocial bases of sensation seeking.* Cambridge: Cambridge University Press.

Section II

Multilevel Analysis

10

Perceived Economic Threat and Anti-Immigration Attitudes: Effects of Immigrant Group Size and Economic Conditions Revisited

Bart Meuleman
University of Leuven

10.1 INTRODUCTION

Since the 1990s, Europe has experienced increasing immigration flows (Hooghe, Trappers, Meuleman, & Reeskens, 2008), and simultaneous electoral successes of anti-immigration parties (Anderson, 1996; Lubbers, 2001). These tendencies have revived scientific attention to the perceptions of ethnic threat and to anti-immigration attitudes. Because of the increasing availability of European cross-national survey data, scholars have started to approach these topics from a comparative point of view. Following the lead set by Quillian (1995), various recent studies have investigated whether or not international variations in the prevalence of negative attitudes toward out-groups are dependent on contextual factors, such as economic conditions and immigrant group size (studies concerning the national level: Coenders, 2001; Meuleman, Davidov, & Billiet, 2009; Scheepers, Gijsberts, & Coenders, 2002; Schneider, 2008; Semyonov, Raijman, & Gorodzeisky, 2006, 2008; Sides & Citrin, 2007; Strabac & Listhaug, 2008; studies concerning the regional or local level: Schlueter & Wagner, 2008; Semyonov, Raijman, Yom Tov, & Schmidt, 2004; Wagner, Christ, Pettigrew, Stellmacher, & Wolf, 2006).

In spite of the rapidly growing amount of empirical research, the impact of context variables is still not an open-and-shut case. Some studies report a benign influence of economic prosperity on out-group attitudes (Coenders, 2001; Quillian, 1995; Semyonov et al., 2006), whereas others are not able to replicate these results (Strabac & Listhaug, 2008). Certain studies conclude that perceived threat from immigration, and anti-immigration attitudes, are more widespread in ethnically diverse contexts (Quillian, 1995; Scheepers et al., 2002; Semyonov et al., 2008), while in other studies, such a relation is not discovered (Coenders, 2001; Semyonov et al., 2004; Semyonov et al., 2006; Strabac & Listhaug, 2008), or even that opposite effects are discerned (Wagner et al., 2006). The inconsistency in this field is perfectly illustrated by the fact that even two studies using identical data (i.e., the 2002–2003 round of the European Social Survey [ESS]) reach opposing conclusions. While Schneider (2008) finds small, but significant, effects of economic conditions and immigrant group size on anti-immigration attitudes, Sides and Citrin (2007) conclude that such effects are absent.

The incompatibility of empirical results suggests that the above-mentioned body of research has to contend with several problems. First, the field suffers from vague theory formulation and a large theoretical gap between contextual indicators and individual attitudes (i.e., the so-called black box problem, Goldthorpe, 1997; see also Western, 1996). Most studies test whether context and attitudes are related, but pay insufficient attention to the social mechanisms (in the sense of Hedström, 2005) that underlie the context-attitudes connection. This failure to unravel various processes at work—processes that might even have opposite effects and could thus cancel each other out—can distort the findings considerably. Second, the inconsistencies might also be due to methodological issues. Most of the above-cited studies* employ multilevel models to analyze cross-cultural data, with countries as the higher-level units. However, statistical tests for context effects are known to be very unreliable given the relatively small numbers of available countries (Meuleman & Billiet, 2009), although more recently, attempts have been undertaken to circumvent these estimation problems by means of bootstrapping techniques (Chapter 12 of this book). Furthermore, previous studies only seldom test the cross-cultural compa-

* The study by Sides and Citrin (2007) is an exception here.

rability of attitude scales in an adequate way (Steenkamp & Baumgartner, 1998; Vandenberg & Lance, 2000).*

Because of the contradictions shown in previous studies, I am convinced that it is useful to revisit the effects of economic conditions and immigrant group size on anti-immigration attitudes. Data from the first round of the ESS offers excellent opportunities for doing this. In several ways, this study attempts to tackle the problems that might be responsible for the confused findings seen in previous research. First, I try to provide a more detailed theoretical specification of the causal chain between context and attitudes. Introducing as many as possible relevant intermediary variables between context and attitudes can bring us a step closer to a test of social mechanisms, even if this test of underlying processes remains indirect. Second, a multigroup structural equation modeling (MGSEM) approach is used, which makes it possible both to avoid the rigorous assumptions made by multilevel models, and to test for measurement equivalence at the same time.

10.2 THEORY: ELABORATION OF MACRO–MICRO LINKS BETWEEN CONTEXT AND ATTITUDES

10.2.1 Anti-Immigration Attitudes as a Response to Perceived Threat

In most of the above-cited studies, group conflict theory (Blalock, 1967; Olzak, 1992) is taken as a starting point to conceptualize the effects of economic conditions and immigrant group size on anti-immigration attitudes. Group conflict theory is used here as a generic term covering various theories that share the central premise that negative attitudes toward other social groups are essentially rooted in perceived intergroup competition for scarce goods (Jackson, 1993). In this line of thinking, anti-immigration attitudes—a particular translation of negative out-group attitudes—stem from the perception that immigrant groups pose a threat to certain interests of the own social group.

* Some studies, for example Coenders (2001), report tests for the cross-cultural equivalence of measurements. However, in these studies only metric equivalence is assessed (i.e., equality of factor loadings), while the use of multilevel models presupposes scalar equivalence (i.e., additional equality of intercepts).

According to the nature of the interest that is felt to be threatened, various types of perceived threat can be distinguished (Stephan, Ybarra, & Bachman, 1999; Stephan, Ybarra, Martínez, Schwarzwald, & Tur-Kaspa, 1998). Perceived economic threat has probably received the widest scientific attention (Citrin, Green, Muste, & Wong, 1997; Dustmann & Preston, 2004; Olzak, 1992; Quillian, 1995). This type of threat refers to the perception that social groups have to compete for scarce economic goods, such as well-paid jobs, affordable housing, or welfare state resources. Perceived economic threat is thus related to the view that majority and minority groups are locked in a zero-sum game for economic resources (Blalock, 1967; Blumer, 1958; Quillian, 1995). Yet, material interests are not the only possible things at stake in intergroup competition. Cultural (Zarate, Garcia, Garza, & Hitlan, 2004) or symbolic threats (Stephan et al., 1999), for example, refer to the perception that out-groups adhering to different cultural traditions, pose a threat to the own worldview that is believed to be morally right (Stephan et al., 1998).*

10.2.2 Contextual Determinants of Perceived Threat

Group conflict theory not only claims that perceptions of threat are the driving forces behind anti-immigration attitudes, but also elaborates on the roots of such threat perceptions. Group conflict theory is particularly useful in conceptualizing context effects, because it looks beyond intra-individual processes, and takes group processes into account (Bobo, 1983). The development of perceived threat is seen as a fundamentally collective process, by which a particular social group comes to define other groups (Blumer, 1958). As a consequence of this supra-individual focus, group conflict theorists primarily look for the origins of perceived threat in the context in which intergroup relations take place.

Blalock's (1967) distinction between actual and perceived competition is crucial to understanding the role played by contexts in shaping perceived threat (see also Semyonov et al., 2004). Actual competition is used to denote objective conditions of competition between members of different groups. Perceived competition, on the other hand, refers to the interpretations of this objective situation made by individual group members; it is

* The different forms of ethnic threat can be expected to be triggered by different antecedents, and therefore imply different theoretical models. In this chapter, however, I confine myself to perceptions of economic threat.

the subjective perception that out-group members pose a threat to in-group interests (Bobo, 1983). Blalock (1967) proposes a connection between actual and perceived competition: The degree of actual competition can determine the extent to which individuals experience ethnic rivalry. Thus, actual competition does not have a direct, but an indirect impact on anti-immigration attitudes, via perceived competition and threat.

The concept of actual competition is usually operationalized by means of two context variables, namely, economic conditions and immigrant group size. In times of a downward economic trend, economic competition intensifies because the material goods that are the object of competition become scarcer, thereby leading to higher levels of perceived threat. In more prosperous times, on the other hand, competition becomes less intense and the perception that majority and minority groups are locked in a zero-sum game is reduced (Blalock, 1967).

Besides economic conditions, the immigrant group size (i.e., the proportion of immigrants in the population) is thought also to have a crucial impact on perceptions of threat. According to group conflict theorists, a more sizeable immigrant population implies a greater number of ethnic competitors, and consequently a more intense struggle for scarce goods. Yet, Blalock (1967) argues that large immigrant groups not only mean more competitors, but also stronger ones, as they generate more potential for ethnic organization and mobilization. For these reasons, feelings of economic threat are expected to be stronger in countries where sizeable immigrant groups are present.

However, group conflict theory is not the only useful theoretical framework to conceptualize the relationship between immigrant presence and anti-immigration attitudes. Contrary to group conflict theory, intergroup contact theory predicts a negative relationship between immigrant group size and threat perceptions. According to this framework, contact between members of different social groups can lead to a decrease in intergroup hostility (Allport, 1958; Pettigrew, 1998; Williams, 1947). Under certain facilitating conditions, for example, cooperation directed at common goals, intergroup contact can make threatening images of the other group dissolve and can trigger positive emotions (Pettigrew & Tropp, 2006). Obviously, the presence of immigrant groups in a country increases the probability of contact with immigrants, thereby creating opportunities to mitigate anti-immigration attitudes.

Thus, conflict and contact theories clearly lead to opposing predictions. According to conflict reasoning, perceived threat is expected to be reinforced when large immigrant groups are present, whereas contact theory precisely predicts that such a presence tempers feelings of threat. Stein, Post, & Rinden (2000, p. 290), point out that both approaches complement, rather than contradict, each other. The two frameworks consider intergroup encounters at different levels. While the abstract presence of minority groups "in the arena of the remote" (Blumer, 1958) can foster perceptions of ethnic threat, close personal contacts can break up negative out-group attitudes. Probably, the existence of these two counteracting processes can explain why empirical evidence of the relationship between minority group presence and out-group attitudes is somewhat mixed (Schlueter & Wagner, 2008). In order to disentangle conflict and contact effects, it is desirable to specify as much as possible the causal chain between immigrant group size and perceived threat. Contact theory, as described above, states that moderating effects on threat follow from personal contacts with immigrants (Wagner et al., 2006). It is somewhat less straightforward to find a variable that mediates the threat-reinforcing effects of immigrant presence. In the lead of Semyonov et al. (2004), I argue that perceived threat is influenced by perceived immigrant presence (i.e., the proportion of the population that is immigrant that individuals perceive to be present in their country).*

In countries with a sizeable immigrant population, individuals are more likely to give a higher estimate of the number of immigrants that live in the country. Accordingly, a higher perceived presence of immigrants could induce threat perceptions. After all, only when individuals are aware of the presence of immigrants, can they perceive them as a threat to certain interests.

The ideas formulated above are summarized graphically in Figure 10.1. This figure corresponds with the following six concrete and testable hypotheses:

Hypotheses 1: Perceived economic threat leads to more negative attitudes toward immigration.

Hypothesis 2: Unfavorable economic conditions (at the country-level) lead to stronger perceptions of economic threat.

Hypothesis 3: The larger the immigrant group size in the country, the higher the perceived immigrant presence.

* One could argue that this relationship also operates in the other direction, and that perceived immigrant presence is caused by, rather than causing, threat perceptions. Unfortunately, the causality of this relationship cannot be tested with the available dataset. The theoretical framework used in this chapter (group conflict theory), however, predicts that this relationship flows predominantly from perceived immigrant presence to perceived threat.

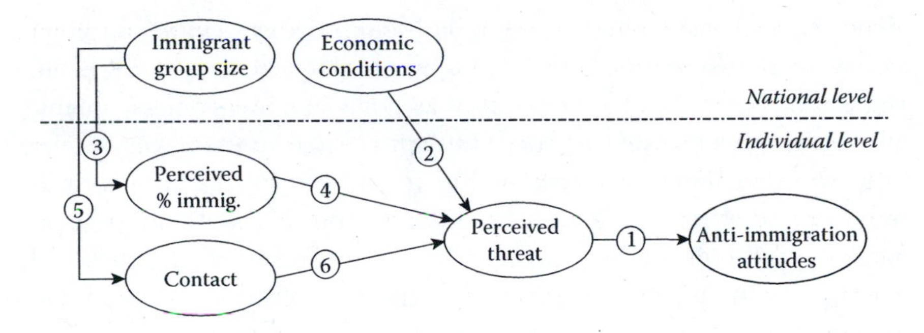

FIGURE 10.1
Conceptual model. The numbers next to the arrows refer to the hypotheses that are represented by these arrows.

Hypothesis 4: High perceived immigrant presence leads to higher levels of perceived economic threat.

Hypothesis 5: The larger the immigrant group size in the country, the more likely majority members are to have contact with immigrants.

Hypothesis 6: Intergroup contact diminishes perceptions of economic threat.

10.2.3 Alternative Explanations

Previous research suggests that threat perceptions and anti-immigration attitudes also depend on various other individual characteristics. For example, self-interest theories predict that negative attitudes toward out-groups are more widespread among strata of the population that hold similar positions as immigrant groups, and are therefore most vulnerable to competition (Scheepers et al., 2002). According to this argument, low-educated persons, low-skilled workers and those at the lower end of the income distribution scale are expected to show higher levels of perceived threat (Citrin et al., 1997; Dustmann & Preston, 2004; Fetzer, 2000; Kluegel & Smith, 1983; Mayda, 2006; O'Rourke & Sinnott, 2006; Scheve & Slaughter, 2001).

Students of religion have repeatedly evidenced that connections exist between religious involvement and out-group sentiments (Billiet, 1995; Cambré, 2002; McFarland, 1989). Those who are strongly involved in a religious community hold less individualistic dispositions and feel less powerless, which would cause a moderating effect on the perception of being threatened (Billiet, 1995). Related to this, previous research has shown that attitudes toward immigration are influenced by human value priorities

(Davidov, Meuleman, Billiet, & Schmidt, 2008). Another research tradition focuses on the association between out-group sentiments on the one hand, and on the other, social attitudes such as political powerlessness, anomy, utilitarian individualism, and social (dis)trust. These attitudes, which refer to social discomfort and alienation, lead to more outspoken negative attitudes toward ethnic minorities. The logic behind this relationship could relate to contra-identification with immigrants, as suggested in the social (contra-)identification theory (Eisinga & Scheepers, 1989). By rejecting ethnic minorities, a positive (collective) identity can be acquired, in which the socially isolated group regains status and recognition.

In order to rule out interference between context effects and these alternative explanations, indicators of self-interest, religiosity, and social trust will be included as control variables in the model.

10.3 DATA AND METHODS

10.3.1 Indicators

To test the expectations formulated above, various data sources are used. The individual-level data is taken from the 2002–2003 wave of the ESS. This international survey was carried out in 21 European countries.* Since the focus is on attitudes among majority group members, respondents that have a foreign nationality (item c18), or consider themselves as part of an ethnic minority (item c24), are dropped. In total, information from 36,443 respondents is included in the analysis.†

Attitudes toward immigration are operationalized through five survey items that question whether respondents prefer their country to grant entrance to many, or to few, immigrants (see Table 10.1 for question wordings). These items constitute the scale REJECT. Higher scores are indicative of a more outspoken rejection of new immigration flows. Perceptions of economic threat are measured by five items gauging the perceived consequences of immigration on different aspects of the economy, such as the

* Israel also participated in round 1 of the ESS. However, I decided to remove the results of this country from the analyses because of large differences in the immigration context.

† If sufficient information was available (i.e., missings on less than one-third of all items used), missing values were imputed by means of the EM-algorithm available in LISREL 8.7.

TABLE 10.1

Question Wording of the ESS Scale Items

	Question Wording	Answer Categories
Reject	To what extent do you think [country] should allow people ... D4. ... of the same race or ethnic group from most [country] people to come and live here? D5. ... of a different race or ethnic group from most [country] people to come and live here? D7. ... from the poorer countries in Europe to come and live here? D8. ... from the richer countries outside Europe to come and live here? D9. ... from the poorer countries outside Europe to come and live here?	1 (many), 2 (some), 3 (a few), 4 (none)
Ecothreat	D19. People who come to live and work here generally harm the economic prospects of the poor more than the rich D21. If people who have come to live and work here are unemployed for a long period, they should be made to leave.	1 (agree strongly) to 5 (disagree strongly)
	D25. Would you say that people who come to live here generally take jobs away from workers in [country], or generally help to create new jobs?	0 (take jobs away) to 10 (create new jobs)
	D26. Most people who come to live here work and pay taxes. They also use health and welfare services. On balance, do you think people who come here take out more than they put in or put in more than they take out?	0 (generally take out more) to 10 (generally put in more)
	D27. Would you say that it is generally bad or good for [country] economy that people come to live here from other countries?	0 (bad for the economy) to 10 (good for the economy)
Social Trust	A8. Would you say that most people can be trusted, or that you can't be too careful in dealing with people?	0 (You can't be too careful) to 10 (Most people can be trusted)
	A9. Do you think that most people would try to take advantage of you if they got the chance, or would they try to be fair?	0 (Most people would try to take advantage of me) to 10 (Most people would try to be fair)

(*Continued*)

TABLE 10.1 (Continued)

Question Wording of the ESS Scale Items

	Question Wording	Answer Categories
	A10. Would you say that most of the time people try to be helpful or that they are mostly looking out for themselves?	0 (Most people look out for themselves) to 10 (Most people try to be helpful)
Religious Involvement	C13. Regardless of whether you belong to a particular religion, how religious would you say you are?	0 (Not at all religious) to 10 (Very religious)
	C14. Apart from special occasions such as weddings and funerals, about how often do you attend religious services nowadays?	1 (Every day) to 7 (Never)
	C15. Apart from when you are at religious services, how often, if at all, do you pray?	

labor market or tax burden (ECOTHREAT). Items were reversed, so that higher scores indicate higher levels of perceived ethnic threat.

The social trust scale (SOCIAL TRUST) contains three items that ask respondents to express whether they think people in general are trustworthy, helpful, and fair. RELIGIOUS INVOLVEMENT refers to the self-reported degree of religiosity and the frequency of prayer and attendance of religious services.

The perceived presence of immigrants is measured by the following question: "Out of every 100 people living in [country], how many do you think were born outside [country]?" The answers of respondents can range between 0 and 100. Contact is a dummy variable with value 1 if respondents state to have at least some immigrant friends (d47) or colleagues (d48), and value 0 otherwise. This contact-variable thus refers in the first place to repetitive and quite close contact that takes place in a friendly and cooperative setting. By consequence, the most crucial conditions for intergroup contact to influence attitudes are fulfilled.

Several individual-level variables that refer to the alternative explanations mentioned in Section 10.2.3 are included as control variables. Age is measured in years, and gender is a dummy variable with the value 0 for males and 1 for females. Education is recoded in a variable with four categories that are based on the international classification scheme ISCED: (0) no or only primary education; (1) lower secondary education; (2) higher secondary education; and (3) tertiary education. Jobs skills are operationalized by means of a dummy variable indicating low-skilled workers and a dummy variable indicating those not in the labor market. High-skilled workers are thus used as a reference category. The distinction between low- and high-skilled jobs is based on the Erikson-Goldthorpe-Portocarero (EGP) scheme for occupations (Ganzeboom & Treiman, 1996). EGP classes 1, 2, 3, 5, 6, and 7 are considered as high skilled. Income is the household's total net income, subdivided into 12 categories. The income variable was standardized per country to allow comparability. Thus, income refers in the first place, to the relative position on the scale of national income distribution.

The national-level context variables were taken from various international databases. In this study, three different indicators of the general economic situation are included: gross domestic product (GDP) per capita in purchasing power parities (PPP), real GDP growth, and the harmonized unemployment rate. Because the latter two variables are quite volatile, 5-year averages are calculated. These economic indicators were taken from the Eurostat Web site (http://ec.europa.eu/eurostat). The context variable immigrant group size is operationalized by various indicators: The proportion of foreign population, the proportion of foreign-born population, and the proportion of population born outside the EU-27. In addition to these stock-variables, the inflow of foreign immigrants relative to the population size is also taken into account. Also for this variable, the 5-year average is taken. The rationale for including immigration flows is especially that recent increases in immigrant population might be relevant to public perceptions. The immigration-related statistics were collected by the OECD, except for the statistics for the non-EU born population, which come from my own calculations based on Eurostat data.

10.3.2 Methodology

This chapter compares attitude patterns across various European countries, in order to assess the influence of national context variables. This cross-cultural approach brings up additional methodological issues that do not arise in single-nation studies. First, respondents with a different cultural background might interpret the content of the items differently. As a result, it is not certain whether the constructs used are measured in a cross-culturally equivalent way, and whether cross-country comparisons could lack validity (Horn & McArdle, 1992; Steenkamp & Baumgartner, 1998; Vandenberg & Lance, 2000). Second, cross-national studies such as this one are usually limited to between 20 and 30 countries. Because the country is taken as a unit of analysis, sample sizes at the macro-level are generally very limited. This small-N problem clearly limits the possibilities for statistical modeling of contextual effects (Goldthorpe, 1997; Meuleman & Billiet, 2009).

To deal with these pressing methodological problems, I choose to analyze the data by means of a so-called two-step approach (Achen, 2005). In the first step, the relationships between all variables at the individual level are estimated, using multigroup structural equation modeling (MGSEM; Jöreskog, 1971). MGSEM provides possibilities to study the cross-cultural comparability of the measurement scales. By constraining certain measurement model parameters to be equal across countries (such as factor loadings and/or indicator intercepts), various levels of measurement equivalence can be tested for (Billiet, 2003; Steenkamp & Baumgartner, 1998; Vandenberg & Lance, 2000). In previous research, partial metric equivalence (i.e., the equality of factor loadings) was shown for the scales used in this analysis, by means of multigroup confirmatory factor analysis (MGCFA). Concretely, this means that (unstandardized) regression coefficients involving latent constructs can meaningfully be compared across countries. However, Hypothesis 2 also implies that country-means of one of the latent constructs (i.e., perceived economic threat) are to be compared. For such comparisons to be valid, the intercepts of the measurement model also need to be equal across countries (i.e., scalar equivalence).* For 14 out of 21 countries, partial scalar equivalent was found (see Meuleman, 2009 for a detailed description of these equivalence tests).†

In the second step, parameters calculated at the individual level, such as latent country-means, are linked to context variables. Macro–micro connections are then studied by means of tools that do not rely as heavily on statistical assumptions as do multilevel models (e.g., graphical techniques or bivariate correlations). This two-step approach thus allows the combining of rigorous process-modeling at the individual level (i.e., the level where sufficient observations are available) with more flexible and exploratory techniques at the highest level.

* Strictly speaking, scalar equivalence is also required for the other endogenous individual-level variables that are directly linked to contextual variables (i.e., perceived presence of immigrants and contact). However, as these are single-indicator concepts, this assumption cannot be tested. (I would like to thank Eldad Davidov for this useful addition.)

† In Section 10.4.2.1, more information is given on how I treat the countries for which partial scalar equivalence is lacking.

10.4 RESULTS

10.4.1 Individual-Level Model

The two-step approach implies that I start by fitting a multigroup SEM with all individual level variables included. This individual model,* depicted in Figure 10.2, follows on, in a straightforward manner, from the theoretical model presented above. The latent factor ECOTHREAT is the pivotal variable of the model. ECOTHREAT is a determinant of

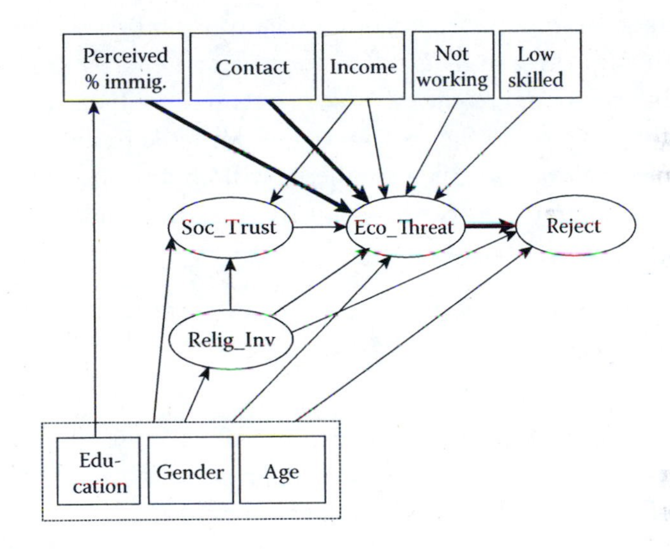

FIGURE 10.2
Estimated model for the individual variables. Only the effects represented by bold arrows are discussed in detail in this chapter.

* Technical specifications: The estimated model is a multigroup model with 21 groups. The mean structure of the data is not taken into account, so that no intercepts or latent means are estimated. All factor loadings are set equally across groups, except for the significant deviations from metric equivalence that were detected during equivalence testing (Meuleman, 2009). Correlations were estimated between all exogenous variables of the model. Because most items are measured on ordinal scales, and various items have a strongly skewed distribution, I used a weighted least squares (WLS) estimation procedure, in which polychoric correlations and asymptotic covariance matrices are used as input rather than regular covariance matrices (Jöreskog, 1990). All models are estimated with LISREL 8.7 (Jöreskog & Sörbom, 1993). In some countries, the direct paths from gender (DK, FI, GB, NL, PT, SI), age (DK, IT), or education (FI, IT, NL, PT) to REJECT were deleted, because they are virtually identically to zero and cause difficulties in the estimation (i.e., large standard errors for some parameters).

REJECT, but is at the same time explained by contact with immigrants, the perceived percentage of immigrants and a number of control variables (age, education, gender, work status, income, social trust, and religious involvement). Judged by a variety of criteria, this model fits the data reasonably well. For 4728 degrees of freedom, the model has a chi-square value 16,527.13, leading to a chi^2/df ratio of approximately 3.5. The root mean square error of approximation (RMSEA; 0.038) is well below commonly accepted cut-off points, and CFI (0.998) is sufficiently close to 1 (Bentler, 1990; Browne & Cudeck, 1992; Hu & Bentler, 1999; Marsh, Hau, & Wen, 2004).

Estimating this model for 21 countries leads to a huge number of parameter estimates (1572 to be exact), containing an enormous amount of relevant information. Presenting these results in a neatly arranged manner is a difficult task. In the sections below, only the parts of the model that are most relevant for the hypotheses will be discussed. A complete overview of all parameters can be obtained from the author.

10.4.1.1 Attitudes Toward Immigration as a Response to Perceived Economic Threat

A first key hypothesis of the theoretical model states that higher levels of perceived economic threat lead to more outspoken anti-immigration attitudes. The estimates (unstandardized as well as standardized) of the effects of ECOTHREAT on REJECT are given in Table 10.2. To compare the size of the effects over countries, it is preferable to use the unstandardized parameters. After all, variances of the latent factors were not tested to be equal across countries, which might give rise to the lack of comparability after standardization. Yet standardized parameters remain useful, as they provide more insight into the strength of effects.

In all 21 countries, a highly significant relationship is found between ECOTHREAT and REJECT. As expected, this effect is positive: Individuals who perceive higher levels of economic threat are more likely to favor immigration restrictions. Not the mere presence of such an effect, but the size of the effect is surprising. Standardized parameters range between 0.55 and 0.74, indicating that the effects are indeed strong to very strong. This analysis can thus be interpreted as robust support for the hypothesis that anti-immigration attitudes are a response to perceived economic threat (Hypothesis 1).

TABLE 10.2

Effects of ECOTHREAT on REJECT—Unstandardized Parameter Estimates and Standardized Effects

	Par. Est.	Std. Par.			Par. Est.	Std. Par.	
CH	1.25	(0.71)	***	ES	1.07	(0.60)	***
IT	1.23	(0.73)	***	DE	1.02	(0.68)	***
LU	1.23	(0.59)	***	CZ	1.00	(0.64)	***
SE	1.22	(0.71)	***	PT	1.00	(0.63)	***
DK	1.18	(0.69)	***	SI	0.99	(0.60)	***
FI	1.17	(0.74)	***	HU	0.98	(0.61)	***
NO	1.16	(0.67)	***	BE	0.93	(0.60)	***
IE	1.11	(0.64)	***	GR	0.93	(0.69)	***
NL	1.11	(0.64)	***	AT	0.91	(0.60)	***
FR	1.09	(0.72)	***	PL	0.84	(0.55)	***
GB	1.08	(0.70)	***				

***$p < .001$.

The presence of a relatively similar economic threat-effect in 21 European countries, indicates the cross-cultural robustness of the relationship between threat perceptions and anti-immigration attitudes. Yet despite these similarities, there also exists some variation in the size of the effect. In countries such as Switzerland, Italy, Luxemburg, and Sweden, feelings of economic threat translate even more rapidly in anti-immigration feelings than they do in Poland, Austria, and Greece. Based on theoretical arguments borrowed from group conflict theory, one could expect that attitudes toward immigration would be especially driven by feelings of economic threat under less favorable economic conditions. However, empirical evidence contradicts this argumentation: The strongest effects are found in countries with a relatively high GDP per capita, such as Luxembourg, Norway, Sweden, and Switzerland. In Poland, The Czech Republic, Hungary, and Greece—countries that are situated at the lower end of the GDP per capita ranking—economic threat only determines immigration attitudes to a somewhat lesser extent. Yet, the main conclusion from Table 10.2 remains that, as expected, anti-immigration attitudes are strongly influenced by threat perceptions in all the countries under study.

10.4.1.2 Contact and Perceived Immigrant Presence

According to the theoretical model, contact with immigrants and the perceived presence of immigrant groups, are crucial elements for an understanding of the effects of ethnic diversity. These two variables are hypothesized to play an intermediary role between immigrant group presence and threat perceptions. Table 10.3 contains estimates of the effects on economic threat perceptions of contact and perceived presence. In all countries with the exception of Luxembourg, contact with immigrants turns out to be significantly related to feelings of economic threat. As expected by intergroup contact theory, the relationship between contact and feelings of threat is negative: Lower levels of perceived threat are found among people having immigrant friends or colleagues.* This finding largely confirms Hypothesis 6.

The perceived presence of immigrant groups also has a significant effect on ECOTHREAT in the vast majority of the countries. Yet contrary to the contact effect, this relation is predominantly positive (in 17 out of 21 countries). The higher someone estimates the proportion of foreign-born population, the stronger their perception that immigrants challenge certain economic interests. Only in Poland, was an inverse relation found. The finding that subjective minority group size influences threat perceptions in almost all countries, lends support to Hypothesis 4. Judging by the size of the standardized parameters, this effect of perceived presence is, however, somewhat smaller that the impact of intergroup contact.

10.4.1.3 Effects of Control Variables

Besides contact and perceived immigrant presence, several other antecedents of ECOTHREAT are included in the model. Because these control variables are only indirectly related to the research questions, the effects of these variables are summarized very briefly.†

Self-interest theory (Citrin et al., 1997; Dustmann & Preston, 2004; Fetzer, 2000; Kluegel & Smith, 1983; O'Rourke & Sinnott, 2006; Scheve &

* For reasons of conciseness, contact is operationalized here as a single dummy variable indicating contact with immigrant friends and/or colleagues. Exploratory analyses with separate indicators for both modalities of contact show that having immigrant friends has a substantially stronger effect than having immigrant colleagues (see also Schneider, 2008). Probably, this finding can be explained by self-selection mechanisms: especially individuals with proimmigration attitudes will select immigrants as friends. However, even contact with colleagues, which is far less a matter of free choice, turns out to temper threat perceptions considerably. I would like to thank Peter Schmidt for drawing my attention to this issue.

† Complete results can be obtained from the author.

TABLE 10.3

Estimated Effects of Contact and Perceived Presence on ECOTHREAT—Unstandardized Parameter Estimates and Standardized Effects

	Contact				Perceived Presence		
	Par. Est.	**Std. Par.**			**Par. Est.**	**Std. Par.**	
FR	−0.17	(−0.28)	***	GR	0.15	(0.21)	***
ES	−0.16	(−0.29)	***	GB	0.13	(0.21)	***
GR	−0.15	(−0.21)	***	NL	0.13	(0.23)	***
PT	−0.15	(−0.23)	***	NO	0.12	(0.22)	***
DE	−0.14	(−0.23)	***	DK	0.11	(0.20)	***
AT	−0.13	(−0.20)	***	IT	0.11	(0.20)	***
DK	−0.13	(−0.24)	***	CH	0.10	(0.19)	***
CH	−0.12	(−0.22)	***	LU	0.10	(0.21)	***
GB	−0.12	(−0.19)	***	CZ	0.08	(0.13)	***
BE	−0.10	(−0.17)	**	BE	0.06	(0.09)	***
CZ	−0.10	(−0.16)	***	AT	0.05	(0.08)	**
FI	−0.10	(−0.16)	***	DE	0.05	(0.07)	**
IT	−0.10	(−0.17)	***	FR	0.05	(0.08)	**
NO	−0.10	(−0.19)	***	FI	0.04	(0.07)	***
SI	−0.09	(−0.15)	***	IE	0.04	(0.08)	***
IE	−0.08	(−0.15)	***	PT	0.04	(0.06)	**
NL	−0.08	(−0.15)	***	SI	0.04	(0.07)	**
SE	−0.07	(−0.12)	***	SE	0.03	(0.05)	
HU	−0.05	(−0.09)	**	ES	−0.02	(−0.03)	
PL	−0.05	(−0.08)	**	HU	−0.02	(−0.03)	
LU	−0.03	(−0.05)		PL	−0.02	(−0.04)	*

*$p < .05$; **$p < .01$; ***$p < .001$.

Slaughter, 2001) postulates that threat perceptions are, in the first place, a function of an individual's economic position. Feelings that immigrants pose a threat to economic interest are thus expected to thrive especially among individuals who are most vulnerable to ethnic competition (i.e., low-skilled workers, people on a lower income, and the lower educated). The ESS data gives only very partial support for self-interest theory. In only five countries (namely, Belgium, Denmark, Great Britain, Hungary, and Ireland), is income found to have a significant impact on economic threat perceptions. In these countries, a higher income is found to temper perceptions of economic threat. In 13 countries, low-skilled workers report stronger feelings of economic threat than do their high-skilled colleagues. Effects of income and work status are relatively small, as most standardized parameters do not exceed 0.10.

Education, on the other hand, has a far more marked effect on threat perceptions. In all countries with the exceptions of France and Britain, a higher education is found considerably to soften perceived economic threat. Yet, this education-effect cannot be unambiguously interpreted as support for self-interest theory. Education also entails an aspect of socialization of values, such as tolerance and understanding that could temper feelings of being threatened by immigrant groups. Besides that, education stimulates cognitive capacities, and therefore decreases the psychological need to classify social objects into a limited number of categories. Education could therefore put the brakes on the processes of social categorization that can eventually trigger perceived threat (Coenders & Scheepers, 2003). Unfortunately, the intermediary variables are lacking, with which to disentangle self-interest, socialization, and categorization effects.

Some interesting effects of religious involvement are found. In four countries, religiosity is found to have the anticipated moderating effect on economic threat (Billiet, 1995; Cambré, 2002). In Germany, Denmark, Great Britain, and Sweden, threat perceptions are found to be weaker among those involved in religious movements. In six other countries, The Czech Republic, Spain, Greece, Ireland, Luxemburg, Poland, and Portugal, exactly the reverse pattern is discovered. In these countries, perceived ethnic threat prevails especially among the more religious. This evident difference in the role of religious involvement could be related to the place of religion in society. The countries where religiosity is found to temper threat have a predominantly protestant, or religiously heterogeneous background, and belong to the most secularized in Europe. Strong religious involvement appears to induce threat predominantly in highly religious, Catholic countries. Further research is needed in order to gain deeper insight into the roots of these country-specific patterns.

Finally, social trust turns out to be a very powerful predictor of threat perceptions. In all countries, individuals who are not trusting of their fellow men, also perceive strong economic threat. Apparently, general societal discomfort plays a more decisive role in the development of subjective economic threat than does individual economic vulnerability.

10.4.2 Macro–Micro Links

10.4.2.1 Economic Conditions and Perceived Threat

Group conflict theory claims that, under unfavorable economic conditions, intergroup competition becomes more intense and that consequently, perceptions of economic threat increase (Hypothesis 2). To test this assertion, I calculate the correlation between three different indicators of the health of national economy on the one hand, and the country-mean on latent variable ECOTHREAT on the other. The country-means are estimated by means of a multigroup structural SEM (again taking measurement equivalence constraints into account). The country-means are controlled for education, gender, and age, so that differences in the composition of population with respect to these variables cannot influence country averages.

Measurement equivalence tests have shown that for seven countries in the ESS data set, partial scalar equivalence for ECOTHREAT is missing (Meuleman, 2009). As a result, country-mean comparisons for these countries could lack validity. However, it was also shown that the bias resulting from this inequivalence is relatively small, and does not substantially affect country rankings.* Therefore, I argue that it is still possible to make comparisons that are based on country rank orders. Concretely, I calculate Spearman rank-order correlations, rather than the more conventional Pearson correlation coefficient. Because the correlations are calculated at the national level, the number of observations (20 or 21, depending on the availability of context indicators) is very small, leading to a lack of statistical power. Therefore, I decided to use $\alpha = .10$ as a significance level. I am aware of the fact that this decision carries an increased risk of falsely rejecting the null hypothesis. The rank-order correlations are given in Table 10.4.

Two out of three economic indicators turn out to be significantly ($\alpha = .10$) related to economic threat perceptions. The strongest effect (–0.60) is found for GDP per capita: Perceptions of economic threat in the first place prevail

* Concretely, I compared latent country-mean rankings of: (1) the model with partial scalar equivalence for all countries and (2) the best-fitting model, where partial scalar equivalence is violated for seven countries. Although the latent mean scores are somewhat different, both models yield almost identical country rankings. Consequently, it can be concluded that the present measurement for inequivalence only biases the results to a limited extent, and that country rankings are largely unaffected.

TABLE 10.4

Spearman Rank-Order Correlations Between ECOTHREAT and Indicators of the Economic Situation

	Spearman Correlation	*p*-Value	*N*
GDP per capita (2002)	–0.60	.0039	21
Real GDP growth (average 1998–2002)	0.32	.1545	21
Harmonized unemployment rate (average 1998–2002)	0.39	.0883	20

in countries with a relatively low GDP per capita, such as Greece, Portugal, and Hungary. In richer European countries, economic threat is less widespread among the population. This analysis also reveals a significant positive correlation between unemployment rates (averaged over 1998 and 2002) and economic threat perceptions. Again in line with group threat theory, perceived threat is stronger where unemployment figures are high. Judging by the nonsignificant correlation coefficient, recent economic growth is less important in understanding the origins of threat perceptions.

Figure 10.3 provides deeper insight into the negative relationship between GDP per capita and threat perceptions, and the specific positions countries take. It becomes clear that in spite of the rather strong correlation, the relationship is far from a perfect one. Countries such as Sweden, Denmark, and Norway, for example, are below the regression line, meaning that economic threat in these countries is even weaker than what could be expected based on GDP per capita alone. The Greeks, on the other hand, feel economically more threatened than what would be predicted by their average economic position. This shows that, although the average wealth of a country has an important influence on feelings of threat, other contextual elements are also at work. Figure 10.3 is also helpful in identifying possible outliers, such as Luxembourg. Because of the strongly developed financial sector in Luxemburg, the GDP per capita overestimates the living standards of inhabitants, which can explain its particular position on the graph. Yet even after excluding Luxembourg, the relation between GDP per capita and ECOTHREAT remains very strong and statistically significant (corr. = –0.55, *p*-value = .0103).

Summarizing, these findings lend support to the expectation that unfavorable economic conditions can induce perceptions of threat among individuals, and hence create a less immigration-friendly climate.

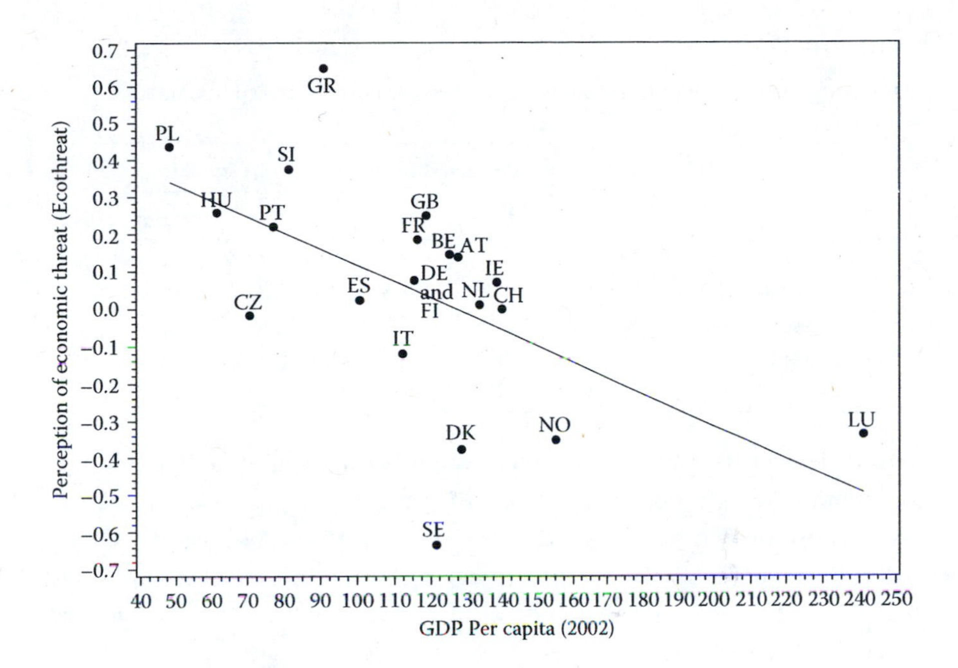

FIGURE 10.3
The relation between GDP per capita and economic threat perceptions.

10.4.2.2 Immigrant Group Size

Besides economic conditions, immigrant group size is also predicted to have consequences for threat perceptions. In the theoretical model, two processes were indentified through which individual attitudes are influenced by the presence of minority groups. First, the presence of a sizeable immigrant population can enhance opportunities for contact with immigrants (Hypothesis 5). At the same time, in societies with larger immigrant groups, individuals will probably give higher estimates of the proportion of foreign-born population (Hypothesis 3). In Section 10.4.1.2, it has already been demonstrated how intergroup contact tempers threat perceptions, while a higher perceived presence of immigrants reinforces feelings of threat.

To test these macro–micro links, correlations are calculated between various indicators of minority presence on the one hand, and country averages on the variables contact and perceived immigrant presence on the other (see Table 10.5).

Despite the small number of observations, all correlations are statistically strongly significant. In ethnically diverse countries, the subjectively perceived presence of immigrants is higher. An almost identical effect is

TABLE 10.5

Correlations Between Immigrant Group Presence Indicators, Perceived Immigrant Presence and Intergroup Contact

	Perceived Presence		Contact		
	Corr.	***p*-value**	**Corr.**	***p*-value**	***N***
Foreign-born population (in %)	0.73	.0002	0.72	.0003	20
Foreign population (in %)	0.70	.0006	0.83	<.0001	20
Population born outside EU 27 (in %)	0.70	.0006	0.55	.0111	20
Inflow of immigrants (average 1998–2002)	0.45	.0410	0.57	.0068	21

found, irrespective of whether the foreign-born population, the foreign population, or the proportion of non-EU immigrants, are used as indicators for minority group presence. Also, recent immigration flows seem to affect threat perceptions in a similar way, although this effect is somewhat weaker. The finding that all diversity indicators have similar consequences for threat perceptions is perhaps not too surprising, as they have quite strong intercorrelations, but it nevertheless illustrates the robustness of the findings.

Figure 10.4 depicts the relationship between actual, and perceived, immigrant presence in greater detail. All data points are situated above the 45° diagonal (dotted line), suggesting that in every country under study, perception bias exists: The population systematically overestimates the proportion of foreign-born population. In most countries, the proportion of foreign-born population is estimated at 5 to 15 per cent points higher than in reality. In France, discrepancy between reality and perceptions is greatest (i.e. almost 20 per cent points). Yet despite the inaccurate assessment of minority presence by the majority populations, public opinion turns out to be not completely disconnected from reality. At the national level, Figure 10.4 illustrates a strong and linear relationship between the actual and the perceived percentages of foreign population. Thus, there is clear evidence that the presence of a sizeable foreign-born population contributes to even higher estimates of immigrant group size.

Also, the degree to which majority group members have contact with immigrants seems to depend on minority group presence. In countries where a substantial portion of the population consists of immigrants, people are found more often to count immigrants among their colleagues and friends. This clearly confirms Hypothesis 3. Again, this effect is significant

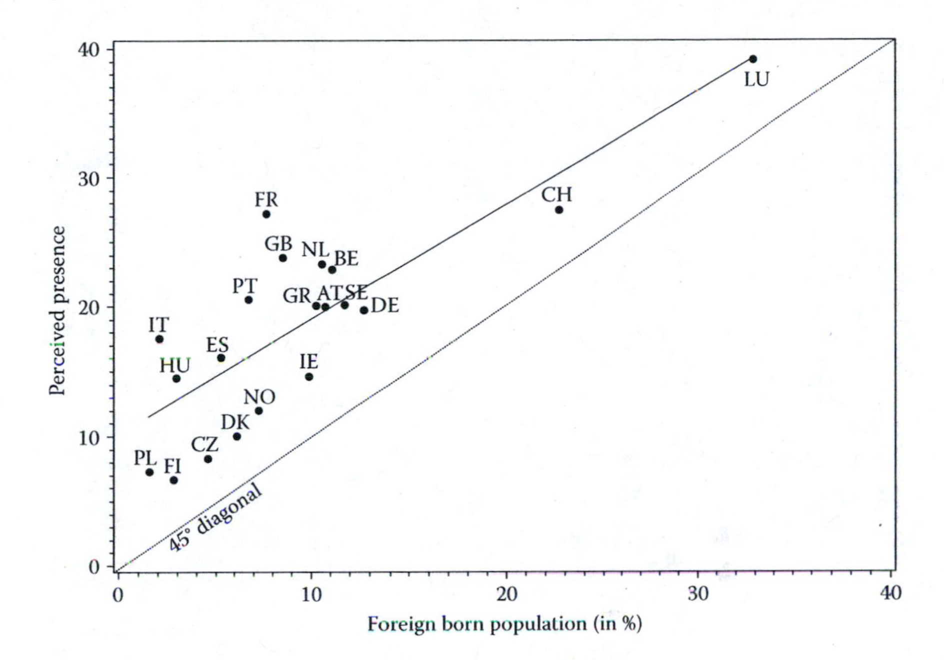

FIGURE 10.4
Foreign-born population versus perceived immigrant presence.

for all four indicators. Also for contact, the relationship with proportion for foreign-born population is graphically illustrated (Figure 10.5). Countries that fall below the regression line on this graph, mostly Southern and European countries, have lower levels of intergroup contact than that which would be expected based on the sizes of their immigrant populations. Northern and Western European countries are more often situated above the regression line. A possible explanation for this pattern could be that immigration flows into Southern and Eastern Europe are more recent, so that processes of social integration are still at an early stage.

If we put this information together with that found earlier in the individual model, the pieces of the jigsaw fall into place. Through subjective estimates of immigrant group size, the actual presence of immigrant groups indirectly reinforces perceptions of economic threat. Individuals living in ethnically diverse countries have the impression that larger immigrant groups are present in their countries, which makes them fear more often that these immigrant-groups threaten their economic interests. Yet at the same time, actual immigrant presence has the result that more people encounter immigrants on a daily basis in their circle of friends, or at work. Such more

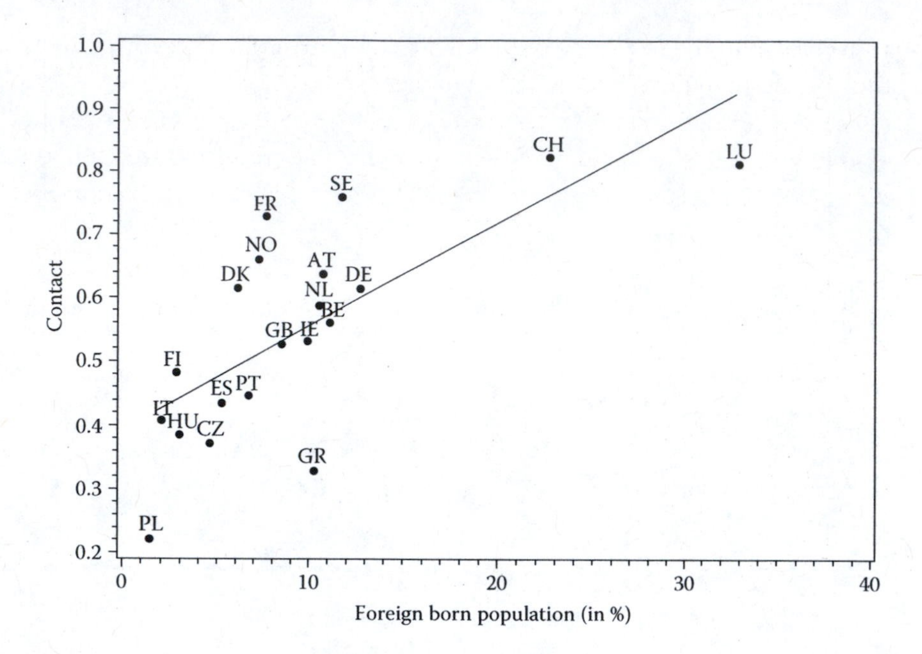

FIGURE 10.5
Foreign-born population versus intergroup contact.

TABLE 10.6

Spearman Rank-Order Correlations Between ECOTHREAT and Indicators of Immigrant Group Size

	Spearman Correlation	*p*-Value	*N*
Foreign born population (in %)	−0.19	.4312	20
Foreign population (in %)	−0.26	.2738	20
Population born outside EU 27 (in %)	0.00	.995	20
Inflow of immigrants per 1000 inhabitants (average 1998–2002)	−0.36	.1078	21

personal contacts were shown to take away threat perceptions. These two processes, one operating at a more distant level (perceived presence), and one in the personal life sphere (contact), have inverse effects and thus cancel each other out, at least partially. Indeed, if we look at direct effect of immigrant group size on ECOTHREAT, nonsignificant correlations are found (see Table 10.6). Though not significant, the total effect of minority group presence on threat perceptions is negative, suggesting that the contact effect is stronger than the perceived presence effect. This finding is in line with a study on German district level data (Wagner et al., 2006).

Only by disentangling contact and perceived presence effects, does it become possible to understand how immigrant group size and threat perceptions are related to each other. Probably because most previous studies (Coenders, 2001; Scheepers et al., 2002; Semyonov et al., 2004, 2006, 2008; Sides & Citrin, 2007; Strabac & Listhaug, 2008) have neglected to specify the causal chain in greater detail, incompatible results have been found.

10.5 CONCLUSIONS

Recently, a number of studies have dealt with the question of whether national context variables affect individual attitudes toward immigration in Europe (Coenders, 2001; Meuleman et al., 2009; Quillian, 1995; Scheepers et al., 2002; Schneider, 2008; Semyonov et al., 2006, 2008; Sides & Citrin, 2007; Strabac & Listhaug, 2008). However, the empirical evidence reported in these studies is far from consistent. While some studies report that anti-immigration attitudes are more prevalent in countries with unfavorable economic conditions and a sizeable immigrant population, others are unable to replicate such effects. Because of these mixed findings, it is useful to revisit the effects on anti-immigration attitudes of economic conditions and immigrant group size. This chapter attempts to tackle several issues that might be responsible for the confused state of the field. On the theoretical level, efforts are made to specify in further detail the causal link between context and attitudes. Methodologically, attention is paid to the cross-cultural comparability of the measurements and to the use of adequate statistical tools for the small sample size at country level.

Usually, group conflict theory is taken as a theoretical starting point from which to conceptualize context effects on anti-immigration attitudes. In this framework, attitudes toward immigration are seen as a response to the perception that certain prerogatives are threatened by immigrant groups. In turn, this perceived threat is thought to be affected by the context in which intergroup relationships take place. Because unfavorable economic conditions, and the presence of sizeable immigrant numbers, would intensify intergroup competition, threat perceptions are hypothesized to become stronger under these conditions. Yet at the same time, immigrant presence enhances opportunities for personal contacts with immigrants. And, according to intergroup contact theory, such encounters can make threat perceptions dissolve. Thus, immigrant group size could have various effects that work in opposite directions. The fact that previous studies have neglected to disentangle the conflict and contact effects of immigrant group size, might partly explain why empirical evidence is unclear.

To test the research hypotheses, data from the first round of the ESS (2002–2003) is used. Instead of the more conventional multilevel model, this study employs a two-step approach. In the first analytical step, a multigroup SEM, including all individual-level variables, was estimated. In the second step, country-level means of individual variables are linked to context variables, in order to study how the national context affects processes of attitude formation. These macro–micro connections are studied by analytical tools (e.g., scatter plots and correlations) that do not rely as heavily on large sample-size assumptions as do multilevel models.

This analysis yields several noteworthy conclusions. First, very strong evidence is found for the hypothesis that perceptions of economic threat are a crucial driving factor behind negative attitudes toward immigration. Those who feel economically threatened by immigrants favor a more restrictive immigration policy. In all countries, the standardized effect parameter is larger than 0.55, which points to very strong and cross-culturally robust effects indeed. This result is in line with a study by Semyonov et al. (2004), who have shown that exclusionist attitudes depend on perceived, rather than actual, threat. Second, the results clearly show that national context plays a role in the development of threat perceptions. Inhabitants of countries with a low GDP per capita and a high unemployment rate, report higher levels of perceived economic threat. Immigrant group size affects threat perceptions via two processes operating at different levels. First, the presence of immigrant groups offers opportunities to have contact with immigrants as friends or colleagues. Such personal intergroup contact appears to temper perceptions of threat. At a less personal and more distant level, immigrant group presence also increases the perception that the population contains a large proportion of immigrants, and this perception therefore indirectly reinforces threat perceptions. These findings are very similar to a study by Schlueter and Wagner (2008), also using ESS data, but focussing on the regional, rather than national, level. Although there is some evidence that the contact effect gains the upper hand, these two opposing effects cancel each other out to a large degree.

This can explain why studies that do not distinguish between contact and conflict mechanisms, such as Semyonov et al. (2004), conclude that immigrant presence is unrelated to perceived threat.

These results support several assertions of group conflict theory. First, a central tenet of this framework; namely that perceived threat is a driving force behind anti-immigration attitudes, is unambiguously confirmed. Second, the finding that contextual indicators of competition are more relevant than indices of individual vulnerability to ethnic competition (e.g., personal income or work skills), supports the idea that the development of threat perceptions transcends the purely individual. The formation of anti-immigration attitudes should be fundamentally understood as a group phenomenon. Yet support for group conflict theory should be qualified in other respects. The finding that immigrant presence mitigates threat perceptions through personal contacts evidences the importance of processes that run counter to group conflict mechanisms. Furthermore, compared to alternative explanations, such as social trust or educational level, the explanatory power of group conflict variables is relatively limited. It should also be borne in mind that these findings by no means imply that intergroup competition for scarce goods is actually taking place. The only conclusion that can be rightfully drawn from this study is that, in certain contexts, the majority population is more likely to interpret ethnic relationships in terms of competition and conflict. Further research is needed to find out whether such a paradigm shift among the general population has its roots in experiences of actual competition, or is rather the result of the dominant discourse in media and politics.*

REFERENCES

Achen, C. H. (2005). Two-step hierarchical estimation: Beyond regression analysis. *Political Analysis, 13*(4), 447–456.

Allport, G. W. (1958). *The nature of prejudice*. New York, NY: Doubleday Anchor.

Anderson, C. J. (1996). Economics, politics, and foreigners: Populist party support in Denmark and Norway. *Electoral Studies, 15*(4), 497–511.

Bentler, P. M. (1990). Comparative fit indexes in structural models. *Psychological Bulletin, 107*(2), 238–246.

* The author would like to thank Jaak Billiet, Marc Swyngedouw, Hideko Matsuo, Eldad Davidov, and Peter Schmidt for comments on earlier versions of this chapter.

Billiet, J. B. (1995). Church involvement, individualism, and ethnic prejudice among Flemish Roman Catholics: New evidence of a moderating effect. *Journal for the Scientific Study of Religion, 34*(2), 224–233.

Billiet, J. B. (2003). Cross-cultural equivalence with structural equation modeling. In J. Harkness, F. Van de Vijver, & P. Mohler (Eds.), *Cross-cultural survey methods* (pp. 247–264). Hoboken, NJ: John Wiley.

Blalock, H. M. (1967). *Toward a theory of minority-group relations.* New York, NY: John Wiley.

Blumer, H. (1958). Race prejudice as a sense of group position. *The Pacific Sociological Review, 1*, 3–7.

Bobo, L. (1983). White's opposition to busing: Symbolic racism or realistic group conflict? *Journal of Personality and Social Psychology, 45*(6), 1196–1210.

Browne, M. W., & Cudeck, R. (1992). Alternative ways of assessing model fit. *Sociological Methods & Research, 21*(2), 230–258.

Cambré, B. (2002). *De relatie tussen religiositeit en etnocentrisme. Een contextuele benadering met cross-culturele data.* [The relationship between religiosity and ethnocentrism. A contextual approach with cross-cultural data.] Leuven, Belgium: Katholieke Universiteit Leuven.

Citrin, J., Green, D. P., Muste, C., & Wong, C. (1997). Public opinion toward immigration reform: The role of economic motivations. *The Journal of Politics, 59*(3), 858–881.

Coenders, M. (2001). *Nationalistic attitudes and ethnic exclusionism in a comparative perspective. An empirical study of attitudes toward the country and ethnic immigrants in 22 countries.* Nijmegen, The Netherlands: Interuniversity Center for Social Science Theory and Methodology.

Coenders, M., & Scheepers, P. (2003). The effect of education on nationalism and ethnic exclusionism: An international comparison. *Political Psychology, 24*(2), 313–343.

Davidov, E., Meuleman, B., Billiet, J., & Schmidt, P. (2008). Values and support for immigration: A cross-country comparison. *European Sociological Review, 24*(5), 583–599.

Dustmann, C., & Preston, I. (2004). *Racial and economic factors in attitudes to immigration.* London: CReAM.

Eisinga, R. N., & Scheepers, P. H. L. (1989). *Etnocentrisme in Nederland: Theoretische en empirische modellen.* Nijmegen, The Netherlands: Instituut voor Toegepaste Sociale Wetenschappen.

Fetzer, J. S. (2000). Economic self-interest or cultural marginality? Anti-immigration sentiment and nativist political movements in France, Germany and the USA. *Journal of Ethnic and Migration Studies, 26*(1), 5–23.

Ganzeboom, H., & Treiman, D. J. (1996). Internationally comparable measures of occupational status for the 1988 International Standard Classification of Occupations. *Social Science Research, 25*, 201–239.

Goldthorpe, J. H. (1997). Current issues in comparative macrosociology: A debate on methodological issues. *Comparative Social Research, 16*, 1–26.

Hedström, P. (2005). *Dissecting the social: On the principles of analytical sociology.* Cambridge: Cambridge University Press.

Hooghe, M., Trappers, A., Meuleman, B., & Reeskens, T. (2008). Migration to European countries. A structural explanation of patterns, 1980–2004. *International Migration Review, 42*(2), 476–504.

Horn, J. L., & McArdle, J. J. (1992). A practical and theoretical guide to measurement invariance in aging research. *Experimental Aging Research, 18*(3), 117–144.

Hu, L., & Bentler, P. M. (1999). Cutoff criteria for fit indexes in covariance structure analysis: Conventional criteria versus new alternatives. *Structural Equation Modeling, 6*(1), 1–55.

Jackson, J. W. (1993). Realistic group conflict theory: A review and evaluation of the theoretical and empirical literature. *The Psychological Record, 43*(3), 395–413.

Jöreskog, K. G. (1971). Simultaneous factor analysis in several populations. *Psychometrika, 36*(4), 408–426.

Jöreskog, K. G. (1990). New developments in LISREL: Analysis of ordinal variables using polychoric correlations and weighted least squares. *Quality and Quantity, 24*(4), 387–404.

Jöreskog, K. G., & Sörbom, D. (1993). *LISREL 8 user's reference guide.* Mooresville, IN: Scientific Software.

Kluegel, J. R., & Smith, E. R. (1983). Affirmative action attitudes: Effects of self-interest, racial affect, and stratification beliefs on White's views. *Social Forces, 61*(3), 797–824.

Lubbers, M. (2001). *Exclusionistic electorates. Extreme right-wing voting in Western Europe.* Nijmegen, The Netherlands: Interuniversity Center for Social Science Theory and Methodology.

Marsh, H. W., Hau, K.-T., & Wen, Z. (2004). In search of golden rules: Comment on hypothesis-testing approaches to setting cutoff values for fit indexes and dangers in overgeneralizing Hu and Bentler's (1999) findings. *Structural Equation Modeling, 11*, 320–341.

Mayda, A. M. (2006). Who is against immigration? A cross-country investigation of individual attitudes toward immigrants. *The Review of Economics and Statistics, 88*(3), 510–530.

McFarland, S. G. (1989). Religious orientations and the targets of discrimination. *Journal for the Scientific Study of Religion, 28*(3), 324–336.

Meuleman, B. (2009). *The influence of macro-sociological factors on attitudes toward immigration in Europe. A cross-cultural and contextual approach.* Leuven, Belgium: Centre for Sociological Research (CeSO).

Meuleman, B., & Billiet, J. (2009). A Monte Carlo sample size study: How many countries are needed for accurate multilevel SEM? *Survey Research Methods, 3*(1), 45–58.

Meuleman, B., Davidov, E., & Billiet, J. (2009). Changing attitudes toward immigration in Europe, 2002–2007: A dynamic group conflict theory approach. *Social Science Research, 38*(2), 352–365.

Olzak, S. (1992). *Dynamics of ethnic competition and conflict.* Stanford, CA: Stanford University Libraries.

O'Rourke, K. H., & Sinnott, R. (2006). The determinants of individual attitudes towards immigration. *European Journal of Political Economy, 22*, 838–861.

Pettigrew, T. F. (1998). Intergroup contact theory. *Annual Review of Psychology, 49*, 65–85.

Pettigrew, T. F., & Tropp, L. R. (2006). A meta-analytical test of intergroup contact theory. *Journal of Personality and Social Psychology, 90*(5), 751–783.

Quillian, L. (1995). Prejudice as a response to perceived group threat: Population composition and anti-immigrant and racial prejudice in Europe. *American Sociological Review, 60*(4), 586–611.

Scheepers, P., Gijsberts, M., & Coenders, M. (2002). Ethnic exclusionism in European countries. Public opposition to grant civil rights to legal migrants as a response to perceived ethnic threat. *European Sociological Review, 18*(1), 1–18.

Scheve, K. F., & Slaughter, M. J. (2001). Labor market competition and individual preferences of immigration policy. *The Review of Economics and Statistics, 83*(1), 133–145.

Schlueter, E., & Wagner, U. (2008). Regional differences matter: Examining the dual influence of the regional size of the immigrant population on derogation of immigrants in Europe. *International Journal of Comparative Sociology, 49*, 153–173.

Schneider, S. L. (2008). Anti-immigrant attitudes in Europe: Outgroup size and perceived ethnic threat. *European Sociological Review, 24*(1), 53–67.

Semyonov, M., Raijman, R., & Gorodzeisky, A. (2006). The rise of anti-foreigner sentiment in European societies, 1988–2000. *American Sociological Review, 71*, 426–449.

Semyonov, M., Raijman, R., & Gorodzeisky, A. (2008). Foreigners' impact on European societies. Public views and perceptions in a cross-national comparative perspective. *International Journal of Comparative Sociology, 49*(1), 5–29.

Semyonov, M., Raijman, R., Yom Tov, A., & Schmidt, P. (2004). Population size, perceived threat, and exclusion: A multiple-indicators analysis of attitudes toward foreigners in Germany. *Social Science Research, 33*, 681–701.

Sides, J., & Citrin, J. (2007). European opinion about immigration: The role of identities, interests and information. *British Journal of Political Science, 37*, 477–504.

Steenkamp, J. E., & Baumgartner, H. (1998). Assessing measurement invariance in cross-national consumer research. *Journal of Consumer Research, 25*, 78–90.

Stein, R. M., Post, S. S., & Rinden, A. L. (2000). Reconciling context and contact effects on racial attitudes. *Political Research Quarterly, 53*(2), 285–303.

Stephan, W. G., Ybarra, O., & Bachman, G. (1999). Prejudice toward immigrants. *Journal of Applied Psychology, 29*(11), 2221–2237.

Stephan, W. G., Ybarra, O., Martínez, C., Schwarzwald, J., & Tur-Kaspa, M. (1998). Prejudice toward immigrants to Spain and Israel. An integrated threat theory analysis. *Journal of Cross-Cultural Psychology, 29*(4), 559–576.

Strabac, Z., & Listhaug, O. (2008). Anti-Muslim prejudice in Europe: A multi-level analysis of survey data from 30 countries. *Social Science Research, 37*, 268–286.

Vandenberg, R. J., & Lance, C. E. (2000). A review and synthesis of the measurement invariance literature: Suggestions, practices, and recommendations for organizational research. *Organizational Research Methods, 3*, 4–70.

Wagner, U., Christ, O., Pettigrew, T. F., Stellmacher, J., & Wolf, C. (2006). Prejudice and minority proportion: Contact instead of threat effects. *Social Psychological Quarterly, 69*(4), 380–390.

Western, B. (1996). Vague theory and model uncertainty in macrosociology. *Sociological Methodology, 26*, 165–192.

Williams, R. M., Jr. (1947). *The reduction of intergroup tensions*. New York, NY: Social Science Research Council.

Zarate, M. A., Garcia, B., Garza, A. A., & Hitlan, R. T. (2004). Cultural threat and perceived realistic group conflict as dual predictors of prejudice. *Journal of Experimental Social Psychology, 40*(1), 99–105.

11

A Multilevel Regression Analysis on Work Ethic

Hermann Dülmer
University of Cologne

11.1 INTRODUCTION

In his book *Modernization and Postmodernization,* Inglehart (1997) embeds his theoretical approach of an intergenerational value change toward postmaterialist value priorities into a broader theoretical approach of social change, whereby two successive phases are distinguished. Modernization is a process that transforms a traditional society into a modern one. Historically, modernization first took place in Protestant countries, where the emergence of the Protestant ethic (Weber, 1992/1930) facilitated the rise of capitalism, which contributed to the Industrial Revolution. During this phase "status-quo", cf. p. 316, p. 320 oriented traditional, usually religious norms were supplanted by achievement-oriented, increasingly secular norms. After World War II, advanced industrial societies have attained unprecedentedly high levels of physiological and economic security. Due to a diminishing marginal utility of further economic accumulation, a postmodern shift takes place in Western Europe and North America. At the individual level, work ethic conducive to maximizing economic gains is assumed to gradually fade from top priority: subjective well-being and the desire for meaningful work are becoming more crucial for a growing segment of the population.

On the background of this theoretical approach, Norris and Inglehart (2004) tested the influence of religious cultures on value orientations in contemporary societies in their book *Sacred and Secular.* All regression analyses in the book were conducted via conventional Ordinary Least Square

Regression (OLS-regression). By ignoring the hierarchical structure of the data—the respondents of a country share country-specific influences on their attitudes and value orientations—the assumption of independence of the observations is almost always violated. As a consequence, the estimates of the standard errors of conventional statistical tests are much too small (cf. Hox, 2002, p. 5). This leads to spuriously significant results: a null hypothesis will be rejected where the alternative hypothesis has to be rejected. Thus, the results of the OLS-regression might not be trustworthy. Multilevel analysis on the other hand allows contextual heterogeneity to be taken into account by including random components for capturing unmeasured contextual influences. If no random components are needed, OLS-regression is adequate. However, an advantage of multilevel analysis is that it tests assumptions that otherwise have to be presupposed.

The purpose of this contribution is twofold: A methodological purpose consists in illustrating the disadvantages of using OLS-regression for international comparisons instead of the more adequate multilevel regression. In their OLS-regression, Norris and Inglehart (2004) used an additive index for work ethic as dependent variable. Computer programs like Mplus allow multilevel confirmatory factor analysis (CFA) to be carried out as well as multilevel structural equation modeling (MLSEM). So, work ethic will be measured in our multilevel analyses by CFA. In a first step I will test whether a one-level CFA or a two-level CFA is empirically more appropriate. In a second step I will try to explain the theoretically expected differences in work ethic as latent dependent variable by including predictor variables into the full multilevel regression model (MLSEM) and comparing the results with those from OLS-regression. A more substantial purpose of this article consists in testing how far Norris and Inglehart's results (2004, p. 166 and p. 179) also hold for multilevel analysis. Finally, a multilevel regression model will be estimated that eliminates fundamental inconsistencies between Norris and Inglehart's theory and their empirical model.

11.2 WORK ETHIC IN MODERNIZING AND POSTMODERNIZING SOCIETIES

According to Inglehart (1997) social change follows a path of two successive processes called modernization and postmodernization. The former process transforms preindustrial traditional societies into modern societies. In preindustrial traditional societies survival of most human beings was precarious. Since the main source of wealth in such economically steady-state societies was land, which is a fixed supply, the only way to become rich was by seizing the land of someone else by violence (i.e., at the expense of someone else). In order to prevent that the survival of the whole society was threatened by internal violence, virtually all traditional societies established cultural, usually religious norms that limited the use of violence and repressed aspirations for social mobility. The value system of such societies encouraged people to accept their hereditary social position in this life by emphasizing that denial of world aspirations will be rewarded in the next life. Duties of sharing and charity helped to compensate the poor for the absence of social mobility and to mitigate the harshness of a subsistence economy. Although such value systems help to maintain social solidarity, they further undermined the legitimacy of economic accumulation (cf. Inglehart, 1997, pp. 30–31 and pp. 70–71).

Breaking cultural constraints on accumulation was historically achieved first by the random emergence of the Protestant ethic (see Weber, 1992/1930, cf. also Inglehart, 1997, p. 27) in Western Europe during the time of the Protestant reformation. A central element of the Protestant ethic was the Calvinist doctrine of predestination (cf. Weber, 1992/1930, pp. 56–61). This doctrine consists in the belief that God, according to the "secret counsel and good pleasure of His will" (Weber, 1992/1930, p. 57), predestinated some people unto everlasting life and foreordained others to everlasting death. In an age in which the afterlife was more important and also more certain than any interests of life in this world, for every believer the all-important question must have arisen whether he or she was one of the chosen and how one can be sure of achieving this state of grace. To disperse religious doubts and to attain self-confidence, restless professional work was advised as the most suitable means. Restless and systematic work was seen as a calling and as the only means of attaining certainty of grace (cf. Weber, 1992/1930, pp. 65–67, p. 116, and p. 121). Since man was seen as only a trustee of the goods given by God, for ascetic Calvinists it was at least hazardous to use any of the goods for a purpose that serves not the glory of God but only one's own enjoyment. These constraints that were imposed upon the consumption of wealth led to increased productive investment of capital and for that reason fostered conditions conducive to private enterprise and capitalism (cf. Weber, 1992/1930, pp. 114–116).

By considering material accumulation no longer as ignoble greed but as evidence for divine favor, the Protestant ethic contributed essentially to supplant status-quo oriented traditional, usually religious norms by achievement-oriented, increasingly secular modern norms (cf. Inglehart, 1997, pp. 70–73). That the achievement-oriented value system of the Protestant ethic did not disappear as it had appeared can be traced back mainly to technical developments that took place at the same time and that made rapid economical growth possible. This cultural-economic syndrome led to the rise of capitalism and eventually to industrialization, which is seen as the material core of modernization (cf. Inglehart, 1997, p. 27 and p. 70). By emphasizing inner worldly material success, however, the Protestant ethic also fostered the emergence of a scientific, rational-legal worldview that contributed to secularization and bureaucratization. The change from traditional, usually religiously based authority to rational-legal authority is seen by Inglehart (1997, p. 73) as the cultural core of modernization. The logical culmination of modernization was the socialist state with a state-regulated or even state-owned mass production (cf. Inglehart, 1997, p. 30 and p. 74). This statement demonstrates that modernization, although concentrated in the West at one point in history, is a global process (cf. Inglehart, 1997, p. 11). Thus, the rise of Protestantism is seen by Inglehart (cf. Norris & Inglehart, 2004, p. 161) only as an example that explained how cultural change contributed to supplant a set of religious norms that are common to most preindustrial societies and that inhibit economic achievement by a set of achievement-oriented modern norms that are conducive to capitalism.

Most advanced societies underwent modernization from the Industrial Revolution until the second half of the twentieth century. Striving for materialistic growth, however, has during the last 35 years in advanced industrial societies increasingly reached a point of diminishing marginal utility and led to a postmodern shift that, according to Inglehart (1997, p. 28, cf. also p. 324), "in some way constitutes the decline of the Protestant Ethic." The turning point for advanced industrial societies came during the 1980s mainly for two reasons, namely, the diminishing functional effectiveness of hierarchic, centralized bureaucratic organizations and their declining mass acceptance due to changes in people's value priorities (cf. Inglehart, 1997, pp. 28–30).. Whereas hierarchical bureaucratic organizations helped to create modern society by mobilizing and organizing the energy of masses of people, hypertrophied bureaucracy paralyzed adaptation and innovation and became less effective in high-technology societies with highly specialized workforces. As a consequence, state-run economies are replaced more and more by market economies. Declining mass acceptance of further modernization is traced back by Inglehart (1997, pp. 76–77) to the postmodern shift in values priorities from maximizing economic growth to maximizing subjective well-being and quality of life concerns.

The key indicator for the broader syndrome of postmodernization is a shift from materialist to postmaterialist value priorities (cf. Inglehart, 1997, p. 35 and p. 103). With his value change thesis Inglehart assumes a long-term shift in prevailing values in industrial welfare societies as older cohorts are replaced by younger cohorts born after World War II in an environment with a historically unprecedented degree of economical and physical security. This assumption of a value change is based on two key hypotheses (cf. Inglehart, 1997, p. 33): The scarcity hypothesis assumes that "one places greatest subjective value on things that are in relatively short supply." This hypothesis is seen as being similar to the principle of diminishing marginal utility in economic theory. The socialization hypothesis states that (Inglehart, 1997, p. 33) "one's basic values reflect the conditions that prevailed during one's preadult years." Whereas the former hypothesis implies that during their whole life people retain a certain capability to adapt their value priorities to short-time changes in their environment (period effects), the latter states that the basic value priorities of an individual are socialized during their formative years and remain quite stable during their whole life (cohort effects). Taken together, value change is expected to be characterized by short-time period effects that are superimposed on long-term cohort effects reflecting the conditions that prevailed while a cohort was growing up (cf. Inglehart, 1990, pp. 79–82, cf. also 1997, p. 34). The direction of the value change is deduced by referring to Maslow's (1954, cf. also Inglehart, 1977, pp. 22–23) hierarchy of needs. Although he does not follow Maslow's need hierarchy in detail, Inglehart (1997, p. 33 and 1990, p. 134) adopts a basic distinction between fundamental materialist needs for economic and physical security, and higher order postmaterialist needs such as belonging, esteem, self-expression, and aesthetic satisfaction. The latter value orientations are assumed to take priority not until the former are taken for granted.

The postmodernization process, in which the postmaterialistic value change is embedded as a core element, gives way to a shift from an emphasis on the disciplined, self-denying, and achievement-oriented norms of industrial society to an increasingly broad latitude for individual choice of lifestyles, individual self-expression, and an emphasis on the quality of life (cf. Inglehart, 1997, p. 28). On the background of this development, Inglehart (1997) expects a gradual shift in what motivates people to work, from "maximizing one's income and job security toward a growing insistence on interesting and meaningful work" (Inglehart, 1997, p. 44), "a process that could be viewed as the decline of the Protestant work ethic in postmodernizing societies" (cf. Inglehart, 1997, p. 218).

11.3 HYPOTHESES

The OLS-regression model for work ethics (work as a duty) presented by Norris and Inglehart (2004) includes a society's type of religious culture, a country's Human Development Index (HDI), and its Level of Political Development (Gastil Index) as macro-level variables and a respondent's age, gender, education, income, and religiosity as micro-level variables.* For each of these variables a linear relationship on work ethic was tested empirically. Since both authors were mainly interested in the impact of religious culture, no hypotheses were derived explicitly for the other predictor variables. Hence, this has to be done in the following.

By assuming that their model reflects their theory adequately, the following hypotheses can be formulated: younger generations grown up in an environment of, all in all, improved economical and physical security should show a weaker work ethic than older generations (H1). Formal education is seen by Inglehart (1997, pp. 151–152, cf. also Abramson & Inglehart, 1996, p. 453) as an excellent indicator of the economic security an individual experienced during the formative years. Hence, better educated people should display a lower work ethic than less well-educated people (H2). By focusing on the present living conditions that are more secure for wealthier than for poorer people, a negative relationship between current income and work ethic should be expected (H3; cf. also Inglehart, 1997, pp. 45–46). Since religiosity is seen by Inglehart (1997, p. 42, 1990, p. 177, or Norris &

* Unfortunately, the b-coefficient for religiosity that was controlled for (cf. Norris & Inglehart, 2004, p. 166) is missing in the Table A7.1 with the complete regression results (p. 179).

Inglehart, 2004, p. 18) as an indicator for security needs that are traditionally satisfied by established religion, importance of religion and work ethic are expected to be positively related (H4). By referring to traditional gender role expectations—in traditional societies the division between male breadwinner and female caregiver is crucial for the survival of children (cf. Inglehart & Norris, 2003, p. 16)—it can be assumed that due to their socialization men may feel a higher duty to work in the paid labor market than women, who may see working in the labor market more as an issue of gender equality and as a means to being economically independent (H5).

Besides these factors, that should account for differences in the work ethic at the individual-level, Norris and Inglehart (2004, pp. 13–17, cf. also Inglehart, 1997, pp. 32–33) also assume that the general living conditions in different countries have an important impact of their own on the values of their citizens. The unprecedentedly high level of economic prosperity and the emergence of the modern welfare state in advanced industrial societies in the decades after World War II have contributed to a greater sense of economic security among all social strata. Since increasing affluence is assumed to weaken work ethic, economic growth should lead to a society-wide decline in work ethic. Since a society's well-being does not depend exclusively on economic affluence, Norris and Inglehart (2004, pp. 48–51) introduced into their regression analysis: the HDI, as a broader summary scale of modernization that combines a society's level of literacy, its level of health, and its per capita GDP, and the Gastil Index (Political Development Index), as a standard measure of political rights and civil liberties. As indicators for a society's well-being, both the HDI (H6) and the Gastil Index (H7) should be negatively related to the citizen's work ethic. Most central for analyzing the impact of the Protestant ethic in current societies is the type of religious culture. By referring to Weber (1992/1930), Norris and Inglehart (2004, p. 162) formulated the hypothesis that "compared with those living in all other religious cultures (especially Catholic societies), Protestant societies should display the strongest work ethic conducive to modern capitalism, exemplified by valuing the virtue of work as a duty." However, although both authors (cf. Norris & Inglehart, 2004, p. 162) share the assumption that the Protestant ethic fostered the emphasis of personal achievement and economic growth, they also assume that the values established by the Protestant ethic tend to fade away under conditions of affluence. The expectation of such a curvilinear relationship was already expressed by Inglehart (1997, pp. 223–224):

> Achievement motivation seems to reflect the transition from preindustrial to industrial value systems, linked with the Modernization process. Materialist/Postmaterialist values, on the other hand, reflect the transition from industrial to postindustrial society, bringing a shift *away* from emphasis of economic growth, toward increasing emphasis ... on the quality of life in general.

Thus, as a result of postmodernization one might expect to find religious cultures that show a higher work ethic than historically Protestant societies (H8).

By having a closer look at the formulated hypotheses it becomes rapidly clear that the theoretically assumed shift in the prevailing direction of value change from modernization to postmodernization cannot be tested adequately via a linear relationship. In order to overcome such inconsistencies between theory and empirical tests, at least the hypothesis of an intergenerational value change (H1) has to be modified. Long-term value change can neither be explained by life cycle nor by short-term period effects but is driven according to Inglehart (1990, pp. 77–83) by cohort effects caused by different socialization conditions. This assumption should not only hold for postmodernization but also for modernization. Hence, intergenerational cohort replacement has to be also the main reason for supplanting status-quo oriented values prevailing in traditional preindustrial societies by an achievement-oriented work ethic prevailing in modern industrial societies. By taking this consideration seriously, H1 has to be restricted to the postmodernization process. Thus, it can be expected that younger cohorts should display a stronger work ethic than older cohorts in modernizing societies and a weaker work ethic than older cohorts in postmodernizing societies (H1a).

A second modification refers to education, which is seen by Inglehart (1997, p. 152) "as an excellent indicator of how economically secure one was during one's formative years." Insofar, estimating a linear relationship is theoretically adequate. However, from the point of view of cognitive psychology, education is indicative of an individual's cognitive capabilities to cope with the requirements of the environment. In a changing environment, higher educated people adapt more easily than less well-educated people to changing functional requirements. Since modernization requires the individual to adapt to an achievement-oriented value system, in modernizing societies the better educated should display a higher work ethic than the less well educated. This tendency will probably also be reinforced by parental socialization influences: because parents' education is positively correlated with their children's education, better educated parents might provide their children with insights and norms that are already better adapted to the changing restrictions or opportunities of the environment. These considerations should not only apply to modernization but also to postmodernization where the environment allows wealthier and better educated people to place higher priority on postmaterialist values like self-fulfillment. If these assumptions are correct, then H2 has to be restricted to postmodernizing societies. Thus, the better educated should show a stronger work ethic than the less well educated in modernizing societies and a weaker work ethic than the less well educated in postmodernizing societies (H2a).

Finally, a further modification might be necessary. If a country's level of development has its own impact on work ethic then the relationship should be a curvilinear one: whereas the level of a society's development should be conducive to an increasing work ethic in modernizing societies, it should contribute to a decreasing work ethic in postmodernizing societies (H3a).

11.4 DATA AND OPERATIONALIZATIONS

The present study is based on the combined dataset of Wave III of the European Values Study (EVS, 1999/2000) and Wave IV of the World Values Survey (WVS, 1999/2000, cf. The European Values Study Foundation and World Values Survey Association, 2006). Wave III of the EVS was carried out between 1999 and 2001, Wave IV of the WVS between 1999 and 2004. The same database was used by Norris and Inglehart (2004), except that both authors had to restrict their analyses of "work as a duty" to the EVS 1999/2000 and to the first countries of the WVS 1999/2000 for which data were already available when they wrote their book. The integrated dataset of both waves embraces 72 countries. Mainly because a number of countries from the WVS did not include the questions on work ethic, I had to restrict the number of countries to 53.* All in all, I was able to include seven

* In this article I will report robust standard errors (cf. Hox, 2002, p. 200). Using robust standard errors for MLSEM requires for reasons of power a minimum number of 40 countries (cf. Meuleman & Billiet, 2009). Inferences based on robust standard errors sacrificing some statistical power in order to be less dependent on the assumption of normality (cf. Hox, 2002, p. 201). For less than 40 countries remains the option to use conventional standard errors.

more societies than Norris and Inglehart (2004, p. 165). Appendix 11.A gives an overview of the countries, both included and excluded.

By using explorative factor analysis, Norris and Inglehart (2004, pp. 163–164) identified three main dimensions of work ethic. For our purposes I will restrict the analyses to "work as a duty" that lies, according to Norris and Inglehart (2004, p. 163) "at the heart of the ascetic forms of Protestantism." This dimension was measured by the items, according to The European values study foundation and world values survey association (2006) "it is humiliating to receive money without having to work for it," "people who don't work turn lazy," "work is a duty towards society," and "work should always come first, even if it means less spare time." The interviewees were asked to indicate their opinion on these items on a scale ranging from 1 (agree strongly) to 5 (disagree strongly). For the reversed answer scales both authors computed an unweighted additive index and standardized it to a range from 1 to 100. For our purposes the original answer scale was transformed into one that reached from 0 (disagree strongly) to 4 (agree strongly). Thereafter, each respondent's mean across the four items was computed. The resulting respondent specific mean will be used as dependent variable for our OLS-regression. A more adequate way to deal with measurement errors than to compute unweighted mean scores is to use CFA in a first step. Theoretically expected differences in the latent factor will be explained in a second step by including the same predictor variables into the multilevel model that were used for the OLS-regression model. The Protestant ethic was thought by Weber "to be pervasive, influencing devout and atheists alike, within Protestant Societies" (cf. Norris & Inglehart, 2004, p. 161). Hence, it seems to be imperative to include besides the individual-level latent factor also a country-level latent factor that captures a society's influence on its citizens' work ethic.

For reasons of maximal comparability the same set of explanatory variables that were used by Norris and Inglehart (2004, p. 179) will be included in our analyses. For the individual-level both authors used age, education, income, importance of religion, and gender. Dummy variables are theoretically more adequate for estimating cohort effects than a single age variable. Since Inglehart (1981, p. 886, cf. similar also 1977, p. 106) assumes a "significant watershed between the postwar generation and the older groups that had experienced the World Wars, the Great Depression and their associated threads," 1946 was chosen as the starting point for distinguishing three cohorts (i.e., born before 1946, born from 1946 to 1965, and born from

1966 to 1987). The middle and the youngest cohort will be distinguished each by a 0–1 coded dummy from the oldest cohort that serves as reference group. Whereas Norris and Inglehart (2004) tested for a linear relationship between education and work ethic, I will use two 0–1 coded dummy variables instead, one for secondary level education and one for tertiary level education. The reference group are respondents with less than secondary education. Income is measured on a 10-point scale, ranging from 0 (low) to 9 (high). Importance of religion in a respondent's life is a 4-point scale ranging from 0 (not at all important) to 3 (very important). Finally, gender is a 0–1 coded dummy variable, with males coded as 1.

At the country-level Norris and Inglehart (2004, p. 166) included in their OLS-regression: a society's type of religious culture, the HDI 1998 (cf. UNDP, 2000), and the Gastil Index 1999 (cf. Freedom House, 2009). For the type of religious culture I followed the classification of societies by their historically predominant major religions as proposed by Norris and Inglehart (2004, pp. 46–47). The classification distinguishes between Catholic, Protestant, Orthodox, Muslim, and Eastern religious cultures, whereby the Eastern religious culture embraces China, India, Japan, South Korea, and Viet Nam. Two of the countries included in our analyses are not listed by the classification: Kyrgyzstan is a historically Muslim society, Singapore an Eastern society. The HDI combines a society's level of educational attainment (adult literacy and the combined gross primary, secondary, and tertiary enrollment ratio), its level of longevity (life expectancy at birth), and its standard of living (real gross domestic product per capita in PPP U.S.$, cf. UNDP, 2000, p. 17). Among the included countries Uganda had the lowest HDI in 1998 (0.409) and Canada the highest one (0.935).* The Gastil Index (Level of Political Development) is computed as the arithmetic mean of the Political Rights Index and the Civil Liberties Index. By following Norris and Inglehart (2004, p. 51 and p. 179) the Gastil index has been reversed for ease of interpretation. Among the analyzed countries Viet Nam had the lowest possible value of 0 (not free society) on our reversed Gastil Index in 1999 and 10 countries reached the highest value of 6 (free society).

All multilevel models reported in this contribution were estimated with Mplus 5. In order to level off different sample sizes a weight was computed

* Appendix 11.A includes the complete information about the type of religious culture and the HDI 1998.

that ensures that each country is represented by the same number of respondents whereby the total number of respondents from all countries remained unchanged.

11.5 EMPIRICAL RESULTS

11.5.1 Work Ethic: One-Level CFA Versus Two-Level CFA

Weber's claim about the Protestant ethic concerned societal-level cultural effects (cf. also Norris & Inglehart, 2004, p. 162). Hence, I will test whether a one-level or a two-level CFA (for the latter case see Hox, 2002, pp. 225–250) results in a better model fit. If social forces inside a society contribute significantly to shape the citizens' work ethic then the latter model should turn out to be the better one.

Carrying out a CFA requires first looking at the correlations and covariances between the indicator variables. If the correlations are very weak then even the latent factor of a good fitting model will only explain much of rather nothing that these indicators have in common. Table 11.1 shows the correlations and covariances for the pooled sample one-level model (left-hand side) as well as for the two-level model where these coefficients are decomposed into their within countries and between countries parts (right-hand side).

For the one-level model, the correlations range between 0.25 ("humiliating" with "work first") and 0.39 ("lazy" with "duty to society"). Thus, the bivariate relationships between the four items are relatively strong. By decomposing the correlations into their within and between parts, the correlations for the within part become somewhat weaker and are now in the range between 0.19 ("humiliating" with "work first") and 0.35 ("lazy" with "duty to society"). The structure of the within correlation matrix remains very similar to the structure of the pooled sample model; that is, the rank order of the correlations has practically not changed. The correlations of the between countries matrix are much stronger, ranging from 0.61 ("lazy" with "work first") to 0.75 ("lazy" with "duty to society"). Furthermore, the between countries correlation matrix deviates somewhat from the structure of the within countries correlation matrix. However, even the weakest correlation of 0.19 is seen as sufficiently strong to carry out a CFA on the basis of all four items.

TABLE 11.1

Correlations, Covariances, Means, and ICC for the Four Indicators of Work Ethic

		Pooled Sample Correlations and Covariances					Within and Between Countries Correlations and Covariances			
		1	2	3	4		1	2	3	4
						within				
1	Humiliating	1.48	*0.37*	*0.30*	*0.25*		1.33	*0.32*	*0.26*	*0.19*
2	Lazy	0.52	1.35	*0.39*	*0.29*		0.40	1.15	*0.35*	*0.22*
3	Duty to Society	0.38	0.47	1.08	*0.37*		0.30	0.37	0.99	*0.33*
4	Work First	0.37	0.40	0.46	1.41		0.23	0.26	0.35	1.15
						between				
1	Humiliating						0.15	*0.73*	*0.68*	*0.70*
2	Lazy						0.13	0.21	*0.75*	*0.61*
3	Duty to Society						0.08	0.11	0.10	*0.71*
4	Work First						0.14	0.15	0.12	0.27
	Means	2.51	2.71	2.76	2.47		2.49	2.68	2.75	2.46
	ICC						0.10	0.16	0.09	0.19

Note: Italic entries in the upper diagonal are the correlations; 54,201 respondents from 53 countries; weighted data.

The means of the items to be found in the lower part of Table 11.1 for the one-level model are nearly exactly the same as for the two-level analysis. All items display a mean above the scale mean of 2. Thus, the respondents at least weakly agree with all four statements. “Duty to society” is not only the item with the highest level of agreement (nearly 2.75) but it is also the least controversial one as indicated by its comparably low variance (pooled sample: 1.08, two-level analysis: 0.99 within and 0.10 between). “Work first” has the lowest mean (slightly above 2.45). Although this item is also most controversial between the countries (0.27), the item “humiliating” turned out to be most controversial at the individual-level as well as in the pooled sample (1.33 and 1.48, respectively).

The last row of Table 11.1 includes each item’s intraclass correlation coefficient (ICC or ρ). As a heterogeneity measure it informs about the proportion of variance in a respective variable that is accounted for by the grouping structure in the population. The ICC is computed by dividing the macro-level variance of an item by its total variance on both levels (cf. Hox, 2002, p. 15 or Snijders & Bosker, 1999, p. 17). The heterogeneity between countries is lowest for “duty to society” and highest for “work first" (ICC = 0.09 and 0.19, respectively). As a rule of thumb, Hox (2002, p. 184) suggests using 0.05, 0.10, and 0.15 as small, medium, and large values for the ICC in general cases, and using the values 0.10, 0.20, and 0.30 in those cases where a much higher ICC appears reasonable on a priori grounds. Independent of which of the two rules is applied, our results can be understood as a first hint that a two-level CFA may fit the data better than a one-level CFA. Figure 11.B.1 (cf. Appendix 11.B) depicts the structure of the two-level CFA. Table 11.2 contains the results of the one-level CFA (Model 1a) and the two-level CFA (Model 1b).

The upper part of Table 11.2 includes two descriptive coefficients for model comparison (AIC and adjusted BIC) and four descriptive goodness-of-fit indices (CFI, TLI, RMSEA, and SRMR, cf. Brown, 2006, pp. 81–88) for evaluating the data fit of a CFA model. The CFI (Comparative Fit Index) and the TLI (Tucker–Lewis Index) both compare a user specified model to the "null" or "independence" model, whereby the CFI compensates for model complexity by including a penalty function for adding freely estimated parameters that do not markedly improve the model fit. Although there is no consensus about which indices and what cutoff criteria should be used, CFI and TLI values in the range of 0.90–0.95 may be indicative of an acceptable model fit (cf. Brown, 2006, pp. 86–87). With respect to the CFI, both CFA models turn out to have a highly acceptable model fit (one-level CFA: 0.970, two-level CFA: 0.956). The recommended minimal value of 0.90 for the TLI is reached by the one-level CFA (0.909) but not by the two-level CFA (0.867). The SRMR (standardized root mean square residuals) and the RMSEA (root mean square error of approximation) are indices for the degree of model misspecification: a low value indicates a better model fit. Conceptually, the SRMR is a measure for the average discrepancy between the observed correlations and the correlations predicted by the model (cf. Brown, 2006, p. 82). Like the CFI, the RMSEA also incorporates a penalty function for the number of freely estimated parameters. According to Hu and Bentler (1999, cf. Brown, 2006, p. 87), a reasonably good fit between the target model and the observed data is given if the SRMR value is close to 0.08 or below and the RMSEA value is close to 0.06 or below. As a rule of thumb, Browne and Cudeck (1993, cf. Brown, 2006, p. 87) suggest that RMSEA values less than 0.08 indicate an adequate fit, and values less than 0.05 a good

TABLE 11.2

Confirmatory Factor Analyses (CFA) for Work Ethic

	Model 1a: One-Level CFA			**Model 1b: Two-Level CFA**		
AIC	6,46,894.195			6,25,090.322		
Sample Size Adjusted BIC	6,46,962.864			6,25,204.770		
CFI	0.970			0.956		
TLI	0.909			0.867		
RMSEA	0.073			0.034		
SRMR	0.022					
SRMR Within				0.028		
SRMR Between				0.027		
Respondent Level (Level 1)	54,201 Respondents			54,201 Respondents		
Country Level (Level 2)				53 Countries		
	b	***z***		***b***	***z***	
Intercept Level 1						
Intercept Level 2						
Humiliating				2.486	44.789**	
Lazy				2.681	40.187**	
Duty to Society				2.751	59.069**	
Work First				2.463	32.327**	
Humiliating	2.507	456.185**				
Lazy	2.706	513.022**				
Duty to Society	2.757	587.369**				
Work First	2.472	460.575**				
Factor Loadings	***b***	***z***	**β**	***b***	***z***	**β**
Humiliating				1.000	-.-	0.834
Lazy				1.210	6.396**	0.846
Duty to Society				0.851	6.388**	0.866
Work First				1.291	7.123**	0.793
Humiliating	1.000	-.-	0.521	1.000	-.-	0.469
Lazy	1.138	82.008**	0.621	1.134	43.322**	0.573
Duty to Society	1.048	61.986**	0.638	1.146	26.729**	0.624
Work First	0.972	60.500**	0.518	0.900	19.839**	0.455

(*Continued*)

TABLE 11.2 (Continued)

Confirmatory Factor Analyses (CFA) for Work Ethic

	Model 1a: One-Level CFA		**Model 1b: Two-Level CFA**	
Residual Variances	**Variance**	***z***	**Variance**	***z***
Humiliating			0.045	4.037**
Lazy			0.060	2.955**
Duty to Society			0.025	2.902**
Work First			0.102	3.953**
Humiliating	1.074	110.268**	1.039	27.968**
Lazy	0.827	86.189**	0.770	23.364**
Duty to Society	0.641	80.093**	0.605	26.725**
Work First	1.030	119.838**	0.910	29.037**
Variance	**Variance**	***z***	**Variance**	***z***
Latent Factor (Work Ethic)			0.103	3.037**
Latent Factor (Work Ethic)	0.401	44.887**	0.293	16.753**

*$p \leq 0.05$; **$p \leq 0.01$

Note: Weighted data; Estimator: Full Maximum Likelihood with robust standard errors (MLR); the beta-coefficients are fully standardized; the scaling correction factor for Model 1b is 8.252.

model fit. The SRMR values of both CFA models are well below the recommended threshold.* Whereas the RMSEA of the two-level CFA (0.034) is well below 0.06, the RMSEA of the one-level model (0.073) is slightly above the value given by Hu and Bentler but remains below the value suggested by Browne and Cudeck. By taking all four goodness-of-fit indices into account, both models can be accepted. Hence, the question of the better fitting model remains.

The answer to this question is given by comparing the respective AIC (Akaike Information Criterion) and the adjusted BIC (Bayesian Information Criterion) of both CFA models. Both indices are based on

* Together with Norris and Inglehart (2004) measurement invariance has been assumed but not tested (for testing measurement invariance see Chapter 7 in this book). Testing measurement invariance with more than 30 countries is "unwieldy at best" (Selig, Card, & Little, 2008, p. 105). However, the very good fit of the SRMR within and the SRMR between of Model 1b might be a hint that measurement invariance is given for the vast majority of countries. In any case, research is needed in order to know more about the relationship between fit measures and measurement invariance in multilevel CFA.

the log-likelihood-function and a lower value indicates a better fitting model. In order to compensate for poor model parsimony, they both include a penalty function for adding freely estimated parameters that do not improve the model fit. Although the two-level CFA (Model 1b) is the more complex model, it reduces both model fit indices of the one-level CFA (Model 1a) by more than 21,500. Thus, Model 1b should be used for our further analyses.

The lower part of Table 11.2 gives an overview of the intercepts, factor loadings, and residual variances of the four work ethic items, as well as the variance of the latent factors. The labels for the indicator variables that were estimated at the country-level are indented to the right. "Humiliating" was chosen as a marker indicator that passes its metric onto the latent factor. The intercepts of both models are identical to the means of Table 11.1. "Lazy" is the item that shows the highest unstandardized factor loading in the one-level CFA ($b = 1.138$); "duty to society" is the one that displays the highest factor loading on the within latent factor for work ethic ($b = 1.146$) but the lowest factor loading on the between latent factor for work ethic ($b = 0.851$). However, the fully standardized beta-coefficients reveal that "duty to society" is nonetheless the item with the strongest factor loading for the one-level CFA (0.638) as well as at both levels of the two-level CFA (individual-level: 0.624, country-level: 0.866). Thus, "work as a duty to society" is the leading indicator for measuring work ethic. The items "lazy," "humiliating," and "work first" follow, ranked two to four. Again, this applies to the one-level CFA as well as to both levels of the two-level CFA. The standardized factor loadings for the country-level latent factor are always much stronger than those for the respondent-level latent factor. The minimum explained variance is estimated for the item "work first": in this case the within latent factor explains nearly 21% ($= 0.455 \times 0.455$) of the observed variance of this item.

A final look at the residual variances of the indicator variables (bottom of Table 11.2) shows that all of them have significant within as well as between residuals. Furthermore, the latent factors also have significant variances. These differences in the latent variable among respondents as well as between countries should—according to our hypotheses—be systematically related to respondent and country characteristics. In the following I will try to reduce these variances by including predictor variables into a multilevel regression model.

11.5.2 OLS-Regression Versus Multilevel Analysis: An Empirical Comparison

Table 11.3 contains the conventional OLS-regression model (Model 2a), the corresponding multilevel structural equation model (MLSEM, Model 2b), and the improved MLSEM (Model 2c). The first part of Table 11.3 (pp. 331–332) includes (besides the intercept of the OLS-regression) the CFA part of both multilevel models; the second part of Table 11.3 displays the regression part of all three models including the respective model fit indices. Since our main interest consists in a model comparison between OLS-regression and multilevel regression, I will restrict the interpretation to the second part of Table 11.3 (pp. 333–334).

The results of our OLS-regression confirm Norris and Inglehart's (2004, p. 179) findings: younger cohorts (H1), the better educated (H2), and people with a higher income (H3) display a significantly lower work ethic than older cohorts, less well-educated respondents, and people with a lower income. The more important religion is in an individual's life, the higher is her or his work ethic (H4); men have a significantly higher work ethic than women (H5). Thus, H1–H5 are corroborated. At the country-level, the HDI is negatively related to work ethic whereas the Level of Political Development (Gastil Index) turned out to be positively related to work ethic. Both effects are highly significant. These results replicate those of Norris and Inglehart (2004, p. 179): H6 is confirmed by OLS-regression whereas the finding for the Level of Political Development disconfirms H7. The results also show that people living in Protestant countries (reference group) today display the weakest work ethic among all major religious cultures (H8), not the strongest. This finding again corroborates that reported by Norris and Inglehart (2004). However, how far do these results also hold for the multilevel regression model?

The b-coefficients of Model 2b are rather similar to those of Model 2a. Huge differences between both models become visible with respect to the *t*-values/*z*-values.* Since OLS-regression ignores potential clustering in

* Mplus uses the *z*- instead of the *t*-distribution. Hence, in cases with comparably few macro-level units and a relatively low number of degrees of freedom for estimating a b-coefficient (say, df < 120) the acceptance region for the null hypothesis might be slightly too small; that is, the null hypothesis might be rejected too easily. This affects in general (a) macro-level main effects if the intercept is estimated with a random component, (b) slopes of micro-level indicators that are estimated with their own random component, and (c) macro-level indicators that interact with a micro-level indicator that is estimated with a random component. The predictor variables of macro-level latent factors are also affected. Substantial differences between both tests affect only borderline effects.

TABLE 11.3

Model Comparison: OLS-Regression Model, Multilevel Structural Equation Model (MLSEM), and Final Improved MLSEM

Respondent Level (Level 1)	Model 2a 54,201 Respondents		Model 2b 54,201 Respondents		Model 2c 54,201 Respondents	
Country Level (Level 2)	**53 Countries**		**53 Countries**		**53 Countries**	
	b	***t***	***b***	***z***	***b***	***z***
Intercept Level 1	4.051	145.297**				
Confirmatory Factor Analysis						
Intercept Level 2						
Humiliating			3.702	21.839**	1.652	2.786**
Lazy			3.905	18.503**	1.894	3.467**
Duty to Society			3.558	19.057**	2.386	9.171**
Work First			4.040	13.252**	1.388	1.868
Factor Loadings			***b***	***z***	***b***	***z***
Humiliating			1.000	-.-	1.000	-.-
Lazy			1.001	5.390**	0.954	5.058**
Duty to Society			0.627	4.480**	0.495	3.892**
Work First			1.315	4.932**	1.269	4.957**
Humiliating			1.000	-.-	1.000	-.-
Lazy			1.106	40.460**	1.107	40.393**
Duty to Society			1.229	31.014**	1.231	31.335**
Work First			1.021	21.847**	1.023	21.767**

(*Continued*)

TABLE 11.3 (Continued)

Model Comparison: OLS-Regression Model, Multilevel Structural Equation Model (MLSEM), and Final Improved MLSEM

	Model 2a		Model 2b		Model 2c	
Residual Variances	**Variance**	*t*	**Variance**	*z*	**Variance**	*z*
Humiliating			0.040	4.693**	0.037	4.523**
Lazy			0.104	2.890**	0.103	2.854**
Duty to Society			0.040	3.517**	0.039	3.513**
Work First			0.086	4.277**	0.081	3.853**
Humiliating			1.063	27.897**	1.064	27.927**
Lazy			0.818	24.928**	0.819	24.981**
Duty to Society			0.584	25.883**	0.584	25.806**
Work First			0.868	28.971**	0.867	28.899**
Predictor variables: Regression	*b*	*t*	*b*	*z*	*b*	*z*
Block 1: Level of Development Indexes						
Human Development Index 1998	−2.068	−56.464**	−1.837	−5.817**	4.178	2.400*
Squared Human Development Index 1998					−3.969	−3.261**
Political Development Index 1999	0.022	7.379**	0.024	0.330		
Block 3: Type of Religious Culture						
Catholic	0.309	39.787**	0.305	3.796**	0.253	3.183**

Orthodox	0.223	20.133**	0.290	1.974*	0.153	1.111
Muslim	0.564	39.581**	0.515	3.644**	0.369	2.636**
Eastern	0.437	35.610**	0.366	2.898**	0.265	2.685**
Block 2: Socio-demography						
Born 1946–1965	−0.235	−28.323**	−0.203	−12.539**	0.194	1.897
Human Development Index 1998					−0.485	−3.847**
Born 1966–1987	−0.358	−41.490**	−0.319	−12.490**	−0.010	−0.082
Human Development Index 1998					−0.375	−2.586**
Education 2nd Level	−0.075	−10.187**	−0.042	−3.290**	0.176	2.982**
Human Development Index 1998					−0.273	−3.579**
Education 3rd Level	−0.188	−19.975**	−0.117	−5.252**	0.475	3.585**
Human Development Index 1998					−0.737	−4.480**
Income	−0.005	−3.938**	−0.005	−2.246*	−0.005	−2.266*
Importance of Religion	0.085	27.407**	0.079	13.686**	0.079	13.701**
Gender (1 = Male)	0.078	12.422**	0.073	5.812**	0.072	5.808**

(*Continued*)

TABLE 11.3 (Continued)

Model Comparison: OLS-Regression Model, Multilevel Structural Equation Model (MLSEM), and Final Improved MLSEM

	Model 2a		Model 2b		Model 2c	
Variance Components Level 2	**Variance**	***t***	**Variance**	***z***	**Variance**	***z***
Intercept Level 2: Work Ethic			-.-	-.-	-.-	-.-
Born 1946–1965			0.009	4.063**	0.007	3.203**
Born 1966–1987			0.024	5.044**	0.022	4.745**
Education 2nd Level			0.004	2.923**	0.002	2.726**
Education 3rd Level			0.015	3.837**	0.007	3.082**
Income			0.000	2.596**	0.000	2.535*
Importance of Religion			0.001	2.012*	0.001	2.089*
Gender (1 = Male)			0.006	6.144**	0.006	6.261**
Level 1: Work Ethic			0.229	16.523**	0.228	16.481**
Fit Indices	**Adj. R^2**	**R^2-Change (F-Test)**	**AIC**	**Sample Size Adj. BIC**	**AIC**	**Sample Size Adj. BIC**
Block 1:	0.105		6,25,052.654	6,25,178.547	6,25,039.620	6,25,165.513
Block 1 + Block 2:	0.167	0.062**	6,20,541.613	6,20,741.899	6,20,462.654	6,20,685.829
Block 1 + Block 2 + Block 3:	0.206	0.039**	6,20,499.105	6,20,722.280	6,20,443.116	6,20,689.181

$^{*}p \leq 0.05$; $^{**}p \leq 0.01$

Note: Weighted data; Estimator: Full Maximum Likelihood with robust standard errors (MLR); Block 1: Work Ethic not fixed; the scaling correction factor for Model 2b is 5.259 and for Model 2c 4.887.

hierarchically structured data, it is highly susceptible to a heavy overestimation of the *t*-values. Multilevel analysis solves this problem by allowing each country to have its own b-coefficients that deviate by a certain amount (by a random u-term) from the respective grand mean. Thus, multilevel regression is less restrictive than OLS-regression and for that reason is also the more general but less parsimonious method. Whether or not a random term is needed has to be decided empirically—the expectation that no random term is needed is also an assumption that has to be tested empirically. The lower part of Table 11.3 shows that all explanatory variables of the respondent-level latent factor for work ethic had to be estimated with a separate variance component (random component; the variance of a u-term is called τ). This also explains why the *z*-values of our multilevel model are much lower than the *t*-values from the corresponding OLS-regression.

Although the *z*-values for the b-coefficients of Model 2b are much lower than the respective *t*-values of Model 2a, this will most often not result in substantial differences between both models. However, two substantial differences exist: firstly, the positive relationship between the Level of Political Development and the country-level latent factor for work ethic failed to become significant in the MLSEM ($z = 0.330$ instead of $t = 7.379$ for the OLS-regression). The b-coefficient of this macro-level variable did not become positive until the dummy variables for the type of religious culture (Block 3) were entered into the OLS-regression. As long as only the level of a country's development (Block 1) or Block 1 together with the socio-demographic variables (Block 2) was included into the OLS-regression, the Level of Political Development turned out to have the assumed significant negative impact on work ethic (H7). Since the Gastil Index is already highly correlated with the HDI ($r = 0.664$), the switch of the sign of the b-coefficient for the former index could be caused by multicollinearity. However, the Variance-Inflation Factor (VIF; cf. Fox, 1991, pp. 11–13) for the Gastil Index is 2.604 and for that reason is much too low to cause a multicollinearity problem. Instead we have to conclude on the basis of the more appropriate MLSEM that the t-value of the OLS-regression is misleading. No relationship exists between the Level of Political Development and work ethic. Thus, H7 has to be rejected. Secondly, the effect of the Orthodox culture is of borderline significance ($z = 1.974$). Since the number of degrees of freedom (df) for estimating the influence of the macro-level predictor variables on the country-level latent factor for work ethic is the number of countries ($N = 53$) minus the number of estimated macro-level predictors including the intercept ($N = 7$), it is advised in this case to carry out the significance test on the basis of the *t*-distribution. The *t*-value for 60 df and a significance level of 5% is 2.000 (tested two sided). Hence, Orthodox and Protestant cultures do not differ significantly with respect to work ethic.

The variance of the country-level latent factor in a CFA becomes the intercept variance component in MLSEM after macro-level predictors are introduced in order to explain the variance of a latent factor. In our case the variance component of the country-level latent factor became insignificant and was fixed for that reason. Thus, we successfully explained the differences in work ethic between the countries that were found in the earlier CFA. A final look at the model fit (bottom of Table 11.3) corroborates Norris and Inglehart's (2004, pp. 166–167) finding that the type of religious culture contributes to explain differences in work ethic. Even after controlling for all other predictor variables (Block 1 and 2), the R^2-change test for the OLS-regression became significant when type of religion (Block 3) was entered. This result is consistent with that of our multilevel model (Model 2b), where one has to rely on descriptive indices like the AIC and the adjusted BIC. Both indices reduced slightly (43 and 20, respectively) after type of religious culture (Block 3) was entered in the final step. Compared with the former two-level CFA model, the AIC has decreased by slightly more than 4500 and the adjusted BIC by slightly less than 4500. Thus, Model 2b has the better fit than the two-level CFA of Table 11.2.

So far it has been illustrated that by using OLS-regression instead of the more appropriate multilevel framework for analyzing hierarchically structured data, one is in danger of drawing wrong conclusions from hypotheses testing. In order to overcome the discrepancies between the theory and the empirical model of Norris and Inglehart (2004, p. 179), in a final step I estimated Model 2c. Since the Level of Political Development turned out to be insignificant, it has been removed from the multilevel model. To test the expected curvilinear relationship between the HDI and work ethic, the squared term of that index was additionally included into the estimated model. Furthermore, I also entered the cross-level interaction terms between the HDI and the cohorts on the one hand and the HDI and education on the other hand. All five additionally estimated b-coefficients are highly significant.

According to H1a, younger cohorts should display a higher work ethic than older cohorts in modernizing societies and a lower work ethic than older cohorts in postmodernizing societies. The main effect of a multiplicative interaction represents the influence of one x-variable of the interaction term under the *condition* that the other x-variable of the interaction term equals zero (cf. Friedrich, 1982, pp. 804–809). Thus, a cohort's main effect ($b = 0.194$ and $b = -0.010$) represents the respective cohort effect under the hypothetical condition that the HDI of a country is zero. To avoid interpreting such (meaningless) extrapolations beyond the observed range, it is recommended inserting the observed extreme values into the equation of the first partial derivative of the regression equation.* Uganda had the lowest HDI in 1998 (0.409), Canada the highest one (0.935). So, the conditional b-coefficients for the middle and the youngest cohort of Uganda as a modernizing country are –0.004 ($= 0.194 - 0.485 \times 0.409$; $z = -0.081$, $p > .05$) and –0.163 ($= -0.010 - 0.375 \times 0.409$; $z = -2.615$, $p < .01$), respectively; the corresponding cohort effects for Canada as a postmodernizing society are –0.259 ($= 0.194 - 0.485 \times 0.935$; $z = -11.675$, $p < .01$) and –0.361 ($= -0.010 - 0.375 \times 0.935$; $z = -11.247$, $p < .01$).† Since younger cohorts in all countries display a lower work ethic than older cohorts (although the difference between the middle cohort born from 1946 to 1965 and the oldest cohort born before 1946 as reference group remains insignificant for Uganda), the theoretically expected, deeply rooted value change of modernizing societies toward a higher work ethic can, at least, not be traced back to cohort replacement. As a consequence, H1a has to be rejected.‡ For Uganda, the conditional b-coefficients for the second and the third level of education are 0.064 ($= 0.176 - 0.273 \times 0.409$; $z = 2.210$, $p < 0.05$) and 0.174 ($= 0.475 - 0.737 \times 0.409$; $z = 2.608$, $p < .01$), respectively. The corresponding effects for Canada are –0.079 ($= 0.176 - 0.273 \times 0.935$; $z = -4.502$, $p < .01$) and –0.212 ($= 0.475 - 0.737 \times 0.935$; $z = -7.354$, $p < .01$). Thus,

* The first partial derivative for the cohort born from 1946 to 1965 is, for instance, $\Delta\check{Y}/\Delta$ Born 1946–1965 = 0.194–0.485 × (HDI 1998).

† The formula for calculating conditional standard errors is given by Friedrich (1982, p. 810). Conditional z-values can be calculated by dividing the conditional b-coefficient by its conditional standard error.

‡ One might try to save H1a by assuming that at least the majority of traditional countries would have not developed or even have suffered from economic decline during the second half of the twentieth century. Hence, modernization would have taken place, at best, in a minority of traditional countries. This assumption, however, clearly contradicts Inglehart's (1997, pp. 229–230, cf. also p. 332) own finding according to that poorer countries showed in the past higher growth rates than wealthier countries.

H2a is confirmed: whereas education contributes significantly to increase work ethic in modernizing societies, it significantly reduces work ethic in postmodernizing societies.

Even after controlling for these interaction effects, the Level of Human Development turned out to be curvilinear related to work ethic. The linear term has a significant positive influence ($z = 2.400$, $p < 0.05$), the squared term a significant negative one ($z = -3.261$, $p < 0.01$). Since the Level of Human Development interacts with cohorts and education, the turning point where the positive impact of the HDI on work ethic changes into a negative one is group specific: for the oldest cohort with the lowest level of education the turning point is reached in societies with a HDI of 0.526; for the age cohort born from 1946 to 1965 with the highest level of education the turning point is already reached in countries with a HDI of 0.372.* For all other possible combinations of cohort and education the turning point is in between. Societies with a HDI of 0.739 or below in 1998 were classified by Norris and Inglehart (2004, p. 247) as agrarian societies.† Thus, the decrease in work ethic already set in during the process of modernization. Whereas the curvilinear pattern per se corroborates H3a, the decreasing work ethic in some modernizing countries is hardly compatible with Inglehart's theory.‡ A final look at the fit indices shows that Model 2c is fitting slightly better than Model 2b: the AIC decreases by roughly 56, the adjusted BIC by nearly 33.

11.6 CONCLUSIONS

A main methodological purpose of this contribution was to illustrate the disadvantages of using OLS-regression for international comparisons instead of the more adequate multilevel analysis. The empirical comparison between both methods revealed tremendous differences in the respective t- and z-values of the b-coefficients that are caused by the much too

* The first partial derivative for HDI 1998 is $\Delta\check{Y}/\Delta$ HDI 1998 = 4.178 – 2 × 3.969 × (HDI 1998) -0.485 (Born 1946–1965)-0.375 × (Born 1966–1987)-0.273 × (Education 2nd Level)-0.737 × (Education 3rd Level).

† Appendix 11.A informs about the relationship between HDI 1998 and type of society.

‡ There are no substantial changes in the other effects (including the conditional effects) if the squared HDI for 1998 would be dropped from Model 2c. The AIC and the adjusted BIC would, however, slightly increase (by less than 10).

small standard errors of the OLS-regression. As a consequence, the null hypothesis will be too often erroneously rejected, and the results might be very misleading. The more substantial purpose of the article consisted in testing whether the results reported by Norris and Inglehart (2004) also hold for multilevel analysis. A somewhat surprising result was that for OLS-regression the Level of Human Development and the Level of Political Development turned out to be related in an opposite direction to work ethic. Multilevel analysis revealed that the latter relationship is spurious. The same applies to the difference between historically Protestant and historically Orthodox societies.

In order to overcome inconsistencies between the theory and the model presented by Norris and Inglehart (2004), interaction effects between the HDI and cohorts as well as between the HDI and education were also tested. The results revealed that intergenerational replacement cannot account for the assumed value change in modernizing societies: the youngest generation in all societies under investigation displays the weakest work ethic. Higher education on the other hand turned out to be positively related to work ethic in modernizing societies and negatively related to work ethic in postmodernizing societies. If education is above all an excellent indicator for formative security then higher educated and younger cohorts should both have been related in the same way to work ethic; that is, the higher educated and the youngest cohort should have displayed a weaker work ethic than the respective reference group. Our results, however, corroborate the expectation that education has a strong cognitive component of its own.

Do the results contradict Weber, as assumed by Norris and Inglehart (2004, p. 163) when they wrote "contrary to Weber's thesis … *those living in Protestant societies today display the weakest work ethic*?" Such a far reaching conclusion can surely not be drawn from the findings, already for the reason that restless professional work was seen by the Calvinist doctrine as a means for the individual believer of attaining certainty of grace. Work was perceived "as a moral duty pursued for its own sake" (cf. Norris & Inglehart, 2004, p. 160) but never had a collectivist imprint like "work as a duty to society." Finally, Weber (1992/1930, pp. 123–124) never expected the Protestant ethic to persist, but rather assumed that the capitalist order, once established in a society, would force the individual to work like the Puritan who wanted to work in a calling.

REFERENCES

Abramson, P. R., & Inglehart, R. (1996). Formative security, education and Postmaterialism: A response to Davis. *Public Opinion Quarterly, 60*, 450–455.

Browne, M. W. & Cudeck, R. (1993). Alternate ways of assessing model fit. In K. A. Bollen & J. S. Long (Eds.), *Testing Structural Equation Models* (pp. 136–162). Newbury Park, CA: Sage.

Brown, T. A. (2006). *Confirmatory factor analysis for applied research*. New York, NY: The Guilford Press.

The European Values Study Foundation and World Values Survey Association. (2006). European and World Values Surveys four-wave integrated data file, 1981-2004, v.20060423. Retrieved from http://www.jdsurvey.net/jds/jdsurveyAnalisis.jsp?ES_COL=131&Idioma=I&SeccionCol=10&ESID=397 (accessed August 1, 2006).

Fox, J. (1991). *Regression diagnostics*. Newbury Park, CA: Sage.

Freedom House. (2009). Freedom in the world comparative and historical data. Country ratings and status 1972–2007. Retrieved from http://www.freedomhouse.org/template.cfm?page=439 (accessed February 18, 2009).

Friedrich, R. J. (1982). In defense of multiplicative terms in multiple regression equations. *American Journal of Political Science, 26*(4), 797–833.

Hox, J. (2002). *Multilevel analysis. Techniques and applications*. Mahwah, NJ: Lawrence Erlbaum.

Hu, L., & Bentler, P. M. (1999). Cutoff criteria for fit indexes in covariance structure analysis: Conventional criteria versus new alternatives. *Structural Equation Modeling, 6*, 1–55.

Inglehart, R. (1977). *The silent revolution. Changing values and political styles among Western publics*. Princeton, NJ: Princeton University Press.

Inglehart, R. (1981). Post-materialism in an environment of insecurity. *American Political Science Review, 74*(4), 880–900.

Inglehart, R. (1990). *Culture shift in advanced industrial society*. Princeton, NJ: Princeton University Press.

Inglehart, R. (1997). *Modernization and postmodernization. Cultural, economic, and political change in 43 societies*. Princeton, NJ: Princeton University Press.

Inglehart, R., & Norris, P. (2003). *Rising tide. Gender equality and cultural change around the world*. Cambridge: Cambridge University Press.

Maslow, A. H. (1954). *Motivation and personality*. New York, NY: Harper & Brothers.

Meuleman, B., & Billiet, J. (2009). A Monte Carlo sample size study. How many countries are needed for accurate multilevel SEM? *Survey Research Methods, 3*(1), 45–58.

Norris, P., & Inglehart, R. (2004). *Sacred and secular. Religion and politics worldwide*. Cambridge: Cambridge University Press.

Selig, J. P., Card, N. A., & Little, T. D. (2008). Latent variable structural equation modeling in cross-cultural research. Multigroup and multilevel approaches. In F. J. R. van de Vijver, D. A. van Hemert, & Y. H. Poortinga (Eds.), *Multilevel analysis of individuals and cultures* (pp. 93–119). New York, NY: Lawrence Erlbaum.

Snijders, T. A. B., & Bosker, R. J. (1999). *Multilevel analysis. An introduction to basic and advanced multilevel modeling*. Thousand Oaks, CA: Sage.

UNDP. (2000). Human development report 1998. Human rights and human development. Retrieved from http://hdr.undp.org/en/media/HDR_2000_EN.pdf

Weber, M. (1992/1930). *The Protestant ethic and the spirit of capitalism*. London: Routledge.

APPENDIX 11.A

Included Countries (and Year of Fieldwork)

European Values Study (Wave III): Belarus 2000 (0.781, IN, O), Belgium 1999 (0.925, PI, C), Bulgaria 1999 (0.772, IN, O), Croatia 1999 (0.795, IN, C), Czech Republic 1999 (0.843, IN, C), Denmark 1999 (0.911, PI, P), Estonia 1999 (0.801, IN, P), Finland 2000 (0.917, PI, P), France 1999 (0.917, PI, C), Germany 1999 (East and West separately; 0.911, PI, P), Great Britain 1999 (0.918, PI, P), Hungary 1999 (0.817, IN, C), Iceland 1999 (0.927, PI, P), Ireland 1999 (0.907, PI, C), Italy 1999 (0.903, PI, C), Latvia 1999 (0.771, IN, P), Lithuania 1999 (0.789, IN, C), Luxembourg 1999 (0.908, PI, C), Malta 1999 (0.865, IN, C), Netherlands 1999 (0.925, PI, P), Northern Ireland 1999 (0.918, PI, P), Poland 1999 (0.814, IN, C), Romania 1999 (0.770, IN, O), Russia 1999 (0.771, IN, O), Slovakia 1999 (0.825, IN, C), Slovenia 1999 (0.861, IN, C), Spain 1999 (0.899, PI, C), Sweden 1999 (0.926, PI, P), Turkey 2001 (0.732, IN, M), Ukraine 1999 (0.744, IN, O).

World Values Survey (Wave IV): Albania 2002 (0.713, AG, M), Argentina 1999 (0.837, IN, C), Canada 2000 (0.935, PI, C), Chile 2000 (0.826, IN, C), China 2001 (0.706, AG, E), India 2001 (0.563, AG, E), Japan 2000 (0.924, PI, E), Kyrgyzstan 2003 (0.706, AG, M), Mexico 2000 (0.784, IN, C), Morocco 2001 (0.589, AG, M), Peru 2001 (0.737, AG, C), Philippines 2001 (0.744, IN, C), Republic of Korea 2001 (0.854, IN, E), Republic of Macedonia 2001 (0.763, IN, O), Republic of Moldova 2002 (0.700, AG, O), Singapore 2002 (0.881, IN, E), South Africa 2001 (0.697, AG, P), Uganda 2001 (0.409, AG, P), United Republic of Tanzania 2001 (0.415, AG, P), United States 1999 (0.929, PI, P), Viet Nam 2001 (0.671, AG, E), Zimbabwe 2001 (0.555, AG, P).

Note: The information in brackets refers to the HDI 1998 (cf. UNDP 2000), the type of society, and to a country's type of religious culture. "PI" refers to Postindustrial countries, "IN" to Industrial countries, and "AG" to Agrarian countries (cf. Norris & Inglehart, 2004, pp. 243–246). "P" refers to Protestant countries, "C" to Catholic countries, "O" to Orthodox countries, "M" to Muslim countries, and "E" to Eastern countries (cf. Norris & Inglehart, 2004, pp. 46–47). Societies with a HDI score over 0.900 were classified as postindustrial countries, societies with a HDI score between 0.739 and 0.899 as industrial countries, and societies with a HDI of 0.739 or below as Agrarian countries (cf. Norris & Inglehart, 2004, p. 247). The classification for the type of society was slightly modified by the authors by separately taking into account the per capita GDP (in PPP $U.S.).

Excluded Countries (and Year of Fieldwork as Well as Reason for Exclusion)

European Values Study (Wave III): Austria 1999 (4-point answer scale for items on work ethic), Greece 1999 (no representative survey), Portugal 1999 (6-point income scale).

World Values Survey (Wave IV): Algeria 2002 (no question on work ethic), Bangladesh 2002 (4-point answer scale for items on work ethic), Bosnia 2001 (no HDI 1998 available), Egypt 2000, Indonesia 2001, Iran 2000, and Iraq 2004 (no question on work ethic), Israel 2001 (only one country for this religious culture), Jordan 2001 (no question on work ethic), Montenegro 2001 (not independent in 2001, no HDI 1998 available), Nigeria 2000 and Pakistan 2001 (no question on work ethic), Puerto Rico 2001 (self-governing unincorporated territory of the United States, no HDI 1998 available), Saudi Arabia 2003 (no question on work ethic), Serbia 2001 (no HDI 1998 available), Venezuela 2000 (no question on work ethic).

APPENDIX 11.B

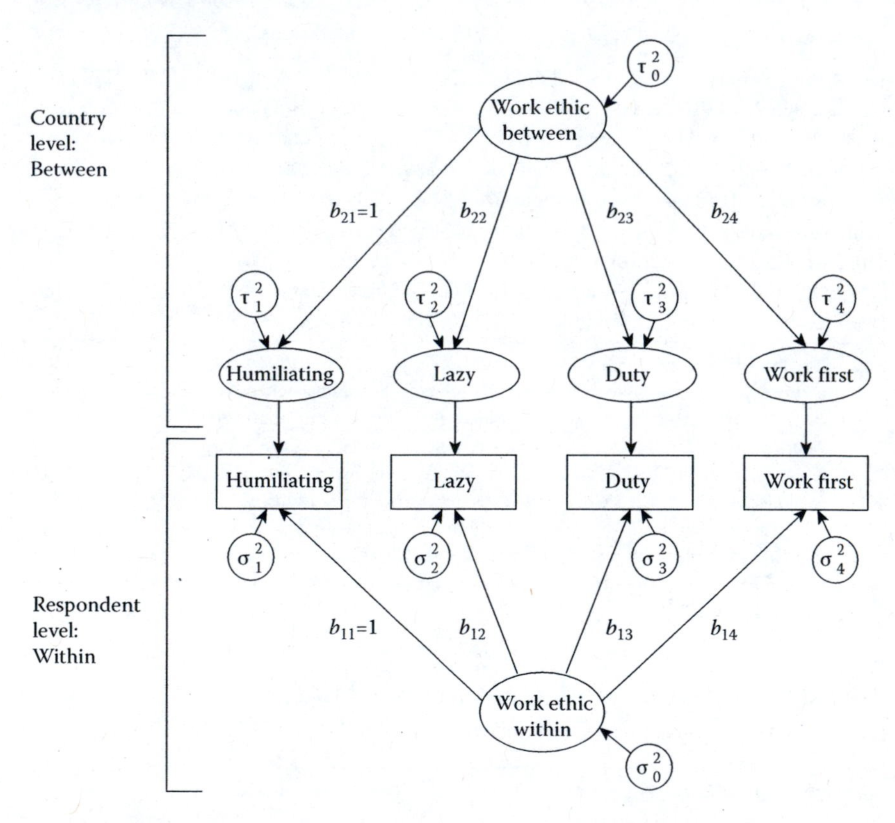

FIGURE 11.B.1
Model of the Two-Level CFA for Work Ethic.

12

Multilevel Structural Equation Modeling for Cross-Cultural Research: Exploring Resampling Methods to Overcome Small Sample Size Problems

Remco Feskens
Utrecht University and IQ Healthcare, UMC St. Radboud Nijmegen

Joop J. Hox
Utrecht University

12.1 INTRODUCTION

Cross-cultural research often deals with hierarchical data structures, either due to the sampling procedure, or to characteristics of sampled units that are related to a grouping variable. Multilevel models offer the possibility to take the resulting dependency between group and individual characteristics into account. In addition to the more traditional technique to deal with hierarchical or nested data, which is multilevel regression analysis, both multigroup structural equation models (SEM) and multilevel SEM are available to analyze such data. Both of these approaches share the well-known advantages of SEM. Among others this means that latent variables can be included in the analysis and that variables can be endogenous (outcomes) as well as exogenous (predictors). This provides very flexible model building possibilities, for instance to model mediation or moderation processes. Multilevel SEM combines the advantages of multilevel analysis and SEM. Compared to multigroup SEM, the sample size of the grouping variable is not limited, and it is possible to include group level variables in the model. An example of a multigroup SEM can be found in Chapter 7 of this book.

Multilevel SEM assumes that a given set of countries is a sample from a larger population. Therefore it does not estimate a unique single parameter value for each country, but instead it assumes a distribution of parameter values. On the other hand, multigroup SEM is a fixed model, generally resulting in a large model with many unique parameter values, one set for each country. For this reason, multilevel SEM is more parsimonious compared to multigroup SEM when the number of countries increases. At the same time, a major drawback of multilevel SEM is that the requirement of a sufficiently large sample size at the group level is often not met. If the sample size at the group level is small, the standard errors of parameters at the group level are likely to be underestimated, which compromises hypothesis testing (Busing, 1993; Hox, 1998). Meuleman and Billiet (2009) show using Monte Carlo simulation studies that multilevel SEM with 20 groups leads to inaccurate estimation of model parameters. In particular, standard errors of between-level parameters tend to be seriously underestimated. Depending on the model complexity they recommend group level sample sizes ranging from 40 to 100. This fits with the conclusions that Hox and Maas (2001) draw from a large simulation study on sample sizes in multilevel SEM. They conclude that for accurate estimation and testing, the group level sample size should be at least 50. Most cross-sectional surveys are, however, limited in the number of participating countries. For instance, the well-known European Social Survey (ESS) now includes 31 participating countries. To overcome this problem of too few cases at the group level while using multilevel SEM, we will investigate the use of resampling methods in order to obtain accurate estimates and standard errors. Resampling methods are frequently used in small sample size research (cf. Yung & Chan, 1999). The bootstrap approach, a popular statistical resampling method is often suggested to deal with the problem of obtaining accurate estimates of errors with small sample sizes. Throughout this chapter we will focus on standard errors as they are the simplest measure of accuracy. As will become clear throughout this chapter—to our knowledge—currently no popular software can generate resampled standard errors in multilevel SEM. In order to assess the accuracy of standard errors in a small group sample multilevel SEM, we will compare these standard errors with combined standard errors from a multigroup analysis.

12.2 USING RESAMPLING METHODS TO OBTAIN ACCURATE STANDARD ERRORS

As described above, often datasets used for multilevel analysis do not have a sufficiently large sample size, which may lead to unstable or biased estimates. In order to obtain robust estimates of standard errors and confidence intervals of population parameters several resampling methods can be used to assess the sampling distribution. Rodgers (1999) defines a sampling distribution as "the distribution of a statistic across all samples of a given size drawn from a specified population" (p. 442). Several different approaches have been developed to empirically assess sampling distributions. Among the most popular are the jackknife and the bootstrap procedures. The jackknife technique uses subsets of the available data to assess the precision of sample statistics. Typically, some version of "leave one out" is used to form N jackknife samples of size N-1 each (N being the total sample size). The variability among these N-1 samples is used as an indication of the sampling variability. The bootstrap generalizes the jackknife by using random subsets of the dataset, typically by drawing with replacement a large number of samples of size N from the original dataset. In this chapter we will use the bootstrap method as a tool to evaluate the precision of multilevel estimates in situations with a small sample size at the group level. In this chapter we will explicitly focus on the bootstrap procedure.

12.2.1 Bootstrap

Introduced by Efron (1979) and expanded upon by Efron and Tibshirani (1993) and Davison and Hinkley (1997), the bootstrap is a computer-based method for estimating the standard errors of a parameter. Assuming that the population and empirical distributions converge with an infinite sample size, it resamples from the sample data in order to obtain a bootstrapped sampling distribution of the parameters of interest. In addition to generating bootstrapped standard errors, the bootstrap procedure can also generate other measures of accuracy, such as bias of estimates. In this chapter we do not investigate parameter bias, since simulations (Hox & Maas, 2001) generally show that these are small, especially when regression coefficients are estimated. Instead, we focus on the standard errors, which are a determinant of the width of the confidence intervals, and in the absence of bias indicative of the coverage. In traditional analyses, estimates of the standard errors heavily lean on the underlying assumptions of the central limit theory. Asymptotically, the standard errors are accurate; with large sample sizes, they are accurate enough to be used for testing. With small sample sizes, however, the asymptotic properties are not reached, and sufficient accuracy is often not met. The bootstrap procedure is less dependent on the assumptions of the central limit theory and provides an alternative for the estimation of standard errors.

Yung and Chan (1999) summarize the bootstrap procedure as follows: (1) Define a pseudopopulation distribution for resampling, usually defined as the distribution of the sample data. (2) Resample with replacement N independent observations, this is called the bootstrap resample, compute the parameters of interest. (3) Repeat Step 2 several times, the generated sets of values form the bootstrap sampling distribution.

In general, it holds that with more observations, it will be more likely that the distribution of a random sample resembles the population distribution. Ideally, the number of observations will go to infinity. This ideal bootstrap has the smallest possible standard deviations among nearly unbiased estimates of the standard error (Efron & Tibshirani, 1993). Of course, practical issues limit the number of observations and Efron and Tibshirani provided the following rule of thumb for a satisfactory number of replications: "very seldom are more than 200 replications needed for estimating a standard error" (p 52).

12.2.2 Jackknife

Just like the bootstrap, the jackknife is a resampling method to estimate bias and standard error of a statistic. In fact, both methods yield the same results in many applications. The jackknife computes a statistic several times by leaving out one observation at each sample moment. The jackknife was originally invented by Quenouille (1956) and developed further by Tukey (1958). Its name introduced by Tukey (1958) is referring to its methodological usefulness and flexibility. Contrary to this methodological advantage, the jackknife is computationally demanding. It does make use (just like the bootstrap method) of the variability between subsamples to estimate bias and standard errors.

Both methods differ in their sampling method: the bootstrap method requires resampling with replacement, whereas the jackknife requires resampling without replacement (Rodgers, 1999). They also differ in the sample size. The bootstrap uses the full sample size of the original data; the jackknife only uses a part of that, which requires adjustments at a later stage when jackknifed standard errors are determined. Furthermore, Efron and Tibshirani (1993) show that the jackknife is a linear approximation of the bootstrap. For linear statistics this is not a problem, but compared to the bootstrap, the jackknife will lead to a loss of information if nonlinear statistics are involved. For these reasons, the bootstrap has replaced the jackknife as the standard resampling method to determine bias and standard errors of estimates when asymptotic statistics are either not available or their assumptions are assumed to be violated.

12.3 APPLICATION EXAMPLE

We will apply the bootstrap method as a tool to obtain accurate standard errors on a small multilevel SEM model using the ESS data. Started in 2001 the ESS is a biannual returning survey, monitoring attitude and value changes in European countries. The fifth round of the survey is officially planned to start in June 2009. We perform this application on ESS data, because the structure of the ESS data illustrates very well the problem of multilevel SEM, a small sample size at the group level (here a limited number of countries). Above that, with already around 24,500 registered users worldwide, the ESS is also a much used database by substantive researchers.

A total of 22 countries participated in the first round (2001–2003), 26 countries took part in round 2, and 25 countries in the third round.*

* The following countries participated in the first round: Austria, Belgium, Czech Republic, Denmark, Finland, France, Germany, Greece, Hungary, Ireland, Israel, Italy, Luxemburg, the Netherlands, Norway, Poland, Portugal, Slovenia, Spain, Sweden Switzerland, and the United Kingdom. The same countries, except Israel, participated in the second round of the ESS, and Estonia, Iceland, Slovakia, Ukraine, and Turkey participated for the first time. In the third round Czech Republic, Greece, Iceland, Israel, Italy, Ireland, Luxemburg, and Turkey did not participate, where Bulgaria, Cyprus, Estonia, Latvia. Romania, Russia participated in this round for the first time.

A record of 31 countries has confirmed their participation for round 4. We will use the available data from the first three rounds to illustrate the bootstrap method. A total of 115,862 responses have been collected during the three rounds. This data has been retrieved from the ESS Web site (January 2009) and consists of data from the following countries: Austria, Belgium, Bulgaria, Cyprus, Czech Republic, Denmark, Estonia, Finland, France, Germany, Greece, Hungary, Ireland, Italy, Latvia, the Netherlands, Norway, Poland, Portugal, Russia, Slovakia, Slovenia, Spain, Sweden, Switzerland, and the United Kingdom. So the total dataset contains responses of a total of 26 countries. This number of participating countries illustrates the dilemma for the analyst. Carrying out a multigroup analysis with a complex SEM on 26 groups is well within the capabilities of current SEM software, but interpreting the output that produces a potentially different set of parameter estimates for each or any of these 26 countries is a daunting challenge. The multilevel approach is more parsimonious, and therefore less intimidating, but a group level sample size of 26 is too small to feel confident about the resulting estimates, and especially about the corresponding standard errors.

Our application example makes use of the following simple multilevel SEM, where the main substantive question is to what degree does the age and educational level of the respondents have an impact on the attitude toward immigration. Figure 12.1 shows a graphical display of the model.

The latent variable "attitude toward immigration" is measured by three manifest variables all about respondents' perceptions of allowing immigration.* These three variables are all questions with a four point answer scale. At the individual level attitude toward immigration is regressed on education level and age. For convergence purposes, age (with by far the largest variance) has been divided by 10. At the country level, attitudes toward immigration are regressed on relative inflow of immigrants. For simplicity, the residual disturbances and measurement errors are omitted from Figure 12.1.

* The exact wording of the questions was: "To what extent do you think [country] should allow people of the same race or ethnic group as most [country's] people to come and live here," "How about people of a different race or ethnic group from most [country] people?" and "How about people from the poorer countries outside Europe?" for items allow 1, 2, 3, respectively. All answer categories are coded as 1 = Allow many to come and live here; 2 = Allow some; 3 = Allow a few; 4 = Allow none. Age is measured in years, divided by 10.

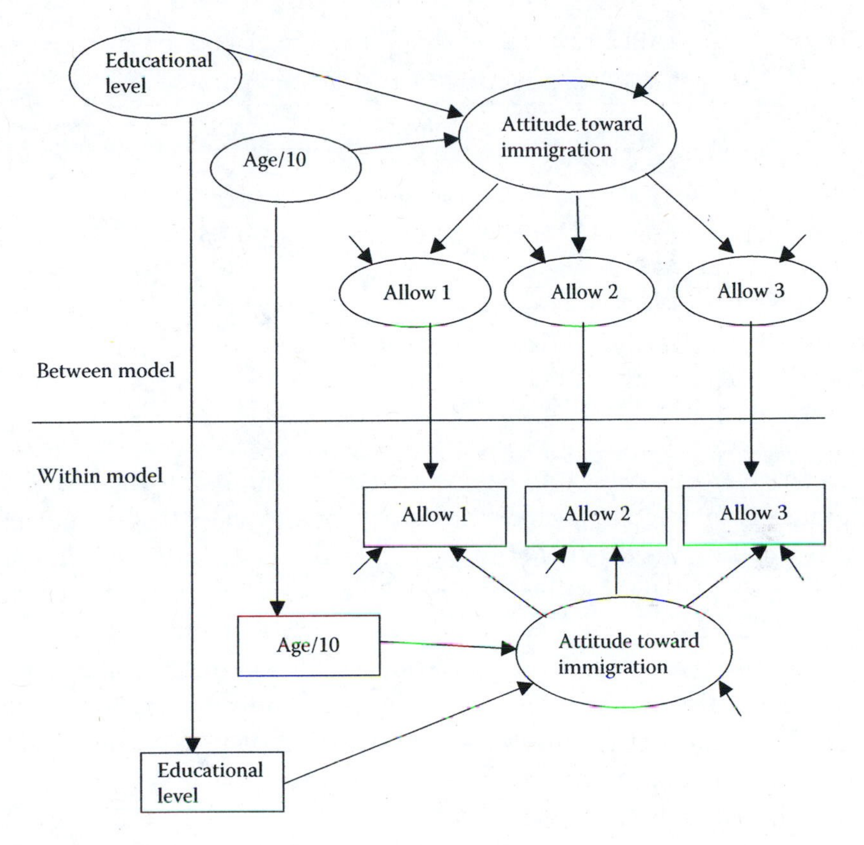

FIGURE 12.1
Illustration of the multilevel structural equation model.

First we have tested if there is a statistically significant time-effect over the three rounds. This was not the case and therefore we have decided to continue our analysis with a model where all respondents over the different round are pooled together. First we conduct a simple one-group SEM analysis, ignoring the hierarchical structure of the sample data. Results are found in Table 12.1.

Since the sample size is very large, the assessment of model fit is mainly based on two goodness-of-fit indices that are less sensitive to sample size: Bentler comparative fit index (CFI; see Bentler, 1990) and the root mean square error of approximation (RMSEA) value (Browne & Cudeck, 1993). The CFI value indicates the proportion in the improvement of the overall fit of the specified model relative to an independence model in which

TABLE 12.1

Simple SEM Results

	Estimates	S.E.
Allow 1	1.000	—
Allow 2	1.260	0.005
Allow 3	1.144	0.005
Age	0.023	0.001
Education	–0.033	0.002

Chi-square test of model fit (chi-square = 159.694, df = 4, *P*-value = .0000).

CFI = 0.998; RMSEA = 0.021; SRMR = 0.006.

the variables are assumed to be uncorrelated (Kline 2005). The RMSEA fit index is an exact fit in which the null hypothesis states that the model corresponds to the data (RMSEA = 0.00). In this case, both the CFI and RMSEA support the data by showing a good model fit, the CFI is 0.998 and the RMSEA is 0.021, which is well within accepted limits for close fit. The standardized root mean square residual (SRMR) value is also satisfactory. This analysis does not take into account that individual responses are nested within countries. The intraclass coefficient (ICC) is an important measure in order to determine to which degree variation at the individual level can be attributed to variation to the national level. In this case the ICC for the dependent variables are 0.073, 0.108, and 0.127 for allow 1, allow 2, and allow 3, respectively. These values are usually not in cross-national research and they indicate that the group structure should be included in the model. Multiple group confirmatory analysis shows that partial measurement equivalence holds, so we can safely continue our multilevel SEM analysis. This claim is supported by earlier research by Davidov, Meuleman, Billiet, & Schmidt (2008) and Meuleman, Davidov, and Billiet (2009).

We have estimated random coefficients in the model, to accommodate the partial measurement equivalence using a random loading, but none of the associated variance components appeared to be statistically significant. For identification reasons we had to constrain the residual variance of allow 2 to zero. This was done in order to prevent that due to the small size at the group level this variance would be estimated as a (small) negative value. Results of the multilevel SEM model can be found in Table 12.2.

TABLE 12.2

Multilevel SEM Results

	Within Level	
	Estimates	**S.E.**
Allow 1	1.000	—
Allow 2	1.238	0.030
Allow 3	1.110	0.021
Age	0.036	0.005
Education	–0.037	0.017
	Between Level	
	Estimates	**S.E.**
Allow 1	1.000	—
Allow 2	1.692	0.306
Allow 3	1.832	0.375
Age	0.016	0.014
Education	–0.080	0.042

Chi-square test of model fit value (31.434, df = 9, *P*-value = .0002).
CFI = 0.994, RMSEA = 0.005; SRMR = value for between model 0.093; value for within model 0.005.

Model fit indices values are excellent again, confirming the model. If we look at the standard errors, we see that these are much larger than the standard errors in the model that does not account for the hierarchical structure of the data. However, these standard errors may still be biased due to small group level size. Here resampling methods can provide a solution.

Our aim is to implement the bootstrap procedure in this multilevel SEM example. Wang, Carpenter, and Kepler (2006, 2007) show how to conduct nonparametric residual bootstrap multilevel modeling. They transform centered level 1 and 2 residuals in such a way that their variance/covariance matrix resembles the original model residual variance/covariance matrix. Bootstrap resamples are drawn from these transformed residuals. Together with the original independent variable they form the bootstrap samples. A multilevel model is then fitted to each of the bootstrap datasets, and the standard deviation from the bootstrapped model is used to estimate a bootstrapped standard error (Wang et al., 2006). In their illustration model they find a modest downward-bias in standard errors. Another approach is introduced by Stapleton (2008). She shows how to implement, among others, the bootstrap procedure in aggregated SEM models using complex sample data. In these aggregated models the researcher is primarily looking for theoretical models at the individual level. Multilevel modeling on the contrary involves the assessment of theoretical models with components at different levels. She estimates standard errors using the original parameter estimates and bootstrapped weights (see Stapleton, 2008). Her application model shows that conventional analysis suffers from a downward bias of standard errors as well. Integrating the approaches of Wang et al. (2006, 2007) and Stapleton (2008) should lead to our goal of bootstrapping standard errors in multilevel SEM. Unfortunately, this is currently not supported in popular SEM software. Multilevel bootstrapping is more complex than single-level bootstrapping. The naïve procedure of resampling groups, followed by resampling subjects within groups does not apply, because it does not correctly preserve the multilevel correlation structure (Goldstein, 2003). Bootstrapping standard errors is therefore, at the moment, not a feasible solution to overcome small sample size at the group level. In order to assess the potential bias in standard errors we have continued our analyses by returning to a multigroup analysis SEM model. Multigroup SEM is contrary to multilevel SEM in a fixed model. With an increasing number of groups, multigroup SEM results in a large model, because it estimates a unique set of parameter values for each group. But, bootstrapping is a technique that is feasible to conduct in multigroup SEM. The bootstrapped standard errors are generated by group, preserving the sample size in each group. Following the rule of thumb of Efron and Tibshirani (1993), 200 bootstrap replications are performed to generate the standard errors. We use the same substantive model to further illustrate this point. As mentioned above, partial measurement invariance was found for the construct attitude toward immigration. The multilevel model did not produce significant variances for the random coefficients of the loadings, and therefore the default Mplus procedure is followed, which constrains factor loadings to be equal across all groups. This results in acceptable model fit measures as shown in Table 12.3.

The multigroup SEM shown in Table 12.3 produces separate parameter estimates for each group, which complicates assessing the amount of bias in standard errors in multilevel SEM. To address this, we use a procedure developed by Rubin (1987) in the context of multiple imputation for combining independent standard errors. By applying this formula we can compare the combined bootstrapped standard errors from the multigroup SEM with the potentially biased standard errors of the multilevel SEM.

TABLE 12.3

Bootstrapped Multigroup Results

			Estimates	S.E.
All countries	Allow 1		1.000	0.000
	Allow 2		1.199	0.005
	Allow 3		1.096	0.004

	Age Estimate	S.E.	Education Estimate	S.E.
Austria	0.048	0.009	0.006	0.002
Belgium	0.052	0.006	−0.107	0.006
Switzerland	0.051	0.006	−0.125	0.007
Czech Republic	0.053	0.008	−0.121	0.018
Germany	0.069	0.005	−0.115	0.009
Denmark	0.088	0.007	−0.146	0.008
Spain	0.025	0.01	−0.098	0.008
Finland	0.075	0.005	−0.077	0.006
France	0.062	0.006	−0.109	0.006
Great Britain	0.032	0.008	−0.007	0.004
Greece	0.064	0.015	−0.09	0.008
Hungary	0.036	0.007	−0.096	0.008
Ireland	0.018	0.005	−0.094	0.007
Italy	0.014	0.008	−0.142	0.013
Luxembourg	0.007	0.006	−0.09	0.011
Netherlands	0.014	0.005	−0.105	0.007
Norway	0.044	0.006	−0.125	0.006
Poland	0.052	0.006	−0.078	0.007
Portugal	0.017	0.005	−0.111	0.007
Sweden	0.031	0.006	−0.072	0.005
Slovenia	0.024	0.006	−0.12	0.009
Bulgaria	0.154	0.043	−0.119	0.032
Cyprus	0.055	0.025	−0.019	0.005
Estland	0.013	0.029	−0.039	0.023
Russia	0.109	0.024	−0.05	0.02
Slovakia	0.011	0.004	−0.044	0.023

Chi-square test of model fit (1999.005, df = 154, *P*-value = .0000).
CFI = 0.998; RMSEA = 0.061; SRMR = 0.038.

Average parameter estimates are calculated as follows:

$$\bar{Q} = \frac{1}{m}\sum_{j=1}^{m}\hat{Q}_j. \tag{12.1}$$

Within component of the variation in parameter estimates:

$$\bar{U} = \frac{1}{m}\sum_{j=1}^{m}\bar{U}_j. \tag{12.2}$$

The between component of the variation in parameter estimates:

$$B = \frac{1}{m-1}\sum_{j=1}^{m}\left(\hat{Q}_j - \bar{Q}\right)^2. \tag{12.3}$$

And combining these components:

$$T = \bar{U} + \left(1 + \frac{1}{m}\right)B. \tag{12.4}$$

As Equations 12.1 through 12.4 show, Rubin's method uses the average of the asymptotic sampling variances in each (bootstrapped) sample, and adds a variance component that reflects the resampling variance. Thus, if the sampling variance is larger than expected by asymptotic methods, the added variance becomes evident in the variance of the bootstrapped samples, and is added to the asymptotic variance using Equation 12.4.

The combined bootstrapped multigroup SEM results show that the standard error of the structural estimates of age and education to the latent variable "attitude toward immigration" are both 0.012 (see Table 12.4). Compared to the standard errors of the same between-model estimates they are somewhat smaller. In the multilevel SEM model these standard errors are 0.014 and 0.042, respectively (see Table 12.2). Inspecting the structural effects of the between-model part of the multilevel SEM show that both paths are underestimated: 0.016 compared to 0.047 and −0.080

TABLE 12.4

Bootstrapped Combined Multigroup Results

		Estimates	S.E.
All countries	Allow 1	1.000	0.000
	Allow 2	1.199	0.005
	Allow 3	1.096	0.004
	Age	0.047	0.012
	Education	−0.088	0.012

compared to −0.088 for age and education, respectively. These differences are consistent with the literature on SEM with small sample sizes (e.g., Bentler & Yuan, 1999).

12.4 CONCLUSIONS

Cross-national research often deals with hierarchical data and the most often used statistical technique to deal with such data is multilevel modeling. Structural equation modeling (SEM) provides a more flexible modeling approach, such as including latent constructs in a model. The conventional approach in the context of SEM is to apply a multigroup model, with countries as groups. This is a powerful model, especially when the number of countries is relatively small, and when the theoretical focus is on pairwise comparisons between countries. When the number of countries increases, multigroup models become unwieldy, and multilevel approaches prevail. Combining SEM with multilevel modeling has gained increased attention in cross-national research. The sample size at the group level is, however, often limited and this can lead to incorrect standard errors estimates and therefore untrustworthy hypothesis testing. Resampling procedures can theoretically help here to obtain robust standard errors. In this chapter we have focused on the bootstrap procedure. In order to assess the potential bias in multilevel SEM dealing with a small group level sample size we have used a small illustrative model from the ESS. The ESS is a frequently used database and has currently a potential group sample size of 31. Although Stapleton (2008) and Wang and colleagues (2006, 2007) provide promising approaches to implement a bootstrap procedure for standard errors in, respectively, SEM models and multilevel models, combining these procedures is currently supported in popular statistical software. Given the added complexity of multilevel bootstrapping, multilevel bootstrapping in the context of SEM is not a simple procedure to implement outside current software, for example, by generating the required bootstrap samples in a computing environment such as R. In order to establish the potential bias in variance components, we have used bootstrapping in a multigroup model. This produces, for each country, estimates and bootstrapped standard errors. Combining the bootstrapped country level standard errors using Rubin's rule results in one set of country level bootstrapped standard errors that can be compared to the corresponding asymptotic standard errors in the multilevel SEM. This comparison shows that in this case the bootstrapped standard errors are smaller compared to the multilevel SEM results. The small group level sample size apparently results in inflated standard errors. Although this does not threaten the statistical validity of the null hypothesis tests, it does result in a decrease in statistical power. One way to deal with this is to argue, based on the comparison between the bootstrapped and the asymptotic standard errors that the criterion for significance can be increased to an alpha level of 0.10 instead of the more usual 0.05.

Although in this example bootstrapped standard errors from the multigroup model were substantially lower compared to the asymptotic standard errors from the multilevel SEM, this does not need to be the case in all situations. Following Meuleman and Billiet (2009), we recommend that substantive researchers interpret the asymptotic estimates with caution. A bootstrap procedure, or if the number of countries is very small, a jackknife, provides an effective method to assess the potential for bias. The bootstrap can also be used to assess whether the standard errors are inflated, as in our case, or whether they are too small. Such bootstrap analyses is a guide when an adjustment to the standard alpha level is considered, as mentioned before.

It should be noted that the accuracy of parameter estimates and standard errors in SEM does not only depend on the sample size, but also on the complexity of the model (Bandalos, 2006). More complex models require larger sample sizes, which in the context of multilevel SEM means that the second level model must be simple unless the second level sample size is large (100–200, cf. Meuleman & Billiet, 2009). A limitation of our study is that we do not address the issue of statistical power. At the country level, where the sample sizes are small, we would expect power to be an issue. Meuleman and Billiet (2009) find exactly that. An analysis by

Hox, de Leeuw, and Brinkhuis (in press) shows that power in intercultural comparisons may depend not only on the second level sample size, but also on the analysis technique employed. Their research suggests that multigroup comparisons have a higher power to detect differences between countries than multilevel modeling of the same data. However, this issue has not been addressed systematically in comparative multilevel research.

ACKNOWLEDGMENT

The authors thank Peter Lugtig for his comments on an earlier version of the chapter.

REFERENCES

Bandalos, D. L. (2006). The use of Monte Carlo studies in structural equation modeling research. In G. R. Hancock & R. O. Mueller (Eds.), *Structural equation modeling: A second course* (pp. 385–426). Greenwich, CT: IAP.

Bentler, P. M. (1990). Comparative fit indexes in structural models. *Psychological Bulletin, 107(2)*, 238–246.

Bentler, P. M., & Yuan, K. H. (1999). Structural equation modelling with small samples: Test statistics. *Multivariate Behavioral Research, 34*, 181–197.

Browne, M. W., & Cudeck, R. (1993). Alternative ways of assessing model fit. In J.S. Long (Ed.), *Testing Structural Equation Models* (pp. 136–162). Newbury Park, CA: Sage.

Busing, F. (1993). Distribution characteristics of variance estimates in two-level models: A Monte Carlo study, Tech. Rep. No. PRM 93-04, Leiden University, Department of Psychometrics and Research Methodology, Leiden, The Netherlands.

Davidov, E., Meuleman, B., Billiet, J., & Schmidt, P. (2008). Values and support for immigration: A cross-country comparison. *European Sociological Review, 24*(5), 583–599.

Davison, A. C., & Hinkley, D. V. (1997). *Bootstrap methods and their application*. Cambridge: Cambridge University Press.

Efron, E. (1979). Bootstrap methods: Another look at the jackknife. *Annals of Statistics, 7*, 1–26.

Efron, E., & Tibshirani, R. J. (1993). *An introduction into the bootstrap*. New York, NY: Chapman and Hall.

Goldstein, H. (2003). *Multilevel statistical models* (3rd ed.). London: Arnold.

Hox, J. J. (1998). Multilevel modeling: When and why. In I. Balderjahn, R. Mathar, & M. Schader (Eds.), *Classification, data analysis and data highways* (pp. 147–154). New York, NY: Springer Verlag.

Hox, J. J., & Maas, C. J. M. (2001). The accuracy of multilevel structural equation modeling with pseudobalanced groups and small samples. *Structural Equation Modeling, 8*, 157–174.

Hox, J. J., de Leeuw, E. D., & Brinkhuis, M. (in press). Analysis models for comparative surveys. In J. A. Harkness, B. Edwards, T. P. Johnson, L. E. Lyberg, P. Ph. Mohler, B.-E. Pennell, & T. Smith (Eds.), *Survey methods in multicultural, multinational, and multiregional contexts*. New York, NY: Wiley.

Meuleman, B., & Billiet, J. (2009). A Monte Carlo sample size study: How many countries are needed for accurate multilevel SEM? *Survey Research Methodology, 3*(1), 45–58.

Meuleman, B., Davidov, E., & Billiet, J. (2009). Changing attitudes toward immigration in Europe, 2002–2007: A dynamic group conflict theory approach. *Social Science Research, 38*, 352–365.

Quenouille, M. (1956). Notes on bias in estimation. *Biometrika, 43*, 353–360.

Rodgers, J. L. (1999). The bootstrap, the jackknife, and the randomization test: A sampling taxonomy. *Multivariate Behavioral Research, 34*, 441–456.

Rubin, D. B. (1987). *Multiple imputation for non-response in surveys.* New York, NY: John Wiley.

Stapleton, L. M. (2008). Variance estimation using replication methods in structural equation modelling with complex sample data. *Structural Equation Modeling, 15*, 183–210.

Tukey, J. W. (1958). Bias and confidence in not-quite large samples (abstract). *Annals of Mathematical Statistics, 29*, 614.

Wang, J., Carpenter, J. R., & Kepler, M. A. (2006). Using SAS to conduct nonparametric residual bootstrap multilevel modeling with a small number of groups. *Computer Methods and Programs in Biomedicine, 82*, 130–143.

Wang, J., Carpenter, J. R., & Kepler, M. A. (2007). Corrigendum to "Using SAS to conduct nonparametric residual bootstrap multilevel modeling with a small number of groups". [*Computer Methods and Programs in Biomedicine 82* (2006), 130–143]. *Computer Methods and Programs in Biomedicine, 85*, 185–186.

Yung, Y.-F., & Chan, W. (1999). Statistical analyses using bootstrapping: Concepts and implementation. In R. Hoyle (Ed.), *Statistical strategies for small sample research* (pp. 82–108). Thousand Oaks, CA: Sage.

Section III

Latent Class Analysis (LCA)

13

Testing for Measurement Invariance With Latent Class Analysis

Miloš Kankaraš
Tilburg University

Guy Moors
Tilburg University

Jeroen K. Vermunt
Tilburg University

13.1 INTRODUCTION

There are three important reasons why latent class (LC) analysis offers a valuable approach for testing measurement invariance in cross-cultural survey research. First, LC analysis can be used to identify latent structures from the relationships among sets of discrete observed variables, and the questions used in survey research have almost always discrete (ordinal or nominal) response categories. Second, different from, for instance, the more popular multigroup confirmatory factor analysis (MCFA), which has been elaborated on in Chapters 2–10, LC models can treat latent variables as nominal, to identify a typological classification from a given set of categorical indicators, as well as ordinal, to investigate the scalability of a set of categorical indicators. These two specifications are sometimes referred to as LC cluster and LC factor models, respectively. Third, multigroup LC analysis offers a flexible alternative to the more commonly used MCFA and multigroup item response theory (IRT) approaches, which both rely on stronger distributional assumptions than LC analysis.

This chapter is organized as follows. We first introduce the basic multigroup LC model, where attention is paid to three possible parameterizations of the model, and subsequently discuss two important extensions of the basic model, that is, an extension for dealing with ordinal indicators and for modeling the latent variables as ordinal variables. We then turn to the analysis of measurement invariance using multigroup LC models, discussing the general procedure as well as methods for parameter estimation and evaluation of model fit. Finally, two examples are presented in which multigroup LC cluster and LC factor models are applied to a set of nominal and ordinal observed variables, respectively, with the aim to assess measurement invariance in a cross-cultural comparative setting.

13.2 MULTIGROUP LATENT CLASS MODELS

The multigroup extension of the standard LC model has been developed for the analysis of latent structures of observed categorical variables across two or more groups (Clogg & Goodman, 1984, 1985). When comparing latent structures across groups, a number of possible outcomes can occur: they may turn out to be completely different (heterogeneous model), partially different (partially homogeneous model), or completely the same (homogeneous model). In this section we focus on the heterogeneous model, in which all of the model parameters are group-specific. We will discuss the classical probabilistic parameterization of the multigroup LC model, as well as its log-linear and logistic parameterizations. We also pay attention to multigroup LC models for ordinal responses and with ordinal latent variables. The next section, which deals with the application of the multigroup LC model in cross-cultural research, discusses models in which some or all parameters are restricted to be equal (invariant) across groups.

13.2.1 The Heterogeneous LC Model

Multigroup LC models assume the presence of three types of categorical variables: observed (indicator) variables; an unobserved (latent) variable that accounts for the relationships between the observed variables; and a grouping variable G, which is a categorically scored, manifest variable that can be associated with both the indicators and the latent variable.

Let us assume an LC model with four observed polytomous variables A, B, C, and D having I ($i = 1, 2, \ldots, I$), J ($j = 1, 2, \ldots, J$), K ($k = 1, 2, \ldots, K$), and L ($l = 1, 2, \ldots, L$) categories, respectively; one latent polytomous variable X with T classes ($t = 1, 2, \ldots, T$); and one grouping variable G with S groups indexed by $s = 1, \ldots, S$. The variables A, B, C, and D are observed in each of these S groups. Thus, we have a set of S four-way ($I \times J \times K \times L$) observable contingency tables, or one five-way table ($I \times J \times K \times L \times S$). Then the multigroup LC model takes the following form:

$$\pi_{ijklts}^{ABCDX|G} = \pi_{ts}^{X|G} \pi_{its}^{A|XG} \pi_{jts}^{B|XG} \pi_{kts}^{C|XG} \pi_{lts}^{D|XG}. \quad (13.1)$$

Here, $\pi_{ijklts}^{ABCDX|G}$ denotes the conditional probability that an individual who belongs to the sth group will be at level (i, j, k, l, t) with respect to variables A, B, C, D, and X. The conditional probability of X taking on level t for a member of the sth group is denoted by $\pi_{ts}^{X|G}$, which determines the LC proportion for the sth group. $\pi_{its}^{A|XG}$ is the conditional probability of an individual taking level i of variable A, for a given level t of the latent variable X and for a given group membership s of the grouping variable G. Parameters $\pi_{jts}^{B|XG}, \pi_{kts}^{C|XG}$, and $\pi_{lts}^{D|XG}$ are similarly defined conditional probabilities.

It should be noted that Equation 13.1 implies that indicator variables A, B, C, and D are independent from each other, given the value of the latent variable X. This is usually referred to as the assumption of local independence (Lazarsfeld & Henry, 1968). The LC and conditional response probabilities are constrained to a sum of 1: $\Sigma_t \pi_{ts}^{X|G} = 1$, $\Sigma_i \pi_{its}^{A|XG} = 1$, and so on.

The model presented in Equation 13.1 can be called a heterogeneous model since all model parameters differ across groups. In fact, it is equivalent to applying a standard LC model (see Equation 13.2) for each group separately (Clogg & Goodman, 1985). Or alterably, the standard LC model can be viewed as a special case of the more general multigroup LC model (Equation 13.1) with the number of groups $S = 1$:

$$\pi_{ijklt}^{ABCDX} = \pi_{t}^{X} \pi_{it}^{A|X} \pi_{jt}^{B|X} \pi_{kt}^{C|X} \pi_{lt}^{D|X}. \quad (13.2)$$

The probabilistic LC model presented in Equation 13.1 can also be parameterized using log-linear terms (Goodman, 1974; Haberman, 1979;

McCutcheon, 2002). The conditional response probabilities from the probabilistic parameterization can be obtained from log-linear terms as follows (Haberman, 1979; Heinen, 1996):

$$\pi_{its}^{A|XG} = \frac{\exp(\lambda_i^A + \lambda_{it}^{AX} + \lambda_{is}^{AG} + \lambda_{its}^{AXG})}{\sum_i \exp(\lambda_i^A + \lambda_{it}^{AX} + \lambda_{is}^{AG} + \lambda_{its}^{AXG})}, \text{etc.} \quad (13.3)$$

While λ_i^A and λ_{it}^{AX} represent the parameters of the standard, single-group LC model, λ_{is}^{AG} and λ_{its}^{AXG} are the log-linear parameters that depict the inter-group variability of the two former parameters. Parameter λ_{its}^{AXG} is sometimes referred to as an interaction effect as it indicates that the latent and grouping variables interact with each other in their effect on the indicator variable. In other words, the relationship between item responses and latent variables is modified by the group membership. In a similar manner, λ_{is}^{AG} refers to a direct effect of the grouping variable *G* on the indicator *A*. Such direct effects are present when group differences in item responses cannot be fully explained by group differences in the latent factors, that is, when the group variable influences indicators independently of the latent variable.

Not only the response probabilities, but also the class membership probabilities $\pi_{ts}^{X|G}$ can be defined in terms of log-linear parameters; that is,

$$\pi_{ts}^{X|G} = \frac{\exp(\gamma_t^X + \gamma_{ts}^{XG})}{\sum_{t=1}^{T} \exp(\gamma_t^X + \gamma_{ts}^{XG})}, \quad (13.4)$$

where the symbol γ denotes a log-linear parameter of the marginal distribution of the latent variable *X* (Magidson & Vermunt, 2001).

Above, we presented two possible parameterizations of the multigroup LC model, which we called the probabilistic and the log-linear parameterizations. A third way of specifying a multigroup LC model is by using a logistic regression-type equation for the item response probabilities. In this logistic parameterization, the model for indicator item A takes on the following form:

$$\pi_{its}^{A|XG} = \frac{\exp(\alpha_{is}^{A|G} + \beta_{its}^{AX|G})}{\sum_i \exp(\alpha_{is}^{A|G} + \beta_{its}^{AX|G})}, \text{etc.,} \quad (13.5)$$

where $\alpha_{is}^{A|G}$ represents the group-specific intercepts and $\beta_{its}^{AX|G}$ the group-specific slope parameters. The slope parameters $\beta_{its}^{AX|G}$ indicates the strength of the relationships between the latent variable and the indicator variable and can thus be interpreted as a factor loading expressed in log-linear terms (Vermunt & Magidson, 2005). Note that there is a straightforward connection between the log-linear and the logistic formulations of the multigroup LC model presented in Equations 13.3 and 13.5:

$$\alpha_{is}^{A|G} = \lambda_i^A + \lambda_{is}^{AG} \tag{13.6}$$

and

$$\beta_{its}^{AX|G} = \lambda_{it}^{AX} + \lambda_{its}^{AXG}. \tag{13.7}$$

In their unrestricted forms, the three parameterizations of the multi-group LC model are essentially equivalent, estimating the same number of parameters and producing identical expected values. However, they allow for slightly different types of model restrictions that have important implications for the procedures to test measurement equivalence. First, in the probabilistic parameterization, equivalence is studied by restricting probabilities to be group invariant, in the log-linear parameterization by eliminating interaction and direct effects, and in logistic formulation by restricting intercepts and slopes to be invariant. Second, the latter two parameterizations are needed to formulate models in which indicator or latent variables are treated as discrete-ordinal. The next two sections focus on ordinal indicators and ordinal latent variables.

13.2.2 Multigroup LC Models with Ordinal Indicators

As noted previously, the log-linear and logistic parameterizations of the LC model allow for the formulation of restricted LC models for ordinal observed and ordinal latent variables. This is achieved by introducing linear restrictions among the parameters for the different categories of the same variable. When applied to the observed variables, these linear restrictions define them as discrete-ordinal variables. This is an important extension of the LC model since in many areas of social sciences, including cross-cultural comparative research, indicator items are often of a discrete-ordinal form (e.g., rating scales).

One straightforward way to define ordinal indicator variables is to assume equidistance between their categories and to modify the log-linear and logistic models for nominal items defined in Equations 13.3 and 13.5 by using equidistant category scores. The resulting response model takes on the form of an adjacent-category ordinal logit model. For example, in the case indicator item A is a five-point rating scale ($i = 1, 2, \ldots, 5$), these scores could be

$$\upsilon_i^A = \{1 \text{ if } i=1, 2 \text{ if } i=2, \ldots, 5 \text{ if } i=5\}. \tag{13.8}$$

In the log-linear specification of Equation 13.3, the υ_i^A is used to restrict λ_{it}^{AX}, as well as the direct and interaction effects (see, e.g., Heinen, 1996)

$$\lambda_{it}^{AX} = \upsilon_i^A \lambda_{*t}^{AX}, \quad \lambda_{is}^{AG} = \upsilon_i^A \lambda_{*s}^{AG}, \quad \text{and} \quad \lambda_{its}^{AXG} = \upsilon_i^A \lambda_{*ts}^{AXG}, \tag{13.9}$$

and the intercepts and slopes of the logistic model defined in Equation 13.5 as

$$\beta_{its}^{AX|G} = \upsilon_i^A \beta_{*ts}^{AX|G}. \tag{13.10}$$

Depending on the parameterization, the conditional response probability for ordinal indicator A becomes

$$\pi_{its}^{A|X} = \frac{\exp(\lambda_i^A + \upsilon_i^A \lambda_{*t}^{AX} + \upsilon_i^A \lambda_{*s}^{AG} + \upsilon_i^A \lambda_{*ts}^{AXG})}{\sum_i \exp(\lambda_i^A + \upsilon_i^A \lambda_{*t}^{AX} + \upsilon_i^A \lambda_{*s}^{AG} + \upsilon_i^A \lambda_{*ts}^{AXG})}, \tag{13.11}$$

or

$$\pi_{its}^{A|XG} = \frac{\exp(\alpha_{is}^{A|G} + \upsilon_i^A \beta_{*ts}^{AX|G})}{\sum_i \exp(\alpha_{is}^{A|G} + \upsilon_i^A \beta_{*ts}^{AX|G})}. \tag{13.12}$$

In Equation 13.11, the loading for variable A on the latent variable X is given by λ_{*t}^{AX}, and λ_{*ts}^{AXG} indicates how it differs across groups. In Equation 13.12, $\beta_{*ts}^{AX|G}$ is the group-specific loading parameter, where $\beta_{*ts}^{AX|G} = \lambda_{*t}^{AX} + \lambda_{*ts}^{AXG}$. It can easily be observed that for ordinal indicators the two parameterizations are no longer equivalent with respect to the part concerning the intercepts and the direct effects. This can be seen by writing $\alpha_{is}^{A|G} = \lambda_i^A + \upsilon_i^A \beta_{*s}^{AG}$. The log-linear model is more parsimonious than the logistic model because it restricts the way in which the intercepts differ across groups by taking the ordinal nature of the response variable into account. As a result, there is only one direct effect parameter in Equation 13.11 (λ_{*s}^{AG}) per additional group, whereas there are $I - 1$ intercept parameters in Equation 13.12 ($\alpha_{is}^{A|G}$) per additional group.

Above we showed how to define multigroup LC models for ordinal items by restricting the log-linear and logistic parameters of the model for nominal items using the category scores for the indicators. This amounts to using an adjacent category ordinal logit specification. Alternative ordinal specifications are, among others, cumulative logit and cumulative probit models. Multigroup LC models using such response models could also be specified either with direct effects and interactions or with group-specific intercepts and slopes.

13.2.3 Multigroup LC Models with Ordinal Latent Variables

LC models with discrete-ordinal latent variables are called LC factor models since they in many ways resemble linear factor analysis (Magidson & Vermunt, 2001; Vermunt & Magidson, 2005). In most aspects multigroup LC factor analysis is equivalent to standard multigroup LC analysis, with the main difference being that instead of comparing typologies it compares latent dimensions of observed discrete variables across groups (Kankaraš & Moors, 2009; Moors, 2003).

Let us restrict ourselves to the situation in which there is a single latent variable. The latent variable is modeled as ordinal by using equidistant category scores υ_t^X between 0 and 1 for the levels of the latent variable X in its relationship with the indicators. For example, in the case of a three-level latent variable X ($t = 1$, 2, and 3) these scores are

$$\upsilon_t^X = \{0 \text{ if } t=1,\ 0.5 \text{ if } t=2,\ 1 \text{ if } t=3\}, \tag{13.13}$$

with the following constraints in the log-linear specification:

$$\lambda_{it}^{AX} = \upsilon_t^X \lambda_{i*}^{AX} \quad \text{and} \quad \lambda_{its}^{AXG} = \upsilon_t^X \lambda_{i*s}^{AXG}, \tag{13.14}$$

and in the logistic specification:

$$\beta_{its}^{AX|G} = \upsilon_t^X \beta_{i^*s}^{AX|G}. \tag{13.15}$$

Note that the two parameterizations are equivalent because $\beta_{i^*s}^{AX|G} = \lambda_{i^*}^{AX} + \lambda_{i^*s}^{AXG}$. It is also possible to define both the latent variable and the indicators to be ordinal, which yields

$$\lambda_{is}^{AG} = \upsilon_i^A \lambda_{*s}^{AG},\ \lambda_{it}^{AX} = \upsilon_i^A \upsilon_t^X \lambda_{**}^{AX},\ \text{and}\ \lambda_{its}^{AXG} = \upsilon_i^A \upsilon_t^X \lambda_{**s}^{AXG}, \tag{13.16}$$

and

$$\beta_{its}^{AX|G} = \upsilon_i^A \upsilon_t^X \beta_{**s}^{AX|G}. \tag{13.17}$$

Similar to the multigroup LC models with ordinal indicators and a nominal latent variable described in the previous subsection, the log-linear and logistic formulations are not completely equivalent anymore, as direct effects and intercepts contain different numbers of parameters. Although LC factor models are typically used with ordinal indicators, multigroup LC factor models with nominally defined indicators can be very useful in cross-cultural research as it allows for simultaneous analysis of measurement invariance and various response styles that can occur in survey responses (Moors, 2004).

13.3 ANALYZING MEASUREMENT INVARIANCE

In the multigroup LC models presented in the previous section, all model parameters were assumed to differ across groups, which makes it difficult to compare the results across groups. However, these are not the types of models a cross-cultural researcher is aiming at since he or she wants to be able to compare results across groups. To determine whether this is possible, the researcher has to check whether LCs have the same meaning in all groups (i.e., whether measurement invariance can be established). In the context of LC analysis measurement invariance is established when the class-specific conditional response probabilities are equal across groups. This implies that it is necessary to impose across-group equality restrictions on these conditional probabilities in order to test for measurement equivalence. As is shown below, using a multigroup LC analysis approach, various levels of homogeneity (i.e., measurement invariance) can be tested, each of which involves restricting specific sets of model parameters to be equal across groups.

13.3.1 The General Procedure of Analyzing Measurement Invariance

The ideal situation for an applied researcher who wishes to compare groups occurs when all measurement model parameters can be set equally across groups. From this perspective, the objective of researching measurement invariance is to find the model with the lowest level of inequivalence possible that fits the data well. The model selection procedure usually starts by determining the required number of LCs or discrete latent factors for each group. How this is determined will be explained later on. If the number of classes is the same across groups, then the heterogeneous model is fitted to the data, followed by a series of nested, restricted models that are evaluated in terms of model fit (Eid, Langeheine, & Diener, 2003; Hagenaars, 1990; McCutcheon, 2002).

Graphical representations of the four prototypical models that differ in the assumed level of measurement invariance are provided in Figure 13.1

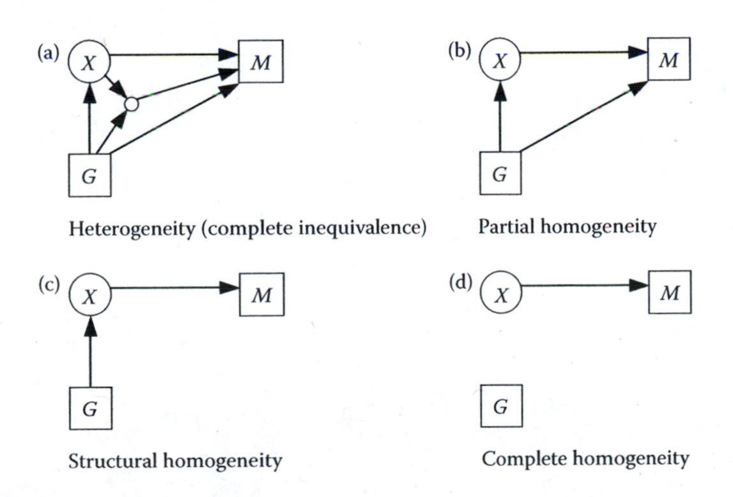

FIGURE 13.1
Relationships between latent variable (X), manifest variable (M), and group variable (G) in four different multigroup LC models.

and explained in the remainder of this section of the chapter. The heterogeneous, unrestricted multigroup LC model, as we have described in the first section of this chapter (cf. Equations 13.1, 13.3, and 13.5) is graphically presented in Figure 13.1a, in which X represents the latent variable, M is the set of manifest variables, and G is the group variable.

The model in Figure 13.1a represents the situation of complete lack of comparability of results across groups as all measurement model parameters are group specific. Comparability is only established if we can impose across-groups restrictions on the model parameters without deteriorating the fit with the data. Imposing restrictions create various nested homogeneous models. If some, but not all, of the model parameters are restricted to be equal across groups; the model is called partially homogeneous (Clogg & Goodman, 1984, 1985).

Among the various possible partially homogeneous models, the one presented in Figure 13.1b with no group-latent variable interaction terms is especially important. This model implies the following restrictions:

$$\lambda_{its}^{AXG} = \lambda_{jts}^{BXG} = \lambda_{kts}^{CXG} = \lambda_{lts}^{DXG} = 0, \tag{13.18}$$

or

$$\beta_{its}^{AX|G} = \beta_{it}^{AX}, \text{etc.,} \tag{13.19}$$

which results in the following equations for the group-specific conditional response probabilities:

$$\pi_{its}^{A|XG} = \frac{\exp(\lambda_i^A + \lambda_{it}^{AX} + \lambda_{is}^{AG})}{\sum_i \exp(\lambda_i^A + \lambda_{it}^{AX} + \lambda_{is}^{AG})}, \text{ etc.} \tag{13.20}$$

or

$$\pi_{its}^{A|XG} = \frac{\exp(\alpha_{is}^{A|G} + \beta_{it}^{AX})}{\sum_i \exp(\alpha_{is}^{A|G} + \beta_{it}^{AX})}, \text{ etc.} \tag{13.21}$$

Thus, this model still allows for direct effects of the grouping variable on the indicator items (λ_{is}^{AG}) or, in second formulation, it allows for group-specific intercept parameters ($\alpha_{is}^{A|G}$). This means that the values of the conditional response probabilities (i.e., their difficulties) are different across populations. However, as there are no group-latent variable interaction effects in the model (as slope parameters are assumed to be equal across groups), relationships between the latent variable and the responses are the same across groups, which makes it possible to compare group differences in LC memberships (McCutcheon & Hagenaars, 1997). It should be noted the partially homogeneous model presented in Equations 13.20 and 13.21 can only be specified with log-linear and logistic parameterizations—distinguishing direct and interaction effects and intercepts and slope parameters, respectively—and thus not with the probabilistic parameterization. This is conceptually similar to the metric equivalence model in MCFA in which factor loadings are equal across groups, but item intercepts may be unequal. Likewise, it resembles the situation of uniform differential item functioning (DIF) in IRT modeling. The partially homogeneous model can be tested against the unrestricted heterogeneous model. If the difference in fit between two models is not significant, a researcher can conclude that interaction effects are not needed in the model and can proceed with the next step in the analysis.

In comparative social research, researchers are typically interested in establishing full comparability of the measurement across groups; that is, they want to attain complete measurement invariance. In order to do so in the context of LC models, it is necessary to establish structural equivalence (McCutcheon, 2002). In a structurally equivalent (homogeneous) model (Figure 13.1c) both direct and interaction effects are excluded from the log-linear model (set to zero), or in the alternative logistic formulation both intercept and slope parameters are set to be equal across groups. This means that the conditional probabilities of items are restricted to be equal across groups (e.g., $\pi_{it1}^{AX|G} = \pi_{it2}^{AX|G} = \ldots = \pi_{itS}^{AX|G}$), making the indicator variables independent of the group variable, when controlled for the latent variable. The structurally equivalent LC model then takes the following form:

$$\pi_{ijklts}^{ABCDX|G} = \pi_{ts}^{X|G} \pi_{it}^{A|X} \pi_{jt}^{B|X} \pi_{kt}^{C|X} \pi_{lt}^{D|X}, \qquad (13.22)$$

or, in log-linear form:

$$\pi_{its}^{A|XG} = \pi_{it}^{A|X} = \frac{\exp(\lambda_i^A + \lambda_{it}^{AX})}{\sum_i \exp(\lambda_i^A + \lambda_{it}^{AX})}, \text{ etc.,} \qquad (13.23)$$

and in logistic terms:

$$\pi_{its}^{A|XG} = \pi_{it}^{A|X} = \frac{\exp(\alpha_i^A + \beta_{it}^{AX})}{\sum_i \exp(\alpha_i^A + \beta_{it}^{AX})}, \text{ etc.} \tag{13.24}$$

Thus, in the structurally equivalent model the relationships between indicator items and the latent variable are identical across groups so that the class memberships have the same meaning in all groups. In other words, measurement invariance is established if this model does not fit the data significantly worse than the partially homogenous and heterogeneous models. The homogeneous model is comparable with the scalar equivalent model in MCFA that defines both factor loadings and item intercepts to be the same across groups. In the IRT approach, it is similar to the model with both difficulty and discrimination parameters invariant across groups.

Finally, if all parameters are restricted to be equal across groups, that is, if aside from conditional response probabilities, LC probabilities are also independent of group membership ($\pi_{t1}^{X|G} = \pi_{t2}^{X|G} = \ldots = \pi_{tS}^{X|G}$), then we have the case of a completely equivalent (homogeneous) model (Figure 13.1d):

$$\pi_{ijklts}^{ABCDX|G} = \pi_{ijklt}^{ABCDX} = \pi_t^X \pi_{it}^{A|X} \pi_{jt}^{B|X} \pi_{kt}^{C|X} \pi_{lt}^{D|X}, \tag{13.25}$$

or, in the log-linear parameterization:

$$\pi_{ts}^{X|G} = \frac{\exp(\gamma_t^X)}{\sum_t \exp(\gamma_t^X)}. \tag{13.26}$$

For researchers in comparative social research, the latter model is of less practical relevance, since the very aim of cross-cultural research is typically to describe country differences in LC membership probabilities or factor means and, hence, to illustrate cross-cultural diversity.

Research is not by definition restricted to comparing the four models described in Figure 13.1. Various combinations of within- and across-groups restrictions and different parameterizations are possible. One of these possibilities is, for instance, to test for equal error rates of the indicator variables by restricting the corresponding conditional probabilities within a group to be equal (McCutcheon & Hagenaars, 1997).

The procedure we just explained includes an analysis at the scale level; that is, all indicator variables in the model are simultaneously modeled with the same set of restrictions. However, multigroup LC analysis of measurement invariance can be conducted at the item-level as well. This is particularly relevant when the scale level analysis indicates inequivalence either in the interaction or in the direct effects. In that case the analysis continues with item-level comparisons in order to check whether all items cause inequivalence. More specifically, equivalence in the slope parameter (presence of interaction effect) for a particular item A is assessed by comparing the unrestricted, heterogeneous model with a model in which this parameter is equated across groups for this item. In order to test for equivalence in intercept parameters (presence of direct effects) at the item-level we need to assume equivalence in the slope parameters. Therefore, testing equivalence of the intercept parameters of item A is based on the comparison of the partially homogeneous model with equal slope parameters for all items (Equations 13.20 and 13.21) with the model, which in addition assumes equal intercept parameters for item A. This procedure is very similar to the one used in MCFA, where it is referred to as partial equivalence (Steenkamp & Baumgartner, 1998; for a discussion on the MCFA approach to partial invariance; see also Chapter 3 in this book). It should be noted that multiple LC analysis differs from MCFA in that it does not require the use of an invariant marker item for identification purposes.

As we have noted before, the first step in a multigroup LC analysis is to determine whether the number of LCs or the number of discrete factors is the same across groups (McCutcheon, 1987; McCutcheon & Hagenaars, 1997). However, it might very well be that a model with an acceptable fit in one group has more LCs than the best-fitting model in another group; and in an LC factor model the best-fitting model in one country may have more factors than in other countries. In MCFA, the latter situation is referred to as a violation of the configural invariance assumption (Steenkamp & Baumgartner, 1998), which limits the possibility of group comparisons. However, multigroup LC analysis with a nominal latent variable is rather flexible in the sense that it can be used to accommodate different numbers of LCs across groups while still assuming measurement invariance.

This involves specifying a model with the same number of classes in each group, but in which are some of the classes are empty (having proportions of 0) in certain groups. An example could be a three-class model with class proportions of 0.2, 0.3, and 0.5 for one group and of 0.4, 0.6, and 0.0 for the other group. The analysis of measurement invariance can proceed as described above.

The flexibility of the multigroup LC approach is also reflected in the fact that not all LCs need to be equivalent in order to validly compare results across groups. In other words, there may be a situation in which only some of the LCs have the same conditional response probabilities across groups, while other LCs in a model do not. If this is the case, it is still possible to compare class sizes of equivalent classes while treating other classes in the model as group-specific and noncomparable. Models of this type can be defined using the probabilistic parameterization of the multigroup LC model.

13.3.2 Parameter Estimation and Assessment of Model Fit

LC models are usually estimated by means of maximum-likelihood (ML) under the assumption of a multinomial distribution for the indicator variables in the model. Maximization of the likelihood function is performed by the use of an expectation-maximization (EM) or a Newton–Raphson algorithm, or a combination of these two.

There are several model fit criteria that are commonly used for model fit evaluation in multigroup LC analysis. The likelihood-ratio chi-square (L^2) statistic is used as a standard measure of discrepancy between observed and expected frequencies in the model. This statistic has one important advantage over the Pearson chi-square (χ^2) test that lays in its partitioning ability. In particular, when two models are nested and the less restricted model fits the data well, then the difference in the likelihood ratios between the two models represents a conditional likelihood ratio (L^2) test on its own, following a chi-square distribution with a number of degrees of freedom equal to the difference between the degrees of freedom of the two nested models. Thus, this conditional likelihood test can be used to compare the fit of successive, nested models and so to investigate the plausibility of (measurement invariance) restrictions included in nested models.

However, the likelihood ratio chi-square test, although extensively used in statistical literature, has a number of important limitations. The major one is its limited use when dealing with sparse tables, that is, when the number of possible response patterns is large and the sample size is small, creating contingency tables with many small and zero observed frequencies. In these cases *p*-values of the chi-square tests cannot be trusted as they might not follow the theoretical chi-square distribution. On the other hand, when sample sizes are large, likelihood-ratio tests tend to be too conservative, indicating misfit even for minimal differences between two models. In addition, the likelihood-ratio statistic does not provide enough control for the number of parameters in a model that can sometimes be very large even for models of modest size (McCutcheon, 2002).

These limitations prompted the recent development and use of several information criteria, such as the Akaike information criterion (AIC), the Bayesian information criterion (BIC), the modified AIC (AIC3), and the consistent AIC (CAIC), each of which is designed to penalize models with larger numbers of parameters. Since more parameters in a model increase its likelihood, the information criteria reduce that likelihood by a certain amount that is a function of the increased number of estimated parameters. They differ in the specific function with which they calculate the penalizing value for each additional parameter in a model. Specifically, AIC and AIC3 rely solely on the number of parameters in the model:

$$\text{AIC} = L^2 - 2\text{df} \quad \text{and} \quad \text{AIC3} = L^2 - 3\text{df}, \tag{13.27}$$

while BIC and CAIC also take into account the sample size:

$$\text{BIC} = L^2 - \text{df}^*[\ln(N)] \quad \text{and} \quad \text{CAIC} = L^2 - \text{df}^*[\ln(N) + 1], \tag{13.28}$$

where N is the sample size. Thus, models with lower values of information criteria have a better fit to the data, for a given number of parameters. Since they also control for sample size, BIC and CAIC are preferred fit statistics in situations when the sample size is large. For small to medium sample sizes, the AIC statistic is most commonly used.

Software packages that can be used to obtain ML estimates and model fit statistics of the LC models are LEM (Vermunt, 1997), Latent GOLD (Vermunt & Magidson, 2005, 2008), Mplus (Muthén & Muthén, 2006), and GLLAMM (Rabe-Hesketh, Skrondal, & Pickles, 2004).

13.4 EMPIRICAL EXAMPLES

In this section we present two examples of the use of LC models for the analysis of measurement invariance. The first example involves a standard multigroup LC analysis as both latent and indicator variables are treated as nominal. Multigroup LC factor analysis is illustrated in the second example with latent and indicator variables defined to be discrete-ordinal. In both examples we used equal size weighting of the samples to a sample size of 1000 per country, which was the size of the smallest country sample. This procedure is often used in cross-cultural research to prevent countries with larger sample sizes to dominate the results.

The analyses of measurement invariance follow the procedures outlined in Section 13.2.1, by first selecting the best-fitting model at the scale level and then testing the invariance of the individual items at the item-level. We use the BIC statistic as our main model selection fit criterion since both the conditional L^2 test and AIC do not provide control mechanisms for sample size and are thus too conservative in their model fit evaluation with sample sizes as large as the ones used in the presented examples. Models were estimated with the syntax version of the Latent Gold 4.5 program (Vermunt & Magidson, 2008). The syntax used in the two examples is reported in Appendix 13.A.

13.4.1 Example 1: Standard Multigroup LC Analysis

The first example involves the analysis of four categorical items on preferences with respect to social developments in different spheres of life taken from the 1999/2000 European Value Survey. Respondents were asked whether it would be a good thing, a bad thing, or whether they didn't mind if in the near future emphasis would be placed on the development of: (1) technology, (2) the individual, (3) family life, and (4) natural lifestyle. Though it is hard to imagine that these four issues refer to a single dimension, it can be that groups of respondents can be identified with different preferences, which is why a traditional LC analysis approach is used. Models are defined using the logistic parameterization presented in Equation 13.5. We compare results between four countries: Belarus, Romania, Luxembourg, and Austria. These countries were chosen because this particular selection allowed us to demonstrate a number of important features of the method.

Separate analyses for each country indicated that a two-class model provides the best fit in terms of BIC statistics. Whether a common two-class structure emerges from the data, that is, whether the data are measurement invariant, can be tested by fitting a two-class model with the pooled dataset. The level of measurement invariance present in data is indicated by the degree of homogeneity in the model that fits the data best. The more homogeneous the best-fitting model is, the more equivalent the data are.

In Section a of Table 13.1, we report the fit statistics for the various multigroup two-class models that were estimated. As can be seen, the partially homogeneous model with equal loadings but different intercept

TABLE 13.1

Fit Statistics of the Estimated two- and three-Class Multigroup LC Models

	Npar[a]	L^2	BIC(L^2)	df
a. H_1: Heterogeneous two-class	**68**	**402.5**	**−1642.4**	**252**
H_2: Partial homogeneity (Figure 13.1b)	44	481.2	−1758.4	276
H_3: Structural homogeneity	20	822.7	−1611.7	300
b. H_4: Heterogeneous three-class	**104**	**241.5**	**−1511.2**	**216**
H_5: Partial homogeneity (Figure 13.1b)	56	352.6	−1789.6	264
H_6: Structural homogeneity	32	512.4	−1824.6	288
c. H_4: Heterogeneous three-class	**104**	**241.5**	**−1511.2**	**216**
H_{4a}: Technology	92	276.8	−1573.4	228
H_{4b}: Individual	92	265.4	−1584.7	228
H_{4c}: Family	92	274.2	−1575.9	228
H_{4d}: Natural lifestyle	92	283.3	−1566.8	228
d. H_5: Partial homogeneity three-class	**56**	**352.6**	**−1789.6**	**264**
H_{5a}: Technology	50	395.7	−1795.3	270
H_{5b}: Individual	50	409.1	−1781.9	270
H_{5c}: Family	50	373.6	−1817.3	270
H_{5d}: Natural lifestyle	50	365.1	−1825.9	270
e. H_7: Selected three-class	**38**	**439.3**	**−1849.1**	**282**
H_7: H_6 with 1 direct effect				
H_{7a}: H_7 with equal class sizes	32	729.3	−1607.8	288

a Number of parameters for heterogeneous models with nominal indicators is calculated in the following way: Npar = $(A-1) + [(A-1) \times (B-1)] + B \times [C + D]$, with $C = (E-1) \times F$ and $D = (A-1) \times (E-1) \times F$, where A is number of clusters, B is number of items, C is number of intercept parameters, D is number of loadings parameters, E is number of response categories, and F is number of countries. For partially homogeneous models, D changes to $D = (A-1) \times (E-1)$; for structurally homogeneous models, C additionally changes to $C = E-1$.

parameters across countries (depicted in Figure 13.1b) fits the data best (BIC = –17,584). This indicates that the estimated class-specific response probabilities for the two classes are not exactly the same across countries.

There is a second route to be explored. It is possible that some LCs can be observed in all countries, whereas other LCs are country specific. In that case, a two-class model for the pooled dataset would not be the best choice, but instead a model with more classes would be better. Hence, an alternative way to investigate the source of invariance is by checking whether the inclusion of (an) additional class(es) improves the model fit. In Section b of Table 13.1, we report the fit statistics of the same three multigroup LC models but now with three instead of two classes. As we can see, the best fitting three-class model is the structurally homogeneous (measurement invariant) model. Obviously, the addition of the third class has accounted for a substantial part of the inequivalence encountered in the two-class model. This indicates that the partial inequivalence found in the two-class model can, at least partially, be explained by selecting a model with too few classes. Once the third class is included in the model, the LCs turn out to be equivalent and comparable.

Whereas the analyses presented so far were at the scale level, it is also useful to perform an item-level analysis to check the invariance of individual items. It could be that some items may turn out to be noninvariant even if the scale-level analysis selects the homogeneous three-class model. In Sections c and d of Table 13.1, we present the fit measures obtained with the item-level analysis for the four items, both in terms of absence of interaction effects or invariance in slope parameters (Section c of Table 13.1) and in terms of absence of direct effects or invariance in intercept parameters (Section d of Table 13.1). As could be expected, all items have invariant slopes as BIC values of models without interaction effects for one item at a time (H_{4a} – H_{4d}) are smaller than that of the heterogeneous model H_4. However, one of the items, that is, "assessing the preferred development of the individual," turns out to be inequivalent in terms of its intercept, as is indicated by a higher BIC for model H_{5b} compared to the partially homogeneous model H_5. In other words, respondents' differences in answering this question were not only determined by membership to given LCs but also by additional group-specific factor(s) that are unrelated to class membership. Therefore, in order to validly compare the class proportions across countries, we will need to include the direct effect of countries on this indicator in the measurement model, that is, to allow the intercept of

TABLE 13.2

Item Response and Class Probabilities for Preferences of Social Development

	Class 1	Class 2	Class 3
a. Response Probabilities			
Technology			
Good	0.947	0.369	0.541
Bad	0.023	0.312	0.027
Don't mind	0.030	0.319	0.432
Individual (average across countries)			
Good	0.985	0.734	0.488
Bad	0.008	0.089	0.032
Don't mind	0.006	0.176	0.480
Family			
Good	0.972	0.917	0.506
Bad	0.003	0.041	0.025
Don't mind	0.025	0.042	0.469
Natural lifestyle			
Good	0.884	0.868	0.235
Bad	0.048	0.073	0.096
Don't mind	0.068	0.059	0.669
b. Latent Class Proportions			
Belarus	0.753	0.134	0.114
Romania	0.843	0.103	0.054
Luxembourg	0.467	0.458	0.075
Austria	0.336	0.578	0.086
Total	0.588	0.329	0.083

this indicator to vary across countries. Thus, the final measurement model is the model H_7 (Section e of Table 13.1) that is equal to the structural homogeneous model H_6 modified by adding the direct effect of the grouping variable "country" on the item "individual." All other parameters in the model are invariant across countries.

Having selected a measurement model that allows for comparison of countries, the next two questions refer to (a) a substantive interpretation of the LCs and (b) the comparison of class sizes across countries. In Table 13.2 we report the item response probabilities and class proportions obtained for the selected H_7 model.

Class 1 comprised 58.8% of respondents with an overwhelmingly positive preference toward all four social developments; 32.9% of people belonging to Class 2 had somewhat more negative and less involved preferences toward the development of technology; 8.3% of respondents belonging to Class 3 were rather indifferent in respect to the given subject (have high percentage "don't mind" answers).

Class sizes differ substantially across countries. Most of the respondents in Belarus and Romania belong to class 1 and have positive preferences for all social developments, whereas in Luxembourg and Austria there is also a considerable number of people belonging to Class 2 with more reserved views on the development of technology. The third class containing the less concerned respondents, is the smallest in all four countries. To test whether class sizes differ significantly across countries we compare the selected model H_7 with a model in which equal class sizes are assumed (model H_{7a}). The fit statistics of this model (H_{7a}), presented in Section e of Table 13.1, shows that it fits much worse than model H_7, which indicates that the obtained differences in class sizes across countries are statistically significant.

13.4.2 Example 2: Multigroup LC Factor Analysis

In this second example we illustrate multigroup LC factor analysis with an application to a set of discrete-ordinal indicators from the 2006/2007 European Social Survey (ESS), which contains information on 23 European countries. The records were weighted in order to yield an equal number of 1000 cases per country. We investigated the measurement invariance of a four-item scale measuring interpersonal feelings that assesses to what extent respondents: (a) feel that people in their local area help one another, (b) feel that people treat them with respect, (c) feel that people treat them unfairly, and (d) feel that they get the recognition they deserve. Answers are given on a seven-point rating scale ranging from "Not at all" to "A great deal." We modeled the indicators and the latent variable (three-levels) as discrete-ordinal, using the logistic parameterization of the LC factor model presented in Equation 13.17.

In Table 13.3, we report the likelihood ratio (L^2) and BIC statistics for various LC factor models. On the scale level (Section a of Table 13.3), we compared three basic LC models: the heterogeneous model H_1; the partially homogeneous model H_2 without interaction effects between the latent and

TABLE 13.3

Fit Statistics for the Estimated Multigroup LC Factor Models

Model	Npar	L^2	BIC(L^2)	df
a. H_1: Heterogeneous model	**668**	**27511.0**	**−179865.0**	**20792**
H_2: Partial homogeneity (Figure 13.1b)	580	28146.1	−180107.6	20880
H_3: Structural homogeneity	52	32336.1	−181183.8	21408
b. H_1: Heterogeneous model	**668**	**27511.0**	**−179865.0**	**20792**
H_{1a}: Item 1	646	27698.6	−179896.7	20814
H_{1b}: Item 2	646	27559.8	−180035.6	20814
H_{1c}: Item 3	646	27691.9	−179903.5	20814
H_{1d}: Item 4	646	27674.6	−179920.7	20814
c. H_2: Partial homogeneity	**580**	**28146.1**	**−180107.6**	**20880**
H_{2a}: Item 1	448	28961.3	−180608.9	21012
H_{2b}: Item 2	448	29362.1	−180208.2	21012
H_{2c}: Item 3	448	29114.0	−180456.3	21012
H_{2d}: Item 4	448	29228.4	−180341.8	21012

grouping variable (with equal slope parameters); and the measurement invariant, homogeneous model H_3 with neither direct nor interaction effects (with equal intercept and slope parameters). As we see, the BIC statistic indicates that the homogeneous H_3 model fits the data that best takes into account the number of parameters and the sample size. However, before drawing a final conclusion about measurement invariance, we need to check whether all individual items are measurement invariant.

In the item-level analysis, we first compare the heterogeneous model H_1 with four models (H_{1a} – H_{1d}) in which the interaction effect between the latent and grouping variable is excluded for one item at a time (Section b of Table 13.3). Since the four models excluding a single interaction term do not fit worse than the unrestricted model H_1, we can conclude that there are no significant interaction effects and the relationship between the latent variable and indicators can be assumed to be the same across countries, which confirms what we found in the scale-level analysis.

The next step involves testing of the need for direct effects at the item-level comparison the four models H_{2a}–H_{2d} that exclude the direct effects of the grouping variable on a single item with the partially homogeneous H_2 (Section c of Table 13.3). The fit measures show that none of these restricted models fits worse than the partially homogeneous model H_2, which indicates that the conditional response probabilities can be assumed to be equal across countries for each of the four items. Thus, our analysis shows that the scale designed to measure interpersonal feelings is measurement invariant. This means that the four indicator items are measuring one latent variable in all of the 23 countries and that the meaning of this latent variable is the same across countries. Having established measurement invariance, a researcher can now proceed with the analysis of substantive differences in latent variables across countries.

Class proportions and discrete factor means for each country are reported in Table 13.4. The latter are calculated by multiplying class proportions with predefined fixed scores 0, 0.5, and 1 of each factor level. The level of positive feelings increases with class number.

TABLE 13.4

Latent Class Proportions and Latent Means for the 23 Countries

	Proportions			
Country	**Class 1**	**Class 2**	**Class 3**	**Means**
Austria	0.314	0.538	0.147	0.417
Belgium	0.314	0.578	0.108	0.397
Bulgaria	0.388	0.441	0.169	0.391
Switzerland	0.134	0.625	0.240	0.553
Cyprus	0.296	0.534	0.169	0.436
Germany	0.321	0.566	0.112	0.395
Denmark	0.088	0.641	0.270	0.591
Estonia	0.345	0.518	0.136	0.395
Spain	0.192	0.586	0.221	0.515
Finland	0.272	0.603	0.123	0.426
France	0.313	0.552	0.134	0.410
United Kingdom	0.419	0.487	0.093	0.337
Hungary	0.219	0.462	0.318	0.550
Ireland	0.215	0.520	0.263	0.524
Netherlands	0.245	0.608	0.145	0.450
Norway	0.106	0.639	0.253	0.574
Poland	0.406	0.495	0.097	0.345
Portugal	0.221	0.571	0.207	0.493
Russian Federation	0.387	0.499	0.113	0.363
Sweden	0.140	0.655	0.203	0.532
Slovenia	0.350	0.512	0.137	0.393
Slovakia	0.550	0.392	0.057	0.253
Ukraine	0.466	0.433	0.100	0.317
Total	**0.290**	**0.543**	**0.166**	**0.437**

The estimates reported in Table 13.4 indicate that respondents from Denmark, Norway, and Switzerland have the most positive, and those from Slovakia, the Ukraine, and United Kingdom the most negative feelings about their relationship with other people.

13.5 CONCLUSIONS

In this chapter we discussed the use of multigroup LC analysis as a tool for investigating measurement invariance. Three parameterizations of the multigroup LC models were presented (i.e., probabilistic, log-linear, and logistic parameterizations). The latter two are used to define the LC model with ordinal indicator variables and the LC factor model. An additional benefit of the log-linear and logistic parameterizations is that they are better suited for testing measurement invariance, as they allow a researcher to test a whole range of partially homogeneous models that are not possible to formulate using probabilistic parameterization. It was shown how to test for strict and less strict forms of measurement invariance by gradually imposing restrictions on the fully heterogeneous unrestricted multigroup LC model and comparing the resulting model fit statistics.

The LC approach is an obvious choice when a researcher wishes to compare typological structures across countries, that is, when analyzing whether there are cross-cultural differences in the frequencies of the different types, taking into account issues of measurement equivalence. With the possibility to define the latent variable as discrete-ordinal, it is shown that the LC approach can also be used for cross-cultural comparisons of dimensional structures, thus presenting an alternative to the more frequently used MCFA and IRT approaches. This is especially true in those situations when some of the modeling assumptions of MCFA and IRT do not hold. With its flexible set of tools, combined with recent developments in software for multigroup LC modeling, the presented approach is a very attractive option for studying measurement invariance in any situation in which the indicators are discrete variables.*

* This work was partially supported by a grant No. BFR06/040 from the "Fonds National de la Recherche" (Luxembourg).

REFERENCES

Clogg, C. C., & Goodman, L. A. (1984). Latent structure analysis of a set of multidimensional contingency tables. *Journal of the American Statistical Association, 79*, 762–771.

Clogg, C. C., & Goodman, L. A. (1985). Simultaneous latent structure analysis in several groups. In N. B. Tuma (Ed.), *Sociological methodology* (pp. 81–110). San Francisco, CA: Jossey-Bass.

Eid, M., Langeheine, R., & Diener, E. (2003). Comparing typological structures across cultures by multigroup latent class analysis. A primer. *Journal of Cross-Cultural Psychology, 34*, 195–210.

Goodman, L. A. (1974). Exploratory latent structure analysis using both identifiable and unidentifiable models. *Biometrika, 61*, 215–231.

Haberman, S. J. (1979). *Analysis of qualitative data: Vol. 2 New developments*. New York, NY: Academic.

Hagenaars, J. A. (1990). *Categorical longitudinal data–Loglinear analysis of panel, trend and cohort data*. Newbury Park, CA: Sage.

Heinen, T. (1996). *Latent class and discrete latent trait models: Similarities and differences*. Thousand Oaks, CA: Sage.

Kankaraš, M., & Moors, G. (2009). Measurement equivalence in solidarity attitudes in Europe. Insights from a multiple group latent class factor approach. *International Sociology, 24*(4), 557–579.

Lazarsfeld, P. F., & Henry, N. W. (1968). *Latent structure analysis*. Boston, MA: Houghton Mifflin.

Magidson, J., & Vermunt, J. K. (2001). Latent class factor and cluster models: Bi-plots and related graphical displays. *Sociological Methodology, 31*, 223–264.

McCutcheon, A. L. (1987). *Latent class analysis*. Sage University Paper. Newbury Park, CA: Sage.

McCutcheon, A. (2002). Basic concepts and procedures in single- and multiple-group latent class analysis. In J. Hagenaars & A. McCutcheon (Eds.), *Applied latent class analysis* (pp. 56–88). Cambridge: Cambridge University Press.

McCutcheon, A. L., & Hagenaars, J. A. (1997). Comparative social research with multi-sample latent class models. In J. Rost & R. Langeheine (Eds.), *Applications of latent trait and latent class models in the social sciences* (pp. 266–277). Münster, Germany: Waxmann.

Moors, G. (2003). Diagnosing response style behavior by means of a latent-class factor approach. Socio-demographic correlates of gender role attitudes and perceptions of ethnic discrimination re-examined. *Quality & Quantity, 37*, 227–302.

Moors, G. (2004). Facts and artefacts in the comparison of attitudes among ethnic minorities. A multi-group latent class structure model with adjustment for response style behaviour. *European Sociological Review, 20*, 303–320.

Muthén, L. K., & Muthén, B. O. (2006). *Mplus user's guide* (4th ed.). Los Angeles, CA: Author.

Rabe-Hesketh, S., Skrondal, A., & Pickles, A. (2004). *GLLAMM manual*. U.C. Berkeley Division of Biostatistics Working Paper Series. Working Paper 160. Berkeley, CA: University of California.

Steenkamp, J. E. M., & Baumgartner, H. (1998). Assessing measurement invariance in cross-national consumer research. *Journal of Consumer Research, 25*, 78–90.

Vermunt, J. K. (1997). *LEM 1.0: A general program for the analysis of categorical data.* Tilburg, The Netherlands: Tilburg University.

Vermunt, J. K., & Magidson, J. (2005). Factor analysis with categorical indicators: A comparison between traditional and latent class approaches. In A. Van der Ark, M. A. Croon, & K. Sijtsma (Eds.), *New developments in categorical data analysis for the social and behavioral sciences* (pp. 41–62). Mahwah, NJ: Erlbaum.

Vermunt, J. K., & Magidson, J. (2005). *Latent GOLD 4.0 user's guide.* Belmont MA: Statistical Innovations.

Vermunt, J. K., & Magidson, J. (2008). *LG-Syntax user's guide: Manual for Latent GOLD 4.5 Syntax Module.* Belmont, MA: Statistical Innovations.

APPENDIX 13.A LATENT GOLD SYNTAX FILES USED IN THE TWO EXAMPLES

In this appendix we present the "variables" and "equations" sections of the Latent GOLD 4.5 syntax files used for the two examples in this chapter. The logistic parameterization of the heterogeneous multigroup LC model with a 3-class nominal latent variable and four nominal indicator variables as used in example 1 is as follows:

```
variables
  caseweight weight;
  dependent item1 nominal, item2 nominal, item3 nominal,
  item4 nominal;
  independent country nominal;
  latent Cluster nominal 3;
  equations
  Cluster <- 1 | country;
  item1 <- 1 | country + Cluster | country;
  item2 <- 1 | country + Cluster | country;
  item3 <- 1 | country + Cluster | country;
  item4 <- 1 | country + Cluster | country;
```

In the "variables" section, one provides the relevant information on the dependent (items), independent (here the grouping variable), and latent (here the latent classes) variables to be used in the analysis. In this analysis, these are all nominal variables, where for the latent variable called "Cluster" one also has to indicate how many categories it has.

The first "equation" defines the logistic model for the class proportions ("1" indicates the intercept), which are assumed to be different across countries (indicated with "| country"). The next four equations define the logistic regression models for the four items. These contain the term "1" referring to the intercept and the term "Cluster" referring to the slope. Both are indicated to differ across countries.

Other more restricted models are obtained with slight modifications of the equations. A model assuming invariant item intercepts and/or slopes across countries is obtained by removing "| country" from the term(s) concerned. Thus, a partially homogeneous model is defined by equations of the form:

```
item# <- 1 | country + Cluster;
```

and the homogeneous model by:

```
item# <- 1 + Cluster;
```

A log-linear parameterization of these models can be defined by writing " + country" instead of "| country" for intercepts and " + Cluster country" instead of "| country" for slope parameters. The item equations of the heterogeneous model would then be as follows:

```
item# <- 1 + country + Cluster + Cluster country;
```

Finally, the only modification needed to obtain a multigroup LC factor model for ordinal items (our second example) is that the dependent and latent variables should be defined to be ordinal instead of nominal:

```
dependent item1 ordinal, item2 ordinal, item3 ordinal,
    item4 ordinal;
latent factor ordinal 3;
```

The "equations" remain exactly the same as with nominal dependent and latent variables, though it should be noted that the log-linear and logistic parameterizations are no longer equivalent with ordinal indicators.

14

A Multiple Group Latent Class Analysis of Religious Orientations in Europe

Pascal Siegers
University of Cologne

14.1 INTRODUCTION

Since 1950, empirical research on religion in Europe was framed in terms of secularization theory. Consequently, the question of whether religion gradually disappears in modern European societies prevailed in the sociology of religion. More recently, proponents of individualization theory have challenged the conclusion from secularization theory that modernization mechanically decreases the individual and social significance of religion. Instead, they argue that contemporary European societies are characterized by increasing pluralism of religious orientations. The main argument of individualization theory is that in modern societies individuals can choose from more religious options than in traditional societies (Taylor, 2007) and that a growing number of Europeans opt for religious beliefs outside the traditional churches.

Numerous studies provide evidence for the existence of alternative beliefs in Europe. According to these authors, one of the most significant alternatives to church religiosity is what they call holistic spiritualities (Heelas & Woodhead, 2005) or spirituality tout court (Knoblauch, 2005, 2006). Because of the wide range of different beliefs and practices referred to by this notion, I will use the plural "alternative spiritualities" throughout this text when addressing these beliefs. Two aspects particularly distinguish alternative spiritualities from church religiosity: (1) the emphasis on religious emotions and (2) the explicit distance to religious organizations and authorities (i.e., the churches).

Studies on alternative spiritualities somehow challenge the validity of conclusions drawn from studies on European secularization. If alternative spiritualities replace church religiosity in Europe, the link between modernization and decreasing importance of religion does not hold. The evidence provided for the growing importance of alternative spiritualities, however, is mainly based on qualitative research. Hence, there is an ongoing debate about the quantitative importance of alternative spiritualities in Europe. Knoblauch, for example, argues that since the 1990s, New Age beliefs have diffused into mainstream culture and thus unfold direct influence on attitudes and behavior of individuals (Knoblauch, 2005, p. 128). On the other hand, Pollack states that "the scope of extra-church religiosity tends to be hugely overestimated due to excessive media coverage" (Pollack, 2008, p. 16).

The evidence supporting the secularization argument, in turn, does not cover the realm of alternative spiritualities because social science surveys only include indicators for church religiosity (e.g., belief in God, Church attendance). However, it is known that a large share of Europeans can be classified neither as highly church religious nor as convinced atheists (Voas, 2009). Hence, the empirical knowledge about religious orientations in Europe is still fragmentary.

It is the aim of this chapter to contribute to the debate about the importance of different religious orientations in Europe by suggesting a measurement model that allows us to distinguish church religiosity, unbelief, and alternative spiritualities, and to compare the relative importance of each religious orientation across 11 European countries. To examine if spiritual beliefs are a significant option for Europeans, the question of how alternative spiritualities can be operationalized for survey research requires particular attention.

The following descriptive questions will guide the research: (1) Which are the relevant religious options for Europeans? (2) Are the patterns of religious orientations comparable across countries? (3) Are alternative spiritualities a significant option for Europeans?

To answer these questions, two challenges for empirical research need to be tackled: (1) A meaningful measurement model for religious orientations has to be devised, and (2) to allow for valid comparisons across countries, it will be necessary to establish the equivalence of the measurement across the countries included in the analysis. To do so, I apply multiple group latent class analysis (MGLCA) to data from 11 European countries.

This chapter is composed of four sections. In the first section, I will introduce the most important religious options available to Europeans. Some expectations about the results of the measurement model will be formulated that will help to guide the process of model selection. In the second section, I will describe the dataset and the operationalization of the concepts. The third section presents the results of the MGLCA-model. In the fourth section, I will discuss the implications of my findings for the discussion about religious orientations in Europe.

14.2 RELIGIOUS ORIENTATIONS IN CONTEMPORARY EUROPE

Studies on religious orientations implicitly or explicitly assume that historically in Europe church religiosity was dominant. Although different denominations coexisted, unbelief, atheism, or alternative religiosities did not constitute a significant religious option.

Within traditional societies, religion is considered to be an important vector of social integration. This view is highly influenced by Durkheim's functionalist approach to religion that assumes religion to be the fundament of social integration. Charles Taylor argues that this functionalist approach to religion does not hold anymore for secular European societies (Taylor, 2007, p. 514). Secularity, he argues, does not mean that religion withers away. It only means that individuals can freely choose whether they have any religious beliefs and what kind of belief they adopt. It is this shift from the societal to the individualistic model of religion that characterizes the modern religious landscape in Europe.

However, the relevance of individual religious choices may diverge across European societies. It is one aim of this chapter to evaluate how heterogeneous the European societies really are with respect to religious orientations. Denominational differences within the broad field of church religiosity are not addressed. My approach is located at the abstract level of different ways to believe, or to put it more technically, I am studying different social forms of religion (see Luckmann, 1991). But which social forms of religion can be expected to be relevant options for individuals in modern Europe?

The increasing importance of individual choices for religious orientations has frequently been raised when referring to the concept of "religious bricolage" (Hervieu-Léger, 2005). This argument suggests that individuals recombine many elements from the most diverse religious traditions to form their own new and syncretistic beliefs. Although this argument is very appealing if one considers the impressive diversity of spiritual groups, centers, and publications, there is no mechanical link between individual choices and individualized contents of nontraditional beliefs (Aupers & Houtman, 2006; Taylor, 2007, p. 516). Qualitative research has identified some leitmotivs of alternative spiritualities that are present for all of the different branches of the "spiritual movement."

The core argument of the spirituality literature is that the social locus of religion has moved from the group to the individual. This has important implications for one of the central problems that each religion has to deal with: how to validate the truth and authenticity of their teachings.

The Christian churches in Europe validate their religious truth through the longstanding tradition of religious teachings and religious institutions. Churches are the traditionalized form of the religious charisma that stems from an original experience of transcendence (Hervieu-Léger, 1990). They claim to be the only legitimate guardians of the religious truth derived from this religious charisma (institutional mode of belief validation). This does not mean that individuals within the church context do not experience the transcendental personally. Rather, these experiences of transcendence are moderated through the church's interpretation of transcendence.

Alternative spiritualities, in contrast, validate religious authenticity only through individual (direct, unmediated) transcendental experiences. The fact that individuals experience the transcendental order allows them to consider the transcendent as real. This is what Danièle Hervieu-Léger calls the mode of auto-validation of religious beliefs (Hervieu-Léger, 1999, p. 187). The validation of religious truth is entirely subjective within this mode of validation, and this has two important implications for distinguishing church religiosity and alternative spiritualities:

- The mode of auto-validation of beliefs emphasizes personal experiences of transcendence. Institutional validation, in contrast, stresses the coherence of religious teachings. To put in other terms: individualized beliefs emphasize the emotional dimension of religion, while church religiosity emphasizes the cognitive dimension.

- Auto-validation strongly emphasizes autonomy of the individual. The mediation of religious truth through religious institutions or a specialized clergy is rejected. Religious authorities cannot be legitimate because the subject is the only relevant instance to judge religious authenticity. This implies that individualized beliefs are to be found first of all, outside of the churches.

The strong emphasis on subjectivity implies that very different spiritual paths are equally legitimate, and this means that a measurement of alternative spiritualities along some beliefs (e.g., reincarnation) or practices (e.g., Yoga, Ayuverda, and Zen meditation) is not possible. Hence, it seems more promising to capture alternative spiritualities based on the very abstract principles that structure this religious orientation.

Despite the diversity of practices within the spiritual movement, a monistic worldview structures spiritual beliefs (Knoblauch, 2006). The conception of the personal God—crucial for all monotheistic traditions—has lost its relevance for spiritual beliefs. The divine is conceived as an impersonal force omnipresent in the world.

In sum, three aspects characterize alternative spiritualities in opposition to church religiosity: (1) Alternative spiritualities emphasize the direct and primarily emotional experience of transcendence, while church religiosity concedes greater significance to religious teachings and tradition; (2) Church religiosity is bound to membership to religious organizations. Alternative spiritualities, in contrast, reject religious authorities. Each individual is responsible for his or her spiritual development; and (3) Alternative spiritualities reject a dualistic perception of transcendental powers.

Church religiosity and alternative spiritualities, however, are only two religious options among others. A large body of evidence shows that unbelief has become a very common religious orientation for Europeans (Voas, 2008). Reasons for the decline of church religiosity are extensively discussed by proponents of secularization theory (for a summary see Bruce, 2002). A detailed discussion of secularization theory is not necessary for the aim of this study. It is useful, however, to point to an important differentiation within the field of unbelief, where strong and weak forms of unbelief coexist (Barker, 2005). The strong form of unbelief in its ideal-typical representation is atheism; that is, the denial of the existence of any metaphysical reality (Pollack, Wohlrab-Sahr, & Gärtner, 2003). Weaker forms of unbelief probably have greater importance for religious orientations in Europe. These embrace agnosticism as well as religious indifference. The latter means that individuals simply have no opinion on religious questions. They do not feel concerned with religious issues and questions, and religion has no relevance for their lives. But this group does not exclude the possibility that a metaphysical reality exists (Pollack et al., 2003, p. 12).

Empirical evidence from the sociology of religion shows that a large share of Europeans can be classified neither as church religious nor as unbelievers (Strom, 2009). Voas (2009) suggests the term "fuzzy fidelity" to address a loose form of identification with a religious tradition (i.e., mostly Christianity in the European context). But, as Voas emphasizes, fuzzy fidelity generally has only a little impact on attitudes and behavior, and the fuzzy beliefs do not have high salience. Consequently, fuzzy fidelity is close to religious indifference.

Grace Davie suggests that although many people turn away from the churches, they do not completely abandon their religious beliefs. This believing without belonging form of religiosity is likely to be less coherent because a continuous contact with religious organization is lacking (Davie, 2008). But the religious beliefs in this group should be largely inspired by Christianity. Thus, within the realm of church religiosity, two different patterns of religious orientations emerge: the first is made up of individuals who are fully integrated into the churches, and the second is comprised of individuals who are somehow religious, even though their religiosity is not closely linked to the churches.

To summarize: overall, five forms of religious orientations are expected to be relevant for religious choices in contemporary Europe: church religiosity, believing without belonging, atheism, religious indifference, and alternative spiritualities.

It is challenging to assume that these five groups are present in all countries included in the analysis especially because cross cultural comparisons require conceptual equivalence across countries. In each case, I do not expect equal distribution of the five groups across countries because of the differences in cultural legacies and socioeconomic development across European societies.

14.3 DATA, OPERATIONALIZATION, AND METHOD

Standard indicators for religiosity in social science surveys are mostly designed with reference to traditional religions in Europe. Hence, these indicators are useful to discriminate church religiosity and unbelief.* Additional questions about respondent's beliefs are scarce, and thus it is rarely possible to assess the significance of alternative spiritualities. The dataset from the Religious and Moral Pluralism Project (RAMP)† included some questions to measure church religiosity, unbelief, and alternative spiritualities. Therefore, the dataset offers a unique possibility to describe religious orientations in Europe and to evaluate if the patterns of religious orientations are conceptually equivalent across countries. The RAMP survey was conducted in 1999 in 11 European countries as a face-to-face interview with a random sampling. Samples from Belgium ($N = 1662$), Denmark ($N = 606$), Finland ($N = 786$), Great Britain ($N = 1466$), Hungary ($N = 2149$), Italy ($N = 2020$), the Netherlands ($N = 1004$), Norway ($N = 503$), Poland ($N = 1134$), Portugal ($N = 986$), and Sweden ($N = 1032$) are available.

Although the RAMP questionnaire includes a large number of items on religious beliefs, a direct measure of alternative spiritualities is not included. Therefore, it is necessary to combine the available indicators in a way that discriminates the five expected patterns of religious orientations. For this purpose, five items are particularly suited. The first item is religious self-assessment. The respondents are asked whether they consider themselves to be a religious person. Responses are given on a 7-point scale. This item has to be interpreted with reference to the everyday life understanding of the term religious: the identification with a religious tradition in a narrow sense (i.e., referring to a traditional church).

The second item is the frequency of church attendance. Church attendance is generally considered to measure religious participation. In the latent class (LC) model that I will present subsequently, I suggest to interpret church attendance as an indicator for integration into the churches. Integration into churches implies sharing the values and norms of the

* The items frequently included in surveys are: frequency of church attendance, the importance of God for respondentís life, religious self-assessment, denominational membership, and frequency of prayer.

† RAMP was coordinated by Wolfgang Jagodzinski (University of Cologne) and Karel Dobbleaere (Catholic University of Leuven). I am grateful to Wolfgang Jagodzinski for providing me the dataset.

religious community. Church attendance thus reflects the belonging part of church religiosity.

The third item included in the model is a forced choice item that asks for respondent's conception of transcendental powers. This item offers five different views: The first is the personal God ("I believe in a God with whom I can have a personal relationship") from the Christian, Muslim, and Jewish traditions (i.e., expressing church religious beliefs). The second and the third options suggest more impersonal views of transcendental power: "I believe in a spirit or life force" and "I believe God is something within each person rather then something out there." Both views reflect an impersonal conception of transcendence typical for alternative spiritualities (Heelas & Houtman, 2009). A fourth option reflects the atheist position ("I don't believe in God or any kind of spirit or life force") and the fifth offers the agnostic view ("I really don't know what to believe").

The three items mentioned so far are particularly suited to distinguish church religiosity and unbelief. They do not provide sufficient information to distinguish between unbelief and alternative spiritualities. Hence, two additional items are included in the model: The first asks respondents whether they have a "spiritual life" (7-point scale). Like the religious self-assessment item, the spiritual life item has to be interpreted with reference to the everyday life meaning of spirituality. Some ambiguity results from the fact that the meaning of religiosity and spirituality is not mutually exclusive. Several empirical studies were conducted in the United States to disentangle the meaning attributed to the terms religiosity and spirituality, respectively. These studies show that there is substantial overlap between both notions (i.e., the reference to a metaphysical reality) though each has its particular emphasis. Religiosity refers to the realm of organized religion, while spirituality grasps the individual connectedness with the divine and/or transcendent (i.e., the subjective element of religion; Hill & Pargament, 2003; Schlehofer, Omoto, & Adelman, 2008; Zinnbauer et al., 1997). Therefore, I argue that the spiritual life item is an adequate measure for the emphasis of religious emotions. In the RAMP dataset, the religious self-assessment and the spiritual life items are moderately correlated. The correlation is highest in Finland ($r = 0.473$) and lowest in Norway ($r = 0.316$).

Alternative spiritualities are expected to be characterized by an emphasis of the spiritual life without being highly religious. But because the boundaries between both terms are fuzzy, it seems not appropriate to measure alternative spiritualities by simply selecting those respondents from the dataset that indicate to have a spiritual life but do not describe themselves as religious. Using this simple classification, Barker finds about 15% of alternative spirituals in the pooled RAMP dataset (Barker, 2005). A number that seems quite high especially when compared to the 1.6% of observant spirituals that Heelas and Woodhead counted (Heelas & Woodhead, 2005).

From a methodological point of view, a LC model is better suited to disentangle both forms of religious orientations. The overlap between the everyday life meanings of religiosity and spirituality implies that items referring to spirituality have to be considered together with indicators for church religiosity to be interpretable. LC analysis is suited to do this without setting arbitrary thresholds on the scales.

Finally, an item is included in the model that asks respondents for the frequency they have transcendental experiences: "Have you ever had an experience of something that exists, but transcends (goes beyond) everyday reality, and which you may or may not call God?" Personal transcendental experiences are of crucial importance for the mode of auto-validation of religious beliefs. Hence, alternative spiritualities should be characterized by relatively high levels of openness for transcendental experiences. Because the wording of the item mentions God, there will be a considerable bias toward church religiosity because experiences of God probably are the most common form of transcendental experience for church religious individuals.

Table 14.1 summarizes the expected outcome of the LC model. The different patterns of religious orientations will not be ordered along a single dimension because on the one hand, atheism and alternative spiritualities share the distance to the churches. On the other hand, alternative spiritualities and church religiosity share the belief in a metaphysical reality. But concrete representations of transcendental power differ for church religiosity and alternative spiritualities. For this reason, again, a LC analysis is more appropriate than dimensional techniques to set up the measurement model.

Before running the analysis, the items have been recoded to reduce the number of categories. This is necessary because some categories gather only very few respondents, and reducing the number of categories eases the interpretation of the model. For the religious self-assessment and the spiritual life items, the extreme points of the scales were collapsed so that

TABLE 14.1

Expected Outcome of the Latent Class Model

	Expected Religious Orientation (Expected Latent Classes)				
Indicator	**Church Religious**	**Believing Without Belonging**	**Alternative Spiritualities**	**Religious Indifference**	**Atheism**
Church attendance	+	–	–	–	–
Religious self-assessment	+	O/+	O/-	O	–
Perceptions of the transcendental	Personal God	Personal God	Impersonal force	Personal or Impersonal	None
Spiritual life	+	O	+	–	–
Experiences of transcendence	+	–	+	–	–

+ = high level expected, O = medium level expected, – = low level expected.

the items have five categories each. The seven categories of the church attendance item were recoded into four categories: (1) never attending, (2) irregular attendance (several times a year/specific holidays), (3) regular attendance (at least once a month), and (4) frequent attendance (once a week and more often). Similarly, the transcendental experience item was recoded into three categories: (1) No transcendental experiences, (2) sometimes experiences, and (3) frequent transcendental experiences.

The LC model presented in this chapter in its simple form can be expressed through Equation 14.1 (McCutcheon, 1987, p. 33):

$$\pi_{ijklmt}^{ABCDEX} = \pi_{it}^{\bar{A}X} * \pi_{jt}^{\bar{B}X} * \pi_{kt}^{\bar{C}X} * \pi_{lt}^{\bar{D}X} * \pi_{mt}^{\bar{E}X} * \pi_{t}^{X}. \tag{14.1}$$

A, *B*, *C*, *D*, and *E* refer to the observed variables, *I*, *J*, *K*, *L*, and *M* to the categories of the observed variables [A = Perceptions of the transcendent ($I = 5$), B = Religious self-assessment ($J = 5$), C = Spiritual life ($K = 5$), D = Frequency Transcendental Experiences ($L = 3$), and E = Church attendance ($M = 4$)]. X refers to the latent variable (with T latent classes). The single sample LC model thus describes the joint distribution of the observed variables of a $5 \times 5 \times 5 \times 3 \times 4$ five-way contingency table (i.e., a table with 1500 cells).

In Equation 14.1, π_{ijklmt}^{ABCDEX} expresses the probability of a particular response profile for individuals (e.g., $i = 1$, $j = 3$, $k = 2$, $l = 2$, $m = 1$) given class membership in a particular class (t; e.g., the church religious class) of the latent variable X (i.e., religious orientations). Consequently, $\pi_{it}^{\bar{A}X}$ is the conditional probability that an individual is located on a particular level (i) of the observed variable (A) given his membership in a particular LC (t) of the latent variable (X). For instance, we expect a high conditional probability (e.g., 0.700) of frequent church attendance within the church religious class of the latent variable religious orientations. In other words: a respondent being in the LC "church religiosity" has a 70% probability to report frequent church attendance. The conditional probabilities define the substantial meaning of the LCs. They indicate whether a category of the observed variables is likely to be reported by members of a class. Hence, the conditional probabilities indicate the strength of the association between each of the LCs and each of the indicator variables. They can be interpreted in analogy to factor loadings in factor analysis (McCutcheon, 1987, p. 33).

It is important to note that LC models assume that at a particular level of the latent variable no further associations between the observed variables persist. This assumption of conditional or local independence means that the classes of the latent variables account for the variation of the observed variables.

Within each of the LCs (t) of the latent variable (X), the conditional probabilities for the categories of the observed variables (e.g., I, with $i = 1$, $i = 2$, $i = 3$, $i = 4$, $i = 5$) sum up to 1. Thus, for an indicator variable with five categories, only four conditional probabilities have to be estimated per class. Analogously, the LC probabilities for each group sum to 1 because each individual is classified into one of the LCs based on the LC that has the highest (posterior) probability for the particular response profile of the individual.

Extending the model to a multiple group LC model means to analyze the associations in the contingency table for each group separately. Formally, this means adding a grouping variable (G) to Equation 14.1 where S is the number of groups. Equation 14.2 expresses the formal multiple group LC model (McCutcheon, 1987):

$$\pi_{ijklmt}^{\bar{A}\bar{B}\bar{C}\bar{D}\bar{E}G\bar{X}} = \pi_{ist}^{\bar{A}GX} * \pi_{jst}^{\bar{B}GX} * \pi_{kst}^{\bar{C}GX} * \pi_{lst}^{\bar{D}GX} * \pi_{mst}^{\bar{E}GX} * \pi_{st}^{G\bar{X}}. \quad (14.2)$$

The interpretation of the conditional probabilities is the same as for Equation 14.1. But now, the probability of LC membership is conditional on group membership ($\pi_{st}^{G\bar{X}}$). In its less restrictive form, each conditional probability is estimated for each group separately. This type of model is generally called the heterogeneous model because no similarities are assumed to exist across groups. For the model presented in this example, this means that for each LC in each country, 17 conditional probabilities are estimated. Consequently, the comparative interpretation across groups rapidly turns out to be difficult.

Comparative analyses, hence, trying to minimize heterogeneity in the model by testing whether equality constraints can be imposed on the model. This is important not only to facilitate the interpretation of coefficients but also to test for measurement invariance; that is, whether the meaning of the LCs is equivalent across groups (Chapter 13 in this volume).

Measurement invariance for LC models means that the conditional probabilities are equal for all groups under consideration (McCutcheon, 2002). In the terminology of LC analysis, these models are called structurally homogeneous models (McCutcheon, 2002). These models are much more parsimonious than heterogeneous models because conditional probabilities are estimated only once for all groups.

Sometimes, distributional homogeneity (or complete structural homogeneity, see Kankaraš et al. in this volume) is discussed in the literature, which means that the sizes of the LCs (i.e., the LC probabilities) are the same across groups. The assumption of distributional homogeneity is unrealistic for religious orientations and hence will not be addressed in this chapter.

Besides heterogeneous and homogeneous models, there is also a broad range of possibilities to test for partially homogenous models. These models are present when some of the measurement parameters are equal across countries, while others are not. Partially homogeneous models are useful to minimize heterogeneity when homogeneous models do not fit the data.

There are various ways to specify partially homogenous LC models (here I refer only to the probabilistic parameterization; see Kankaraš et al. in this volume): (1) by fixing the conditional probabilities for some observed variables to be equal across groups while conditional probabilities for other indicators are estimated freely across groups or (2) by fixing conditional probabilities for some classes while estimating parameters for other classes free across countries. For the latter case, the measurement of classes estimated with equal conditional probabilities across countries is invariant and the classes can easily be compared.

The strategy to select an appropriate multiple group LC model suggested in textbooks (McCutcheon & Hagenaars, 1997) is to determine, first, the number of classes required for each of the groups separately. If the number of classes is the same for all groups, in a second step, measurement invariance can be tested. This procedure, however, might be inappropriate for the comparison of religious orientations because the countries can be expected to differ with respect to the diversity of religious orientations. While in countries like Poland and Italy, which are known to be highly integrated with respect to religious orientations, only a few classes might be sufficient to describe religious orientations, other countries (e.g., the Netherlands, Great Britain, and the Scandinavian countries) might show greater diversity of religious orientations (i.e., secular attitudes and alternative spiritualities coexist with church religiosity). Although a different number of LCs are needed to describe the religious orientations, measurement invariance can be tested for the classes in the model (Kankaraš et al. in this volume). For instance, the church religious and the atheistic classes could be present in all countries and be invariant. At the same time, in some of the countries an alternative spiritualities class might be added, while in other countries this class does not exist.

Several criteria are available to guide model selection: (1) Chi-square based tests for model fit, such as the likelihood ratio or the Pearson's chi square, statistics are available. In complex models like the one presented in this study, the use of chi-square based tests is not recommended because in contingency tables with sparse cells, the test statistics are not chi-square distributed and cannot be used to evaluate the model fit (Nylund, Asparouhov, & Muthen, 2007); (2) Descriptive information criteria are very common for model selection. They allow comparing the relative fit of different models against each other (Eid, Langheine, & Diener, 2003). According to a simulation study by Nylund et al. (2007), the Bayesian Information Criterion (BIC) and the sample-size-adjusted BIC (adj. BIC) perform best to identify the appropriate number of classes, while the Akaike Information Criterion tends to overestimate the number of classes (Nylund et al., 2007). Consequently, the model selection will be based on BIC and adj. BIC; and (3) LC models can be evaluated on the classification quality (entropy). This measure is based on the posterior probabilities of each respondent for each class. The sharper the posterior probabilities distinguish the different LC memberships, the better the value for the entropy of the model. I will rely on a measure of relative entropy that is reported by Mplus and takes a value of 0 when classification is highly uncertain and 1 if classification is certain.

Experience shows that the different criteria often contradict each other. For this reason, substantial considerations always have to guide the process of model selection. Models that are clearly interpretable and correspond to theoretical expectations might be preferred, although other models show a better fit to the data.

14.4 RESULTS

The model selection proceeds in three steps; (1) I run heterogeneous models to determine the number of classes needed to appropriately describe the data if no equality constraints are imposed across countries; (2) I compare heterogeneous models with homogenous models to test whether it is appropriate to fix estimates to equality across countries; and (3) I examine whether partially homogeneous models are better suited to describe religious orientations in Europe than homogeneous or heterogeneous models. In the following, I will concentrate on BIC and adj. BIC because the entropy values from Table 14.2 show that classification quality is satisfying (around 0.9) for all models.

The BIC and adj. BIC values for the heterogeneous models, reported in the first block of Table 14.2, indicate that a 3-class model should be selected (M2 in Table 14.2).* This is only partly in line with results from single group LC models run for each country separately (not reported here). Here, the BIC values also point to 3-class models, but adj. BIC shows that for most of the countries, 4- or 5-class models should be selected.

When running the homogeneous models, I explicitly considered the possibility that some LCs are present in some countries, but not in all countries. Technically, a class does not exist in a country when the LC

* All models reported here are estimated with Mplus Version 5.2. Missing cases were excluded listwise. Overall, 10,809 cases are included in the analysis.

TABLE 14.2

Fit Measures for Latent Class Models

	BIC	Adj. BIC	Entropy	Number of Parameters	Fixed Latent Class Probabilities
Heterogeneous models					
M1: 2 classes	1,82,513	1,81,258	0.951	395	0
M2: 3 classes	1,81,521	1,79,637	0.923	593	0
M3: 4 classes	1,82,257	1,79,744	0.902	791	0
Homogeneous models (no distributional homogeneity assumed)					
M4: 3 classes	1,81,855	1,81,591	0.921	83	0
M5: 4 classes	1,80,173	1,79,833	0.914	107	4
M6: 5 classes	1,79,266	1,78,844	0.909	133	6
M7: 6 classes	1,79,011	1,78,525	0.899	153	14
Partially homogeneous models					
M8: 5 classes with experience and attendance free across countries for class I	1,79,113	1,78,535	0.898	182	7
M9: 5 classes with experience and attendance free for class I and experience free for class III across countries	1,79,001	1,78,359	0.896	202	7

probability is 0. If during model estimation the LC probabilities turned out to be zero or very close to 0, I fixed them to 0 upon the condition that fixing the parameter decreased BIC and adj. BIC values because this indicates that the restricted model is more appropriate. For example, altogether 14 LC probabilities of the 6-class homogeneous model (M7 in Table 14.2) can be fixed. This results in a 4-class model for 7 countries, whereas for 3 countries I estimated a 6-class model.

The information criteria for homogeneous models (second block in Table 14.2) reveal that more classes are needed to attain data fit equivalent to the heterogeneous models. The 3-class heterogeneous model (M2) fits better than the 3-class homogeneous model (M4). The homogeneous 4-class model (M5), however, should be preferred to the 4-class heterogeneous model (M3). Four LC probabilities of M5 are fixed to 0 resulting in a 4-class model for eight countries and a 3-class model for four countries. The 5-class homogeneous model (M6, with six 0 LC probabilities) has lower BIC and adj. BIC values than the heterogeneous 3-class model (M2). This means that if we allow the number and meaning of classes to differ across countries, the homogeneous models do better than the heterogeneous models because differences in the LCs absorb some of the heterogeneity across countries.

The homogeneous 6-class model (M7, with fourteen 0 LC probabilities) fits even better than the homogeneous 5-class model (M6). As mentioned earlier, M7 is in fact a 4-class model for seven countries (Denmark, Finland, Hungary, Italy, Norway, Poland, and Sweden) and a 6-class model for four countries (Belgium, Great Britain, the Netherlands, and Portugal). A detailed comparison of models M6 and M7 reveals that at least two different classes cover the realm of church religiosity: One class gathers respondents that are frequently attending but report no transcendental experiences. This class has a 0 LC probability in Denmark, Finland, Hungary, Norway, and Sweden. The other is marked by frequent experiences but only moderate church attendance. This class is important in Scandinavian countries and Hungary but absent in Poland and Italy (conditional probabilities not reported). It is plausible to argue that theological differences between Protestantism and Catholicism cause differences in the profile of church religiosity. Nevertheless, both can be assigned to the church religious type of religious orientations. As the chapter has the primary descriptive aim to distinguish different basic forms of religious orientations, it is not necessary to include further distinction of subtypes of church religiosity. To collapse both classes, I run a partially homogeneous 5-class model where the conditional probabilities for church attendance and transcendental experiences are estimated freely across countries for the church religious class (M8 in the third block of Table 14.2). This procedure allows collapsing the two church religious classes without losing information about its country-specific characteristics. Seven LC probabilities can be fixed to 0 resulting in a 4-class model for Denmark, Finland, Hungary, Norway, Sweden, Italy, and Poland and a 5-class model for Belgium, Great Britain, the Netherlands, and Portugal. According to adj. BIC, the models M7 and M8 are rather equivalent in model fit. But BIC shows that M7 fits better than M8.

From a substantial point of view, M8 is a less convincing model because two classes for religious indifference emerge that differ only with respect to the frequency of transcendental experiences (conditional probabilities not reported here). An alternative spiritualities class that was evident in M7 disappears in M8. For the aim of this research, it is not crucial to distinguish among different forms of religious indifference but highly relevant to identify the alternative spirituality class. Consequently, an additional partially homogeneous model is estimated where the conditional probabilities for frequency of church attendance and transcendental experiences in the church religious class and the conditional probabilities for the frequency of transcendental experiences in the religious indifference class are estimated for each country separately (M9 in Table 14.2). M9 has lower BIC and adj. BIC values than M7. Although two classes of the model are not invariant, it is appropriate to interpret this model because it uncovers interesting country-specific characteristics of religious orientations across European countries.

The conditional probabilities for model M9 are reported in Tables 14.3 and 14.4. Table 14.3 shows the homogeneous part of the model; that is, the conditional probabilities that are fixed for all countries. Table 14.4 shows the heterogeneous part of the model (i.e., the country-specific conditional probabilities).

The first class in Table 14.3 is the church religious class. The pattern that appears is rather clear: this class is characterized by the Christian tradition of the personal God (0.750) and a strong religious self-assessment. Respondents in this class also have a high probability to report an intense spiritual life.

The two remaining indicator variables were not invariant for the church religious class. The transcendent experiences item reveals particularly interesting differences (see the first block of Table 14.4): in the Scandinavian countries the church religious class is characterized by frequent experiences of transcendence, whereas in the Catholic countries church religious respondents report less frequent experiences of transcendence. The remaining countries are in between. With respect to the frequency of church attendance, the pattern is inversed (see second block of Table 14.4): frequent church attendance is much stronger in Catholic countries than in Protestant countries. Here again, the mixed countries are in between. At least, irregular church attendance is evident for the church religious class in Protestant countries, suggesting that a link to the churches persists.

TABLE 14.3

Conditional Probabilities for M9 (Homogeneous Part)

	Conditional Probabilities				
Latent Class Indicator	**Class I Church Religious**	**Class II Moderate Religious**	**Class III Atheism**	**Class IV Religious Indifference**	**Class V Alternative Spiritualities**
Perceptions of transcendence					
Personal God	0.750	0.500	0.008	0.189	0.078
Spirit or life force	0.035	0.129	0.144	0.232	0.471
God within each person	0.212	0.346	0.177	0.464	0.378
No God	0.001	0.003	0.412	0.008	0.017
Don't know what to believe	0.002	0.021	0.258	0.107	0.057
Religious self-assessment					
Not religious at all (1)	0.010	0.003	0.902	0.151	0.256
(2)	0.007	0.053	0.066	0.208	0.129
(3)	0.079	0.317	0.028	0.395	0.240
(4)	0.264	0.409	0.001	0.197	0.265
Very religious (5)	0.640	0.218	0.003	0.048	0.110
Having a spiritual life					
No spiritual life (1)	0.070	0.254	0.679	0.380	0.000
(2)	0.028	0.151	0.075	0.156	0.021
(3)	0.105	0.361	0.099	0.233	0.150
(4)	0.208	0.187	0.066	0.143	0.243
Very spiritual life (5)	0.589	0.047	0.081	0.087	0.587
Transcendental experiences					
No experiences	Free across groups	0.790	0.839	Free across groups	0.055
Sometimes	Free across groups	0.143	0.127	Free across groups	0.330
Often	Free across groups	0.067	0.034	Free across groups	0.615

(Continued)

TABLE 14.3 (Continued)

Conditional Probabilities for M9 (Homogeneous Part)

Latent Class Indicator	Class I Church Religious	Class II Moderate Religious	Class III Atheism	Class IV Religious Indifference	Class V Alternative Spiritualities
	Conditional Probabilities				
Frequency of church attendance					
No attendance	Free across groups	0.009	0.946	0.596	0.714
Irregular attendance	Free across groups	0.290	0.046	0.353	0.250
Regular attendance	Free across groups	0.310	0.005	0.045	0.035
Frequent attendance	Free across groups	0.390	0.003	0.006	0.000

This pattern suggests that the mechanisms of integration into church religiosity operate in different ways depending on the religious context: in Catholic countries, integration into church religiosity proceeds through integration into the religious community, whereas in Protestant countries individual experiences of transcendence are of greater importance for the maintenance of individuals beliefs.

Although measurement invariance could not be established, I argue that the church religious class covers equivalent concepts in Catholic and Protestant countries. The particular shape of church religiosity, however, differs somewhat across countries with different religious traditions. In so far, it is justified to interpret the partial homogeneous class instead of opting for a 6-class model with different classes for church religiosity in Protestant and Catholic countries.

The second class from Table 14.3 is best described as a moderate religious class (Strom, 2009). This class was not expected in Table 14.1 and is nonexistent in Denmark, Finland, Hungary, Norway, and Sweden. Overall, this class is characterized by a firm self-description as religious and a medium-level intensity of the spiritual life, both, however, at lower levels than that of the church religious class. Individual experiences of transcendence do not play a role for this class (the conditional probability

TABLE 14.4

Conditional Probabilities for M9 (Heterogeneous Part of the Model)

	Country										
	BEL	**DEN**	**FIN**	**GB**	**HUN**	**IT**	**NL**	**NOR**	**POL**	**SWE**	**POR**
Church religious class: Frequency of transcendental experiences											
No experiences	0.436	0.088	0.108	0.120	0.049	0.685	0.418	0.003	0.530	0.027	0.428
Sometimes	0.250	0.222	0.283	0.210	0.133	0.144	0.228	0.119	0.186	0.139	0.139
Often	0.314	0.690	0.609	0.670	0.818	0.171	0.354	0.878	0.284	0.834	0.432
Church religious class: Frequency of church attendance											
No attendance	0.118	0.174	0.185	0.172	0.174	0.089	0.288	0.000	0.033	0.163	0.057
Irregular attendance	0.171	0.421	0.363	0.194	0.177	0.163	0.051	0.395	0.009	0.201	0.156
Regular attendance	0.094	0.255	0.209	0.129	0.171	0.176	0.161	0.237	0.094	0.242	0.097
Frequent attendance	0.617	0.150	0.243	0.504	0.478	0.573	0.500	0.368	0.865	0.393	0.690
Religious indifference class: Frequency of transcendental experiences											
No experiences	0.813	0.449	0.507	0.546	0.318	0.921	0.862	0.443	0.552	0.234	0.705
Sometimes	0.122	0.467	0.448	0.301	0.349	0.032	0.104	0.224	0.241	0.610	0.147
Often	0.065	0.084	0.045	0.153	0.332	0.047	0.034	0.333	0.207	0.156	0.148

of reporting no experiences of transcendence is systematically higher than for the church religious class). This expresses the lower extent of individual involvement into religion. In the same vein, the conditional probabilities of church attendance confirm the lower level of integration into the churches but regular or frequent church attendance are still obvious for this class.

It is interesting to note that two conceptions of transcendental powers characterize the moderate religious class: the personal God (0.500) and the God within (0.346). The personal God expresses the link to traditional core beliefs of the churches. Thus, it is somewhat surprising that the God within has a substantial share for this group. According to Heelas and Houtman (2009), the God within category is not a priori in conflict with church religious convictions in southern European countries.

It is the church attendance item that defines the difference between the moderate religious pattern found here and the believing without belonging pattern expected in Table 14.1. The moderate religious class represents a subtype of the more general realm of church religiosity as a social form of religion.

The third class from Table 14.3 corresponds to the expected atheist class. This class reflects great distance of religion and spirituality for all the indicator variables included in the model. Only the item on transcendental consciousness indicates that this group not only gathers convinced atheists who answer that there is no God or any transcendental power but also the agnostic answer category (0.258). Hence, this class gathers not only individuals who reject all metaphysical realities but also weaker forms of unbelief characterized by a strong distance to any religious concerns. The atheist class is invariant across all countries.

With respect to the transcendental consciousness, the fourth class is characterized by impersonal conceptions of transcendence with a clear preference for the God within (0.464), which is the most metaphorical category of this item. In each case, the zero conditional probability for the no God category shows that respondents in this class do not exclude the existence of transcendental realities. In addition, individuals in this class describe themselves as at least somewhat but not highly religious (categories 2, 3, or 4 of the self-assessment scale). Obviously, respondents in this class consider their spiritual life to be less intense than their religious self-assessment; that is, the no spiritual life category has the highest conditional probability (0.380).

Conditional probabilities for church attendance show that respondents worship only irregularly (if at all), which expresses a much greater distance to the churches than the moderate religious or church religious class.

The freely estimated conditional probabilities for the frequency of transcendental experiences (third block in Table 14.4) reveal great differences across countries: For Belgium, Italy, the Netherlands, and Portugal the no experiences category best describe this class. In Denmark, Finland, and Sweden, the sometimes and no experiences categories taken together describe the pattern fairly well. In Norway and Hungary, the conditional probabilities for the often category exceed 0.300 and thus point to a stronger spiritual involvement within this class. A similar statement is true for Poland where the often category has a probability of 0.207 to occur and where the no experiences category has only a 0.552 probability. To interpret these level differences, it is useful to compare the importance of transcendental experiences with those of the church religious and, if applicable, to the moderate religious class. A fairly consistent pattern emerges for eight out of 11 countries: the respondents are most likely to report frequent transcendental experience for the church religious class followed by the moderate religious class (that is absent in Denmark, Finland, Hungary, Norway, and Sweden) and then the fourth class. In Portugal, there are no differences between the moderate religious and the fourth class. Only two countries deviate from this pattern: in Great Britain and Poland, the probabilities of reporting some or frequent experiences of transcendence are higher than for the moderate religious group but still lower than for the church religious group. These differences, obvious in Table 14.4, complicate the interpretation of the fourth class in the cross country comparison. For the Catholic countries (with the exception of Poland) and the Netherlands, the combination of an impersonal conception of the transcendent, a medium strength of religious self-assessment, no spiritual life, irregular or no church attendance, and the absence of any transcendental experience leads to the conclusion that this class is best described as the religious indifference class.

In the Protestant countries, Poland and the United Kingdom, the transcendental experience item expresses higher probabilities for individuals to report emotional involvement into religion, although outside the churches. This class could stand for the Protestant version of moderate religiosity because experiences of God are an important vector of integration into church religiosity. Consequently, the class is not comparable across Protestant and Catholic countries.

The overall pattern of the fifth class from Table 14.3 fits the expectations about the shape of alternative spiritualities drawn from the literature in the first section. This picture is manifest in the conditional probabilities: (1) Individuals in the fifth class have an impersonal perception of the transcendent with a slight preference for the spirit or life force (0.471), which is less metaphorical than the God within. (2) The conditional probability for never attending church is around 0.760 indicating that individuals in this class do not worship regularly or even frequently. (3) Not surprisingly, the conditional probabilities indicate an emphasis of the spiritual life. The probability to be located on the very spiritual life pole of the scale is about 0.600. (4) The probability to report frequent experiences of transcendence is around 0.600 and for sometimes it is 0.330. Hence, individuals in the alternative spiritualities class have a probability higher than 0.900 to report experiences of transcendence. (5) This said, it is interesting to note that the religious self-assessment scale does not fit the expectation formulated in Table 14.1. The conditional probabilities indicate that individuals in the alternative spirituality class are equally likely to describe themselves either as religious or not religious. This finding confirms that being religious and being spiritual is not mutually exclusive even from the perspective of the spiritual milieu. It is not implausible that a significant share of alternative spirituals claim to be religious because they might consider spirituality as an equivalent of church religiosity. Consequently, the measurement of alternative spiritualities through classification of respondents that describe themselves as spiritual but not religious is inappropriate. Latent class analysis is a better method to identify alternative spirituals. Further research on this point is needed to improve the measurement of alternative spiritualities. The alternative spirituals class is absent in Italy and Poland.

Finally, Table 14.5 shows the LC distributions across countries obtained from M9. Several elements are noteworthy: (1) Poland, Italy, and Portugal are the only countries where church religiosity (Classes I and II) gathers the largest proportion of the sample and hence can be considered the reference model for religious orientations. Less than 10% of the population are atheists; (2) In most countries, religious indifference is the modal class. The only exceptions are Italy, Poland, and the Netherlands. The Netherlands is the only country where atheists outnumber indifferents; and (3) Overall, it turns out that about 60–70% of Europeans do not have firm religious beliefs (Classes III and IV). (4) Finally, the model shows

TABLE 14.5

Latent Class Distributions

	Country										
Classes	**BE**	**DK**	**FI**	**GB**	**HU**	**IT**	**NL**	**NO**	**PL**	**PT**	**SE**
Church religious	12.8%	14%	30%	18.8%	28.1%	43.2%	11.9%	15.9%	32.2%	27.5%	9.7%
Moderate religious	14.4%	0%	0%	4.4%	0%	26.4%	14.2%	0%	56.5%	20.1%	0%
Atheism	29.5%	27.3%	17.7%	26.6%	30.1%	7.6%	34.5%	33.4%	2.7%	9.6%	35.4%
Religious indifference	37.7%	48.6%	43.5%	38.9%	34.6%	22.8%	29.6%	42.2%	8.7%	36.9%	42.4%
Alternative spiritualities	5.6%	11.8%	8.0%	11.4%	7%	0%	9.8%	8.4%	0%	5.9%	12.4%

BE, Belgium; DK, Denmark; FI, Finland; GB, Great Britain; HU, Hungary; IT, Italy; NL, Netherlands; NO, Norway; PL, Poland; PT, Portugal; SE, Sweden.

that alternative spiritualities are indeed a significant religious option for Europeans. Although they are not relevant in the highly religiously integrated Catholic countries, the share of alternative spirituals exceeds 10% of the sample in Denmark, Great Britain, and Sweden.

14.5 CONCLUSIONS

This chapter aims to draw a comprehensive picture of religious orientations in Europe. Five patterns of religious orientations were expected to be found in the data: church religiosity, believing without belonging, atheism, religious indifference, and alternative spiritualities. The question whether alternative spiritualities are a significant religious option for Europeans guided the construction of the measurement model. A multiple group LC model was chosen for measurement of religious orientations. This allowed testing for measurement invariance across groups. It emerged that a partially homogeneous 5-class model appropriately describes religious orientations in Europe when the number of classes is allowed to differ across countries.

Some interesting conclusions can be drawn from the analysis.

1. Integration into church religiosity operates through different mechanisms in Protestant and Catholic countries. Protestants emphasize experiences of transcendence, while Catholics emphasize church attendance. This means that the institutional mode of beliefs validation is stronger for Catholic countries and church attendance is not an equivalent measurement for church religiosity across countries. The church religious class was found to be not invariant.
2. A believing without belonging form of religious orientations is not evident in the data analysis. Individuals in Catholic countries tend to be in the moderate religious class, while in Protestant countries they tend to be indifferent.
3. Alternative spiritualities are a significant religious option for Europeans. As expected by the theory, this class is characterized by a strong emphasis on personal experiences of transcendental powers, big distance to the churches, and impersonal perceptions of

transcendental powers. The LC distributions show that about 10% of the samples can be classified as alternative spirituals. In the Catholic countries, alternative spiritualities are not relevant. The development of alternative spiritualities thus might be conditional on religious individualism that has a stronger tradition in Protestant countries. The measurement of alternative spiritualities by simply classifying individuals that are spiritual but not religious is inappropriate because both terms have huge intersections from the perspective of the spiritual movement.

Further research is needed to validate the findings from the MGLCA model. As a first step, it is necessary to improve the indicators for different forms of religion. Particularly, the emotional aspects of religion are underdeveloped in survey research but will gain increasing attention. Second, it has to be tested if alternative spirituals develop in place of church religiosity or in place of unbelief. Only if this question is answered it is possible to say whether the existence of alternative spiritualities challenges secularization theory. The study shows that in each case, alternative spiritualities have to be considered by empirical research on religion in Europe.

REFERENCES

Aupers, S., & Houtman, D. (2006). Beyond the spiritual supermarket: The social and public significance of new age spirituality. *Journal of Contemporary Religion, 21*(2), 201–222.

Barker, E. (2005). Yet more varieties of religious experiences. Diversity and pluralism in contemporary Europe. In H. Lehmann (Ed.), *Religiöser Pluralismus im vereinten Europa. Freikirchen und Sekten* (pp. 156–172). Gšttingen, Germany: Wallstein Verlag.

Bruce, S. (2002). *God is dead. Secularization in the West*. Oxford: Blackwell.

Davie, G. (2008). From believing without belonging to vicarious religion: Understanding the patterns of religion in modern Europe. In D. Pollack & D. V. A. Olson (Eds.), *The role of religion in modern societies* (pp. 165–176). New York, NY: Routledge.

Eid, M., Langheine, R., & Diener, E. (2003). Comparing typological structures across cultures by multigroup latent class analysis. *Journal of Cross-Cultural Psychology, 34*(2), 195–210.

Heelas, P., & Houtman, D. (2009). RAMP findings and making sense of the "God within each person, rather than out there." *Journal of Contemporary Religion, 24*(1), 83–98.

Heelas, P., & Woodhead, L. (2005). *The spiritual revolution. Why religion is giving way to spirituality*. Oxford: Blackwell.

Hervieu-Léger, D. (1990). Renouveaux émotionnels contemporains. Fin de la sécularisation ou fin de la religion? [Contemporary renewals of emotion. The end of secularization or the end of religion?] In F. Champion & D. Hervieu-Léger (Eds.), *De l'émotion en religion. Renouveaux et traditions* [Emotion in religion. Renewals and traditions] (pp. 217–248). Paris, France: Centurion.

Hervieu-Léger, D. (1999). *Le pèlerin et le converti. La religion en mouvement.* [The pilgrim and the converted. Religion in movement] Paris, France: Flammarion.

Hervieu-Léger, D. (2005). Bricolage vaut-il dissémination? Quelques réflexions sur l'opérationnalité sociologique d'une métaphore problématique. [Does bricolage merit dissemination? Some reflections on the sociological usefulness of a problematic metaphor]. *Social Compass, 52*(3), 295–308.

Hill, P. C., & Pargament, K. I. (2003). Advances in the conceptualization and measurement of religion and spirituality. Implications for physical and mental health research. *American Psychologist, 58*(1), 64–74.

Knoblauch, H. (2005). Einleitung: Soziologie der Spiritualität. *Zeitschrift für Religionswissenschaft, 5*(2), 123–131.

Knoblauch, H. (2006). Soziologie der Spiritualität. In K. Baier (Ed.), *Handbuch Spiritualität. Zugänge, Traditionen, interreligiöse Prozesse* (pp. 91–111). Darmstadt, Germany: Wissenschaftliche Buchgesellschaft.

Luckmann, T. (1991). *Die unsichtbare Religion*. Frankfurt am Main, Germany: Suhrkamp.

McCutcheon, A. L. (1987). *Latent class analysis*. Newbury Park, CA: Sage.

McCutcheon, A. L. (2002). Basic concepts and procedures in single- and multiple-group latent class analysis. In J. A. Hagenaars & A. L. McCutcheon (Eds.), *Applied latent class analysis* (pp. 56–88). Cambridge: Cambridge University Press.

McCutcheon, A. L., & Hagenaars, J. A. (1997). Comparative social research with multiple-sample latent class models. In J. Rost & R. Langeheine (Eds.), *Applications of latent trait and latent class models in the social sciences* (pp. 266–277). New York, NY: Waxmann.

Nylund, K. L., Asparouhov, T., & Muthen, B. O. (2007). Deciding on the number of classes in latent-class analysis and growth mixture modeling: A Monte Carlo simulation study. *Structural Equation Modeling, 14*(4), 535–569.

Pollack, D. (2008). Religious change in modern societies—Perspectives offered by the sociology of religion. In D. Pollack & D. V. A. Olson (Eds.), *The role of religion in modern societies* (pp. 1–22). New York, NY: Routledge.

Pollack, D., Wohlrab-Sahr, M., & Gärtner, C. (2003). Einleitung. In D. Pollack, M. Wohlrab-Sahr, & Gärtner, C. (Eds.), *Atheismus und religiöse Indifferenz* (pp. 9-20). Opladen, Germany: Leske und Budrich.

Schlehofer, M. M., Omoto, A. M., & Adelman, J. R. (2008). How do "Religion" and "Spirituality" differ? Lay definitions among older adults. *Journal for the Scientific Study of Religion, 47*(3), 411–425.

Strom, I. (2009). Halfway to heaven: Four types of fuzzy fidelity in Europe. *Journal for the Scientific Study of Religion, 48*(4), 702–718.

Taylor, C. (2007). *A secular age*. Cambridge, MA/London: The Belknap Press of Harvard University Press.

Voas, D. (2008). The continuing secular transition. In D. Pollack & D. V. A. Olson (Eds.), *The role of religion in modern societies* (pp. 25–48). New York/Milton Park, NY: Routledge.
Voas, D. (2009). The rise and fall of fuzzy fidelity in Europe. *European Sociological Review, 25*(2), 155–168.
Zinnbauer, B. J., Pargament, K. I., Cole, B., Rye, M. S., Butter, E. M., Belavich, T. G., ... Kadar, J. L. (1997). Religion and spirituality: Unfuzzing the fuzzy. *Journal for the Scientific Study of Religion, 36*(4), 549–564.

Section IV

Item Response Theory (IRT)

15

Using a Differential Item Functioning Approach to Investigate Measurement Invariance

Rianne Janssen
Katholieke Universiteit Leuven

15.1 INTRODUCTION

As an illustration of the topic of the present chapter, consider a questionnaire on depression in which respondents are asked to indicate whether they experienced certain emotions or performed certain behaviors during the last week. For example, it is asked whether the person felt lonely, experienced lack of energy, suffered somber thoughts, had trouble in falling asleep, and failed to work efficiently. Suppose further that it is also asked whether the respondent cried or felt like crying. A depression score is obtained by the sum of all the items endorsed. If one would find that the average sum score is higher for women than for men, the interpretation would be that in the studied sample, women are more depressed than men. However, generally speaking, crying has a lower threshold for women than for men (e.g., Schaeffer, 1988). This implies that if you have a man and a woman of a comparable level of depression, the probability of crying is higher for the woman than for the man. Consequently, if crying items are included in a depression questionnaire, the average sum score for women may turn out to be higher than for men. However, this finding may be due to fact that crying items function differently for both genders and not to the fact that women are more depressed than men. Hence, when comparing test scores between groups, it seems necessary to investigate whether or not the test items function in the same way across the groups. This screening of items is called the study of differential item functioning or shortly DIF.

The present chapter discusses basic models from item response theory (IRT) to investigate DIF among different groups taking the test. These psychometric models are able to disentangle DIF from the main effect of group on the variable measured by the test (e.g., the effect of gender on depression). DIF in itself can be seen as an interaction effect of group and specific items in the test, as was illustrated in the crying example. Figure 15.1 gives a graphical representation of the crying example and illustrates the difference between a main effect and an interaction effect of a group. The depression test is represented with seven items with Item 6 being the crying item. All items are assumed to measure the latent variable depression (labeled *W*), which is represented by the arrows from the observed item responses to *W*. Gender is represented as a possible violator *V*. First, the arrow from *V* to *W* indicates the main effect of gender on depression. Second, the arrow from *V* to Item 6 indicates the interaction effect of gender on crying.

In the following, the basic IRT models are presented first. Afterward, the IRT definition of DIF is introduced and it is shown how DIF can be modeled within an IRT framework. In the next section, different methods for the detection of DIF are presented, followed by an example of

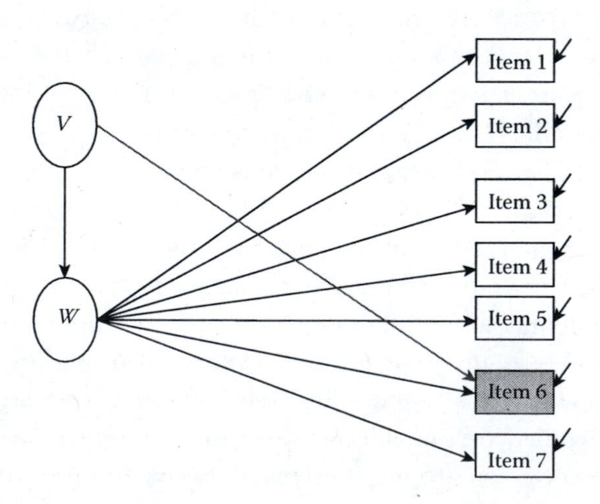

FIGURE 15.1
Graphical representation of DIF in the crying example.

application. A discussion of the DIF approach to measurement invariance concludes the chapter.

In the following, DIF will be presented for the case of comparing the performance on an item by members of some focal group compared to the members of some reference group. This is just for conceptual simplicity, as the study of DIF is certainly not restricted to two groups only.

15.2 BASIC IRT MODELS

15.2.1 The IRT Approach

IRT models belong to the family of the so-called latent variable models. These models assume that discrete item responses on a test are the observable manifestations of a hypothesized trait, which is not directly observed, but which is assumed to be behind the response process. The latent trait may refer to various kinds of underlying person attributes, such as a cognitive ability (e.g., intelligence), a personality trait (e.g., verbal aggression), a state (e.g., emotional distress), or the severity of a disorder (e.g., depression). Characteristic for IRT models is that they model the relationship between the latent variable and the response behavior at the level of the item responses themselves, and not at the level of the aggregated test score. More specifically, IRT models describe the probability of endorsement of a person on each item in the test. For a comparison of IRT and structural equation modeling see, for example, Glöckner-Rist and Hoijtink (2003).

In the present chapter we focus on a subset of IRT models only. Firstly, we discuss IRT models where the relationship between a positive response on the item and the latent variable is strictly monotonously increasing. This implies that one can expect that the higher the person scores on the latent variable, the higher the probability of a positive response is on the item. These IRT models are not suitable for measuring for attitude items that are of the proximity type and not of the dominance type. For example, when asking a respondent the proximity item, “Are you in favor of the present regulations concerning smoking in public places?” a negative response is ambiguous with respect to the position of the person on the latent variable as it could indicate that the person finds the present regulations either too prohibitive or not prohibitive enough. For such proximity items other IRT models exist (e.g., Hoijtink, 1991), which can also be tested on DIF (Hoijtink & Molenaar, 1992). If one would rephrase the above item into a dominance item (e.g., "Are you in favor of banning smoking in public places?" and/or "Are you in favor of allowing smoking in public places?"), then the attitude item can be modeled with standard IRT models. Secondly, the present chapter is confined to parametric IRT models where the relationship between the latent variable and the response probability is described by a specific mathematical function. In nonparametric IRT (see, e.g., Sijtsma & Molenaar, 2002) item response data are studied in a more flexible way without fully committing to a particular functional form. Finally, only IRT models for dichotomously scored items or dichotomized item scores are discussed. In IRT models for polytomous items (see, e.g., Ostini & Nering, 2005), the probability of choosing a certain score given the latent variable is modeled. For these polytomous IRT models, Thissen, Steinberg, and Wainer (1988) presented a methodology to study patterns of differential response among the item's response alternatives, hence, generalizing the concept of DIF to the investigation of differential alternative functioning (DAF).

15.2.2 The Rasch Model

15.2.2.1 Model

The Rasch model or one-parameter logistic (1PL) model is the simplest IRT model (see, e.g., Fischer & Molenaar, 1995). In this model, the probability of endorsement for a person j on an item i is modeled on the basis of a person parameter θ_j and an item threshold or difficulty parameter β_i. More specifically, the probability of a correct response is function of the difference between θ_j and β_i:

$$P(X_{ij}=1)=f(\theta_j-\beta_i), \tag{15.1}$$

where θ_j and β_i are rational numbers. In the original formulation of the model by Rasch (1960), the function f was the logistic function. This S-shaped function transforms any value on the real line into a value between 0 and 1. Also a probit link function can be used, where f equals the cumulative normal distribution. Parameter equivalence among logistic and normal ogive IRT models can be ensured by including a scaling parameter (see, e.g., Camilli, 1994). In order to identify the model in

Equation 15.1, the origin of the scale has to be fixed. This can be done by restricting the mean of the item or person parameters to zero. Another way of identifying the model is to set $\beta_1 = 0$.

One can infer from Equation 15.1 that the higher the value of θ_j, the higher the probability of success, and the higher β_i, the lower the probability of success. When θ_j equals β_i, the probability of success is .50. The person and item parameters refer to the same latent continuum. This latent continuum is thus defined in two ways: as the dimension on which the persons are located in increasing order and as the dimension on which the items are located in increasing order of their threshold. Hence, individual differences in the probability of a correct response are reflected in the θ-parameter and differences in the probability of a correct response among the items are reflected in the β-parameter.

A distinguishing characteristic of the Rasch model in comparison to other IRT models is that it has the feature of specific objectivity (Rasch, 1960). This feature implies that comparisons among individuals are independent of the set of items that were used to estimate their ability (given that these items refer to the same measurement scale). In a symmetrical way, the feature of specific objectivity also implies that comparisons among items are independent of the particular sample of individuals who took the items (given that the same Rasch model holds in all samples). From a practical point of view, the characteristic of specific objectivity is attractive as one can obtain the estimates of the item parameters β_i even in nonrepresentative samples of the population. However, not all samples may contain the same information about the items' position on the latent scale, and, hence, the standard error of estimation of the item parameters may differ across different samples.

15.2.2.2 Example of Application

De Bonis, Lebeaux, De Boeck, Simon, and Pichot (1991) developed a Rasch scale for measuring the severity of depression. The θ-parameter refers to the individual's level of depression. The higher the score of a person on the scale, the more severe the experienced depression is. The β-parameter refers to the severity of the symptoms of depression expressed in the items. At the lower end of the scale were items like "I work less easily than before" and "I feel blue." At the higher end of the scale were items like "I feel useless" and "I have had enough of life and wish it were ended." Hence, the

IRT model can be used at the level of the persons as a measurement device to assess the position of a person on the latent variable of depression. Likewise, at the level of the items, the IRT model indicates which items are symptoms of severe depression (as only persons high on the measurement scale tend to endorse the item), and which items are indicators of mild forms of depression (as also persons low on the measurement scale tend to endorse the item).

15.2.2.3 Graphical Representation

Figure 15.2a gives a graphical representation of the Rasch model. For three items the probability of a correct response expressed in Equation 15.1 is plotted as a function of the latent trait. Such a graph is called the item characteristic curve (ICC) of an item. The three ICC in Figure 15.2a differ only in location, which corresponds to their different threshold values.

Given the ICC for each item, also a test characteristic curve (TCC) can be constructed. This curve gives the expected test score result as a function of θ. It is calculated by taking the sum of the item probabilities of the items in the test:

$$T_j = \sum_{i=1}^{I} P(X_{ij} = 1). \tag{15.2}$$

Within the framework of classical test theory, T_j refers to the true score for examinees with ability level θ_j. Figure 15.2b shows the TCC for the

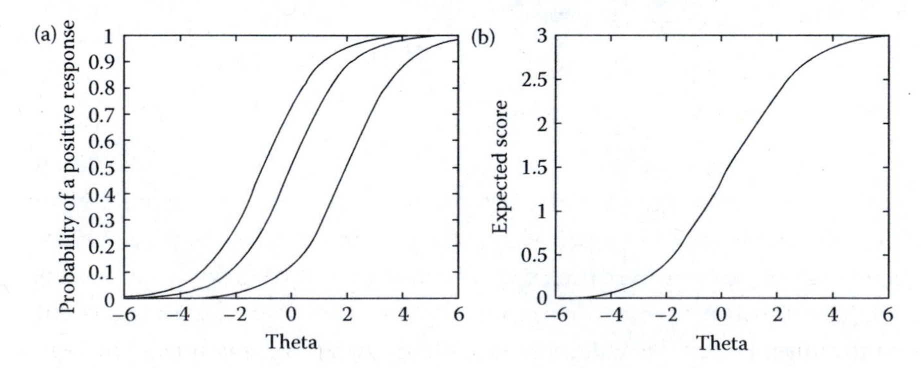

FIGURE 15.2
(a) The ICC and (b) the corresponding TCC of three items in the Rasch model.

three example items. The relationship between the latent trait θ and the expected test score is curvilinear.

15.2.3 The Two-Parameter Logistic Model

15.2.3.1 Model

The Rasch model assumes that all items differentiate equally well among persons. This assumption is commonly too strong for a set of items. In the two-parameter logistic (2PL) model a second item parameter is therefore included, namely, an item discrimination parameter. Formally, the 2PL reads as:

$$P(X_{ij} = 1) = f(\alpha_i(\theta_j - \beta_i)), \tag{15.3}$$

where α_i refers to the item discrimination. Like in the Rasch model, the threshold parameter β_i is the point where the probability of endorsement equals .50. The parameter α_i is a quantitative index of the degree to which the item is related to the latent continuum. It can therefore be compared to the value of a factor loading on a common factor in classical factor analysis (Takane & de Leeuw, 1987). In order to identify the model, one needs to fix the origin and scale of the latent dimension. The latter is commonly accomplished by fixing the α_i of one particular item. Another way to identify the scale is to set the variance of the person parameters to a constant when adding a model for the θ_j to the 2PL, for example, by stating that the person parameters come from a standard normal distribution.

15.2.3.2 Graphical Representation

Figure 15.3a presents the ICC of three items according to a 2PL. Items a and b have the same threshold, but they differ in discrimination. Given its higher discrimination, Item a has an ICC with a steeper slope than Item b. Item c has the same slope as Item a, but it has a higher threshold. Note that due to the inclusion of the discrimination parameter, the ICC of different items cross each other. This implies that the ordering of the items according to their probability of endorsement switches across the latent continuum. For example, although Items a and b have the same threshold parameter, respondents with an ability lower than the corresponding β_i value have a higher probability of endorsement to Item b than to Item a,

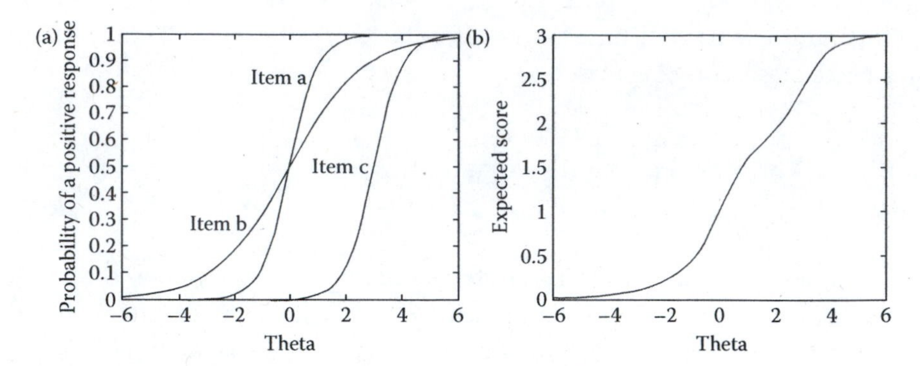

FIGURE 15.3
(a) The ICC and (b) the corresponding TCC of three items in the 2PL model.

while respondents with an ability higher than β_i have a higher probability of endorsement to Item b than to Item a.

Also for the 2PL, a TCC can be constructed. Figure 15.3b shows the TCC for the three 2PL items shown in Figure 15.3a. Like for the Rasch model, the shape of the TCC for a test that is modeled with the 2PL is always monotonically increasing, but its specific form depends on a number of factors, like the number of items and the values of the item parameters. In the present example, the TCC levels off a bit for the persons in the ability region where the expected score on the test equals between 1.5 and 2. This is because of the interplay of the difference in discrimination and of the fact that the third item has a higher threshold. Consequently, a score larger than 2 can only be expected for persons with a high level of the latent trait.

15.2.4 The Three-Parameter Logistic Model

In educational measurement also a three-parameter logistic model (3PL) has been proposed. In this model, the possibility of getting a correct response through guessing is taken into account. More specifically, a guessing parameter g_i is added to the 2PL:

$$P(X_{ij}=1)=g_i+(1-g_i)f[\alpha_i(\theta_j-\beta_i)]. \tag{15.4}$$

The parameter g_i functions as the lower bound of the ICC. Through the inclusion of g_i persons with a low value on the latent dimension have a certain probability to give a positive response. The 3PL was especially devised to model response behavior on multiple-choice items.

15.3 MODELING DIF

15.3.1 IRT Definition of DIF

Lord (1980) provided an IRT definition of DIF:

> If each test item in a test had exactly the same item response function in every group, then people of the same ability or skill would have exactly the same chance of getting the item right, regardless of their group membership. Such a test would be completely unbiased. If on the other hand, an item has a different item response function for one group than for another, it is clear that the item is biased. (p. 212)

Lord's definition of DIF is frequently translated formally. If the different groups are categories of the variable V, then for a DIF item the following inequality holds:

$$P(X_{ij}=1|\theta_j, V_j = v) \neq P\,(X_{ij}=1|\,\theta_j). \tag{15.5}$$

Three important implications can be drawn from the definition if DIF. First, Lord's formulation of DIF indicates that DIF can be discerned from the fact that the ICC of the item for the focal and the reference group differ. Mellenbergh (1982) distinguished between two types of DIF. Figure 15.4a shows an item that has a higher threshold for the focal group in comparison with the reference group. This type of DIF is called uniform DIF, as it only involves a difference in item location between the focal and the reference group. In the case of uniform DIF, the sign and approximately the size of the

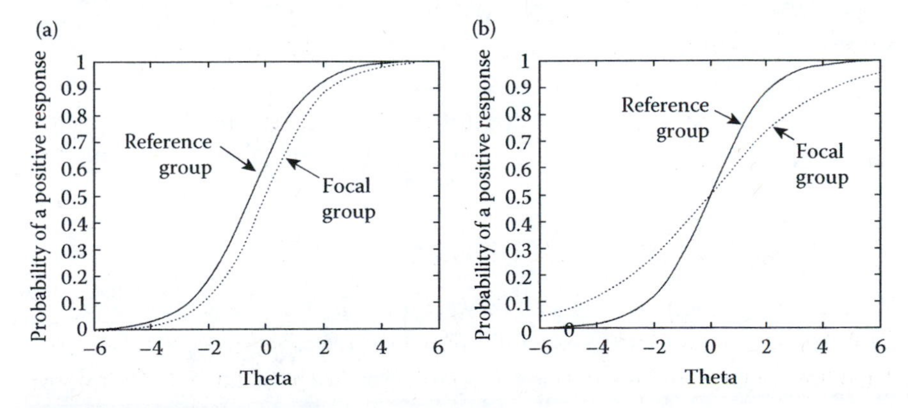

FIGURE 15.4
Example of (a) uniform and (b) nonuniform DIF.

differences in success probability between the two groups is the same within a certain range of the latent continuum. Figure 15.4b shows an item that discriminates less in the focal group. This type of DIF is called nonuniform DIF, as it involves the slope and possibly the location of the ICC. If an item shows nonuniform DIF, the sign and size of the difference in probability of endorsement between the focal and the reference group varies across the latent trait.

A second implication from Lord's definition of DIF was already pointed out in the introductory example. DIF refers to a difference in item performance between groups after the members of the groups have been matched with respect to the dimension that the test purportedly measures. Therefore, Equation 15.5 is conditional on the ability level. DIF does not refer to a difference in the ability distribution of θ between the focal and reference group. Such a difference is called the impact (Dorans & Holland, 1993). Of course, a difference in mean ability between the two groups may lead to overall differences in item performance across groups. However, in such cases, if there is no DIF, the item will still have the same ICC for focal and reference group.

A final implication of the IRT approach to DIF is that by looking at the TCC one can see the cumulative effect of DIF at the item level on the expected test score. As Shealey and Stout (1993) observed, "small and perhaps undetectable amounts of bias at the item level can be translated into a substantial amount of bias expressed at the test level" (p. 238). Hence, the study of DIF may end up in finding differential test functioning (DTF). Like for DIF, DTF may be either uniform across the ability range, advantaging one group above the other, or nonuniform, when the expected test score may be higher for the focal group for a certain range of θ, but lower for another part of the continuum. However, finding DIF items does not necessarily imply that DTF will be found. It may be the case that the DIF works in two directions: advantaging the reference group over the focal group on some items, while the opposite is the case for other items. In such cases the DIF at the item level cancels out at the expected test score level.

15.3.2 Formal Modeling of DIF and Impact

Given the one-to-one relationship between the ICC and the item parameters, differences in the ICC between the focal and the reference group can be translated into a change in the model parameters, as is shown in Table 15.1. Uniform DIF corresponds to a change in the location parameter of the item. In particular, the item location of the focal group is obtained by adding the parameter δ_i^{β} to the location parameter of the reference group. In the 2PL-model, also nonuniform DIF can be detected. In this case, the slope parameter of the focal group is obtained by adding the parameter δ_i^α to the slope of the reference group. In the 2PL model, both δ_i^α and δ_i^β can be nonzero. Note that when the slopes are not equal, the ICC of the focal and reference group must cross. The value of δ_i^β then indicates whether the crossing is near β_i (in which δ_i^β is approximately zero) or not (in which case $|\delta_i^\beta| > 0$). Modeling of DIF in the 3PL is commonly restricted to looking at the differences in item location and slope. In principle, it is possible to model differences in the guessing parameter as well.

Impact can be modeled by including assumptions about the distribution of θ. For example, in the 2PL one may assume that $\theta \sim N(0,1)$ for the reference group and that $\theta \sim N(\mu,\sigma^2)$ in the focal group. In the Rasch model the variance of θ can be estimated for both the focal and the reference group.

15.4 DIF DETECTION

Given the parametric approach to DIF presented in Table 15.1, the detection of DIF corresponds to testing hypotheses about parameters in a model. In particular, presence of DIF corresponds to rejecting the null hypotheses that the DIF parameters δ_i^β and/or δ_i^α equal zero against the alternative hypotheses that they differ from zero. For individual items, presence of DIF can be tested with a Wald test comparing the value of the estimate of the DIF parameter (δ_i^α or δ_i^β) to its standard error. For a set of items, Thissen and his colleagues (Thissen, Steinberg, & Gerrard, 1986; Thissen, Steinberg, & Wainer, 1988, 1993) proposed to test the null

TABLE 15.1

Logit of the Success Probability on Anchor Items and DIF Items for the Rasch and 2PL Model

Model	Group	G	Anchor Items	DIF-Items
Rasch	Reference	0	$\theta_p - \beta_i$	$\theta_p - \beta_i$
	Focal	1	$\theta_p - \beta_i$	$\theta_p - (\beta_i + \delta_i^\beta)$
2PL	Reference	0	$\alpha_i(\theta_p - \beta_i)$	$\alpha_i(\theta_p - \beta_i)$
	Focal	1	$\alpha_i(\theta_p - \beta_i)$	$(\alpha_i + \delta_i^\alpha)[\theta_p - (\beta_i + \delta_i^\beta)]$

hypothesis of jointly having no DIF with a likelihood ratio (LR) test that compares a compact model without DIF parameters to an augmented model that includes DIF parameters for the set of items under consideration. If the LR test turns out to be significant, it is concluded that the studied items show DIF.

However, as Table 15.1 indicates, the testing of DIF for items suspected of DIF presupposes a set of so-called anchor items where the location and slope parameters are forced to be equal between focal and reference groups. In fact, the models in Table 15.1 are only identified if there is at least one anchor item in the test. When an a priori set of unbiased or anchor items is not available, one can follow an exploratory approach to detect DIF. Meulders and Xie (2004) distinguished between a forward and a backward approach. In a forward approach, DIF is first estimated for each single item separately with the other items as anchor items. Afterward, all significant DIF parameters are included in one model. In a backward approach, DIF is allowed simultaneously for all items but one, and subsequently nonsignificant DIF parameters are dropped from the model. The soundness of starting with a particular item as anchor item can be investigated by carrying out a second DIF detection procedure that starts with another anchor item.

Other approaches to screen the items on possible DIF (and to select anchor items) use the sum score on all the items as a proxy for the latent variable. Holland and Thayer (1988) proposed the Mantel–Hanszel approach to the detection of uniform DIF. In this approach, an item is flagged as a DIF-item if the odds of getting an item correct across different levels of the sum score differs between the focal and the reference group. A related method is the standardization approach to DIF detection (Dorans & Holland, 1993; Dorans & Kulick, 1986) that is based on the (weighted) average difference between the expected item scores (proportion endorsed) across score levels. A variation of the standardization approach is the simultaneous item bias test (SIBTEST) of Shealy and Stout (1993) that uses an adjusted estimate of the difference between the expected item scores, weighted by the distribution of scores in the reference group or the focal group or a combination. Finally, Swaminathan and Rogers (1990) suggested using a logistic regression of the binary item responses on the sum score, group membership, and the interaction between those two variables to detect DIF.

The selection of anchor items is the Achilles' heel of the current DIF methods. One needs to choose at least one anchor item for which one is sure that it is DIF-free before being able to apply a DIF procedure. Defining items as DIF-free when they actually contain DIF is not without consequences. Finch (2005) showed that the type-I error of the Mantel–Haenszel procedure and the LR approach increases when the chosen anchor items are not completely free of DIF. Navas-Ara and Gomez-Benito (2002) showed that when there are items exhibiting DIF in the anchor set, the estimates of the persons' position on the latent variable are biased. In their review of DIF procedures, Millsap and Everson (1993) also warned that the use of observed scores may not always be adequate proxies for the latent trait, and may result in false DIF detection, particularly in shorter scales.

15.5 EXAMPLE OF APPLICATION

Chapter 16 in the current volume describes an application of DIF in the analysis of comparative social science data. In this application, the different groups refer to people belonging to different nations. In the present chapter, a short example of DIF research is given coming from research on the equivalence of a paper-and-pencil test and a computerized version of it. This kind of DIF research is comparable to comparing interview mode groups, and it is maybe a somewhat atypical application of DIF detection. Another difference of the present application with applications on cross-cultural comparisons is that social surveys usually work with larger population samples, but with much shorter tests. Finally, the current application illustrates a global DIF-detection procedure, whereas more analytical (item by item) procedures are more common in cross-cultural comparison research.

Empirical research sometimes found a mode effect when comparing a paper-and-pencil test to a computerized test administration, but not always (e.g., Clariana & Wallace, 2002; Parshall, Spray, Kalohn, & Davey, 2002). Volckaert and Janssen (2005) investigated the mode effect for a test on biology for pupils from Grade 8. The test consisted of 70 items, which were split in two parallel halves. When the items were prepared for the computer mode, care was taken that no scrolling was needed within one item. The test was administered to 436 pupils according to an incomplete design presented in Table 15.2. Each pupil answered to the full set of items, which were presented either all on paper, all on computer, or partly on paper and on computer. The design has the advantage that a

TABLE 15.2

Schematic Representation of the Design of Administration of the Computer and Paper-and-Pencil Tests

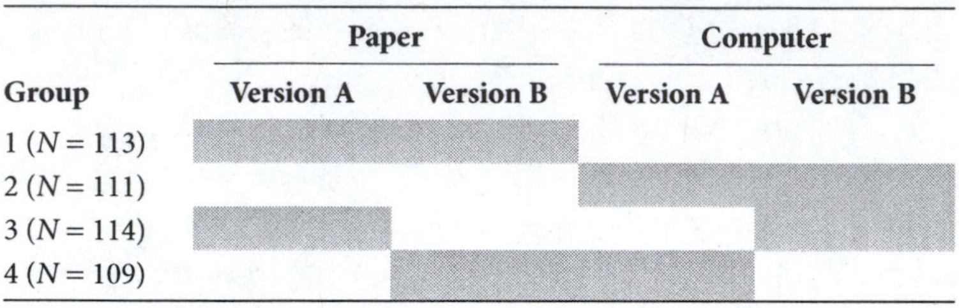

	Paper		Computer	
Group	**Version A**	**Version B**	**Version A**	**Version B**
1 ($N = 113$)	■	■		
2 ($N = 111$)			■	■
3 ($N = 114$)	■			■
4 ($N = 109$)		■	■	

pupil never received the same item twice and that the items administered on computer and on paper can be put on the same scale. One of the strengths of IRT models is indeed that they are applicable for incomplete designs.

Various specialized software packages exist for estimating IRT models and doing DIF research (e.g., Bilog, Multilog, OPLM). However, given that IRT models can be seen as nonlinear mixed models (e.g., Rijmen, Tuerlinckx, De Boeck, & Kuppens, 2003), these models can also be estimated with general statistical software. For example, De Boeck and Wilson (2004) provide computer commands from the SAS package to estimate various kinds of IRT models, including DIF models. They also give sample commands for other major computer packages.

The current DIF-analyses were performed with the procedure NLMIXED of SAS. A 2PL IRT model was used. Its scale was fixed by assuming that the pupils' abilities came from a standard normal distribution. The impact of the test mode was modeled by including a main effect for the items in the computer mode. One item was chosen as an anchor item. All other items were considered as potential DIF items. Table 15.3 gives an overview of the different models that were estimated with their corresponding AIC-value. Judging from the AIC-values there was no clear evidence for uniform or nonuniform DIF, given that the AIC was the smallest for the model with no DIF. However, inspection of the model with equal β_i and unequal α_i showed that three items had a significant DIF for the discrimination parameter. Including DIF for these three items resulted in the best fitting model. It was difficult to see a common feature in these three items, but they all used a graphical presentation in the item stem (like other items), and for two of the three items the test taker also had to scroll down in the computer-based version to see the multiple-

TABLE 15.3
Results of the Different DIF-Models

Model	AIC
Equal β_i, equal α_i	34,591
Equal β_i, unequal α_i	34,628
Equal β_i, equal α_i except for three items	34,575
Unequal β_i, equal α_i	34,628
Unequal β_i, unequal α_i	34,649

choice question, whereas the full item was on one page in the paper test. The effect of these three items on the TCC was negligible. There was also no main effect of the test mode. Hence, for the test under investigation there was no evidence for a mode effect between a paper-and-pencil and a computer test.

15.6 CONCLUSIONS

The investigation of DIF is concerned with the investigation of measurement invariance in a rather analytical way. In the DIF approach, measurement invariance is studied at the item level, and not at level of a composite score. DIF corresponds to a lack of constancy of the item threshold and/or the item discrimination parameters across groups. Despite these differences in item functioning, it is assumed that the test as a whole measures the same latent variable in the different groups. However, multidimensionality of the items is frequently proposed as an explanation for the occurrence of DIF (e.g., Ackerman, 1992). In this view, DIF is caused by a nuisance dimension in the test on which the different groups of respondents differ in ability. For example, a test on general reasoning ability may show DIF for gender on items that can also be solved by using a strategy based on spatial representations. As men are on the average better in spatial orientation, they have an advantage over women on these items, regardless of the gender differences in general reasoning ability. Apart from multidimensionality, DIF may also be caused by a common feature in the DIF items. In such a case, one may summarize the DIF of several items, by including an interaction between an item property or item facet and a group parameter (Meulders & Xie, 2004), which is called differential feature functioning (DFF).

DIF research has a long tradition in educational measurement where matters of fairness and equity were paramount. In this context, DIF was commonly referred to by the notion of item bias. Concerns about test bias typically centers around the differential performance by groups based on gender or race. Currently, the scope of DIF research is much wider. Apart from issues on equity and fairness and apart from investigating lack of invariance, Zumbo (2007) discerned other general uses of DIF, such as the investigation of the comparability of translated or adapted measures, or the use of DIF as a method to help understand the cognitive and/or psychosocial process of item responding and test performance.

REFERENCES

Ackerman, T. A. (1992). A didactic explanation of item bias, item impact, and item validity from a multidimensional perspective. *Journal of Educational Measurement, 29*, 67–91.

Camilli, G. (1994). Origin of the scaling constant d = 1.7 in item response theory. *Journal of Educational and Behavioral Statistics, 19*, 293–295.

Clariana, R., & Wallace, P. (2002). Paper-based versus computer-based assessment: Key factors associated with the test mode effect. *British Journal of Educational Technology, 33*, 593–602.

De Boeck, P., & Wilson, M. (Eds.). (2004). *Explanatory item response models: A generalized linear and nonlinear approach*. New York, NY: Springer.

de Bonis, M., Lebeaux, M. O., De Boeck, P., Simon, M., & Pichot, P. (1991). Measuring the severity of depression through a self-report inventory: A comparison of logistic, factorial and implicit models. *Journal of Affective Disorders, 22*, 55–64.

Dorans, N. J., & Holland, P. W. (1993). DIF detection and description: Mantel-Haenszel and standardisation. In P. W. Holland & H. Wainer (Eds.), *Differential item functioning* (pp. 35–66). Hillsdale, NJ: Lawrence Erlbaum.

Dorans, N. J., & Kulick, E. (1986). Demonstrating the utility of the standardization approach to assessing unexpected differential item performance on the scholastic aptitude test. *Journal of Educational Measurement, 23*, 355–368.

Finch, H. (2005). The MIMIC model as a method for detecting DIF: Comparison with Mantel-Haenszel, SIBTEST, and the IRT likelihood ratio. *Applied Psychological Measurement, 29*, 278–295.

Fischer, G., & Molenaar, I. (1995). *Rasch models: Foundations and recent developments*. New York, NY: Springer.

Glöckner-Rist, A., & Hoijtink, H. (2003). The best of both worlds: Factor analysis of dichotomous data using item response theory and structural equation modeling. *Structural Equation Modeling, 10*, 544–565.

Hoijtink, H. (1991). The measurement of latent traits by proximity items. *Applied Psychological Measurement, 15*, 153–170.

Hoijtink, H., & Molenaar, I. W. (1992). Testing for DIF in a model with single peaked item characteristic curves: The PARELLA model. *Psychometrika, 57*, 383–398.

Holland, P. W., & Thayer, D. T. (1988). Differential item performance and the Mantel-Haenszel procedure. In H. Wainer & H. Braun (Eds.), *Test validity* (pp. 129–145). Hillsdale, NJ: Lawrence Erlbaum.

Lord, F. M. (1980). *Applications of item response theory to practical testing problems.* Hillsdale, NJ: Lawrence Erlbaum.

Mellenbergh, G. J. (1982). Contingency table models for assessing item bias. *Journal of Educational Statistics, 7*, 105–118.

Meulders, M., & Xie, Y. (2004). Person-by-item predictors. In P. De Boeck & M. Wilson (Eds.). *Explanatory item response models: A generalized linear and nonlinear approach* (pp. 213–240). New York, NY: Springer.

Millsap, R. E., & Everson, H. T. (1993). Methodology review: Statistical approaches for assessing measurement bias. *Applied Psychological Measurement, 17*, 297–334.

Navas-Ara, M. J., & Gomez-Benito, J. (2002). Effects of ability scale purification on the identification of DIF. *European Journal of Psychological Assessment, 19*, 9–15.

Ostini, R., & Nering, M. L. (2005). *Polytomous item response theory models.* Thousand Oaks, CA: Sage.

Parshall, C. G., Spray, J. A., Kalohn J. C., & Davey T. (2002). *Practical considerations in computer-based testing.* New York, NY: Springer.

Rasch, G. N. (1960). *Probabilistic models for some intelligence and attainment tests.* Copenhagen, Denmark: Danish Institute for Educational Research.

Rijmen, F., Tuerlinckx, F., De Boeck, P., & Kuppens, P. (2003). A nonlinear mixed model framework for item response theory. *Psychological Methods, 8*, 185–205.

Schaeffer, N. C. (1988). Application of item response theory to the measurement of depression. In C. C. Clogg (Ed.), *Sociological methodology* (Vol. 18, pp. 271–308). Washington, DC: American Sociological Association.

Shealy, R. T., & Stout, W. (1993). A model-based standardization approach that separates true bias/DIF from group ability differences and detects test bias/DIF as well as item bias/DIF. *Psychometrika, 58*, 159–194.

Sijtsma, K., & Molenaar, I. W. (2002). *Introduction to nonparametric item response theory.* Thousand Oaks, CA: Sage.

Swaminathan, H., & Rogers, H. J. (1990). Detecting differential item functioning using logistic regression procedures. *Journal of Educational Measurement, 27*, 361–370.

Takane, Y., & de Leeuw, J. (1987). On the relationship between item response theory and factor analysis of discretized variables. *Psychometrika, 52*, 393–408.

Thissen, D., Steinberg, L., & Gerrard, M. (1986). Beyond group mean differences: The concept of item bias. *Psychological Bulletin, 99*, 118–128.

Thissen, D., Steinberg, L., & Wainer, H. (1988). Use of item response theory in the study of group difference in trace lines. In H. Wainer & H. Braun (Eds.), *Test validity* (pp. 147–169). Hillsdale, NJ: Lawrence Erlbaum.

Thissen, D., Steinberg, L., & Wainer, H. (1993). Detection of differential item functioning using the parameters of item response models. In P. Holland & H. Wainer (Eds.), *Differential item functioning* (pp. 67–113). Hillsdale, NJ: Lawrence Erlbaum.

Volckaert, B., & Janssen, R. (2005, May). *Differential Item Functioning als methode om de equivalentie tussen computerondersteunde en papieren toetsen te achterhalen* [Differential item functioning as a method to investigate the equivalence between a computerbased and a paper-and-pencil test]. Paper presented at the ORD conference of the Dutch and Flemish society for educational research, Gent, Belgium.

Zumbo, B. D. (2007). Three generations of DIF analyses: Considering where it has been, where it is now, and where it is going. *Language Assessment Quarterly, 4*, 223–233.

16

Using the Mixed Rasch Model in the Comparative Analysis of Attitudes

Markus Quandt
GESIS, Leibniz Institute for the Social Sciences

16.1 INTRODUCTION

When the comparability of social science scales in international surveys is to be assessed, current survey researchers almost habitually think of multi-group confirmatory factor analysis (MGCFA) as the method of choice (He, Merz, & Alden, 2008; Schmitt & Kuljanin, 2008). Alternative methodological approaches do however exist, with conceptual and practical advantages of their own. Recently, international educational attainment testing surveys such as the Program for International Student Assessment (PISA; OECD, 2005) have given some visibility to models collectively known under the name of item response theory (IRT), which have their origin in educational testing research.* Among these, the Rasch model (Rasch, 1960) is the most basic, but due to its parsimony perhaps also the most elegant approach. Originally designed for dichotomous questions, it has long been extended to also handle the polytomous ordinal response formats more common in attitude research (Andrich, 1978; Masters, 1982). The present chapter will, from an applied perspective, explore the use of a particular version of the polytomous Rasch model to investigate measurement equivalence in comparative research settings. This particular version is the combination of the polytomous Rasch model with latent class analysis in the so-called mixed Rasch model (von Davier & Rost, 1995).

* IRT modeling has rapidly followed the statistical advances of the last decades, among them Bayesian methods and hierarchical or multilevel modeling. Chapter 17 demonstrates an elaborate hierarchical IRT approach with PISA data.

16.2 THE POLYTOMOUS RASCH MODEL

To understand the potential benefits of the mixed Rasch model for comparative analysis, it is necessary to understand the type of information that Rasch models provide on the individual items of a multiitem measurement instrument. In the dichotomous Rasch model, the probability of choosing either the response $x = 0$ or $x = 1$ is a function of the person ability parameter θ_j and an item difficulty parameter β_i, for person j and item i, both parameters being on the same logit scale:

$$P(X_{ij} = x) = \frac{\exp[x_{ij}(\theta_j - \beta_i)]}{1 + \exp(\theta_j - \beta_i)}. \tag{16.1}$$

To arrive at the most general polytomous Rasch model for ordinal items, the partial-credit model (Masters, 1982), the perspective is changed in a simple way. The difficulty parameter β_i is now understood to be a parameter for passing the threshold between two adjacent categories. These categories happen to be 0 and 1 in the dichotomous case, but they can be any pair of adjacent categories of a multicategory item. For better distinction from the dichotomous model, β_i is exchanged against τ_{it}, with an index x for the category of item i, index m for the number of categories of item i, and index t for the number of thresholds separating these categories. Taking into account that the probability of choosing category x reflects the cumulated difficulty of all previously passed category thresholds of the item, which condensates to $\sigma_{ix} = \sum_{s=0}^{x} \tau_{it}$, the model equation for the partial-credit Rasch model becomes:

$$P(X_{ji} = x) = \frac{\exp(x\theta_j - \sigma_{ix})}{\sum_{s=0}^{m} \exp(s\theta_j - \sigma_{is})} \; with\, \sigma_{i0} = 0. \tag{16.2}$$

Note that, in order to reflect the postulated ordinality of the item categories, the estimated item thresholds should be ordered; that is, passing the threshold between categories 1 and 2 should be easier than passing the threshold between categories 2 and 3. In the partial-credit model, there is however no restriction that mathematically enforces such an ordering.

Empirically, disordered thresholds can occur, pointing to problems of the item—or more precisely, problems of certain of its category pairs—to discriminate between different positions of the respondents on the latent trait. The other aspect of item ordinality is that there need not be a constant latent trait interval between pairs of adjacent items. So, not only the positions of the thresholds, but also the distances between thresholds can vary freely, reflecting the lack of interval scale quality of the manifest item.*,†.

A good way to study the relationship of the latent trait held by the respondents and the observed item responses is therefore to look at the threshold profile of an item. Figure 16.1 shows the threshold profile of a well-behaved item with five categories. The categories are separated by four ordered thresholds. This example shows an item for which most categories are below the average difficulty of all the item parameters in the model (this is the zero line), but the difficulty of switching to a higher category increases progressively, in a more-than-linear fashion.

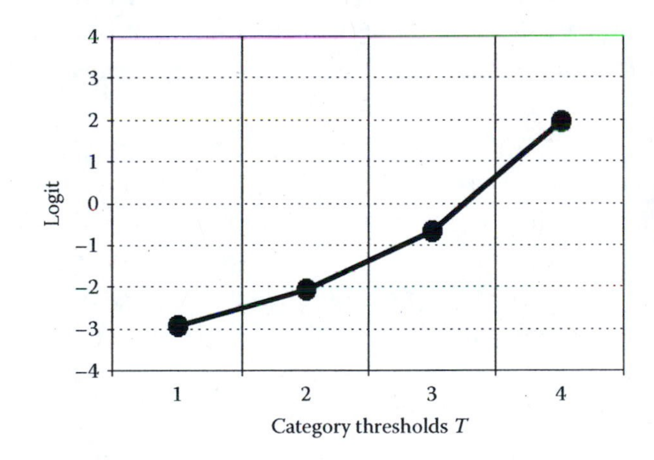

FIGURE 16.1
Partial-credit category thresholds for a five-category item.

---

* In turn, restricting the threshold distances of the same item to be equal can serve to actually test the interval scale quality of items (Andrich, 1978; Rost, 2004).

† One consequence of this is that the concept of differential discriminatory power of different items indirectly appears in the Rasch model, although the individual logistic item characteristic curves (ICC) are still estimated with constant slope, and a single location parameter per ICC. This often goes unnoticed, because no explicit discrimination parameter is used as, for example, in the two parameter logistic model.

16.3 RASCH SPECIFICS RELEVANT FOR COMPARATIVE ANALYSIS

Beyond the general aspect of IRT models being theoretically most appropriate for manifest indicators with ordinal response categories, the Rasch model has some features that make it attractive for comparative analyses from a methodological point of view (Salzberger, Holzmüller, & Souchon, 2009). First, the Rasch model being a unidimensional model, its latent variable yields person scores that are unambiguous, easily interpretable, and can be readily saved for manipulation and analyses outside the latent variable model. Second, these scores have a scale level equivalent to interval scaling: The difference scale that Rasch models produce for the latent trait has constant intervals. While not having a natural origin, it has, by virtue of the model's construction on item characteristic curves, respectively, category probability functions with identical slopes for all items, and a common zero point for all subsets of a population for which a given Rasch model holds. Third, as a result of the first two features, once that a measurement instrument (a set of items) has been shown to have Rasch properties for a given population, a measurement performed with that instrument on any subsample of the same population will yield scores that can be validly compared to any other subsample with regard to levels of the trait measured. This property of specific objectivity can be understood to be the Rasch equivalent to scalar invariance (Salzberger et al., 2009). It is unique to Rasch models, also in contrast to other IRT models such as the two or three-parameter logistic IRT models (Bond & Fox, 2001, p. 195; Chapter 15 in this volume describes 2PL and 3PL models). In other words, the Rasch model achieves for testing measurement invariance what only the most restricted MGCFA models achieve.

16.4 BASIC STRATEGIES FOR (IN-)EQUIVALENCE TESTING USING THE RASCH MODEL

As mentioned above, one way of establishing measurement invariance across samples is to show that the data from different samples fit the same Rasch model. This can be approached from two angles: One is to test each sample separately for compliance with the Rasch model and then inspect the estimated item parameters for differences across samples. Many variations of this approach lead to analyses of differential item functioning (DIF) presented elsewhere in detail (Thissen, Steinberg, & Wainer, 1993; Chapter 15 in this volume; see also Zumbo (2007) for a recent review of approaches and developments in DIF analysis). A second approach is to collect all subsamples into one pooled data file and to run a single Rasch analysis over that pooled file, which implies consciously ignoring the potential between-sample differences. A well-fitting Rasch model—this being a model without violations of the assumptions that the item characteristic curves all follow logistic functions with the same slope, of unidimensionality, and of absence of DIF—should then per assumption provide unbiased latent trait estimates for all segments of the sample. Individual item misfit can be easily assessed within the Rasch model. Interestingly, the same holds for misfit of respondents, or rather, of response patterns (Andrich (1988) or Bond & Fox (2001) describe standard Rasch methodology for both). Unidimensionality is sometimes also assessed in a preliminary way via principal components analysis or CFA before a battery of items is subjected to Rasch scaling for reasons of convenience, and clearly problematic items are then removed in advance (Rasch and factor analytic methods usually come to similar conclusions about lack of unidimensionality at the level of data screening, see Wright (1996) for an example). Differences between both methods often start to show up only after further elaboration, see Salzberger & Sinkovics (2006). However, explicit DIF tests are recommended by Rasch analysts anyway as part of the fit testing routine. This again involves splitting the pooled sample by some criteria, which would typically include the subsample distinction. Salzberger et al. (2009) have recently provided a useful primer on how to combine the pooled sample approach and the separate samples approach to apply Rasch models in a comparative setting.

There is, however, one characteristic of the traditional DIF testing methods in IRT, which they share with MGCFA that can be seen as a limitation from certain viewpoints.* This characteristic is that explicit DIF testing is inevitably based on preexisting groups. In many cases, such groupings are indeed straightforward: There is an evident interest to test for the absence

* See Stark, Chernyshenko, and Drasgow (2006) and Ewing, Salzberger, and Sinkovics (2005) for overviews of commonalities and differences of IRT and MGCFA.

of method effects such as those of interview mode, questionnaire translation, sample selection, and so on, all of those relating to groups well-defined by application of this or that interview mode, of this or that language questionnaire, of being in one or the other sample. The same does apply to some extent to cross-national analyses, where the existence of different country samples provides an apparently natural grouping criterion. One drawback, however, is that such grouping criteria may be used for DIF/inequivalence testing simply because they are there, similar to the way in which gender or age brackets seem sometimes to be used when DIF analyses are routinely performed. Not finding DIF on these criteria may lead researchers to conclude that there is no DIF or measurement inequivalence in the sample at all. This need not be true, there can be as many reasons for DIF as there are social or psychological reasons for perceiving and understanding questions differently for different groups of respondents, but few of them lend themselves to easy observation in clear-cut groups. Some of them are considered to be methodological effects, such as response sets or response styles, acquiescence, and so on. Others can stem from more substantive reasons. If it is, for example, cultural diversity that causes respondents from different countries to react differently to the same question, then it is easy enough to think of manifold cultural delineations within a country's population that may have the same power: the difference of urban versus rural lifestyles, educational background, or any other socialization or cognitive factors that may combine in hard-to-predict ways. It is not even evident a priori that such factors are less relevant than those of nationality and language. Arguably, the within-country heterogeneity could sometimes be larger than the between-country heterogeneity, and groupings like, for example, respondents with distinct response sets, members of a religious group, or an urban life-style group, could be comparably homogeneous across country borders in terms of their distinct understanding of certain items. In brief, DIF need neither follow, nor stop at, national borders.

Therefore, proposals to use explorative methods for the detection of DIF that operate without predefined grouping criteria seem attractive. One such method is the mixed Rasch model proposed by von Davier and Rost (1995).*
As a discrete mixture model, the mixed Rasch model can distinguish latent

* A number of related model variations have been proposed before and after that, see for an overview of recent developments the volume edited by von Davier and Carstensen (2007).

classes or subgroups with different item or threshold parameter sets, for the same items, in a more or less exploratory fashion. With the index c for a latent class, the dichotomous Rasch equation (for the sake of simplicity, only this is shown) looks like this (von Davier & Yamamoto, 2007):

$$P\left(X_{ij}=x\middle|\theta,c\right)=\prod_{i=1}^{I}\frac{\exp\left[x_{ij}(\theta_j-\beta_{ic})\right]}{1+\exp(\theta_j-\beta_{ic})}. \tag{16.3}$$

A typical result of a mixed Rasch analysis is that a few different subpopulations are scaled with structurally identical, but not identically parameterized Rasch models. The number of latent classes is largely an empirical matter and not subject to strong hypotheses. Although the number of classes is not a parameter of the mixed Rasch model, the ideal number of classes is usually found by sequentially testing nested models in an explorative manner, with an increasing number of classes. The differences between the class-specific parameter sets thus obtained for each of the subpopulations are a very direct expression of DIF. It is then up to the researcher to interpret those parameter differences in a meaningful way, be that interpretation founded on methodological or on substantive reasons. Ideally, any interpretation would finally be supported by some kind of external validation.

Can the mixed Rasch model still fully deliver on the promise of measurement equivalence made by the homogeneous Rasch model? It is tempting to just rely on the property of specific objectivity, regardless of having differently parametrized Rasch models in several classes. For example, Biswas-Diener, Vittersø, and Diener (2009) and Vittersø, Biswas-Diener, and Diener (2005), in their applications of mixed Rasch analysis to comparative data on life-satisfaction, explicitly assume that this can be done. Although the trait values of independently estimated Rasch models for different samples cannot be assumed to be on the same scale and thus cannot be compared across samples (Rupp & Zumbo, 2006), inspection of Equation 16.3 shows that this is indeed possible for the mixed Rasch model: the θ parameter of the latent trait, or the person parameters, is not class specific. In contrast, the norming of the scale for the item parameters is determined separately in each class, by summing all class-specific item parameters (Rost, 2004, p. 242; von Davier & Yamamoto, 2007, p. 103). Therefore, it is not useful to compare absolute item difficulties across classes.

Even the comparison of the person parameters across classes may be risky, however. Rost, Carstensen, and von Davier (1997, pp. 331–332) caution that the substantive meaning of the scale might change from one class to another, and that we can only compare person parameters when we have reason to assume that a change of meaning did not happen. One example when comparisons remain valid could be that the threshold distances for all items are on average narrower and more irregular in, say, class A than in class B, with all else being equal across classes. This would indicate a particular response style in terms of scale use, members of class A would be distinguishing less well between adjacent categories, and we would only know with some certainty what position they have on the latent trait if we happened to find them on the extreme ends of the response scale. That would usually be considered as a reliability problem, but if the induced loss of reliability is not too severe, it would be less consequential for the substance of the scale. Rupp and Zumbo (2006) further demonstrate that moderate DIF usually has little consequences for the level of the latent trait values, even for individual cases.

If, however, the profiles of difficulties of all items assume different shapes across classes, this means that respondents from class A find different substantive statements harder to agree with than respondents from class B. That points to a differential understanding of the content of one or more of the items, in other words, to multidimensionality. In this case, the mixed Rasch model would resolve multidimensionality not into groupings of items, as done by, for example, principal component analysis, but into groupings of respondents.

It must further be noted that the mixed Rasch approach has conceptual limitations of its own, compared to DIF analysis with fixed groups. In the latter, there is a statistical test for DIF in each individual item. Thus, it can be used to detect and then perhaps remove, perhaps modify single problematic items in the phase of measurement instrument design. This cannot be done so easily in the more holistic mixed Rasch approach. Identification of DIF per distinction of latent classes always works on the full set of items in the model, and properties of several items will usually combine to mark out the different latent classes, so there is no implied significance test for individual item DIF.* On the other hand, using all items simultaneously for DIF detection circumvents the issue of having to select one or more, presumably

* However, it is possible to compute confidence intervals around threshold parameter estimates per class, and check whether these overlap across classes.

nonbiased, anchor items for DIF diagnosis (Chapter 15 of this volume for the conventional strategies of DIF identification in IRT. Chapter 17 of this volume presents an advanced approach that also obliterates the need to define anchor items).

The remainder of this chapter demonstrates an application of the mixed Rasch model and discusses its interpretation.

16.5 DATA

The data to be analyzed here have been collected for the International Social Survey Program (ISSP) of 2003 on national identity, using a battery of items on the objects of general national pride. The ISSP is an on-going, high-quality survey series with annually changing topics, administered in many countries around the world (see http://www.issp.org/). The topical module for the year 2003 covered aspects of the respondents' national pride, subjective identification with the nation state and other entities, attitudes toward foreigners, and a number of related topics. The integrated international data file of this study contains representative samples from 34 countries and can be obtained via the GESIS Data Archive (ZA No. 3910).

The construct of national pride or nationalism describes the positive affect toward, and evaluation of, one's own country (Smith & Kim, 2006), including feelings of superiority in relation to other countries. It is, for example, relevant to explaining attitudes toward foreigners, of identity, or of loyalty toward the country's institutions (Arts & Halman, 2005). Of the seven items of the original battery, the following five items were selected for subsequent Rasch analysis:*

- citz: I would rather be a citizen of [COUNTRY] than of any other country in the world.
- betw: The world would be a better place if people from other countries were more like the [COUNTRY NATIONALITY].

* The battery has seven items in ISSP 2003. One item was not included because it was not a replication from a previous application of this instrument in ISSP 1995 (ZA No. 2880), although comparison of both ISSP modules over time is not in the scope of this paper. Another item was dropped after a principal component analysis. Both items appear to have somewhat lower face validity in the judgment of this author, and incidentally, they are the only negatively worded items of the battery.

- betc: Generally speaking, [COUNTRY] is a better country than most other countries.
- ctrw: People should support their country even if the country is in the wrong.
- ctrs: When my country does well in international sports, it makes me proud to be [COUNTRY NATIONALITY].

All questions were asked in an agree/disagree format with five response categories. Responses have been recoded to a range of 0–4 such that high scores indicate high-national pride.

Davidov (2009) has used two of these items: "betc: The world would be a better place if ... " and "betw: ... [COUNTRY] is a better country than most other countries," to test the construct of nationalism (and simultaneously, a related construct with four indicators) for invariance over all 34 countries of the ISSP 2003, using MGCFA. Davidov confirms metric invariance, but finds lack of scalar invariance over this large set of countries. However, his contribution does not look at the reasons of misfit in much detail. The present chapter being more focused on methodological demonstration than on substantive issues, only five samples (four countries) from ISSP 2003 are used here. This is done partly for ease of presentation, partly for limiting the set of factors potentially affecting equivalence or DIF: Germany (separate samples for West- and East-Germany, 850 and 437 cases, respectively), Great Britain (873), Sweden (1186), and the United States (1216). This selection is insofar intentional as both German subsamples and Sweden rank rather close to the lower end of the list of 34 ISSP country raw scores over the five national pride items, whereas the United States are on the second position of that rank order (the very top is held by Venezuela), and Great Britain marks a medium position.* In spite of all these countries being wealthy western democracies, and although there are only three different languages used in the five (sub)samples, the countries' historical trajectories and cultural backgrounds are certainly diverse enough to have effects on how feelings of national pride and identity develop (Hjerm (1998) analyzes this for three of our four countries; Tilley & Heath (2007) specifically address Great Britain). Hence, we can

---

* Although we have not yet shown scalar invariance for the battery, we know enough about the quality of the item battery that it would be a surprise if the country ranks changed by more than a few positions when using latent trait estimates instead of raw scores.

expect very substantial variation in the range of the latent trait to be measured, and culturally specific interpretations of individual items, or sets of items, are not excluded.* Thus, there is ample room for DIF.

16.6 ANALYSES AND RESULTS

The software used for estimating the (mixed) Rasch model is WinMira 1.45 (von Davier, 2001). Although the Rasch model generally does not require that missing data be dropped (Bond & Fox, 2001), a major drawback of this otherwise powerful program is that the data are subjected to listwise deletion of cases with missing values. Of the 4562 cases in the full sample, 4031 valid cases remain.

The testing strategy applied was this: a first run tried to fit the model under the assumption of a homogeneous sample, with the partial-credit approach (Masters, 1982) being used for modeling the polytomous responses.† For this initial fit test, global Chi^2 fit statistics were the main criterion. Because the observable response pattern table that this fit statistic assesses is very sparse, the number of possible response patterns is far higher (3125) than the number of distinct response patterns observed in our data file (917), the usual Chi^2 statistics cannot be applied and have to be replaced by a bootstrapping approach (von Davier, 1997). For each analysis, 150 bootstrap samples were drawn, and fit was assessed by looking for (non)significance of the bootstrapped Pearson Chi^2 and Cressie-Read statistics.

Although the overall results even for the single class model indicate rather good results, with all items having good discrimination, only one single and very marginal threshold order reversal, and no individual item under-fitting significantly, the global fit statistics show highly significant deviations of the observed response patterns from those expected under

---

* One reason for selecting this subset of countries is that all used self-administered questionnaires, with many other countries using face-to-face interviews for the ISSP survey. Interview mode effects could be plausible sources of DIF, which would however mandate a more systematic investigation than can be provided here.

† Other options for handling polytomous responses available in the software would be the rating scale, dispersion, and equidistance models, which pose different additional restrictions on the distance of the category thresholds (von Davier, 2001). Being more restrictive, they are less likely to fit the data and also less prone to uncover aberrant item category profiles. The relatively poorer fit was confirmed by according model runs (not reported).

the Rasch model. After confirming lack of fit for the homogeneous Rasch model, model selection proceeded by sequentially increasing the number of latent classes until satisfactory fit was reached, indicated by non-significant *p*-values of the Cressie-Read and Pearson Chi^2 statistics. For every new model, bootstrapped fit statistics and the BIC statistic (Bayesian Information Criterion, cf. Bozdogan, 1987) were recorded (see Table 16.1). Already the 2-class model shows a marginal level of fit, as indicated by the *p*-value of .1 (>.05) for the Pearson Chi^2. However, fit further improves on all statistics for the 3-class model, even though the *p*-value for Cressie-Read remains below the conventional .05 level. Unfortunately, there is no clear methodological rule for deciding between conflicting measures of best fit. Such a conflict is found here for the 3-class model, which is to be preferred by the higher *p*-values of the Pearson and Cressie-Read statistics, versus the 4-class model, which is to be preferred if we go by the lower BIC value and the (just marginally) higher geometric mean likelihood. As there may be some risk of over-fitting the data with too high a number of classes, the more parsimonious 3-class model was selected here as the starting point for interpretation and detailed inspection of scaling results. Choosing the boot-strapped Pearson, respectively, Cressie-Read statistics over the information criteria is also in line with a recommendation given by von Davier (2001).[*,†]

TABLE 16.1

Fit Statistics for Homogeneous and Mixed Rasch Models (Partial Credit)

Model	Number of Parameters	BIC	Geom. Mean Likelihood	Significance of Cressie-Read (Bootstrapped)	Significance of Pearson Chi^2 (Bootstrapped)
Saturated model	3124	/	0.29,492,014	/	/
1 class	21	52,888.84	0.27,043,386	0.000	0.000
2 class	43	52,287.05	0.27,574,806	0.013	0.100
3 class	65	52,118.35	0.27,816,192	0.020	0.153
4 class	87	52,060.16	0.27,982,879	0.013	0.080

Note: BIC = Bayes information criterion.

* A 5-class model did not converge after 1200 iterations and its preliminary estimates showed no improvement in fit over the 4-class model.

† The number of parameters is determined by the number of observed response patterns for the saturated model. For the Rasch models, every item requires one parameter each for estimating its category thresholds, plus two parameters for a logistic function that approximates the distribution of response scores. For each additional class, one parameter for the class size has to be included.

The three classes are of rather uneven sizes (cf. Table 16.2). We will first look at class-specific patterns of category thresholds, then at the class-specific item difficulty profiles, and then at country-specific frequency distributions of items. Only then we will begin looking at item contents again for a more substantive interpretation.

Beginning with the largest Class 1, which comprises 62.3% of the pooled sample, Figure 16.2 reveals an almost ideal set of threshold profiles. No threshold disordering occurs, and all items except ctrw show rather regular intervals between thresholds. Not only does each item cover a substantial range of the latent variable with five to seven logit units, but also do the overall items vary in terms of their average difficulty (this is also called item location and is the arithmetical mean of the threshold values of each item) by around two logit units. A good spread of the measurement instrument's stimuli over the latent trait increases reliability. Indeed, reliability as assessed by coefficient α (0.679) is acceptable for a scale of five items.*

Figure 16.3 shows the threshold profiles found in Class 2, with 24.2% of the sample. None of the items covers much of the latent trait range, and all except betc show some threshold disordering, but four items show at least

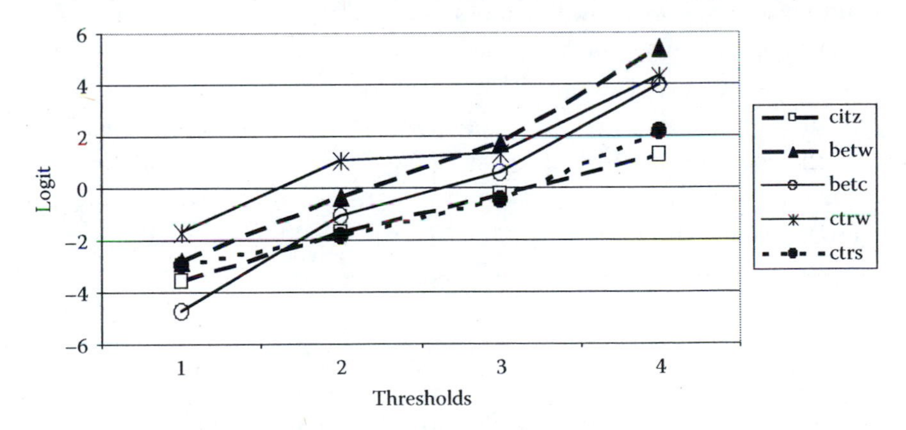

FIGURE 16.2
Item threshold profiles for Class 1.

* To avoid some complexity, the explanation and reporting of certain Rasch-specific measures computed by WinMira, such as Andrichís index of person separability, which is largely equivalent to coefficient α (Andrich, 1988, p. 84), is omitted here. Results are available from the author on request.

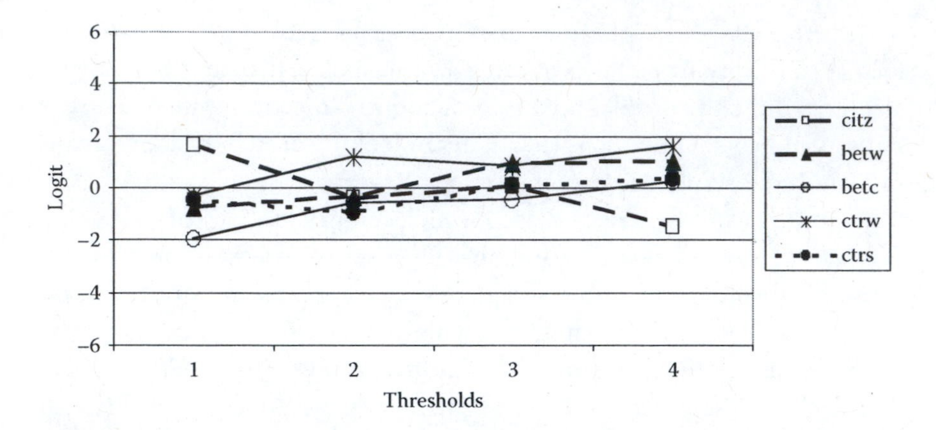

FIGURE 16.3
Item threshold profiles for Class 2.

discrimination between the bottom and the top thresholds. For item citz, the last threshold is even below the first one. The likely interpretation of this will become transparent when the relative frequency distributions of the individual items are shown and discussed below. The general pattern could be interpreted to be a case of low-discriminatory power for these respondents, going along with low reliability of the responses. This is in line with Alpha reliability, which only assumes the hardly acceptable value of 0.274.

The smallest Class 3 comprises 13.5% of the sample. Again, we observe poor discrimination and some disordering between threshold values, but here, the final threshold stands out as being clearly higher than all the preceding ones for four items (cf. Figure 16.4). The exception is once more the item citz, where the increase for the final threshold is minimal. Overall, reliability remains low at $\alpha = 0.296$.

Looking at the results for all three classes, we so far have indications that class 1 consists of respondents for whom the measurement instrument worked without notable problems. More than 60% of the pooled sample clearly appears to be scalable with a Rasch model. How do classes 2 and 3 differ from that reference class, apart from displaying low-threshold spread and low reliability? Figure 16.5 gives the class-specific profiles of the item locations.

As noted before, the item location profiles displayed here do not lend themselves to judging absolute trait level differences between classes; rather, it is the relative difficulty of items within each class that is of interest. The location profiles of classes 1 and 2 differ mostly on items citz and betw. Class

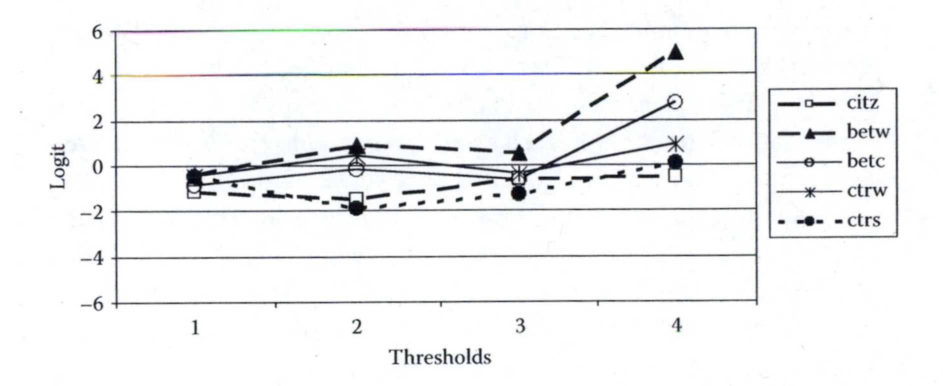

FIGURE 16.4
Item threshold profiles for Class 3.

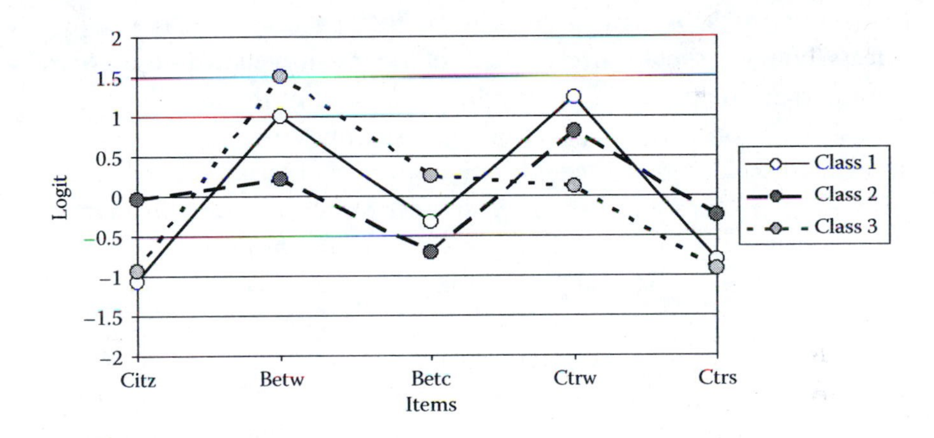

FIGURE 16.5
Item location profile over classes.

3 deviates from the other two most clearly in the relative position of ctrw, which is relatively easy to agree with in Class 3. For Classes 1 and 3, items betw and ctrw are those that respondents find it most difficult to agree with. betw is probably relatively difficult because it not only asks respondents to express an explicit sentiment of superiority over other countries; this it has in common with betc, which is generally rather easy, but additionally demands that citizens of other countries should be or become more similar to the respondent. ctrw introduces a different kind of hurdle to agreement, namely, the possibility that one's own country's actions could be morally wrong. Its high level of difficulty in Classes 1 and 2 makes its relatively

intermediate position in Class 3 appear all the more striking. Further, betc is relatively more difficult in Class 3, compared to the other classes.

These somewhat confusing results can be better understood by taking the levels of the latent trait in each class into account. In class 1, the average person parameter is 0.44, which is relatively close to the center (0) of the distribution (item raw score 11.38, with a range from 0 to 20). Class 2 is in contrast marked by very high levels of national pride (person parameter 1.08, raw score 15.79), and Class 3 by very low levels (person parameter –0.83, raw score 7.17). One possible conclusion could be that Class 2 is affected by ceiling effects of the items, with most of the items generally being too easy for the members of this class.

The result would be a compression of threshold ranges per item as well as of item location ranges, which we indeed have observed above. Class 3 could likewise be somewhat affected by floor effects. Floor and ceiling effects, however, should affect all items of the instrument in a similar way, with perhaps reducing the outstanding character of the items that have already had more extreme locations in Class 1. Thus, they are not sufficient to explain the differential item location profiles of Classes 2 and 3. The profiles of Classes 2 and 3 are more distinct from each other than any of them is distinct from Class 1. In other words, respondents in Class 2, with a very high level of national pride, seem to have a different perception of some items than respondents in Class 3, with a low level of national pride. If we abandon the option that the segmentation is due alone to floor/ceiling effects, two possible interpretations remain: There could be either a substantive relationship between understanding of items and level of trait, which would be the most undesirable outcome from a methodological point of view; or the segmentation procedure has confounded aspects of multidimensionality of the instrument with the methodological problem of floor/ceiling effects. Under both interpretations, it would be questionable to compare scale values across classes.

A way to shed more light on the question of floor/ceiling effects is of course to scrutinize the frequency distributions of individual items. Since already the ranking of the raw scores induced the conclusion that the trait levels are very different across some of our country samples, this will be investigated in country-specific displays. This must however be seen on the background of the distribution of classes across countries, which is displayed in Figure 16.6. Both German subsamples have a very similar distribution, with class 2 being far less relevant than in the pooled sample.

In Great Britain, it is Class 3 that is hardly of importance. Most striking is the distribution observed for the United States, where Class 1 and Class 2 have the same weight, and Class 3 is even smaller than in Great Britain. Sweden is again similar to the German samples.

As far as the small set of country samples used here allows any conclusions, it appears from Figure 16.6 that a country's position on the rank order of raw scores is related to the internal distribution of classes (low rank and Class 2 small: DE-W, DE-E, SE; medium rank and Class 2 intermediate: Great Britain; high rank and Class 2 large: United States). That picture has to be completed with a look at the class-specific estimated trait levels, which should allow a more robust assessment than the raw scores. Figure 16.7 shows how the class-specific trait means vary across countries. In all cases, Class 2 has the highest average trait level, Class 1 the second highest, and Class 3, by a very large margin, the lowest level. Using the latent trait estimates, it still appears that, for example, the high average U.S. raw score could relate to the very large share of Class 2 in the U.S. sample by way of a composition effect. This would still hold despite of the trait average of the U.S. Class 2 cases being marginally lower than that of

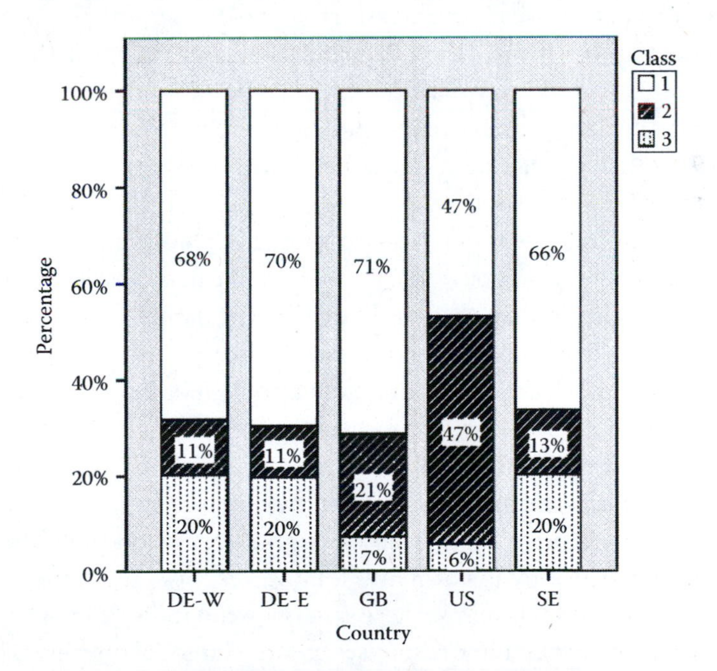

FIGURE 16.6
Distribution of latent classes over countries.

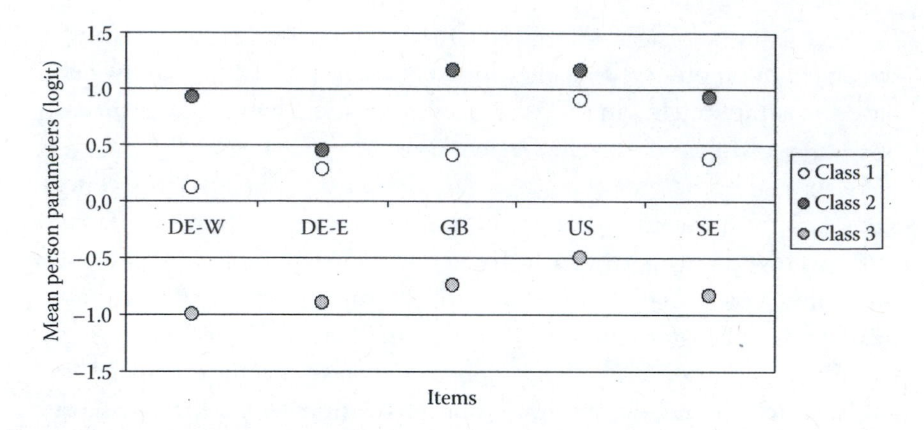

FIGURE 16.7
Latent trait means by class and country.

Class 2 in the UK sample. However, in Class 1 the U.S. trait level stands out most clearly from the other countries' levels. In other words, the use of class-specific trait estimates does not remove country-specific differences in the absolute trait levels, and even within the same class can the trait distribution vary massively over countries.

With the country-specific class sizes and trait values in mind, the inspection of the item frequency distributions can be rather selective. To save space, only the distributions for citz and betw are reported in Figures 16.8 and 16.9 (with the other items lying between the rather distinct general pictures provided by these).

The distributions in Class 1 are nicely unimodal for all items, with the weight usually being on one of the three central categories. This indicates that the items are rather well calibrated to the sample, as was already apparent by the reliability values for Class 1.

Figure 16.8 very clearly shows that item citz is indeed affected by ceiling effects in Class 2, in particular for the United States and Great Britain. The threshold order reversals observed above can obviously be attributed to some categories being practically empty: if hardly any respondents use the lower categories, there is not enough information to derive stable parameter estimates for them. Only for the very few respondents from East Germany in this class (39), there also is a weak indication of a general tendency to use only extreme responses, per the bimodal distribution seen here. Only for the United States, the distribution of citz is heavy on the right tail in all classes. In contrast, the distribution in Class 3 shows little

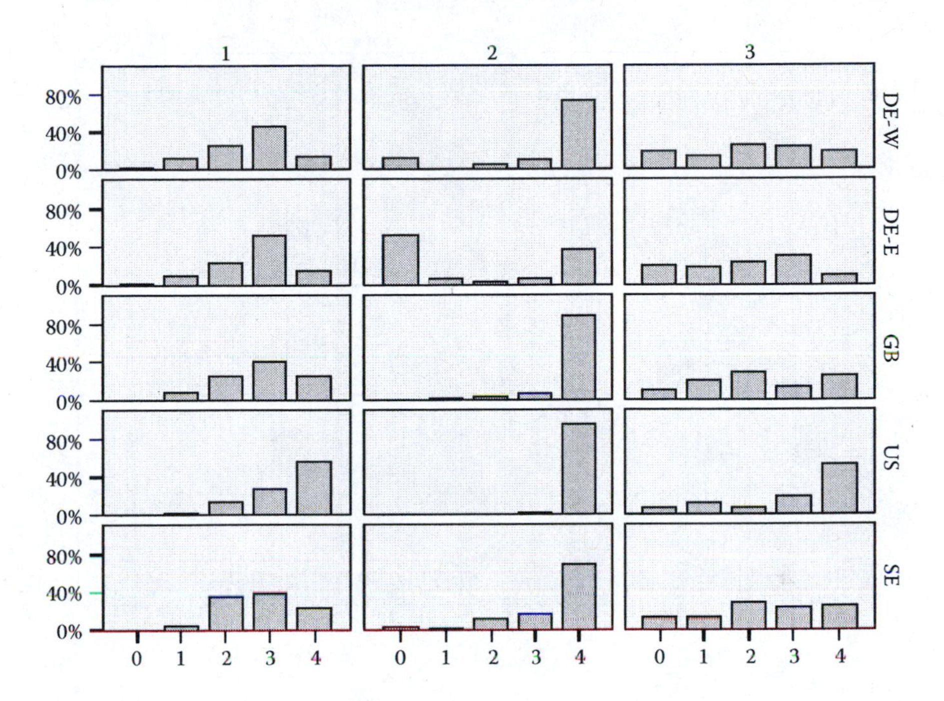

FIGURE 16.8
Rather be a citizen of [...] than of any other country.

structure for any of the countries, so we cannot clearly conclude that a floor effect is reducing the quality of this item here.

Item betw, displayed in Figure 16.9, is in all classes one of the two most difficult items. Accordingly, its frequency distribution is either far less heavy on the right tail (Class 2) than that of citz, or even distinctly skewed toward the left tail (Class 3). These tendencies are reflected in Class 1 having almost no responses on either of the extreme categories of the item. Here, it is Class 2 that shows no particular structure, but the threshold reversals were also not very severe for this item.

In summary, the item distributions corroborate the presence of clear ceiling and some floor effects in Classes 2 and 3, respectively, but it seems unlikely that such effects are the only reason behind the class distinction. Going back to Figure 16.7 and Table 16.2, it is apparent that the Rasch estimates have somewhat dampened the extremity of the raw scores in Class 2, through estimation of lower threshold parameters for items with extremely high degrees of agreement. Apart from the general tendency to high-item response categories in the United States, which generally corresponds very

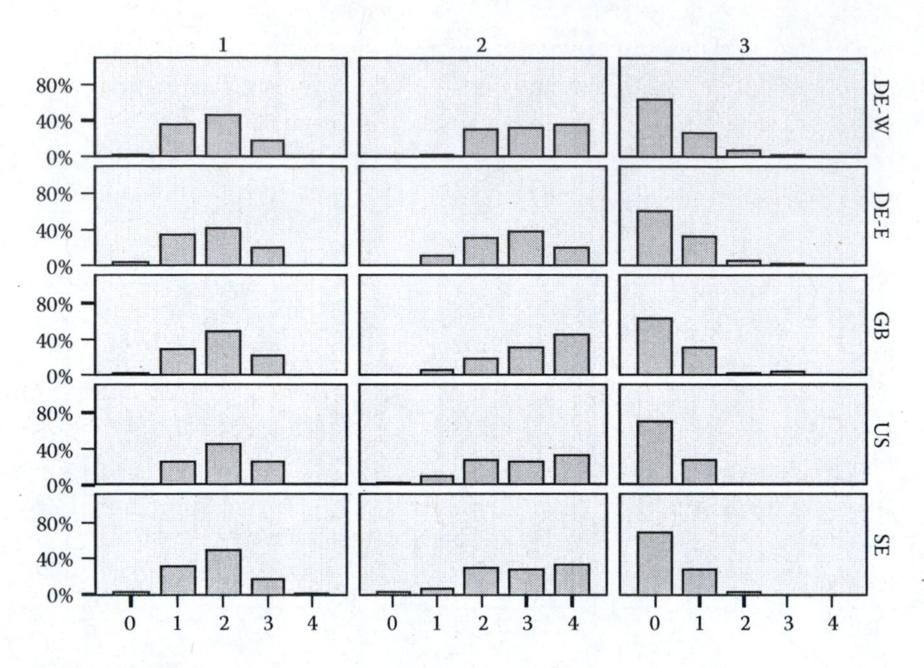

FIGURE 16.9
World a better place if people from other countries were more like [...].

TABLE 16.2
Overview of Latent Class Descriptives

	Class 1	Class 2	Class 3
Size (% of pooled sample)	62.3	24.2	13.5
Mean of latent trait	0.44	1.08	–0.83
Raw score	11.38	15.79	7.17
Reliability (α)	0.68	0.27	0.30
Std. deviation of latent trait	1.13	0.72	0.56
Std. deviation of raw score	2.75	2.46	2.92

well with the high-trait values estimated for that sample, almost no country-specific particularities have become visible in the raw item data.

16.7 INTERPRETATION

The interpretation that multidimensionality may be also driving the class distinction cannot be fully explored here, as this would require an in-depth analysis with many potential covariates of the class assignment. Still, it should be noted that some multidimensionality in this item battery is not unlikely, since the strategy for its construction obviously was to widen its scope by using different referents in each item: citz uses the personal preference for the place of residence; betw uses the notion of an ideal world; betc is referring to the quality of a country and therefore the most general item; ctrw sets the importance of the nation against that of moral virtue; ctrs introduces international sports (with two implied risks: that respondents do not necessarily care about sports at all, or not about its international varieties, and even if they do, it could be that a country rarely figures in international sports).* Thus, the challenge for any scaling procedure is to isolate nationalism as the hopefully dominant dimension from some expectable nonrandom disturbances; and eventually, the strategy of dropping the majority of the items as chosen by Davidov (2009) may be seen as the only route to obtaining an internationally comparable subset of the national pride battery of the ISSP 2003 module.

Except for the U.S. sample with its outstanding distribution of latent classes, the recommendation could albeit be a different one as well. For four out of five subsamples, between 66 and 71% of the respondents fell in class 1, which proved to be scalable under the Rasch model with good reliability. In such a case, it might be worth considering limiting analyses to those cases with validated scalability. Classes 2 and 3 would then be regarded as more or less residual categories, which collect cases with problematic measurement properties. If one included them in further analyses at all, one would certainly look at such cases with less confidence in the latent trait estimates, and accordingly, in the raw scores. To this author, such a differential treatment of cases with low-measurement quality is intuitively at least as appealing as dropping items with supposedly poor quality. (In the present analysis, no indications of poor quality of individual items were found that were consistent over all classes.) Both methods of excluding sources of misfit from measurement models sacrifice data, but the number of individual data points lost is often much higher when full columns of the data matrix are dropped than when selected rows of the data matrix are dropped. The disadvantage of excluding cases obviously is

* Together with the distribution of classes over countries, the item location profiles provide one bit of information that could be pursued for further interpretation: just by the size of Class 2 in the U.S. sample, the higher relative difficulty of items citz and ctrs in that class appears to be almost a U.S. specialty.

that the representativeness of the sample is at stake, but the disadvantage of excluding items always is that the theoretical content domain of the measurement is reduced or changed, in a possibly arbitrary way.

With the share of Class 2 respondents being so high in the U.S. sample, the case-selection strategy does however not look too convincing for the present case. Even without further detail analyses, it seems unlikely that nearly half of the U.S. sample are of a quality too low to be useful. To the contrary, only for this sample, the segmentation into classes in fact decreases the value of the consistency coefficient α in every single class, compared to the situation without segmentation (α for full U.S. sample: 0.68, U.S. Class 1: 0.62, U.S. Class 2: 0.26, U.S. Class 3: 0.47). By separating many cases with extreme positive responses into class 2, the segmentation has obviously created a class with reduced internal variation, and it has removed some systematic variation from the top end of the scale in the other classes.

Even if the present analyses cannot disentangle the probable confounding of substantive and methodological problems in Classes 2 and 3, some cautious methodological conclusions about the item battery still seem possible. The first is that some items display clear ceiling effects in Class 2, while the floor effects in Class 3 are less pronounced and Class 3 is much smaller. At least one or two of these items: citz, betc, and ctrs, should therefore be modified to become more difficult in terms of the latent trait, so that even for the samples from populations with an extraordinary high-trait level, such as the United States, precise measurement remains possible.

Secondly, another reason for some reversals of category threshold order could be that respondents did not use the category distinctions of the five-point scale very systematically. Using fewer categories might make the items easier to handle for many respondents in Classes 2 and 3, without noticeable loss of precision for respondents in Class 1. Split-ballot experiments would be required to show that the item battery could work equally well if only four or three response categories were offered to respondents.

16.8 CONCLUSIONS

Rasch models are not very popular among survey researchers in sociology or political science. In contrast, these models are widely used in educational attainment testing or physical ability evaluation in medical research.

The reasons behind this may be partly of a historical kind, ability testing being the field where the first applications were implemented (Rasch, 1960), and where most of the terminology comes from. A more profound reason could be that those fields provide more homogeneous and controllable settings for measurement. Individual traits can be assessed with much longer instruments in the survey practice of those fields. Also, it is probably easier to define clear-cut unidimensional latent traits and their corresponding indicators for cognitive or physical abilities as for attitudes, which are usually held to be composites of cognition, affect, and tendencies to act [for a typical definition from a social psychology textbook, see Krech, Crutchfield, and Ballachey (1962, p. 139)].

Further, it is not always clear whether certain attitude items can be expected to produce the monotonically increasing item characteristic curves that the Rasch model requires. Some attitude items may be answered according to an ideal point process, not according to a dominance relationship between respondent and category threshold (Jacoby, 1991). Ideal point processes do however produce nonmonotonical item characteristics, which should usually not fit the Rasch model. So-called unfolding models exist to deal with ideal point-data. Some of these models can also reveal response styles [e.g., Javaras & Ripley (2007) analyze the national pride data of ISSP 1995], but these are inherently complex and not yet readily available in user-friendly software.

A final plausible reason for the popularity of Rasch models in ability tests is that such tests often are connected to high stakes for the persons tested. Having test results used for, for example, recruiting decisions, or for therapeutical measures, puts high demands on the objectivity and reliability of the instrument and its scoring mechanism. Comparing competing persons to each other by some test score certainly requires scalar invariance of that test, and it certainly justifies utmost strictness in testing the measurement instrument itself. Whether, however, the absence of such high-personal stakes in other social sciences justifies much weaker demands on measurements has been fiercely questioned (Michell, 1997). The most popular uses of, for example, cross-cultural survey results certainly are not correlational analyses requiring only metric invariance, but comparisons of means. Therefore, testing for scalar invariance should be demanded as a matter of course in comparative research.

The Rasch model and its extension to the mixed Rasch model, in principle, provide a straightforward approach to this type of problem. In the example used here, it was possible to obtain fit of the multicountry data on national pride and the mixed Rasch model, but not of the initial simple Rasch model. The outcome that simple Rasch modeling does not confirm a high level of measurement quality and equivalence more often than similarly demanding methods such as MGCFA do can hardly be surprising. If we want to look at the glass as being half-full, a tentative conclusion is this: There is one dominant class of respondents that can be measured with great validity and reliability across four out of five subsamples. The mixed Rasch analysis has allowed distinguishing these respondents from a minority of respondents with different measurement problems in a very parsimonious way, without even referring to fixed country borders. Of course, this preliminary conclusion asks for replications with larger numbers of countries and different data.

However, the results of the present mixed Rasch analysis also come with some ambiguities and are thus not fully satisfactory. A skeptical interpretation of the suspicious class distribution in the U.S. sample and the generally difficult interpretation of Classes 2 and 3 could be that the segmentation of the mixed Rasch model was over-sensitive to response distribution differences, such that an extreme response style could not consistently be separated from a very skewed distribution of the latent variable. The introduction of new parameters via additional classes potentially gives room to the over-fitting of such aberrations, in particular if these concern smaller subsets as is the case with class 3. It is obviously desirable to investigate whether Classes 2 or 3 of our solution are associated with individual factors susceptible of driving extreme response behavior, such as low motivation or limited cognitive abilities of respondents. However, the data at hand do not contain reliable indicators for such factors.*

What else, then, can be gained by using Rasch models instead of, or in addition to, MGCFA? As this contribution has tried to demonstrate, the mixed Rasch model invites looking at the item response profiles at a very detailed level. While the potential for identifying substantive intergroup differences or multidimensionality could not be exhausted here, this option proved useful for identifying response distribution problems.

* Analyses with education and (high) age as proxies did not prove useful. One problem is that these proxies are also correlated with the substantive scale. Presentation has been omitted for want of space. An application of hierarchical IRT methods focused on explicitly estimating respondents' propensity to extreme response styles can be found in De Jong, Steenkamp, Fox, and Baumgartner (2008).

In the present case, these were limited mostly to ceiling effects, but generally, response sets or styles can equally well be identified [for an application, see Rost et al. (1997); for a similar approach using conventional Rasch methodology, see Curtis (2004)]. At the least, it could prove to be useful to perform mixed Rasch analysis in conjunction with (MG)CFA in particular in the phase of developing measurement instruments and pretesting surveys.*

REFERENCES

Andrich, D. (1978). Rating formulation for ordered response categories. *Psychometrika, 43*(4), 561–573.

Andrich, D. (1988). *Rasch models for measurement.* Sage University Paper Series on Quantitative Applications in the Social Sciences, 07-068. Newbury Park, London, New Delhi: Sage Publications.

Arts, W., & Halman, L. (2005). National identity in Europe today—What the people feel and think. *International Journal of Sociology, 35*(4), 69–93.

Biswas-Diener, R., Vittersø, J., & Diener, E. (2009). The Danish effect: Beginning to explain high well-being in Denmark. Social Indicators Research. Online publication date: 19-Jun-2009. doi: 10.1007/s11205-009-9499-5

Bond, T. G., & Fox, C. M. (2001). Applying the Rasch model. *Fundamental measurement in the human sciences*. Mahwah, NJ; London: Lawrence Erlbaum Associates.

Bozdogan, H. (1987). Model selection and Akaike's information criterion (AIC): The general theory and its analytical extensions. *Psychometrika, 52*(3), 345–370.

Curtis, D. D. (2004). Misfits: People and their problems. What might it all mean? *International Education Journal, 2*(4), 91–99.

Davidov, E. (2009). Measurement equivalence of nationalism and constructive patriotism in the ISSP: 34 countries in a comparative perspective. *Political Analysis, 17*, 64–82.

de Jong, M. G., Steenkamp, J.-B. E. M., Fox, J.-P. & Baumgartner, H. (2008). Using item response theory to measure extreme response style in marketing research: A global investigation. *Journal of Marketing Research, XLV*, 104–115.

Ewing, M. T., Salzberger, T., & Sinkovics, R. R. (2005). An alternate approach to assessing cross-cultural measurement equivalence in advertising research. *Journal of Advertising, 34*(1), 17–36.

He, Y., Merz, M. A., & Alden, D. L. (2008). Diffusion of measurement invariance assessment in cross-national empirical marketing research: Perspectives from the literature and a survey of researchers. *Journal of International Marketing, 16*(2), 64–83.

Hjerm, M. (1998). National identities, national pride and xenophobia: A comparison of four western countries. *Acta Sociologica, 41*(4), 335–347.

* I am indebted to a reviewer for helpful hints and comments. All remaining errors are my own.

Jacoby, W. G. (1991). *Data theory and dimensional analysis.* Sage University Paper Series on Quantitative Applications in the Social Sciences, 07-078. Newbury Park, London, New Delhi: Sage.

Javaras, K. N., & Ripley, B. D. (2007). An "unfolding" latent variable model for Likert attitude data: Drawing inferences adjusted for response style. *Journal of the American Statistical Association, 102*(478), 454–463.

Krech, D., Crutchfield, R. S., & Ballachey, E. L. (1962). *Individual in society. A textbook of social psychology*. New York, NY: McGraw-Hill.

Masters, G. N. (1982). A Rasch model for partial credit scoring. *Psychometrika, 47*(2), 149–174.

Michell, J. (1997). Quantitative science and the definition of measurement in psychology. *British Journal of Psychology, 88*(3), 355–383.

OECD—Organization for Economic Cooperation and Development. (2005). *PISA Technical Report*, Paris, France: OECD Publications.

Rasch, G. (1960). *Probabilistic models for some intelligence and attainment tests.* Copenhagen, Denmark: The Danish Institute of Educational Research

Rost, J. (2004). Lehrbuch Testtheorie, Testkonstruktion. 2. [Test theory and test construction: a textbook. 2nd edition] Auflage. Bern u.a.: Hans Huber.

Rost, J., Carstensen, C., & von Davier, M. (1997). Applying the mixed Rasch model to personality questionnaires. In J. Rost & R. Langeheine (Eds.), *Applications of latent trait and latent class models in the social sciences* (pp. 324–332). Münster, Germany: Waxmann.

Rupp, A. A., & Zumbo, B. D. (2006). Understanding parameter invariance in unidimensional IRT models. *Educational and Psychological Measurement, 66*, 63–84.

Salzberger, T., Holzmüller, H. H., & Souchon, A. (2009). Advancing the understanding of construct validity and cross-national comparability: Illustrated by a five-country study of corporate export information usage. *Advances in International Marketing, 20*, 321–360.

Salzberger, T., & Sinkovics, R. R. (2006). Reconsidering the problem of data equivalence in international marketing research. Contrasting approaches based on CFA and the Rasch model for measurement. *International Marketing Review, 23*(4), 390–417.

Schmitt, N., & Kuljanin, G. (2008). Measurement invariance: Review of practice and implications. *Human Resource Management Review, 18*, 210–222.

Smith, T. W., & Kim, S. (2006). National pride in comparative perspective: 1995/96 and 2003/04. *International Journal of Public Opinion Research, 18*(1), 127–136.

Stark, S., Chernyshenko, O. S., & Drasgow, F. (2006). Detecting differential item functioning with confirmatory factor analysis and item response theory: Toward a unified strategy. *Journal of Applied Psychology, 91*(6), 1292–1306.

Thissen, D., Steinberg, L., & Wainer, H. (1993). Detection of differential item functioning using the parameters of item response models. In P. W. Holland & H. Wainer (Eds.), *Differential item functioning* (pp. 67–113). Mahwah, NJ: Lawrence Erlbaum

Tilley, J., & Heath, A. (2007). The decline of British national pride. *British Journal of Sociology, 58*(4), 661–678.

Vittersø, J., Biswas-Diener, R., & Diener, E. (2005). The divergent meanings of life satisfaction: Item response modeling of the satisfaction with life scale in Greenland and Norway. *Social Indicators Research, 74*, 327–348.

von Davier, M. (1997). Bootstrapping goodness-of-fit statistics for sparse categorical data—Results of a Monte Carlo study. *Methods of Psychological Research Online, 2*, 29–48.

von Davier, M. (2001). *WinMira 2001, version 1.41*. Computer software. Retrieved from http://winmira.von-davier.de/wmira/index.html

von Davier M., & Carstensen, C. (Eds.). (2007). *Multivariate and mixture distribution Rasch models*. New York, NY: Springer.

von Davier, M., & Rost, J. (1995). Polytomous mixed Rasch models. In G. H. Fischer & I. W. Molenaar (Eds.), *Rasch models: Foundations, recent developments, and applications* (pp. 371–379). New York, NY: Springer.

von Davier, M., & Yamamoto, K. (2007). Mixture-distribution and HYBRID Rasch models. In M. von Davier and C. H. Carstensen (Eds.), *Multivariate and mixture distribution Rasch models* (pp. 99–115). New York, NY: Springer.

Wright, B. D. (1996). Comparing Rasch measurement and factor analysis. *Structural Equation Modeling, 3*, 3–24.

Zumbo, B. D. (2007). Three generations of DIF analyses: Considering where it has been, where it is now, and where it is going. *Language Assessment Quarterly, 4*(2), 223–233.

17

Random Item Effects Modeling for Cross-National Survey Data

Jean-Paul Fox
University of Twente

Josine Verhagen
University of Twente

17.1 INTRODUCTION

Item response theory (IRT) methods are standard tools for the analysis of large-scale assessments of student's performance. In educational survey research, the National Assessment of Educational Progress (NAEP) is primarily focused on scaling the performances of a sample of students in a subject area (e.g., mathematics, reading, science) on a single common scale, and measuring change in educational performance over time. The Organization for Economic Cooperation and Development (OECD) organizes the Program for International Student Assessment (PISA). The program is focused on measuring and comparing abilities in reading, mathematics, and science of 15-year-old pupils in 30 member countries and various partner countries every 3 years and started in 2000. Another example is the Trends in International Mathematics and Science Study (TIMSS) conducted by the International Association for the Evaluation of Educational Achievement (IEA) to measure trends in students' mathematics and science performance.

Large-scale (educational) survey studies can be characterized by: (1) the ordinal character of the observations, (2) the complex sampling designs with individuals responding to different sets (booklets) of questions, (3) booklet effects are present (the performance on an item depends on an underlying latent variable but also on the responses to other items in the booklet), and (4) presence of missing data. The presence of booklet effects and missing data complicates an IRT analysis of the survey data. The analysis of large-scale survey data for comparative research is further complicated by several measurement invariance issues (e.g., Meredith & Milsap, 1992; Steenkamp & Baumgartner, 1998), as assessing comparability of the test scores across countries, cultures, and different educational systems is a well-known complex problem. The main issue is that the measurement instrument has to exhibit adequate cross-national equivalence. This means that the calibrations of the measurement instrument remain invariant across populations (e.g., nations, countries) of examinees.

It will be shown that a random item effects model is particularly useful for the analysis of cross-national survey data. The random item effects parameters vary over countries, which leads to noninvariant item characteristics. Thus, cross-national variation in item characteristics is allowed and it is not necessary to establish measurement invariance. The random item effects approach supports the use of country-specific item characteristics and a common measurement scale. Further, the identification of the random item effects model does not depend on marker or anchor items. In current approaches to measurement invariance, at least two invariant marker items are needed to establish a common scale across countries. In theory only one invariant item is needed to fix the scale, but an additional invariant item is needed to be able to test the invariance of this item. Further, a poorly identified scale based on one marker item can easily jeopardize the statistical inferences. Establishing a common scale by marker items is very difficult when there are only a few test items and/or when there are many countries in the sample.

The focus of the current study is on exploring the properties and the possibilities of the random item effects model for the analysis of cross-national survey data. After introducing the model, a short description of the estimation method will be given. Then, in a simulation study, attention is focused on the performance and global convergence property of the estimation method by reestimating the model parameters given simulated data. Subsequently, an illustration is given of a real-data application using PISA 2003 data.

17.2 RANDOM ITEM EFFECTS MODELING

IRT methods provide a set of techniques for estimating individual ability (e.g., attitude, behavior, performance) levels and item characteristics from observed discrete multivariate response data. The ability levels cannot be observed directly but are measured via a questionnaire or test. The effects of the persons and the items on the response data are modeled by separate sets of parameters. The person parameters are usually referred to as the latent variables, and the item parameters are usually labeled item difficulties and item discrimination parameters.

Assume a normal ogive IRT model for binary response data for $k = 1,\ldots,$ K items and $I = 1,\ldots, n$ respondents. The overall item characteristics are denoted as $\xi_k = (a_k, b_k)^t$ representing item difficulty and item discrimination parameters, respectively. The individual ability level is denoted as θ_i. The probit version of the two-parameter IRT model also known as the normal ogive model is defined via a cumulative normal distribution,

$$P(Y_{ik} = 1 \mid \theta_i, a_k, b_k) = \Phi(a_k\theta_i - b_k) = \int_{-\infty}^{a_k\theta_i - b_k} \phi(z)dz, \tag{17.1}$$

where $\Phi(.)$ and $\varphi(.)$ are the cumulative normal distribution function and the normal density function, respectively. The a_k is referred to as the discrimination parameter and the b_k as the item difficulty parameter.

In Equation 17.1, the item parameters apply to each country and can be regarded as the international item parameters. Without a country-specific index, cross-national variation in item characteristics is not allowed. Following the modeling approach of De Jong, Steenkamp, Fox (2007) and Fox (2010), country-specific item characteristics are defined. Let $\tilde{a}_{kj}$ and $\tilde{b}_{kj}$ denote the discrimination and difficulty parameters of item k in country j ($j = 1, \ldots, J$). As a result, the success probability depends on country-specific item characteristics, that is,

$$P\left(Y_{ijk} = 1 \mid \theta_i, \tilde{a}_{kj}, \tilde{b}_{kj}\right) = \Phi(\tilde{a}_{kj}\theta_i - \tilde{b}_{kj}). \tag{17.2}$$

The country-specific or nation-specific item parameters are based on the corresponding response data from that country. When the sample size per country is small and response bias (e.g., extreme response style, nonrepresentative samples) is present, the country-specific item parameter estimates have high-standard errors and they are probably biased. This estimation problem can be averted by a random item effects modeling framework in which the country-specific item parameters are considered random deviations from the overall item parameters. The main advantage of this hierarchical modeling approach is that information can be borrowed from the other country-specific item parameters. Therefore, a common population distribution is defined at a higher level for the country-specific item parameters. As a result, a so-called shrinkage estimate comprises the likelihood information at the data level and the information from the common assumed distribution. Typically, the shrinkage estimate of country-specific item parameters has a smaller standard error and gives a more robust estimate in case of response bias.

For each item k, assume an exchangeable prior distribution for the country-specific item parameters. This means that the joint distribution of the country-specific item parameters is invariant under any transformation of the indices. A priori there is no information about an order of the country-specific item characteristics. That is, for each k, for $j = 1, \ldots, J$ holds that:

$$\tilde{\xi}_{kj} = (\tilde{a}_{kj}, \tilde{b}_{kj})^t \sim N\left[(a_k, b_k)^t, \Sigma_{\tilde{\xi}}\right], \tag{17.3}$$

where (a_k, b_k) are the international item parameter characteristics of item k and $\Sigma_{\tilde{\xi}}$ is the cross-national covariance structure of country-specific characteristics. This covariance structure is allowed to vary across items. Here, a conditionally independent random item structure is defined with $\Sigma_{\tilde{\xi}}$ a diagonal matrix with elements $\sigma^2_{a_k}$ and $\sigma^2_{b_k}$.

In most cases there is not much information about the values of the international item parameters. Without a priori knowledge to distinguish the item parameters it is reasonable to assume a common distribution for them. A multivariate normal distributed prior is assumed for the item parameters. It follows that,

$$\xi_k = (a_k, b_k)^t \sim N(\mu_\xi, \Sigma_\xi), \tag{17.4}$$

where the prior parameters are distributed as:

$$\Sigma_\xi \sim IW(\nu, \Sigma_0) \tag{17.5}$$

$$\mu_\xi \mid \Sigma_\xi \sim N(\mu_0, \Sigma_\xi / K_0), \tag{17.6}$$

for $k = 1, \ldots, K$. The multivariate normal distribution in Equation 17.4 is the exchangeable prior for the set of K item parameters ξ_k. The joint prior distribution for (μ_ξ, Σ_ξ) is a normal inverse Wishart distribution, denoted as IW, with parameters $(\mu_0, \Sigma_0 / K_0; \nu, \Sigma_0)$ where K_0 denotes the number of prior measurements, and ν and Σ_0 describe the degrees of freedom and scale matrix of the inverse-Wishart distribution. These parameters are usually fixed at specified values. A proper vague prior is specified with $\mu_0 = 0$, $\nu = 2$, a diagonal scale matrix Σ_0 with elements 100 and K_0 a small number.

To summarize, the random item effects model can be specified as a normal ogive IRT model with country-specific item parameters, in Equation 17.2. The country-specific item parameters are assumed to have a common population distribution with the mean specified by the international item parameters (Equation 17.4). At a higher level, conjugated proper priors are specified for the international item prior parameters.

In different ways and for different purposes IRT models with item parameters defined as random effects have been proposed. Albers, Does, Imbos, and Janssen (1989) defined a Rasch model with random item difficulty parameters for an application where items are obtained from an item bank. De Boeck (2008) also considered the Rasch model with random item difficulty parameters. Janssen, Tuerlinckx, Meulders, and De Boeck (2000) defined an IRT model where item parameters (discrimination and difficulty) are allowed to vary across criterions in the context of criterion-referenced testing. Glas and Van der Linden (2003) and Glas, Van der Linden, and Geerlings (2010) considered the application of item cloning. In this procedure, items are generated by a computer algorithm given a parent item (e.g., item shell or item template). De Jong, Steenkamp, Fox, and Baumgartner (2008) used cross-national varying item parameters (discrimination and difficulty) for measuring extreme response style.

17.3 MODELING RESPONDENT HETEROGENEITY

In large-scale survey research, the sampled respondents are often nested in groups (e.g., countries, schools). Subsequently, inferences are to be made at different levels of analysis. At the level of respondents, comparisons can be made between individual performances. At the group level, mean individual performances can be compared. To facilitate comparisons at different hierarchical levels, a hierarchical population distribution is designed for the respondents.

Common IRT models assume a priori independence between individual abilities. Dependence of results of individuals within the same school/country is to be expected, however, since they share common experiences. A hierarchical population distribution for the ability of the respondents can be specified that accounts for the fact that respondents are nested within clusters. The observations at level-1 are nested within respondents. The respondents at level-2 are nested within groups (level-3) and indexed $i = 1,\ldots,n_j$ for $j = 1, \ldots, J$ groups. Let level-2 respondent-specific covariates (e.g., gender, SES) be denoted by $\mathbf{x}_{ij}$ and level-3 covariates (e.g., school size, mean country SES, type of school system) by $\mathbf{w}_{qj}$ for $q = 0, \ldots, Q$.

A hierarchical population model for the ability of the respondents consists of two stages: the level-2 prior distribution for the ability parameter θ_{ij}, specified as:

$$\theta_{ij} \mid \beta_j \sim N\left(\mathbf{x}_{ij}^t \beta_j, \sigma_\theta^2\right), \tag{17.7}$$

and the level-3 prior, specified as:

$$\beta_j \sim N\left(\mathbf{w}_j \gamma, \mathbf{T}\right). \tag{17.8}$$

An inverse-gamma (IG) prior distribution and an inverse-Wishart prior distribution are specified for the variance components σ_θ^2 and **T**, respectively. The extension to more levels is easily made.

This structural hierarchical population model is also known as a multilevel model (e.g., Aitkin & Longford, 1986; Bryk & Raudenbush, 1992; de Leeuw & Kreft, 1986; Goldstein, 1995; Snijders & Bosker, 1999).

17.4 IDENTIFICATION AND ESTIMATION

The common IRT model (assuming invariant item parameters) with a multilevel population model for the ability parameters is called a multilevel IRT model (MLIRT; e.g., Fox, 2007; Fox & Glas, 2001). In empirical multilevel studies, estimated ability parameters are often considered to be measured without an error and treated as an observed outcome variable. Ignoring the uncertainty regarding the estimated abilities may lead to biased parameter estimates and the statistical inference may be misleading.

Several comparable approaches are known in the literature. Zwinderman (1991) defined a generalized linear regression model for the observed responses with known item parameters at the lowest level of hierarchy. Adams, Wilson, and Wu (1997), Raudenbush and Sampson (1999), and Kamata (2001), defined a generalized linear regression model for the observed responses with item difficulty parameters at the lowest level. This model consists of a Rasch model for the observed responses and a multilevel regression model for the underlying latent variable. Note that a two-parameter IRT model extended with a multilevel model for the latent variable leads to a more complex nonlinear multilevel model since the conditional density of the responses given the model parameters is not a member of the exponential family that seriously complicates the simultaneous estimation of the model parameters (Skrondal & Rabe-Hesketh, 2004).

In the MLIRT modeling framework the multilevel population model parameters are estimated from the item response data without having to condition on estimated ability parameters. In addition, this modeling framework allows the incorporation of explanatory variables at different levels of hierarchy. The inclusion of explanatory information can be important in various situations, this can, for example, lead to more accurate item parameter estimates. Another related advantage of the model is that it can handle incomplete data in a very flexible way.

Here, the MLIRT model is extended with a random item effects measurement model. In fact, this is the MLIRT model with noninvariant item parameters as the item parameters are allowed to vary across countries. This MLIRT model with random item effects is not identified since the scale of the latent variable is not defined. When the item parameters are invariant, the model is identified by fixing the mean and variance of the latent scale. In case of noninvariant item parameters, in each country, there is indeterminacy between the latent country-mean (parameterized by a random intercept) and the location of the country-specific item difficulties (parameterized by random difficulty parameters). This indeterminacy is solved by restricting the sum of country-specific difficulties to be zero in each country. The variance of the latent scale can be defined by restricting the product of international item discrimination parameters to be one, or by imposing a restriction on the variance of the latent variable.

The model parameters are estimated simultaneously using a Markov chain Monte Carlo (MCMC) algorithm that was implemented in Fortran that will be made available in the MLIRT R-package of Fox (2007). The MCMC algorithm consists of drawing iteratively from the full conditional posterior distributions. The chain of sequential draws will converge such that, after a burn-in period, draws are obtained from the joint posterior distribution. These draws are used to make inferences concerning the posterior means, variances, and highest posterior density (HPD) intervals of parameters of interest.

17.5 SIMULATION STUDY

The estimation method for the MLIRT model with random item effects is evaluated by investigating convergence properties and by comparing true and estimated parameters for a simulated data set. Different priors for the cross-national discrimination parameter variances are used to investigate the prior influence on the estimation results.

17.5.1 Data Simulation

A data set was simulated with 10,000 cases, 15 items, and 20 groups of 500 students. The ability parameters were generated in two steps. First, the mean group ability parameters β_j were generated from a normal $N(0, \tau^2)$ distribution, with τ^2 from an IG(1, 1) distribution. The individual ability parameters θ_{ij} were subsequently generated from a normal $N(\beta_j, \sigma_\theta^2)$ distribution, with σ_θ^2 equal to 1.

International item parameters a_k and b_k were sampled independently from a lognormal distribution with mean $\mu_a = 1$ and standard deviation $\sigma_a = 0.15$, and a normal distribution with mean $\mu_b = 1$ and standard deviation $\sigma_b = 0.30$, respectively. Subsequently group specific parameters a_{kj} and b_{kj} were sampled independently from a lognormal distribution with mean a_k and between group standard deviation $\sigma_{a_k} = 0.20$, and a normal distribution with mean b_k and between group standard deviation $\sigma_{b_k} = 0.40$, respectively. As a result the group-specific discrimination parameters ranged from 0.32 to 1.79 and the group-specific difficulty parameters from −1.16 to 1.32.

Responses were generated by applying the random effects normal ogive IRT model to acquire the success probabilities, comparing this probability with a random number *r* from a uniform distribution on (0,1) and assigning a value 1 when $P(Y_{ijk} = 1|\theta_{ij}, \xi_{kj}) < r$ and a value 0 otherwise.

17.5.2 Procedure

The model was estimated using an MCMC algorithm implemented in Fortran that will be made available in the MLIRT Package (Fox, 2007). To be able to use an MCMC algorithm, prior distributions and initial values for the estimated parameters need to be specified. The initial values were generated from a standard normal distribution for the individual ability parameters and set to zero for the group-specific ability parameters. International and country-specific difficulty parameters were set to zero and the discrimination parameters were set to one. All initial values for the variances were set to one. There were 20,000 iterations run, of which the first 1000 were discarded as burn-in period. As an indication of the accuracy of the estimation, correlations between true and estimated parameters, the mean absolute difference between the true and the estimated parameters and the root mean of the squared differences between the true and estimated parameters were computed, all over items and countries.

17.5.3 Investigating Cross-National Prior Variance Dependence

The noninformative priors for the variance components should have as little impact as possible on the final parameter estimates. It is not desirable that cross-national differences in item characteristics are implied by the prior settings. In this section, the sensitivity of the prior for the cross-national item discrimination variances is investigated. Analyses showed that prior settings were highly influencing the results.

To examine the prior sensitivity of the cross-national variance of the discrimination parameters $\sigma^2_{a_k}$, several IG priors with different scale and shape parameters (1, 1; .1, .1; .01, .01; 1, .1; 1, .01) were investigated for this parameter. The similar correlations between the true and the estimated parameters ($\rho_a = 0.89 - 0.91$, $\rho_b = 0.95$), the similar root mean squared differences ($\text{RMSD}_a = 0.11 - 0.13$, $\text{RMSD}_b = 0.17$) and the mean absolute differences ($\text{MAD}_a = 0.09$, $\text{MAD}_b = 0.13$) across different priors show that the choice of prior does not affect the difficulty parameter estimates at all and the discrimination parameter estimates only slightly. The cross-national item parameter variance estimates are influenced, however. Tables 17.1 and 17.2 show that an IG(1, 1) prior resulted in estimates of the cross-national item parameter variances that were consistently too high, and the IG (1, 0.01) prior resulted in estimates that were consistently slightly lower than the original variances, but within the range of the 95% HPD interval. The 95% HPD interval is the interval over which the integral of the posterior density is 0.95 and the height of the posterior density for every point in the interval is higher than the posterior density for every point outside the interval. Because the posterior density is the distribution of the estimated parameter, the interpretation of this interval is that given the observed data this interval contains the parameter with 95% probability. The other priors performed almost equally well in this respect. With exception of the IG(1, 1) prior, all IG prior settings gave almost equal results, so unless a too informative prior is taken the results are not dependent on the choice of prior.

TABLE 17.1

True and Estimated Cross-National Discrimination Variances for Different Priors

	True	**IG(1, 1)**		**IG(1, 0.1)**		**IG(1, 0.01)**	
Item	$\sigma^2_{a_k}$	**Mean**	**SD**	**Mean**	**SD**	**Mean**	**SD**
1	0.03	0.15	0.05	0.05	0.05	0.03	0.01
2	0.04	0.16	0.06	0.05	0.05	0.04	0.02
3	0.04	0.14	0.05	0.04	0.04	0.02	0.01
4	0.03	0.13	0.04	0.03	0.03	0.02	0.01
5	0.02	0.13	0.04	0.03	0.03	0.02	0.01
6	0.04	0.15	0.05	0.05	0.05	0.04	0.01
7	0.06	0.15	0.05	0.05	0.05	0.04	0.01
8	0.05	0.16	0.06	0.06	0.06	0.05	0.02
9	0.03	0.17	0.06	0.06	0.06	0.04	0.02
10	0.06	0.16	0.06	0.06	0.06	0.05	0.02
11	0.05	0.16	0.05	0.05	0.05	0.04	0.02
12	0.03	0.14	0.05	0.04	0.04	0.03	0.01
13	0.07	0.17	0.06	0.07	0.07	0.06	0.02
14	0.05	0.15	0.05	0.05	0.05	0.03	0.01
15	0.04	0.16	0.05	0.06	0.06	0.04	0.02

TABLE 17.2

True and Estimated Cross-National Difficulty Variances for Different Gamma Priors

	True	IG(1, 1)		IG(1, 0.1)		IG(1, 0.01)	
Item	$\sigma^2_{b_k}$	**Mean**	**SD**	**Mean**	**SD**	**Mean**	**SD**
1	0.19	0.24	0.08	0.14	0.14	0.13	0.05
2	0.17	0.26	0.09	0.17	0.17	0.16	0.06
3	0.13	0.23	0.08	0.13	0.13	0.12	0.04
4	0.12	0.23	0.08	0.13	0.13	0.12	0.04
5	0.11	0.20	0.07	0.10	0.10	0.09	0.03
6	0.12	0.22	0.07	0.12	0.12	0.11	0.04
7	0.13	0.22	0.07	0.12	0.12	0.11	0.04
8	0.12	0.20	0.07	0.10	0.10	0.09	0.03
9	0.17	0.29	0.10	0.19	0.19	0.18	0.06
10	0.15	0.19	0.07	0.09	0.09	0.08	0.03
11	0.15	0.25	0.08	0.15	0.15	0.14	0.05
12	0.11	0.20	0.07	0.10	0.10	0.09	0.03
13	0.13	0.22	0.07	0.12	0.12	0.11	0.04
14	0.19	0.26	0.09	0.17	0.17	0.16	0.05
15	0.13	0.23	0.08	0.13	0.13	0.12	0.04

17.5.4 Convergence and Parameter Recovery

To check whether the MCMC chains have converged, convergence diagnostics and trace plots are inspected for both the cross-national item parameter variances and the international item parameters. The Geweke Z convergence diagnostic is computed by taking the difference between the mean of (a function of) the first n_A iterations and the mean of (a function of) the last n_B iterations, divided by the asymptotic standard error of this difference that is computed from spectral density estimates for the two parts of the chain (Cowles & Carlin, 1996). The result is approximately standard normally distributed. A large Z means that there is a relatively big difference between the values in the two parts of the chain, which indicates the chain is not yet stationary. The autocorrelation is the correlation between values in the chain with a certain lag between them.

The traceplots show a homogeneous band around a mean that after a burn-in-period stays more or less the same, without trends or large-scale fluctuations. The international difficulty parameters and the cross-national variances of the difficulty parameters showed good convergence, with an autocorrelation below 0.15 and Geweke Z values under 3. This was similar for most discrimination parameters except for the discrimination parameter for item 9, which had an autocorrelation of 0.31. In Figure 17.1, examining the traceplot of this parameter some trending is observed, but not in an extreme way. The high discrimination parameter corresponds with high information in a small region of latent scores. As the latent scores in some groups will fall predominantly outside this area, parameter estimates for the item are difficult to make for these groups. In similar situations higher autocorrelations have been found (e.g., Wollack, Bolt, Cohen, & Lee, 2002). In general, estimation is better when the highest item information is matched to the latent trait distribution in the sample.

The true item parameters that were used to simulate the dataset were recovered well, as is illustrated in Figure 17.2. The correlations between the true and estimated country-specific and international item parameters were all larger than 0.91. All true values fall into the 95% HPD intervals, and all estimated parameters were in the right direction. The cross-national item parameter variances and the group means of the ability parameters were also very accurately estimated.

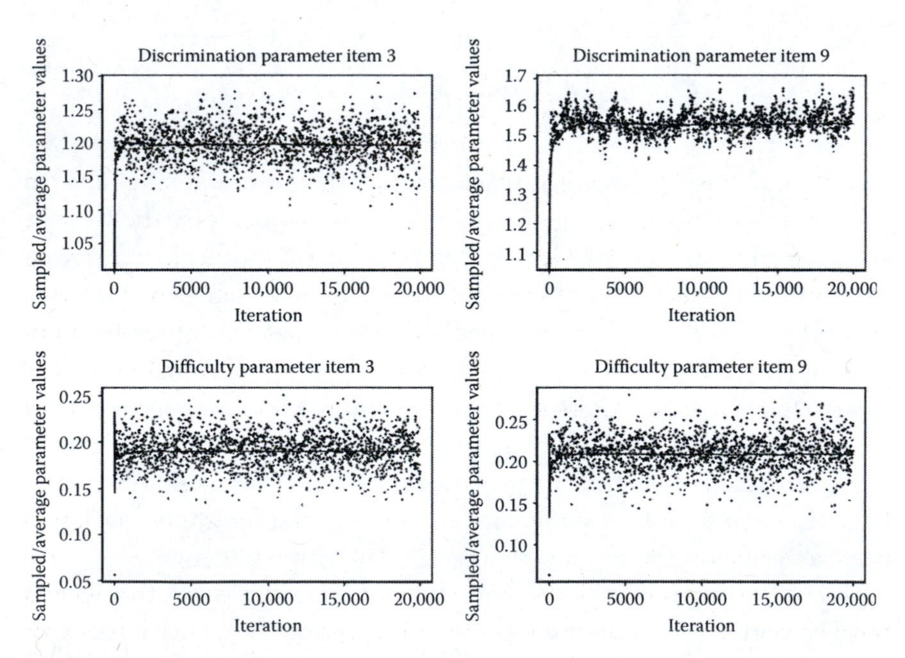

FIGURE 17.1
Traceplots and moving averages for the item parameters of item 3 and 9.

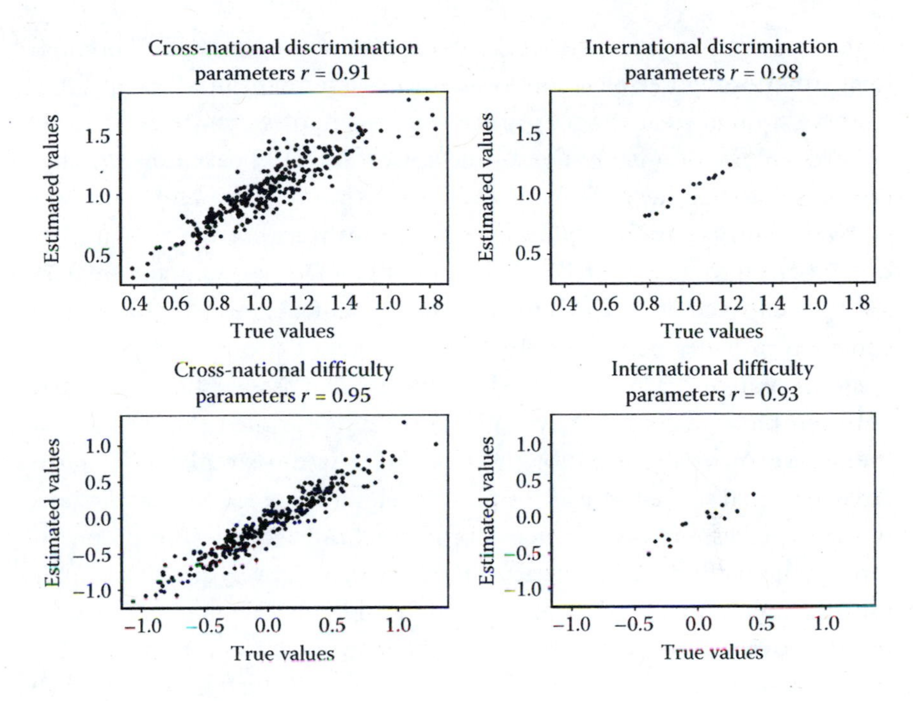

FIGURE 17.2
Plots of true and estimated international and cross-national item parameters.

17.6 PISA 2003: MATHEMATICS DATA

In this section the random item effects (MLIRT) model will be applied to a data set collected by the PISA in 2003. PISA is an initiative of the OECD. Every 3 years PISA measures the literacy in reading, mathematics, and science of 15-year-old students across countries, where literacy refers to "the capacity to apply knowledge and skills and to analyze, reason and communicate effectively as problems are posed, solved and interpreted in a variety of situations" (OECD, 2004, p. 20). In each data collection round one subject area is emphasized. In 2003 this was mathematic literacy, which resulted in four subdomains for mathematic performance. In addition to subject-specific knowledge, cross-curricular competencies as motivation to learn, self-beliefs, learning strategies, and familiarity with computers were measured. Furthermore the students answered questions about their background and their perception of the learning environment, while school principals provided school demographics and an assessment of the quality of the learning environment.

The current practice in PISA for items that show signs of differential item functioning between countries is to delete them in all or in some countries, or to treat them as different items across countries. Item by country interaction is used as an indication for DIF, based on whether the national scaling parameter estimates, the item fit, and the point biserial discrimination coefficients differ significantly from the international scaling values (OECD, 2005). The (international) item parameters are then calibrated for all countries simultaneously, in order to create a common measurement scale. In practice, cross-national differences in response patterns are present, which makes the assumption of invariant item parameters unlikely. Goldstein (2004) argued that the Rasch measurement model used for the PISA data is too simplistic for such cross-national survey data as the multilevel nature of the data and country-specific response differences are not acknowledged. The proposed random item effects model deals with these problems by simultaneously including a multilevel structure for ability and allowing item parameters to differ over countries while at the same time a common measurement scale is retained. In addition, covariates can be included in the model to explain within and between country variance in ability and item parameters. We hypothesize that a random item effects model will acknowledge the real-data structure more and therefore will fit the data better than the Rasch model.

We chose to use items from the domain that measured skills in quantitative mathematics, which consists essentially of arithmetic or number-related skills applied to real life problems (e.g., exchange rates, computing the price of assembled skateboard parts). PISA works with a large item pool, from which students receive only limited clusters of items. In this way testing time is reduced, while at the same time the full range of topics is covered. Fourteen booklets with different combinations of item clusters were used, equally distributed over countries and schools. Due to this (linked) incomplete design the test scores can later be related to the same scale of estimated ability using IRT. To avoid booklet effects and simultaneously keep all countries well represented, we chose to use the first booklet, in which eight quantitative mathematics items were present. Due to a lack of students, the data from Liechtenstein were removed. This resulted in test data from 9769 students across 40 countries on eight quantitative mathematics items.

As covariates we used gender, index of economic, social, and cultural status, minutes spend on math homework, mathematical self-concept, and school student behavior. Gender differences and social economic status are generally known to be predictors of mathematical performance. The index of economic, social, and cultural status was a combined measure of parental education, parental occupational status, and access to home educational and cultural resources. A student questionnaire measured engagement in mathematics, self-beliefs concerning mathematics, and learning strategies in mathematics. As all the latter measures correlated strongly with self-beliefs in mathematics, we chose to include self-concept in mathematics (belief in own mathematical competence). A school questionnaire was given to the school principals to assess aspects of the school environment. From these questions, student behavior (absenteeism, class disruption, bullying, respect for teachers, alcohol/drug use) was the best predictor for mathematical performance. In addition, from the time spent on total instruction, math instruction, and math homework, minutes spent on math homework was the best predictor of mathematical performance. Missing values in the covariates (ranging from 5 to 22%) were imputed by the SPSS missing value analysis regression procedure based on 20 variables. This procedure imputes the expected values from a linear regression equation based on the complete cases plus a residual component chosen randomly from the residual components of the complete cases.

17.6.1 PISA 2003: Results

Three random item effects models were estimated with the MLIRT package. The most general model, denoted as *M*3, allows for random item effects and random intercepts and covariates on the ability parameters. The other two models are nested in this model. Model *M*3 is presented as:

$$P\left(Y_{ijk}=1 \mid \theta_{ij}, \tilde{a}_{kj}, \tilde{b}_{kj}\right)=\Phi\left(\tilde{a}_{kj}\theta_{ij}-\tilde{b}_{kj}\right) \tag{17.9}$$

$$\left(\tilde{a}_{kj}, \tilde{b}_{kj}\right)^t=(a_k, b_k)^t+(\varepsilon_{a_k}, \varepsilon_{b_k})^t,$$

where the residual cross-national discrimination and difficulty effects are normally distributed with variance $\sigma^2_{a_k}$ and $\sigma^2_{b_k}$, respectively, and

$$\theta_{ij} = \gamma_{00} + \beta_1 \text{HOMEWORK}_{ij} + \beta_2 \text{BEHAVIOR}_{ij} +$$

$$\beta_3 \text{SELF-CONCEPT}_{ij} + \beta_4 \text{ESCS}_{ij} + \beta_5 \text{FEMALE}_{ij} + u_{0j} + e_{ij}, \quad (17.10)$$

where $e_{ij} \sim N(0, \sigma_\theta^2)$ and $u_{0j} \sim N(0, \tau^2)$. The restricted model *M*1 only allows for random intercepts on the ability parameters and restricted model *M*2 allows for country-specific item parameters in addition to *M*1. Model *M*1 is identified by restricting the mean and variance of the latent ability scale to zero and one, respectively. Model *M*2 and *M*3 are identified by restricting the variance of the latent ability scale to one and by restricting the sum of country-specific item difficulties to zero in each country. There are no restrictions specified for the discrimination parameters, since the models assume factor variance invariance.

The first 1000 iterations were discarded, the remaining 19,000 iterations were used for the estimation of the model parameters. The program took approximately 2.5 hours to complete the estimation. To check whether the chains reached a state of convergence, trace plots, and convergence diagnostics were examined. The diagnostics and trace plots did not indicate convergence problems, except for a somewhat high autocorrelation for the discrimination parameter of item 2 in both random item effects models, model *M*2 and *M*3. The high autocorrelation results from the fact that this item has both a high discrimination and a high difficulty parameter. Since the item information function for this item is very steep and centered on the difficulty parameter value, the parameters of this item will be very hard to estimate, especially in countries where the ability level is low. In Brazil, for example, only 13 out of the 250 selected students had an estimated ability that was higher than the difficulty level of the item, which indicates that there was very little information to base the estimated parameters on in this country. For the three models, the estimated international item parameter estimates are given in Table 17.3. For model *M*2 and *M*3, the estimated cross-national discrimination and difficulty standard deviations are also given.

17.6.1.1 Cross-National Variance

The estimated international discrimination parameters of *M*1 and *M*2 are very similar. The estimated international difficulty parameters of model *M*2 are higher, because the identification rules for the two models differ. However, the estimated difficulty parameters of model *M*1 can be

TABLE 17.3

Parameter Estimates of the MLIRT Model and Two Random Item Effects Models

	Model $M1$		Model $M2$				Model $M3$			
Item	$\hat{a}_k$	$\hat{b}_k$	$\hat{a}_k$	$\hat{\sigma}_{a_k}$	$\hat{b}_k$	$\hat{\sigma}_{b_k}$	$\hat{a}_k$	$\hat{\sigma}_{a_k}$	$\hat{b}_k$	$\hat{\sigma}_{b_k}$
1	0.81	−0.59	0.82	0.09	0.00	0.14	0.78	0.08	−0.02	0.14
2	1.06	0.19	1.10	0.24	0.99	0.12	1.16	0.20	1.03	0.15
3	0.73	−0.04	0.72	0.07	0.48	0.11	0.69	0.06	0.46	0.11
4	0.69	−0.36	0.70	0.12	0.14	0.11	0.70	0.10	0.14	0.11
5	0.56	−0.02	0.58	0.12	0.40	0.08	0.61	0.13	0.41	0.09
6	0.37	−1.51	0.40	0.16	−1.26	0.10	0.38	0.16	−1.26	0.10
7	0.69	−0.78	0.69	0.10	−0.29	0.10	0.66	0.09	−0.30	0.10
8	0.66	−0.94	0.69	0.12	−0.46	0.08	0.67	0.11	−0.46	0.08

	Mean	HPD	Mean	HPD	Mean	HPD
γ_{00}	0.01	[−0.14, 0.15]	0.73	[0.58, 0.88]	1.01	[0.88, 1.14]
σ^2	0.79	[0.77, 0.82]	0.79	[0.77, 0.82]	0.57	[0.54, 0.59]
τ^2	0.22	[0.13, 0.33]	0.22	[0.13, 0.33]	0.14	[0.08, 0.21]
β_1 (Homework)					−0.37	[−0.44, −0.30]
β_2 (Behavior)					0.07	[0.05, 0.09]
β_3 (Self-concept)					0.28	[0.25, 0.30]
β_4 (ESCS)					0.33	[0.31, 0.36]
β_5 (Female)					−0.07	[−0.11, −0.03]
−2 LL IRT		−36,129.56		−35,642.12		−35,813.18
−2 LL ML		−12,897.95		−12,901.53		−11,261.54
DIC MLIRT		1,05,431.03		1,04,481.66		10,1973.38

transformed to the scale of model $M2$. For item 1, the transformed estimated item difficulty of $M1$ resembles the estimated item difficulty of $M2$ ($0.73 \cdot 0.82 \cdot 0.59 \approx 0.01$). Note that the estimated variances of both ability scales are approximately equal.

In Table 17.3, the estimated −2 log-likelihood of the IRT part and the structural multilevel part are given. Both terms are used to estimate a DIC that also contains a penalty function for the number of model parameters. When comparing model $M1$ with $M2$, the log-likelihood of the IRT part is improved and the log-likelihood of the multilevel part is almost equal. The DIC also shows a clear improvement in fit due to the inclusion of random item effects. This supports the hypothesis of noninvariant item parameters.

The estimated cross-national variance in item discriminations and item difficulties supports the hypothesis of cross-national item parameter variance.

Item 6 does not discriminate well between students with lower and higher ability in math, probably because the item is too easy. The estimated country-specific discrimination parameters of model *M*2 show that in some countries (e.g., Japan: 0.614), the item discriminates better, while in other countries (e.g., Switzerland: 0.149 and Belgium: 0.192) the item hardly discriminates at all. Item 2 is the most discriminating item, the estimated country-specific discriminations range from 0.634 (Indonesia) and 0.751 (Tunisia) to 1.415 (Hungary) and 1.602 (Japan). The estimated difficulty parameters for this item range from 0.784 (United States) to 1.127 (Ireland). Figure 17.3 shows the item characteristic curves (ICCs) for item 8. The relatively low discrimination parameters for Denmark, Indonesia, and the Netherlands make the curves for those countries relatively flat, while their difficulty parameters separate their curves in horizontal directions. The relatively high discrimination parameters for Thailand and Japan make their curves very steep.

The data supports the grouping of respondents in countries. The estimated intraclass correlation coefficient shows that 21% of the total variance in latent ability is explained by mean ability differences across countries.

17.6.1.2 Covariates on the Ability Parameters

Model *M*2 is extended with explanatory information at the individual-level and this leads to model *M*3. It is to be expected that the estimated

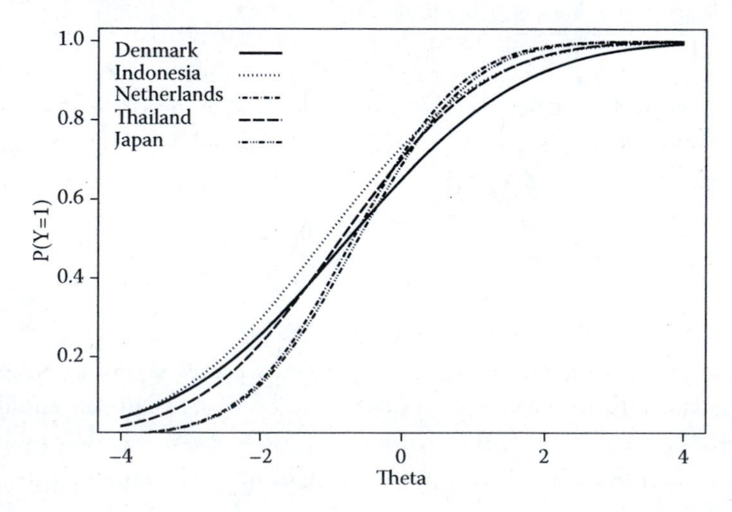

FIGURE 17.3
Cross-national item specific curves for item 8.

international item parameters and the estimated cross-national item variances of model *M*2 and *M*3 are equal since individual-based explanatory information is incorporated. From Table 17.3, it can be seen that the estimated international item parameters and estimated cross-national item variances are approximately the same. Thus, the covariates do not explain cross-national item variance.

The log-likelihood of the IRT part did not change much, but the log-likelihood of the multilevel part shows a clear improvement of model fit. The DIC shows that model *M*3 fits the data better than the other two models, indicating that the inclusion of explaining covariates on the individual level is an improvement of the model.

The covariates explain around 28% of the level-2 variance in ability between students and around 36% of the level-3 variance in ability between countries. The explained variance is within as well as between group variance, the conditional intraclass correlation stays almost the same at 0.20. The parameter γ_{00} is no longer the general latent mean, but the intercept in a regression equation that predicts the latent scores for the individuals conditional on the covariate effects.

The effects of all five covariates were strong, as can be seen from the estimated HPD intervals. Time spent on math homework and being female were predictive of a lower ability and a higher self-concept in mathematics, a higher economic, social, and cultural status and absence of negative student behavior at the school of a student had a positive effect on math ability. The negative effect of time spent on math homework can be explained by the fact that weak math students spend more time on their homework. This is in line with results found in PISA (OECD, 2004) and in other studies about predictors for math performance (e.g., Chiu & Klassen, 2010).

17.7 CONCLUSIONS

A random item effects model was introduced for cross-national item response data. The model supports the use of country-specific item parameters. Further, a structural multilevel population model for the respondents was specified where cross-national differences in mean abilities are allowed. As a result, cross-national differences in item characteristics and respondents' abilities can be modeled and measurement invariant items are not needed. The corresponding identifying restrictions make the often difficult search for common invariant items unnecessary. The object is to explain the variation using covariate information at the item, individual, and group level. The model discussed here gives the opportunity to include covariates to predict ability, which gives the opportunity to estimate explanatory effects simultaneously with the IRT parameters, taking into account the measurement error in the ability parameters.

The simulation study showed accurate recovery of the simulated parameters, although the estimates were a bit unstable for high-discrimination parameters. The convergence criteria showed that MCMC draws are obtained from the joint posterior (target) distribution and they can be used to make posterior inferences. The prior choices can be evaluated via a prior sensitivity analysis to evaluate whether the prior choices substantially affect inferences. Here, the IG prior of the cross-national discrimination variances was investigated. It was shown that an informative prior (IG prior with a shape and scale parameter of one) can lead to significant cross-national variation in item discriminations. The study also showed that stable results were obtained for smaller prior parameter values.

The PISA data supported the hypothesis that large-scale educational response data are more accurately analyzed with a random item effects model as this model fitted the data better. Substantial cross-national item parameter variance was detected. In PISA 2003, each item was selected and tested to be measurement invariant, however, the present analysis showed that the item characteristics were not invariant across countries. To avoid this complex issue of establishing partial or full measurement invariance, the proposed methodology for handling complex cross-national response data takes a different approach and provides a flexible framework for making meaningful cross-national comparisons.

REFERENCES

Adams, R. J., Wilson, M., & Wu, M. (1997). Multilevel item response models: An approach to errors in variable regression. *Journal of Educational and Behavioral Statistics, 22*, 47–76.

Aitkin, M., & Longford, N. (1986). Statistical modelling in school effectiveness studies. *Journal of the Royal Statistical Society A, 149*, 1–43.

Albers, W., Does, R. J. M. M., Imbos, Tj., & Janssen, M. P. E. (1989). A stochastic growth model applied to repeated tests of academic knowledge. *Psychometrika, 54*, 451–466.

Bryk, A. S., & Raudenbush, S. W. (1992). *Hierarchical linear models.* Newbury Park, CA: Sage.

Chiu, M. M., & Klassen, R. M. (2010). Relations of mathematics self-concept and its calibration with mathematics achievement: Cultural differences among fifteen-year-olds in 34 countries. *Learning and Instruction, 20,* 2–17.

Cowles, M. K., & Carlin, B. P. (1996). Markov chain Monte Carlo convergence diagnostics: A comparative review. *Journal of the American Statistical Association, 91,* 883–904.

De Boeck, P. (2008). Random item IRT models. *Psychometrika, 73,* 533–559.

De Jong, M. G., Steenkamp, J. B. E. M., & Fox, J.-P. (2007). Relaxing cross-national measurement invariance using a hierarchical IRT model. *Journal of Consumer Research, 34,* 260–278.

De Jong, M. G., Steenkamp, J. B. E. M., Fox, J-P., & Baumgartner, H. (2008). Using item response theory to measure extreme response style in marketing research: A global investigation. *Journal of Marketing Research, 104,* 104–115.

De Leeuw, J., & Kreft, I. G. G. (1986). Random coefficient models for multilevel analysis. *Journal of Educational and Behavioral Statistics, 11,* 57–86.

Fox, J.-P. (2007). Multilevel IRT modeling in practice. *Journal of Statistical Software, 20,* 1–16.

Fox, J.-P., & Glas, C. A. W. (2001). Bayesian estimation of a multilevel IRT model using Gibbs sampling. *Psychometrika, 66,* 269–286.

Fox, J.-P. (2010). *Bayesian item response modeling: Theory and applications.* New York: Springer.

Glas, C. A. W., & Van der Linden, W. J. (2003). Computerized adaptive testing with item cloning. *Applied Psychological Measurement, 27,* 247–261.

Glas, C. A. W., Van der Linden, W. J., & Geerlings, H. (2010). Estimation of the parameters in an item-cloning model for adaptive testing. In W. J. Van der Linden & C. A. W. Glas (Eds.), *Elements of Adaptive Testing* (pp. 303–331).

Goldstein, H. (1995). *Multilevel statistical models* (2nd ed.). London, New York: Springer. Edward Arnold.

Goldstein, H. (2004). International comparisons of student attainment: Some issues arising from the PISA study. *Assessment in Education, 11,* 319–330.

Janssen, R., Tuerlinckx, F., Meulders, M., & De Boeck, P. (2000). A hierarchical IRT model for criterion-referenced measurement. *Journal of Educational and Behavioral Statistics, 25,* 285–306.

Kamata, A. (2001). Item analysis by the hierarchical generalized linear model. *Journal of Educational Measurement, 38,* 79–93.

Meredith, W., & Millsap, R. E. (1992). On the misuse of manifest variables in the detection of measurement bias. *Psychometrika, 57,* 289–311.

Organization for Economic Cooperation and Development. (2004). *Learning for tomorrow's world: First results from PISA 2003.* Paris, France: OECD Publications.

Organization for Economic Cooperation and Development. (2005). *Pisa technical report.* Paris, France: OECD Publications.

Raudenbush, S. W., & Sampson, R. J. (1999). Ecometrics: Toward a science of assessing ecological settings, with application to the systematic social observation of neighborhoods. *Sociological Methodology, 29,* 1–41.

Skrondal, A., & Rabe-Hesketh, S. (2004). *Generalized latent variable modeling: Multilevel, longitudinal, and structural equation models.* Boca Raton, FL: Chapman and Hall-CRC.

Snijders, T. A. B., & Bosker, R. J. (1999). *Multilevel analysis: An introduction to basic and advanced multilevel modeling.* Thousand Oaks, CA:Sage.

Steenkamp, J. B. E. M., & Baumgartner, H. (1998). Assessing measurement invariance in cross-national consumer research. *Journal of Consumer Research, 25*, 78–90.

Wollack, J. A., Bolt, D. M., Cohen, A. S., & Lee, Y.-S. (2002). Recovery of item parameters in the nominal response model: A comparison of marginal maximum likelihood estimation and Markov chain Monte Carlo estimation. *Applied Psychological Measurement, 26*, 339–352.

Zwinderman, A. H. (1991). A generalized Rasch model for manifest predictors. *Psychometrika, 56*, 589–600.

Contributors

Nick Allum is Senior Lecturer in Empirical Sociology at the University of Essex. He obtained his PhD from the London School of Economics and Political Science. His graduate work was on the public perception of risk in relation to gene technology. He has published risk perception and attitudes toward science and technology in numerous articles and books. He has also researched and published on survey methodology.

Luis Arciniega is Professor of Organizational Behavior (OB) and Human Resources Management (HRM) at ITAM Business School in Mexico City. He received his PhD in Organizational Psychology from the University of Salamanca in Spain. His research interests focus on studying the influence of personal values on work attitudes and team processes. He has published in leading academic journals and presented several papers in international conferences. He worked as a practitioner in HRM for more than a decade at Televisa Group, one of the largest media corporations in the world and as a consultant for multinational organizations.

Achilles Armenakis (D.B.A., 1973, Mississippi State University) is the James T. Pursell, Sr. Eminent Scholar in Management Ethics and Director of the Auburn University Center for Ethical Organizational Cultures. Achilles's research has focused on diagnosis, implementation, and assessment of organizational change. He is currently involved in research on ethics-related topics in organizational change.

Rasa Barkauskiene, PhD is an Associate Professor at the Department of Clinical and Organizational Psychology at Vilnius University, Lithuania. Her research interests include personality psychology and developmental psychopathology.

Mahmut Bayazit is currently an Assistant Professor of Organizational Studies at Sabanci University where he teaches courses on organizational behavior and leadership. He received his PhD from the School of Industrial and Labor Relations, Cornell University. His research focuses on the social psychology of unions and the impact of leadership on employee motivation and attitudes. His research has been published in journals such as

Journal of Applied Psychology, *Journal of Occupational Health Psychology*, and *Small Group Research*.

Jaak Billiet, PhD was a Professor in Social Methodology at the Katholieke Universiteit Leuven, Belgium, and is now Professor Emeritus with research tasks. His main research interest in methodology deals with validity assessment and the modeling of measurement error in social surveys. His substantial research covers longitudinal and comparative research in the domains of ethnocentrism, political attitudes, and religious orientations. Recent publications appeared in *Methodological Methods & Research*, *European Sociological Review*, *Social Science Research*, *Survey Research Methods*, and *Journal of Social Issues*.

Nikos Bozionelos, PhD is Professor of Organizational Behavior and International Human Resource Management in Durham Business School, Durham University, UK. His interests include cross-cultural psychology and management, careers, and emotion work. He is Associate Editor for *Career Development International*, member of the Editorial Review Board of *Group and Organization Management*, and has been member of the Steering Committee of the Careers Division of the Academy of Management. He belongs to the small proportion of academics with individual impact factor h_I above 10 in the *Publish or Perish Index* (http://www.harzing.com/pop.htm).

Georg Datler is a PhD candidate at the Institute of Sociology, University of Zurich, Switzerland. His research interests are in political sociology, European integration, the methodology of the social sciences, and the application of structural equation modeling in a comparative perspective.

Eldad Davidov, PhD is Professor of Sociology at the University of Zurich, Switzerland. His research interests are applications of structural equation modeling to survey data, especially in cross-cultural and longitudinal research. Applications include human values, national identity, and attitudes toward immigrants and other minorities.

Alain De Beuckelaer, PhD is Assistant Professor of International Management at Radboud University Nijmegen, the Netherlands, and Senior Researcher at Ghent University, Belgium. His scientific work is interdisciplinary including management, psychology, and organizational behavior. Most of his research deals with methodological issues in cross-cultural comparative research.

Hermann Dülmer, PhD is Assistant Professor of Sociology at the Institute for Data Archiving and Data Analysis (former Central Archive for Empirical Social Research) of the University of Cologne. His substantive research interests include comparative value research, including value change, and electoral research, with a particular emphasis on right-wing extremism. His methodological interests focus on multilevel analysis and factorial surveys.

Ivana Ferić earned her PhD in Social Psychology from the Department of Psychology at University of Zagreb. Since 1998 she has been employed at the Institute of Social Sciences Ivo Pilar in Zagreb, where she is now a Research Associate. She specialized in methodology of scientific research, and her current interests include human values, attitudes, and beliefs.

Remco Feskens, PhD is a researcher at IQ Healthcare Department at the University Medical Centre St. Radboud Nijmegen. His current research projects are multilevel research and survey methodology. Recent publications include "Difficult Groups in Survey Research and the Development of Tailor-Made Approach Strategies" (PhD thesis, 21/10/2009, Utrecht University) and publications in *Journal of Official Statistics, Field Methods,* and *Survey Research Methods.*

Jean-Paul Fox, PhD is Associate Professor in the Department of Research Methodology, Measurement, and Data Analysis, at the University of Twente, Enschede, the Netherlands. His areas of specialization include developing and applying Bayesian techniques and statistical models in test theory and other scientific disciplines.

Yuka Fujimoto received her PhD from Monash University and is a Senior Lecturer at Deakin University within the School of Management and Marketing. Her research interest lies in the diversity and justice oriented, decision-making process and diversity inclusiveness in organizations. She is a recipient of Best Paper Proceedings at the Academy of Management and Asia Academy of Management conferences. She has also coauthored a textbook, Human Resource Management (2nd Edition) published by Pearson Education in June 2010.

Luis González is Professor of Human Resource Management and Work and Organizational Psychology in the Faculty of Economics and Management at the University of Salamanca, Spain. He received his PhD in Social Psychology from the University of Salamanca. He has served as

Director of the Master on Human Resource Management of University of Salamanca. His research interests include the development of evaluation instruments in work and organizational psychology, methodological issues in structural equation modeling, work motivation and work redesign, organizational commitment, and human resources management.

Jian Han, PhD is an Assistant Professor of Management at China Europe International Business School. Han's research interest mainly focuses on how to integrate HR management with characteristics of different levels (individual, team, and corporate) in an effort to improve organizational performance. Han obtained her PhD degree from the ILR School, Cornell University.

Hilde Hetland, PhD is an Associate Professor at the Department of Psychology at the University of Bergen, Norway. Her research areas are organizational psychology and educational psychology. She has published articles in various international journals.

Joop J. Hox is a Full Professor of Social Science Methodology at the Department of Methodology and Statistics of the Faculty of Social Sciences at Utrecht University. As Methodology Chair, he is responsible for the research, development, and teaching carried out at the faculty in the field of social science methods and techniques. His research interests focus on two lines of work: data quality in social surveys and multilevel modeling. In survey methodology, he has written articles on nonresponse problems and the effects of data collection mode and interviewers on various aspects of data quality. In multilevel modeling, he has written numerous articles, book chapters, and an introductory handbook, with a newly written monograph currently in press.

Martina Hřebíčková received her PhD from Charles University of Prague and she is currently Senior Scientist at the Institute of Psychology, Academy of Science of the Czech Republic in Brno. Her research interests include personality structure and measurement, with a special interest in the psycholexical and dispositional approach to trait psychology.

Rianne Janssen received her PhD in psychology from the Katholieke Universiteit Leuven (Belgium). Currently, she is employed as an Assistant Professor at the Faculty of Psychology and Educational Sciences at the same university.

Nerina Jimmieson is an Associate Professor and is the Centre and Program Director for Organizational Psychology at the University of Queensland,

Australia. She teaches undergraduate and postgraduate courses in organizational behavior, personnel selection, and organizational change. Her research interests are concerned with stress and coping in the workplace, employee adaptation to organizational change, and the role of employee attitudes and behaviors in the prediction of client satisfaction.

Miloš Kankaraš is a PhD student in the Department of Methodology and Statistics at Tilburg University, the Netherlands. He holds a MSc in Psychology from the University of Belgrade, Serbia. His research interests are in the areas of cross-cultural comparative research, measurement equivalence, and attitudes and values.

Jana Kordačová, PhD holds the position of senior research fellow at the Institute of Experimental Psychology of the Slovak Academy of Sciences. Her long-term interest lies in functional and dysfunctional aspects of cognition and emotion relations (until late it was specifically irrational beliefs) and at present in the context of positive psychology as well.

Marina Kotrla Topić received her BA in Psychology in 2002 and since 2003 she has been completing her PhD at the graduate study Language Communication and Cognitive Neuroscience at the University of Zagreb. Since 2004 she has been employed at the Institute of Social Sciences Ivo Pilar in Zagreb.

Jaehoon Lee, PhD is a Research Associate at the Center for Research Methods and Data Analysis at the University of Kansas. His primary research interests are in applications of structural equation modeling and item response theory to practical measurement problems, including measurement equivalence, differential item functioning, and matching/anchoring. An additional interest is the use of Monte Carlo analysis for educational and organizational research.

Todd D. Little, PhD is Professor of Quantitative and Developmental Psychology at the University of Kansas. He also serves as the Director of the Center for Research Methods and Data Analysis at the University of Kansas. He was elected President of Division 5 (dedicated to research methods and practices) of the American Psychological Association for the 2010 term and has been a member of the Society of Multivariate Experimental Psychology (SMEP) since 2006. His quantitative research interests include psychometrics, structural equation modeling, the analysis of repeated measures/longitudinal data, and cross-cultural data analysis.

Bart Meuleman is Professor of Sociology at the University of Leuven (Belgium), where he teaches social research methodology. His main research interests involve cross-cultural comparisons of attitude and value patterns, such as welfare attitudes, ethnocentrism, religiosity and basic human values. In his work, he mainly applies multi-level and structural equation models. Recent publications appeared in Social Science Research, European Sociological Review and International Migration Review.

Hitoshi Mitsuhashi is an Associate Professor in the Faculty of Business and Commerce at Keio University. He received his PhD from the New York State School of Industrial and Labor Relations at Cornell University. His research interests include the evolutionary dynamics of interorganizational relations and the path dependency of organizational behavior.

Boris Mlačić earned his PhD in Personality Psychology from the Department of Psychology, Faculty of Philosophy at University of Zagreb. He has been employed since 1992 at the Institute of Social Sciences Ivo Pilar in Zagreb where he is now a Senior Research Associate. He was a recipient of the Croatian Annual National Award for Science for 1999. In his research he focuses on individual differences, the lexical approach in personality psychology, the Big-Five model, and personality development.

Guy Moors is an Assistant Professor in the Department of Methodology and Statistics at Tilburg University, the Netherlands. He holds a PhD in Social Sciences from the Free University of Brussels. His publications are in the field of social demography, survey methodology, cross-cultural comparative research, attitudes, and values research.

Sandra Ohly is currently an Assistant Professor in Industrial and Organizational Psychology at the University of Frankfurt. She earned her PhD at the Technical University of Braunschweig. Her research focuses on creativity at work, proactive behavior, and suggestion making. She is also interested in the effects of time pressure on motivation and in emotions, organizational change, and resistance to change.

Shaul Oreg earned his PhD in Organizational Behavior from Cornell University. In 2003 he joined the Department of Sociology and Anthropology at the University of Haifa, where he is now a Senior Lecturer.

In his research he focuses on individual differences in social and organizational contexts. In particular, he studies traits and values and their effect on individuals' attitudes and behaviors. He specializes in quantitative methods, including scale development, advanced factor analytic techniques, and cross-level analyses.

Per Øystein Saksvik is at present a Professor at the Department of Psychology, Norwegian University of Science and Technology where he also received his PhD in 1991 in Occupational Health Psychology. He has seven years of experience as a Researcher at the Institute of Social Research in Industry, Trondheim, Norway. He does research in occupational health and safety, organizational interventions, sickness absenteeism and presenteeism, and organizational change.

Kristopher J. Preacher, PhD is an Assistant Professor of Quantitative Psychology at the University of Kansas. His research concerns the use of structural equation modeling and multilevel modeling to analyze longitudinal and correlational data. Other interests include developing techniques to test mediation and moderation hypotheses, and improving model selection in the application of multivariate methods to social science questions.

Markus Quandt, PhD is a Senior Researcher and acting Head of Department at the GESIS Data Archive in Cologne, Germany. He has rich experience in dealing with comparative survey data from his involvement in the data integration work of the International Social Survey Programme. He has also worked in the analysis of political attitudes and electoral research.

Sanna Read has a PhD in Psychology. She works as a Research Fellow at the London School of Hygiene and Tropical Medicine and the Helsinki Collegium for Advanced Studies. Her research interests are motivation, trust, social networks, and health in adulthood and old age.

Ingvild Berg Saksvik is a PhD student at the Department of Psychology at the University of Bergen in Norway. Her research areas are personality, stress, sleep, and shift work.

Willem E. Saris is a professor at Universitat Ramon Llull and Universitat Pompeu Fabra (UPF), Spain. He is the director of the Research and Expertise Centre for Survey Methodology at the department of Politics and Social Sciences (UPF). He is a laureate of the Descartes Prize 2005, for the best collaborative research. In 2009 he received the Helen Dinerman Award by the World Association of Public Opinion Research in recognition to his extensive contributions to the fields of public opinion research and development of survey research methods. He is also the president and founder of the European Survey Research Association and a member of the central coordinating team (CCT) of the European Social Survey.

Peter Schmidt, PhD is Professor of Sociology at the University of Marburg and Professor Emeritus of Social Research Methods and Political Science at the University of Giessen, Germany. His research interests are the foundations and applications of structural equation models, analysis of panel data, and empirical testing of rational choice theory. Applications include national identity, immigration, and environmental behavior, topics on which he has published several important books and papers.

Shalom H. Schwartz, PhD is the Sznajderman Professor Emeritus of Psychology at the Hebrew University of Jerusalem, Israel. His recent work concerns two topics: the nature and sources of basic human values and their role as bases of attitudes and behavior, and the nature and sources of cultural value orientations as expressions of and influences on the institutional structures, policies, and prevailing norms and practices in different societies.

Pascal Siegers graduated in Social Sciences from SciencesPo Bordeaux (France) and the University of Stuttgart (Germany). He is currently a postgraduate student at the research training group "Social Order and Life Chances in International Comparison" at the University of Cologne. His main research interests are the causes and consequences of alternative religiosity in contemporary Europe.

Holger Steinmetz is a work psychologist and works as a Scientific Assistant at the Faculty of Economics and Business Administration at the University of Giessen, Germany. His research interests are structural equation modeling, cross-cultural research, and work psychology.

Patrick Sturgis obtained his PhD in Psychology at London School of Economics and Political Science, and is Professor of Research Methodology in the Division of Social Statistics at the University of Southampton and Director of the U.K. National Centre for Research Methods. His research focuses on survey methodology, the dynamics of opinion formation and change, and the analysis of panel data.

Gilbert Swinnen, PhD is Professor of Marketing at Hasselt University, Belgium. His scientific work within the marketing field has a strong emphasis on retailing and consumer behavior. He has also published numerous papers on multivariate statistical analysis techniques and data mining techniques.

Maria Vakola is an Organizational Psychologist and is currently working as an Assistant Professor at the Athens University of Economics and Business in Greece. She earned her PhD in change management and organizational behavior from the University of Salford, UK. Her main research interests focus on individual differences and reactions to organizational change. She has published in academic journals such as *Journal of Applied Psychology, Journal of Organizational Change Management*, and *Communications of the ACM* to name a few.

Karen van Dam is an Associate Professor of Personnel Psychology at Tilburg University, the Netherlands. She received her PhD at the University of Amsterdam. Her research focuses on how employees adapt to changes in the work situation, including employability, employee learning, job changes, retirement, and resistance to change.

William M. van der Veld is assistant professor at the department of developmental psychology at the Radboud University Nijmegen, The Netherlands. He is a specialist in the field of survey research and structural equation modeling with a special interest in model testing. He received his PhD, Cum Laude, from the University of Amsterdam. His latest achievement is the development of a software program called JRule, which simplifies model evaluation using an approximate test and taking the power of the test into account. He is a member of the coordinating team of the Dutch Association for Survey Research (NPSO).

Fons J. R. van de Vijver, PhD holds a Chair in Cross-Cultural Psychology at Tilburg University, the Netherlands; in addition, he is Extraordinary Professor at North-West University, South Africa. He is the past Editor-in-Chief of the *Journal of Cross-Cultural Psychology.* He has published about 325 publications, mainly in the domain of cross-cultural psychology (methods, intelligence, acculturation, and multiculturalism).

Josine Verhagen is a PhD student in the Department of Research Methodology, Measurement, and Data Analysis, at the University of

Twente, Enschede, the Netherlands. Her research project is focused on the Bayesian modeling of heterogeneity for large-scale comparative research.

Jeroen K. Vermunt is a Professor in the Department of Methodology and Statistics at Tilburg University, the Netherlands. He holds a PhD in Social Sciences from Tilburg University. He has published extensively on categorical data techniques, methods for the analysis of longitudinal and event history data, latent class and finite mixture models, and latent trait models.

Author Index

C

D

E

F

I

J

K

N

O

P

Q

R

S

T

U

V

W

X

Y

Z

Subject Index

In lieu of a subject index the editors supplied Table 0.1 in the Preface to indicate the most important concepts dealt with per chapter.